Forecasting Financial and Economic Cycles

WILEY FINANCE EDITIONS

Forecasting Financial and Economic Cycles

MICHAEL P. NIEMIRA
PHILIP A. KLEIN

CLARKSTON CENTER

John Wiley & Sons, Inc.

New York • Chichester • Brisbane • Toronto • Singapore

Library of Congress Cataloging in Publication Data:

Niemira, Michael P., 1955–
    Forecasting financial and economic cycles / Michael P. Niemira,
Philip A. Klein.
        p.   cm. — (Wiley finance editions)
    Includes index.
    ISBN 0-471-84544-2
    1. Business cycles—United States.   2. Economic forecasting-
-United States.   3. United States—Economic conditions—1918–1945.
    4. United States—Economic conditions—1945–   5. Business cycles.
    6. Economic forecasting.   I. Klein, Philip A.   II. Title.
    III. Series.
    HB3743.N53   1994
    338.5'442—dc20   93-27196

Foreword

For more than a century, economists have been developing and analyzing measures of financial and other economic fluctuations. They have sought to distinguish patterns, such as seasonal movements, from long-term trends and from the less regular but highly important cyclical swings. This book takes a further step along this path. Many individuals will find it interesting for a variety of reasons.

An investor who wants to learn how to avoid some of the risks attached to investments and how to detect new opportunities may find answers here. A policymaker who wants to adopt policies that may abbreviate recessions or extend recoveries can find out here how and when to do it. The business executive or advisor who wants to pick the best time to launch a new enterprise or enlarge an existing one may find decision-making assistance here. Finally, the economist who wants to make a further contribution to this field would be well advised to read this book first, just to learn what puzzles have been solved and what remains to be done.

In addition to dealing with the history of business cycles and the application of forecasting methods to that history, this book is completely up to date in terms of both the data and the methods used. Hence, readers who become concerned with business or financial cycles later in this century or in the next will be able to compare them with events as recent as the 1990–1991 recession or the 1991–1993 recovery. In these respects, the book is somewhat like an encyclopedia, which may be consulted for a long time to come.

For students and professors in the field of economic forecasting, this book has many of the attributes of a classic textbook. It covers the subject thoroughly, explains and illustrates the methods, provides references to other sources, and raises questions requiring further study. My own forecast, therefore, is that these features will place the book on a rising growth trend in academic circles (not cycles).

GEOFFREY H. MOORE

Director, Center for
International Business
Cycle Research, Columbia
University

Preface

It is our view that a comprehensive book on the measuring, monitoring, and forecasting of economic cycles was long overdue. As such, our intention was to put together a comprehensive reference on the rhythm of business activity—chockfull of information on types of cycles, measurement techniques, cycle theory, historical perspective, and forecasting applications. It is a practitioner's book of economic and financial cycles. But although it takes a cycle perspective, the reader should recognize that it is really a practical discussion of the many facets of economic growth.

For readers who want to delve into topics in more depth, the book is rich with references as well as examples and techniques for their own analysis. It is our contention, in the words of Wesley Mitchell, that "the quickest way to attain reliable results is to take great care in measuring the phenomena exhibited by business cycles." Moreover, since there are so many diverse theories on the business cycle, it is necessary to use the empirical evidence to judge the business cycle theories based on the regularity with which those "alleged stresses" recur and the degree of adjustment that they attain. In many respects, this empirical research does not require the latest statistical technique. It is more important—and a goal of this book—to recognize what questions to ask and which technique or type of techniques might be appropriate to a given application. In today's literature, unfortunately, applications and analysis seem to be more technical, but not necessarily more informative. Our perspective is to start with the basics and refine the techniques later—if needed. The message from the analysis is more important than the technical messenger. Moreover, these same techniques and theories can be useful in analyzing specific problems such as international economies, regions, industries, and financial cycles.

Over the years, several people have provided useful comments on various sections of this book, sometimes before it was in book form. We especially would like to acknowledge and thank Gary Ciminero, Samuel Kahan, Geoffrey Moore, Salih Neftçi, Monroe Newman, Richard Weiss, Victor Zarnowitz, and Gerald Zukowski. A special word of thanks goes to Karl Weber, Wendy Grau, and Myles Thompson of John Wiley & Sons, Inc., for their patience and encouragement in this long project. Additionally, we acknowledge Nana Prior at John Wiley and Nancy Marcus Land and Denise Netardus and the staff at Publications Development Company of Texas for their superb editing, admirable emphasis on accuracy, and an all around excellent job in the production of this book.

Although it may be unusual for one author to acknowledge another, it is appropriate that I thank Philip Klein for agreeing to come aboard on this project late in its evolution. Professor Klein not only brought to this book his unparalleled experience on international business cycles but quickly and without any doubt improved numerous sections, not the least of which was the chapter on business cycle theories. He also brought a tremendous knowledge and real-world understanding of measuring, monitoring, and forecasting the business cycle.

A special acknowledgment goes to Andrew Niemira—to whom this book is dedicated.

MICHAEL P. NIEMIRA

I have been teaching Business Cycles courses at Penn State for many years. Since the path-breaking text of Robert Aaron Gordon, my teacher of business cycles at the University of California, became hopelessly outdated, there has not been a large selection of texts covering business fluctuations in all the areas I have thought essential: measurement and monitoring, business cycle theories, and history. While stabilization policy may be the ultimate objective, that subject is covered thoroughly in most advanced undergraduate macroeconomics courses. Students also need a concentrated course in fluctuations. For many years, I thought that writing my own text (a project I kept postponing) was the only answer to the problem of finding a suitable text.

At the same time, my many years of work with Geoffrey H. Moore (first at the National Bureau of Economic Research and later at the Center for International Research on Business Cycles at Columbia University) has made me keenly conscious that proper measurement of instability has myriad applications in the business and financial worlds.

When I encountered Michael Niemira's manuscript for this book, I felt that he was well on the way to producing both the rounded text that I had longed for and a volume that highlights the many applications of modern business cycle measurement and analysis techniques to the business world. It was, accordingly, a great pleasure for me to accept when he more than generously invited me to join him as coauthor. The format of the work was set long before I became involved. I added chapters in areas of my specialization.

I would like to acknowledge the influence of my many years of working with Geoffrey H. Moore. Most of what I know about this important subject I learned-by-doing from him.

Finally, I would add my granddaughters, Justine and Maya, to the dedication. It is right that this book be dedicated to young people—to those in the generation that will most fully reap the benefits, or suffer the distresses of the economy we are now striving to set on a strong but stable growth path.

PHILIP A. KLEIN

Contents

PART THREE   ECONOMIC HISTORY

CHAPTER 4   U.S. BUSINESS CYCLE HISTORY   245

PART FOUR   APPLICATION OF CYCLE TECHNIQUES

CHAPTER 5   INDUSTRY CYCLES   311

CHAPTER 6   REGIONAL BUSINESS CYCLES   327

Regional Monthly Production Indexes in the United States   329
Zoltan Kenessey

Part One

Cycle Types and Theory

1 The Nature of Economic Cycles

MEASURING BUSINESS FLUCTUATIONS

In December 1959, Arthur F. Burns gave the presidential address to the American Economic Association in which he said, "[T]he American people have of late been more conscious of the business cycle, more sensitive to every wrinkle of economic curves, more alert to the possible need for contracyclical action on the part of government, than ever before in history. Minor changes of employment or of productivity or of the price level, which in an earlier generation would have gone unnoticed, are nowadays followed closely by laymen as well as experts."[1] If this was true in 1959, then it certainly is an even more appropriate description of the public today. In the 1960s, however, economists questioned whether the business cycle was finally dead, only to find out the hard way that it was alive and well. What is meant by the term "business cycle," and what causes it? Why should an economist or businessperson be concerned about it? How is the cycle explained, measured, monitored, and forecasted? These are only some questions that will be addressed in this and later chapters.

Description of the "Typical Business Cycle"

Although most people may not fully understand the formal definitions, theories, interactions, and distinctions among economic cycles, the effects of these swings are felt all around us. Witness the layoffs in certain industries when business activity slows and the swings in mortgage interest rates at different times in the business cycle. Observe, too, that labor strikes seem more prevalent when economic growth is healthy. These and many similar occurrences are all related to the business cycle. Between 1948 and 1991, the U.S. economy has experienced nine major business cycle contractions and four minor slowdowns in the rate of economic growth. The average duration of these business cycle swings has been 3 to 4 years. Nonetheless, certain activities

3

seem dominated by longer-term swings in demographics. Some colleges, for example, have expressed concern that their enrollment may decline sharply in the years ahead because of slower population growth. On the other hand, fluctuations can be quite short such as the interyear or seasonal swings in business activity.

Many of these seemingly separate occurrences interact and cause or affect macroeconomic cycles of the 3- to 4-year variety. So, even though no two business cycles are exactly alike, these 3- to 4-year cycles display many similar tendencies in the aggregate. With this in mind, the typical characteristics in the 3- to 4-year cycle will be sketched out since this cycle will be the core and reference point of much of the following discussion. The main features include expansion phases lasting about 3 years and contractions lasting about 1 year with an average decline of about 2.5% in real output. These swings tend to be a result of shocks—monetary or real, inventory swings, and/or some imbalance in the economy. Generally, the following are observable: (1) Output is affected across many sectors, (2) production/consumption of consumer durable goods exhibit a higher degree of volatility than nondurable goods and services, (3) inflation and interest rates tend to decline during recessions and increase during expansions, and (4) employment moves in the same direction as the overall phase of the business cycle. In summary, the business cycle is a consensus of cycles in many specific activities, which have a tendency to peak and trough around the same time.

NBER Method of Cycle Delineation

Business Cycles.   When business activity declines in absolute levels and then rebounds, this is called a "classical business cycle"; more frequently, it is simply referred to as a "business cycle." In the United States, these business cycle periods of contractions from rebounds are delineated by the Business Cycle Dating Committee of the National Bureau of Economic Research (NBER). The U.S. Commerce Department accepts the conclusion of this Committee as the official U.S. business cycle turning point dates. The standard set of dates provides economists with a common point of reference for analyzing economic activity. The rationale for this is the same as for selecting a standard for electricity in the United States. If economists did not agree on a common set of business cycle reference dates, it would create a situation similar to that found in the computer industry, which currently does not have a standard operating system for the microcomputer; a person buying one system is often unable to use software written for a different system.

Empirical work that started in 1920 is responsible for a large part of the influence on business cycle measurement methodology that the National Bureau of Economic Research exerts today. In that year, a group of economists including

N. I. Stone, Edwin Gay, John Commons, and Wesley Clair Mitchell banded together and formed the NBER to address measurement problems in economics.[2] The Bureau's first concern was the development and improvement of measures of national income. Their second endeavor was the study of business cycles, and today, the NBER is involved in research in all areas of economics. But because of their pioneering work on quantitative economics, the NBER's basic methodology for analysis of the empirical business cycle has remained a standard for examining fluctuations in business activity. Therefore, it is useful to begin the discussion of business cycles with the characterization distilled from many years of analysis at the Bureau. In 1946, Wesley C. Mitchell and Arthur F. Burns presented the following working definition of the business cycle:

> Business cycles are a type of fluctuation found in the aggregate economic activity of nations that organize their work mainly in business enterprises: a cycle consists of expansions occurring at about the same time in many economic activities, followed by similarly general recessions, contractions, and revivals which merge into the expansion phase of the next cycle; this sequence of changes is recurrent but not periodic; in duration business cycles vary from more than one year to ten or twelve years; they are not divisible into shorter cycles of similar character with amplitudes approximating their own.[3]

This classic description can be restated and summarized essentially with four factors:

1. *Depth and Rebound (Amplitude).* To be considered a cycle, economic activity must show a pronounced decline followed by a rebound. Yet, the magnitude of this decline in business activity remains vague[4] in this definition.

2. *Length of Recessions and Recoveries (Duration).* The duration of a business cycle—which includes the length of adjacent recovery and recession phases—is at least one year. This immediately rules out any seasonal fluctuation. The maximum length observed was about 12 years. Also, this definition rules out fixed-length cycles.

3. *Impact on the Economy (Diffusion).* A business cycle must be broadly based throughout many industries and economic activities. The actual quantification of this concept will be examined later, when business cycle measurement methods are discussed.

4. *Displacement and Utilization.* Displacement can help classify business cycles by degree of severity and strength. Displacement measures the degree of economic disruption from recessions or the degree of utilization during expansions. Two common measures of displacement are the unemployment rate and capacity utilization.

In and of itself, the Burns and Mitchell definition is not a theory of the business cycle but simply a description. Philip A. Klein[5] has argued that this definition was a result of Wesley Mitchell's fundamental institutionalism. An institutional explanation of the business cycle attempts to explain economic fluctuations as they exist rather than to develop a simplified or abstract model and claim that it explains the cyclical behavior. The strength of the Mitchell (and Burns) approach is that it provides standard analytical tools to study the business cycle devoid of a particular theory.

Once the characteristics of the cycle have been defined, it is possible to delineate phases within the cycle. The Burns and Mitchell approach distinguishes two critical points in the cycle: the peak and the trough. This reference scale for distinguishing periods of increasing and decreasing business activity rests on two assumptions: (1) Business cycles are continuous—an expansion turns into a recession that is followed by a contraction and then a revival that, in turn, begins the process all over; and (2) it is sufficient to mark off turning points in business activity simply based on peaks and troughs.

The popular terminology often retains only three of the four segments that Burns and Mitchell posited: recession, recovery, and expansion. The term *recession* refers to the period from the upper turning point (the initial peak) to the lower turning point (the trough). *Recovery* refers to the period from the trough to the point at which business activity returns to its previous peak level. *Expansion* refers to the period when the economy increases beyond previous boundaries.

Growth Cycles.   A second National Bureau definition of the business cycle is termed the *deviation cycle* or, more commonly, the *growth cycle*. A growth cycle is a pronounced deviation around the trend rate of change. Thus this definition portrays periods of accelerating and decelerating rates of growth in the economy, a type of fluctuation that also has a long-standing history. In fact, Burns and Mitchell noted:

> If secular trends were eliminated at the outset as fully as are seasonal variations, they would show that business cycles are a more pervasive and a more potent factor in economic life. . . . For when the secular trend of a series rises rapidly, it may offset the influence of cyclical contractions in general business, or make the detection of this influence difficult. In such instances [the classical business cycle method] may indicate lapses from conformity to contractions in general business, which would not appear if the secular trend were removed.[6]

As shown in Table 1.1 and noted in the comment by Burns and Mitchell, growth cycles are more common and encompass classical business cycles. Research on growth cycles at the National Bureau of Economic Research has

Table 1.1   U.S. Business and Growth Cycles in the Post-World War II Period.

Business Cycles		Growth Cycles	
Peak	Nov. 1948	High	July 1948
Trough	Oct. 1949	Low	Oct. 1949
Peak	—	High	Mar. 1951
Trough	—	Low	July 1952
Peak	July 1953	High	Mar. 1953
Trough	May 1954	Low	Aug. 1954
Peak	Aug. 1957	High	Feb. 1957
Trough	Apr. 1958	Low	Apr. 1958
Peak	Apr. 1960	High	Feb. 1960
Trough	Feb. 1961	Low	Feb. 1961
Peak	—	High	May 1962
Trough	—	Low	Oct. 1964
Peak	—	High	June 1966
Trough	—	Low	Oct. 1967
Peak	Dec. 1969	High	Mar. 1969
Trough	Nov. 1970	Low	Nov. 1970
Peak	Nov. 1973	High	Mar. 1973
Trough	Mar. 1975	Low	Mar. 1975
Peak	Jan. 1980	High	Dec. 1978
Trough	July 1980	Low	—
Peak	July 1981	High	—
Trough	Nov. 1982	Low	Dec. 1982
Peak	—	High	July 1984
Trough	—	Low	Jan. 1987
Peak	July 1990	High	Feb. 1989
Trough	Mar. 1991	Low	

Sources: National Bureau of Economic Research and Center for International Business Cycle Research.

been particularly useful for examining fluctuation in business activity of foreign economies that may be dominated by trends. This was especially evident for the Japanese economy during the post-World War II period.

A growth cycle has many of the same characteristics as the classical business cycle. Growth cycles are a short-term fluctuation in aggregate economic activity characterized by periods of high and low growth; they must meet the same duration criteria applied to business cycles.

Figure 1.1 shows the relationship between growth and business cycles. Although no cycle follows as smooth a path as is shown, it is nonetheless useful to examine the phases of this growth cycle. The solid horizontal line represents

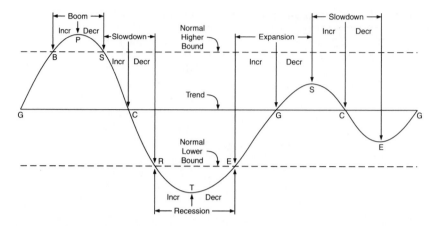

Figure 1.1 Phases in the Deviation Cycle. Letters distinguish the beginning and middle of the various phases. While they are not to be taken literally, the letters stand for various economic conditions generally associated with the phases to which they refer: *G* (Growth), *B* (Boom), *P* (Peak), *S* (Slowdown), *C* (Contraction), *R* (Recession), *T* (Trough), *E* (Expansion), Incr (Increasing Rate), Decr (Decreasing Rate). (*Source:* E. Haywood, "The Deviation Cycle: A New Index of the Australian Business Cycle, 1953–1973," *The Australian Economic Review,* Fourth Quarter, 1973, p. 34.)

the trend rate of growth in the series and the dashed horizontal lines represent one standard deviation around this trend rate. These standard deviation lines are a way of capturing the cyclical amplitude and distinguish growth cycles from business cycles.[7] Points *P* and *T* correspond to growth cycle periods that became business cycle peaks and troughs, whereas points *S* and *E* measure growth cycle highs and lows.

As an example of the differences between measuring cycles on a growth cycle versus a classical business cycle basis, consider the economic data series, labor cost per unit of manufacturing output, shown in Table 1.2. The Commerce Department calculated this series with and without a trend adjustment. The series with trend adjustment captures the essence of this growth cycle idea. What is apparent here and true in general, is that the high in the trend-adjusted series is earlier than the corresponding peak in the actual data. Unfortunately, examining the monthly pattern of this unit labor cost data shows that the real-world contours in these data may not be as clear-cut as the ideal cycle portrayed in Figure 1.1. So, this leads to using other data transformation methods to amplify the cycle while suppressing the irregular component. This is the goal of many of the methods to be discussed in Chapter 3.

Table 1.2 Cyclical Highs in Unit Labor Cost Data Index of Labor Cost per Unit of Output, Total Manufacturing (1967 = 100) (Actual and Trend-Adjusted Data).

Period		Actual	Trend-Adjusted
1969	Jan.	104.7	99.6
	Feb.	104.6	99.4
	Mar.	105.2	100.0
	Apr.	106.0	100.7
	May	106.9	101.5
	June	106.8	101.4
	July	106.9	101.4
	Aug.	107.7	102.1
	Sept.	108.0	102.3
	Oct.	108.2	102.4
	Nov.	108.6	102.7
	Dec.	109.8	103.8
1970	Jan.	111.8	105.4—High
	Feb.	111.5	104.8
	Mar.	112.4	105.4
	Apr.	112.2	104.9
	May	112.1	104.5
	June	112.6	104.7
	July	112.8	104.6
	Aug.	112.9	104.4
	Sept.	112.9	104.1
	Oct.	112.9	103.8
	Nov.	112.8	103.5
	Dec.	112.8	103.2
1971	Jan.	113.1	103.2
	Feb.	113.3	103.1
	Mar.	113.6	103.1
	Apr.	113.3	102.5
	May	113.4	102.3
	June	113.1	101.7
	July	112.8	101.1
	Aug.	114.2—High	102.0
	Sept.	112.4	100.1
	Oct.	112.0	99.4
	Nov.	111.9	99.0
	Dec.	113.3	99.8
1972	Jan.	112.5	98.8
	Feb.	113.7	99.5

Source: U.S. Department of Commerce.

Why do these competing approaches between growth and classical cycles exist for measuring short-term cycles? Is one approach more useful than the other? Ilse Mintz provided this answer to these questions:

> Distinguishing between two types of periods of differing economic experience, i.e., between business cycle phases, has proved eminently useful for the analysis of economic change. But this usefulness is diminished when one of the two phases occurs quite rarely and briefly. As long as absolute declines are frequent, drawing the line between absolute rises and falls is a most useful distinction. But when absolute declines are an exception, a different dividing line becomes more useful.[8]

Whereas Mintz gives one reason for studying growth cycles as opposed to business cycles, other reasons also exist. Four important reasons to monitor the stage of the growth cycle are:

1. Growth cycles are closely tied to inflation cycles.[9] On average, directional swings in the growth rate of the economy lead swings in the inflation rate by 7 months. With the mild growth cycles of 1951 and 1962, however, there was either no effect or essentially a coincidental effect.

2. Growth cycle peaks lead their comparable business cycle peaks. Growth cycle highs are reached, on average, 7 months before business cycle peaks occur. (This point was shown in Figure 1.1.)

3. Growth cycles are more symmetric in length and amplitude than business cycles.[10] Between 1948 and 1982, the average growth cycle upswing phase lasted 22 months, whereas the downswing phase lasted 21 months. There is a wide variation around the average—but adjacent phases tend to be quite similar in duration. For example, the March 1975 to December 1978 upswing lasted 45 months, and the next phase of the growth cycle lasted 48 months. This sharply contrasts with business cycle experience. Business cycle recessions between 1948 and 1982 lasted, on average, 11 months, whereas recoveries/expansions lasted more than three times as long (36 months without the 106-month 1960s expansion, or 46 months including all periods).

4. The Commerce Department's composite index of leading indicators has a better track record for forecasting growth cycles than business cycles. Declines in the composite index of leading indicators have been associated with all 10 growth cycle declines between 1948 and 1982.

Although these factors suggest reasons to look at growth cycles as well as business cycles, the question still arises, Why a dividing line at all? The pioneering empirical research done over the past half century by the National Bureau more than adequately demonstrates that the dynamics of the business cycle become clearer by measuring economic development against some reference point. Indeed, a knowledge of repetitive economic processes is a vital source of information for businesses, investors, and government policymakers.

Alternative Classification of Cycle Experience

Joseph Alois Schumpeter (1883–1950) has helped shape thinking on the process of economic change. Although his ideas are still controversial, he has offered the economics profession a broad view of the cause of the business cycle. Consistent with this view, he suggested his own idea for dating business cycles. Schumpeter held that inflection points are the key concept for cycle dating, unlike the Burns and Mitchell view that delineated peaks and troughs of business cycles. He called these inflection points neighborhoods of equilibrium, and they marked off periods of above-equilibrium growth from below-equilibrium growth. Schumpeter further distinguished four cycle phases similar to the Burns and Mitchell approach. Figure 1.2 shows these four phases: the above-equilibrium phases—upswing and recession—and the below-equilibrium phases—depression and revival. Schumpeter, however, did not rule out the possibility of noncontinuous cycle sequences as did Burns and Mitchell. Unfortunately, two major problems exist with Schumpeter's approach to empirically testing and monitoring the business cycle: (1) The equilibrium point is a vague concept; and (2) because of the possibility of noncontinuous phases, it becomes difficult to determine what phase the economy is in,

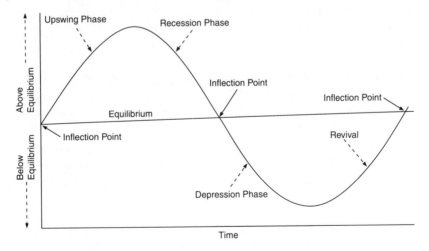

Figure 1.2 Schumpeter's View of the Business Cycle.

although additional empirical studies might yield some concrete rules for cycle phase classification. Maurice Lee aptly summarized his criticism of the Schumpeter idea as follows:

> Difficulty confronts us in attempting to evaluate his unorthodox marking-off of cycles from equilibrium to equilibrium, with his emphasis that the revival phase has no necessary connection with the recovery phase which follows but belongs rather in the next cycle (if there is one?). There is more to this than just a matter of taste, for the clear implication of Schumpeter's thinking is that these cyclical movements are not continuous processes. Presumably, the economy, according to this line of thought, might return through a period of revival to an equilibrium and then mark time until some innovator sets in motion the forces of a new prosperity and cycle.[11]

Schumpeter's business cycle theory is weaved around this equilibrium and incorporates an interaction of various cycles of varying length. More will be said about this later in the chapter.

Despite Schumpeter's unorthodox cycle dating method, it might be possible to restate his concept in terms of the NBER's growth cycle methodology. It would mean however, that the equilibrium point would have to be replaced with a trend-growth rate—a much more quantifiable idea. Nonetheless, a fundamental disagreement still would exist regarding the continuous cycle phase issue. Whether or not this assumption is critical to Schumpeter's own theory is questionable; yet others have implicitly followed Schumpeter in holding to this view.

A prominent cycle dating methodology in the Schumpeter tradition and in that of the NBER was advocated by John R. Meyer, a former president of the NBER, and Daniel H. Weinberg. Their four-stage taxonomy for phase classification of business cycles includes recession, recovery, demand-pull inflation, and stagflation. Each phase was defined as follows:

1. *Recession.* A period of decline in aggregate activity lasting at least one year with widely diffused effects on the economy.

2. *Recovery.* The rebound period in economic activity characterized by relatively stable prices, expanding output, and productivity gains.

3. *Demand-Pull Inflation.* A period during the expansion whereby capacity constraints result in rising prices and declining productivity.

4. *Stagflation.* A period when growth slows considerably but inflation remains relatively high.[12]

Meyer and Weinberg used discriminant analysis, a statistical classification technique, to develop their cycle chronology for the period 1947 to 1973. Table 1.3 shows the results. First, their recession and recovery dates tend

Table 1.3   Meyer and Weinberg Classification of Cycle Experience.

Phase	Description	Starting Date
IV	Stagflation	May 1948
I	Recession	Dec. 1948
II	Recovery	Nov. 1949
III	Demand-Pull	July 1950
IV	Stagflation	Jan. 1951
I	Recession	Nov. 1953
II	Recovery	Aug. 1954
III	Demand-Pull	Mar. 1955
IV	Stagflation	—
I	Recession	Sept. 1957
II	Recovery	May 1958
III	Demand-Pull	—
IV	Stagflation	—
I	Recession	June 1960
II	Recovery	Feb. 1961
III	Demand-Pull	May 1965
IV	Stagflation	Dec. 1967
I	Recession	Jan. 1970
II	Recovery	Dec. 1970
III	Demand-Pull	Jan. 1973

Source: National Bureau of Economic Research 55th Annual Report, New York, p. 3, September 1975.

to lag the NBER/Commerce Department dates by a month to as much as 4 months, but this is not significantly different. More importantly, the demand-pull and stagflation periods did not always exist over this historical period. They argue the reason these phases may or may not exist is tied to government monetary and fiscal policy. Although their point may be valid, it nonetheless calls into question the advantage of their cycle taxonomy. In fact, they concluded:

> Classification is, of course, simply a reflection of the current status of many different series and variables that one might expect those making policy decisions to scrutinize. Given the ambiguities of translating these data into a taxonomy, the policymaker would seem well advised to go back to the primary sources instead of relying on any secondary classification derived from these underlying data. The moral is surely obvious: An aggregate label of the economy as being in a recession or not in recession really does not convey all that much information. The policymaker, with a variety of different policy options at his disposal, must go beneath simple dichotomous labels to determine a sensible selection from these options.[13]

While these researchers tended to be negative on the entire approach except for historical analysis, they missed an important point—policy can be tied to the stage of the cycle in a quantifiable manner. Recognition of the business cycle phase can be determined by examining a market basket of economic indicators. If, as a group, these indicators begin to signal a recession, government policy-makers may be able to avert it or lessen its effect. Similarly, investment policy during recessions can differ greatly from that during expansions. So, classification can be important for understanding and responding to economic change.

To quickly recognize the stage of the cycle, one alternative is to rely on a single broadly based measure of activity in which a reference business cycle can be tracked. In August 1960, the Japanese government's Economic Planning Agency (EPA) selected this approach. They constructed a single measure of the breadth of the cycle using a cumulative diffusion indicator. Later, the construction of this type of measure will be discussed, but for now it is more important to understand that this is a different idea for selecting turning points and knowing when you have reached one. Figure 1.3 shows the EPA business cycle peaks and troughs as measured by their cumulative diffusion index. This index comprises 11 components:[14]

1. Index of industrial production.
2. Index of producer's shipments.
3. Index of capacity utilization ratio.
4. Index of consumption of raw materials.
5. Electric power consumption of large users.
6. Quantum index of imports.
7. Construction started, floor space.
8. Ratio of job offers to applicants.
9. Sales at department stores.
10. Net profits.
11. Sales of small and medium-size enterprises.

The Japanese EPA approach for selecting turning points in the business cycle is very objective or mechanical (a slowdown begins when the monthly diffusion index increases by less than 50%, which means that less than half of the composite indicators are expanding) as opposed to the NBER approach, which dates the reference cycle in terms of a whole set of indicators weighing each judgmentally and deciding by committee on the turning point dates about 6 months after the fact.

Another variant for dating cycles is the Australian Deviation Cycle approach, which is a cross between the Japanese EPA method and the NBER

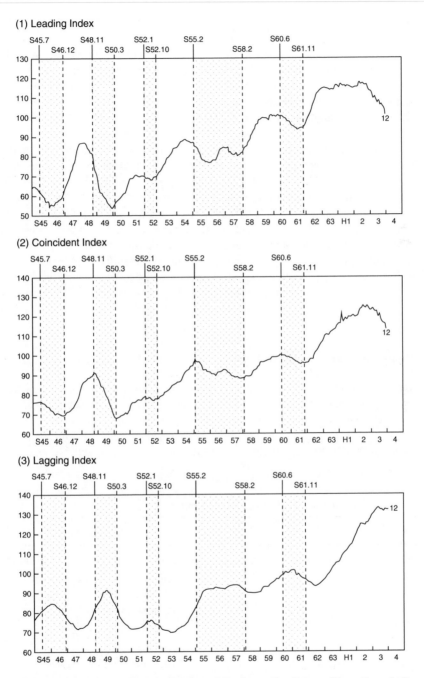

Figure 1.3 Japanese Diffusion Indexes of Business Conditions (Data through December 1991). "S45" corresponds to 1970, or the 45th year of the emperor; similarly, "H1" corresponds to the first year of the new emperor, or 1989. (*Source:* Economic Planning Agency, Japanese government, February 1992.)

growth cycle method. The Australian approach measures the deviation cycle with 52 indicators covering industrial production, money and credit, domestic activity, foreign trade, employment, and government activity. It uses the same methodology as the growth cycle approach but derives the reference cycle index by dating highs and lows in a composite index of these 52 indicators after they are individually trend adjusted. This method is objective and broad based but may be less timely than the EPA method because the calculation of the growth cycle extrapolates a trend that may not be accurate once the data become available. Therefore, this cycle dating technique requires a passage of time before dates can accurately be determined.

To summarize, we have discussed five methods for selecting business cycle dates, as shown in Table 1.4. Each method has strengths and weaknesses but each also characterizes stages of economic change. In and of themselves, these dates are meaningless; they become useful only when analysis of various stage activity is examined and compared. Although every business cycle is unique, there are, nonetheless, many similarities in the cyclical fluctuation of underlying components within the economy. A knowledge of these similarities and differences helps in monitoring and forecasting the business cycle.

Measuring Business Cycle Time

Implicit in the previous discussion of business cycle turning points is a view that dividing the cycle into recession and expansion phases provides more insight into how the economy operates than simply looking at economic time series over calendar periods. This also is the perspective of subsequent chapters. Yet, there are critics of this Burns and Mitchell, or traditional NBER, approach. For example,

Table 1.4 Various Cycle Dating Methodologies.

Approach	Critical Points
Burns and Mitchell (classical cycles)	Peaks and troughs in absolute levels
Growth cycles	High and low points in trend-adjusted cycle
Schumpeter	Equilibrium points
Japanese EPA	50% of composite expanding, on a monthly basis
Australian Deviation Cycles	High and low growth rates
Meyer and Weinberg	Peaks and troughs in real and price sectors

Irving Fisher stated that he saw "no reason to believe in the business cycle. It is simply a fluctuation about its own mean. And yet the cycle idea is supposed to have more content than mere variability."[15] Sargent[16] who measured and defined the business cycle using a statistical method known as spectral analysis, concluded that most economic time series did not display the typical pattern that would be consistent with the conventional or NBER definition of the business cycle. However, Sargent cautioned that this lack of the expected spectral pattern within economic time series should not necessarily imply the absence of a business cycle. But Stock[17] forcefully argued:

> "[T]here is strong evidence that the aggregate [economic] variables evolve on an economic time scale other than business cycle or calendar times. The two key variables determining these time scales are the rate of interest and the growth rate of GNP: when interest rates are high and GNP growth is strong, economic time appears to 'speed up.'[18]

The Stock conclusion, based on his statistical "deformation" model, provided strong criticism of the NBER chronology. Therefore, before proceeding, it is essential to ask; Is there information in dividing the business cycle into recession and expansion phases?

As shown in Table 1.5, the average growth rate in real GNP is quite distinct between recessions and expansions. To examine this issue formally, however, the Wilcoxon two-sample statistical test will be applied. The null hypothesis to be tested is that the business cycle periods—marked off by the NBER's peak and trough dates—have statistically similar average values.[19] Accepting that hypothesis would lead to rejecting the usefulness of the NBER's recession and expansion periods. Fortunately, the Wilcoxon test provides a statistical justification for using the business cycle as a measure of economic time and for rejecting the Stock assertion.

Although the result of this statistical test supports distinguishing recession from expansion periods using the traditional NBER criteria, the Stock research raises a second question. Stock suggested that additional delineation of recession and expansion into *growth phases* (also known as NBER or Burns and Mitchell's *business cycle stages*) does not provide any meaningful information. To test this claim, the Wilcoxon statistical test again was applied to the stages of the business cycle. (For more details on how to determine business cycle stages using the Burns and Mitchell methodology and the logic, see Chapter 3.) The question addressed was, Does real GNP growth show statistically distinctive growth rates over the course of these business cycle stages?

The Wilcoxon statistical test was far less supportive of the usefulness in dividing the business cycle into the traditional NBER business cycle stages, which conceptually measure the internal growth dynamic within the business cycle.

Table 1.5   Real GNP Changes over the Business Cycle (Average % Change over Recession and Expansion Periods).

Recession Beginning	Average Real GNP % Change per Quarter
1948	−0.9%
1953	−1.6
1957	−2.4
1960	0
1969	−0.6
1973	−2.3
1980	−1.6
1981	−1.8

Expansion Beginning	Average Real GNP % Change per Quarter
1950	+8.5%
1954	+3.5
1958	+5.9
1961	+4.6
1971	+4.8
1975	+4.2
1980	+3.9

The real problem, however, in subdividing the business cycle into growth phases is that the NBER method is implemented using calendar rules (e.g., one-third of the expansion duration falls into the first stage of the business cycle expansion). These rules divide the expansion and recession phases into business cycle stages as a proxy for differing growth phases (i.e., the concern is primarily between stages II through IV and stages VI and VIII of the traditional NBER nine stages of the business cycle). Hence, the conclusion from the Wilcoxon test was that further division of the business cycle into supposed growth rate phases using calendar rules would fall short of its goal at least for real GNP. Therefore, examining growth rates over the stages of the cycle only should be suggestive of how the cycle unfolds and not necessarily representative of the "true" nature of the individual growth cycle phases. Yet, with a recognition of this limitation, business cycle stage analysis still can be helpful in understanding the cycle.[20]

To be sure, the NBER chronology has its limitations, but examining the business cycle using the NBER-defined recession and expansion phases can be informative; and conceptually, further division of the cycle into growth phases can help shed light on the business cycle dynamic.

FIVE TYPES OF CYCLES

Cycles exist throughout many aspects of business activity. Some cycles are of short duration such as the 2- to 4-year inventory cycles, whereas other cycles, such as those tied to demographic swings, unfold over longer periods of time. The specific nature of the activity determines the duration of the cycle. In this section, five types of cycles will be explored. Each of these represents specific cycles that may or may not be pervasive enough to cause business or growth cycles. Furthermore, even if these activities have such a potential, they may or may not influence any given business cycle. The five types of cycles are:

1. Agricultural or Cobweb Cycles.
2. Inventory or Kitchin Cycles.
3. Fixed Investment or Juglar Cycles.
4. Building or Kuznets Cycles.
5. Kondratieff (Kondratyev) Cycles.

Agricultural Cycles

Probably the best-known sector cycle in economics is the classic agricultural commodity cycle. This type of fluctuation followed what Nicholas Kaldor called the *cobweb pattern,* which is discussed further in Chapter 2. Additional theoretical work was done by Mordecai Ezekiel on this type of pattern, and it is his name that is most often associated with this cyclical process. The theory suggests that regular fluctuations occur in agricultural production because (1) the following period's production is determined by current or past prices, and (2) the current price is determined by current production. Conceptually, the agricultural cycle can be triggered by a drought or any other natural disaster at home or abroad that would reduce supply and raise the price of the commodity. In turn, the high price would cause producers to increase production in the subsequent period, which then would cause the price to fall, and thus the process would go on. The length of this cycle, again conceptually, is determined by the time required to produce a new generation of a crop or livestock.

Empirical work on the agricultural production cycle, however, found that the theoretical model does not fully capture the actual agricultural cycle. For example, the hog cycle is about four years long though a new generation of hogs can be produced in 12 months. Moreover, Tomek and Robinson argue that "the amplitude and length of livestock production cycles are by no means uniform . . . There has been more uniformity in the upward phase of the cycle than the downward phase. The upward phase is constrained biologically by the time it takes to produce more [animals, while] the downward or liquidation phases, in contrast, is determined by economics. It can be short or long, depending on price incentives."[21] Finally, those researchers also found that the cyclical behavior of agricultural prices was even more irregular than the production cycle.

Inventory Cycles

With the widespread application of computerized inventory control systems it might seem that inventory cycles should become less and less a problem in the future. Yet, at an NBER conference on business cycles held in March 1984, Alan Blinder and Douglas Holtz-Eakin reached the opposite conclusion. They observed that inventory fluctuations now are relatively more important to the economy than in earlier times because the other components of real output tend to be far less volatile.[22] This circumstance highlights the need to examine the inventory cycle.

In the 1920s, Joseph Kitchin, a British statistician, suggested that the business cycle (or the British term, the "trade cycle") can be viewed as consisting of two or three minor cycles that last about 40 months in duration and make up the major wave. Kitchin attributed these minor cycles to psychological reasons, but his theoretical explanation seemed insufficient. Interest in this minor cycle was renewed by Joseph Schumpeter who incorporated this Kitchin cycle into his theories. But the real interest grew out of research by Moses Abramowitz at the NBER in the late 1940s. Today, many economists consider the American business cycle to be essentially an inventory cycle—although this was not so before the 1940s.

Figure 1.4 shows the inventory cycle for the nonfarm sector of the U.S. economy. Using quarterly data, the turning point dates are given in Table 1.6. The average length of the inventory cycle between 1951 and 1991 was 28 months or 2.3 years. But what causes the fluctuation in the inventory cycle?

Many reasons have been suggested for holding inventories such as (1) to smooth production, (2) to produce more cost-effective lot sizes, (3) to buffer stock thereby preventing lost sales because of insufficient stock (a transaction motive), and (4) to take advantage of a lower price (speculative motive). But can this behavior be responsible for business cycles?

In 1941, Lloyd A. Metzler[23] offered some possible answers to this question. He developed a model of the inventory process. A simplified version of his model made the following assumptions: (1) The marginal propensity to consume is 0.6; (2) the system is in equilibrium, and the second period shows a exogenous increase in other investment; (3) income is the sum of production for expected sales and for inventory and other investment; and (4) current period desired inventories are equal to the difference between actual and expected sales in the preceding period. The key ideas derived from his example are (1) the cycle is damped, that is, total income approaches an equilibrium and remains there, and (2) inventories

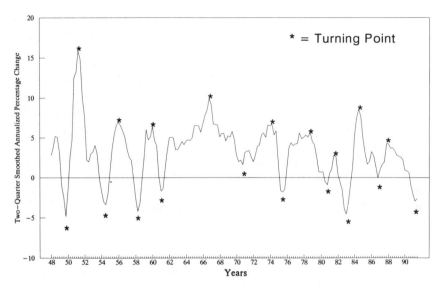

Figure 1.4 The Nonfarm Inventory Cycle.

Table 1.6 Cyclical Turning Points in the Inventory Cycle (Percentage Change in Nonfarm Inventories, Two-Quarter Smoothed Rate).

Peak		Trough		Duration	
				Quarters	Months
1951	2Q	1954	3Q	13	39
1956	1Q	1958	2Q	9	27
1960	1Q	1961	1Q	4	12
1966	4Q	1970	4Q	16	48
1974	2Q	1975	3Q	5	15
1978	4Q	1980	4Q	8	24
1981	3Q	1983	1Q	6	18
1984	3Q	1986	4Q	9	27
1987	4Q	1991	2Q	14	42
		Average		9.3	28
		Standard Deviation		3.9	11.8

lag behind income. A variant on the Metzler example is shown in Table 1.7. In this example, noninventory investment is held constant and the marginal propensity to consume, that is the share of each incremental dollar of income that is spent for goods and services, is 0.75. This produces a pronounced but stable cycle. Notice the following: The cyclical turning points in total income and sales are coincident with one another, inventory turns lag behind sales and income, and the inventory to sales ratio also lags turning points in income and sales as well as inventories. This example highlights some of the logic behind the actual selection of cyclical indicators by the Commerce Department.

In 1961, Klein and Popkin[24] argued that 75% of all business cycle fluctuation was from inventory swings and that the likelihood of future business cycles would be lowered if inventory swings could be controlled. As Blinder[25] noted, these inventory swings can have ripple effects on the rest of the economy. He observed

Table 1.7   A Variant on the Metzler Pure Inventory Model with a Marginal Propensity to Consume = 0.75.

Period	Production for		Other Investment	Total Income	Sales (actual)	Stock of Inventories	I/S Ratio
	Expected Sales	Inventories					
1	600	0	500	1100	825	1500	1.818
2	600	0	500	1100	825	1275	1.545
3	825	225	500	1550	1163	1163	1.000
4	1163	338	500	2000	1500	1163	.775
5	1500	338	500	2338	1753	1247	.711 T
6	1753	253	500	2506	1880	1373	.731
7	1880	127	500	2506 P	1880 P	1500	.798
8	1880	0	500	2380	1785	1595	.894
9	175	−95	500	2190	1642	1642	1.000
10	1642	−142	500	2000	1500	1642 P	1.095
11	1500	−142	500	1858	1393	1607	1.153
12	1393	−107	500	1786	1340	1553	1.159 P
13	1340	−53	500	1786 T	1340 T	1500	1.120
14	1340	0	500	1840	1380	1460	1.058
15	1380	40	500	1920	1440	1440	1.000
16	1440	60	500	2000	1500	1440 T	.960
17	1500	60	500	2060	1545	1455	.942 T
18	1545	45	500	2090	1568	1477	.943
19	1568	23	500	2090 P	1568 P	1500	.957
20	1568	0	500	2068	1551	1517	.978

P = Peak.
T = Trough.

from a review of Keynesian models that a slowing in the pace of inventory accumulation or an outright decumulation of final goods inventories is likely to depress the demand for labor. From an entirely different perspective, Hoagland, Buddress, and Heberling[26] argue that the source of that inventory fluctuation can be traced to purchasing managers' buying practices. They argue that a rational buying policy at firms could have a destabilizing macroeconomic impact by forcing industries to shift purchasing strategies from a "current need plus two months" additional supply to a "current need plus four months" supply. Reasons for this shift include supply shortages, potential strikes, and other types of shocks. In a more detailed discussion of how purchasing behavior could trigger an inventory cycle, Mather[27] provides a real-life example. Mather begins from the same perspective as does Hoagland et al., in hypothesizing that millions of inventory decisions, which are not necessarily tied to changes in demand, can trigger a pickup or decline in the new order flows. Two common buying systems used in business are order-point planning and material requirements planning, each of which has the potential to *cause* a cycle. Mather shows how buying decisions tied to delivery lead times can generate a cycle when a steady state order flow is either temporarily increased or decreased. He further argued that computerized buying systems will not necessarily moderate this inventory cycle and even have the potential of aggravating the problem. The Mather model provides a significant contribution to the understanding of the inventory cycle.

To demonstrate the Mather delivery lead-time model, consider the following example with the initial conditions:

Industry Capacity = 4 units per week

Industry Demand = 4 units per week

Initial Backlog = 12 units

Quoted Lead Time = 3 weeks

where production or supplier lead time is defined as backlog divided by capacity. In the second period, assume that the producer receives 4 new orders and can produce and ship to its capacity of 4 units. Hence, the lead time in period 2 remains at 3 weeks. But what if 5 new orders are received in period 3? Then during period 3, the following occurs:

Industry Capacity = 4 units per week

Period 3 Industry Demand = 5 units per week

Period 3 Backlog = 13 units

Quoted Lead Time = 4 weeks

where the new backlog is defined as the prior period's backlog (12 units) plus the difference between new orders and shipments (5 minus 4) and the quoted lead time then is 13 units divided by 4 units and expressed in full weeks—the industry practice is to round to the next integer. In week 4, however, business will unleash another week's worth of orders—now out to four weeks because of the increase in lead time. Assuming that the underlying demand holds at 4 units per week, then new orders have to be increased from 4 units to the current weekly need of 4 units plus another week's need of 4 units for a total increase of 8 new orders. While the underlying demand has not changed, *the order flow appears to have increased.* (However, orders per lead time remain constant.) In week 4, the new backlog becomes 13 units + (8 new orders − 4 shipments), or 17. As a result, the lead time increases to 17 units divided by 4 units and is quoted as 5 weeks.

Industry Capacity = 4 units per week

Period 4 Industry Demand = 8 units per week

Period 4 Backlog = 17 units

Quoted Lead Time = 5 weeks

In the subsequent week, more new orders again amplify the cycle. This process will continue until something changes the other conditions such as an increase in capacity. Once capacity is increased, this will burst the bubble and cause the lead times to decline; the order flow will then contract. The contraction in the orders in the current week is solely an adjustment for shorter lead times and not a change in underlying demand. The contraction also feeds on itself as the lead time is adjusted downward week after week. Mather then concludes: "[B]y itself the lead-time syndrome is a critical disturber of the industrial sector of our economy. But because of its ramifications, lead time is a major contributor to the amplification of small real-demand changes into large, but largely false, changes in order-flow rates and backlogs."[28]

Although inventory swings contribute to the business cycle, it still has not been established whether these swings are the sole cause of the business cycle or just a result of it. It is our contention, however, that the evidence is more supportive of the inventory cycle being a result of final demand changes and not a catalyst in and of itself. Nevertheless, the inventory cycle can and often does help to determine the overall amplitude of business cycle fluctuations.

The Fixed Investment Cycle

Fixed investment (business expenditures on equipment and structures) has a longer life span than inventories and consequently, a longer cycle duration.

Before World War II, the fixed investment cycle varied from 7 to 11 years and was considered the main influence for the business cycle. This type of cycle was named after Clement Juglar (1819–1905), a French physician who was one of the first to examine a cycle of that length. Yet, Juglar's insights and work in this area in the late nineteenth century contributed little to the theory of the investment cycle. Juglar's contribution is that ever since he "definitely established the existence of wave-like movements which pervade economic life within the institutional framework of capitalist society, the work of finding, linking-up, measuring relevant fact, has been steadily progressing."[29]

Table 1.8 presents two chronologies, one by Joseph Schumpeter and the other by Burns and Mitchell, of the prewar Juglar cycle. The cycle's relatively stable duration led Schumpeter to posit that every Juglar cycle he had observed was divisible into three shorter business cycles. Burns and Mitchell examined the Schumpeter hypothesis and rejected it, arguing instead that the duration of Juglar cycles generally could not be viewed as a triplet of business cycles.

Have fixed investment cycles persisted into the postwar period? Empirical evidence suggests that investment cycles are still very much alive. However, the dating and definition of this type of cycle vary widely. For example, Robert J. Gordon and John M. Veitch, in an article entitled "Fixed Investment in the American Business Cycle, 1919–1983," defined investment as private expenditures on durable goods, equipment, and structures.[30] This is a nontraditional definition because it added consumer durable goods to the traditional concept. These economists reasoned that because consumer durable goods have an extended life span similar to business fixed investment, they should follow the same economic stimuli. However, van Duijn[31] narrowly defined investment as

Table 1.8   Pre-World War II Juglar Cycles in the United States.

Dates Assigned by Schumpeter			Dates Assigned by Burns and Mitchell			Business Cycles Occurring
Peak	Trough	Duration (Yrs)	Peak	Trough	Duration (Yrs)	
1848	1858	10	1848	1858	10	2
1858	1866	8	1858	1867	9	2
1866	1876	10	1867	1878	11	2
1876	1885	9	1878	1885	7	1
1885	1895	10	1885	1894	9	3
1895	1904	9	1894	1904	10	3
1904	1914	10	1904	1914	10	3
1914	1922	8	1914	1921	7	2
1922	1932	10	1921	1932	11	3

Source: Burns and Mitchell, 1946, p. 441.

producers' durable equipment (PDE). Using PDE data alone, he calculated the Juglar cycle as a deviation from trend in a 3-year moving average (to eliminate any short-term fluctuation). Updating his results suggested that between 1948 and 1991, there were five complete investment cycles (as measured from peak to peak or from trough to trough) with an average duration of about 7 years. These results are shown in Table 1.9.

However, with the use of a more comprehensive measure of investment, including both producers' durable equipment and nonresidential structures (which van Duijn would argue are part of the building cycle), and quarterly examination instead of annual data, the post-World War II investment cycle duration appears closer to 6 years with a range of 4 to 10 years. This conclusion seems to suggest a shorter investment cycle now exists than during the prewar period and provides even more evidence against the Schumpeter hypothesis that three business cycles were encompassed by one Juglar cycle. Table 1.10 shows the turning points in the investment cycle.

If a shorter investment cycle now exists as a stylized economic fact, then the question is, Why did the cycle length shorten in the postwar period? A possible reason is that the duration of the cycle can be influenced by government fiscal and monetary policy, which may have been more aggressive than in the past. A second possible reason is that information is much more quickly disseminated today. Businesses may jump on investment opportunities or technological advances faster than in the past, which could compress the duration of the cycle. Alternatively, more rapid improvement in technology could shorten the replacement cycle. In any event, the shorter nature of the investment cycle remains a phenomenon to be reckoned with.

Table 1.9   Juglar Cycles in the United States, 1948–1991 (Based on Real Producers' Durable Equipment).

Annual Turning Points			
Peak	Trough	Peak	Duration (Yrs)
1948	1955	1956	8
1956	1961	1967	11
1967	1971	1973	6
1973	1975	1978	5
1978	1982	1985	7
1985	1991ᵀ		—
		Average	7.4

Source: J. J. van Duijn, *The Long Wave in Economic Life*, George Allen & Unwin, London, 1983, p. 14. Updated by authors, 1975–1991.

T = Tentative.

Table 1.10 A More Traditional View of the Juglar Cycle (Based on Real Nonresidential Fixed Investment—Adjusted for Short-Term Cycles).

Peak		Trough		Peak		Total Duration (Qtrs)	P-T-P (Yrs)
1951	3Q	1952	3Q	1955	4Q	17	4.3
1955	4Q	1958	3Q	1966	1Q	41	10.3
1966	1Q	1971	3Q	1973	3Q	30	7.5
1973	3Q	1975	2Q	1978	2Q	19	4.8
1978	2Q	1983	1Q	1985	2Q	28	7.0
1985	2Q	1987	1Q	1989	3Q	17	4.3
1989	3Q	1991	2Q^T			—	—
				Average		25.3	6.3
				Standard Deviation		8.7	2.2

Note: These dates are based on the deviation from a 12-quarter (3-year) moving average of total business fixed investment in inflation-adjusted terms. This is consistent with the van Duijn methodology. The last date for 1991 is tentative.

The Building Cycle

The building, or Kuznets, cycle is both a long-term and short-term phenomenon. The short-term fluctuation is tied to the credit markets, whereas the long-term wave is primarily a function of demographics. Because Simon Kuznets was the first person to examine this long building cycle in the United States, his name often is associated with this construction activity. But, research on this type of fluctuation dates from an 1881 German study by Conrad. Gottlieb in describing the Conrad study noted:

> This wavelike tendency was traced back to the eighteenth century by Conrad, who studied the city of Freiburg for twenty selected years from 1755 to 1875. He found that waves in the rate of growth of population and of buildings tended to be about thirty years in length, whereas the rate of change in prices was about half that length, but of greater intensity.[32]

The basic logic for this specific cycle has not changed. Easterlin formulated a model for the Kuznets cycle: During prosperous economic times the demand for labor increases, which puts upward pressure on wages. In turn, the improved economic environment causes an increase in new family formations, sparking the demand for new housing units. This then boosts the nation's output some more, and the process begins again. Unfortunately, the dating of this cycle seems more controversial than the logic for the building cycle.

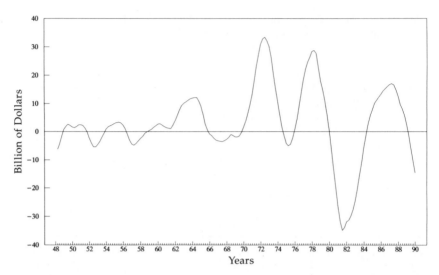

Figure 1.5   Residential Investment Cycle. Deviation from Trend—Growth in Real Investment.

Figure 1.5 portrays the cycle in residential investment adjusted for trend growth and smoothed by a 3-year (12-quarter) centered moving average used to remove the effect of the short-term cycle. van Duijn argues that both residential and nonresidential structures should be included in the building cycle concept, but it is unclear why industrial and commercial buildings necessarily coincide with any demographic development except through a lagged output effect. Burns and Mitchell observed that the long building cycle is characterized by a regular duration, and Dauten and Valentine[33] and van Duijn calculate the average length of the Kuznets cycle (1861–1975) measured from trough to trough or peak to peak to be about 16 years while Klotz and Neal[34] confirm this using spectral analysis. Figure 1.5 however, does not visually confirm a 16-year cycle. Too much of the short cycle effect is still present in these data making the results difficult to prove heuristically.

Nonetheless, the usefulness of examining the building cycle is unquestionable. Witten[35] applied a cycle framework to understand the residential real estate market. He argued that knowing the phase of the real estate cycle gives the real estate professional an important investment edge—timing. Witten divides the building cycle into four phases: (1) development, (2) overbuilding, (3) adjustment, and (4) acquisition. To distinguish each phase, he suggested monitoring a "supply" and "demand" cycle, as represented by home sales (which represent the demand side of the market) and housing starts (which represent the upcoming supply of new homes).

In the *development stage* of the building cycle, demand picks up and an increase in housing starts follows. This phase, characterized by low vacancy rates and rising rents, reaches maturity after about 3 to 5 years; a signal of this turning point is the aggressive bidding up of land prices. When housing starts consistently outpace home sales (in some smoothed basis), this is a signal of the *overbuilding* stage. The *adjustment* phase of the cycle occurs when builders react to the declining demand and curtail housing starts. When this occurs, occupancy rates slip further and rental concessions are commonplace. Builder pessimism is generally high. Finally, the *acquisition* phase of the cycle occurs when starts continue to decline while home sales firm. In the acquisition phase, pessimism is still high and building activity is reduced further, although vacancy rates have peaked and rent concessions have ceased. Witten argued that a separate investment strategy should be tailored to each phase of that cycle. His approach is a popular application of the research on the building cycle.

The Kondratieff Cycle

Nikolai Dmitriyevich Kondratyev, or Kondratieff, is noted for his studies on the long wave, which he claimed had a duration of between 45 and 60 years. Kondratieff is considered one of the first to study the long wave, but earlier work on the long cycle was done by Schumpeter in 1911 and by a Dutch economist named J. van Gelderen (using the pen name "J. Fedder") in 1913. Wesley Mitchell in his review of the early work on long duration cycles wrote:

> A [Dutch] compatriot, S. de Wolff, confirmed van Gelderen's results in 1924 by the use of more technical statistical analysis. Meanwhile the Russian investigator, N. D. Kondratieff, had developed the same idea independently in 1922. Not content with his first results, Kondratieff collected and analyzed all the time series he could find which covered long periods. The results of his work, which agree substantially with those of van Gelderen and de Wolff, were published in Russian in 1925.[36]

Today, the long wave is as controversial an idea as when Kondratieff proposed it in Russia as an explanation of capitalist economic development. Kondratieff never set forth any theory for the long wave, and his Russian colleagues were critical of his long wave idea at that time, in part because of this lack of theory (but they were more critical because it did not fit well with Marxist doctrine). Although Kondratieff cited several empirical characteristics of his long wave, the most relevant observation for subsequent theoretical work was that "during the recession of the long waves, an especially large number of important discoveries and inventions in the technique of production and communication are made, which, however, are usually applied on a large scale only at the beginning of the next long upswing."[37]

This observation led to a theoretical explanation of the long wave—yet, it was never made by Kondratieff. Others including Joseph Schumpeter, W. W. Rostow, George Ray, and Jacob van Duijn all have developed this *innovation theory* of the long wave. Unfortunately, most empirical evidence does not support the long wave lasting about 50 years and resulting from a clustering of innovation. For example, Edwin Mansfield observed: "Although it is likely that some clustering occurs in the number of innovations, the evidence supporting the view that well-defined clusters occur every forty to sixty years seems limited and open to serious criticism. . . . The hypothesis that severe depressions trigger and accelerate innovations is also questionable."[38]

Without categorically trying to resolve this issue of the existence of the long wave, it is worth simply examining the data for the U.S. gross national product (GNP) with the effects of inflation removed. These data are shown in Table 1.11 for the period 1909 through 1984. Even if a 9-year centered moving average of the data is calculated, as Kondratieff suggested, it is difficult to see a pronounced long wave in this data over this period. Granted, if the cycle searched for is as long as 60 years, it is unlikely to be clearly spotted with such a short span of data. However, the long wave turning point dates found by several authors (see Table 1.12) would suggest that a cycle low should be observable, at least in the 9-year moving average, somewhere between 1938 and 1948 and a cycle high should be seen between 1968 and 1973. If anything—and it is quite questionable—a long-wave peak occurred in 1939 and maybe a low in 1978 (a 39-year cycle?). But these observations contradict the basic tenets of the long wave view that a low point in the wave occurred around the 1940s and not a high as these data suggest. A major problem with most of these chronologies of the Kondratieff cycle between the 1700s and early 1900s is that they were based on price movements and not on real output as most analysts tend to view the state of the economy today. Thus, if the long cycle exists in price movements, it does not necessarily imply that a long cycle exists in physical volume measures. Even so, the long wave in prices also seems implausible based on the data in Table 1.13 for the implicit price deflator. Table 1.13 presents the price cycles in the raw price series, in the 9-year moving average growth, and finally in the price cycle adjusted for population, which is a proxy for the cost per capita. These price data also provide insufficient evidence of a long cycle in inflation. Finally, it also has been argued from a methodology standpoint that the use of moving averages could introduce a cycle of a predetermined periodicity where none really exists. This is known as the Slutsky–Yule effect, and although it should not be viewed as rejecting the use of moving averages, it does highlight a potential bias in some empirical results.

So what can be concluded? Unfortunately, this cursory review cannot settle the issue of the existence of the Kondratieff wave. A formal statistical analysis, however, was undertaken by Solomou[39] of Cambridge University. Solomou

Table 1.11 In Search of the Long Wave.

Year	Real GNP (Bil. $)	% Change	Nine-Year Moving Average	% Change	Growth minus 3.0%	Population (Million)	GNP per Capita (c.1/c.6)	GNP per Cap. Sm. (c.3/c.6)	% Change	Possible Long Wave Turns
1909	180.4	—	—	—	—	90.6	199.1	—	—	
1910	185.6	2.9	—	—	—	92.2	201.2	—	—	
1911	191.4	3.1	—	—	—	93.6	204.5	—	—	
1912	200.9	5.0	—	—	—	95.0	211.5	—	—	
1913	202.9	1.0	196.4	—	—	96.4	210.6	203.8	—	
1914	195.5	−3.6	203.3	3.5	.5	97.7	200.0	208.0	3.5	
1915	192.9	−1.3	208.0	2.3	−.7	99.1	194.6	209.8	2.3	
1916	207.3	7.5	210.5	1.2	−1.8	100.5	206.3	209.4	1.2	
1917	210.6	1.6	210.2	−.1	−3.1	101.9	206.7	206.4	−.1	
1918	243.0	15.4	213.1	1.4	−1.6	103.3	235.3	206.4	1.4	
1919	227.6	−6.3	219.5	3.0	.0	104.6	217.5	209.8	3.0	
1920	213.4	−6.2	226.5	3.2	.2	106.0	201.3	213.6	3.2	
1921	199.0	−6.7	234.1	3.3	.3	107.8	184.7	217.2	3.3	
1922	228.7	14.9	243.0	3.8	.8	109.5	208.8	221.9	3.8	
1923	253.4	10.8	248.5	2.3	−.7	111.3	227.7	223.3	2.3	
1924	255.6	.9	256.0	3.0	0	113.0	226.2	226.5	3.0	
1925	275.2	7.7	267.3	4.4	1.4	114.8	239.8	232.9	4.4	
1926	290.9	5.7	277.0	3.6	.6	116.5	249.7	237.7	3.6	
1927	292.3	.5	280.8	1.4	−1.6	118.3	247.2	237.4	1.4	
1928	295.2	1.0	277.9	−1.0	−4.0	120.0	246.0	231.5	−1.0	
1929	315.7	6.9	274.2	−1.3	−4.3	121.8	259.3	225.2	−1.3	
1930	285.6	−9.5	270.2	−1.5	−4.5	123.2	231.8	219.3	−1.5	Low?
1931	263.5	−7.7	266.7	−1.3	−4.3	124.1	212.2	214.8	−1.3	
1932	227.1	−13.8	267.1	.1	−2.9	124.9	181.8	213.8	.1	

Table 1.11 (*Continued*)

Year	Real GNP (Bil. $)	% Change	Nine-Year Moving Average	% Change	Growth minus 3.0%	Population (Million)	GNP per Capita (c.1/c.6)	GNP per Cap. Sm. (c.3/c.6)	% Change	Possible Long Wave Turns
1933	222.1	-2.2	268.8	.6	-2.4	125.7	176.7	213.8	.6	
1934	239.1	7.7	266.6	-.8	-3.8	126.5	189.0	210.8	-.8	
1935	260.0	8.7	270.4	1.4	-1.6	127.4	204.1	212.3	1.4	
1936	295.5	13.7	279.4	3.3	.3	128.2	230.5	218.0	3.3	
1937	310.2	5.0	298.7	6.9	3.9	129.0	240.5	231.6	6.9	
1938	296.7	-4.4	325.3	8.9	5.9	130.0	228.3	250.3	8.9	
1939	319.8	7.8	357.8	10.0	7.0	131.0	244.1	273.1	10.0	High?
1940	344.1	7.6	392.1	9.6	6.6	132.6	259.5	295.7	9.6	
1941	400.4	16.4	421.6	7.5	4.5	133.9	299.0	314.8	7.5	
1942	461.7	15.3	440.2	4.4	1.4	135.4	341.1	325.2	4.4	
1943	531.6	15.1	459.5	4.4	1.4	137.3	387.3	334.8	4.4	
1944	569.1	7.1	478.4	4.1	1.1	138.9	409.7	344.4	4.1	
1945	560.4	-1.5	494.9	3.4	.4	140.5	399.0	352.3	3.4	
1946	478.3	-14.7	509.8	3.0	.0	141.9	337.0	359.2	3.0	
1947	470.3	-1.7	522.9	2.6	-.4	144.7	325.0	361.4	2.6	
1948	489.8	4.1	530.6	1.5	-1.5	147.2	332.7	360.4	1.5	
1949	492.2	.5	536.6	1.1	-1.9	149.8	328.6	358.3	1.1	Low?
1950	534.8	8.7	542.8	1.2	-1.8	152.3	351.2	356.5	1.2	
1951	579.4	8.3	562.7	3.7	.7	154.9	374.1	363.3	3.7	
1952	600.8	3.7	585.1	4.0	1.0	157.6	381.3	371.4	4.0	
1953	623.6	3.8	606.6	3.7	.7	160.2	389.3	378.7	3.7	
1954	616.1	-1.2	627.6	3.5	.5	163.0	377.9	385.0	3.5	
1955	657.5	6.7	648.4	3.3	.3	165.9	396.2	390.8	3.3	
1956	671.6	2.1	665.9	2.7	-.3	168.9	397.6	394.3	2.7	

Year										High?/Low?
1957	683.8	1.8	683.2	2.6	-.4	172.0	397.6	397.3	2.6	
1958	680.9	-.4	702.9	2.9	-.1	174.9	389.3	401.9	2.9	
1959	721.7	6.0	726.9	3.4	.4	177.8	405.8	408.8	3.4	
1960	737.2	2.1	751.2	3.3	.3	180.7	408.0	415.8	3.3	
1961	756.6	2.6	779.9	3.8	.8	183.7	411.9	424.5	3.8	
1962	800.3	5.8	813.3	4.3	1.3	186.5	429.0	436.0	4.3	
1963	832.5	4.0	850.0	4.5	1.5	189.2	439.9	449.2	4.5	High?
1964	876.4	5.3	887.4	4.4	1.4	191.9	456.7	462.5	4.4	
1965	929.3	6.0	926.3	4.4	1.4	194.3	478.3	476.7	4.4	
1966	984.8	6.0	962.9	3.9	.9	196.6	501.0	489.9	3.9	
1967	1,011.4	2.7	998.7	3.7	.7	198.7	509.0	502.6	3.7	
1968	1,058.1	4.6	1,037.9	3.9	.9	200.7	527.2	517.1	3.9	
1969	1,087.6	2.8	1,079.9	4.0	1.0	202.7	536.6	532.8	4.0	
1970	1,085.6	-.2	1,115.2	3.3	.3	205.1	529.4	543.8	3.3	
1971	1,122.4	3.4	1,142.6	2.5	-.5	207.7	540.5	550.2	2.5	
1972	1,185.9	5.7	1,174.4	2.8	-.2	209.9	565.0	559.5	2.8	
1973	1,254.3	5.8	1,209.1	2.9	-.1	211.9	591.9	570.6	2.9	
1974	1,246.3	-.6	1,248.1	3.2	.2	213.9	582.8	583.6	3.2	
1975	1,231.6	-1.2	1,291.8	3.5	.5	216.0	570.3	598.1	3.5	
1976	1,298.2	5.4	1,331.0	3.0	.0	218.0	595.4	610.5	3.0	
1977	1,369.7	5.5	1,367.3	2.7	-.3	220.2	621.9	620.8	2.7	
1978	1,438.6	5.0	1,392.3	1.8	-1.2	222.6	646.3	625.5	1.8	Low?
1979	1,479.4	2.8	1,424.4	2.3	-.7	225.1	657.4	632.9	2.3	
1980	1,475.0	-.3	1,469.7	3.2	.2	227.7	647.7	645.3	3.2	
1981	1,512.2	2.5	—	—	—	230.0	657.4	—	—	
1982	1,480.0	-2.1	—	—	—	232.3	637.0	—	—	
1983	1,534.7	3.7	—	—	—	234.5	654.4	—	—	
1984	1,639.3	6.8	—	—	—	236.7	692.6	—	—	

Table 1.12 Kondratieff Chronologies Based on Various Studies.

	Lower	Upper	Lower	Upper	Lower	Upper	Lower	Upper
Kondratieff (1926)	ca. 1790	1810–1817	1844–1851	1870–1875	1890–1896	1914–1920		
De Wolff (1929)	—	1825	1849–1850	1873–1874	1896	1913		
Von Ciriacy-Wantrup (1936)	1792	1815	1842	1873	1895	1913		
Schumpeter (1939)	1787	1813–1814	1842–1843	1869–1870	1897–1898	1924–1925		
Clark (1944)	—	—	1850	1875	1900	1929		
Dupriez (1947; 1978)	1789–1792	1808–1814	1846–1851	1872–1873	1895–1896	1920	1939–1946	1974
Madison (1977)	—	—	—	—	1870	1913	1950	1970
Rostow (1978)	1790	1815	1848	1873	1896	1920	1935	1951
Kahn (1979)	—	—	—	—	1885	1913	1947	1973
Mandel (1980)	—	1826	1847	1873	1893	1913	1939–1948	1967
van Duijn (1983)	—	—	1845	1872	1892	1929	1948	1973

Source: J. J. van Duijn (1983), *The Long Wave in Economic Life*, London: George Allen & Unwin, p. 163.

Table 1.13   In Search of the Long Price Wave.

Year	GNP Deflator 1972 = 100	% Change	Nine-Year Moving Average	% Change	Population (Million)	Cost per Capita Smoothed (c.3/c.5)	% Change
1909	18.5	—	—	—	90.6	—	—
1910	19.1	3.2	—	—	92.2	—	—
1911	18.7	-2.1	—	—	93.6	—	—
1912	19.6	4.8	—	—	95.0	—	—
1913	19.5	-.5	20.9	6.9	96.4	21.7	5.4
1914	19.7	1.0	22.3	8.9	97.7	22.8	7.4
1915	20.7	5.1	24.3	11.1—High	99.1	24.5	9.5—High
1916	23.3	12.6	27.0	6.3	100.5	26.8	4.9
1917	28.7	23.2—High	28.7	5.0	101.9	28.2	3.6
1918	31.4	9.4	30.1	5.2	103.3	29.2	3.8
1919	37.0	17.8	31.7	4.4	104.6	30.3	3.0
1920	42.9	15.9	33.1	3.6	106.0	31.2	1.9
1921	35.0	-18.4—Low	34.2	1.5	107.8	31.8	-.1
1922	32.4	-7.4	34.8	.4	109.5	31.7	-1.2
1923	33.7	4.0	34.9	-1.3	111.3	31.4	-2.8
1924	33.2	-1.5	34.4	-3.3—Low	113.0	30.5	-4.7—Low
1925	33.9	2.1	33.3	-1.1	114.8	29.0	-2.6
1926	33.4	-1.5	32.9	-1.2	116.5	28.3	-2.7
1927	32.5	-2.7	32.6	-2.7	118.3	27.5	-4.2
1928	32.9	1.2	31.7	-2.8	120.0	26.4	-4.2
1929	32.8	-.4	30.8	-2.4	121.8	25.3	-3.5
1930	31.8	-3.1	30.0	-2.0	123.2	24.4	-2.8
1931	28.9	-9.1	29.4		124.1	23.7	

Table 1.13 *(Continued)*

Year	GNP Deflator 1972 = 100	% Change	Nine-Year Moving Average	% Change	Population (Million)	Cost per Capita Smoothed (c.3/c.5)	% Change
1932	25.7	-11.1	28.9	-1.7	124.9	23.1	-2.3
1933	25.1	-2.1	28.5	-1.4	125.7	22.7	-2.0
1934	27.3	8.6	28.1	-1.6	126.5	22.2	-2.2
1935	27.9	2.1	27.7	-1.3	127.4	21.7	-2.0
1936	28.0	.4	27.7	.1	128.2	21.6	-.6
1937	29.3	4.6	28.3	2.2	129.0	22.0	1.6
1938	28.7	-2.2	29.4	3.6	130.0	22.6	2.8
1939	28.4	-.8	30.3	3.3	131.0	23.2	2.5
1940	29.1	2.2	31.4	3.3	132.6	23.6	2.1
1941	31.2	7.5	32.5	3.5	133.9	24.2	2.5
1942	34.3	9.9	34.1	5.0	135.4	25.2	3.9
1943	36.1	5.3	36.4	6.8	137.3	26.5	5.3
1944	37.0	2.4	39.1	7.5—High	138.9	28.2	6.2—High
1945	37.9	2.4	41.7	6.7	140.5	29.7	5.5
1946	43.9	15.7—High	44.2	5.9	141.9	31.1	4.9
1947	49.6	12.9	46.7	5.7	144.7	32.3	3.7
1948	53.0	6.9	49.2	5.2	147.2	33.4	3.4
1949	52.5	-.9	51.6	4.9	149.8	34.4	3.1
1950	53.6	2.0	54.0	4.7	152.3	35.5	2.9
1951	57.1	6.6	55.9	3.5	154.9	36.1	1.7
1952	57.9	1.5	57.3	2.6	157.6	36.4	.9
1953	58.8	1.6	58.7	2.3	160.2	36.6	.6
1954	59.6	1.2	60.2	2.6	163.0	36.9	.8

Year							
1955	60.8	2.2	61.7	2.6	165.9	37.2	.8
1956	62.8	3.2	63.0	2.1	168.9	37.3	.3
1957	64.9	3.4	64.3	2.0	172.0	37.4	.2
1958	66.0	1.7	65.6	2.0	174.9	37.5	.3
1959	67.6	2.4	66.9	2.1	177.8	37.6	.4
1960	68.7	1.6	68.3	2.0	180.7	37.8	.4
1961	69.3	.9—Low	69.6	1.9	183.7	37.9	.2—Low
1962	70.6	1.8	70.9	1.9—Low	186.5	38.0	.3
1963	71.7	1.5	72.3	2.0	189.2	38.2	.6
1964	72.8	1.5	74.0	2.3	191.9	38.6	.9
1965	74.4	2.2	76.0	2.7	194.3	39.1	1.4
1966	76.8	3.2	78.4	3.2	196.6	39.9	2.0
1967	79.1	3.0	81.3	3.6	198.7	40.9	2.5
1968	82.5	4.4	84.4	3.9	200.7	42.1	2.8
1969	86.8	5.1	88.1	4.3	202.7	43.5	3.3
1970	91.5	5.4	92.6	5.1	205.1	45.2	3.9
1971	96.0	5.0	98.1	5.9	207.7	47.2	4.6
1972	100.0	4.2	104.0	6.0	209.9	49.5	4.9
1973	105.8	5.8	110.4	6.1	211.9	52.1	5.1
1974	115.1	8.8	117.4	6.4	213.9	54.9	5.4
1975	125.8	9.3	125.4	6.8	216.0	58.1	5.8
1976	132.3	5.2	134.6	7.3	218.0	61.7	6.3
1977	140.1	5.8	145.2	7.9—High	220.2	65.9	6.8—High
1978	150.4	7.4	156.5	7.8	222.6	70.3	6.6
1979	163.4	8.6	167.6	7.1	225.1	74.5	5.9
1980	178.4	9.2	178.5	6.5	227.7	78.4	5.2
1981	195.6	9.6—High	—	—	230.0	—	—
1982	207.4	6.0	—	—	232.3	—	—
1983	215.3	3.8	—	—	234.5	—	—
1984	223.4	3.8	—	—	236.7	—	—

performed an exhaustive statistical analysis of production, productivity, investment, prices, and invention trends in the United States, England, Germany, and France. He found little evidence to support the Kondratieff wave. This study was quite thorough and tested a key statistical question: Given those turning point dates by various authors, is there evidence that the upswing and downswing periods of the alleged wave showed statistically different growth patterns? Solomou's research provided very damaging evidence against the existence of the Kondratieff wave. The author, however, believed there was evidence for a Kuznets cycle that researchers confused with the Kondratieff wave.

It is possible to reject the Kondratieff wave while still believing in a long cycle. In the next section, long wave views will be presented that blend cycles of different lengths.

LONG WAVES IN ECONOMIC DEVELOPMENT

In 1978, former Federal Reserve Chairman Paul Volcker said in a speech on the business cycle, "[W]e can . . . see in historical experience a pattern of relatively long periods of generally favorable economic conditions followed by deeper than average contractions and relatively sluggish recoveries."[40] This view represents a long-wave hypothesis; there are three schools of economic thought on the existence of long waves in economic activity. These approaches are (1) the Schumpeter school, (2) the Forrester school, and (3) the Mitchell-Burns school.

Each school incorporates a subset of the following five types of economic fluctuations discussed earlier: the Kondratieff, Kuznets, Juglar, Kitchin, and business cycle.

Schumpeter's Three-Cycle Schema

Joseph Schumpeter proposed a long-wave schema consisting of a short inventory cycle, that is, the Kitchin cycle, superimposed on an investment cycle (the Juglar cycle), which in turn forms the Kondratieff wave. His basic philosophy was, "[T]here is no ground to believe that there should be just one wave-like movement pervading economic life. On the contrary, it stands to reason that some processes covered by [Schumpeter's] concept of innovation must take much longer time than others to have a full effect.[41] Schumpeter's set of cycles were developed on this premise. Further, Schumpeter claimed, "[I]t is possible to count off, historically as well as statistically, six Juglars to a Kondratieff and three Kitchins to a Juglar—not as an average but in every individual case."[42] As noted earlier, further work at the National Bureau of Economic Research in the 1940s rejected this assertion of a rigid relationship.

Forrester's "System Dynamics"

More recent research in the 1970s by Jay W. Forrester approaches the long wave by hypothesizing that long-term economic development is the sum of three types of cycles: the business, Kuznets, and Kondratieff cycles. This idea is conceptually different from Schumpeter's notion of the set of cycles. Forrester posits instead that these three cycles are independent of one another and writes:

> The short-term business cycle can result from interactions between backlogs, inventories, production, and employment without requiring involvement of capital equipment. The Kuznets cycle is consistent with policies governing production and the acquisition of capital equipment. The fifty-year Kondratieff cycle can arise from the structural setting of the capital equipment sector, which supplies capital to the consumer goods sectors but also at the same time must procure its own input capital equipment from its own output.[43]

According to Forrester, the Kondratieff cycle is largely caused by a fluctuation in the capital stock of the country that is a result of overinvestment. Although this explanation is theoretically plausible, the empirical evidence seems sketchy as noted earlier.

Burns and Mitchell's "Cycle of Cycles"

Arthur F. Burns and Wesley C. Mitchell proposed a more promising view of the long wave that consisted of a sequence of cycles. This sequence has two phases—the industrial phase and the speculative phase. Burns and Mitchell described their view as follows: "After a severe depression industrial activity rebounds sharply, but speculation does not. The following contraction in business is mild, which leads people to be less cautious. So, in the next two or three cycles, while the cyclical advances become progressively smaller in industrial activity, they become progressively larger in speculative activity. Finally, the speculative boom collapses and a drastic liquidation follows, which ends this cycle of cycles and brings us back to the starting point.[44] During Dr. Burns's tenure as chairman of the Federal Reserve Board, he applied this reasoning to the 1961–1974 period. Burns characterized 1961 to 1965 as the industrial phase marked by productivity increases, an unemployment rate drop, and price stability. The period from 1965 to 1974 he called the speculative phase, marked by a wave of corporate mergers, a wave of speculation in real estate, greater stock market speculation, and a buildup in inventories. This idea of the long wave is interesting and flexible, and does not require a fixed length for this cycle of cycles.

Rostow's Stages of Long-Term Economic Growth

W. W. Rostow has formulated a classification system to summarize the phases of long waves in economic growth. His hypothesis, a worldwide extension of Schumpeter's own theory, is based on the interaction of several processes. The major interactions are the impact of leading sectors of economic activity, the relative profitability of producing foodstuffs and raw materials versus industrial goods, and waves of migration that are linked to investment in housing and infrastructure.[45] These factors tend to be catalysts for economic growth that Rostow suggests can be characterized by the following stages:

1. *Traditional Society.* A period in the economic activity limited by technology that also tends to be limited to the immediate region.

2. *Preconditions for Takeoff.* The occurrence of agricultural improvements and development of commerce.

3. *Takeoff.* Activity marked by rapid growth in limited areas.

4. *Drive to Maturity.* A diffusion of modern technology to many sectors of the economy.

5. *Age of High Mass Consumption.* A shift to consumer goods and services by the leading sectors of the economy.

6. *Search for Quality (or beyond Consumption).* An emphasis in the economy on quality over quantity.

Rostow's description of growth goes beyond the simple boom and slump cycle (though this is certainly part of it) and attempts to provide a far-reaching view of growth. Criticism of this view, however, centers on the realism of these stages and the usefulness of the description as a theory of growth.[46] Whether or not these stages exactly describe the typical sequences of growth over the long term, they challenge the business cycle forecaster to put current business activity into a historical context.

CYCLES AS A SEQUENCE OF CRISES

Throughout this chapter, we have discussed methods and techniques of dating turning points in *statistical cycles*. Wesley Mitchell was extremely influential in shaping the early foundations of that approach. Moreover, Mitchell's view of the business cycle was a distinct break with most cyclical analysis up until the early twentieth century. John Hicks[47] put this point into perspective when he argued, "[W]e need however to understand that the cycles, which Jevons [in the 1870s] and his immediate successors had in mind, were not the statistical cycles so well known to the modern economist."[48] Hicks further argued, "I want to insist that [the statistical cycle] is *not* what Jevons and his contemporaries can have had in mind; for the statistical apparatus of trend-fitting had not in their time come into use. They were thinking of the sequences of trade *crises* which had marked the preceding half-century."[49] Morgan echoed this observation[50] when she noted that during the first half of the twentieth century, "[C]ycle theories had been recast twice: The theory of crises had given way to the theory of business cycles and this in turn had given way to macroeconomic theory."[51] But those distinctions were and still are blurred. For example, in an interesting account of the U.S. postwar period, Wolfson[52] intertwined the theory of the business cycle with the theory of crisis. Wolfson argued that financial crises, which are sudden events, often occur after a business cycle peak. He developed a model along those lines to help explain the persistence of financial crises such as the collapse of the Bank of New England in 1991 and the stock market crash in 1987. Although this book's approach is along the lines of the business cycle, this should not be viewed as a limiting device for understanding business activity. As Wolfson has shown, the business cycle framework is flexible enough to incorporate other frameworks into it.

2 Business Cycle Theory

Even though we have convincing evidence that the major industrial market economies have suffered business fluctuations virtually without exception, since they industrialized, most efforts to develop business cycle theory have come in this century. (Some explanations emerged in the nineteenth century, from what Robert Heilbroner once called "the underworld of economics.")[1] We shall need to ask why possible explanations of business cycles were so slow in being proffered, particularly since we have dated business cycles in the United States back to 1790, in the United Kingdom back to 1792, in Germany back to 1866, and in France back to 1840.[2] But the mainstream of economic theorists developed classical economic theory by making at least two simplifying assumptions that precluded worrying very much about instability. First, they assumed that Say's law of markets was correct—that the process of producing output created the income necessary to purchase it. Second, they assumed that full employment of all resources was the economy's natural condition.

Taking these two assumptions at face value would suggest that the economy could never produce more than could be sold, and that what the economy produced would be determined by what full employment could turn out at any given time relative to the stage of technological development and the amount of resources—including human resources—that existed. So viewed, it would be difficult indeed to suffer instability. And in any case, whatever small perturbations the economy might experience would be short run and self-correcting—hardly requiring the development of an elaborate theory or interventionist policy.

One of Keynes's great insights was to assert that Say's law of markets could not really save the economy from instability, given the way competitive (flexible) prices work. While the market value of output would be equal to the income generated in its production, no automatic regulator guarantees that people in the economy would necessarily choose to buy what had been produced.[3]

Uncertainty about future sales is considered part of the justification of profits in a capitalist system. Entrepreneurs take chances. Moreover, the whole process of correctly coordinating increases in capacity of various lines of work with future demands is a vastly complicated affair and errors can easily occur. Many of the theories surveyed here emanate from essentially these problems in one form or another. Table 2.1 provides an outline of our classification of business cycle theories, along with the major economists associated with each theory. (We shall be discussing only representatives of each group.)

Before we begin our review of business cycle theories, we want to stress that we are not reviewing theories in order to pick a winner. Business cycle theories are not like beauty pageant contestants, where only one can win. Some of the theories are new, but some, we shall see, are quite old. The justification for looking at alternative explanations of instability must always be to try to increase our

Table 2.1   Classification of Business Cycle Theories.

I. Relatively simple unicausal theories
   A. Agricultural (W. S. Jevons, H. S. Jevons, H. L. Moore)
   B. Psychological (Mills, Pigou)
   C. Purely monetary (Hawtrey)

II. Business economy theories
   A. Price/cost relations, profit margins (Mitchell, Lescure)
   B. Inventory cycles (Abramowitz, Stanback)

III. Theories emphasizing the savings-investment process
   A. Pre-Keynesian
      1. Overinvestment
         a. Monetary (Wicksell, Hayek, Mises, Machlup, Robbins, Ropke, Strigel)
         b. Nonmonetary
            (1) Shortage of capital (Tugan-Baranowsky, Spiethoff, Cassel)
            (2) Innovation (Schumpeter)
      2. Underconsumption (Lauderdale, Malthus, Major, Douglas, Sismondi, Foster and Catchings, Lederer, Hobson)
      3. Marxian
   B. Keynesian
   C. Post-Keynesian
      1. Dynamic models
         a. Multiplier-accelerator interaction (J. M. Clark, Aftalion, Samuelson, Fellner)
         b. Growth-Cycle (Harrod, Hicks, Domar, Lundberg, Kalecki, Kaldor)
         c. Neo-Marxian (Sherman, Evans)
         d. Chaos (Baumol and Quandt, Brock and Sayers)

IV. New classical theories
   A. Monetarist (Friedman, Brunner, Meltzer, Schwartz, Cagan)
   B. "Real" business cycle (King, Ploesser, Walsh)
   C. "Supply side" (Laffer, Craig, et al.)
   D. Political business cycle (Kalecki, Nordhaus, MacRae, Meiselman)
   E. Rational expectations (Muth, Lucas, Sargent, Wallace, Barro)

understanding of what is happening currently and what may happen in the fore-seeable future. Thus we always ask, can this theory shed any light on the current causes of economic instability? Except for a few bows in the direction of well-known theories (like the "sunspot theory"), all these theories can be potentially instructive in understanding the current causes of instability. And in any given crisis, one or another factor may be the primary cause of the downturn—the straw that breaks the camel's back, so to speak. Many students of the business cycle today believe that instability is "partly endogenous and partly exogenous," and so a large number of factors can be viewed as helping to explain overall instability.

RELATIVELY SIMPLE UNICAUSAL THEORIES

Agricultural Theories

Throughout much of our life as a nation, agriculture was the largest sector. In the twentieth century, agriculture has constituted a declining percentage of GNP/GDP (gross national or domestic product), but it remains a critical sec-tor. Accordingly, it is appropriate to consider briefly the stability of this facet of the economy. Moreover, some of the earliest efforts to explain instability were devoted to agriculture.

In Haberler's classic work on business cycles, *Prosperity and Depression,* [4] he suggested that the so-called agricultural theories of the cycle could be divided into three groups: The first argued that periodicity in agricultural cycles caused business cycles elsewhere. He placed W. S. Jevons, H. S. Jevons, and Henry L. Moore in this category. The second category consisted of theorists who did not assume there was in fact a crop cycle, but rather that, on occasion, fluctuations in agricultural crops could act like an exogenous starter and set off a cumulative cyclical response in the rest of the economy. He classified A. C. Pigou and Dennis Robertson in this group. The last group, which included Alvin Hansen and J. M. Clark, argued that agriculture was a passive element but one that could respond disproportionately to fluctuations originating elsewhere in the economy. [5]

W. S. Jevons, the Englishman known for "the sunspot theory," promulgated his views in "Solar Periods and the Price of Corn," published in 1875. [6] He ar-gued that the chain of causation went from changes in the weather and meteoro-logical conditions to agricultural crop production to business activity in general. Concluding that sunspots recurred periodically producing a $10\frac{1}{2}$-year cycle, he was obviously trying to account for what today we call a "major" cycle. His son, H. S. Jevons, revised his father's work (but not his theory) and concluded that the crop cycle was $3\frac{1}{2}$ years long. [7] He was attempting via agriculture to explain what today we would probably call "inventory" or "minor" cycles.

In the United States, the same view was held by H. L. Moore, who wrote a book titled *Economic Cycles: Their Law and Cause* (published in 1914).[8] He, too, developed the view that weather conditions cause crop cycles. He described the result of crop cycles in particularly vivid language:

> . . . these cycles in crops constitute the natural, material current which drags upon its surface the lagging rhythmically changing values and prices with which the economist is more immediately concerned.[9]

Moore thought the cycles he found were 8½ years long.

Today, no one would claim that crop cycles exist in so mechanical a form, and certainly no one would attribute modern business fluctuations to this cause. We can conclude only that agriculture was a much larger percentage of GNP in those days and that at least these economists were trying to explain instability rather than merely assuming it away.

Pigou, typifying the second group, asked a useful question: What is the economic consequence of an unusually large harvest? He developed a restricted and quite artificial model to answer the question, but using the customary tools and concepts of conventional price theory, he demonstrated that in the case of agricultural products, where the demand is relatively inelastic and the supply relatively elastic, the consequence of a large harvest is likely to be a decrease in agricultural income. (And if agriculture is a significant part of the economy, the consequence is that the value of aggregate economic activity will decrease.)[10]

Dennis Robertson factored in the "marginal disutility of work" and the "marginal utility of food" and concluded that the impact of a large harvest would be particularly disastrous when the economy was at or near full employment.[11] In any case, Pigou and Robertson correctly anticipated a number of the difficulties that were recognized much later as affecting agriculture adversely over the cycle. These effects led to efforts to stabilize farm incomes through price supports and other schemes introduced in the United States in the 1930s and later in Western Europe as well. The challenge of stabilizing agricultural incomes over the cycle, particularly for small farmers, is still largely unmet.

Growing out of recognition of the relative inelasticity in the demand for agricultural products is the third position—that far from being a cause of business cycles, the agricultural sector is likely to bear disproportionate hardship during recessions, certainly in comparison with the manufacturing or service sector. The well-known statistician, Mordecai Ezekial, developed an explanation for agricultural instability that incorporated not only the inelastic demand but the fact that the "gestation period" in agriculture (that is, the period between the decision to produce and the appearance in the market of the product produced) is quite long—a full harvest cycle. See Figure 2.1, which depicts an "exploding cobweb." He noted that farmers in competitive unregulated markets would

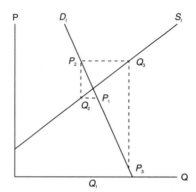

Figure 2.1   Cobweb Effect—an "Exploding Cobweb."

decide how much to produce according to the market price prevailing at the time of planting (a past time) $S_t = \text{fn}(P_{t-1})$, and that they would sell in a market in which the price was determined by the demand-and-supply conditions at this later date. $D_t = \text{fn}(P_t)$ (in Figure 2.1, demand in time t is a function of price in time t, but supply in time t is a function of price in $t - 1$.) Because the demand is more inelastic than the supply for most agricultural products, the effort to adjust production to available prices would lead farmers to move further from the market-clearing price and hence to make activity in agricultural markets more and more unstable.

Figure 2.1 shows the results, called an "exploding cobweb."[12] (Were supply less elastic than demand, a condition unlikely to prevail, the cobweb would be "converging" rather than "exploding" and eventually the profit-seeking farmers would reestablish a stable equilibrium.)

Today, the income of small farmers is still highly vulnerable to cyclical instability. Most government programs to alleviate farmer distress over the cycle aid large farmers disproportionately, because these programs are tied to output (e.g., a subsidy per bushel produced) rather than based on the minimal income needs of individual farmers.

Although some of these theories are highly unrealistic, and the early ones are relatively simple, they remind us that even though agriculture is a steadily declining fraction of GNP, it remains a critically important sector of our economy and is particularly sensitive to economic fluctuations.

Psychological Theories

It is arguable that a theory of instability based solely on "psychological factors" might be viewed, like the "sunspot" theory, as a unicausal and relatively simple (if not simplistic) explanation of business fluctuations.

In fact, while many theorists have included psychological factors, few theories revolve totally around these factors. Gottfried Haberler comments that many theories of instability note the intensifying effect of psychological considerations on other factors. Theorists who mentioned this possibility include Pigou, Taussig, Robertson, Spiethoff, and Tugan-Baranowsky. Haberler summarizes the latter's approach in these words: "Expansion creates optimism which stimulates investment and intensifies expansion. Contraction creates pessimism, which increases contraction."[13] In a similar vein, Pigou emphasized that "errors of judgment" as influenced by alternating "waves of optimism and pessimism" played a significant role in accounting for instability.[14]

While none of these explanations can fully account for the instability observed in modern market economies, many of the theories we shall be considering emphasize psychological factors. For example, Keynes's explanation of instability in aggregate economic activity assigns a significant role to psychological factors.

More generally, economists increasingly have recognized the importance of psychological factors. Recent studies have focused heavily on the role of expectations and anticipations in influencing economic decision making (e.g., stock market behavior). The attention being paid to how economic agents respond to uncertainty is at bottom a question concerning the psychological aspects of economic responses.

We may conclude, therefore, that how economic agents react to various stimuli—the heart of what is meant by psychological factors—is important in many explanations of the cycle. Typically, however, these explanations are classified by the factors influenced rather than by their psychological precursors.

Purely Monetary Theory

This theory is customarily associated with the English economist, R. G. Hawtrey, who developed his views in a series of books published between 1913 and 1937.[15] As Haberler tells us, Hawtrey believed the cycle was caused by purely monetary factors because changes in "the flow of money" alone can account for the cycles we observe. Hawtrey begins by developing his own terminology to make the point that the only way aggregate income and output can diverge arises from the activities of the banking system in creating money. Searching for a stage in economic activity that would be highly sensitive to interest rate changes, he settles on "the trader" (i.e., wholesaler). Needing little capital stock, the trader survives with short-term, "self-liquidating" loans that cover the period between paying the producer for output and receiving payment from retailers whose orders he fills. In the concept of the trader, Hawtrey has the ideal participant in economic activity for his purposes. Arguing that the only way traders can spend more than their income—if they do not reduce their own consumption—is by borrowing, he states that during expansion, traders borrow and so increase output relative to income. Their efforts to build up their stocks stimulate economic activity but are self-defeating as they lead to increased demands (via increased income). (This is one of the "vicious circles" with which business cycle explanations are replete.) Increasing orders leads to increased sales, which nullify the effort to increase inventories. This process is initially stimulated by the availability of bank credit (hence the label "purely monetary" theory), but once it is underway, the banks need do nothing further to stimulate expansion. In effect, Hawtrey is able to charge the trader with excessive stimulation of effective demand, made possible by expansion of bank credit. He does charge the decisions on the part of banks to stop credit expansion with bringing on the upper turning point.

Hawtrey's theory permits him to utilize the quantity theory of money, derived from the Marshallian or Cambridge equation of exchange. This equation, $M = kY$ (where M is cash balances, Y is nominal income, and k is a fairly constant ratio), forms the basis for much of the modern approach to monetary instability. In its most rigid version, in which prices are assumed passive, the money supply is exogenous, and k is fixed, it provides a precise, but unfortunately rather unrealistic, guide to monetary policy. In a less restrictive reading, it provides support for the activities of our central bank. Changing the conditions that govern changes in the supply of money is assumed after some period to move nominal economic activity in the same direction, but not by a precisely specifiable amount.

Hawtrey can conclude that changing the discount rate would be an adequate method to control the destabilizing proclivities of profit-seeking banks.

Hawtrey can explain downswings by reversing his argument—the effort of traders to reduce their inventories sets up a cumulative process that in the end reduces income and sales and so is self-defeating.

Modern economists would criticize Hawtrey's theory on several grounds: He exaggerated the importance of the traders (or wholesalers); he probably exaggerated their sensitivity to interest rate changes (certainly they would be as sensitive to changes in their expected profit rates as to changes in current interest rates); he failed to realize that business fluctuations are likely to be more than merely monetary phenomena; he may have overemphasized the "inherent instability in credit"; and he did not appreciate that modern monetary policy probably is a good deal more flexible and useful than he thought or than the record of the 1920s and 1930s would imply.[16]

On the positive side, Hawtrey underscored a matter we need to consider even today: Left to their own devices, profit-seeking banks will exacerbate rather than mitigate instability because they will be most inclined to lend in the later stages of expansion when interest rates are high and profit opportunities seem best, and least likely to lend in recessions when interest rates are low and profit opportunities seem bleakest.

Finally, if Hawtrey's theory seems overly simple, at least he was attempting to explain the instability visible on all sides rather than simply assuming it away as so many of his contemporaries did.

BUSINESS ECONOMY THEORIES

Price/Cost Relations, Profit Margins

A second broad group of theories that attempt to explain endemic instability in market-oriented economies may be termed the "business economy theories." The French economist, Jean Lescure, is often classified in this group.[17] By far, however, the most important member of this category is Wesley Clair Mitchell, the founder of the National Bureau of Economic Research, and the single person who did the most to promulgate the view that sound (i.e., useful) theoretical explanations could only emerge by carefully deriving hypotheses from the empirical record of an economy over long periods of time.[18] In a famous review (entitled "Measurement without Theory") of Burns and Mitchell's book, *Measuring Business Cycles,* which laid out their approach to studying fluctuations, Tjalling C. Koopmans leveled a serious charge. He argued that no progress in understanding business fluctuations could emerge from the Mitchellian approach, which consisted of searching the empirical record for "empirical regularities."

Rather, insisted Koopmans, one must develop a hypothesis concerning the cause of cycles, and then collect and test relevant data. In a famous debate of the time, Rutledge Vining sided with Mitchell and Burns in arguing that "hypothesis seeking" is a necessary stage in scientific analysis of business cycles. In effect, Vining claimed that until some "empirical regularities" are discerned, there can be no meaningful development of hypotheses to test. As such, the Mitchell analysis played a valuable role. Eventually, Koopmans determined that given the current state of understanding of instability, the Mitchell-Burns approach might be a "reasonably efficient" way to use data.[19] In general, Mitchell's perspective toward cycles and their study was the most widely accepted in the period before Keynes; it is still widely accepted by many students of business fluctuations as an explanation of how instability develops.

Mitchell himself put his explanation as follows:

The very conditions that make business profitable gradually evolve conditions that threaten a reduction of profits. When the increase in business, at first a cause and later both a cause and a consequence of rising profits, taxes the productive capacity of the existing industrial equipment, the early decline of supplementary costs per unit of output comes gradually to a standstill. Meanwhile, the expectation of making satisfactory profits induces active bidding among business enterprises for materials, labor, and loan funds, and sends up their prices. . . . Thus the prime costs of doing business become heavier. After these processes have been running cumulatively for a while, it becomes difficult to advance selling prices fast enough to avoid a reduction of profits by the encroachment of costs.[20]

This explanation for the business cycle elevated the quest for profits—presumably the prime incentive for business entrepreneurs in market capitalist economies—to the central position: hence the name, business economy theory. As we have seen, the expansion is dominated by growth in business demand based on rising profit expectations. This inevitably leads sooner or later to shortages and rising prices, which squeeze profit margins. As profit growth diminishes, so, too, does the business expansion, ultimately resulting in recession.

Cost-cutting measures (layoffs, reduced hours of employment, cutbacks in nonlabor expenses) come to be dominant in recession; this in turn improves productivity and increases profit margins.[21] The improved outlook for profits sparks recovery as firms step up the pace of capital spending and hiring. In this theory, costs lag prices during both early expansion and early contraction but catch up as the next turning point approaches. This progression permits the recurring squeezing and widening in profit margins that produce the entrepreneurial reactions which characterize the business fluctuations. Although the theory is quite general, it can account for a variety of specific causes of cyclical changes including credit crunches, oil price shocks, and even exogenous shocks, all through the profit link.[22]

Arthur F. Burns has said of Mitchell's work: "No other work between Marshall's *Principles* and Keynes' *General Theory* has had as big an influence on the economic thought of the Western World."[23] Robert Lucas echoed a similar view when he wrote:

> It is easy to forget the remarkable character of the regularities that Mitchell succeeded in discovering and documenting . . . we have lived with them for so long that they seem not so much the product of an imaginative and abstract way of organizing economic time series as simply "facts" that "everyone knows."[24]

Inventory Cycles

Lloyd Metzler, an economist at the University of Chicago, developed a simple explanation of short business cycles that is, interestingly, not unlike Hawtrey's theory of a monetary cycle caused by traders' self-defeating efforts to build or reduce inventories.[25] In Hawtrey's theory, the availability of bank credit finances the trader's self-defeating efforts. While Metzler's theory is not monetary at all, but "real," he, too, argues that efforts by the business community to alter its inventory levels will, for a time, be self-defeating. According to Metzler, entrepreneurs have a fixed notion of their desired inventory/sales ratio. When their demands rise in an expansion, they find their inventories reduced.

Their efforts to return their inventory levels to the established inventory/sales ratio lead to a rise in new orders and thus to increases in employment and income. Since the latter effects increase sales, the inventory/sales ratio still falls short. For Metzler, the upper turning point is the result of the marginal propensity to consume, which is positive, but less than one. Therefore, the increases in sales will be smaller than the increases in income. During late expansion, the desired inventory/sales ratio gradually can be restored, eliminating the stimulus to the economy via efforts to increase inventory levels. As a result, the imbalances that caused the expansion eventually are removed.

In contraction, the reverse process occurs: The entrepreneurs try to reduce their inventory levels and their sales fall, and the effort further reduces incomes and so prevents the fall in the ratio. However, the rate of decline in sales is lower than the rate of decline in income, and so over time, the entrepreneurs reestablish the desired inventory/sales ratio and the contraction bottoms out.

Metzler argues that because of inventory behavior, short cycles are self-correcting. His theory has been criticized on the grounds that rational profit-seeking entrepreneurs would not incessantly have a rigid inventory/sales ratio in mind but would in fact want the ratio itself to vary over the cycle. Moreover, Metzler virtually ignored the impact of changes in expectations, which could prove even more significant in affecting entrepreneurs' behavior than the changes in past sales. Finally, inventories are undoubtedly important, but whether, by themselves, they are sufficiently pivotal to account for all short-run instability is problematical at best.

THEORIES EMPHASIZING THE
SAVINGS-INVESTMENT PROCESS

Pre-Keynesian Theories

Overinvestment Theories

Monetary Theories. Monetary overinvestment explanations of the business cycle are closely related to the purely monetary explanations. The major difference is that, as their name suggests, these theories relate the credit-expanding proclivities of the banking system to investment.

All these theories, including Hawtrey's purely monetary theory, were greatly influenced by the Swedish economist, Knut Wicksell.[26] He was the first, perhaps, to contemplate the impact that the existence of an elastic monetary system could have on the classical economists' view of equilibrium. The latter implied acceptance of Say's law of markets and the assumption of flexible wages and prices, which led to the conclusion that full employment operation of the economy with all output being purchased (production would equal consumption) was the long-run natural result. At worst, business fluctuations were minor self-correcting phenomena. Into this conceptual Garden of Eden, Wicksell introduced a snake in the form of the cyclical expansion of the money supply by profit-seeking bankers. He thereby distinguished between what he called the natural and the market rate of interest. (See Figure 2.2.) At the natural rate of interest ($i_{natural}$), the supply of savings would equal the demand for loanable funds, which was determined by what entrepreneurs wished to invest. Since the natural rate thus ensured that all expenditures in the circular flow not utilized by consumption would be saved and invested, there could be no market glut of unsold goods and services.

Wicksell argued that the market rate of interest (i_{market}) equated the demand for funds with the bank-inflated supply of loanable funds. Hence, the impact of the operation of the banking system was to drive the market rate of interest below the natural rate. This in turn led investors to increase their activities, causing the economy to expand to levels not sustainable in terms of what consumers were willing to purchase. The contraction that resulted might well drive the market rate of interest below the natural rate of interest. Only when the two rates were the same could the economy achieve equilibrium. The influence of Wicksell's distinguishing between the real and the monetary system enabled subsequent students of the business cycle to consider the destabilizing impact of the profit-seeking banking system in a variety of ways.

Perhaps the best known monetary overinvestment theory was that of Friedrich von Hayek, an Austrian economist who has been on the faculty at the University of Chicago for many years.[27] But Ludwig von Mises[28] developed a similar monetary overinvestment theory.

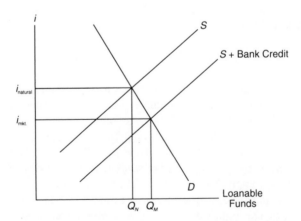

Figure 2.2   Impact of Bank Credit on Interest (Wicksell).

Hayek began by asking an important question. Why is it that producer goods industries exhibit much greater amplitude over the cycle than consumer goods industries? Many students of the business cycle have noted the greater volatility to be found in the "higher" (that is, earlier) stages of production. There are better explanations now than the one Hayek developed (for example, the way in which the accelerator affects the stages of production over the cycle), but at least Hayek began with a useful question.

Hayek argued that the banking system makes loans available to entrepreneurs during the upswing, causing the market rate of interest to fall below the natural rate (this Hayek took from Wicksell). Hayek's major addition was to claim that the banks lent to the higher stages of production, thereby enabling them to expand (why only to the higher stages is not clear). If bank credit enabled the higher stages to bid resources away from the lower stages, (particularly as the economy approached full employment), expansion would lead to higher income, whereas consumer goods output would not have increased—and might even decrease. This situation would necessarily lead to an increase in consumer prices. The demand for consumer goods would presumably represent the same proportion of the now higher income, but consumer demand (related to "voluntary saving") would be unchanged. The result would be higher prices for consumer goods, and with higher prices, consumers could not buy as much out of any level of nominal income. This is what Hayek meant by "forced saving." The consumers had not voluntarily chosen to purchase less. They were forced to purchase less by virtue of the rise in consumer prices. Out of a given level of nominal income, consumers could purchase a smaller volume of consumer products, in effect, forcing up the real saving rate.

Consumers would wish to buy as before, but fewer goods would now be available. As these shortages led to higher prices, profit rates in the consumer sector might well rise, enabling the lower stages once more to bid resources back down to the consumer level. Higher consumer prices could offset the cost advantages of lower interest rates (lower by virtue of still more bank credit being available) in the higher stages. This process could continue—luring resources up and then down—as long as the banking system was able to expand credit.

In effect, then, Hayek's boom consisted of an abnormally rapid rate of capital formation (in the higher stages) under the artificial stimulus of the bank injection of new credit. The upper turning point partly results from the limits to the expansion of bank credit and partly from the collapse of the capital spending boom in the face of the falling real consumer demand occasioned by higher prices (the forced saving). The resultant recession, among other things, restores the original balance between consumer and producer sectors ratified by the consumers prior to the increase in bank credit that set off the original expansion.

This rather elaborate explanation has the virtue of trying to explain the empirically observable difference in volatility between the producer and the consumer goods industries noted earlier. But the theory, though elaborate, is based on a simplistic view of how banks perform. Its weaknesses would include its failure to appreciate that real as well as monetary factors can lead to capital formation (changes in profit expectations, technological changes, etc.). In general, it has been criticized for overemphasizing the importance of monetary factors (changes in interest rates) and its relatively unrealistic view of the investment process in general. Most particularly, Hayek pays no attention to the impact of changes in expectations on the behavior of entrepreneurs. (We earlier made the point that psychological factors are important even if by themselves they constitute an inadequate theory of instability.) As we shall see, most notably when considering Keynes' contribution to understanding instability, fluctuations of profit expectations are in principle at least as important as fluctuations of costs—including interest rates—in accounting for investment changes. Finally, while Hayek could explain, however inadequately, the upper turning point, the theory has relatively little to say about the lower turning point. Hayek's theory, while offering an interesting rationale for the fixed investment cycle, is ultimately an inadequate explanation of modern business cycles because it ignores too many critical factors. Business cycles are complex, and in the end, no relatively simple theory can adequately explain them.

Nonmonetary Theories

Shortage of Capital Theories. There are two general explanations for fluctuations in modern market economies that can be termed nonmonetary overinvestment theories. The first (sometimes called the "shortage of capital" theory) is associated with the Russian economist Michael Tugan-Baranowski, the German economist Arthur Spiethoff, and the Swedish economist Gustav Cassel. The theories are called "nonmonetary" because while they recognize that the financial system has a role to play in the investment process, the cyclical difficulties arise quite independently of that connection. The financial system merely transmits the disturbances.

Tugan-Baranowsky captured the attention of his readers by likening the problem of overinvestment to the pressure in a steam engine.[29] Just as the pressure of steam builds up in an engine cylinder, eventually overcoming the resistance of the piston and setting it in motion, so in the economy, loan capital builds up and forces its way into industry "setting it in motion."[30] What the loan capital permits, in Spiethoff's view, is a rate of expansion of investment that literally outruns the ability of the economy to make resources available for use in the sectors not devoted to current consumption goods production (durable or semi-durable consumer or capital goods, materials for producing durable goods, etc.).[31] The rate of investment is too rapid given the resources devoted to consumption (investment is disproportionate to the rate of saving).

Cassel is in essential agreement on this point.[32] The rate of investment is too high relative to the resources devoted to consumption rather than saving. The shortage of capital in late expansion is thus a real shortage, brought about not by inadequate income but by conflicting demands for the resources required for increased production of plant and equipment. As Cassel put it, "What is over-estimated is the capacity of capitalists to put savings in sufficient quantity at the disposal of producers."[33]

Schumpeter's Innovation Theory. In the theories we have just considered, the cause of the upper turning point is that the rate of investment during expansion has exhausted the resources available for investment; that is, the rate of investment has outrun savings. We shall shortly consider the opposite view—that investment outruns not savings but consumption. These "under-consumption theories" date back at least to Malthus in the early years of the nineteenth century. Before considering them, however, we need to look at a variant of the overinvestment approach that finds the difficulty not in the constraint of limited savings but in the entrepreneur's perceptions of invest-ment opportunities. This theory was developed by Joseph Schumpeter, an Austrian economist who spent the last part of his career as a professor of eco-nomics at Harvard University. Schumpeter's theory is indeed a nonmonetary overinvestment theory, but it is far broader than the theories of Spiethoff or Cassel and is sometimes called a "partial-overinvestment" theory. Schumpeter finds the cause of major expansions in the investment opportuni-ties provided by a major technological breakthrough. More particularly, Schumpeter distinguished between "inventions" and "innovations." He defined inventions as the discovery of new ways of producing. These occur more or less continuously in modern market economies (people are always discovering new ways of producing, better ways of producing).[34] However, in-ventions become economically significant only when they are actually intro-duced into economic activity. This he called "innovation," and Schumpeter argued that such is the nature of modern economies that innovations occur only discontinuously. They tend to be bunched or clustered, and this cluster of investment opportunities exploited more or less at the same time produces an expansion.

In general, innovation for Schumpeter meant a change in production severe enough to cause a discontinuity in a production function. The most basic kind would be the introduction of a new product with a new production process, par-ticularly one requiring the construction of a new plant or equipment to carry it out. The introduction of the assembly line to produce Henry Ford's new auto-mobiles is the clearest historical example of an innovating entrepreneur. There have been other kinds of innovation involving new sources of raw materials, new markets for products, or new methods of organization in an industry. But whatever the type, the distinctive character of innovation for Schumpeter was that it required introducing fresh ideas into the production process and these involved investment outlays to bring them into being. Schumpeter argued that to innovate successfully an entrepreneur must have "broader horizons," his term for the range of new possibilities that any entrepreneur felt comfortable contemplating. Significant innovations were, therefore, associated with the rise to leadership of new entrepreneurs. These infrequent leadership changes occurred only when dissatisfaction with old ways reached a critical level. This level was associated with the building up of tension in the firm caused by slow or nonexistent progress under old leadership, and the consequent willingness of those who decide on entrepreneurial fates to take a chance on new leaders.

Innovation in one industry or firm tended to result in other firms taking a chance in what Schumpeter called "imitation waves." The introduction of new techniques and inventions was thus customarily bunched—the cluster of innovations about which Schumpeter wrote:

> Progress—in the industrial as well as in any other sector of cultural or social life—not only proceeds by jerks and rushes but also by one-sided rushes productive of consequences other than those which would ensue in the case of coordinated rushes. In every span of historic time it is easy to locate the ignition of the process and to associate it with certain industries and, within these industries, with certain firms, from which the disturbances spread over the entire system.[35]

Schumpeter, therefore, developed a broad theory to account for instability in modern industrialized market-oriented economies. It focuses on the profit-motivated activity of entrepreneurs who operate within a given culture and are heavily influenced by all the experiences that shape as well as limit their perspective and vision.

Much of Schumpeter's actual explanation of the interrelated processes occurring during expansion and contraction is not unique. Once beyond his distinctive view of what starts expansion, Schumpeter, in common with many students of the cycle, finds a role for factors such as the banks, the operation of wages and prices, and the difficulties of adapting changes in capacity to anticipated changes in demand. In all of this, Schumpeter's thinking is consonant with a number of the views we have already surveyed. While explanations of the upper turning point distinguish most theories of business fluctuations, Schumpeter's theory, however, is most distinctive in his explanation of the onset of expansion. From this viewpoint, innovation and the investment that it brings on overstrain the adaptive power of the economy. Innovation stimulates expansion; adjustment to the consequences of innovation brings on contraction.

Finally, Schumpeter goes beyond most theorists of the cycle in looking to the future. He asked, "Can capitalism survive?" Unlike the Marxists, who argued that capitalism would not survive because it was a failure (it would "collapse because of its own internal contradictions"), Schumpeter thought that in time capitalism would collapse because of its successes. He distinguished "competitive capitalism" from "trustified capitalism." Competitive capitalism was his name for the environment in which the vigorous efforts of profit-motivated entrepreneurs blossomed into better means of production and so more effective ways to increase firm profits. Sooner or later, the entrepreneurs, looking at their past successes, would begin to ask, "Why take chances?" Instead of fearlessly trying new things, they would become timid and fearful and eventually would settle into a "Why rock the boat?" attitude that marked them as "trustified capitalists."

In the final analysis, the process of innovation required what Schumpeter called "creative destruction"—the willingness to supersede old methods and products with innovations producing genuine efficiencies. This meant increasingly that "trustified capitalists" would refuse to subject themselves and their productive processes to "the perennial gale of creative destruction" (Schumpeter's colorful term for the progress through innovation required of entrepreneurs).[36]

There is much more to Schumpeter's views on instability. In many ways, his theory anticipated the modern "real business cycle theory" in the sense that, while banks could exacerbate instability, they were not necessarily responsible for it. Schumpeter's thinking about the causes of economic instability in modern capitalist economies represents one of the most complete explanations for business fluctuations. As such, it was more than a narrowly economic explanation, but a full-fledged consideration of how modern firms and their leaders cope with technological change as they seek to maximize their profits. Schumpeter's views were more complex and sophisticated than those of many economists who considered the causes of instability long after he wrote.

Underconsumption Theories.   The underconsumption theories are among the oldest explanations for cyclical instability.[37] They are interesting for a number of reasons, not the least of which is that they illustrate how earlier theories on occasion can be both more sophisticated and more satisfactory than later ones.

The history of underconsumption theories goes back all the way to Thomas Robert Malthus, whose explanation of instability was essentially underconsumptionist. In contrast to mainstream nineteenth-century macrotheory (which assumed that Say's law of markets held and that full employment of all resources, both human and nonhuman, was the usual condition for the economy), these theories attempted to explain business fluctuations of the sort on display in the nineteenth century, rather than assuming them away.

Underconsumption theories, therefore, are the principal occupants of Robert Heilbroner's "underworld" of nineteenth-century economics. The distinctive characteristic of underconsumption theories is that the cause of the

upper turning point is the decreasing ability of the economy to continue consuming what it produces during expansion.

In general, underconsumptionists fall into three broad groups in terms of
the development and sophistication of their theories. Interestingly, the most
satisfactory theories (in the sense of being dynamic and realistic) are not necessarily the most recent ones.

The English economist, C. H. Douglas proposed the most naive underconsumptionist position.[38] Major Douglas, as he was known, argued that the economy suffers recurring crises because of its failure in expansion to generate
sufficient purchasing power to buy all that is being produced. Why should this
be the case? Major Douglas offered various explanations. The simplest was his
notion that interest paid to banks for loans reduced purchasing power. Failing
to understand the modern banking system, Douglas assumed that interest paid
to banks by firms originated in the production process but would leave the re-
cipients of factor payments with less income than the market value of the
goods and services produced by the amount of interest that the producing firms
had to pay. However, interest payments to banks can get back into the income
flow by way of new bank loans, and so forth.

Douglas's most famous explanation was known as the "A plus B theorem."
In the process of production, firms incur two types of costs. A payments represent outlays for wages and dividends paid to individuals. B payments represent
expenditures to other firms for raw materials and other essentials. The prices
at which produced goods are offered for sale reflect both A payments and B
payments, but the individuals in the economy possessed only the A payments.
Thus purchasing power would be deficient in the amount of the B payments.

In addition to failing to appreciate the impact of modern banking on the
economy, Douglas did not realize that payments for materials generate income
quite as surely as payments for wages or dividends and can be utilized to buy
the output of consumer goods and services.

On occasion, Douglas argued that "people save," which is essentially the
customary underconsumptionist argument (oversaving is perforce underconsumption) rather than a failure to generate purchasing power.

Douglas did not just diagnose the end of expansion as being caused mostly by
inadequate purchasing power. He recommended a solution: The government
should offer "social credit" in the amount of the inadequacy in purchasing power
so that the economy could continue to consume what was being produced. Why
is Douglas's work remembered today if his analysis of the modern industrialized
market economy was so deficient? We can do no better than to offer the views of
John Maynard Keynes:

> Major Douglas is entitled to claim, as against some of his orthodox adversaries,
> that he at least has not been wholly oblivious of the outstanding problem of our

economic system. Yet he has scarcely established an equal claim to rank—a private, perhaps, but not a major in the brave army of heretics—with Mandeville, Malthus, Gesell, and Hobson, who, following their intuitions, have preferred to see truth obscurely and imperfectly rather than maintain error, reached indeed with clearness and consistency and by easy logic, but on hypotheses inappropriate to the facts.[39]

The work of the American economists, W. T. Foster and Waddell Catchings,[40] illustrates a second, perhaps more respectable, underconsumptionist position. Unlike Douglas, they do not argue that expansion generates insufficient purchasing power, but only that any saving will get the economy into trouble. If unconsumed income is what is meant by saving, it follows that saving represents income not spent on consumption. The problem is not too little purchasing power, but too little spending. Foster and Catchings asserted that entrepreneurs were faced with "the dilemma of thrift." This dilemma suggested that without saving there could be no investment, but with saving, it was inevitable that sooner or later the economy could not consume what it had produced. There was, in short, no way to avoid an underconsumption crisis, and in the end, this was the cause of the upper turning point.

Foster and Catchings made their case with a simple illustration. Suppose a company manufactured watches, which sold for a dollar apiece and that the price reflected costs of 80 cents and a profit of 20 cents. If the company manufactured 100 watches, it would offer the market $100 of watches but only $80 of income to be spent. The watch company's activity would result in an underconsumption problem of $20. What could be done? If they declared a $10 dividend, they could get the underconsumption imbalance down to $10. If they plowed the other $10 back into watch production the result would be that, at costs of 80 cents a watch, they would produce 12 extra watches. In an effort to get enough spending to clear the original 100 watches from the market they would end up with 12 unsold watches instead of the 10 they had before!

At this point, Foster and Catchings introduced the concept of "the period of gestation," a notion found in many underconsumption explanations. The idea was that if the watch company plowed the $10 back into their company not for immediate production, but to increase their capacity to produce, they could get all their original watches sold, and could avoid an underconsumption crisis so long as the new plant was in process of construction. When the plant was completed, however, and the "period of gestation" ended, their problems would be even worse. Just when their ability to employ workers would go down because construction would end, the capacity of their total operations to produce would go up. Capacity would increase just when ability to buy was shrinking. Underconsumption could not be avoided.

It must be said that Foster and Catchings did manage to capture the attention of their fellow economists. They offered a substantial monetary prize to anyone who could show them any errors in their analysis. Unfortunately (for them), it was not really difficult to do so. For one thing, production in a plant of any size—the new enlarged one quite as much as the old one—is not costless. New income would be generated hiring workers to produce in the new plant, for example. Moreover, the notion that undistributed profits must mean a shortage in ability to consume total produced output fails to comprehend, among other things, the functioning of a modern banking system. These profits would show up in banks in the form of excess reserves and could lead to lending in other areas of the economy that could make possible buying all that had been produced (assuming there were households wishing to purchase). Finally, the period of gestation cannot be interpreted in so mechanical a way. As we shall see a bit later, periods of gestation for the entire macroeconomy need not come to an end. There can always be jobs at all stages of production, provided the economy is not in recession. To take but one simple example, workers who specialize in digging foundations for plants are not unemployed when a given foundation is completed. They move on to other foundation-digging projects. The critical factor is the perceived availability of investment opportunities. So if Foster and Catchings did not err as Major Douglas did in arguing that purchasing power would be inadequate, they erred in assuming that all saving led—sooner or later—to inadequate ability to spend.

A more sophisticated version of the underconsumption argument than either of the two previously considered is that of John A. Hobson, who wrote before either Major Douglas or Foster and Catchings. Hobson, achieved this sophistication because his version was also the most dynamic. He argued that saving was both necessary and not troublesome provided it was not greater than the "optimum rate of savings."[41] Unfortunately, he insisted, saving greater than the optimum rate was unavoidable. Why was this?

To answer this question, it is first necessary to ask, What for Hobson was the optimum rate of saving? Hobson's answer was that the optimum rate represented the maximum rate of saving which, when productively invested, resulted in a flow of increased output not too great for consumers to take off the market. The optimum rate was, therefore, the fastest rate of growth an economy could sustain in the sense that it would and could continue to purchase the increased rate of output.

Hobson argued that the culprit spoiling expansions lay in the unequal distribution of income. As expansion continues, a disproportionate percentage of the increase flows to those in the upper-income groups, who tend to use rather a smaller percentage of their income on consumption (Keynes would have said they have a lower marginal propensity to consume). Thus, the longer the boom goes on, less and less of the newly formed income flows to lower-income groups—who will spend the most on consumption—and more and more of the increase flows to the high-income groups—who will spend relatively little.

The result is that the economy will gradually become unable to increase its rate of consumption as much as it will increase its rate of production of the new output. A market glut is inevitable. And what is a market glut except unconsumed (or unconsumable) output.

Hobson was not without some policy recommendations to redress the economic impact of the unequal distribution of income operating in expansion by means of progressive taxation, encouragement of trade unions, and regulation of monopolies. If all else failed, he advocated social ownership of the means of production to avoid extreme income inequality.

If Hobson's theory thus far seems a sophisticated and reasonably dynamic look at the challenge of maintaining an economy's ability to increase its consumption as rapidly as it could increase its rate of production, he then went one step further. He argued that as mature market economies continued to expand and to search for places to sell their market glut, the competition would provoke capitalist wars to obtain colonies where excess production could be dumped. This explanation of how and why imperialism was inevitable provided a more pessimistic model than Marx's in the sense that Marx thought capitalism would fail because of its internal contradictions. Hobson thought the contradictions were so vast that they would push capitalist countries into wars with each other. Probably few readers wholly agreed with him.

Although Hobson's theory seems extreme, it was, despite its "logical" conclusion in *Imperialism,* the most dynamic, and in this sense, the most realistic and relevant, theory of the problems that beset a market economy in attempting to appropriately coordinate the rate of increase in capacity with the rate of increase in aggregate demand. As such, Hobson speaks to difficulties that modern market economies still face.

Marxian Theory.   Marx is best known for his diagnosis of the overall operation of a capitalist system and for his "laws of motion"—long-run tendencies that capitalist countries, in his view, could not avoid because of the system's internal contradictions.[42] These laws included the belief that tensions between workers and capitalists (those who owned the means of production), would inevitably heighten, and that successive crises would get worse until the proletariat revolted, overthrowing the bourgeoisie (the owners) in the process. This system was driven by its internal difficulties to become more and more unstable until it collapsed. One manifestation of this growing instability was business fluctuations, which Marx forecast would get ever worse.

This progression was, therefore, historically inevitable and unavoidable. In his famous *Communist Manifesto,* which appeared in 1848, Marx wrote:

> Modern bourgeois society with its relations of production, of exchange and of property, a society that has conjured up such gigantic means of production and of

exchange, is like the sorcerer, who is no longer able to control the powers of the nether world whom he has called up by his spells. . . . It is enough to mention the commercial crises that by their periodical return put on its trial, each time threateningly, the existence of the entire bourgeois society. In these crises a great part not only of the existing products, but also of the previously created productive forces, are periodically destroyed. In these crises there breaks out an epidemic that, in all earlier epochs, would have seemed an absurdity—the epidemic overproduction.[43]

Marx's view of instability has strong underconsumption connotations. Interestingly, his analysis led him to predict that the revolution would come first in the most mature capitalist country (where presumably the internal contradictions were most advanced as well). Thus, the revolution should have occurred in Germany (or possibly England). Instead it happened in Russia.

Keynesian Theory

One of the ironies of twentieth-century economic thought is that Keynes, who probably had a larger impact on thinking about instability in market-oriented economies than any other single person, never really developed his own full-fledged theory of the cycle. He never analyzed what happened during typical cyclical fluctuations with anything like the detail, say, of a Wesley Clair Mitchell.[44]

Repeating the entire macroeconomic theory that Keynes developed in his general theory would take us too far afield, so we will comment only on the unique aspects that bear particularly on his explanation of business fluctuations.

Keynes began by specifically rejecting the two assumptions that formed the cornerstones of classical and neoclassical thought (and which not incidentally enabled them to regard business fluctuations as "short-run, self-correcting" disturbances for which no special policies needed to be developed). These assumptions were (1) Say's law of markets, and (2) full employment. The former suggested that the process of producing output created the income to purchase it, so there could never be market gluts or serious overproduction. The second suggested that, provided wages and prices were flexible, there was always a price at which any market—including most particularly the labor market—could be cleared.

Besides rejecting these assumptions, Keynes broke with the classical tradition by arguing that savings and investment originate in different sectors of the economy (savings result from the household decision concerning how much of its income should be devoted to consumption, whereas investment is the province of the entrepreneurs). In classical or neoclassical economics, fluctuations in the interest rate equated savings and investment. Thus any divergence between savings and investment would affect the interest rate so as to reestablish equality between savings and investment. In effect, the two were equated by market forces.

Keynes emphasized effective demand—the demand of consumers for consumer goods, of firms for investment goods, and (in a complete system) of the government for public goods. Private demand consisted of the first two. (In Figure 2.3, equilibrium income, Y, would equal consumption (C) plus investment (I), or what is the same thing, savings (S) equals investment.) Of these, consumption was relatively stable, being influenced primarily by the size of income itself. (The consumption function, representing the functional relationship between income changes and consumption changes was, Keynes asserted, one of the more stable relationships to be found. Household budget studies as well as studies over time of the relationship between national income and national consumption support his view.) Investment, on the other hand, was determined by the profit expectations of the entrepreneurs and the cost of investment (the interest rate). Investment was the volatile factor over the cycle, and Keynes emphasized that investment could be affected as much or more by changing profit expectations as by changes in the interest rate. In our judgment, Keynes's investment theory was realistic. Investors can find out how much they have to pay for

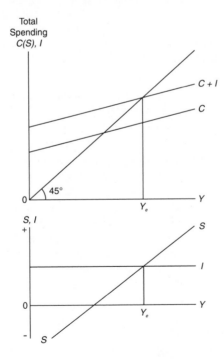

Figure 2.3 Keynesian Equilibrium Income.

a given loan. The interest rate is, therefore known. Entrepreneurs decide whether to invest or not by asking themselves whether, if they borrow the money, they will, over the life of the investment, make at least as much from the stream of expected profits as they will need to pay out in interest payments on the loan. Investment decisions are, therefore, based on entrepreneurs' decisions about investment. They compare known interest rates (the known cost of investment) with anticipated or expected profit rates. (If they contemplate plowing profits back into the firm, the consideration is the same. They can either invest in their own firm, or lend in the open market to others).

One of his major insights was that equilibrium income (the sum of what was earned producing consumer goods (*C*) plus what was earned producing investment goods (*I*) plus government spending (*G*)) was a sum measurable either as income or output and that it need not employ all available resources. As Keynes stated:

> . . . given what we shall call the community's propensity to consume, the equilibrium level of employment . . . will depend on the amount of current investment. The amount of current investment will depend, in turn, on what we shall call the inducement to invest; and the inducement to invest will be found to depend on the relation between the schedule of the marginal efficiency of capital and the complex of interest rates on loans of various maturities and risks.
>
> Thus, given the propensity to consume and the rate of new investment, there will be only one level of employment consistent with equilibrium . . . . This level cannot be greater than full employment . . . . But there is no reason in general for expecting it to be equal to full employment.[45]

Therefore, the size of *C* plus *I* plus *G* determined equilibrium income or output, but there was nothing necessarily "good" about it. As Figure 2.4 shows, it could occur with massive unemployment as it clearly did in the 1930s in both the United States and the United Kingdom (a deflationary gap) or massive inflation (an inflationary gap). Equilibrium simply meant a stable level of (nominal) income or output that the economy would continue to generate unless or until the determinants of *C, I,* or *G* change. The determinants of *C* change over time little if at all. But the determinants of investment change all the time. The important question is the relation of equilibrium income to "full employment" income.

So for Keynes, business cycles were largely the result of instability in private investment. The demand for investible funds (Keynes called it the "marginal efficiency of capital," changed by subsequent Keynesian economists to the "marginal efficiency of investment" (MEI) to stress the crucial role in any given year of additions to the existing stock of plant and equipment) reflects entrepreneurs' current profit expectations.

What caused a Keynesian crisis—that is, brought on a depression? His answer was that it could be produced by a sudden and more or less complete collapse in the marginal efficiency schedule (see Figure 2.5). In the immediate

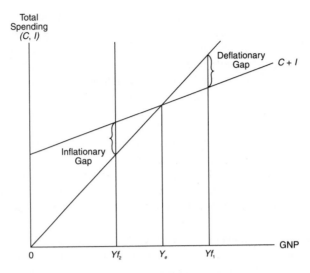

Figure 2.4 Underemployment Equilibrium, OYf_1; Overemployment Equilibrium, OYf_2 (Keynes).

aftermath of such a collapse, there might be little sensitivity in the economy to changing interest rates (i). Profit expectations might be so low as to preclude investment in the eyes of the entrepreneur, even at low interest rates. An implication of Keynes's analysis, therefore, is that equilibrium has no normative implications. In recent years, there has been much debate about Keynes's theory. There are those who argue that "underemployment equilibrium" is possible only

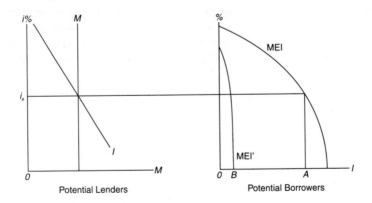

Figure 2.5 Keynesian Explanation of Upper Turning Point—Collapse of the MEI Function (M = money supply).

if wages and prices are "sticky." If prices (and wages) are flexible—then there is always a market price which will equate demand and supply. Presumably this should apply as well to the labor market. In modern economies, we have concerns about the minimum wage, but beyond that, it is questionable whether full employment always is possible even with flexible wages. During the Great Depression, could the 25% of the labor force unemployed have had jobs? Were there positions to be had at wages lower than workers were willing to accept? This does not appear to have been the case.

Keynes stressed that entrepreneurs' willingness to hire labor depended on the perceived prospect for sales and hence profits. Thus these expectations are subsumed in Keynes's marginal efficiency of investment. Arguably, many vicious circles are at work during business cycles and one of them may well be the unwillingness of entrepreneurs to take a chance and hire workers because they fear they could not sell the output.

There are policy implications to Keynes's theory as well. Monetary policy—designed to encourage greater or less activity in the private sector—may not be adequate, particularly during severe recession, when entrepreneurs' profit expectations could be so low that any interest rate seems too high. A fiscal policy of stimulating or depressing economic activity by direct government expenditures and taxes had a place in the overall scheme of things. Keynesian fiscal policy would call for balancing the federal budget over the cycle rather than over an arbitrary 12-month period. Only if historically over the long run, had bad times in the United States been more abundant than good times, could it be argued that "Keynesian fiscal policy" might lead to ever larger deficits. We mention this only to underscore that the recent high annual deficits in the United States have their origins in other factors not related simply to stabilizing the macroeconomy.

We may conclude that both in what it rejected (Say's law, and the assumption of the normality of full employment) as well as what it put forth (the critical role of profit expectations, the possibility of underemployment equilibria) Keynes's work had a profound impact on thinking about instability by later macroeconomists. We shall consider some current reconsiderations of Keynes a bit later.

Post-Keynesian Business Cycle Theory

In the years since Keynes wrote, theories of instability have generally moved in one of two directions. The first direction was an effort by a number of theorists to make explanations of instability more dynamic. The second, the "new classical theories," represented efforts to argue that Keynesian conclusions were a special case, and that theorists who did not make the special assumptions that lie beneath Keynesian theory could in effect restore thinking about instability to the pre-Keynesian perspective. We shall consider each in turn.

Dynamic Models: Multiplier-Accelerator Interaction.   Arguably, the single dynamic element in Keynes's theory—the only element that explains the path of change of the economy over time—is the multiplier.[46] And in Keynes, the multiplier is really "instantaneous:" Given the marginal propensity to consume, a change in investment will immediately result in a multiplied change in the equilibrium income level. Because in Keynes the economy moves with a change in investment from one equilibrium income level to another, many feel his theory was at best a comparative statics approach.

The first major addition to Keynes's insights was provided by Paul A. Samuelson in a famous article exploring the implications for macroeconomic stability of a model that included not only the multiplier but the accelerator.[47] (The notion of the accelerator had been introduced in an article by John M. Clark published in 1917.[48]) Samuelson asked what would happen to the path of change of an economy if it were subject to both the multiplier and the accelerator. The multiplier (k), based on the psychological factors that determine the marginal propensity to consume (MPC) tells us that a change in investment will lead to a larger change in investment. It can of course also be expressed in terms of the marginal propensity to save (MPS). Actually,

$$k \times \Delta I = \Delta Y, \text{ where } k = 1/(1\text{-MPC}) \text{ or } 1/\text{MPS}.$$

The accelerator, on the other hand, is based not on the psychology of household behavior, but on the technology of production in a modern industrialized economy. In such an economy, the demand for consumer goods can change incrementally, but the supply of producer goods must increase in discontinuous fashion because of the economies of large scale production. The precise size of the accelerator will depend on the technology governing particular industrial processes. But in general we may write:

$$\beta \Delta C = \Delta I$$

This tells us that a small change in consumer demand can lead to a relatively large change in investment. The accelerator helps explain why producer goods industries are more volatile than consumer goods industries. (Hayek asked the same question but gave a less satisfactory answer.)

What, Samuelson asked, happens to the path of change of the macroeconomy if both the multiplier and the accelerator are assumed to be operating?

In general, the impact of a multiplier on a change in investment is $k\Delta I = \Delta Y$. But with a change in Y we may expect a change in C (ΔC) (determined by the marginal propensity to consume). Thus the ΔC will activate the accelerator ($\Delta C \times \beta = \Delta I$). The change in investment could in turn stimulate further multiplier effects, which in turn would produce more accelerator effects, and so forth.

The interaction of the multiplier and the accelerator can help to explain in a general way why small disturbances in aggregate economic activity (either increases or decreases) lead to larger disturbances, rather than producing offsetting pressures that would return the economy to a stable growth path as pre-Keynesian economists would have argued. The interaction of the multiplier and the accelerator suggests why business cycles might not be short-run, self-correcting episodes.

Samuelson's unique contribution was to calculate the path the economy would take with multipliers and accelerators of various sizes. Specifically, the multiplier is based on the marginal propensity to consume (Samuelson called it α), which could vary from 0 (no part of a change in income is consumed) to 1 (the entire change in income is devoted to consumption). The size of the accelerator is not so easily calculated and as noted depends on the technology governing a production process at any given time. Samuelson demonstrated that by the time the accelerator got as large as 5, one could account for all the kinds of movement an economy could take through time.

As can be seen in Figure 2.6, small βs can be combined with αs to give the case Keynes stressed (field A) the multiplier effect only. All that this adds is the suggestion that the multiplied new equilibrium will be reached in a series of stages rather than instantaneously. At the other extreme, large βs combined with fairly large αs give growth at compound interest rates (field D). In between, one gets cycles. Specifically in field B, there are damped cycles; in field C, there are explosive cycles; while finally the line between fields B and C is made up of combinations of α and β that give cycles of unchanging amplitude.

This simple Samuelson model was the basis of much consideration and further analysis. It was clear early that the accelerator would produce these results only when the economy had no excess capacity. The presence of such excess permits the economy to adjust to varying demands for consumer goods without having any impact on demand in the producer goods industries. Hence, excess capacity will reduce the size of the accelerator forces at work in the economy at any given time.

On the other hand, there are forces at work that make the accelerator's impact potentially greater than Samuelson anticipated. William Fellner, for one, introduced the notion of "investment for further investment," and argued that any change in output could induce accelerator consequences, not just changes in consumer demand.[49] Investment is required to change capacity quite as much as to change the output of consumer goods. To the extent that this principle prevails, the impact of the accelerator on the instability of the system would be greater than Samuelson calculated. In fact, with a "total output accelerator" instead of just a "consumption accelerator," it has been calculated that a much larger part of the fields shown in Figure 2.6 would be unstable, and, all the possibilities for change in the economy over time that Samuelson envisaged could be found in a multiplier-accelerator field with an accelerator no larger than four, rather than five.

Growth-Cycle Models.   Many other models of instability incorporating the accelerator appeared in the 1950s including models by Michael Kalecki,[50] Nicholas Kaldor,[51] Richard Goodwin,[52] Evsey Domar,[53] Roy Harrod,[54] and John R. Hicks.[55] We should note at the outset that, increasingly, business cycles and the underlying trends are not analyzed separately. From the perspective of these dynamic theories, the modern industrial economy appears more likely to be confronting irregular growth rates than suffering from recurrent business cycles. As such, these theories harken back to Schumpeter's view that "progress is fluctuation." Instability and economic growth seem to be inextricably intertwined.

Domar's Model.   A major shift in perspective from thinking about business cycles as separate phenomena to thinking of business cycles as part of the overall problem of unacceptably irregular growth rates occurred with the work of Harrod and Domar. Often linked together as "the Harrod-Domar Growth Model," the two actually take quite different approaches. Domar was concerned with a fairly limited question: At what rate would the U.S. economy have to grow to keep its resources more or less continuously employed? Domar

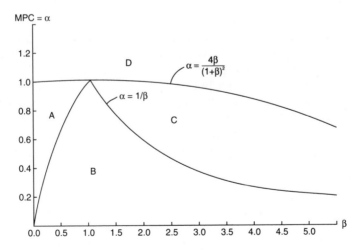

Figure 2.6   Interaction of Multiplier and Accelerator—Possible Results (Samuelson).

made a number of simplifying assumptions (the marginal propensity to save was constant and equal to the average propensity to save; he ignored both government and the rest of the world). His critical notion involving investment was (σ), the increase in output that resulted from a dollar's worth of increase in capacity via investment. (He called this the potential social average productivity of investment.)[56] Under these highly restrictive assumptions, Domar was able to conclude that the rate of growth of the aggregate economy necessary to keep its resources fully employed is equal to ($\alpha \times \sigma$). This is the rate determined by the MPS and what that savings stream when productively invested will add to income and output.

A full employment equilibrium rate of growth such as Domar's is far more distinctive than the rate that would be considered by simply asking, "What is the rate of growth going to be?" The latter is really the question Harrod asked.

Harrod's Growth Theory.   In 1936, Harrod developed a trade cycle model including both the multiplier and the accelerator (he called it the relation). By 1948, he was prepared to elaborate his trade cycle model into a growth-cycle model. Underlying all Harrod's consideration of instability is his view of the underlying long-run growth of the economy. This is determined by technological change and the increments to income and output made possible by the growth rate of capital they produce.

Harrod's system essentially revolves around the analysis of three different growth rates. The first, known as the actual growth rate, may be written:

$$GC = s,$$

where $G = \Delta Y/Y$—the rate of growth of income, $C = I/\Delta I$—the capital coefficient (i.e., the growth of capital produced by the investment that is occurring); and $s = S/Y$—the rate of savings (savings, S, divided by income, Y) in fact occurring at whatever level of income the economy achieves.

The equation, therefore, simply tells us how fast the economy can grow, recognizing that the rate of savings determines the rate of resource availability for investment and the rate of investment determines the growth in the capital stock (the level of technological development being assumed known).

If one considers what G, C, and s represent, it will be immediately clear that this is merely the Keynesian $I = S$, but now written for every possible level of income that the economy might have achieved. It represents a dynamic version of the Keynesian static income level. The equality, moreover, represents a truism.

The second Harrod growth rate, known as the warranted rate of growth (G_w), is the equilibrium rate of growth and is written $G_w C_r = s$, to suggest that the capital growth rate (C_r) necessary to produce a growth rate is such that the entrepreneurs' expectations will not be disappointed. It is thus the rate of growth that persuades the entrepreneurs they made the right decisions. Harrod carries this one step further and asserts that the warranted rate of growth not only validates past entrepreneurial decisions but will therefore be continued by the decisions of the entrepreneurs in the coming period. It is thus an equilibrium rate of growth and is also correctly indicated by the equality symbol.

The third rate of growth is the natural rate of growth (G_n), and represents the rate of growth with population and technological changes as they in fact are. This rate of growth, G_n, is one which may or not be achieved, so we must say that $G_n C_r =$ (or does not $=$) s. G_n is "full employment" rate.

For the rest, Harrod considers various relationships among the three growth rates. Thus, at full employment, G must fall to G_n. In revival, G is less than G_n. When G_n is below G_w, a business slump is inevitable (expectations are doomed to disappointment). When G is greater than G_w, a boom develops (and when G is less than G_w, a slump will be produced). If G_w is greater than G_n, G must be lower than G_w—a situation called secular stagnation.

Obviously, the objective of sound macropolicy must be to get G_w up to G_n. Harrod's world is still a very simplified world (for example, it involves a version of the accelerator that cannot be; it requires increasing capacity at the same time as the output that required the new capacity increases). Nonetheless, despite its limitations, it presents a way of looking at cycles as a part of overall growth and so was an important step toward greater realism in contemplating the challenge of irregular growth.

Hicks' Dynamic Cycle. John R. Hicks began his consideration by noting that Harrod's warranted rate of growth was mathematically unstable in the sense that it would break down in the face of a change (discontinuity) in the savings rate. If the savings rate were to increase abruptly, the warranted rate of growth would have to increase to absorb the increased flow of savings, whereas in fact a new equilibrium rate would likely have to be lower, reflecting the lower rate of consumption and the attendant fall in the rate at which required capacity would increase. Historically, the rate of savings has not changed abruptly, although there is evidence of a slightly decreased rate in the late 1980s, at least in the United States.

Hicks considered the growth rate of the economy assuming that savings was a lagged function of income, that the accelerator would be nonlinear, and that the Keynesian multiplier would actually not operate in instantaneous fashion, but through a number of periods during which investment would exceed savings and the income level would continue to increase toward the new, but as yet unattained, equilibrium level. The notion that equilibrium levels can be useful, even if not attained, in showing the direction and force with which the economy would move was highly instructional in assessing forces leading to instability.

Hicks developed his growth model with a series of preliminary cases—a single change in investment, continuous changes in investment of unvarying magnitude, and ultimately the case shown in Figure 2.7. The vertical scale measures

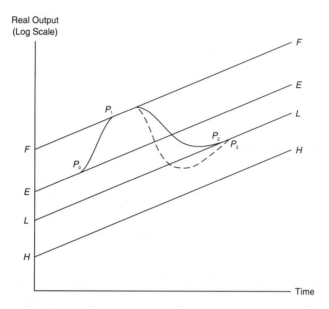

Figure 2.7   Equilibrium Path—Economic Activity (Hicks' Model).

real output change, whereas the horizontal scale represents time. The lowest growth rate shown, *HH*, represents the rate at which the economy will grow over time due to changes in the autonomous rate of investment. It is the fundamental long-run growth rate of the economy. The next growth rate, *LL*, the lower equilibrium growth rate, represents the rate of growth the economy would achieve over time due to the impact of the multiplier on the change in investment that forms the basis for *HH*. The third growth rate, *EE*, represents the upper equilibrium growth rate and indicates the impact on growth not only of autonomous investment but also of induced investment. This latter reflects the operation of the accelerator. But it is more than this. The *EE* rate of growth represents the combined impact on growth of autonomous growth (the *HH* rate), the multiplier effect on the underlying investment increase lying back of *HH*, the changes in investment induced by *LL* (the accelerator), and the multiplier effect not only of autonomous investment, but also of this induced investment. (Hicks called this the "supermultiplier".) Hence the three rates of growth, *HH*, *LL*, and *EE*, must be found in the order shown. The last growth rate, *FF*, need not lie above the other three, but here that position is assumed. It represents the rate of maximum growth possible if all resources are fully employed. It corresponds to Harrod's G_n. *EE* would correspond to Harrod's G_w, and represents the rate of growth that persuades the entrepreneurs they made the correct decisions.

The actual rate of growth is suggested in the movement from P_0 to P_1 and so forth. Assume that the economy is moving at its equilibrium growth rate, *EE,* when for some reason, there is a greater than average increase in autonomous investment (e.g., an exogenous shock to the economy). The actual rate of growth would veer upward, the precise rate depending on the degree to which the change in investment shocked the system. But however great the rate might be, when the economy reaches *FF,* by definition it cannot grow any faster. It has hit the "full employment ceiling." All greater-than-average multiplier and accelerator forces that may have been unloosed at P_0 would, therefore, at P_1 have to fall. Any new multiplier or accelerator forces launched in the economy after P_1 would be no greater than those that, on the assumptions of the model, would keep the economy moving along *EE.* Thus at some point, the economy would veer off *FF* and begin moving toward *EE,* which represents declining output for a time. Hence, after the economy moves away from *FF,* the negative forces affecting economic activity would include negative multipliers, and accelerator forces rendered impotent by the increasing appearance of excess capacity. These negative forces, therefore, would produce a recession. What ends the recession is that the negative forces will be weakened somewhat by factors such as the marginal propensity to consume (as income declines, consumption will decline but at a lower rate), as well as by the gradual reappearance of the positive forces associated with the long-run underlying growth rate implied by *HH.* In the usual recession, the economy would gradually approach *LL* and ultimately turn positive (increase) as the positive multiplier and accelerator forces associated with *LL* overcome the steadily weaker negative forces associated with the recession. In cases of severe recession (Hicks called it a slump equilibrium—P_3), the economy might fall below *LL* but would ultimately see the contractionary forces spent, and then would begin responding to the underlying positive growth factors associated with *HH.*

In this way, Hicks's model shows cyclical activity within a growth context. The expansions are limited by the ceiling imposed on growth by full employment and whatever long-run rate of technological advance is assumed. The contractions are limited by the floor imposed by the long-run growth rate produced by the rate of technological development.

While this approach is unrealistic and many aspects are overly mechanical, Hicks nonetheless moved thinking about instability forward by focusing on how destabilizing forces impinge on the underlying growth rate of the economy. It pushed thinking about instability into a more dynamic context.

Chaos Models and the Business Cycle. Chaos models, which represent one of the latest mathematical ways of describing cyclical fluctuation, are in many ways an extension of the interaction of the accelerator and multiplier idea.[57] Chaos is defined as a seemingly disorderly behavioral pattern that is generated from a deterministic model (i.e., order and disorder can be generated from the same model). Chaos models have two basic properties: (1) there are sudden breaks in the behavioral pattern, and (2) the model parameters are extremely sensitive to small changes. This type of model can be used to explain recessions and recoveries from a technical standpoint. For example, under this framework, a recession could result from the interaction of seemingly stable economic variables and conditions, which under certain conditions or thresholds will propel the economic system into chaos. These models are relatively new to economics, and their full dimensions have not yet been explored. In one statistical test, Brock and Sayers found that evidence of business cycle instability due to "low-level deterministic chaos" was rejected.[58] However, they cautioned that their test may have been too weak to determine the presence of chaos in the business cycle.

NEW CLASSICAL THEORIES

Monetarism

The dynamic growth-cycle models just reviewed represented the major direction that research on cycles took between Keynes's *General Theory* and the late 1950s. Thereafter, macroeconomists in general began to design various models that returned the theory of business cycles or at least the policy implications of that theory, to its pre-Keynes perspective. Several approaches were formulated, the first being the monetarist movement led by Milton Friedman.[59] Other economists who played prominent roles were Anna Schwartz[60] Karl Brunner and Allan Meltzer[61] and Phillip Cagan.[62]

Modern monetarism represents a return to the general approach taken by the purely monetary theories described earlier, including a reconsideration of the quantity theory of money derived from the equation of exchange, $MV = PQ$. This truism tells us that the average money supply in a period multiplied by the average number of times it changes hands equals the average volume of output produced multiplied by the average price. That is, the volume of money spending equals the value of the volume of what it was spent on. This is not very profound, but pre-Keynesian economists turned this identity into the quantity by theory of money. They assumed that the money supply was exogenous, that V and Q changed only very slowly, and that P was always positive. Hence, small changes in the money supply will result in precisely proportional changes in prices. The modern version of the quantity theory is considerably more sophisticated than its predecessor, but it, too, concludes that the money supply is exogenous and that changes in the money supply are the principal determinant of changes in subsequent aggregate economic activity, albeit with a "long and variable lag." Although they view velocity as being more variable than do the older quantity theorists, it is still not subject to much variability. Moreover, modern monetarists argue that price is customarily passive, and that the chain of causation, therefore, is invariably from changes in the supply of money to changes in real economic activity. Their analysis, principally at the hands of Friedman, leads them to conclude that interventionist monetary policy is unnecessary. More often than not, they argue, it will exacerbate rather than mitigate cyclical fluctuations because it is so difficult to get the timing correct. Friedman, therefore, urges adoption of a "simple monetary rule"—strive to have the real money supply (ΔM) grow at the same rate as the average real growth rate of economic activity (ΔQ). The corollary is that it is better to tolerate the inflation (ΔP) and the unemployment (ΔQ) that may result than to try offsetting them with discretionary policy.

Modern Keynesians and modern monetarists both agree that changes in the money supply affect aggregate economic activity. For Keynesians, the relationship is indirect and depends on the responsiveness of the financial sector to changes in the money supply and the responsiveness of the entrepreneurs to changes in the interest rate, both somewhat imponderable as to degree and predictable only as to direction of influence. In this scheme, the impact of changes in the money supply is indirect and not precisely predictable. For monetarists, the relationship is direct and reasonably precise if the long and variable lags are taken into account. In any case, there is no way to improve the precision of this relationship. The policy implications of all this suggest that monetary changes are the major influence on aggregate economic activity.

Real Business Cycle Theories

More than once in the history of ideas, old ideas have been put in new terms or in new settings and gained recognition as "new" ideas. This would appear to be the case with a "new" theory of the business cycle known now as the "real business cycle" theory.[63] Real business cycle theories assert that the primary cause of business fluctuations is real (as opposed to monetary) shocks to the economy. In a sense then, real business cycle theories refute the influence that monetarists attribute to changes in the money supply. This, we said earlier, was also the view of Joseph Schumpeter, who developed a "nonmonetary overinvestment" theory well before World War II. Modern real business cycles theories also have something in common with the model Richard Goodwin developed in the 1940s. That effort combined growth and cycle in a single explanation derived from a "great burst of investment" (both innovational and accelerational). Goodwin's theory, like Schumpeter's, was very much a real business cycle theory.[64] At best, this approach would appear, therefore, to be a reformulation of old ideas. It is a far less rounded or complete theory than that of Schumpeter—hence, we could quite appropriately have classified it among the "unicausal" explanations and discussed it at the outset. But it is a recent theory, and like other recent theories, it has been proffered to counter the Keynesian view that interventionism can stabilize economic activity. Monetarists argue that only monetary changes are really important and they cannot be sufficiently controlled to justify discretionary policy. Real business cycle theorists, coming from the opposite direction, also conclude that discretionary monetary policy is inappropriate. The modern version was no doubt launched in the aftermath of the oil price shocks of 1973 and 1980 and the food shock of 1972. These events are widely used to explain the instability of recent times. But since such explanations revolve around unique occurrences, they lack the generality that any theory requires. Moreover, the channel of influence from such events to the real economy is by no means clear.

"Supply-Side" Theories

Another modern variant of classical theory goes by the name of "supply-side theories." These theories are customarily associated with the name of Arthur Laffer.[65] If monetarism is based on a refurbished version of the quantity theory of money, then supply-side economics is based on a refurbished version of Say's law of markets. Laffer's notion was that the best way to achieve stable growth would be to make it as easy as possible for entrepreneurs to increase aggregate supply. This meant increasing entrepreneurs' incentives to invest. In his view, the major deterrent to investment was high corporate tax rates. Arguing that a 100% tax rate would yield no tax revenues because there would be no incentive to invest or work, he concluded that high taxes yielded no more than low taxes. He concluded this on the basis of his famous "Laffer curve" (Figure 2.8). This curve suggests that an intermediate tax rate yields the highest revenues, and that a high rate (say 80%) yields no more tax revenues than a low rate (say 30%) because of the disincentive to work and invest associated with the high rate. Except

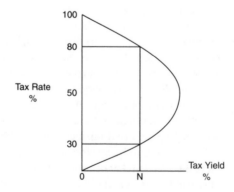

Figure 2.8   Laffer Curve.

for the extremes, the Laffer curve is difficult to quantify. How strong are the disincentives implied in this curve?

In point of fact, encouraging supply along with stimulating aggregate demand was always part of the Keynesian view for achieving optimal growth and stability. Keynes stated:

> I should readily concede that the wisest course is to advance on both fronts at once. Whilst aiming at a socially controlled rate of investment . . . I should support at the same time all sorts of policies for increasing the propensity to consume.[66]

But in the midst of a deep recession, as in the 1930s, Keynes thought the possibilities for improvement lay principally on the demand side. Recall that his explanation for the onset of depression was a collapse in the marginal efficiency of investment—that is, in profit expectations. If expectations are virtually nonexistent, no reduction in interest costs of borrowing can be expected to help much, a major conclusion of our earlier consideration of Keynes's theory. Therefore, when profit expectations are most bleak, it may be easier to affect the propensity to consume than to stimulate investment. Other than that, there is much to be said for encouraging both. Insofar as business cycles are concerned, the major drawback to supply-side economics is that, in common with monetarism, this position argues that fluctuations in the costs of investment (either taxes or interest rates) are far more critical than fluctuations in expected rates of return. Arguably, the latter can be critical as well, and there may be times when expectations cannot be influenced at all. Hence, the door for fiscal action is opened.

Political Business Cycle

Another explanation for business fluctuations, also essentially unicausal, but more recent, is known as the political business cycle.[67] However, today's political business cycle models have their origins in William Nordhaus,[68] who sets out his model in conventional terms as a maximizing problem in which the government attempts to maximize its plurality at the next election. A contribution by Mosley, not ordinarily associated with the political business cycle literature, probably offers a better way of formulating this approach.[69] Mosley develops a "satisficing" model of economic policy. This approach is more appealing in the sense that Mosley's model assumes that the policymaker has several desired targets for various economic and social measures. It does not assume a specific policy will maximize votes.[70]

The basis of the theory of the political business cycle is the notion that governments adapt their policies (primarily monetary and fiscal policies) so as to maximize their chances for reelection. The cycle is roughly the same duration as the term of office of the policymakers. Prior to an election, the government will do all in its power to stimulate the economy. However, the negative consequences of these stimulative actions will not be felt until more than a year after the election, so the policies must be reversed. The main conclusions of this approach are that an electoral-economic cycle can be discerned in real, (inflation-adjusted) disposable income and the unemployment rate.

Tufte carried this a bit further, arguing that a 2-year cycle in the pace of real disposable income per capita is observable, which accelerates before Congressional election years. As for the unemployment rate, it has a 4-year cycle, turning down before each presidential election, and turning up 12 to 18 months after the election.[71] He considered his hypotheses in 27 other countries and concluded there was, on balance, sufficient evidence to support his hypothesis.

While economic conditions undoubtedly affect the popularity of elected officials, the government may not have sufficient control over the economy to fine-tune economic policy so that it can time the impact of interventionist policies precisely. (In recent years, U.S. countercyclical fiscal policy has in effect been nullified because of the huge size in the public debt, and monetary policy continues nominally under the "independent" control of the Federal Reserve Board.)[72] Proponents of the rational expectations school, (considered in the following section) strongly object to the approach of the political business cycle school, on the grounds that all announced or accurately anticipated policy interventions are futile, so the government could not so affect the economy even if it wanted to.[73] More recently, Meiselman[74] has tried to substantiate the presence of a political monetary cycle, which he can explain verbally even though the statistical techniques to test it are hard to produce. Thus it becomes a difficult hypothesis to accept. He argues that there are three discernible stages in the growth rate of the money supply since 1960. Stage I, characterized by a slowing in the growth rate, occurs about a year and a half before a presidential election. Stage II, which begins in the election year, is characterized by an acceleration in the rate of growth in the money supply. Finally, Stage III occurs after the election and is characterized by slower growth rates in the money supply as the Fed tries to counter the inflationary tendencies loosed by the preelection policies. The evidence in support of all this is not very convincing. Nonetheless, the debate continues over whether or not policy makers have created a political business cycle in their periodic efforts to appeal to the voters.

Rational Expectations

The final variant of "new classical macroeconomics" is the rational expectations theory. This approach had its roots in the work of John Muth,[75] who asserted that expectations are rational "since they are informed predictions of future events [and] are essentially the same as predictions of the relevant theory."[76] Muth's approach was incorporated into the work of Robert Lucas, who is generally regarded as the progenitor of the rational expectations move-ment.[77] This approach is based on several fundamental assumptions. The first is that markets clear rapidly. This amounts to arguing that prices and wages are highly flexible, an assumption that Keynes questioned, and that flies in the face of much of the empirical record. (It requires assuming that the Great Depression lasted for 12 years—that is, that the low unemployment levels achieved before the stock market crash in 1929 were not reattained until the rearming that accompanied our entry into World War II—because that is how long it can take for "markets to clear"). If all unemployment of more than very short duration is regarded as "voluntary," this is where the logic of the argu-ment would lead the user.

The second assumption is that economic agents utilize all the information at their disposal in an efficient manner. Agents are thus not systematically wrong. Rational expectations are, therefore, to be contrasted with "adaptive expectations" in which economic agents mostly expect that the future will be like the past, except that they change their expectations when they find they have forecast wrong—they do "adapt" their expectations to past mistakes. In Lucas's view, fluctuations result from the failure of economic agents to have complete information. This lack of information produces the movement in eco-nomic variables associated with business cycles.

Far-reaching conclusions flow from the two basic assumptions. Intervention-ist policy is useless as indeed are all interventions, except for those that constitute "surprises." The others are useless because they have already been discounted by participants in economic decisions. In this respect, the monetarists, who blame the Federal Reserve and its mistakes for most of the instability, differ from ratio-nal expectations adherents, who argue that because everyone knows the Fed will pursue countercyclical monetary policy, they will have already discounted such actions in planning their behavior, so the policy would be totally ineffectual. (Like monetarists, therefore, "RATEXERs" favor fixed and presumably "simple" rules for managing the money supply and its growth.)

The other consequence of the rational expectations movement has been the generation of the "equilibrium business cycle" view. In this perspective, the busi-ness cycle, or the manifestations of the cycle that disturb macroeconomists, are regarded as perfectly normal manifestations of the process by which the econ-omy adjusts to change. Business cycles, far from being disturbances requiring in-tervention, are part of the normal growth process of the economy.

If the business cycle is part of a normal adjustment process, it cannot be ef-fectively altered by interventionist policies. Needless to say, the notion of equi-librium business cycles is controversial. It makes monetary and fiscal policy ineffective normally. Only if agents misinterpret announced policy changes could there be any effects, and they would be only temporary. Tests of rational expectations models are inconclusive, although few studies have supported the hypothesis.[78] The conclusion of a comprehensive review of the hypothesis was, ". . . *a priori* consideration of the marginal costs and benefits of information facing agents in a typical advanced economy leads us to suppose that the rational expectations hypothesis cannot be taken as literally true."[79] Moreover, Arthur Okun no doubt spoke for many economists when he asserted that despite its logic, the model simply did not explain the business cycle.[80]

CONCLUSION

The current state of business cycle explanations largely reflects the basic schism among macrotheorists.[81] In the view of modern classical economists, resource allocation, as it emerges from market deliberations, produces an essentially stable economy. Disturbances are temporary, and when left to its own devices, the economy will grow in a stable way based on its potential output, given the state of technology and resource availability.

Modern Keynesians or neo-Keynesians do not regard the state of either stability or economic growth, as it might emerge from the considerations of economic agents in unfettered markets, to be necessarily satisfactory. This debate has produced a variety of approaches leading to the conclusion that we do not need to develop better interventionist policy. At stake in the debate is the fundamental premise in the development of any theory in the social sciences. This premise is that good theory is needed so that better policy can be devised, which will enable us to achieve more satisfactory performance. In economics, this means greater stability and more rapid growth as market economies move toward the future.

Absent the wish to improve economic performance, the development of theories such as the "new classical theories" become little more than exercises in rationalizing explanatory failures in basic theory. If the new classical economists argue that business cycles are due to misperceptions, imperfect information, or random shocks, other students of the cycle, who persevere in the tradition of both Keynes and Mitchell, argue that modern cycles are not unicausal in explanation but the result of a complex interaction among both real and nominal variables that make the reasons for current instability partly endogenous, partly exogenous, and in any case not unicausal but complex. As such, the research agenda for the immediate future is crowded indeed.

Part Two

Measurement Methods

3 Measuring, Monitoring, and Forecasting Cycles

Between the 1920s and 1940s, the National Bureau of Economic Research (NBER) business cycle dating and analysis techniques have been criticized as measurement without theory. The pros and cons of this criticism are well documented in the literature. Nonetheless, the techniques survived, thrived, and are now well founded in economic theory. That these techniques stood the test of time reflects the usefulness of this approach for business and policymakers.

Today, the tables have turned: Many large-scale econometric models are now being criticized as representing measurement without theory.[1] The pendulum is swinging back to a point where the indicator approach will rightly attain equal stature with other forecasting tools, and theorists are according it new insights, new applications, and new respectability.

This chapter will address measurement economics. It will describe various methods and tools in the context of measuring economic fluctuations and will discuss practical economic statistics, many of which are demonstrated in this and other chapters. The techniques and methods in this chapter provide a *handbook of cycle tools*.

EXPLORATORY DATA ANALYSIS—SOME BACKGROUND TECHNIQUES

Exploratory data analysis (EDA) is a way of summarizing and displaying data to gain the greatest insights. This section first reviews basic growth rate concepts and then discusses methods of calculating trends, cycles, and seasonal patterns. Although the methods discussed here are popular techniques, readers readily will recognize that there can always be another variant on any method proposed. Nonetheless, EDA serves an important role in helping the analyst judge how best to understand and interpret a particular economic time series (a sequence of data representing the same event arranged in chronological order). No one method is right or wrong, some methods just provide more insight than others and consequently should be more helpful in the forecasting process.

Moving Averages, Moving Differences, and Moving Medians

In the analysis of a time-series pattern, it is often difficult to discern clear cyclical, seasonal, or trend movement. The most popular way to bring out these underlying patterns while ignoring the noise in the movement is to use certain forms of moving averages or moving medians, or in some cases to eliminate a trend, a moving difference. The selection of the form of the moving average/ median/difference is, in many respects, ad hoc. Nonetheless, two desirable features in the selection of a smoothing routine are (1) the smoothing process should not distort the original pattern, and (2) the smoothed pattern should not be adversely affected by an outlier, that is, the method should be robust.

There are many elaborate smoothing routines.[2] Some of the more common ones include (1) the Spencer moving average, (2) the Alexander moving average, (3) moving differences, (4) moving medians, and (5) tapered (moving trimmed) means or medians. But they all share a common purpose—to bring out the underlying pattern (sometimes referred to as a *signal*) while reducing the random fluctuation (sometimes referred to as *noise*).

In 1904, Spencer proposed a method to remove a trend in a time series.[3] This method was to use a sequence of moving averages. Spencer's formulation resulted in a 15-term moving average where the weights (see Figure 3.1) are negative on

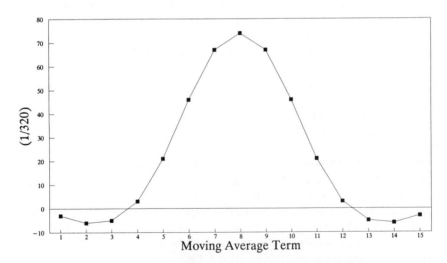

Figure 3.1 Spencer 15—Term Weighting Scheme.

each end of the average. Specifically, the Spencer curve is calculated by using a $5 \times 5 \times 4 \times 4$ moving average, that is, a 4-term moving average of a 4-term moving average of a 5-term moving average of a 5-term moving average with the final moving averages being assigned the weights $-\frac{3}{4}$, $+\frac{3}{4}$, 1, $+\frac{3}{4}$, $-\frac{3}{4}$. The following steps will show how the Spencer curve is derived:

1. *Calculate a Four-Term Moving Average.* The notational form is as follows:

$$MA4_1 = (x_1 + x_2 + x_3 + x_4) / 4 \tag{1}$$

$$MA4_2 = (x_2 + x_3 + x_4 + x_5) / 4 \tag{2}$$

$$MA4_3 = (x_3 + x_4 + x_5 + x_6) / 4 \tag{3}$$

$$MA4_4 = (x_4 + x_5 + x_6 + x_7) / 4 \tag{4}$$

where, $MA4_i$ equals a moving four-term average and x_i is the time series value.

2. *Calculate a Four-Term Moving Average of MA4.* This takes the same form as formulas 1 to 4:

$$MA4 \times 4 = (MA4_1 + MA4_2 + MA4_3 + MA4_4) / 4 \tag{5}$$

Substitute (1) to (4) into (5) and collect terms:

$$MA4 \times 4 = ((\tfrac{1}{4})x_1 + (\tfrac{2}{4})x_2 + (\tfrac{3}{4})x_3 + (\tfrac{4}{4})x_4 + (\tfrac{3}{4})x_5 + (\tfrac{2}{4})x_6 + (\tfrac{1}{4})x_7) / 4$$

$$= (x_1 + 2x_2 + 3x_3 + 4x_4 + 3x_5 + 2x_6 + x_7) / 4$$

Then perform this calculation on all the observations of the time series.

3. *Calculate a Five-Term Moving Average of MA4 $\times$ 4.* The five-term moving average is:

$$MA5 \times 4 \times 4 = (MA4 \times 4_1 + MA4 \times 4_2 + MA4 \times 4_3$$

$$+ MA4 \times 4_4 + MA4 \times 4_5) / 5 \tag{6}$$

Without going through all the intermediate calculation of substituting (5) into (6), the result for the first term is:

$$MA5 \times 4 \times 4_1 = (\tfrac{1}{80})(x_1 + 3x_2 + 6x_3 + 10x_4 + 13x_5 + 14x_6$$

$$+ 13x_7 + 10x_8 + 6x_9 + 3x_{10} + x_{11})$$

This same process is calculated for the other expressions, $MA5 \times 4 \times 4_2$ through $MA5 \times 4 \times 4_5$.

4. *Take a Weighted 5-Term MA of MA5 $\times$ 4 $\times$ 4.* The final step is to calculate a five-term moving average of (6), which have assigned weights. This expression is written as:

$$MA_{Spencer} = (-\tfrac{3}{4})\, MA5 \times 4 \times 4_1 + (\tfrac{3}{4})\, MA5 \times 4 \times 4_2 + MA5 \times 4 \times 4_3$$

$$+(\tfrac{3}{4})\, MA5 \times 4 \times 4_4 - (\tfrac{3}{4})\, MA5 \times 4 \times 4_5 \tag{7}$$

Again, substituting (6) into (7) yields the sequence, for the first term:

$$MA_{Spencer} = (-\tfrac{3}{320})x_1 + (-\tfrac{6}{320})x_2 + (-\tfrac{5}{320})x_3 + (\tfrac{3}{320})x_4 + (\tfrac{21}{320})x_5$$

$$+(\tfrac{46}{320})x_6 + (\tfrac{67}{320})x_7 + (\tfrac{74}{320})x_8 + (\tfrac{67}{320})x_9 + (\tfrac{46}{320})x_{10}$$

$$+(\tfrac{21}{320})x_{11} + (\tfrac{3}{320})x_{12} + (-\tfrac{5}{320})x_{13} + (-\tfrac{6}{320})x_{14}$$

$$+(-\tfrac{3}{320})x_{15}$$

Figure 3.1 presents the resulting weights from this smoothing process.

Once these weights have been derived, only the final formula needs to be known to calculate the Spencer curve. While the derivation process is tedious, it illustrates a technique that can be applied to derive any other type of smoothing process. Finally, all these moving averages are centered (i.e., the resulting value is placed in the midpoint of the time range of the observations), which prevents distortion in the timing of the cycle.

Another elaborate smoothing formula is a 7-term moving average by Alexander.[4] His formula can be written as:

$$(5x_t + 4x_{t-1} + 3x_{t-2} + 2x_{t-3} + x_{t-4} - x_{t-6}) / 14$$

and corresponds to fitting a second-order polynomial to seven consecutive observations. This moving average has been applied to diffusion indexes that tend to be volatile.

Besides moving averages, moving medians and moving differences can also be used to bring out a cyclical pattern. An advantage of a moving median over a moving average is that a median is less affected by outliers than is the average. Moving differences can also be useful at times, especially when there is a secular trend. Moving differences provide one way of eliminating the effect of that trend.

Another robust estimate of central tendency is the trimmed (or in a moving sense, tapered) mean or median. To calculate the trimmed average, the values of the series are rank ordered from low to high and then a preset proportion of the series is trimmed or dropped. This method is useful for eliminating the effect of extreme values (resulting from strikes, weather, political events, and other disruptions) on measures of central tendency.

The Variable-Length Moving Average

A variant on the standard moving average concept requires adjusting the span of the moving average over time. This smoothing process is known as the variable-length moving average (VLMA).[5] The logic for the VLMA is that if the latest changes are significantly different from its historical average change, this may be a sign that the trend has changed and consequently, it is necessary to adjust the span of the moving average. The calculation of the VLMA requires more thought and effort but the effort may pay off in yielding a more realistic trend.

To construct a VLMA requires the following steps:

1. Determine the bounds over which an adjustment will be made to the span of the moving average. This may be determined judgmentally or by historical data sifting, which for example, can be a moving average ranging say, between 40 and 85 months.

A useful application of this methodology is in determining the trend for the NBER's growth cycle. The growth cycle, which is a deviation from trend, conceptually, should incorporate a flexible trend. A variable-length moving average could meet that goal, where the growth cycle trend could use moving averages that would range from the shortest to the longest growth cycle duration and would change based on some preset criteria.

2. Calculate the mean and standard deviation for the data. The sample size should at least equal the longest moving average span.

3. Determine the threshold or trigger points when the span of the moving average would change. One such rule to determine the trigger points is to use the mean plus or minus one standard deviation as the criterion for adjusting the variable span up or down. It is also possible to set a maximum and minimum acceptable span.

4. Set the framework for determining the partition boundaries. An example of four boundaries might be:

$$\text{Partition Bound A} = \text{mean} - (1.5 \times \text{standard deviation})$$

$$\text{Partition Bound B} = \text{mean} - (0.5 \times \text{standard deviation})$$

$$\text{Partition Bound C} = \text{mean} + (0.5 \times \text{standard deviation})$$

$$\text{Partition Bound D} = \text{mean} + (1.5 \times \text{standard deviation})$$

The selection of the number of partition boundaries is somewhat arbitrary, but it is possible to statistically test whether the boundary points maximize the deviation between segments.

5. Preset the amount of observations that the moving average will change when each partition is exceeded. The logic for varying the moving average span might be based on the new observation's distance from the mean. A shorter moving average might be useful when the new observation is considerably different from the mean since this would increase the moving average's sensitivity. Alternatively, when the new observation falls within the normal bounds around the mean, the moving average could be lengthened to reduce its sensitivity.

6. For each period, calculate the new length of the moving average, based on the updated *moving* mean and standard deviation.

7. Then recalculate the partition boundaries and use that information to calculate the next period's span of the moving average. Loop around Steps 6 and 7 until all the data are used.

With the basic procedure described, consider a simple example to calculate a VLMA for housing starts data to determine its *trend*. The series mean and standard deviations are calculated. The average percentage change between 1959 and 1991 was 0.3% per month with a standard deviation of 8.6 percentage points. The break points were set at mean plus or minus one-half the standard deviation and mean plus or minus the standard deviation. In our example, the following boundaries were calculated:

Partition Bound A = mean − (1.5 × standard deviation) = −8.3

Partition Bound B = mean − (0.5 × standard deviation) = −4.0

Partition Bound C = mean + (0.5 × standard deviation) = +4.6

Partition Bound D = mean + (1.5 × standard deviation) = +8.9

This then establishes areas 1, 2, and 3 (as shown in Figure 3.2) for some action.

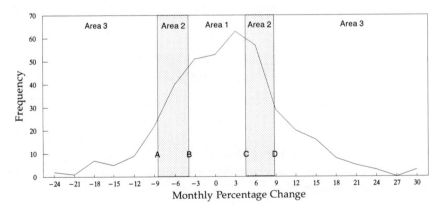

Figure 3.2   Area Partitions in Distribution of Housing Starts.

As a simplifying assumption, no maximum or minimum span was established, and the initial span of the moving average was 18 months. Additionally, when the series would cross into area 3 (when the monthly change was less than -8.3% or greater than 8.9%), the span was reduced by 2 months. When the monthly change fell in area 1 (between -4.0% and $+4.6\%$), the span would lengthen by 2 months. In area 2, no action would be taken. Table 3.1 illustrates how the VLMA was updated over a 4-year period. The VLMA trend and actual data are shown in Figure 3.3.

Calculating Growth Rates

The simplest growth rate is calculated by:

$$G1 = (100(X_t / X_{t-1}) - 1)$$

where G1 is the simple growth rate and X_t is the value of the series at time t. For example, the annual growth rate of gross national product, in constant (1982) dollars, between 1980 and 1981 is calculated as follows:

$$G1 = (100((GNP1981 / GNP1982) - 1))$$

$$= (100((3248.8 / 3187.1) - 1))$$

$$= (100(1.019359 - 1))$$

$$= 1.9\%$$

However, if the span of time is more or less than 1 year, then annual rate comparisons become useful. Growth rates expressed as annual rates, allow direct comparison of quarterly, monthly, and multiyear growth. This formula is:

$$G2 = (100((X_t / X_{t-n})^{(m/n)}) - 1)$$

where G2 is the annualized growth rate, m is the number of periods within the year and n is the number of periods spanned. For example, $m = 12$ (12 periods per year) if monthly data are being annualized, $m = 4$ if quarterly data are being annualized, and so forth. Calculating the annualized growth rate in real GNP between the first quarter of 1985 and the second quarter is done as follows:

$$G2 = (100((GNP1985:Q2 / GNP1985:Q1)^{(4/1)}) - 1)$$

$$= (100((3557.4 / 3547.8)^4) - 1)$$

$$= (100((1.0027)^4 - 1))$$

$$= (100(1.01087 - 1))$$

$$= 1.1\%$$

Table 3.1 Calculating a Variable-Length Moving Average.

Date	Housing Starts (Units)	Monthly % Change	Area	VLMA Length	Average % Change	Updated Moving Standard Deviation	VLMA	Parameter Bounds			
								A	B	C	D
198801	1271	−9.2	3	38	−0.4	6.0	1712.3	−6.4	−3.4	2.7	5.7
198802	1473	15.9	3	36	−0.2	5.9	1709.2	−6.1	−3.1	2.8	5.8
198803	1532	4.0	2	36	0.1	5.9	1706.5	−5.8	−2.9	3.0	6.0
198804	1573	2.7	1	38	0.0	5.7	1701.1	−5.7	−2.8	2.9	5.7
198805	1421	−9.7	3	36	−0.4	5.7	1689.5	−6.1	−3.3	2.4	5.2
198806	1478	4.0	2	36	−0.1	5.5	1684.1	−5.6	−2.9	2.6	5.4
198807	1467	−0.7	1	38	−0.3	5.5	1678.4	−5.8	−3.1	2.4	5.2
198808	1493	1.8	1	40	−0.2	5.5	1677.3	−5.8	−3.0	2.5	5.3
198809	1492	−0.1	1	42	0.0	5.6	1675.9	−5.6	−2.8	2.8	5.6
198810	1522	2.0	1	44	−0.1	5.9	1671.5	−6.0	−3.0	2.9	5.9
198811	1569	3.1	2	44	0.1	5.9	1670.1	−5.8	−2.8	3.1	6.0
198812	1563	−0.4	1	46	0.0	6.5	1667.0	−6.5	−3.2	3.2	6.5
198901	1572	0.6	1	48	0.1	5.9	1666.0	−5.8	−2.8	3.1	6.1
198902	1423	−9.5	3	46	−0.3	6.8	1657.7	−7.1	−3.7	3.1	6.5
198903	1398	−1.8	1	48	−0.1	6.8	1655.3	−6.9	−3.5	3.3	6.7
198904	1344	−3.9	2	48	−0.4	6.8	1646.0	−7.2	−3.8	3.0	6.4
198905	1317	−2.0	1	50	−0.2	7.0	1642.6	−7.2	−3.7	3.3	6.8
198906	1420	7.8	3	48	−0.2	7.0	1630.4	−7.2	−3.7	3.4	6.9
198907	1431	0.8	1	50	−0.3	7.0	1627.5	−7.3	−3.8	3.2	6.8
198908	1339	−6.4	2	50	−0.3	7.0	1620.8	−7.3	−3.8	3.3	6.8
198909	1275	−4.8	2	50	−0.3	7.0	1612.9	−7.4	−3.9	3.2	6.7
198910	1435	12.5	3	48	−0.1	6.9	1603.9	−7.0	−3.6	3.4	6.8
198911	1353	−5.7	2	48	−0.4	7.0	1594.1	−7.4	−3.9	3.1	6.5

198912	1267	−6.4	2	48	−0.4	6.9	1585.3	−7.3	−3.9	3.1	6.5
199001	1543	21.8	3	46	−0.2	6.4	1563.0	−6.6	−3.4	3.1	6.3
199002	1459	−5.4	2	46	−0.3	6.6	1554.1	−6.9	−3.6	3.0	6.3
199003	1298	−11.0	3	44	−0.5	6.6	1526.8	−7.2	−3.8	2.8	6.1
199004	1217	−6.2	2	44	−0.6	6.6	1514.3	−7.2	−3.9	2.7	6.1
199005	1208	−0.7	1	46	−0.7	−6.5	1513.4	−7.2	−3.9	2.6	5.9
199006	1187	−1.7	1	48	−0.7	6.7	1513.6	−7.4	−4.0	2.7	6.1
199007	1155	−2.7	1	50	−0.8	6.7	1513.2	−7.5	−4.1	2.6	6.0
199008	1131	−2.1	1	52	−0.7	6.8	1513.9	−7.6	−4.2	2.7	6.1
199009	1106	−2.2	1	54	−0.7	6.9	1513.1	−7.6	−4.2	2.7	6.2
199010	1026	−7.2	2	54	−0.9	7.3	1497.7	−8.1	−4.5	2.8	6.4
199011	1130	10.1	3	52	−0.7	7.0	1469.2	−7.7	−4.2	2.8	6.4
199012	971	−14.1	3	50	−0.8	6.9	1442.4	−7.7	−4.3	2.6	6.0
199101	847	−12.8	3	48	−1.3	7.5	1413.7	−8.8	−5.1	2.5	6.2
199102	992	17.1	3	46	−0.9	7.4	1382.6	−8.2	−4.6	2.8	6.5
199103	907	−8.6	3	44	−0.9	7.1	1356.7	−8.0	−4.4	2.6	6.1
199104	977	7.7	3	42	−0.9	7.1	1329.1	−8.0	−4.5	2.6	6.2
199105	983	0.6	1	44	−0.8	7.1	1329.6	−7.8	−4.3	2.8	6.3
199106	1034	5.2	2	44	−0.8	6.8	1314.9	−7.6	−4.2	2.6	6.1
199107	1049	1.5	1	46	−0.6	6.8	1317.3	−7.4	−4.0	2.8	6.2
199108	1056	0.7	1	48	−0.5	6.8	1317.9	−7.3	−3.9	2.9	6.3
199109	1017	−3.7	1	50	−0.6	6.8	1317.0	−7.3	−4.0	2.8	6.2
199110	1089	7.1	3	48	−0.6	6.9	1293.5	−7.5	−4.0	2.8	6.3
199111	1066	−2.1	1	50	−0.5	7.2	1296.9	−7.7	−4.1	3.1	6.7

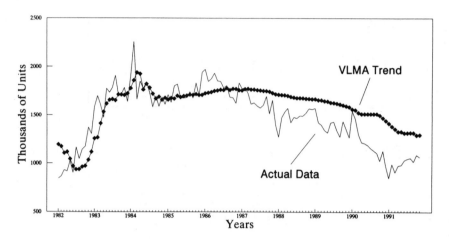

Figure 3.3   Housing Starts: Actual and VLMA.

Similarly, to calculate the annualized growth rate for GNP between the fourth quarter of 1985 and the fourth quarter of 1982 the formula is:

$$G2 = (100((GNP1985:Q4 / GNP1982:Q4)^{(4/12)}) - 1)$$

$$= (100((3605.0 / 3159.3)^{(1/3)}) - 1)$$

$$= (100((1.14108)^{(.333)} - 1))$$

$$= (100(1.04497 - 1))$$

$$= 4.5\%$$

In this case, m remains 4 because it is quarterly data while n is equal to 12 quarters.

Another variant on the growth rate calculation is to average the growth rate over a span of time. The formula for the geometric mean is:

$$G3 = \sqrt[n]{R_1 \times R_2 \times \ \ldots \ \times R_n}$$

where R_i's are the growth rates that are multiplied together and the nth root is taken. While this calculation looks formidable, it is easy to perform with most hand calculators. Alternatively, formula G3 can be approximated by transforming it into logarithms. This variant is calculated using formula G3', and in some cases, it is easier to work with.

$$G3' = (1/n)(\ln R_1 + \ln R_2 + \ldots + \ln R_n) = (1/n) \sum_{i=1}^{i=n} \ln R_i$$

In equation G3', the Greek letter sigma (Σ) is the mathematical notation for the summation of the natural logarithms (ln) of the growth rates (R). As an example of this method, consider calculating the average growth rate for GNP between the fourth quarter of 1982 and the fourth quarter of 1985.

Calculating a Geometric Mean

Period		Real GNP (Growth)	Ratio
1982	Q4	0.6%	1.006
1983	Q1	4.0	1.040
	Q2	8.9	1.089
	Q3	5.5	1.055
	Q4	6.7	1.067
1984	Q1	11.4	1.114
	Q2	5.1	1.051
	Q3	2.1	1.021
	Q4	0.6	1.006
1985	Q1	3.7	1.037
	Q2	1.1	1.011
	Q3	3.0	1.030
	Q4	2.4	1.024

To average the growth rates that appear in column 1, first convert all the rates into a ratio by adding the entries in column 1 to the value 1. For example, the 0.6% growth rate becomes (1 + .006) or 1.006. The reason for this is that if one entry is negative, the product of the multiplication is negative and consequently an nth root would mathematically result in an imaginary number. This method then prevents that situation by converting that negative number into a positive number less than 1 (for example, if the growth rate was -5% this becomes (1 + (−0.05)) or .95). The 13th root of the product of all the column 2 entries is 1.042 or 4.2%.

An advantage of calculating a geometric average for all points is that it provides a more realistic reading of the average percentage change than simply selecting two levels in time and calculating the average percentage change between those points. In the latter case, the selection of the starting and ending points can influence the result. The second advantage of using a geometric average versus a simple arithmetic average (though they would yield the same results in this example) is that the geometric average eliminates a mathematical bias that would be present in the arithmetic average of growth rates.

Another variant on calculating growth rates is the smoothed growth rate. Geoffrey H. Moore and Victor Zarnowitz[6] have devised this method as a way of smoothing out some of the volatility inherent in percentage changes while attempting to preserve the cycle. The formulas for these smoothed rates are:

$$G4 = 100 \times ((X_t / \sum_{i=t-1}^{i=t-13} X_i)^{(12/6.5)} - 1), \textit{for monthly data}$$

$$G5 = 100 \times ((X_t / \sum_{i=t-1}^{i=t-5} X_i)^{(4/2.5)} - 1), \textit{for quarterly data}$$

The monthly smoothed growth rate is expressed as a 6-month smoothed annualized rate (SMSAR) where the average lag is 6.5 months (the formula spans 13 months and half of that is the average lag); consequently, this is the divisor in the exponent. Similarly, formula G5 is expressed as a 2-quarter smoothed annualized rate (TQSAR), where the average lag is 2.5 quarters.

Consider the following example to calculate the SMSAR growth rate (using formula G4) for the Consumer Price Index (CPI). The data and steps in the calculation are shown in Table 3.2. Column 1 lists the data for the CPI-U, while column 2 shows the standard annualized growth rate (using formula G2). Column 2 is shown only for the sake of comparison, so as to observe how different the growth rates can be for any given month. For example, the March 1986 value of the SMSAR growth rate is 1.3% while the G2 formula would yield −5.0%. The remaining columns (3 to 6) detail the steps for calculating the trailing moving average (the moving average calculation is placed in the final month for that span of time) and then deriving the SMSAR growth rate.

An important fact about the various moving average growth rate formulas used to smooth the economic signal is that cyclical turning points can be distorted unless the moving average is centered in the middle period of the span of the average. However, the drawback of a centered moving average is that it reduces the currency of the observation. Hence, there is a tradeoff between currency and smoothness that must be balanced.

Growth Rate Distributions

Once a particular growth rate has been chosen, it is useful to examine some summary statistics about the growth rate distribution. What is the high or low growth rate? What is the average tendency? What are normal bounds around the central tendency? These statistics, as simple as they may seem, provide some overview of the economic series.

Table 3.2   Calculating Six-Month Smoothed Growth Rates (SMSAR).

Month/ Year	(1) CPI-U (1967 = 100)	(2) Annual Rate	(3) 12-Month Trailing Moving Average	(4) Calculating SMSAR Ratio: (1)/(3)	(5) Col. (4) Raised to (12/6.5) Power	(6) Col. (5) Minus One Times 100
1983 Jan.	293.7					
Feb.	293.6	−0.4				
Mar.	293.8	0.8				
Apr.	295.8	8.5				
May	296.9	4.6				
June	297.8	3.7				
July	298.9	4.5				
Aug.	299.9	4.1				
Sept.	301.0	4.5				
Oct.	302.1	4.5				
Nov.	303.1	4.0				
Dec.	304.0	3.6				
1984 Jan.	305.8	7.3	298.4	1.025	1.046	4.6
Feb.	307.0	4.8	299.4	1.025	1.047	4.7
Mar.	307.8	3.2	300.5	1.024	1.045	4.5
Apr.	309.0	4.8	301.7	1.024	1.045	4.5
May	309.5	2.0	302.8	1.022	1.041	4.1
June	310.3	3.1	303.8	1.021	1.040	4.0
July	311.3	3.9	304.9	1.021	1.039	3.9
Aug.	312.6	5.1	305.9	1.022	1.041	4.1
Sept.	313.7	4.3	307.0	1.022	1.041	4.1
Oct.	314.7	3.9	308.0	1.022	1.040	4.0
Nov.	315.3	2.3	309.1	1.020	1.038	3.8
Dec.	316.1	3.1	310.1	1.019	1.036	3.6
1985 Jan.	316.7	2.3	311.1	1.018	1.034	3.4
Feb.	317.7	3.9	312.0	1.018	1.034	3.4
Mar.	319.2	5.8	312.9	1.020	1.038	3.8
Apr.	320.3	4.2	313.8	1.021	1.038	3.8
May	321.0	2.7	314.8	1.020	1.037	3.7
June	321.8	3.0	315.7	1.019	1.036	3.6
July	322.4	2.3	316.7	1.018	1.033	3.3
Aug.	323.1	2.6	317.6	1.017	1.032	3.2
Sept.	323.7	2.3	318.5	1.016	1.030	3.0
Oct.	324.9	4.5	319.3	1.017	1.032	3.2
Nov.	326.7	6.9	320.2	1.020	1.038	3.8
Dec.	327.9	4.5	321.1	1.021	1.039	3.9
1986 Jan.	329.0	4.1	322.1	1.021	1.040	4.0
Feb.	327.7	−4.6	323.1	1.014	1.026	2.6
Mar.	326.3	−5.0	324.0	1.007	1.013	1.3

The method to calculate the average growth rate uses the geometric mean formula described earlier in this chapter. Consider monitoring monthly movements in U.S. industrial production. It is useful to plot the growth rate distribution of monthly percentage changes, as shown in Figure 3.4. A further aspect of the visual distribution is to calculate the average monthly growth rate and determine normal bounds around this rate. This can be useful in developing tracking systems to provide early warning when the growth rate dips below a normal bound. This concept is similar to a quality control chart that places acceptable bounds around the specific target variable. In this example, the normal bounds around the average growth rate are calculated by adding and subtracting one-half of the average absolute deviation around the mean growth rate. The formulas for these calculations are:

$$B_{\text{upper}} = G3 + (½) \, ((1/n) \, | \sum_{i=1}^{i=n} \{R_i - G3\} \, |)$$

$$B_{\text{lower}} = G3 - (½) \, ((1/n) \, | \sum_{i=1}^{i=n} \{R_i - G3\} \, |)$$

where the symbol $|$ is the designation for the absolute value (the value of the expression is always positive).

These normal high-low bands provide a monitoring range for quick evaluation of an economic indicator. More sophisticated bands can be developed depending on the variability of the series and the ultimate purpose of the monitoring system.

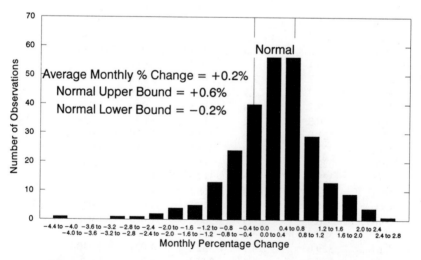

Figure 3.4 Distribution of Industrial Production Percentage Changes.

PERSONS METHOD OF TIME SERIES DECOMPOSITION

One of the earliest methods of analyzing time series data was to decompose the series into various types of movement. Warren M. Persons was among the first to suggest that a time series could be divided into four components: the seasonal, the trend, the cyclical movement, and the residual or irregular component.[7] This time series decomposition approach also has become the basis for the Census Bureau's X-12 seasonal adjustment method (which has just superseded the X-11 method). Conceptually, the series can be defined as either the sum of $T + C + S + I$ or the product of $T \times C \times S \times I$, where T is the trend, C is the cycle, S is the seasonal, and I is the irregular component. Dividing a time series into these component parts is not just an exercise in futility. Forecasting methodologies have been formulated around time series decomposition. In some cases, statistical techniques for forecasting a trend or cycle separately are more reliable than for the entire indicator. Although time series decomposition methods can get elaborate, the following example offers a simple introduction to the concept. Consider the following data for monthly U.S. retail chain store sales, as shown in Table 3.3. In and of itself, it is difficult to discern any meaningful patterns within these data, other than that December sales tend to be strong because of Christmas. Decomposition, however, helps bring out the character of the data. The following illustration, as simple as it is, shows conceptually how to segment the trend, cycle, seasonal, and irregular components from each other.

1. *Calculate the Seasonal Ratio.* The easiest method to calculate a seasonal component of a time series is the ratio-to-moving-average method, which uses a 12-month trailing moving average (or 4-quarter trailing average if the frequency of the data is quarterly etc.). This is done by dividing the current observation by its 12-month trailing moving average. To illustrate, the January 1981 value is:

$$\frac{81.7}{126.784} = 0.607$$

where the value 126.784 is the average of the current plus previous 11 months. The results of that calculation for all months appear in Table 3.4.

2. *Normalize Seasonal Factors to One.* Table 3.4 shows that these seasonal factors do not average to one over the given year. Seasonal factors must be neutral; by definition, they must average to one over the year since a seasonal pattern only is present during the year. To adjust for this, divide each month's seasonal factor by the average seasonal factor for that year (from Table 3.4). The normalized seasonal factors are shown in Table 3.5.

Table 3.3 U.S. Retail Chain Store Sales Index (Unadjusted).

Year	Jan.	Feb.	Mar.	Apr.	May	June	July	Aug.	Sept.	Oct.	Nov.	Dec.	Average
1970	25.8	31.2	45.0	39.5	43.1	53.2	40.3	46.1	52.6	44.7	57.3	67.5	45.5
1971	27.9	33.2	47.4	44.6	47.0	60.4	45.0	50.8	58.5	48.8	63.9	74.4	50.1
1972	31.1	36.9	55.3	47.3	52.6	65.3	51.1	57.8	65.9	56.9	72.0	87.2	56.6
1973	34.8	42.9	63.2	60.1	60.9	78.8	59.5	66.6	75.3	63.0	81.8	98.7	65.5
1974	39.9	47.5	70.9	68.3	69.8	85.6	65.5	73.8	83.7	71.0	86.0	106.6	72.4
1975	42.4	49.7	75.3	67.8	75.4	91.9	69.9	79.2	90.6	76.3	95.4	124.3	78.2
1976	49.6	57.2	83.2	80.7	80.7	101.0	76.2	87.3	100.2	86.3	105.9	141.5	87.5
1977	55.9	63.0	94.5	90.8	92.1	112.6	88.7	99.3	115.3	99.1	119.4	169.4	100.0
1978	61.2	71.1	107.3	100.8	105.2	131.5	100.4	109.5	126.6	108.2	128.5	186.5	111.4
1979	67.7	75.1	110.1	107.7	111.6	135.9	105.8	117.0	135.4	115.0	139.5	201.6	118.5
1980	76.2	82.9	117.0	110.5	117.9	142.3	111.9	123.4	142.1	123.7	145.5	222.4	126.3
1981	81.7	90.5	129.2	133.9	132.0	164.5	125.1	137.2	158.0	133.7	153.7	249.0	140.7
1982	85.7	95.1	136.4	138.7	144.9	169.3	131.1	141.4	163.2	139.2	162.6	226.2	144.5
1983	96.0	103.4	153.2	148.6	160.3	195.4	146.2	162.9	190.1	162.9	191.7	317.9	169.0
1984	112.1	119.9	161.7	174.3	180.0	217.7	159.9	178.5	211.8	178.6	209.2	349.2	187.7
1985	121.2	130.1	178.5	184.7	190.9	229.4	170.3	194.2	222.6	187.0	215.9	360.4	198.8

Table 3.4 Seasonal Pattern, Using 12-Month Moving Averages.

Year	Jan.	Feb.	Mar.	Apr.	May	June	July	Aug.	Sept.	Oct.	Nov.	Dec.	Average
1970	N.A.	N.A.	N.A.	N.A.	N.A.	N.A.	N.A.	N.A.	N.A.	N.A.	N.A.	N.A.	N.A.
1971	0.610	0.724	1.029	0.959	1.004	1.273	0.942	1.054	1.201	0.995	1.288	1.484	1.047
1972	0.617	0.727	1.075	0.917	1.010	1.244	0.964	1.079	1.216	1.037	1.296	1.541	1.060
1973	0.611	0.747	1.088	1.016	1.018	1.292	0.965	1.068	1.191	0.989	1.267	1.508	1.063
1974	0.606	0.717	1.059	1.010	1.022	1.242	0.944	1.054	1.184	0.995	1.199	1.473	1.042
1975	0.584	0.683	1.030	0.927	1.025	1.241	0.938	1.057	1.201	1.005	1.243	1.590	1.044
1976	0.629	0.720	1.039	0.995	0.989	1.226	0.919	1.045	1.188	1.014	1.230	1.618	1.051
1977	0.635	0.712	1.056	1.006	1.010	1.221	0.952	1.054	1.207	1.027	1.223	1.694	1.066
1978	0.609	0.704	1.050	0.979	1.010	1.244	0.942	1.019	1.167	0.991	1.168	1.674	1.046
1979	0.604	0.669	0.979	0.952	0.982	1.193	0.924	1.017	1.170	0.988	1.190	1.701	1.031
1980	0.639	0.692	0.972	0.915	0.973	1.169	0.915	1.005	1.152	0.997	1.168	1.760	1.030
1981	0.644	0.710	1.006	1.027	1.003	1.233	0.930	1.012	1.153	0.970	1.110	1.770	1.047
1982	0.607	0.672	0.961	0.974	1.010	1.176	0.908	0.977	1.124	0.956	1.111	1.566	1.003
1983	0.661	0.708	1.039	1.002	1.072	1.288	0.956	1.052	1.211	1.024	1.188	1.880	1.090
1984	0.658	0.698	0.937	0.998	1.021	1.222	0.892	0.989	1.162	0.973	1.130	1.860	1.045
1985	0.643	0.687	0.936	0.964	0.992	1.186	0.876	0.992	1.132	0.948	1.091	1.813	1.022

Table 3.5 Final Seasonal Factors (Divide Raw Data by These Factors).

Year	Jan.	Feb.	Mar.	Apr.	May	June	July	Aug.	Sept.	Oct.	Nov.	Dec.	Average
1970	N.A.	N.A.	N.A.	N.A.	N.A.	N.A.	N.A.	N.A.	N.A.	N.A.	N.A.	N.A.	
1971	0.583	0.691	0.982	0.916	0.959	1.216	0.900	1.007	1.147	0.950	1.230	1.418	1.000
1972	0.582	0.685	1.014	0.865	0.952	1.174	0.910	1.018	1.147	0.978	1.222	1.453	1.000
1973	0.575	0.702	1.023	0.955	0.958	1.215	0.907	1.004	1.120	0.930	1.192	1.418	1.000
1974	0.582	0.688	1.016	0.969	0.981	1.192	0.906	1.012	1.136	0.955	1.150	1.414	1.000
1975	0.560	0.655	0.986	0.888	0.982	1.189	0.899	1.013	1.150	0.963	1.191	1.524	1.000
1976	0.599	0.685	0.989	0.947	0.941	1.167	0.874	0.994	1.130	0.965	1.171	1.539	1.000
1977	0.596	0.667	0.991	0.943	0.947	1.145	0.893	0.988	1.132	0.963	1.147	1.588	1.000
1978	0.582	0.672	1.004	0.935	0.965	1.189	0.900	0.974	1.115	0.947	1.117	1.600	1.000
1979	0.586	0.649	0.949	0.924	0.953	1.157	0.897	0.987	1.135	0.959	1.154	1.650	1.000
1980	0.621	0.672	0.944	0.889	0.945	1.135	0.889	0.976	1.118	0.968	1.134	1.709	1.000
1981	0.615	0.678	0.961	0.981	0.958	1.178	0.888	0.966	1.101	0.926	1.060	1.690	1.000
1982	0.605	0.670	0.957	0.971	1.006	1.172	0.905	0.973	1.120	0.952	1.107	1.560	1.000
1983	0.606	0.649	0.953	0.919	0.983	1.181	0.877	0.965	1.111	0.940	1.090	1.725	1.000
1984	0.630	0.668	0.897	0.955	0.977	1.170	0.854	0.946	1.112	0.931	1.081	1.780	1.000
1985	0.629	0.673	0.916	0.944	0.971	1.160	0.858	0.971	1.108	0.928	1.068	1.775	1.000

3. *Divide the Seasonal Factor into Raw Data.* Divide each observation from Table 3.3 by the corresponding observation in Table 3.5. The result of this procedure yields a crude seasonally adjusted series, which is shown in Table 3.6.

4. *Calculate the Trend Component.* The method used here to establish the trend component is to calculate a geometric average growth rate of the monthly percentage change in the seasonally adjusted series, as shown in Table 3.7. The geometric average is 0.81% per month, which establishes the trend.

5. *Calculate the Cycle and Irregular Components.* The combined cycle and irregular components are determined by the relationship: CI% = Raw% − Seasonal% − Trend%, where CI% is the percentage change in the cycle and irregular components, Raw% is the percentage change in the raw or unadjusted series, Seasonal% is the seasonal component percentage change, and Trend% is the trend component percentage change, each as defined earlier. Table 3.8 presents the results of this calculation.

6. *Isolate the Cycle from the Irregular Component.* A 5-month moving centered average growth rate is used to define the cyclical component by the relationship, Cycle% = Moving Average (CI%), where Cycle% is the percentage change in the cyclical component and CI% is as defined earlier. These results are shown in Table 3.9.

7. *Calculate the Irregular Component.* Finally, the irregular or unexplained component is derived by the additive decomposition identity: Irregular% = Total% − Seasonal% − Trend% − Cycle%; Table 3.10 shows those results.

While this technique is a useful introduction to decomposition methods, it also highlights some of the limitations of simple methods. The visual inspection of the data shows that some monthly observations in the seasonally adjusted series still are extremely volatile such as the surge in January 1983 or the plunge in January 1984. Numerous techniques have been devised to correct for volatile monthly fluctuation due to moving holidays and other anomalies in the data. Some of these more elaborate techniques will be discussed later in this chapter but for now, it is useful to think in terms of the four components of a time series—the cycle, the seasonal, the trend, and the irregular component. The following sections will explore techniques for measuring trends, cycles, and seasonal patterns.

MEASURING TRENDS

Numerous methods exist to calculate trends in time series, but the objective of all of them is to summarize the long-term pattern of development. The simplest method is to compute a growth rate between the initial point of the series

Table 3.6 Final Seasonally Adjusted Series.

Year	Jan.	Feb.	Mar.	Apr.	May	June	July	Aug.	Sept.	Oct.	Nov.	Dec.
1970	N.A.	N.A.	N.A.	N.A.	N.A.	N.A.	N.A.	N.A.	N.A.	N.A.	N.A.	N.A.
1971	47.8	48.0	48.2	48.7	49.0	49.6	50.0	50.5	51.0	51.3	51.9	52.5
1972	53.5	53.8	54.5	54.7	55.2	55.6	56.2	56.8	57.5	58.2	58.9	60.0
1973	60.5	61.1	61.8	62.9	63.6	64.8	65.6	66.4	67.2	67.7	68.6	69.6
1974	68.7	69.1	69.7	70.4	71.2	71.8	72.3	73.0	73.7	74.4	74.8	75.4
1975	75.8	76.0	76.4	76.3	76.8	77.3	77.7	78.2	78.8	79.3	80.1	81.6
1976	82.8	83.5	84.2	85.3	85.8	86.5	87.1	87.8	88.6	89.5	90.4	91.9
1977	93.8	94.4	95.4	96.2	97.3	98.3	99.4	100.5	101.8	103.0	104.2	106.6
1978	105.1	105.8	106.9	107.8	108.9	110.6	111.6	112.5	113.5	114.3	115.1	116.6
1979	115.4	115.7	116.0	116.6	117.1	117.5	117.9	118.6	119.3	119.9	120.9	122.2
1980	122.8	123.5	124.0	124.3	124.8	125.4	125.9	126.5	127.0	127.8	128.3	130.1
1981	132.8	133.5	134.5	136.6	137.8	139.7	140.9	142.1	143.5	144.4	145.1	147.4
1982	141.5	141.9	142.5	142.9	144.0	144.4	144.9	145.3	145.7	146.1	146.9	145.0
1983	158.4	159.2	160.7	161.6	163.0	165.4	166.8	168.7	171.2	173.3	175.9	184.3
1984	178.0	179.5	180.2	182.5	184.2	186.1	187.3	188.7	190.6	191.9	193.5	196.2
1985	192.6	193.5	194.9	195.8	196.7	197.7	198.6	199.9	200.9	201.6	202.1	203.1

Table 3.7 Monthly Percentage Changes in Seasonally Adjusted Series.

Year	Jan.	Feb.	Mar.	Apr.	May	June	July	Aug.	Sept.	Oct.	Nov.	Dec.
1970	N.A.	N.A.	N.A.	N.A.	N.A.	N.A.	N.A.	N.A.	N.A.	N.A.	N.A.	N.A.
1971	N.A.	0.4	0.4	0.9	0.7	1.3	0.8	0.8	1.0	0.7	1.1	1.2
1972	1.8	0.6	1.3	0.4	0.9	0.8	1.0	1.1	1.2	1.2	1.2	1.9
1973	0.8	0.9	1.2	1.8	1.2	1.9	1.1	1.2	1.2	0.8	1.3	1.5
1974	-1.4	0.6	1.0	1.0	1.1	0.8	0.7	0.9	1.0	0.9	0.5	0.9
1975	0.4	0.3	0.5	-0.1	0.6	0.7	0.5	0.6	0.8	0.6	1.0	1.9
1976	1.5	0.8	0.8	1.3	0.5	0.9	0.6	0.8	0.9	1.0	1.0	1.7
1977	2.1	0.5	1.1	0.9	1.1	1.1	1.1	1.1	1.3	1.1	1.2	2.4
1978	-1.4	0.7	1.1	0.8	1.1	1.5	0.9	0.8	0.9	0.7	0.7	1.3
1979	-1.0	0.3	0.2	0.5	0.5	0.3	0.4	0.5	0.6	0.5	0.8	1.1
1980	0.5	0.5	0.5	0.2	0.4	0.4	0.4	0.4	0.5	0.6	0.4	1.4
1981	2.1	0.5	0.8	1.5	0.9	1.4	0.8	0.9	1.0	0.6	0.5	1.6
1982	-4.0	0.3	0.4	0.3	0.8	0.3	0.3	0.2	0.3	0.3	0.5	-1.3
1983	9.3	0.5	1.0	0.6	0.9	1.5	0.8	1.2	1.4	1.3	1.5	4.7
1984	-3.4	0.8	0.4	1.2	0.9	1.1	0.6	0.7	1.0	0.7	0.8	1.4
1985	-1.8	0.5	0.7	0.5	0.5	0.5	0.4	0.7	0.5	0.4	0.3	0.5

Overall Trend = 0.81%

Table 3.8 Measuring the Cycle and Irregular Components (in Growth Rate Terms).

Year	Jan.	Feb.	Mar.	Apr.	May	June	July	Aug.	Sept.	Oct.	Nov.	Dec.
1970	N.A.	N.A.	N.A.	N.A.	N.A.	N.A.	N.A.	N.A.	N.A.	N.A.	N.A.	N.A.
1971	N.A.	-0.4	-0.2	0.0	-0.1	0.8	-0.2	0.1	0.3	-0.2	0.6	0.5
1972	-0.6	-0.1	1.1	-0.4	0.2	0.2	-0.1	0.4	0.5	0.3	0.7	1.5
1973	-0.6	0.3	0.9	0.9	0.4	1.6	0.0	0.5	0.6	-0.1	0.8	1.0
1974	-0.5	-0.1	0.6	0.2	0.3	0.2	-0.3	0.2	0.3	-0.0	-0.2	0.3
1975	-0.7	-0.5	-0.0	-0.9	-0.1	0.1	-0.4	-0.1	0.1	-0.3	0.5	1.6
1976	-0.5	0.1	0.4	0.5	-0.3	0.3	-0.3	0.1	0.3	0.0	0.4	1.4
1977	-0.6	-0.2	0.8	0.1	0.2	0.5	0.1	0.4	0.7	0.1	0.6	2.5
1978	-0.7	-0.0	0.8	-0.0	0.3	1.1	-0.1	0.1	0.2	-0.2	0.0	1.0
1979	-0.6	-0.5	-0.5	-0.3	-0.3	-0.4	-0.5	-0.2	-0.1	-0.4	0.1	0.7
1980	-0.6	-0.2	-0.1	-0.6	-0.3	-0.3	-0.5	-0.3	-0.3	-0.3	-0.3	1.3
1981	-0.7	-0.3	0.3	0.7	0.1	0.9	-0.2	0.1	0.3	-0.3	-0.2	1.7
1982	-0.7	-0.5	-0.2	-0.5	-0.0	-0.5	-0.5	-0.6	-0.5	-0.5	-0.2	-2.6
1983	-0.6	-0.3	0.6	-0.3	0.1	0.9	-0.2	0.5	0.9	0.3	1.0	6.7
1984	-0.5	0.0	-0.3	0.5	0.2	0.4	-0.3	-0.0	0.4	-0.2	0.1	1.5
1985	-0.7	-0.3	0.2	-0.3	-0.3	-0.2	-0.5	-0.0	-0.3	-0.5	-0.5	-0.0

Table 3.9 Measuring the Cyclical Component (in Growth Rate Terms).

Year	Jan.	Feb.	Mar.	Apr.	May	June	July	Aug.	Sept.	Oct.	Nov.	Dec.
1970	N.A.	N.A.	N.A.	N.A.	N.A.	N.A.	N.A.	N.A.	N.A.	N.A.	N.A.	N.A.
1971	N.A.	N.A.	N.A.	0.0	0.1	0.1	0.2	0.2	0.1	0.3	0.1	0.0
1972	0.3	0.1	0.0	0.2	0.2	0.1	0.2	0.3	0.4	0.7	0.5	0.4
1973	0.5	0.6	0.4	0.8	0.8	0.7	0.6	0.5	0.4	0.5	0.3	0.2
1974	0.3	0.2	0.1	0.2	0.2	0.1	0.1	0.1	-0.0	0.1	-0.1	-0.2
1975	-0.2	-0.4	-0.4	-0.3	-0.3	-0.3	-0.1	-0.2	-0.1	0.3	0.3	0.3
1976	0.4	0.4	0.0	0.2	0.1	0.1	0.0	0.1	0.1	0.4	0.3	0.2
1977	0.4	0.3	0.1	0.3	0.3	0.2	0.4	0.4	0.4	0.9	0.7	0.5
1978	0.6	0.5	0.1	0.4	0.4	0.2	0.3	0.2	-0.0	0.2	0.1	-0.1
1979	-0.1	-0.2	-0.5	-0.4	-0.4	-0.4	-0.3	-0.3	-0.2	0.0	-0.0	-0.1
1980	-0.0	-0.2	-0.4	-0.3	-0.4	-0.4	-0.3	-0.3	-0.3	0.0	-0.1	-0.1
1981	0.1	0.3	0.0	0.4	0.4	0.3	0.2	0.2	-0.1	0.3	0.2	-0.0
1982	0.0	-0.0	-0.4	-0.3	-0.4	-0.4	-0.4	-0.5	-0.5	-0.9	-0.9	-0.9
1983	-0.6	-0.6	-0.1	0.2	0.2	0.2	0.4	0.5	0.5	1.8	1.6	1.5
1984	1.4	1.3	-0.0	0.2	0.1	0.2	0.1	0.1	-0.0	0.4	0.2	0.1
1985	0.2	0.1	-0.3	-0.2	-0.2	-0.3	-0.3	-0.3	-0.4	-0.3	-0.3	-0.3

Table 3.10 Measuring the Irregular Component (in Growth Rate Terms).

Year	Jan.	Feb.	Mar.	Apr.	May	June	July	Aug.	Sept.	Oct.	Nov.	Dec.
1970	N.A.	N.A.	N.A.	N.A.	N.A.	N.A.	N.A.	N.A.	N.A.	N.A.	N.A.	N.A.
1971	N.A.	N.A.	N.A.	0.0	-0.2	0.7	-0.4	-0.1	0.2	-0.5	0.5	0.5
1972	-0.9	-0.2	1.1	-0.6	-0.0	0.1	-0.3	0.2	0.1	-0.4	0.3	1.0
1973	-1.1	-0.3	0.5	0.1	-0.4	0.9	-0.6	-0.0	0.2	-0.7	0.5	0.8
1974	-0.9	-0.3	0.5	-0.1	0.1	0.1	-0.4	0.1	0.3	-0.1	-0.2	0.5
1975	-0.5	-0.2	0.4	-0.6	0.2	0.4	-0.3	0.0	0.1	-0.7	0.2	1.4
1976	-0.9	-0.3	0.4	0.3	-0.4	0.3	-0.4	0.0	0.2	-0.4	0.1	1.2
1977	-0.9	-0.5	0.7	-0.2	-0.1	0.2	-0.3	0.0	0.3	-0.7	-0.1	2.0
1978	-1.3	-0.5	0.7	-0.5	-0.1	0.8	-0.4	-0.1	0.2	-0.4	-0.1	1.1
1979	-0.5	-0.3	-0.1	0.1	0.1	-0.1	-0.2	0.1	0.1	-0.4	0.2	0.8
1980	-0.6	-0.1	0.2	-0.3	0.0	0.1	-0.1	0.0	0.1	-0.3	-0.3	1.3
1981	-0.7	-0.5	0.3	0.4	-0.3	0.6	-0.4	-0.1	0.4	-0.6	-0.4	1.8
1982	-0.7	-0.5	0.2	-0.2	0.3	-0.1	-0.1	-0.0	-0.0	0.3	0.7	-1.8
1983	0.1	0.3	0.7	-0.5	-0.1	0.7	-0.6	0.0	0.4	-1.6	-0.7	5.2
1984	-1.9	-1.2	-0.2	0.3	0.0	0.3	-0.5	-0.1	0.4	-0.6	-0.1	1.4
1985	-0.8	-0.4	0.5	-0.1	-0.1	0.1	-0.2	0.3	0.1	-0.2	-0.2	0.3

and its end point. However, although this method is easy to calculate, the result may not be very representative of the trend since the calculation is strongly influenced by the selection of the two points. A much more desirable alternative is to calculate a geometric average of growth rates for all periods, which is more representative of the average trend growth. Nonetheless, there are limitations to this method as well, since it assumes that the trend remains constant over the entire period. This same assumption is implicit in fitting a linear regression line to the sample to determine the trend path. If the trend varies over time, then a moving average or a higher order polynomial regression might be more desirable to determine the trend.

In determining growth cycle turning points, the NBER has found a 75-month centered moving average could be useful to eliminate a trend in a series. While the selection of the span of the moving average is somewhat arbitrary, the thought was that 75 months was long enough to remove most of the cyclical fluctuation while leaving the underlying secular pattern intact. But even this method is not without its limitation. In particular, the use of a 75-month fixed length cycle to measure the trend of the growth cycle would encounter a problem in fully eliminating the impact of the 1961–1969 cycle on the trend, since that cycle exceeded 75 months. Consequently, the trend calculation inevitably picked up some of the cyclical swing. An alternative, as noted earlier, would be to use a variable-length moving average of some long duration.

Another distinct method for calculating a trend is the *high-low midpoint method*. The steps to apply this method are as follows: (1) select the high and low values in the original time series, (2) interpolate between adjacent pairs of high and low values, and (3) average the high and low values for interpolated series. The following example uses housing data to demonstrate this method.

Because of changes in demographic patterns housing data represent a fluctuating long-term trend; the housing sector is unlikely to have a single trend rate of change. Therefore, this method of segmenting trends is particularly suitable for housing starts data. Table 3.11 lists annual housing starts data from 1959 through 1991. The first step in isolating the various trends is to identify the respective alternating high and low values in the series. All high values are placed in column 2 and the low values in column 3. Linear interpolation is used to fill in the intervening periods between two adjacent highs and lows. To calculate the values between the first high (1517.0) and the next (1603.2), compute the growth rate between these two periods ($[1603.2/1517.0] = 1.0568$) and adjust the growth rate to an annualized rate. Since there is a span of 4 years between these successive high observations, that is, 1959 through 1963, raise the value 1.0568 to the one-fourth (¼) power, which equals 1.0139. Between 1960 and 1962, use the resulting factor (1.0139) to multiply each previous year's value. Thus, the 1960 value equals 1.0139 times 1517.0 or, 1538.1, and the 1961 value equals 1.0139

Table 3.11 High-Low Trend Line Calculations for Housing Starts (in Thousands of Units).

Year	Housing Starts		High Path	Low Path	Average
1959	1517.0	High	1517.0	—	—
1960	1252.2	Low	1538.1	1252.2	1395.2
1961	1313.0		1559.5	1237.2	1398.4
1962	1462.9		1581.2	1222.4	1401.8
1963	1603.2	High	1603.2	1207.8	1405.5
1964	1528.8		1583.6	1193.3	1388.5
1965	1472.8		1564.3	1179.0	1371.6
1966	1164.9	Low	1545.1	1164.9	1355.0
1967	1291.6		1526.3	1226.9	1376.6
1968	1507.6	High	1507.6	1292.3	1399.9
1969	1466.8		1685.7	1361.1	1523.4
1970	1433.6	Low	1884.9	1433.6	1659.2
1971	2052.2		2107.6	1374.2	1740.9
1972	2356.6	High	2356.6	1317.3	1837.0
1973	2045.3		2296.9	1262.8	1779.8
1974	1337.7		2238.7	1210.5	1724.6
1975	1160.4	Low	2182.0	1160.4	1671.2
1976	1537.5		2126.7	1145.8	1636.3
1977	1987.1		2072.8	1131.5	1602.1
1978	2020.3	High	2020.3	1117.2	1568.8
1979	1745.1		1992.1	1103.2	1547.7
1980	1292.2		1964.3	1089.4	1526.8
1981	1084.2		1936.9	1075.7	1506.3
1982	1062.2	Low	1909.8	1062.2	1486.0
1983	1703.0		1883.2	1055.1	1469.1
1984	1749.5		1856.9	1048.1	1452.5
1985	1741.8		1831.0	1041.0	1436.0
1986	1805.4	High	1805.4	1034.1	1419.7
1987	1620.5		1780.2	1027.2	1403.7
1988	1488.1		1755.3	1020.3	1387.8
1989	1381.2		1730.8	1013.5	1372.2
1990	1202.6		1706.7	1006.7	1356.7
1991	1000.0	Low	1682.9	1000.0	1341.4

Note: Shaded data are extrapolated from prior high-point trend.

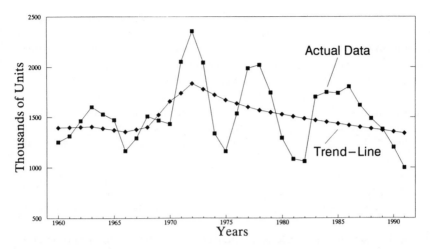

Figure 3.5   Housing Starts, Trend Line Calculated by High—Low, Midpoint Method.

multiplied by 1538.1 and so on. Finally, the result of averaging columns 2 and 3 is shown in column 4. The resulting trend is displayed in Figure 3.5 with the actual yearly data.

There are many variations on these methods to determine a trend. Each method or variation has its own strengths and limitations. Therefore, choosing the appropriate method requires a good deal of judgment.

MEASURING CYCLES

There are two fundamental approaches for investigating cyclical behavior. The first way is to scour the data for a particular cycle duration, while the second approach searches for cycles of varying duration. In many ways, fixed-length cycles provide an easier way of summarizing the past cyclical patterns and presumably extrapolating that pattern into the future. Unfortunately, fixed-length cycles have limited application in economics.

Fixed-Length Cycles

Harmonic Analysis.   The existence of fixed-length cycles can be examined using several statistical techniques. One of the simplest of these techniques to describe and forecast these purely deterministic cycles is to estimate a *harmonic* or *sinusoidal model.* Research work in the agricultural area suggests that these models can be applied to the supply of hogs, broilers, and fish.[8] The basic form of the harmonic model is $Y_t = \text{fn}(\cos wt, \sin wt)$, where Y is a function of cosine and sine functions, w is the frequency defined as $2\pi/p$, and p is the fixed-length periodicity of the cycle, and where t is a time index.

These harmonic models can be estimated using ordinary least squares. An example of this type of model is to estimate housing starts as a function of sine and cosine terms; this is a purely empirical relationship with no particular logical basis. Using annual data between 1947 and 1989 (43 observations), the estimated equation was:

$$\text{Housing Starts} = 1400 + 172.62 \sin(2\pi t/7) + 125.62 \cos(2\pi t/7) + 5.64t$$
$$[5.86] \quad [3.38] \qquad\qquad [2.40] \qquad\qquad [1.91]$$

where the numbers under the coefficients are t-statistics, and t is a time index set to 1 in the initial year and is incremented by 1 unit per year. The actual and fitted values from this linear regression are shown in Figure 3.6. Although the visual relationship appears reasonably supportive of a 7-year cycle, the R-squared statistic is only 0.344, which suggests very little statistical confidence should be put into this 7-year housing starts cycle. Moreover, the shaded area in Figure 3.6 is an extrapolation of that fixed-length cycle for 1990 and 1991. The fixed-length cycle would have suggested improvement in the housing cycle during those 2 years, although the actual performance continued to deterio-

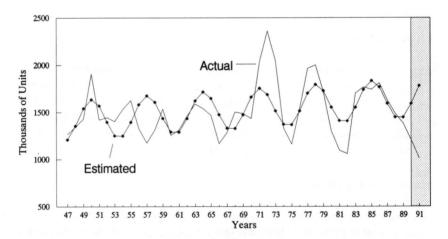

Figure 3.6   Housing Starts Harmonic Model (Estimated 1947–1989, Out of Sample Forecast 1990–1991).

rate. This shows that caution must be exercised in using fixed-length cycles for forecasting, even if the cycle appears to describe the broad trends of the data over history. For forecasting purposes, it is important to ask what fundamental factors have been in play during that period when a fixed-length cycle appeared to be operative and have or could those factors change? In essence, this technique may be a useful summary tool for history, but without understanding the dynamics of the process itself, there is little reason to expect that it will provide a reliable forecast.

Periodogram Analysis. Although this example demonstrated one technique of searching for a fixed-length cycle, other techniques, such as *periodogram analysis,* are more widely used.[9] To apply this method, the data must be arrayed in rows with the number of columns corresponding to the assumed periodicity of the cycle. For example, assume as the political business cycle theorists do, that a 4-year election cycle exists in the unemployment rate. The political business cycle theorists claim that the unemployment rate declines before an election and then increases about a year after the election. This is a clear application of a fixed-length cycle.

Table 3.12 displays the arrayed unemployment rate with column averages. Even allowing for anomalies in the data by excluding high and low values in the columns, a cursory look at the pattern of the unemployment rate, as shown in Figure 3.7, seems to confirm the claim of those analysts arguing for an election-year cycle in the unemployment rate. Although it may be tempting to stop here, the test of the validity of this 4-year cycle must be judged against the possibility of a 2- or 3- or 5- or some other alternative length cycle. A simple statistical test to assess the alternative hypotheses is the *range of means test.* Application of this test is straightforward; it requires that the range of the means be the largest at the assumed periodicity, which would imply that the cycle with the largest amplitude was the most likely periodicity.

The unemployment rate data was arrayed for 24-, 36-, 60-, 72-, 94-, and 108-month spans, and the same calculations were performed to determine the range of the means. The test results are displayed in Figure 3.8. The conclusion from this test was less supportive of the 4-year cycle since the range of the means was larger as the span of time increased. The implication of this was (1) there was an upward trend in the unemployment rate that might bias the political business cycle results, and (2) the data did not necessarily support the 4-year cycle.

In all fairness to the election/economic cycle concept, the analysis can be modified to allow for fixed cycles centered around presidential election dates. This offers a slightly different hypothesis than set forth earlier, which assumed that fixed-length cycles existed every *n* years from the starting point of the data. Alternatively, the time series can be indexed to the election dates and the intercycle trend removed. In this second test, the range of means test is somewhat less

Table 3.12 Periodogram Analysis of the Unemployment Rate.

Election Year	Months prior to Election																							
	−24	−23	−22	−21	−20	−19	−18	−17	−16	−15	−14	−13	−12	−11	−10	−9	−8	−7	−6	−5	−4	−3	−2	−1
1948	3.8	3.8	3.7	3.8	3.8	3.7	3.7	3.6	3.6	3.5	3.5	3.5	3.5	3.5	3.4	3.8	4.0	3.9	3.5	3.6	3.6	3.9	3.8	3.7
1952	4.2	4.3	3.7	3.4	3.4	3.1	3.0	3.2	3.1	3.1	3.3	3.5	3.5	3.1	3.2	3.1	2.9	2.9	3.0	3.0	3.2	3.4	3.1	3.0
1956	5.3	5.0	4.9	4.7	4.6	4.7	4.3	4.2	4.0	4.2	4.1	4.3	4.2	4.2	4.0	3.9	4.2	4.0	4.3	4.3	4.4	4.1	3.9	3.9
1960	6.2	6.2	6.0	5.9	5.6	5.2	5.1	5.0	5.1	5.2	5.5	5.7	5.8	5.3	5.2	4.8	5.4	5.2	5.1	5.4	5.5	5.6	5.5	6.1
1964	5.7	5.5	5.7	5.9	5.7	5.7	5.9	5.6	5.6	5.4	5.5	5.5	5.7	5.5	5.6	5.4	5.4	5.3	5.1	5.2	4.9	5.0	5.1	5.1
1968	3.6	3.8	3.9	3.8	3.8	3.8	3.8	3.9	3.8	3.8	3.8	4.0	3.9	3.8	3.7	3.8	3.7	3.5	3.5	3.7	3.7	3.5	3.4	3.4
1972	5.9	6.1	5.9	5.9	6.0	5.9	5.9	5.9	6.0	6.1	6.0	5.8	6.0	6.0	5.8	5.7	5.8	5.7	5.7	5.7	5.6	5.6	5.5	5.6
1976	6.6	7.2	8.1	8.1	8.6	8.8	9.0	8.8	8.6	8.4	8.4	8.4	8.3	8.2	7.9	7.7	7.6	7.7	7.4	7.6	7.8	7.8	7.6	7.7
1980	5.9	6.0	5.9	5.9	5.8	5.8	5.6	5.7	5.7	6.0	5.9	6.0	5.9	6.0	6.3	6.3	6.3	6.9	7.5	7.6	7.8	7.7	7.5	7.5
1984	10.7	10.7	10.4	10.4	10.3	10.2	10.2	10.1	9.4	9.5	9.2	8.8	8.5	8.2	8.0	7.8	7.8	7.8	7.5	7.2	7.4	7.5	7.4	7.3
Average	5.2	5.3	5.3	5.3	5.3	5.2	5.1	5.1	5.1	5.1	5.1	5.2	5.2	5.1	5.0	4.9	5.0	5.0	5.0	5.1	5.2	5.2	5.0	5.1
Maximum	6.6	7.2	8.1	8.1	8.6	8.8	9.0	8.8	8.6	8.4	8.4	8.4	8.3	8.2	7.9	7.7	7.6	7.7	7.5	7.6	7.8	7.8	7.6	7.7
Minimum	3.6	3.8	3.7	3.4	3.4	3.1	3.0	3.2	3.1	3.1	3.3	3.5	3.5	3.1	3.2	3.1	2.9	2.9	3.0	3.0	3.2	3.4	3.1	3.0
Average less high & low	4.7	4.7	4.6	4.6	4.5	4.4	4.4	4.3	4.3	4.4	4.4	4.5	4.5	4.4	4.4	4.3	4.4	4.4	4.4	4.6	4.6	4.5	4.4	4.5

Table 3.12 (*Continued*)

Election Year	0	1	2	3	4	5	6	7	8	9	10	11	12	13	14	15	16	17	18	19	20	21	22	23	24	Cycle Avg.
1948	3.8	4.0	4.3	4.7	5.0	5.3	6.1	6.2	6.7	6.8	6.6	7.9	6.4	6.6	6.5	6.4	6.3	5.8	5.5	5.4	5.0	4.5	4.4	4.2	4.2	4.6
1952	2.8	2.7	2.9	2.6	2.6	2.7	2.5	2.5	2.6	2.7	2.9	3.1	3.5	4.5	4.9	5.2	5.7	5.9	5.9	5.6	5.8	6.0	6.1	5.7	5.3	3.7
1956	4.3	4.2	4.2	3.9	3.7	3.9	4.1	4.3	4.2	4.1	4.4	4.5	5.1	5.2	5.8	6.4	6.7	7.4	7.4	7.3	7.5	7.4	7.1	6.7	6.2	4.9
1960	6.1	6.6	6.6	6.9	6.9	7.0	7.1	6.9	7.0	6.6	6.7	6.5	6.1	6.0	5.8	5.5	5.6	5.6	5.5	5.5	5.4	5.7	5.6	5.4	5.7	5.8
1964	4.8	5.0	4.9	5.1	4.7	4.8	4.6	4.6	4.4	4.4	4.3	4.2	4.1	4.0	4.0	3.8	3.8	3.8	3.9	3.8	3.8	3.8	3.7	3.7	3.6	4.8
1968	3.4	3.4	3.4	3.4	3.4	3.4	3.4	3.5	3.5	3.5	3.7	3.7	3.5	3.5	3.9	4.2	4.4	4.6	4.8	4.9	5.0	5.1	5.4	5.5	5.9	3.9
1972	5.3	5.2	4.9	5.0	4.9	4.9	4.9	4.9	4.8	4.8	4.8	4.6	4.8	4.9	5.1	5.2	5.1	5.1	5.1	5.4	5.5	5.5	5.9	6.0	6.6	5.5
1976	7.8	7.8	7.5	7.6	7.4	7.2	7.0	7.2	6.9	7.0	6.8	6.8	6.8	6.4	6.4	6.3	6.3	6.1	6.0	5.9	6.2	5.9	6.0	5.8	5.9	7.3
1980	7.5	7.2	7.5	7.4	7.4	7.2	7.5	7.5	7.2	7.4	7.6	7.9	8.3	8.5	8.6	8.9	9.0	9.3	9.4	9.6	9.8	9.9	10.1	10.4	10.7	7.5
1984	7.2	7.2	7.4	7.3	7.3	7.3	7.3	7.3	7.3	7.1	7.1	7.1	7.0	6.9	6.7	7.3	7.2	7.1	7.3							8.1
Average	5.1	5.1	5.1	5.2	5.1	5.2	5.2	5.3	5.3	5.3	5.3	5.5	5.4	5.5	5.7	5.8	5.9	6.0	5.9	5.9	6.0	6.0	6.0	5.9	6.0	
Maximum	7.8	7.8	7.5	7.6	7.4	7.2	7.5	7.5	7.2	7.4	7.6	7.9	8.3	8.5	8.6	8.9	9.0	9.3	9.4	9.6	9.8	9.9	10.0	10.0	11.0	
Minimum	2.8	2.7	2.9	2.6	2.6	2.7	2.5	2.5	2.6	2.7	2.9	3.1	3.5	3.5	3.9	3.8	3.8	3.8	3.9	3.8	3.8	3.8	3.7	3.7	3.6	
Average less high & low	4.5	4.5	4.5	4.5	4.4	4.5	4.4	4.5	4.4	4.3	4.4	4.3	4.3	4.4	4.6	4.7	4.8	5.0	5.0	4.9	5.1	5.1	5.2	5.0	5.1	

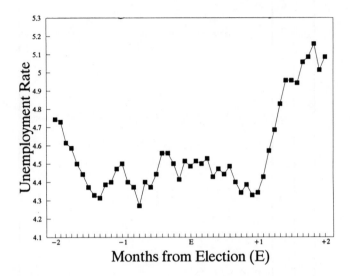

Figure 3.7   The Unemployment Rate during Presidential Election Cycles.

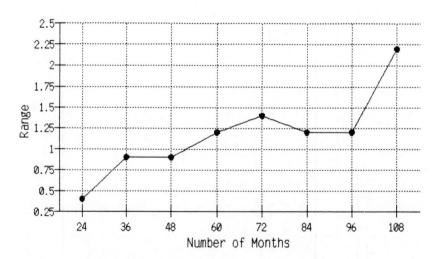

Figure 3.8   Periodogram Analysis: Range of Means.

conclusive, as shown in Figure 3.9, which highlights that the 4-year cycle was more likely than a 2- or 3-year cycle but was equally as likely as a 5- or 6-year cycle.

Spectral Analysis. Another widely used method to determine the length of a fixed-length cycle is *spectral* or *spectrum analysis.* [10] This technique is a cousin of the periodogram analysis and shares many common traits. However, its biggest drawback is that it is more complicated to calculate and the results are far more obscure to interpret. Nonetheless, many researchers have found this method useful in revealing cyclical patterns. (This method also has been used to find seasonal patterns, which seems appropriate for this technique since seasonal patterns are far more regular.) The objective of this method is to search for fixed-length cycles by transforming the search process into an amplitude-frequency domain versus the typical amplitude-time domain. A spectral representation describes the cycle in terms of a frequency and amplitude. The frequency is defined as the inverse of the cycle length, whereas amplitude is the range between peak and trough values.

To apply spectral analysis, Granger and Hatanaka[11] argue that a desirable minimum number of observations is 200. Another condition is that the series must be stationary; the mean and variance of the series must remain constant over time. If the series is not stationary, as most economic time series tend

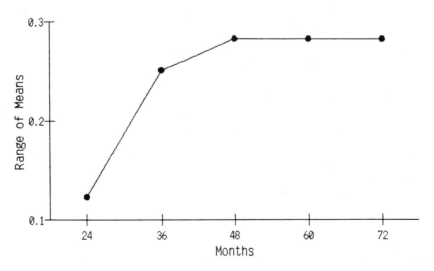

Figure 3.9 Periodogram Analysis: Using Election Cycle Turning Points.

not to be, a first (or higher) difference of the series would be necessary until the differenced series meets the criterion of a stationary mean and variance.

This chapter provides a heuristic discussion of measurement and forecasting techniques instead of the underlying statistical theory. For a more theoretical treatment of spectral analysis, the interested reader should refer to the sources mentioned in the endnotes. Before considering any applications, some of the basic concepts underlying the technique must be reviewed. It is a well-known mathematical property that any set of data points can be exactly replicated with some high order polynomial or some combination of sine and cosine functions. Another point worth noting is that the spectral densities are conceptually similar to the amount of variance explained at a particular cycle frequency. This point will be shown later. Finally, the sinusoidal model forms the starting point for the analysis. This can be represented as:

$$X_t = A_0 + 2\sum_m [A_m \cos(2\pi mt / N) + B_m \sin(2\pi mt / N)] \qquad (8)$$

where t is a time index ranging from 1 to N (the sample size), $N = 2n$, and $m = 1$ to n. The highest possible frequency is n/N where the frequency is defined as the inverse of the length of the sample, that is, $1/N$.

To calculate the coefficients the following formulas are used:

$$A_0 = \bar{x} \text{ (the average of all observations)} \qquad (9)$$

$$A_m = (1/n) \sum_{t=1}^{t=N} x_t \cos(2\pi mt / N), \text{ for } m = 1, \ldots ,n* \qquad (10)$$

$$B_m = (1/n) \sum_{t=1}^{t=N} x_t \sin(2\pi mt / N), \text{ for } m = 1, \ldots ,n* \qquad (11)$$

*or, $n - 1$ if N is odd.

As a side note, if ordinary least squares were used to estimate these coefficients, the R^2 would be equal to one since this formulation exactly replicates the historical observations.

Now consider applying this method to a subset of the housing starts data used earlier to determine the duration of a fixed-length cycle in the annual data. This example will not meet the Granger and Hatanaka criterion for a desirable minimum number of observations, but it will be useful and less cumbersome to demonstrate the method. In this example, the sample size, N, equals 28 and based on the period 1959 to 1986.

1. *Calculate the Average of the Sample.* The average of the housing starts data between 1959 and 1986 was 1560.5 (A_0).

2. *For m = 1 to n, Calculate Each A_m.* In this example, A_1 is calculated for $t = 1, \ldots ,28$ (or, 1959 to 1986) and $m = 1$.

For $t = 1$, $\cos(2\pi mt /N) \times$ Observation 1
    $= \cos((2 \times 3.141595 \times 1 \times 1)/28) \times 1517.0 = 1479.0$

For $t = 2$, $\cos(2\pi mt /N) \times$ Observation 2
    $= \cos((2 \times 3.141595 \times 1 \times 2)/28) \times 1252.2 = 1128.2$

Continue this process for each observation in the sample. After accomplishing this for each observation, sum the 28 calculations; in this case, the sum equals -1519.1. Then divide this result by the sample size:

$$A_1 = (1/N) \times \text{Sum} = (1/28) \times (-1519.1) = -54.3$$

Table 3.13 shows the other A_m values.

3. *For m = 1 to n, Calculate Each B_m.* This is a repeat of the operations in step 2, except that the sine function is substituted for the cosine. The results of this step also appear in Table 3.13.

Table 3.13   Calculated A and B Values for the Spectral Analysis Example Using Housing Starts.

A		B	
A_1	$= -54.3$	B_1	$= -36.4$
A_2	$= 73.4$	B_2	$= 21.4$
A_3	$= -1.9$	B_3	$= 12.6$
A_4	$= 107.0$	B_4	$= -117.4$
A_5	$= -75.4$	B_5	$= -45.9$
A_6	$= 49.0$	B_6	$= 47.0$
A_7	$= -33.5$	B_7	$= -1.4$
A_8	$= 29.3$	B_8	$= 13.4$
A_9	$= 10.6$	B_9	$= 21.6$
A_{10}	$= 7.5$	B_{10}	$= -1.7$
A_{11}	$= 15.8$	B_{11}	$= -5.5$
A_{12}	$= 5.9$	B_{12}	$= -9.3$
A_{13}	$= 0.8$	B_{13}	$= -1.6$
A_{14}	$= -24.0$	B_{14}	$= 0.0$

4. *Calculate the Spectrum.* The spectrum of a sample is defined as: $N(A_m^2 + B_m^2)$ for $m = 1$ to n. In the example, the spectrum are:

Frequency	Years/Cycle	Spectrum
1/28	28.0	119533.5
2/28	14.0	163878.2
3/28	9.3	4567.2
4/28	7.0	706310.7 *Peak*
5/28	5.6	218237.4
6/28	4.7	129192.4
7/28	4.0	31433.3
8/28	3.5	29116.1
9/28	3.1	16196.3
10/28	2.8	1675.0
11/28	2.5	7863.1
12/28	2.3	3377.7
13/28	2.2	86.5
14/28	2.0	16132.8

5. *Smooth the Spectrum (optional).* A whole set of literature has developed on smoothing methods for the spectral density function, which are referred to as *spectral windows.* Care, however, must be exercised (just as with any time-domain smoothing routine) not to introduce a cyclical peak solely due to the smoothing technique.

6. *Interpret the Results.* These results suggest that a 7-year cycle appears in the data, which is observable in Figure 3.10 as a peak in the spectral density. This example is relatively consistent with the regression equation, previously described, suggesting the presence of a 6-year cycle. Clemhout and Neftçi[12] also have found a 6- to 7-year cycle in housing starts data using monthly data between 1947 and 1977. In the final analysis, the usefulness of spectral analysis in *finding* cycles of some fixed duration comes down to assessing its statistical accuracy. *Bartels' test*[13] is one such statistic to measure that accuracy. The test is applied by calculating individual cycle coefficients (the A_m and B_m values for each cycle) and comparing the individual cycle coefficients with the average of all cycles of that given duration.

Finally, the Foundation for the Study of Cycles[14] has been using a spectral analysis variant since 1941. Based on that method, they have cataloged many economic cycles and report their findings in their journal, *Cycles.* In their work, they have identified such short-term movement as a 17-week stock market cycle as well as long-duration waves such as a 54-year cycle in wholesale prices (the Kondratieff wave). Projections of cyclical patterns are made using

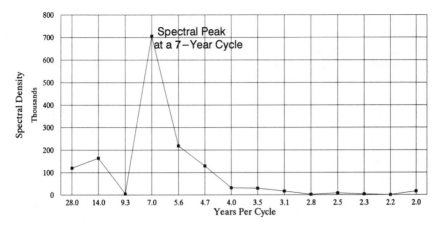

Figure 3.10 Spectral Analysis of Housing Starts: 1959–1986.

an *ideal cycle,* that is, assuming the amplitude and duration of the cycle follows its historical pattern.

The NBER Cycle of Experience

The National Bureau of Economic Research under the leadership of Wesley Mitchell pioneered the cycle of experience concept. Mitchell felt that while it might be desirable to isolate the trend from the cycle in a time series, it was just too ad hoc a procedure to provide a robust solution. In particular, Burns and Mitchell cited a study by Edwin Frickey to support this claim. The Frickey study[15] experimented with 23 different trend lines for the same series and found that the resulting cycle could range from 3 to 4 years to more than 10 times that duration. The solution to this problem, Burns and Mitchell felt was not to trend-adjust the series. This led to a different way of looking at the time series—according to business cycle stages and compared with previous recession–recovery patterns, which eliminated some of the problems associated with trend-adjusting the data.

Recession–Recovery Monitoring.   Recession and recovery analysis, or *recrec* analysis, was a method devised by Geoffrey H. Moore to compare similar business cycle experiences.[16] The technique serves as a current business cycle monitoring tool that compares current economic activity with previous cyclical expansions (or contractions). This time-oriented comparison is best described by example.

Basically, the procedure is a straightforward presentation and interpretation that answers the question: How is the economy performing relative to past business cycles?[17] The actual calculation can be done on the basis of the specific cycle (dating the turning points in the series under consideration) or the reference cycle (using the aggregate business cycle dates) for either the business or growth cycle. Consider the following example where the objective is to assess the performance of the 1990 business cycle recession compared with past cycles and to determine whether the 1990 recession followed the cyclical average pattern or was below or above average. To illustrate this method, industrial production is used as a representative series of the business cycle. The technique is applied as follows:

1. *Assemble the Time Series Data by Business Cycle Dates.* Decide on the span of the comparison, say 1 year before the turning point and 2 years after, and assemble the data in columns for each business cycle episode.

2. *Index Each Cycle by the Initial Turning Point.* Using the monthly industrial production data, each business cycle episode is indexed to 100 at its business cycle peak (or trough, if that is the comparison). For example, the cycle index for January 1990 is derived by dividing the January 1990 observation by its associated value at its cyclical peak, July 1990, and the same is done for the entire span of time as well as for each business cycle episode. The result of this procedure for the industrial production series appears in Table 3.14. Observe that the turning point value for each business cycle period will be 100 and the average of all those cycles also will be 100.

3. *Average the Historical Growth Pattern.* The average cycle pattern can be derived as a simple arithmetic average, the median, or any other measure that seems most representative of the central tendency.[18] The 1948–1981 cyclical average, as shown in Table 3.14, is calculated as an arithmetic average of the business cycle episodes. Although at times it may be desirable to truncate the period if another turning point is encountered before the span (in this example, 24 months after the peak) is completed, that was not done in this example. The logic for truncating the segment would be that the focus was simply on the recession or recovery, and hence, an average of a recovery with a recession episode would bias the result. However, if timing comparisons alone are the focus, then the individual cycle segments would not be truncated after reaching a subsequent turning point. More often than not, the series is likely to be truncated.

4. *(Optional) Calculate the Range for the Individual Cycles.* The high and low growth profile per period also was included for comparison in Table 3.14. The high and low represent the high and low of any cycle for a given month from a turning point. Alternatively, the high or low path might represent a specific cycle. Again, the choice of the presentation and calculation depends on the purpose.

Table 3.14 Industrial Production Cyclical Comparisons from One Year before Business Cycle Peak to Two Years After.

Months from Turning Point	Year and Month Recession Began									1948–1981		
	1948/11	1953/07	1957/08	1960/04	1969/12	1973/11	1980/01	1981/07	1990/07	Low	Averages	High
−12	98.7	84.6	96.7	98.4	98.3	94.5	99.1	93.2	97.6	84.6	95.4	99.1
−11	98.7	90.1	98.9	100.0	98.9	95.3	99.9	94.6	98.0	90.1	97.1	100.0
−10	99.6	93.2	99.7	100.0	99.5	95.5	100.2	95.9	98.0	93.2	98.0	100.2
−9	99.6	94.1	98.9	97.7	100.3	96.8	99.2	96.4	97.6	94.1	97.9	100.3
−8	98.7	96.0	100.3	94.3	99.8	96.8	100.3	98.2	97.9	94.3	98.1	100.3
−7	98.7	96.6	100.0	94.3	99.5	97.1	100.2	98.6	98.4	94.3	98.1	100.2
−6	100.4	96.9	100.8	93.5	100.5	97.6	99.7	97.8	97.4	93.5	98.4	100.8
−5	101.7	97.5	100.8	94.0	100.9	98.3	99.3	98.0	98.3	94.0	98.8	101.7
−4	101.7	98.1	99.4	100.0	101.3	98.9	99.5	98.4	98.6	98.1	99.7	101.7
−3	101.3	98.8	99.2	102.6	101.3	98.8	100.1	97.6	98.6	97.6	99.9	102.6
−2	100.4	99.4	99.4	101.6	101.3	99.6	99.8	98.3	99.1	98.3	100.0	101.6
−1	101.3	98.8	100.0	100.8	100.3	100.0	99.7	98.9	99.7	98.8	100.0	101.3
BC Peak 0	100.0	100.0	100.0	100.0	100.0	100.0	100.0	100.0	100.0	100.0	100.0	100.0
1	99.2	99.4	99.2	99.7	98.1	98.4	100.3	99.8	100.1	98.1	99.3	100.3
2	98.3	97.5	97.5	98.7	98.1	97.1	100.3	99.3	100.2	97.1	98.4	100.3

Table 3.14 *(Continued)*

	Year and Month Recession Began									1948–1981		
	1948/11	1953/07	1957/08	1960/04	1969/12	1973/11	1980/01	1981/07	1990/07	Low	Averages	High
3	97.0	96.6	95.3	98.2	97.9	96.7	98.4	98.5	99.5	95.3	97.3	98.5
4	95.3	94.4	93.6	98.2	97.8	97.1	96.0	97.4	98.1	93.6	96.2	98.2
5	94.9	92.0	91.7	97.2	97.6	96.9	94.9	96.6	97.1	91.7	95.2	97.6
6	93.6	91.4	89.7	96.9	97.3	98.1	94.5	94.6	96.6	89.7	94.5	98.1
7	93.2	91.7	88.6	95.6	97.5	98.4	95.9	96.7	95.7	88.6	94.7	98.4
8	93.2	91.0	87.2	93.8	97.3	97.9	97.2	96.1	95.1	87.2	94.2	97.9
9	94.1	90.4	88.1	94.0	96.7	97.6	97.8	95.5	95.6	88.1	94.3	97.8
10	94.9	91.0	90.6	93.8	94.8	98.0	99.5	94.9	96.4	90.6	94.7	99.5
11	91.5	91.4	91.7	94.3	94.2	97.3	100.0	94.6	97.2	91.4	94.4	100.0
12	94.1	91.4	93.6	96.4	96.4	94.5	99.2	94.1	97.9	91.4	95.0	99.2
13	95.8	91.4	94.4	97.7	97.2	90.6	99.4	93.7	97.8	90.6	95.0	99.4
14	97.0	91.4	95.6	99.2	96.8	88.2	99.8	93.0	98.2	88.2	95.1	99.8
15	97.5	92.6	98.3	100.3	96.8	86.8	99.0	92.2	98.0	86.8	95.4	100.3
16	100.8	94.1	98.6	101.3	97.3	85.2	99.7	91.8	97.8	85.2	96.1	101.3
17	104.2	95.4	100.0	101.0	97.8	86.0	100.2	91.0	97.6	86.0	97.0	104.2
18	106.8	97.5	101.9	103.1	98.3	85.8	101.4	92.8	NA	85.8	98.4	106.8
19	109.7	98.8	103.3	104.7	97.9	86.8	101.2	92.7	NA	86.8	99.4	109.7
20	113.1	100.9	105.6	105.4	97.5	87.4	100.7	93.3	NA	87.4	100.5	113.1
21	116.9	102.2	107.2	104.7	99.1	89.0	99.9	94.5	NA	89.0	101.7	116.9
22	116.1	104.0	107.2	106.5	99.7	89.9	98.7	95.5	NA	89.9	102.2	116.1
23	116.9	104.0	104.7	107.0	100.2	90.3	97.9	96.1	NA	90.3	102.1	116.9
24	116.5	104.9	101.1	107.3	101.3	91.2	95.9	97.9	NA	91.2	102.0	116.5

In the industrial production example, the summary information in Table 3.14 leads to the conclusion that the contraction in industrial production during the 1990 recession was more modest than the average cyclical contraction, as is shown in Figure 3.11. How the question is poised will determine how the recrec analysis will be crafted, but the basic method is the same as demonstrated here.

Cyclical Forecasting of Economic Indicators.   Recession–recovery patterns can be used to forecast the path of the current cycle. One such model for forecasting is the Average Recovery–Recession Model (ARRM).[19]

The ARRM approach is easy to understand and simple to apply. It builds on the recession–recovery patterns just described. This model, however, goes the next step and answers the question: What would the path of the economic variable be if it followed the average cyclical contour? This model is useful if for no other reason then to set up a strawman to discuss the probable expansion or contraction path.[20] To make use of ARRM, all that is necessary is to extrapolate from the latest observation by using the average growth path or the path of a particular cycle episode. This method can be particularly useful to construct a forecast profile for a given series, assuming the current cycle were to follow some past cyclical experience.

Business Cycle Stage Analysis.   Business cycle stage analysis is a technique to consolidate economic time series data into nine standardized segments over a complete cycle measured from peak to peak or trough to trough. This technique of dividing a cycle into nine stages was suggested by Wesley C. Mitchell

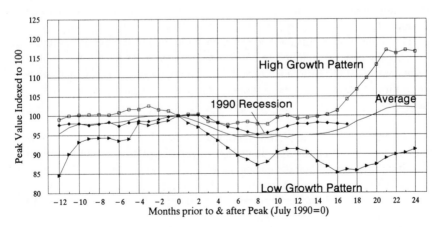

Figure 3.11   Cycle Patterns for Industrial Production, One Year Prior to Peak and Two Years After.

and was utilized at the National Bureau of Economic Research (NBER) as a method to analyze economic processes and to summarize the basic pattern of cyclical behavior. While stage analysis is used primarily for examining the cyclical patterns of economic activities, it also provides some forecasting insights that are generally not available from other business cycle tools.

Pattern or stage analysis has a lot in common with recession–recovery monitoring. Recession–recovery monitoring divides the business cycle into either peak-to-trough or trough-to-peak swings and permits a comparison between the average cycle pattern and the current cycle. However, these recession–recovery comparisons of business cycle changes, from the turning point dates, are time oriented—comparisons are always made the same number of months after the turning point date regardless of the total length of the business cycle. While this is quite useful, it also hides information. Cycle lengths are not identical, and it is easy to lose sight of the business cycle dynamics with recession–recovery monitoring alone. Business cycle stage analysis solves this problem.

Business cycles can be divided into periods of similar development. This type of division is not time-oriented like the recession–recovery technique, but is growth oriented. Unfortunately, it is no small task to divide the economic indicator into growth segments of similar magnitude without regard to timing. Since no two business cycles are identical, it is difficult, if not impossible, to accurately sift through an economic indicator to match corresponding growth phases across numerous irregularly shaped business cycles. Therefore a working solution to this problem is to divide the cycle into a set number of segments or stages and compare its current development with its historical growth pattern per stage. This approximation to standardized growth segments works reasonably well as a tool for analysis, monitoring, and forecasting of the cyclical nature of economic indicators but is not without its limitations, as noted in Chapter 1.

The application of this method is somewhat tedious, but it yields new cyclical insights. Indeed, a variant on this method was used by Richard Katz for investment analysis at the Boston Company.[21] There are two steps in the analysis process: First, "create" the business cycle segments, and then propose "what if" questions.

The Technique.   To apply this technique, some initial cycle parameters must be selected. These parameters include the type of cycle to be analyzed (either specific or reference) and the dating method (classical or growth). The choice is dependent on the aim of the research. Reference cycle stage comparisons allow series to be evaluated against the same standard time frame, whereas this is not the case with specific cycle stages.

After deciding on the cycle parameters, the next step is to determine the turning point dates in the individual series or to use the reference classical or growth cycle dates. Examining the cyclical pattern of price behavior, as represented by the spot price index, provides an example of this technique as well as shows how this method can be used as a supplemental forecasting tool. The spot price index is a leading cyclical indicator of business cycles as well as of inflation cycles. This indicator serves as a sensitive measure of demand in auction or flex-price markets. Current macroeconomic analysis tends to distinguish between two price responses in the marketplace: (1) flexible price markets where price is the adjusting mechanism for balancing supply and demand, and (2) administered or fix-price markets where output is used as the adjusting mechanism to bring supply and demand into equilibrium. The spot price index represents a market basket of prices in the auction market and hence is susceptible to cyclical swings. This series consequently serves as a good example for the application of pattern analysis.

The spot price index was analyzed in terms of its own specific cycle. While more elaborate methods exist for dating cyclical turning points, this example simply relied on visual inspection to select turning points. Based on these turning points, nine complete cycles (trough to trough) were isolated. Each cycle was then divided into nine stages or phases based on the following rules:

1. *The value at a turning point date is calculated as a three-month centered average on that turning point.* The logic for a turning point *zone* is that the NBER's concept of turning points are not a statistical phenomenon but an economic phenomenon and the averaging helps to ensure against statistical quirks.

2. *The expansion and contraction phases of the complete cycle are divided as equally as possible into three segments.* When this is not possible, the middle third is used as the adjusting stage.

3. *The intercycle trend is eliminated.* This is accomplished by first calculating the cycle base which is the average value over the complete cycle. Then the stage averages are divided by their relevant cycle base.

These NBER rules are straightforward and easy to apply. Additionally, they have a long tradition and provide a standard for business cycle analysis.

Table 3.15 shows the turning point dates that have been identified in the spot price index specific cycle. Since trough-to-trough cycles are being examined, nine complete cycles are available for analysis.

Once the cycle dates were identified, the next step was to determine the length of the various stages. The calculation of cycle 1 will be looked at in detail; the calculation of the remaining eight cycles follow the same approach. Table 3.16 shows the stage divisions and the associated length for cycle 1.

Several conventions used in Table 3.16 should be noted. First, it has become traditional to designate the cycle stages in Roman numerals. Second, as already noted, the turning point dates are averaged over a three-month span and

Table 3.15   Cyclical Turning Point Dates Spot Price Index (1967 = 100).

Cycle	Initial Trough	Peak	Terminal Trough	Duration (Months)
1	June 1949	Feb. 1951	Oct. 1953	53
2	Oct. 1953	Dec. 1955	Apr. 1958	55
3	Apr. 1958	Nov. 1959	Dec. 1960	33
4	Dec. 1960	May 1961	June 1963	31
5	June 1963	Mar. 1966	July 1968	62
6	July 1968	Feb. 1970	July 1971	37
7	July 1971	Apr. 1974	July 1975	49
8	July 1975	Feb. 1980	Dec. 1982	90
9	Dec. 1982	May 1984	Apr. 1986	41

centered on the turning point date. Third, although it may not be obvious from the table, stages I and IX for adjacent cycles are the same. For example, stage IX in cycle 1 covers the three months' period from September through November 1953. Stage I of cycle 2 covers this same period—the terminal trough and the next initial trough are always identical. If peak-to-peak stages were being examined, then the terminal peak would be identical to its next cycle's initial peak. Moreover, while these two stages cover the same period, the cycle averages adjusted for intertrend movement would not be the same.

Table 3.16   Stages of Cycle 1, Spot Price Index.

Stage Number	Name of Stage	Period Covered	Duration (Months)
I	Initial revival	May 1949 –July 1949	3
	Period of Expansion		
II	First third	July 1949 –Dec. 1949	6
III	Second third	Jan. 1950 –July 1950	7
IV	Last third	Aug. 1950–Jan. 1951	6
V	Recession	Jan. 1951 –Mar. 1951	3
	Period of Contraction		
VI	First third	Mar. 1951–Dec. 1951	10
VII	Second third	Jan. 1952 –Nov. 1952	11
VIII	Last third	Dec. 1952 –Sept. 1953	10
IX	Terminal revival	Sept. 1953–Nov. 1953	3

Table 3.17 Business Cycle Patterns or Stage Analysis Average in Specific Cycle Relatives at Stages. Spot Price Index (Burns and Mitchell Approach).

Specific Cycle Dates Trough-Peak-Trough (1)	I Three Months Centered on Initial Trough (2)	Expansion			V Three Months Centered on Peak (6)	Contraction			IX Three Months Centered on Ending Trough (10)	Business Cycle Stage Base (11)
		II First Third (3)	III Middle Third (4)	IV Last Third (5)		VI First Third (7)	VII Middle Third (8)	VIII Last Third (9)		
June 49–Feb. 51–Oct. 53	75.5	79.0	83.7	130.1	147.0	125.1	96.9	84.2	78.7	117.20
Oct. 53–Dec. 55–Apr. 58	90.5	92.1	97.5	104.5	111.0	106.7	105.3	94.8	89.1	101.80
Apr. 58–Nov. 59–Dec. 60	90.5	94.3	100.1	103.3	104.8	103.6	102.4	99.8	96.9	100.20
Dec. 60–May 61–June 63	99.1	98.9	102.9	105.8	104.9	103.4	98.5	96.8	95.9	98.00
June 63–Mar. 66–July 68	89.1	92.0	102.9	110.2	115.7	106.5	95.2	93.0	89.6	105.50
July 68–Feb. 70–July 71	86.8	90.2	100.1	106.6	109.1	106.7	99.7	99.1	96.9	109.00
July 71–Apr. 74–July 75	64.0	68.5	83.0	119.2	141.9	136.0	115.9	110.0	106.0	164.90
July 75–Feb. 80–Dec. 82	70.9	79.4	87.0	114.0	129.2	119.1	114.7	98.9	93.3	246.50
Dec. 82–May 84–Apr. 86	89.6	95.6	103.4	111.2	112.2	106.4	97.1	91.1	86.0	256.77
Average (9 cycles)	84.0	87.8	95.6	111.7	119.5	112.6	102.9	96.4	92.5	144.4
Avg. (8 cycles, 1949–82)	83.3	86.8	94.7	111.7	120.5	113.4	103.6	97.1	93.3	130.4
Average Absolute Deviation (9 cycles)	9.2	8.1	7.4	6.3	13.2	9.4	6.1	5.0	5.9	52.2
Normal Upper Bound	88.6	91.8	99.3	114.8	126.1	117.3	105.9	98.9	95.4	170.53
Normal Lower Bound	79.4	83.7	91.9	108.5	112.9	107.9	99.8	93.9	89.5	118.33

The next step in this procedure was to average the series values for each cycle stage. In this example, 90 averages were calculated (9 cycles times 9 stages, plus 9 complete cycle averages). This is a tedious process but can be computerized to expedite the analysis.

The complete cycle averages are termed the *cycle base*. These values are used to calculate the average cycle relatives. Dividing each cycle stage average value by the cycle base results in the cycle relatives which measure the percentage change per stage during the cyclical expansion and contraction sequences. These cycle relatives are generally expressed as an index (ratio multiplied by 100). Table 3.17 on page 127 shows the final calculations for the spot price index, which also is portrayed in Figure 3.12.

Using Business Cycle Stages for Monitoring and Forecasting.   Once the stages are calculated, this method can be used for current monitoring and forecasting. Although this framework was never devised as a forecasting tool, it is possible to examine possible growth paths for the indicator under study. To illustrate, consider three "what if" scenarios that were developed in April 1984 to forecast spot prices. The three paths considered were (1) what if the length of the current stage is equal to the average cycle stage length? (2) what if the series is still in stage II? and (3) what if the growth rate per stage is equal to the stage averages without regard to the length of time? Table 3.18 documents these forecasts from the perspective of April 1984 when only the first eight cycles were known.

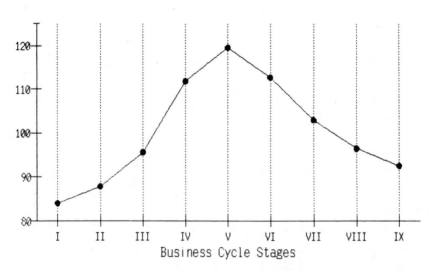

Figure 3.12   Business Cycle Pattern for the Spot Price Index.

Table 3.18   Cycle Stage Monitoring and Forecasting Spot Price Index.

(Ex-Post Forecast Made from April 1984) Current Cycle Monitoring	II/I	III/II	IV/III	V/IV	
A. Growth from prior stage (%)	7.7	12.3	2.9		← Average Months
Months from prior stage	7	8	4		
B. Growth from prior stage (%)	16.8				
Months from prior stage	19				← All in Stage II
C. Growth from prior stage (%)	4.7	6.9	7.5	3.2	← Median Stage Growth
Months from prior stage	3	6	2	8	

Cumulative Expansion	Average % Change	Cumulative % Change	Current as % of Avg.
Eight-Cycle Median (1949–1982)	27.8		
December 1982– April 1984		20.7	74.4

The first scenario, case A, assumed that the current cycle was expanding in line with the average (median) number of months per stage. If this was true, then the spot prices would have the second highest growth rate at 12.3% for that stage of the cycle. This case was rejected because it appeared inconsistent with other information available at the time. The second scenario, case B, assumed that the spot price growth was still in stage II of the cycle. This would be a worst scenario case since it pointed toward historically rapid inflation. Again, this case was rejected since it appeared unrealistic. The third scenario, case C, assumed that the growth in spot prices was consistent with the median growth per stage. This case appeared to be the most plausible. It showed, however, that the rebound in the spot price index—in terms of months—had been faster than previous experience would have suggested. Moreover, this scenario argued that the increase in spot prices was slowing and possibly a peak growth rate was in sight. With the benefit of hindsight, the spot price index peaked in May 1984.

Business cycle stage analysis is a powerful tool for analysis. While it can be used for forecasting, as shown in this example, it should not be viewed as an independent tool but only as a supplemental method.

Business Cycle Summary Statistics.   Burns and Mitchell[22] in their classic work, *Measuring Business Cycles,* offer researchers a host of summary measures to compare and evaluate business cycles and cycle stages. Some of their methods already have been described, although it is worth noting a few other summary statistics.

The simplest way of presenting a measure of central tendency of business cycle activity is to use the mean and the average deviation to capture dispersion. Additionally, Burns and Mitchell propose a shorthand gauge to measure how closely the specific cycle mirrors the reference business cycle. This measure, called an *index of conformity,* is computed as follows: when a series increases during the reference cycle expansion, the series gets a score of +100; if the series remains unchanged, it is scored 0, and if the series declines, it is marked −100. The index of conformity is then calculated as the arithmetic average of these individual cycle scores.[23]

Consider the following example to summarize the average pattern of short-term interest rate movement over the business cycle. The interest rate cycle can be summarized by the Burns and Mitchell nine-cycle stages and this example also can be used to illustrate some other business cycle summary measures. The standard approach, as previously described, consolidates the information into cycle relatives as shown in Table 3.19. Each stage is averaged and the average absolute deviation is calculated, which yields the *normal* upper and lower bounds.

This analysis shows that the duration of the expansion periods exceeds the contraction periods by a ratio of five to one. Another aspect of stage analysis is to look at changes between adjacent cycle phases. This is demonstrated in Table 3.20, which shows the movement between stages of the three-month Treasury bill rate. The summary measures are indicated at the bottom of Table 3.20. From those results, it can be concluded that as the economy comes out of a recession, interest rates increase until the onset of the next recession.

A better alternative to the Burns and Mitchell cycle relative method for summarizing the business cycle is to use the percentage change variant of their method. To do this, geometric averages of monthly percentage changes are calculated for the periods indicated in Table 3.21. An advantage in using percentage change is that less information is lost in summarizing the movement of the time series over the cycle. Although the percentage change variant yields the same conclusion as with the original Burns and Mitchell framework (see Table 3.22,

Table 3.19 Business Cycle Stage Analysis Three-Month Treasury Bill Rate (Burns & Mitchell Approach).

Reference Cycle Dates Trough–Peak–Trough (1)	I Three Months Centered on Initial Trough (2)	II Expansion First Third (3)	III Expansion Middle Third (4)	IV Expansion Last Third (5)	V Three Months Centered on Peak (6)	VI Contraction First Third (7)	VII Contraction Middle Third (8)	VIII Contraction Last Third (9)	IX Three Months Centered on Ending Trough (10)	Business Cycle Stage Base (11)
Oct. 49–July 53–May 54	71.0	79.7	102.5	125.9	137.3	115.6	93.6	65.7	52.4	1.50
May 54–Aug. 57–Apr. 58	36.2	51.2	104.4	136.9	154.1	163.4	134.4	65.3	51.2	2.18
Apr. 58–Apr. 60–Feb. 61	40.6	67.8	107.0	144.8	119.6	98.0	86.2	83.5	85.8	2.74
Feb. 61–Dec. 69–Nov. 70	54.1	64.6	95.1	123.4	175.9	166.0	152.2	141.4	123.1	4.34
Nov. 70–Nov. 73–Mar. 75	92.5	76.1	67.6	113.8	129.7	133.6	140.7	117.0	95.7	5.78
Mar. 75–Jan. 80–July 80	77.4	75.6	76.7	129.0	172.1	196.3	184.7	109.5	113.2	7.15
July 80–July 81–Nov. 82	69.4	96.0	129.5	124.5	129.2	112.3	108.5	82.6	67.8	11.66
Average	63.0	73.0	97.6	128.3	145.4	140.7	128.6	95.0	84.2	5.05
Average Absolute Deviation	16.6	10.1	15.2	7.3	18.8	28.2	27.9	23.7	23.2	2.70
Normal Upper Bound	71.3	78.0	105.2	132.0	154.8	154.8	142.5	106.8	95.7	6.40
Normal Lower Bound	54.7	67.9	90.0	124.7	136.0	126.6	114.7	83.1	72.6	3.70

Table 3.20 Rate of Change from Stage to Stage of Reference Cycles Three-Month Treasury Bill Rate.

Reference Cycle Dates	Expansion				Contraction			
	I – II	II – III	III – IV	IV – V	V – VI	VI – VII	VII – VIII	VIII – IX
Trough – Peak – Trough	Trough to First Third (2)	First to Middle Third (3)	Middle to Last Third (4)	Last Third to Peak (5)	Peak to First Third (6)	First to Middle Third (7)	Middle Third to Last Third (8)	Last Third to Trough (9)
Oct. 1949 – July 1953 – May 1954	1.4%	2.0%	1.6%	1.0%	−5.3%	−6.3%	−10.0%	−6.8%
May 1954 – Aug. 1957 – Apr. 1958	5.2	8.3	2.5	1.6	2.4	−7.1	−20.6	−8.6
Apr. 1958 – Apr. 1960 – Feb. 1961	12.1	7.7	4.7	−3.2	−6.0	−4.0	−1.0	0.9
Feb. 1961 – Dec. 1969 – Nov. 1970	1.0	1.3	0.9	2.2	−1.9	−2.4	−2.0	−4.3
Nov. 1970 – Nov. 1973 – Mar. 1975	−2.4	−1.0	5.9	1.9	0.8	1.1	−3.4	−4.6
Mar. 1975 – Jan. 1980 – July 1981	−0.2	0.1	3.6	3.0	5.6	−3.9	−27.1	1.3
July 1980 – July 1981 – Nov. 1982	11.0	10.0	−1.1	1.1	−3.3	−0.7	−4.8	−4.5
Average Percentage Change per Month	3.8	3.9	2.5	1.1	−1.2	−3.4	−10.9	−3.9
Average Absolute Deviation	1.0	0.4	0.4	0.9	4.8	7.0	20.7	8.3
Normal Upper Bound	4.3	4.1	2.7	1.6	1.2	0.1	−0.5	0.3
Normal Lower Bound	3.3	3.7	2.3	0.7	−3.6	−6.9	−21.3	−8.1

Table 3.21 Business Cycle Stage Analysis Three-Month Treasury Bill Rate (Geometric Averages of Monthly Data).

Reference Cycle Dates Trough – Peak – Trough (1)	I Three Mo. Centered on Initial Trough (2)	Expansion			V Three Months Centered on Peak (6)	Contraction			IX Three Mo. Centered on Ending Trough (10)	Business Cycle Stage Base, % Change (11)
		II First Third (3)	III Middle Third (4)	IV Last Third (5)		VI First Third (7)	VII Middle Third (8)	VIII Last Third (9)		
Oct. 1949 – July 1953 – May 1954	1.3%	1.6%	1.2%	1.9%	-1.9%	-12.2%	-5.1%	-6.6%	-14.7%	-0.55%
May 1954 – Aug. 1957 – Apr. 1958	-14.7	4.9	4.9	1.9	2.4	3.1	-12.0	-27.0	-16.1	0.34
Apr. 1958 – Apr. 1960 – Feb. 1961	-16.1	11.9	2.1	0.4	-6.0	-10.7	0.0	-0.8	2.0	1.79
Feb. 1961 – Dec. 1969 – Nov. 1970	2.0	1.1	1.0	1.1	4.0	-5.3	-0.7	-2.9	-7.3	0.73
Nov. 1970 – Nov. 1973 – Mar. 1975	-7.3	-1.9	1.1	3.6	-3.5	1.2	-0.7	-7.4	-3.6	-0.14
Mar. 1975 – Jan. 1980 – July 1981	-3.6	-0.6	1.4	3.4	2.9	12.5	-13.2	-26.8	2.1	0.59
July 1980 – July 1981 – Nov. 1982	2.1	14.2	2.5	-0.1	-1.6	-6.2	2.2	-8.6	0.1	0.46
Average Percentage Change per Month	-5.5	4.3	2.0	1.7	-0.6	-2.8	-4.4	-12.1	-5.6	0.46
Average Absolute Deviation	6.5	5.0	1.0	1.1	3.1	6.9	5.1	9.1	6.3	0.49
Normal Upper Bound	-2.2	6.8	2.5	2.3	1.0	0.6	-1.8	-7.5	-2.5	0.70
Normal Lower Bound	-8.7	1.8	1.5	1.2	-2.1	-6.3	-6.9	-16.6	-8.8	0.21

133

Table 3.22 Conformity to Reference Business Cycles Three-Month Treasury Bill Rate.

| Reference Cycle Dates | Changes in Reference Cycle Relatives During | | | | | | | |
| | Reference Expansion | | | | Reference Contraction | | | |
Trough – Peak – Trough (1)	Total Change (2)	Interval in Months (3)	Average Change Per Month (4)	Geometric Average of II – IV (5)	Total Change (6)	Interval in Months (7)	Average Change Per Month (8)	Geometric Average of VI – VIII (9)
Oct. 1949 – July 1953 – May 1954	66.3	45	1.47	1.59	–85.0	10	–8.50	–8.03
May 1954 – Aug. 1957 – Apr. 1958	118.0	39	3.02	3.85	–102.9	8	–12.87	–12.84
Apr. 1958 – Apr. 1960 – Feb. 1961	79.0	24	3.29	4.67	–33.8	10	–3.38	–3.96
Feb. 1961 – Dec. 1969 – Nov. 1970	121.8	106	1.15	1.05	–52.7	11	–4.79	–2.99
Nov. 1970 – Nov. 1973 – Mar. 1975	37.2	36	1.03	0.90	–34.0	16	–2.13	–2.33
Mar. 1975 – Jan. 1980 – July 1980	94.7	28	1.63	1.38	–59.0	6	–9.83	–10.57
July 1980 – July 1981 – Nov. 1982	59.8	12	4.99	5.37	–61.4	16	–3.84	–4.32
Average Change Per Month	82.4	45.7			–61.3	11.0		
Index of Conformity								
Expansions (E)			+100	+100				
Contractions (C)							+100	+100
Overall (E+C)/2	+100							

134

which summarizes amplitudes by the two methods), the percentage change method helps reveal other interesting information about the cycle pattern. For example, during the initial stages of the business cycle recovery, interest rates show their largest upward movement. These stylized facts can be useful for forecasting.

Table 3.22 indicated that the three-month Treasury bill rate had a 100% conformity with the reference cycle during the expansion, contraction, and overall cycle. This high degree of conformity held regardless of whether the cycle relatives (column 4) or the percentage change method (column 5) was used.

Finally, among the Burns and Mitchell potpourri of summary statistics, one that stands out is the *duration of run* measure. This statistic records the number of times a like stream of observations occurs. For example, if the concern was to determine the duration of the run of positive numbers in a string of data from Table 3.23, then the highest run in that series is four. This statistic might be a useful measure of volatility in summarizing the profile of a time series during recessions and expansions.

Many of the simple concepts introduced in this section often were used in the business cycle literature of the 1950s through the early 1960s. Although many of these techniques have been neglected in recent years, the ultimate purpose in dusting off any of these techniques is to gain a better understanding of how the economy operates; descriptive analysis frequently provides the best starting point.

Table 3.23 Duration of Runs in the Percentage Change in Retail Sales.

Date		% Change	Runs	Duration
1985	Jan.	0.4	+	1
	Feb.	1.3	+	2
	Mar.	0.3	+	3
	Apr.	2.3	+	4
	May	−0.3	−	1
	June	−0.6	−	2
	July	0	0	0
	Aug.	1.6	+	1
	Sept.	2.4	+	2
	Oct.	−3.6	−	1
	Nov.	0.6	+	1
	Dec.	1.2	+	2
1986	Jan.	0.4	+	3
	Feb.	0.1	+	4
	Mar.	−0.8	−	1

NBER Cycle Dating Rules.   The criteria for cycle dating described in Burns and Mitchell's *Measuring Business Cycles* remains the cornerstone of the traditional NBER method of determining cyclical turning points in a time series. As mentioned earlier, the NBER distinguishes between specific and reference cycles. Both cycle dating approaches will be discussed.

A specific cycle is a set of turning points observable in a particular series; these turns may or may not correspond to the overall business cycle turning point dates. The selection of a turn must meet the following criteria:

1. The cycle duration must be at least 15 months, as measured from either peak to peak or trough to trough.

2. If the peak or trough zone is flat, then the latest value is selected as the turn.

3. Strike activity or other special factors generally are ignored, if their effect is brief and fully reversible.

In 1971, these decision rules were formalized by Bry and Boschen[24](B-B) and incorporated into a computerized routine for determining cyclical turning point dates. Although the original version of the Bry and Boschan computer program did not include an amplitude criterion for the selection of turning points, one has been suggested by Haywood. The Haywood amplitude criterion is based on a moving standard deviation.[25]

The main steps in the B-B computerized routine to select specific cycle turning point dates are:

1. Smooth the data after first adjusting the time series for any outliers.

2. Select preliminary turning points using the smoothed series and then search for turning points in the raw series around the dates found in the smoothed series.

3. Once these tentative dates are selected in the raw series, a check is made of the duration. If the duration criteria are not met, then one pair of cycle dates is eliminated.

4. Although it is not part of the B-B methodology, a final check of the amplitude can be made using the Haywood amplitude criterion, which is based on a moving standard deviation of the series.

5. After the series has passed through all these tests, a statement of the turning point dates is given.

Although the NBER turning point selection method has largely been done by visual inspection or can be done using a computer program (the NBER program or some expert system), the NBER concept of a turning point—however selected—is no less effective in summarizing the cyclical movement of a time series than turning points from spectral analysis or some other purely statistical technique. The NBER selection process uses broad-based measures of current economic activity although an argument also can be made to include measures of specific industries and activities in the selection process. In an early day when economic statistics were less prevalent, Wesley Mitchell observed that "the only safe way of dating a [turning point was] to accept the consensus of opinion among men intimately familiar with business conditions of the time."[26] And to some extent, this still is the thinking in force for dating the German business cycle by the IFO-Institute in Munich, which bases its analysis on business surveys.

A related concept in the selection of specific cycle turning points dates is the determination of the reference business cycle. The conceptual basis for the reference cycle is to select turning point dates from a basket of economic indicators that represent the central tendency of a group of indicators reflecting aggregate supply-and-demand conditions. This group of indicators is dubbed the *coincident indicators*. Some of the economic indicators that serve this role include[27] (1) real (inflation-adjusted) gross national product or gross domestic product, (2) real disposable personal income, (3) real final sales, (4) real manufacturing and trade sales, (5) industrial production, and (6) employment. A reference cycle chronology is then established based on the central tendency of the individual turning points in the basket of coincident economic indicators.

The actual selection of reference cycle turning point dates for the United States is done by the NBER's Business Cycle Dating Committee. Although the turning point selection process may seem mysterious—it is not. Members of the committee have from time to time described the process as a search, a compromise, and a determination, allowing for special factors.[28] The actual selection of turning point dates is not without its critics.[29] But the final selection of dates does provide a framework for future analysis and forecasting.

Shiskin's Rules of Thumb for Spotting a Recession. There is a widely referenced rule of thumb that two consecutive quarters of contraction in real GNP or real GDP signal a recession. Unfortunately, this shortcut for determining the reference business cycle is not totally accurate (in fact, the 1980 recession, for example, only had one quarter when real activity contracted). What is often neglected in this rule of thumb is that it is part of a sequence of rules posited by Julius Shiskin.[30] The complete statement of those rough rules for spotting a recession include: (1) Real GDP or GNP should decline for two successive quarters and industrial production should decline for a 6-month period; (2) real GNP/GDP should decline by at least 1.5% and payroll employment by at least 1.5%, and there should be at least, a two-point rise in the unemployment rate; and (3) for 6 months or longer, less than 25% of the industries are expanding when measured by the employment diffusion index using 6-month spans. Although the Shiskin rules provide a quick means of tracking the reference business cycle, the amplitude and duration criteria probably should be adjusted for more recent business cycle experience. Hence, here are a set of adjusted rules of thumb to spot a recession: (1) Real GDP should decline at least one-quarter and industrial production contract for at least 4 to 6 months. (2) There should be a contraction, for at least 4 to 6 months, in one or more of the following series: (a) industrial production, (b) real disposable personal income, (c) employment, and/or (d) aggregate hours worked. (3) The employment diffusion index should decline below 40% of all industries expanding their work force, on a 1-month change basis, and remain below that point for at least 4 to 6 months. The unemployment rate criteria seems less useful since it can be impacted by demographic influences. For example, during the 1990 recession, the unemployment rate was held down by a *demographic bonus*—a shrinking or very slowly growing labor force.

Measuring Recession Length—A Model of Business Cycle Duration.
Once an economy enters a recession, one inevitable question that always seems perplexing is, *How long will the recession last?* The length of a recession is dependent on a number of factors including (1) how quickly the Federal Reserve responds to the weak economy; (2) the state of fiscal policy—whether policy is relatively easy, tight, or neutral; and (3) the degree of imbalance in various sectors of the economy such as the amount of inventory or building overhang or degree of problems facing the banking sector. Arthur Burns observed: "[I]f the onset of the contraction is marked by a financial crisis or if one develops somewhat later, there is a substantial probability that the decline of aggregate activity will prove severe and perhaps abnormally long as well."[31]

While numerous potential factors will influence the duration of a recession, the Federal Reserve controls the quickest *policy trigger*—short-term interest rates that could impact the economy and consequently the length of the cycle. To test this hypothesis, a business cycle duration model has been constructed that incorporates (1) the speed of response of the Federal Reserve to the onset of a recession as measured by the number of months between when the business cycle peaked and the peak in the federal funds rate, (2) the previous low-high change in the federal funds rate, and (3) the funds rate three months subsequent to the business cycle peak. This model explains 82% of the cycle-to-cycle variation in duration and appears to be a reasonable explanation for the ultimate duration of recessions. The results of this model are presented in Figure 3.13. The negative sign associated with the coefficient on the change in the federal funds rate (in the period prior to the recession) appears

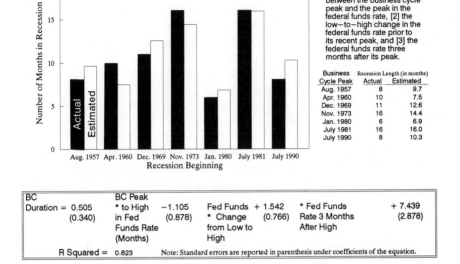

Determinants of business cycle duration model include: [1] the span of months between the business cycle peak and the peak in the federal funds rate, [2] the low–to–high change in the federal funds rate prior to its recent peak, and [3] the federal funds rate three months after its peak.

Business Cycle Peak	Recession Length (in months)	
	Actual	Estimated
Aug. 1957	8	9.7
Apr. 1960	10	7.5
Dec. 1969	11	12.6
Nov. 1973	16	14.4
Jan. 1980	6	6.9
July 1981	16	16.0
July 1990	8	10.3

BC
Duration = 0.505   BC Peak   −1.105   Fed Funds   + 1.542   * Fed Funds   + 7.439
(0.340)   * to High   (0.878)   * Change   (0.766)   Rate 3 Months   (2.878)
in Fed   from Low to   After High
Funds Rate   High
(Months)

R Squared = 0.823   Note: Standard errors are reported in parenthesis under coefficients of the equation.

Figure 3.13 Business Cycle Duration Model. Determinants of business cycle duration model include [1] the span of months between the business cycle peak and the peak in the federal funds rate, [2] the low-to-high change in the federal funds rate prior to its recent peak, and [3] the Federal funds rate three months after its peak.

somewhat at odds with what might have been expected. In particular, on the surface it might seem that the larger the increase in interest rates *before* the recession, the longer the duration. But this equation suggests the reverse is true, possibly because higher interest rates before a recession could cause a correction in some imbalances faster than otherwise, which would ultimately yield a shorter recession. While this result should be viewed as tentative, it does suggest a cause-and-effect reason for the duration of recessions.

Other models of business cycle duration have developed along the lines of *hazard functions*.[32] That approach previously had been used for estimating the probability of the ranks of the unemployed—a conditional probability that an individual will no longer be unemployed in week n given that the individual was unemployed in week $n - 1$. That type of *hazard* model has a natural extension to the business cycle phases. For example, the hazard model could be used to calculate the probability that the economy will enter an expansion in the next period, given that the economy was in its nth month of recession.

MEASURING SEASONAL PATTERNS

This section takes a closer look at the seasonal adjustment process. By definition, seasonal patterns are recurring interyear fluctuations, and the objective of all the seasonal adjustment methods is to smooth out those typical patterns. In some cases, special problems occur in doing this, for example, when a holiday does not have a fixed date, such as Easter. A simple method will be described to handle the effects of these moving holidays.

Earlier in this chapter, an example of series decomposition was illustrated. The centerpiece of that method as well as most seasonal adjustment techniques is the *ratio-to-moving average*. [33] Basically, it was demonstrated that a seasonal factor can be calculated by taking a ratio of the current value to the previous 12 months (or, four quarters, 52 weeks, etc.) and normalizing the 12 monthly seasonal factors to one. More elaborate methods use higher-order smoothing, but the concept remains the same. Before presenting more developed techniques, it may be helpful to expand on the earlier discussion and describe some modifications in the basic methodology to handle special problems.

Early in the development of the seasonal adjustment methodologies, it was noted that certain seasonal patterns can shift from year to year depending on when an event or holiday occurs. The Easter seasonal adjustment illustrates the logic and method used to address this problem. This adjustment is particularly important for retail sales data, which can surge before Easter, because the date of that holiday can vary between late March and late April. One of the most straightforward methods to adjust for a moving holiday is the Piser method.[34] Again consider the U.S. retail chain store sales index shown in Table 3.3. To adjust these data for Easter, the following is done:

1. *Express the March and April Data as a Percentage of the 12-Month Moving Average.* The moving seasonal can be calculated using the simple ratio-to-moving average method (as was done demonstrated earlier) or some more elaborate method.

2. *Take the Difference between the Ratio of the March and April Values Relative to their Moving Averages and the Seasonal Index.* The computation shown in Table 3.24 represents the March and April Easter residuals (the variation after accounting for the typical seasonal pattern). As in most cases, however, this residual also picks up the irregular component.

3. *Subtract the March Residuals from the April Residuals.* This calculation is shown in Table 3.24.

4. *Exclude the Irregular Movement from the Easter Residual.* Table 3.24 also shows the associated Easter residual. One caveat in using these adjustment factors is that the irregular component obscures a determination of a precise Easter correction factor. At this point, it is possible to approximate the

Table 3.24 Computation of Easter Residuals for U.S. Retail Chain Store Sales Index.

	March			April			Easter
	% of Moving			% of Moving			
Year	Average	Seasonal	Difference	Average	Seasonal	Difference	Residual
1971	1.029	0.982	0.046	0.959	0.916	0.043	−0.003
1972	1.075	1.014	0.061	0.917	0.865	0.052	−0.009
1973	1.088	1.023	0.065	1.016	0.955	0.061	−0.004
1974	1.059	1.016	0.043	1.010	0.969	0.041	−0.002
1975	1.030	0.986	0.044	0.927	0.888	0.039	−0.004
1976	1.039	0.989	0.050	0.995	0.947	0.048	−0.002
1977	1.056	0.991	0.066	1.006	0.943	0.063	−0.003
1978	1.050	1.004	0.046	0.979	0.935	0.043	−0.003
1979	0.979	0.949	0.029	0.952	0.924	0.028	−0.001
1980	0.972	0.944	0.028	0.915	0.889	0.026	−0.002
1981	1.006	0.961	0.046	1.027	0.981	0.047	0.001
1982	0.961	0.957	0.004	0.974	0.971	0.003	0.000
1983	1.039	0.953	0.086	1.002	0.919	0.083	−0.003
1984	0.937	0.897	0.040	0.998	0.955	0.043	0.003
1985	0.936	0.916	0.020	0.964	0.944	0.020	0.001

Note: Results rounded to three decimal places.

Easter correction factor visually by plotting the data and drawing a line through the midpoint of the scatter diagram and reading the daily Easter residual off the chart—this is demonstrated in Figure 3.14. Alternatively and more systematically, a daily factor can be interpolated as presented in Table 3.25.

5. *Divide the Easter Correction by Two.* The Easter correction, as shown in Table 3.25, illustrates the correction factor, which is half the total since the factor is calculated over 2 months.

6. *Adjust the Seasonal Factors to Incorporate the Correction Factor.* The final adjustment is to incorporate the moving holiday correction into the existing March and April seasonal factors. The adjusted March seasonal factor equals the old factor minus the correction factor while the adjusted April seasonal factor equals the old factor plus the correction factor. Consequently, this adjustment does not affect the full-year seasonal pattern but simply makes allowances between March and April to account for when Easter occurs. The adjusted seasonal factors are shown in Table 3.26.

This example demonstrates how the existing methodology can be modified to handle special problems such as a moving holiday. But it also opens up a conceptual window to some problems that the more elaborate seasonal adjustment methods must deal with. The derivation of the seasonal cycle may not be as simple to account for as might be thought. Moreover, even elaborate seasonal adjustment methods—many of which simply use variants on the method demonstrated—still

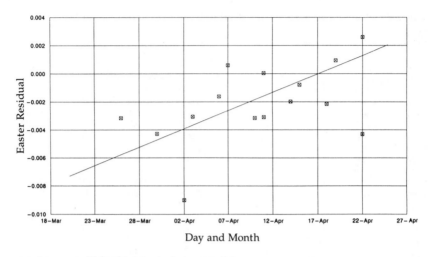

Figure 3.14 Easter Residual Factors Based on U.S. Retail Chain Store Sales, 1970–1985.

face difficult conceptual problems in attempting to model and predict the seasonal cycle. One such problem that has not been adequately handled by the seasonal adjustment methods is the alteration of the seasonal pattern by a weather anomaly, but more will be said about this later.

The Census X-12 Method

In 1954, the U.S. Bureau of the Census first introduced a computer program to seasonally adjust time series. This program was later replaced in 1955 by a program called Census Method II. Then in October 1965, the X-11 version of Method II[35] was introduced. With each evolution, new techniques and procedures were included in the seasonal adjustment procedure. Today, version X-12 stands as the basic method to remove seasonal patterns from times series. The X-12 decomposition of a time series begins with a slightly more elaborate identity, which could be additive or multiplicative, and takes the form:

$$O = TC \times S \times TD \times H \times I, \text{ or}$$

$$O = TC + S + TD + H + I$$

where O is the original series, TC is the trend cycle, S is the seasonal factor, TD is the trading-day factor, H is the holiday factor, and I is the irregular component. The new features of this identity with the original Persons formulation include a *trading day* and a *holiday* factor. The trading-day adjustment is used

Table 3.25   Easter Correction Factors for U.S. Retail Chain Store Sales.

Date of Easter		Easter	Net
Month	Day	Residual	Correction
March		−0.005	−0.003
April	1	−0.005	−0.002
	2	−0.004	−0.002
	3	−0.004	−0.002
	4	−0.003	−0.002
	5	−0.003	−0.001
	6	−0.003	−0.001
	7	−0.002	−0.001
	8	−0.002	−0.001
	9	−0.001	−0.001
	10	−0.001	−0.000
	11	−0.001	−0.000
	12	−0.000	−0.000
	13	0.000	0.000
	14	0.001	0.000
	15	0.001	0.001
	16	0.001	0.001
	17	0.002	0.001
	18	0.002	0.001
	19	0.003	0.001
	20	0.003	0.002
	21	0.003	0.002
	22	0.004	0.002
	23	0.004	0.002
	24	0.005	0.002
	25	0.005	0.003

Table 3.26   Seasonal Factors Adjusted to Easter Occurrence.

	Date of Easter		Net	March Seasonal Factor		April Seasonal Factor	
Year	Month	Day	Correction	Uncorrected	Corrected	Uncorrected	Corrected
1971	April	11	0.000	0.982	0.982	0.916	0.916
1972	April	2	−0.002	1.014	1.016	0.865	0.863
1973	April	22	0.002	1.023	1.021	0.955	0.957
1974	April	14	0.000	1.016	1.016	0.969	0.969
1975	March	30	−0.005	0.986	0.991	0.888	0.883
1976	April	18	0.001	0.989	0.988	0.947	0.948
1977	April	10	0.000	0.991	0.991	0.943	0.943
1978	March	26	−0.005	1.004	1.009	0.935	0.930
1979	April	15	0.001	0.949	0.948	0.924	0.925
1980	April	6	−0.001	0.944	0.945	0.889	0.888
1981	April	19	0.001	0.961	0.960	0.981	0.982
1982	April	11	0.000	0.957	0.957	0.971	0.971
1983	April	3	−0.002	0.953	0.955	0.919	0.917
1984	April	22	0.002	0.897	0.895	0.955	0.957
1985	April	7	−0.001	0.916	0.917	0.944	0.943

to account for a varying number of working days in a given month, which can be important for retail and financial transactions. The holiday adjustment was demonstrated earlier. This adjustment accounts for pattern shifts associated with the timing of holidays such as Easter, Labor Day, and Thanksgiving. The main steps in the X-12 procedure are:

1. *Calculate the Holiday Factors.* This concept was shown earlier. However, the X-12 seasonal adjustment procedure handles the calculation more mechanically.

2. *Compute the Trading-Day Factors.* The trading-day adjustment of the X-12 program computes these factors by regressing the number of each day of the week per month on the irregular component. Although this procedure may lead to conceptual problems (e.g., changes in the *blue laws* may have altered the proportion of retail sales on Sundays), the method is (1) less time consuming than establishing an independent pattern of daily activity, and (2) it is claimed it can provide better adjustment because it is correcting for the net effect of several factors. To get a feel for how the trading-day factors are derived, consider this example. Assume that independent information established that the average pattern of retail sales[36] has the following percentage of weekly sales per day of the week:

Sunday	14.3%	$(1/7)$
Monday	10.7	$(.75/7)$
Tuesday	10.7	$(.75/7)$
Wednesday	10.7	$(.75/7)$
Thursday	10.7	$(.75/7)$
Friday	14.3	$(1/7)$
Saturday	28.6	$(2/7)$

Given this average sales pattern per day, it is possible to calculate any month's trading-day adjustment by summing up the number of Sunday's per month multiplied by its weekly share of sales plus the same weighted share calculation for each of the other days of the week. Table 3.27 shows a hypothetical calculation of the trading-day adjustment for July.

3. *Compute the Preliminary Seasonal Factor.* Once the entire time series for every period is adjusted for the trading-day variation, the remaining components can be expressed as:

$$\frac{O}{(TD \times H)} = TC \times S \times I$$

The X-12 process then separates the seasonal component from the trend cycle and irregular components by calculating a 2-month moving average of a

Table 3.27   Calculation of Trading-Day Adjustment for the Month of July.

Year	Number of Trading Days	Percentage of Average Monthly Trading Days	Raw Data	Data after Adjustment
1979	34	34/31.556 = 1.0775	1000	1000/1.0775 = 928
1980	28	28/31.556 = 0.8873	1250	1250/0.8873 = 1409
1981	30	30/31.556 = 0.9507	1300	1300/0.9507 = 1367
1982	37	37/31.556 = 1.1725	1800	1800/1.1725 = 1535
1983	29	29/31.556 = 0.9190	1350	1350/0.9190 = 1469
1984	28	28/31.556 = 0.8873	1400	1400/0.8873 = 1578
1985	32	32/31.556 = 1.0141	1600	1600/1.0141 = 1578
1986	31	31/31.556 = 0.9824	1700	1700/0.9824 = 1730
1987	35	35/31.556 = 1.1092	1950	1950/1.1092 = 1758
Average = 31.556				

12-month centered moving average of the original series, O, which yields the trend cycle. To remove the effects of random events such as strikes, extreme values are replaced when a value in a three-period average of a 3-month moving average (3×3 MA). A value that falls outside this limit is substituted with an average of the value before and after that point; an end value is substituted with the average of three preceding values, and, three succeeding values are used for the beginning of the series.

After the extreme values have been replaced, the preliminary seasonal factors are adjusted as follows: Lost values at the beginning and end of the series due to the centered 12-month moving average (which means six values are lost on each side) are replaced with seasonal factors from the following year for the beginning of the series and the earlier year for the end of the series. These preliminary factors are then adjusted so that the sum of the seasonal factors for each year equals 1200 (for monthly observations), which means the average of any 12 months will equal the average of the unadjusted data for a full year.

The next step is to use these preliminary seasonal factors to adjust the raw data (divide factor into the raw or original data to be seasonally adjusted, as shown in Table 3.27).

4. *Determine the Final Seasonal Adjustment Factors.* In this final step, the preliminary seasonally adjusted series undergoes additional smoothing to remove any latent seasonal or irregular influences. The final adjustment factor then combines the seasonal, trading-day, and holiday adjustments.

5. *Compute the Year-Ahead Seasonal Factors.* Year-ahead seasonal factors are then extrapolated (in their simplest form) using the formula:

$$SF_{n+1} = SF_n + ((1/2) \times (SF_n - SF_{n-1}))$$

where *SF* is the seasonal factor for year *n;* year *n* − 1 is the same period (month, quarter, week, etc.) 1 year earlier. For example, the January seasonal factor for the current year would equal its previous year's value plus one-half the change from 2 years ago to last year.

The X-12 seasonally adjustment procedure includes some new features for extrapolating year-ahead seasonal patterns, which provides a key difference between it and its predecessor the X-11 method.

Statistics Canada's X-11 ARIMA Variant

Estela Bee Dagum of Statistics Canada extended the X-11 program to better compute seasonal factors one year beyond the end of the time series. This variant of the X-11 program basically incorporates a Box-Jenkins Autoregressive Integrated Moving Average (ARIMA) process or statistical model to replicate the unadjusted time series. Then a forecast of the unadjusted series is made using the ARIMA model and these forecasted values are treated as *actual* data in determining the seasonal factors with the standard X-11 procedure. Empirical studies have found that seasonal factors calculated in this manner are less subject to revision.[37]

Bell Labs Method (SABL)

A relatively new entry into the field of seasonal adjustment methods is SABL (Seasonal Adjustment-Bell Labs).[38] SABL shares the same conceptual iterative framework as is present in the X-12 program, however, SABL utilizes *resistant smoothing* techniques to downplay the effects of outliers. An earlier section of this chapter discussed robust smoothing techniques, and this is a particular application of those methods.

SABL additively decomposes a time series into a trend, seasonal components, and irregular components. The trend is similar to the trend cycle in the X-12 procedure. A thumbnail sketch of the SABL method is shown in Table 3.28.

Empirical evidence suggests that SABL provides similar results to the X-11 procedure when the series is not affected by outliers. However, SABL provides more consistent seasonal factors (from year to year) when the data is not stable.

Other Seasonal Adjustment Methods

Because of the popularity of the X-11 program (and now its successor, X-12), it is easy to forget that other seasonal adjustment methods are in use around the world. Some of the lesser known programs include the Burman method developed by the Bank of England, SEABIRD and DAINTIES developed by the European Economic Community, the Berlin ASA-III method developed at the

Table 3.28   SABL Decomposition of a Time Series.

Input	Operation
Raw Data	Transform the series using power functions to eliminate the dependence of seasonal amplitudes on the trend.
Transformed Series (TS)	Calculate a trend using a linear polynomial. This smoothed trend is subtracted from TS to yield the seasonal and irregular components.
Seasonal and Irregular Components	Using tapered means and medians, an initial set of seasonal factors is determined.
Preliminary Seasonal Component	A final set of operations smooths the preliminary factors and yields refined resistant (robust) seasonal factors.

German Institute for Economic Research and the Central Planning Method (of The Netherlands). In evaluating many of these techniques, Kuiper[39] concluded that all the methods seemed suitable and similar for historical analysis; however, some methods were more suitable for current analysis. In particular, Kuiper found that the X-11 ARIMA method performed best (based on a criterion of less revision) when comparing the projected seasonal to the actual historical factors.

Weekly Seasonal Adjustment

Weekly seasonal adjustment is a variant on the standard monthly adjustment methods; however, it amplifies many of the problems of shifting holidays, weather impacts, and so forth. One of the standard approaches for deriving weekly seasonal factors is by interpolating the monthly factors for each week, and as such, weekly factors pose no special problem from a calculation standpoint. The method that gained general acceptance was proposed by Piser[40] and has been incorporated into the X-11 weekly seasonal adjustment program is used by the Federal Reserve Board.[41] Generating weekly seasonal factors by using the ARIMA methodology has become more common. Methodologies continue to evolve and to address more and more special problems.

The Seasonal Cycle: Another Look

Previously the discussion of the seasonal cycle has been limited to how to adjust time series data to remove its influence. The underlying assumption for that view was that it was a recurrent phenomenon, which was essentially unnecessary to study. But recent research suggests that the seasonal cycle and the business cycle share a common dynamic that may be important to account for in understanding the business cycle.

At the heart of this concern with the seasonal cycle is whether or not lost sales or output from a shock is "permanent" or "transitory" in nature. This concern is especially evident when unseasonable weather impacts consumer spending. Are retail sales permanently lost or simply shifted into some future date? Linden[42] observed that those retail sales *can be* permanently lost due to unseasonable weather. Moreover, his study concluded that "weather has a powerful effect on demand." If this is the case, then it is extremely important to adjust economic data for these effects, as suggested by Maunder,[43] or at least to evaluate the data in the context of abnormal weather. Economists generally, have ignored this issue, except for its obvious impact on agriculture, but the effect of unseasonable weather on broad-based economic activity may be more significant than widely perceived. It must be recognized, however, that unseasonable weather impacts are different at different times of the year as suggested by the U.S. Commerce Department's qualitative assessment (as compiled by Maunder) and shown in Table 3.29. Moreover, if the economic impact from adverse weather is permanently lost sales or output, then economists and policymakers need to be aware of the role weather plays as an economic *shock*. Weather impacts can extend beyond the *real sector* to the financial sector as well. Witness that municipal bonds yields in California were expected to be higher than otherwise due to the drought that was plaguing the state.[44]

Some economic theories can easily accommodate "weather shocks," such as the real business cycle hypothesis that conceptually captures weather anomalies in the same way as any other type of shock.[45] However, weather is not the key tenet of the real business cycle theory or, for that matter, any other theory. Although weather effects can be included in all business cycle theories, the prevalent thinking is to treat weather as "noise" and simply to ignore it. Arthur Burns[46] exemplified the prevailing view that seasonal and very short-term cycles have little significant impact on the economy since they are transitory and/or periodic in nature. Burns observed:

> [B]usiness cycles have a more powerful tendency to synchronize industrial, commercial, and financial processes than do the shorter cycles. Thus, the daily and weekly cycles in total production have no counterpart in inventories, bank loans, or interest rates, while seasonal fluctuations vary widely from one business activity to another. . . . Although custom has left its imprint on the daily and annual cycles, they are part of the natural environment of man. Business cycles, on the other hand are a product of culture.[47]

But Burns's view has been challenged.

Table 3.29 Sensitivity of Gross National Product Components to Widespread Anomalies in Weather Patterns.

	Weather Unusually					
GNP Component	Hot in Summer	Cold in Winter	Dry in Summer	Stormy/ Rainy	Snowy	Mild
1. Personal Consumption Expenditures						
(a) Gasoline and oil	-	-	-	-	-	+ +
(b) Electricity	+ +	+	?	+ +	?	-
(c) Natural gas, fuel oil, coal	?	+ +	?	+ +	+	-
(d) Furniture and appliances	-	-	-	?	-	+ +
(e) Food at home	+ +	+	+ +	+	+ +	--
(f) Food away from home	--	--	?	?	--	+ +
(g) Apparel	-	+	?	?	-	+
(h) New and used cars	-	-	-	-	-	+ +
(i) Housing	-	--	?	?	-	+ +
(j) Transportation	-	-	?	-	-	+ +
(k) Other	?	?	?	?	?	?
2. Nonresidential Fixed Investment	?	?	?	?	?	?
3. Residential Investment	-	-	-	?	-	+ +
4. Change in Business Inventories	+	+	+	+	+	--
5. Net Imports	+	+ +	+	+	+	--
6. Federal Government Purchases	+	+	+	+	+	-
7. State and Local Government Purchases	+	+	+	+	+	-

Scale: +   = increase
+ + = major increase
-   = decrease
--   = major decrease
?   = indeterminant

Source: W. J. Maunder, *The Uncertainty Business,* Methuen, London, 1986, p. 91.

Related to the impact of weather on business activity is the more general link between seasonal and business cycles. Barsky and Miron,[48] Miron,[49] Beaulieu and Miron[50] have found that the seasonal cycle displays similar characteristics to the business cycle in the United States and internationally. In particular, some of the key findings from that research are:

1. More than 85% of the quarterly fluctuation in U.S. real GNP can be explained solely by seasonal fluctuations; there is a large decrease in real GNP in the first quarter (down 8.1% quarter to quarter, at a quarterly

   rate) followed by a 3.7% rebound in the second quarter, a 0.5% decline in
   the third quarter, and a boom of 4.9% in the fourth quarter.

2. The seasonal cycle appears to have a similar pattern (though magni-
   tudes may differ) throughout the world—including both Northern and
   Southern Hemisphere countries.

3. The business and seasonal cycles share common traits:

   a. Sector output is highly correlated

   b. Production smoothing appears absent

   c. Labor productivity is procyclical

   d. Real output and nominal money supply fluctuations move together

   e. Output is far more volatile than prices and wages.

Barsky and Miron suggest that "weather plays an important role in the [sea-
sonal] recovery of GNP from the first to the second quarter."[51] The assumption
behind what we will refer to as the *Miron Hypothesis* (MH) is that the seasonal
cycle has reasonably fixed attributes such as the timing of holidays, weather
patterns, factory shutdown periods, and auto model production changeover
schedules. This is a correct assumption for holidays such as Christmas, but it is
not true of other holidays such as Easter.[52] The retail industry has long observed that the earlier in the year Easter occurs, the smaller the sales impact
is; in many cases, *the seasonal cycle is not neutral.* In recent years, moreover,
numerous special factors have shifted the timing of production and sales: abnormal weather, changes in tax accounting (e.g., elimination of the so-called
6-month convention, whereby firms were allowed to deduct 6 months' worth of
depreciation from their federal taxes even if the item was purchased in the final, or sixth, month of the accounting period), changes in pricing strategies by
auto companies, and so forth. This raises a broader issue about the role of
"shocks" or "noise" on the economy.[53]

   Robert E. Hall[54] has offered an explanation for the interaction of the seasonal and business cycles. He posits that aggregate activity is explained by
a *temporal agglomeration theory* characterized by a thick-market externality
(which is a heavy concentration of producers or merchants). In essence, Hall
argued that there is a bunching of business activity in certain times of the year
and in certain places of the country to capture economies of scale. However, it
is not clear that Hall's theory has captured the true essence of why the seasonal
and business cycles would interact, and it certainly does not accommodate
other types of shocks. A second explanation of how and why these factors impact the economy might be called the *purchasing manager theory,* as discussed
in Chapter 1. This view, as suggested by Hoagland, Buddress, and Heberling[55]
and by Mather,[56] argues that the source of cyclical fluctuation is attributable,

in large part, to a change in industrial buyer behavior. This purchasing behavior results in Mather's *lead-time syndrome,* which is a *new orders accelerator effect* that reinforces any pickup or deceleration in demand through inventories. This view appears to be a more plausible and promising explanation for the interaction of seasonal and business cycle forces than Hall's model, and it is founded in the actual behavior of the firm. This new orders accelerator effect also is consistent with the MH finding that there is an absence of production smoothing within industries. According to the purchasing manager theory, a rational buying policy at firms could have a destabilizing macroeconomic impact if companies were forced to shift purchasing strategies from say a, "current need plus two months" of additional supply to a "current plus four months" supply. Reasons for this shift include weather, supply shortages, potential strikes, and other types of shocks; this hypothesis also could explain why sector output is highly correlated at the seasonal and cyclical frequencies. Industries that are large purchasers, such as the automotive industry, can have a dominate role in triggering that seasonal pattern.[57]

Although it is not the aim of this section to develop an integrated theory of weather and the business cycle, some issues related to that interaction will be explored. The objectives are (1) to examine whether business and growth cycle turning points are influenced by the seasons, (2) to determine if abnormal weather can shift or impact turning points in business and growth cycles, and (3) to reassess the relationship of sunspots and the business cycle.

The Timing of Growth and Business Cycle Turning Points. A simple chi-square statistical test was applied to determine whether there is any significant seasonal impact on business and growth cycle turning points. The test was applied on quarterly turning point dates. Between 1948 and 1990, there was only one business cycle peak in the first quarter, two in the second quarter, and three each in the third and fourth quarters. For business cycle peaks, the chi-square test suggested that the distribution of peak dates was not significantly different, at the 5% level of significance, from equal occurrences per quarter. A similar inference was drawn for the business cycle trough dates. This suggested that a residual seasonal effect was not obvious at the occurrence of business cycle peaks or troughs. However, a similar test applied to the growth cycle turning point dates since 1948 suggested a different conclusion. There were seven growth cycle highs since 1948 in the first quarter, two in each of the second and third quarters and only one in the fourth quarter. On the surface, this hinted at some seasonal impact. The chi-square confirmed that at a 10% level of significance that the observed distribution of growth cycle peak dates was significantly different from an equal distribution of peak dates by quarter. Although there appeared to be an undue clustering of growth cycle trough dates in the fourth quarter of the year, the statistical test suggested it was not significant. Table 3.30 presents the statistical test results. Unfortunately, the statistical power of this test is limited. Two possible reasons could explain the statistical evidence of a seasonal influence on growth cycle peak dates. One explanation is that a true seasonal impact was present, but a second equally valid possibility for this seasonal clustering could be that the trend-adjustment method used to determine growth cycle dates may be unduly influenced by a residual seasonal effect.

The Weather Impact on Turning Point Dates.   Is there a weather impact on turning point dates? To examine this issue, national temperature, precipitation, and insured loss data were examined around turning point dates.[58] Insured loss data is an indirect measure of the degree of damage from natural phenomenon. The data capture only reimbursable losses and hence provide an incomplete measure of total disruption or damage from nature. But the information does serve as a proxy for the broader measure, which is not available. Again, the chi-square statistical test was applied to measure the significance of the weather impact on turning points. The results were reported only for growth and business cycles peaks since the question was whether a weather shock could contribute to a cyclical downturn. The data were examined in four segments: (1) 6 months before the turning point, (2) 3 months before the turning point, (3) 3 months before to 3 months after the turning point, and (4) 6 months after the turning point. An observation was considered larger than normal for our purpose when it was: (1) larger than its average value before and after the turning point for the insurance loss data, (2) greater than its historical mean plus or minus one-half its standard deviation for the temperature data, and (3) greater than its historical mean plus one-half its standard deviation for the precipitation data. Only the *wetter-than-normal* hypothesis was examined with the precipitation data. This test measured the occurrence of abnormality rather than the magnitude of the weather shock.[59] In all cases, unfortunately, the chi-square test failed to reject the null hypothesis that the

Table 3.30   Chi-Square Statistical Test Applied to Occurrence of Quarterly Business and Growth Cycle Turning Point Dates, 1948–1990.

	Chi-Square Statistic	Level of Significance	
		10%	5%
Business cycle peaks	1.22	6.25	7.82
Business cycle troughs	1.00	6.25	7.82
Growth cycle peaks	7.33	6.25	7.82
Growth cycle troughs	5.36	6.25	7.82

observed occurrence was different from its historical average. If there is no aggregate short-term weather impact on cyclical turning points, could there instead be a longer-term weather dynamic impacting the cycle?

Sunspots Revisited and the New Decade Business Cycle Anomaly. Galileo has been credited with discovering sunspots around 1610. Ever since that time, people have debated, at times intensely, about the effect of solar activity on humans, weather, agriculture, and the whole economy. The cycle in sunspot activity, however, was not fully appreciated until Schwabe published a paper on the subject in 1844 and concluded that there was a reasonably periodic cycle in sunspot activity. Hence, the sunspot cycle is often dubbed the *Schwabe cycle*. But when the magnetic characteristics of the cycle are considered, then the cycle spans two Schwabe cycles and is called the *Hale cycle* after the researcher who observed that fact in 1908. Based on a thorough review of the scientific literature on the sun and its impact on weather, Herman and Goldberg[60] concluded: (1) "[T]he amount of annual rainfall . . . exhibits a dependence on the 11 year sunspot cycle in many land areas of the world,"[61](2) "long-term variations in surface temperature show some relationship with [the] sunspot cycle,"[62] and (3) "sunspots are either a barometer for changes in solar [activity] or reflect direct processes related to solar activity which interact with the Earth's atmosphere to affect weather and climate."[63] Moreover, Herman and Goldberg suggest that the consensus of spectral analysis studies is that the major periodicities in sunspots are at average cycle durations of 5.5, 8.1, 9.7, 11.2, 100, 180 years.

An early comprehensive attempt to incorporate the Schwabe cycle into a business cycle framework was suggested by William Stanley Jevons (1835–1882), who early in his career was a practicing meteorologist. In his *Investigations in Currency and Finance,* he discussed economic fluctuations and isolated three components of economic activity—seasonal fluctuation, business cycles, and trends. Jevons attempted to link the business cycle statistically with fluctuations in sunspot activity.[64] After additional research, his son, H. S. Jevons, observed, "[A]mong other meteorological cycles, there exists a three-and-one-half-year period in solar radiation and barometric pressure," which might help to explain the shorter-term business cycle.[65] But despite the ongoing scientific research on sunspots, the economics profession has generally dismissed sunspots as a factor influencing the business cycle, largely because of some statistical problems with the early Jevons study.[66] The recent revival of a sunspot theory in economics only is used as a catchword for an exogenous shock on the economy; hence, that nomenclature is misleading.[67] The intention here, however, is to test whether the *original* sunspot/business cycle linkage, which has long been dismissed by the economics profession, might be valid under certain conditions.

Some motivation for examining this issue is the *new decade business cycle anomaly.* Since the National Bureau of Economic Research started chronicling the business cycle in 1860, there have been recessions around the turn of the new decade 79% of the time, as shown in Table 3.31. While there is no clear-cut reason why this has occurred, it is a curious phenomenon. Moreover, since the average duration of the cycle in this period was about four years, statistically this new decade business cycle effect should occur 50% of the time by chance alone. However, the new decade business cycle effect is more prevalent than happenstance would suggest. A possible explanation for the new decade business cycle effect is tied to the sunspot cycle—which curiously has a similar duration.

The cycle in sunspots is often linked to a climatic cycle that has four major phases: warm-wet, warm-dry, cold-wet, and cold-dry. Between the mid-1930s and the mid-1950s, Raymond H. Wheeler, who was a professor of psychology at the University of Kansas, examined the role that those climatic phases had on human activities including business activity. Zahorchak[68] summarized the Wheeler evidence as follows: While the causes of the business cycle vary, the common thread throughout all cycles is weather; no economic theory is complete without a weather component that can contribute a stimulating and debilitating affect on the economy. Wheeler did not advocate weather as the only cause of the business cycle but as a significant contributing factor. Wheeler's

Table 3.31   U.S. Recessions Associated with a New Decade.

Decade Beginning	Associated Recession Began
1860	Oct. 1860
1870	June 1869
1880	NCR
1890	July 1890
1900	June 1899
1910	Jan. 1910
1920	Jan. 1920
1930	Aug. 1929
1940	NCR
1950	NCR
1960	Apr. 1960
1970	Dec. 1969
1980	Jan. 1980
1990	July 1990

Note: Over the 130 years shown here, the percentage of recessions that started or continued into the start of a new decade was a phenomenally high 11 out of a possible 14 cases or, 79% of the time.

NCR = No Corresponding Recession.

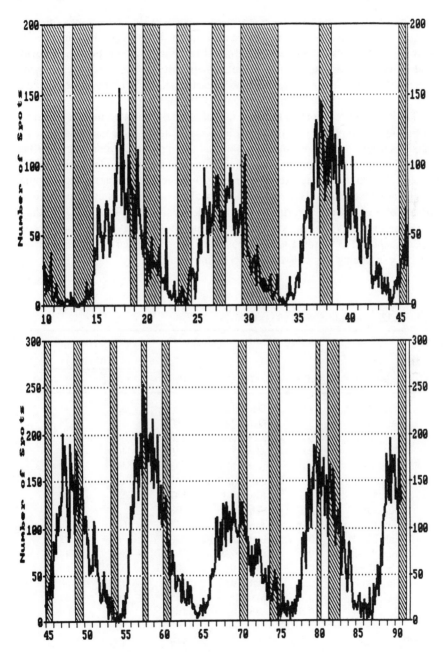

Figure 3.15 Sunspots and the Business Cycle. (*Source:* National Oceanic and Atmospheric Administration, Department of Commerce.)

work is an extension of earlier research by Ellsworth Huntington, who in 1919 suggested that variations in health caused the business cycle; Huntington felt that weather and solar radiation had a critical influence on health. Wheeler and Huntington downplayed the weather/agricultural cycle connection with the economy and instead argued that "weather trends affect people directly, and [people are affected] only incidentally through crops."[69]

The sunspot data from 1910 to the end of 1990 is presented in the two panels of Figure 3.15 on page 155. By visual inspection alone, some business cycle recessions have occurred at sunspot peaks—as the hypothesis would suggest—but some also occur at troughs in sunspot activity. The sunspot cycle is presented in Table 3.32. On the surface, the high in the sunspot cycle appears to lead turning points at new decades. However, sunspot peaks lead business cycle peaks only 54.5% of the time at the turn of a new decade, as shown in Table 3.33. Without much more than visual inspection, the sunspot/business cycle link still seems questionable and will remain so, at least until the scientific research establishes a more convincing link between sunspots and weather.

Table 3.32   Sunspot Cycle, 1833–1990.

				Cycle Duration (Months)	
Low	Value	High	Value	L→H	H→L
June 1833	1.0	Dec. 1836	206.2	42	
Feb. 1843	3.5	Oct. 1847	180.4	56	74
Sept. 1855	0.0	July 1860	116.7	58	95
Jan. 1867	0.0	May 1870	176.0	40	78
Aug. 1878	0.0	Apr. 1882	95.8	44	99
Nov. 1889	0.2	Aug. 1893	129.2	45	91
Apr. 1901	0.0	Nov. 1905	107.2	55	92
Oct. 1906	17.8	Feb. 1907	108.2	4	11
Feb. 1912	0.0	Aug. 1917	154.5	66	60
Aug. 1923	0.5	Dec. 1929	108.0	76	72
Aug. 1933	0.2	July 1938	165.3	59	44
Apr. 1944	0.3	May 1947	201.3	37	69
Jan. 1954	0.2	Oct. 1957	253.8	45	80
July 1964	3.1	Mar. 1969	135.8	56	81
Dec. 1974	0.5	Sept. 1979	188.4	57	69
June 1986	1.1	Aug. 1990	200.3	50	81
Average	1.8		157.9	49.4	73.1

Source: National Oceanic and Atmospheric Administration, U.S. Department of Commerce.

Table 3.33   Sunspots and Business Cycle Peaks at New Decades.

Sunspot Activity Peak	Business Cycle Peak	Sunspots vs. Business Cycle Turning Points
July 1860	Oct. 1860	Plausible Lead
May 1870	June 1869	Lag
Aug. 1893	July 1890	Substantial Lag
NCT	June 1899	No Relationship
Feb. 1907	Jan. 1910	Substantial Lead
Aug. 1917	Jan. 1920	Substantial Lead
Dec. 1929	Aug. 1929	Slight Lag
Oct. 1957	Apr. 1960	Substantial Lead
Mar. 1969	Dec. 1969	Plausible Lead
Sept. 1979	Jan. 1980	Plausible Lead
Aug. 1990	July 1990	Roughly Coincident
Percent Leading	54.5%	
Percent Lagging	27.3%	
Percent Coincident	9.1%	
Percent Missed	9.1%	

NCT = No Corresponding Turn.

Edward Dewey[70] aptly summarized the state of sunspot–economic cycle link when he wrote: "[I]n spite of numerous allegations and widespread folklore, there is, as yet, no conclusive evidence that the dominant 11-year sunspot cycle, or the double sunspot cycle of 22 years, or any of the subsidiary solar cycles that have been alleged, have any economic or sociological repercussions."[71] And that is where the evidence still stands.

The Interaction of Weather and the Business Cycle.   Although weather and seasons may have some impact on business and growth cycles, a quantitative macroeconomic assessment is very difficult. Weather impacts are often measured indirectly by data on national average temperatures, precipitation, insurance losses, and so forth; but in many respects, those measures are not the best statistics to assess the impact of weather on the economy, and they certainly are not the most refined measures for the analysis. Indeed the conclusion from this review is similar to a Commerce Department "study made some years ago, [which] attempted to isolate the impact of weather conditions on the irregular factor of retail sales, [only to find that] the geographic dispersion was too great and no practical application was possible."[72]

THE IRREGULAR COMPONENT—MORE THAN JUST NOISE?

Before leaving the discussion about time series decomposition, it is worthwhile to mention the often neglected and never understood irregular component of a time series. The random or irregular component of a time series may contain some of the most interesting historical information about an economic process. Yet, in practice, this component has been totally ignored as meaningless. The rationale goes that if the irregular component is thought of as an error term after modeling the secular, cyclical, and seasonal influences, then it is simple to assume that its expected value or mean is zero, which would imply that over time, the term is not a statistical problem. But is that a correct assumption? Even if the irregular term does not pose a statistical problem, could it still be an economic problem? There are two conceptual approaches to address this unexplained fluctuation: (1) redefine the secular, cyclical, and seasonal components to include it, or (2) treat it as containing information about one-time events and anomalies and try to understand it.

The first approach calls for a conceptually different model than those previously discussed. With the burgeoning of statistical pattern recognition techniques, techniques such as neural networks or chaos models have become a popular way to explain recurrent patterns. In a nonlinear chaos system, for example, there is no unique solution to the problem but rather an *area of solution*. The same type of output comes from neural network systems. For example, with neural networks, a simple "one plus one" would most likely produce a sum of *around* two—but not necessarily exactly two. This digression is important since these models in essence would eliminate the conceptual need for an irregular component.

The second approach is intriguing from the standpoint of economic understanding. For example, it might be asked: Why does that irregular component blip up in say, May 1988? To understand that is, in part, a challenge to understand economic history. Otto Eckstein, the late founder and head of Data Resources, Inc. (DRI), once made a unique economic forecast presentation in the early 1980s in which he did just that. In his presentation, he discussed the reasons for forecast errors using the DRI model. He ascribed some of the errors to tax law changes and other special events. Finally, it is at least useful to plot the irregular component since it could hint at errors in modeling the other subcomponents of the economic time series.

The irregular component should *not* be overlooked but used. Most definitely, it is more than just noise—to understand the irregular term is to understand economic history.

In the 1920s, Warren Persons suggested that a time series could be segmented into a trend, a cycle, a seasonal component, and an irregular component. His view is still prevalent. The measurement of each of those time series segments continues to be refined, and each segment tends to be analyzed separately. But conceptually, the trend, seasonal, cycle, and irregular components are not distinct no matter how analysts attempt to disentangle those processes; each segment of a time series has some impact on the other. Hence, although the isolation of each segment is a useful paradigm, the absolute segmentation of an economic time series into these processes should not be taken to the extreme. This caution also holds for the alternative paradigm to the Persons method, which segments a time series into its *permanent* and *transitory* components. Joseph Schumpeter's observation about the Persons method (which holds equally for any alternative paradigm) was that making the subconscious assumption that a series can be separated into component parts was tantamount to a theory or the "backbone" of one.[73] He warned it was dangerous to make such an assumption without understanding its implication. Since many of the time series segmentation approaches indeed are an initial attempt to formulate a theory, Schumpeter's alert is important for the user.

PRESSURE INDICATORS

Pressure indicators are a class of cyclical indicator and are formed as ratios, differences, or rates of change of existing measures. These new measures can be fundamental or technical. Fundamental means that the indicator has some quasi-theoretical basis, whereas a technical indicator is developed from some internal dynamic, such as a rate of change.

An example of a theoretically based pressure indicator is the capital-output ratio (or, the change in capital over the change in output), which is derived from a theory that holds an optimal level of capital will produce a fixed amount of output, holding technology constant. This concept is implicit in the Harrod and Domar growth models,[74] discussed in Chapter 2. Unfortunately, with constantly changing technology, it is difficult to empirically assess what the optimal level of that ratio should be.

Probably the most popular pressure indicator is the ratio of inventories to sales. Other less familiar measures can be useful to monitor the business cycle. The ratio of real business fixed investment to real consumption expenditures provides an example of a derived statistical indicator. This ratio, which is shown in Figure 3.16, has a pronounced cyclical pattern and also has been suggested as a possible policy target.[75] Similarly, the Sutro index[76] is a variant on this investment-consumption ratio. The original Sutro index was devised as the ratio of consumer goods to business equipment and provided a *long lead* over business cycle turning points. However, the turning points in that ratio were more closely associated with the preceding cycle, which meant that the Sutro index was an inverted lagging indicator of the business cycle. The reciprocal of the Sutro

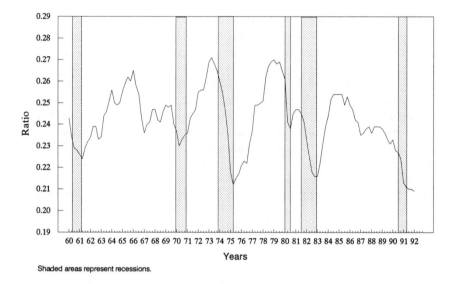

Figure 3.16   Ratio, Real Consumption to Nonresidential Investment (1987 Dollars).

index (business equipment divided by consumer goods), as shown in Figure 3.17, clearly lagged business cycle turning points. Nonetheless, the basic logic for this ratio is that the consumer sector leads the investment sector and the ratio is a more sensitive indicator of that process.

Two of the more elaborate fundamental pressure indicators are the Duncan and Blomster measures. Both of these cyclical indicators are considered leading indicators by their creators. The Duncan leading indicator (DLI) was developed by Wallace H. Duncan at the Federal Reserve Bank of Dallas and later modified.[77] It is calculated from quarterly National Income and Product Account data as follows:

$$DLI = \frac{\dfrac{(CD87_t + CD87_{t-1})}{2} + INVEST87_t}{SALES87_t - EXPORT87_t}$$

where CD87 is durable goods consumption in 1987 dollars, INVEST87 is real business fixed investment, SALES87 is real final sales and EXPORT87 is real exports of goods and services. Figure 3.18 displays the performance of the DLI since 1959. The DLI is mainly a demand-oriented measure and appears to be less of a leading indicator since the 1980s when it either lagged or was coincident with the business cycle peaks since that time. The Duncan indicator does not distinguish between growth and classical recessions and

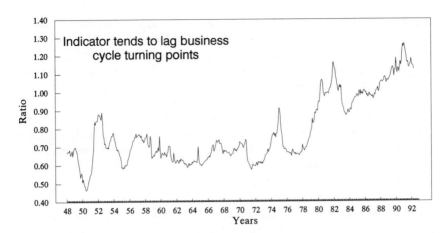

Figure 3.17   Ratio, Consumer Goods to Business Equipment (Industrial Production Components).

was, on average, nearly coincident at growth cycle turnings between 1947 and 1986. Nonetheless, this indicator still may have some use as an indicator of demand imbalances. However, demand imbalances may not be the only cause of the cycle.

The Blomster leading indicator (BLI) was derived using a *naive yield curve model.* [78] The Blomster model, which also can be thought of as a financial leading

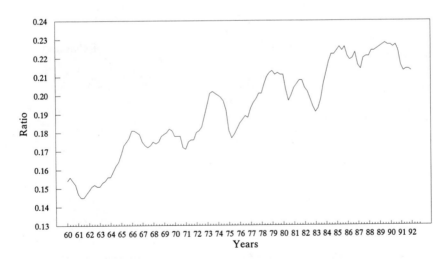

Figure 3.18   Duncan Leading Indicator (1987 Dollars).

indicator (and hence is included in this section), was used to explain and forecast year-over-year percentage change in real domestic final sales (GDP minus inventory change) by relating sales to the interest rate spread between Moody's AAA corporate bond rate and the three-month Treasury bill rate. The interest rate spread was lagged one year in the Blomster formulation. The historical track record is shown in Figure 3.19. Interestingly, the relationship seems to go astray with the 1990 recession. This deviation seems to reflect a concern that the 1990 recession was different from previous experience—at least in how the economy reacted to interest rates. Whether the BLI will again reassert its historical link between the interest rates and the real economy, remains to be seen. Nonetheless, the BLI is another type of pressure indicator worth monitoring.

On the technical side, some examples of pressure indicators are the 3/12 and 12/12 pressure curves and McLaughlin's paired indexes. The 3/12 and 12/12 pressure curves, which are smoothed growth rates, were made popular by the Institute for Trend Research. To illustrate, consider calculating a 3/12 and 12/12 pressure curve for a volatile time series such as durable goods orders. The original data and calculations are shown in Table 3.34 and Figure 3.20. To calculate the two pressure curves, sum 3- or 12-month spans of data (that is, trailing moving sums) and divide the current moving total by the moving total from a year ago. The 12/12 pressure curve value for November 1991, as shown in Table 3.34, is calculated as follows: Calculate a 12-month moving trailing total (1,443,678), then take a year-over-year change in that new series (1,442,678/1,510,102) multiplied by 100, which yields 94.8. A similar calculation is done for the 3/12

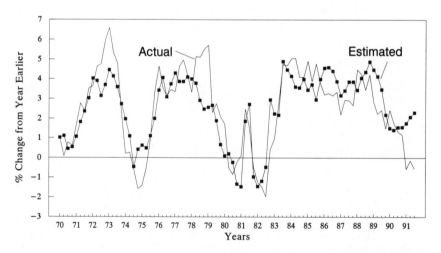

Figure 3.19   Blomster Naive Yield Curve Model, Actual and Year—Ahead Forecast of Real Final Sales.

Table 3.34 Calculating Pressure Curves for Durable Goods Orders.

		Original Data	Twelve Months Moving Total	Pressure Curve, 12/12	Three Months Moving Total	Pressure Curve, 3/12
1989	Jan.	132582	1472103	109.6	389737	112.6
	Feb.	127061	1482165	109.4	394015	112.9
	Mar.	127504	1493677	109.7	387147	110.6
	Apr.	130556	1506964	110.0	385121	110.0
	May	124526	1512723	109.8	382586	108.7
	June	127608	1519012	109.5	382690	107.1
	July	125335	1523335	109.3	377469	104.5
	Aug.	127556	1527131	108.5	380499	103.9
	Sept.	129855	1534501	108.2	382746	104.2
	Oct.	124650	1534388	107.4	382061	103.0
	Nov.	131562	1543167	107.4	386067	104.3
	Dec.	133181	1541976	105.9	389393	102.0
1990	Jan.	121419	1530813	104.0	386162	99.1
	Feb.	122468	1526220	103.0	377068	95.7
	Mar.	131030	1529746	102.4	374917	96.8
	Apr.	125603	1524793	101.2	379101	98.4
	May	129936	1530203	101.2	386569	101.0
	June	127057	1529652	100.7	382596	100.0
	July	129387	1533704	100.7	386380	102.4
	Aug.	129020	1535168	100.5	385464	101.3
	Sept.	126893	1532206	99.9	385300	100.7
	Oct.	130875	1538431	100.3	386788	101.2
	Nov.	116193	1523062	98.7	373961	96.9
	Dec.	120221	1510102	97.9	367289	94.3
1991	Jan.	117789	1506472	98.4	354203	91.7
	Feb.	117547	1501551	98.4	355557	94.3
	Mar.	112116	1482637	96.9	347452	92.7
	Apr.	116139	1473173	96.6	345802	91.2
	May	118434	1461671	95.5	346689	89.7
	June	117128	1451742	94.9	351701	91.9
	July	130827	1453182	94.7	366389	94.8
	Aug.	125482	1449644	94.4	373437	96.9
	Sept.	120144	1442895	94.2	376453	97.7
	Oct.	123325	1435345	93.3	368951	95.4
	Nov.	124526	1443678	94.8	367995	98.4

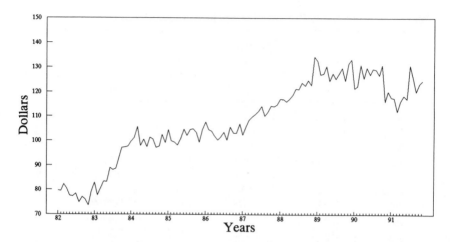

Figure 3.20   Durable Goods Orders (Millions of Dollars).

pressure curve and both curves are shown in Figure 3.21. These pressure curves represent smoothed growth rates, and an interpretation scheme has been suggested for the 12/12 and 3/12 curves.

- *Phase 1.* The volume of sales, production, or orders is lower than a year earlier but getting less unfavorable. In this phase, management should be putting into place a strategy to expand production. This phase is signaled when the 3/12 pressure curve exceeds the 12/12 pressure curve yet both are below 100.

- *Phase 2.* The volume of activity is higher than its level a year ago, and momentum is building. In this phase, activity and conditions are the best. Management should be reaping the benefit of the cyclical upturn with improving profits. This phase is signaled when the 3/12 pressure curve exceeds the 12/12 pressure curve and both are above 100.

- *Phase 3.* Activity remains robust; however, comparisons are turning more unfavorable. Management must begin to plan for the eventual contraction in activity, even though there is no indication of actual weakness at the moment. This phase is signaled when the 12/12 pressure curve exceeds the 3/12 pressure curve and both are greater than 100.

- *Phase 4.* The final phase of the cycle is when the pressure curve falls below its year-ago level, which suggests that a contraction is in place. Management should be well positioned for this if they heeded the warning in Phase 3, and it is an opportunity for management to look to Phase 1 again. This phase is signaled when the 12/12 pressure curve exceeds the 3/12 pressure curve and both are less than 100.

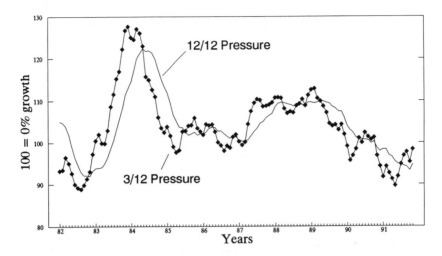

Figure 3.21 Pressure Curves for Durable Goods Orders.

Another method for constructing technical pressure indicators is McLaughlin's paired index concept.[79] This method can best be shown by example. Consider a time series and the same series lagged so that one is an exact leading indicator of the other. In practice, this method would use bona fide leading and coincident indicators, such as the Commerce Department's composite indexes but these constructed data better demonstrate the cyclical timing relationships. The original data are shown in Figure 3.22, where LI represents the leading indicator (which simply is the original series) and CI represents the coincident indicator (which is the lagged series). By design, the target or coincident series cycle peaked in period 9 while the leading indicator peaked in period 8. McLaughlin calculates the rate of change of each series and expresses the results as indexes by adding 100 to that percentage change. Mathematically, the rate of change series (%LI and %CI in Figure 3.23) lead their original counterparts. Additionally, McLaughlin *pairs* the leading and coincident indicators in levels and rates of change. These pressure indicators lead even the rates of change, as shown in Figure 3.24. Table 3.35 summarizes the timing relationship between the various series. In essence, McLaughlin makes use of a mathematical principle to derive these technical pressure indicators.

COMPOSITE INDICATORS

This section will show how and why composite indicators are formed and how they can be used to their fullest potential. Additionally, this section should give

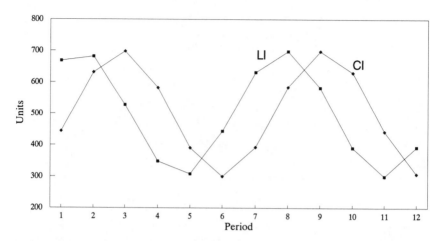

Figure 3.22 McLaughlin's Paired Indicator Concept, Leading (LI) and Coincident Indicators (CI).

readers the knowledge to form their own composite indicators and decision rule systems for interpreting the indicators. Although composite indicators usually have been used to present cyclical measures, the method is general enough for secular, seasonal, or other specialized indicators. Indeed, it is easy to envision a research agenda to develop a composite leading indicator of the long wave using these composite indicator techniques.

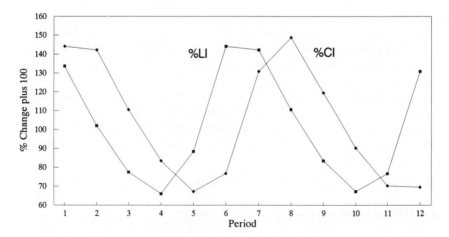

Figure 3.23 McLaughlin's Paired Indicator Concept, Percentage Change in Leading (%LI) and Coincident Indicators (%CI).

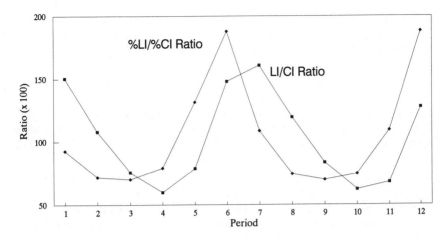

Figure 3.24 McLaughlin's Paired Indicator Concept, Paired Indicators: (LI/CI) and (%LI/%CI).

Arthur Burns has offered a rationale for using composite indicators in his discussion of forecasting principles. He wrote, "[S]ince the cyclical timing of single processes cannot be implicitly trusted, a measure of protection against surprises of the individual cases may be won by combining the indications of numerous series."[80] But even with this safeguard, composite indicators can still give false signals. Therefore, decision-rule systems have been devised to screen the information.

Leading, Coincident, and Lagging Indicators

"As Maine goes, so too does the nation" is the political counterpart of economic leading indicators. An economic indicator can anticipate moves in an

Table 3.35 Timing Relationship among Paired Indicators.

Series	Period Peak Occurred
Coincident Indicator (CI)	9
Leading Indicator (LI)	8
Growth Rate in Coincident Indicator (%CI)	8
Growth Rate in the Leading Indicator (%LI)	6
Ratio of Leading to Coincident Indicators (LI/CI)	7
Ratio of Leading to Coincident Indicator Growth Rates (%LI/%CI)	6

economic process because it has a causal, reporting, or mathematical lead. Theory can help select the causal leading indicators; practical considerations, however, govern the selection of indicators based on their reporting or mathematical lead.

One of the earliest leading indicator systems was developed before World War I.[81] This approach was known as the Harvard ABC curves (we will take another look at them in Chapter 4) and classified cyclical indicators into one of three classes: speculation (curve A), business activity (curve B), and money markets (curve C). The speculative series included industrial stock prices and New York City bank debits. The business series included bank debits outside New York City and commodity prices. The monetary series included commercial paper rates. The selection of those series was based on a review of data between January 1903 and July 1914. Over that time period, it was found that Curve A led cyclical fluctuations in Curve B by 4 to 10 months, whereas Curve B led changes in Curve C by 2 to 8 months. While the Harvard ABC curves did not survive the test of time, the process did.

In the fall of 1937, Henry Morgenthau, Jr., the Secretary of the Treasury, requested the NBER to develop a system of indicators to anticipate cyclical changes in the economy. The National Bureau provided the Treasury with a list of cyclical indicators based on timing; with this action, the system of leading, coincident, and lagging indicators got their start. Previously, the timing classification was viewed as a by-product of the NBER's research to find the cause of the business cycle. Now, however, the system of cyclical indicators was established as a product unto itself.

By October 1961, the Commerce Department began publishing *Business Cycle Developments (BCD),* a comprehensive statistical review of the cyclical indicators identified by the NBER. While this publication later changed its title to *Business Conditions Digest* and was subsequently rolled into the *Survey of Current Business,* neither the content nor the approach lost its appeal—though some observers thought the business cycle analytical techniques would surely fade away. Today, the indicator approach has an even greater following with numerous foreign governments beginning to publish their own countries' leading indicators.

Since no indicator or indicator composite is ever perfect, a periodic review of cyclical indicators (as would be true for any forecasting methodology) is necessary to ensure that the indicators are still representative of the economic process and are still good indicators technically, as well as to add or substitute new indicators to the composite.

Finally, numerous leading indicators have been developed over the past 10 to 15 years, including the Center for International Business Cycle Research's (CIBCR) leading indicator of employment, a leading indicator of British Columbia industrial employment, PaineWebber's leading indicator of automobile sales,

Business Week's weekly leading indicator of production, *Chemical Week*'s leading indicator of the chemical industry's output, the National Association of Home Builders' leading indicator of the housing starts. All these indicators have been developed since 1980 giving tribute to the NBER's methods.

Theory of the Index Model.   The *theory of leading indicators* has two distinct parts: a mathematical foundation and an economic component. Sargent and Sims posited a general mathematical theory of the index model in which the National Bureau's business cycle indicator approach formed a special case.[82] Even earlier, Milton Friedman[83] tried to provide a theoretical structure to the NBER's cyclical indicators by showing how the NBER indicators could be interpreted in terms of standard Keynesian concepts. But more recently, the economic content has been developed around a loosely formulated *expectation theory of the business cycle.* [84]

Since the economic theory behind cyclical indicators is not rigid, the selection of cyclical indicators tends to be an empirical question. The selection of indicators to compile into a composite indicator is similar to direct specification of an equation model or estimation of a reduced-form model. In a sense, that the NBER method does not advocate any one theory is a benefit since it allows many theories to attempt to explain these cyclical processes. In the final analysis, a theory is only as good as it predicts the future. Business cycle theories have come and gone, but interest in the empirically selected indicators has remained strong.

Selecting Cyclical Indicators.   The process of determining a cycle in some relevant measure of business activity (in the overall economy, at the state level, for an industry, etc.) has been discussed earlier. However, the next step in forming a composite indicator is to determine reliable cyclical indicators of the target measure of economic activity, which will anticipate moves in that process, move with it, or follow it. The selection of indicators requires some judgment and a knowledge of data sources—traits needed for any type of econometric model building. Conceptual problems are faced at each turn. For example, should interest rates be a leading or a lagging indicator of the general cyclical fluctuation in the economy? The U.S. Department of Commerce/NBER method classifies most interest rates as lagging indicators. But the United Kingdom's Central Statistical Office uses the rate of interest on three-month prime bank bills (inverted) as a leading indicator. (Burns and Mitchell observed that bond yields could conform positively or inversely to the business cycle.) Further, what may be a good leading indicator for one industry, country, state, or company may not work for another for either conceptual or data reasons. Despite all these potential problems, a good starting point is to replicate some of the concepts already used in existing composite cyclical indicators. While many of these concepts are likely to work in other applications, data limitations may cause insurmountable problem in attempting to follow the identical specification of existing measures. Therefore, it is difficult to say what should or should not be included in a composite indicator. Later in this book, numerous specialized indicators will be discussed.

For now, some useful rules for screening cyclical indicators are:

1. Search for leading and lagging indicators based on a causal relationship—they are most likely to be robust over numerous cycles.
2. Look for data with the highest frequency; for example, if there is an option, use monthly rather than quarterly data.
3. Look for series with the longest history.
4. Do not overlook reliable coincident indicators or lagging indicators. While these coincident and lagging indicators, by themselves, will not help to forecast, they can confirm and forecast when used in other forms.

Generating Leading Indicators from Lagging Indicators. Geoffrey Moore has proposed using the inverse of the composite index of lagging economic indicators as a long-leading indicator.[85] The rationale for this is that the lagging indicators generally represent costs of doing business and as long as costs continue to decline, the risk of an aborted recovery is small. Alternatively, the inverse lagging indicator can reflect the view that the seeds of the current downturn usually are determined in the previous cycle.

Forming Composite Indicators

Simple Method. A composite indicator is a basket of economic time series drawn together in a systematic manner to track a specific economic activity. The selection of indicators to be included in a composite should be based on theoretical and empirical grounds. Most composites are formed to capture the cyclical nature of the economy, industry, or other economic activity. A simple method exists to form this market basket of indicators, which will be discussed first, then the more elaborate method used by the Commerce Department will be described.

A composite index can be formed by summing the change in the individual composite while accounting for the component's importance and volatility.[86] This can be written as:

$$\Delta\%(\text{Composite}) = \Sigma w_i s_i \Delta\%(\text{Component}_i)$$

where $i = 1$ to n (n being the maximum number of components), w is the component's weight, which represents the component's relative importance, and s

is the factor that adjusts the component's volatility to a standardized amplitude for all the components. The reason it is necessary to use the standardization weight (s), which equalizes the percentage change among the individual components, is that it minimizes the influence from any single component dominating the overall index change simply because the component happens to be very volatile. As an illustration of this method, consider forming a composite index of three components—real disposable personal income, industrial production, and employment.

1. *Assign Relative Importance Weights.* In this example, assume that the relative importance weights are assigned such that employment and income each are 1.25 and industrial production is assigned a weight of 0.50 because production is a less comprehensive measure of the nation's activity. The sum of the weights equals the number of components. If there is no reason to expect one indicator to be any more or less important, then equal weighting ($w_i = 1$ for all components) is desirable. The Commerce Department's composite cyclical indexes currently weight the components equally, although this has not always been true.

2. *Determine the Volatility.* In this example, the average absolute deviation around the average growth rate is calculated for each of these indicators and is shown in column 3 of Table 3.36.

3. *Determine the Component Weights.* Convert the three entries in column 1 of Table 3.36 into a relative importance weight by dividing each assigned weight by the sum of all weights. For example, the relative importance weight for employment, in this example, is $100 \times (1.25/3)$. Then determine the standardizing weight, which can be derived from column 3 volatility measures. To do this, divide each volatility by the sum of column 3. The result is shown in column 4. Then take the inverse of column 3 entries and place these results in column 5. Finally, the standardization weights are the entries of column 5 as a share of the total, and the result is shown in column 6. The combined relative importance and standardization factor is determined by multiplying entries in column 2 by those in column 6 (and shown in column 7) and then taking the ratio of each entry in column 7 to the sum of all entries in that column. This determines the final weights shown in column 8.

4. *Calculate the Composite Index.* The composite index is calculated by using the weights determined in the previous step and using the equation:

Composite = 0.597 × Employment + 0.072 × Production + 0.331 × Income.

Although this example has just demonstrated how easy it is to form a composite index, why should one bother? The rationale for forming an index model is in part a pragmatic concern about the quality of the statistical indicators themselves. Composite indicators provide a more reliable gauge of economic activity

Table 3.36 Weighting Components of a Composite Indicator (Basic Method).

Series	(1) Assigned Weight	(2) % of Column 1 Sum	(3) Average Deviation	(4) % of Column 2 Sum	(5) Inverse of Column 3	(6) % of Column 5 Sum	(7) Column 2 × Column 6	(8) % of Column 7 Sum
Employment	1.25	41.67	0.25	16.34	4.00	53.86	2244	59.66
Production	0.50	16.67	0.83	54.25	1.20	16.22	270	7.19
Income	1.25	41.67	0.45	29.41	2.22	29.92	1247	33.15
Column Totals*	3.00	100.00	1.53	100.00	7.43	100.00	3761	100.00

* The sum of the columns may not add to the totals shown due to rounding.

since they can be more comprehensive and hence, are less dependent on any single measure even if that measure has a comprehensive coverage. This is particularly helpful when some components are subject to a lot of revision or when one indicator runs counter to several other measures.[87]

Commerce Department/NBER Method. The Commerce Department/ NBER method of forming a composite indicators uses a refinement on the simple method just described. The main steps followed by the Commerce Department in compiling their composite indexes are to (1) compute the standardized and weighted average changes, (2) modify the average changes and cumulate these changes into an index, and (3) trend-adjust the index, which was eliminated with the December 1993 revision but is described here for conceptual completeness. Here is a step-by-step guide to the Commerce methodology:

1. *Calculate the Symmetrical Percentage Change.* Julius Shiskin noted that when forming an index built on percentage changes, an arithmetic average of growth can introduce a bias if nothing is done to correct for the situation.[88] Shiskin's example of this point is shown in Table 3.37.

Shiskin proposed an alternative method to calculate the growth rate, which was defined as $200\,(X_t - X_{t-1})\,/\,(X_t + X_{t-1})$, where X is the value of the time series at time period t. This expression will be referred to as c_i, where i is the number of series. As Shiskin observed, the average of growth rates from the traditional formula for period-to-period percentage change was +25.0%, while his alternative formula averaged to 0%. Hence, the Shiskin alternative eliminated the arithmetic bias. In fact, as also shown in Table 3.37, the easier way to average the standard percentage changes would have

Table 3.37   Symmetric versus Asymmetric Growth Rates (Shiskin Example).

Data	Asymmetric (Traditional) Percentage Change	Symmetric (Shiskin) Percentage Change
40	—	—
80	+100.0	+66.7
40	−50.0	−66.7
80	+100.0	+66.7
40	−50.0	−66.7
80	+100.0	+66.7
40	−50.0	−66.7
Arithmetic Average	+25.0	0.0
Geometric Average	0.0	−4.9

been to use a geometric average—not an arithmetic average—which would eliminate that bias. Nonetheless, the Shiskin method is used by the Commerce Department to calculate percentage change in the components of the series. However, if the time series is already expressed as a ratio or percentage change, then the change is calculated as a first difference: $c_i = X_t - X_{t-1}$.

2. *Amplitude-Adjust Changes or Percentage Changes.* The values derived from step 1 are standardized by dividing each observation by the mean absolute change, calculated using the formula: $s_{it} = (c_{it}/A_i)$, where:

$$A_i = \frac{\Sigma \, | \, c_{it} \, |}{(N - 1)}$$

and N equals the number of observations. The A's do not change from period to period, but are fixed for a given period. The effect of this calculation is to amplitude-adjust the components of the index so that each component's change over the long run equals one. This will ensure that no single indicator will dominate movement in the indicator.

3. *Weight Amplitude-Adjusted Changes.* Individual indicators are scored according to a scheme devised by Moore and Shiskin.[89] This scoring system, which is not really used any longer by the Commerce Department, rates statistical indicators based on their economic significance (their importance in business cycle theory or broadness of coverage), statistical adequacy (how good the indicator is from a technical standpoint), conformity to the business cycle, consistency in its timing relationship with the business cycle, the promptness of reporting the data, and the smoothness of the series.[90] Based on these criteria, each indicator can be assigned a composite score, which is used as a second weight on each individual indicator included in the composite. The formula for this process is:

$$R_t = \frac{\Sigma s_{it} W_i}{\Sigma W_i}$$

where W is the weight assigned to each component.

4. *Adjust the Weighted Monthly Averages in the Leading and Lagging Indexes.* Calculate the average absolute change for the sum of the components of the leading, coincident, and lagging composites. Then determine the ratios of the average absolute change for the leaders relative to the average absolute change in the coincident composite. Do the same for the lagging indicator. This can be expressed as:

$$F = [(\sum_{t=2}^{n} | \, R \, |) / (N - 1)] / [(\sum_{t=2}^{n} | \, P \, |) / (N - 1)]$$

where P is the coincident index counterpart of R, which was defined in Step 3. Note that adjustment is calculated only for the leading and lagging indicators since $F = 1$ for the coincident index.

Next derive the adjusted weighted monthly changes (r_t) as follows: $r_t = R_t / F$. Once this is done, accumulate the standardized average changes (r_t) into an index using this formula: $I_t = I_{t-1}[(200 + r_t)/(200 - r_t)]$, where the initial value of I is arbitrarily set equal to 100. This then yields the raw index, which will be subject to two further adjustments.

5. *Reverse Trend Adjustment.* The purpose of the leading and lagging indicators is to provide the forecaster with information on the status of the coincident series. Julius Shiskin proposed a method known as reverse trend adjustment, which reduced the number of false signals in the leading indicators.[91] His method was to impose a second trend adjustment to the leading and lagging composites, so that they would have the same trend as the coincident composite (or growth in real GNP/GDP per month). This is accomplished by deriving a trend growth rate between the initial (C_I) and the terminal (C_T) specific cycle peaks, using the formula:

$$T = (\sqrt[m]{(C_T/C_I)} - 1) \times 100$$

where m is the number of months between the initial peak and the terminal peak. Previously, this was calculated for the individual components of the coincident indicators and then averaged. However, the current Commerce Department methodology performs this calculation on real GNP and uses the result (G) as the *target trend* instead of the average of the individual component trends. The target trend (G) is constant for all three composite leading, coincident, and lagging indexes.

A trend-adjustment factor is then determined as the difference between the target trend (G) and the trend in the raw index (T)—where T exists for each raw composite index (r). Then the trend-adjusted composite (r') equals $r_t + (G - T)$. Finally, the r' observations are cumulatively summed over time to form an index, and the result is rebased to a specific desirable base period. The complete process is summarized in Table 3.38.

Tracking the Commerce Department's Leading Indicator. Economists often track the leading indicator composite on an ongoing basis to forecast the upcoming number on a monthly basis. To anticipate the leading indicator report, the methodology described earlier can be condensed into a few steps. Table 3.39 presents a leading indicator worksheet that can be used to track the Commerce Department's (or your own) leading indicator. The Commerce Department's composite index of leading indicators tends to be reported at the

Table 3.38   Summary of Steps to Form a Composite Index.

	For Percentage Change and Differences
For Levels	

For Individual Components of Index

Step 1	$C = 200 (X_t - X_{t-1})/(X_t + X_{t-1})$	or,	$(X_t - X_{t-1})$
Step 2	A = Mean absolute change of C		Same
Step 3	$S = C/A$		Same

For Sum of Components in Index

Step 4 R = Average of all S per period with weighting factors

Step 5 r = R adjusted for coincident index standard change

Step 6 $I = (200 + r)/(200 - r)$ multiplied by lagged value of the composite index with the initial value set equal to 100

For Sum of Components with Trend Adjustment

Step 7 T = Composite index trend from initial cycle peak to terminal cycle peak

Step 8 G = Average of monthly trends of individual components of the composite, called the "target trend"

Step 9 $r' = r + (G - T)$, which yields the trend-adjusted change

Step 10 $I' = (200 + r')/(200 - r')$ multiplied by the lagged value of the composite index with the initial value set equal to 100

For Base Year Changes

Step 11 B = Calendar year mean of I' for new base year

Step 12 $I^B = (I'/B) \times 100$, which yields the new base year composite

end of the month for the period a month earlier. However, various components are known with certainty several weeks in advance of the official leading indicator release. For example, the stock price average is known immediately following the last trading session of the month, or vendor performance is known on the first business day of the next month. With these and other indicators that are released late in the same month or shortly into the next month, it is possible to keep tabs on the leading indicators on an ongoing basis using the worksheet shown in Table 3.39.

Vendor performance, change in sensitive prices, change in unfilled orders, and consumer expectations are calculated as a difference before entering the leading index while the remaining seven components enter the composite as standardized percentage change. To derive the net contributions per component, take the difference or percentage change, divide by the standardization

Table 3.39 Leading Indicator Worksheet.

BCD Series	Series Title	Previous Month	Current Month	Std. Factor	Weight	Change	Std. Change	Contribution	Net Contribution
1	Average Weekly Hours	40.7	41.0	0.477	1.00	0.73	1.53	1.53	0.22
5	Average Initial Unemployment Claims	399	419	−5.236	1.00	4.88	−0.93	−0.93	−0.13
8	Mfg. New Orders, Consumer and Materials	92.80	92.54	2.714	1.00	−0.28	−0.10	−0.10	−0.01
32	Vendor Performance	50.4	48.8	3.423	1.00	−1.60	−0.46	−0.46	−0.06
20	Contracts & Orders for Plant and Equipment	47.85	43.55	6.110	1.00	−9.40	−1.53	−1.53	−0.22
29	Housing Permits	80.1	76.0	5.095	1.00	−5.25	−1.03	−1.03	−0.14
92	Change in Mfg. Unfilled Orders	−1.55	−0.86	0.459	1.00	0.68	1.50	1.50	0.21
99	Change in Sensitive Material Prices	−0.52	−0.61	0.174	1.00	−0.09	−0.51	−0.51	−0.07
19	Index of Stock Prices, S&P 500	380.23	389.40	2.640	1.00	2.38	0.90	0.90	0.13
106	Money Supply, M2, 1982 $	2402.3	2396.7	0.440	1.00	−0.23	−0.53	−0.53	−0.07
83	Index of Consumer Expectations	74.4	75.3	3.931	1.00	0.90	0.22	0.22	0.03

Summary		
A.	Sum of Contributions	−0.948
B.	Sum of Weights	11.000
C.	Ratio of A/B	−0.086
D.	Standardization Factor	0.625
E.	Standardization Change (C/D)	−0.138
F.	Trend Constant	0.142
G.	Monthly Percentage Change (E + F)	0.004

Note: As of December 1993, the Commerce Department eliminated the trend adjustment and updated the standardization factors. However, the computation remains the same as shown. (George R. Green and Barry Beckman, "Business Cycle Indicators: Upcoming Revision of the Composite Indexes," *Survey of Current Business*, October 1993, 44–51.)

factor, and multiply the result by the assigned weight (since 1989, all the leading indicator components are equally weighted; however, this example allows for unequal weights). Then divide the contribution by the overall standardization factor (0.625) and divide by the sum of the components. For example, the average workweek contribution equals:

$$200 \times \{[(41.0 - 40.7) / (41.0 + 40.7)] / 0.477\} = +1.54$$

and the net contribution equals:

$$(+1.54 / 0.625) / 11.000 = +0.22$$

The derivations of the other components are presented in Table 3.39.

Alternatives to the Commerce Department Method.   One alternative to the Commerce Department method of forming composite indicators, which might be dubbed the *geometric average method,* would be to do the following:

1. Compute the traditional percentage change (or difference).
2. Determine the median average absolute deviation from the geometric average of all observations in the growth rate.
3. Divide the monthly change by the median average absolute deviation and then multiply the result by the assigned significance weight.
4. Sum the component changes derived in step 3 and cumulate the changes into an index using weights derived for the leading and lagging composites from an optimal relationship between the individual component and the target or forecast variable.

As shown in Tables 3.40 and 3.41, the various technical factors used in the calculations would be relatively identical. Other things equal, the higher the standardization factors from the Commerce method versus this alternative, the larger is the downward bias in the Commerce Department's series. To some extent, however, the trend adjustment could correct for this.

The final step in this method for compiling an index is to derive the individual component weights for the leading and lagging composites using correlations between the forecast variable and the component. The specific component weight is based on its relative correlation at all points and not only at turning points where the component with the highest correlation would be given the highest weight and so forth. This final set of weights helps to optimize the index to forecast all observations of the target variable.[92]

A second formulation for composite indexes, which might be called the *neural network method,* uses a hybrid between the Commerce Department

Table 3.40   Comparison of Target Trend Computations Using the Commerce Department's Method and the Geometric Average Method (Components of Coincident Indicator).

Component	Monthly Trend Factors*	
	Commerce	Geometric Average
Payroll employment	0.186	0.169
Personal income less transfer payments in 1982 dollars	0.281	0.255
Industrial Production Index (1987 = 100)	0.334	0.290
Manufacturing and trade sales in 1982 dollars	0.282	0.260
Target trend (average)	0.271	0.244
GNP target trend	0.261	

* Individual series trend adjustments were calculated by the U.S. Department of Commerce between initial and terminal peaks in the specific cycles over the period 1948–1981. With the 1989 revision to the composite index, these factors were no longer used to derive the target trend for the composite indexes. Real GNP trend growth replaced the average of the individual trend factors as the target trend. In the geometric average case, the period used for the trend factors was 1948 through 1991. The personal income data were revised to include a 1987 dollar base period, but these data were not available historically at the time of this calculation.

Table 3.41   Comparison of Standardization Factors Using Commerce Department's Method and the Geometric Average Method (Components of Coincident Indicator).

Component	Commerce Factors		Alternative
	Current*	All Periods	
Payroll employment	0.318	0.302	0.244
Personal income less transfer payments in 1982 dollars	0.481	0.477	0.415
Industrial Production Index (1987 = 100)	0.901	0.844	0.795
Manufacturing and trade sales in 1982 dollars	1.000	0.981	0.958

* The "current period" used for estimation of standardization factors by the U.S. Department of Commerce was 1948 to 1985 (or beginning with the first year after 1948 for which data were available). The "all period" calculations were done by the authors and covered 1948 through 1991. The "alternative" is the average absolute deviation around the geometric mean and was calculated between 1948 and 1991.

methodology and a nonparametric neural network model. A neural network is a form of artificial intelligence where a computer algorithm determines the optimal relationship between a set of inputs and an output. An analogy to an ordinary least squares (OLS) regression might be useful in understanding the concept of a neural network, even though the computations are more involved than OLS. The coefficients of the OLS regression are fixed, whereas the coefficients of a neural network are not and vary based on a complex relationship between the input and the output. This makes the neural network model more flexible and potentially better suited for this application. Hence, the input data of the composite index can be preprocessed—assuming there is some target output variable to forecast. For example, it is possible to optimize the individual relationship between the input and the output using a neural network model and then take an average of all the optimized inputs as a composite projection. In this manner, the rationale for a broad-based composite indicator is maintained without sacrificing the forecast precision from other statistical methods. An example of this neural network method will be demonstrated in Chapter 8.

Some Final Thoughts on Forming Composite Indicators.   A natural question that is often asked about composite indicators is, Why go through this procedure when a simple regression model would establish the associated coefficients based on an optimal statistical relationship compared with some dependent variable of interest? It is a fair question. The key differences between the two approaches—a regression model and an indicator model—are subtle. A composite index is often a turning point indicator with no true "dependent" variable. This, however, has been a source of criticism of this approach; namely, *What is it supposed to measure?* On the other hand, supporters of this approach note that this could in fact be a strength, in that the business cycle is not simply fluctuation in one indicator, no matter how broadly based. The second key difference is that a regression model normally would assume a fixed timing relationship between a dependent variable and an independent variable. The indicator approach, however, accepts the unfortunate fact for forecasting that the timing relationship between indicators changes over time and between business cycles. Hence, the indicators are entered with a concurrent relationship, which assumes that the information is simply *today's information* about the future or present. Although the two approaches have subtle differences, they should be viewed as complementary and not competitive. Each technique has its strengths and weaknesses but when it comes to forecasting and monitoring the economy the diversity of the techniques should only add to an understanding.

Evaluating the Leading Indicators

Finally, the bottom line in developing a good leading indicator comes down to selecting appropriate leading indicators that are timely, stable, and significant. Niemira and Fredman[93] evaluated the Commerce Department's leading indicators. They studied 15 economic indicators that tend to lead the U.S. business cycle using a technique known as the *Neftçi criterion* (discussed later in this chapter). The question they asked was, How well do those components work individually, in a probability sense, to signal a business or growth cycle turning point? Their evaluation covered the 11 components of the U.S. Commerce Department's composite index of leading indicators as well as 4 additional financial indicators. These indicators were judged individually and relative to two composite indicators. They concluded that some of the components of the Commerce Department's composite leading indicator have a very low accuracy rate in calling turning points in the economy. Several conclusions were drawn:

1. The composite index contains more reliable cyclical turning point information than most of the individual indicators of the composite alone.

2. The Commerce Department's composite index of leading indicators would benefit by some component substitutions.

3. The ratio of the coincident to lagging composite indicators is more reliable in calling a recession than the composite of leading indicators, but that ratio had a poor track record in calling growth cycles.

4. Most of the individual components of the composite index of leading indicators signal growth cycle turning points better than business cycle turning points. If these conclusions can be generalized, then the value of composite indicators might be summarized as the *whole is greater than the sum of the individual parts.*

Phase Average Trend (PAT) Adjustment for Trend-Adjusting Composite Indicators. The NBER/CIBCR methodology for trend-adjusting composite indexes measures trends between successive cyclical phases and has similarities with the high-low trend measure described earlier in this chapter. This method, which is known as phase average trend (PAT) adjustment, was proposed by Boschan and Ebanks[94] and is applied as follows:

1. *Calculate a 75-Month (25-Quarter) Moving Average of the Series.* This moving average is centered, which means that 37 monthly observations are lost at each end of the time series.

2. *Extend Trend for Lost Observations.* Use the first and preceding two years' growth rate in the centered 75-month moving average (or 25 quarters) to extrapolate forward and backward to extend the trend.

3. *Compute Deviations from the Trend.* Subtract the original series from the moving average series.

4. *Determine the Cyclical Turning Points in the Deviation from the Trend Series.* Apply the Bry and Boschan computerized (or the Burns and Mitchell) criteria to determine the high and low turning points in the deviation series.

5. *Average Adjacent Contraction and Expansion Phases.* Using the turning point dates determined in the previous step, calculate the phase averages in the original series. For example, if a turning point is found in the deviation series at January 1969, a low at November 1970, and another high at March 1973, then the phase averages are computed for the following periods: January 1969 through November 1970 and November 1970 through March 1973.

6. *Calculate a Three-Term Moving Average of the Phase Averages.* To approximate gradual changes in phase trends, a two-term moving average of the triplets (high-low-high averages) was used. This dampened the discontinuity in moving from one PAT to the next.

7. *Connect the Midpoints of the Three-Term Moving Average of the Phase Average.* This step converts the smoothed phase averages to a time series and is the second approximation of the trend.

8. *Level-Adjust Phase Averages to the Original Series.* This adjustment puts the series calculated in the previous step on the same footing as the change in the original series.

9. *Extrapolate Forward and Backward to Calculate the Trend over the Missing Observations.* This is the trickiest part of the calculation, especially in the most recent period when policy decisions might be tied to the analysis. The beginning period trend is extrapolated using the first observation in the original series and the first turning point by using a linear trend (a straight line). The end period trend is extrapolated from the last triplet or phase average.

10. *Smooth the Second Approximation of the Trend.* A 12-month moving average of the second approximation of the trend yields the final trend.

Most trend-adjustment methods, no matter how elaborate, appear somewhat arbitrary. The PAT method also has this drawback, but it does provide an acceptable way of calculating a trend. Any trend-adjustment approach only can be evaluated against competing trend-adjustment methods since each one can be conceptually as good as the next but yield different results. Maybe the best alternative to using the trend-adjusted level of a time series is to use growth rates and *step cycles,* which generally eliminates the need to adjust composite indexes and other time series for trends. But care must be taken in interpreting these growth rate cycles since growth rates tend to be relatively high in the early phases of any expansion and peak before the *high growth rate phase* is over.[95]

Higgins-Poole Method of Trend Adjustment.   Another alternative to PAT is what might be called the Higgins-Poole method of comparing actual values to an extrapolated trend.[96] Of course, the same arbitrariness arises in determining how to extrapolate the variable. As an example of this method, consider deriving a growth cycle chronology using the composite index of coincident indicators compiled by the U.S. Department of Commerce and exponential smoothing to determine the projected trend. Then the trend-adjusted composite index can be defined as the ratio of the actual to extrapolated values (A/E). This trend-adjusted composite can be used to determine the turning points in the growth cycle, subject to minimum duration criteria. Table 3.42 presents these results compared with the NBER growth cycle turning points. Generally, the Higgins-Poole method tends to call turning points slightly earlier than the NBER growth cycle methodology, but it compares quite favorably with it.

Beveridge-Nelson Method. Another alternative to PAT is the Beveridge and Nelson[97] method used to measure business and growth cycles based on a decomposition technique. The logic behind the Beveridge-Nelson method is similar to the Higgins-Poole technique, though more elaborate. Beveridge and Nelson identified and estimated an ARIMA model for the first differences of nonstationary business cycle indicators, where the *cyclical* or *transitory component*

Table 3.42   Growth Cycle Turning Point Dates from a Trend-Adjusted Composite Index of Coincident Indicators Using the Higgins-Poole Method and the NBER/CIBCR Chronology.

NBER/CIBCR Growth Cycle		Higgins-Poole Method	
High	Low	High	Low
July 1948	Nov. 1949	Oct. 1948	July 1949
Mar. 1951	July 1952	Jan. 1951	July 1952
Mar. 1953	Aug. 1954	Mar. 1953	May 1954
Feb. 1957	Apr. 1958	Dec. 1955	Apr. 1958
Feb. 1960	Feb. 1961	June 1959	Feb. 1961
May 1962	Oct. 1964	—	—
June 1966	Oct. 1967	Mar. 1966	Oct. 1967
Mar. 1969	Nov. 1970	Mar. 1969	Nov. 1970
Mar. 1973	Mar. 1975	Feb. 1973	Mar. 1975
Dec. 1978	Dec. 1982	Dec. 1978	Oct. 1982
June 1984*	Jan. 1987*	July 1984	July 1986
Feb. 1989*		Oct. 1988	

Sources: Columbia University's Center for International Business Cycle Research; authors.

* Based on trend-adjusted coincident indicator and subject to revision.

Note: The Higgins-Poole method as applied here used single exponential smoothing with the alpha equal to 0.05 to extrapolate the trend in the coincident indicator. The highs and lows in the ratio of the actual to extrapolated value were used as turning point dates.

was a function of past observations only. This flexibility allows the cyclical component of the time series to be stripped away from the trend or permanent component without the restrictive assumption of a fixed-length centered moving average, which is an integral part of the NBER method. But there are implicit assumptions in this type of model as well.

Beveridge and Nelson then formed an *index of business conditions*. This composite index of indicators was formed from coincident measures as classified by using the authors' own methodology. The weights for this index were selected by principal components analysis to maximize the variance of the index.[98] Unfortunately, not all the components had the *correct sign* (not all the indicators moved in the same direction as the phase of the business cycle). One example was manufacturers' new orders for consumer goods in constant dollars, which Beveridge and Nelson classified as a coincident indicator of the business cycle when in fact it is a leading indicator. Because of this conceptual misspecification, new orders might have had a negative weight (a countercyclical influence). Consequently, this might call into question why new orders were included in the index even though it had the *incorrect* relationship with the business cycle. Nonetheless, their results are still interesting. As shown in Table 3.43, the Beveridge-Nelson approach to trend adjustment yields more growth cycles than the NBER method found, and the dates tend to lead the NBER turning point dates as well. Moreover, the main advantage of trend adjustment using either the Beveridge-Nelson or Higgins-Poole method is that the current period extrapolation is more timely.

Since there is no clear-cut best method for determining trend-adjusted composites, it is likely new experimental methods will continually be proposed. Furthermore, the jury is still out as to whether it is better to form composite indexes from individually trend-adjusted components or to trend-adjust the overall composite. More empirical work is necessary to determine the appropriate path.

Interpreting Movement in the Composite Indicators

Beatrice Vaccara and Victor Zarnowitz[99] concluded in their evaluation of the composite index of leading indicators that the index is valuable as a forecasting tool though not foolproof. Its biggest disadvantage, they felt, was that it can be extremely sensitive to "random or short-lived changes in economic movement."[100] Moreover, the appearance of these *extra cycles* in the leading indicator mislead the public about the likelihood of a recession or recovery. However, Moore[101] has observed that those false signals generally were associated with growth cycle declines and rebounds. But this raises the question: How should fluctuation in the composite index of leading indicators be interpreted? Over the years, several methods have been developed—some simple and others complex—to gauge the user in making the most of composite leading indicators. It is useful to review some of these methods, as applied to the

Table 3.43   Growth Cycle Turning Point Dates of the NBER Chronology and the Beveridge-Nelson Decomposition Method.

NBER/CIBCR Growth Cycle		Beveridge-Nelson Method	
High	Low	High	Low
July 1948	Nov. 1949	Nov. 1947	Apr. 1949
Mar. 1951	July 1952	Aug. 1950	July 1951
Mar. 1953	Aug. 1954	Nov. 1952	Dec. 1953
—	—	Mar. 1955	July 1956
Feb. 1957	Apr. 1958	Dec. 1956	Feb. 1958
—	—	Nov. 1958	Aug. 1959
Feb. 1960	Feb. 1961	Jan. 1960	Feb. 1961
May 1962	Oct. 1964	Dec. 1961	Dec. 1962
June 1966	Oct. 1967	Feb. 1966	Feb. 1967
Mar. 1969	Nov. 1970	Dec. 1967	Nov. 1970
Mar. 1973	Mar. 1975	Feb. 1973	Jan. 1975
—	—	Aug. 1975	Oct. 1976
Dec. 1978	Dec. 1982		
June 1984*	Jan. 1987*		
Feb. 1989*			

Sources: Columbia University's Center for International Business Cycle Research; Beveridge and Nelson (1981).

* Based on trend-adjusted coincident indicator and subject to revision.

Commerce Department's leading index, since they can illustrate techniques that also can be applied to specialized sets of indicators developed by the user. At the heart of this review is the age-old tradeoff between the timeliness of the signal and its accuracy.

Some of the simplest rules for spotting turning points in the economy based on the Commerce Department's composite index of leading indicators include watching when the indicator declines (for recessions) or increases (for expansions) for 2 or more consecutive months. These rules are data *filtering screens* that are intended to eliminate noise or random fluctuation while providing a signal of turning points.[102] But how well do these simple rules work?

Consider the following rules for spotting a turning point in either the growth or classical business cycles based on the Commerce Department's composite index of leading economic indicators and occurrence of the following turning point signals: (1) a 2-month reversal in the direction of the indicator, (2) a 2-month reversal in direction and breaking of a minimum threshold level, (3) a 3-month reversal in direction, and finally, (4) a 3-month reversal rule plus a threshold criterion. Based on a method discussed earlier in this chapter, threshold or zones of indifference in monthly change were derived by calculating the average (geometric mean) percentage change and the average absolute deviation. Normal upper and lower bounds are determined as the mean growth rate plus or minus one-half the average absolute deviation. For the composite leading indicator, normal monthly fluctuation in the composite index was between -0.1% and $+0.7\%$ (as calculated between 1948 and 1991). Any monthly movement within this zone of indifference would not be considered signaling a reversal of the previous turning point. Only when the percentage change exceeded those bounds was the change considered significant. This, then forms the basis of a threshold criterion, which was superimposed on the consecutive month change rule. An alternative to this decision rule with threshold levels is to use a duration of run criterion (not just a sign rule). In this case, a run above or below the *normal bounds* could be the basis for a decision. For example, if the change in the composite index of leading indicators falls within the normal percentage band (-0.1% to $+0.7\%$), then this change can be assigned a value of 2; if it is above the normal upper bound, then the change can be assigned a value of 3; and if it is below the normal lower bound, then it can be assigned a value of 1. Then a run of 2 or 3 months of a "3" reading could be used to signal a lower turning point, or similarly, a 2- or 3-month run of the value "1" could signal a peak. Although the duration of the run rule example showed a symmetric rule, there is no reason to be bound by that framework. The duration of run could be different for peaks and trough without sacrificing the basic framework.

The conclusions from this simple test of decision rules are not really surprising: (1) the longer the span of months used in the decision rule, the longer the lag in turning point recognition, (2) the threshold criterion also lengthens the recognition time but improves the reliability of the signal, and (3) the shorter the span of time in the decision rule, the sooner it will call growth cycle turning points prior to the turn. Tables 3.44 through 3.47 show the individual turning point performance of these decision rules. Here is a summary of each of the rules tested:

- *Two-Month Decline/Increase Rule.* As might have been expected, of the four rules tested, this one had the highest number of extra turning point calls. Against the classical business cycle, this rule provided a correct turning point signal less than half the time, or slightly better than 50-50 accuracy against the growth cycle (see Table 3.44).

- *Two-Month Decline/Increase Rule with a Threshold Criterion.* Adding an amplitude criterion as discussed earlier, greatly improved the 2-month rule. The accuracy jumped to 62% for classical cycles versus 44% without the amplitude criterion and 76% accuracy compared with growth cycle turning points (see Table 3.45).

- *Three-Month Decline/Increase Rule.* The 3-month rule for interpreting the leading indicator changes without an amplitude criterion was little better than the 2-month rule with an amplitude criterion. Moreover, the 3-month rule increased the recognition lag compared the 2-month rule with the threshold criterion (see Table 3.46).

- *Three-Month Decline/Increase Rule with a Threshold Criterion.* As might have been expected, the 3-month rule with the amplitude criterion performed the best based on accuracy (see Table 3.47) though the recognition lag was increased.

Table 3.44   Two-Month Decline/Rebound Turning Point Rule Using the Composite Index of Leading Economic Indicators for Spotting Turning Points in Economic Cycles (1948–1991).

Economic Cycle \a/				Leading Indicator Signal and Timing \b/					
High	Peak	Low	Trough	High/Peak	High	Peak	Low/Trough	Low	Trough
July 1948	Nov. 1948			Aug. 1948	+1	−3			
		Oct. 1949	Oct. 1949				Aug. 1949	0	0
Mar. 1951	− − −			Mar. 1951	0	− −			
		July 1952	− − −				Jan. 1952	−6	− −
Mar. 1953	July 1953			Apr. 1953	+1	−3			
		Aug. 1954	May 1954				Feb. 1954	−6	−3
Feb. 1957	Aug. 1957			Jan. 1957	−1	−7			
		Apr. 1958	Apr. 1958				Apr. 1958	0	0
Feb. 1960	Apr. 1960			Aug. 1959	−6	−8			
		Feb. 1961	Feb. 1961				Jan. 1961	−1	−1
May 1962	− − −			May 1962	0	− −			
		Oct. 1964	− − −				Sept. 1963	−13	− −
June 1966	− − −			May 1966	−1	− −			
		Oct. 1967	− − −				May 1967	−5	− −
Mar. 1969	Dec. 1969			Mar. 1969	0	−9			
		Nov. 1970	Nov. 1970				June 1970	−6	−6
Mar. 1973	Nov. 1973			July 1973	+4	−4			
		Mar. 1975	Mar. 1975				Mar. 1975	0	0
Dec. 1978	Jan. 1980			Dec. 1978	0	−13			
		− − −	July 1980				July 1980	− −	0
− − −	July 1981			July 1981	− −	0			
		Dec. 1982	Nov. 1982				May 1982	−7	−6
July 1984	− − −			June 1984	−1	− −			
		Jan. 1987	− − −				Dec. 1984	−25	− −
Feb. 1989	July 1990			Mar. 1989	+1	−16			
				Averages	−0.2	−7.0	Averages	−6.3	−2.0

False Signals

Classical Cycles: 23 out of 41 (Percent Correct: 43.9%)
Growth Cycles: 19 out of 41 (Percent Correct: 53.7%)

Notes
\a/ Based on turning points in the growth (high to low) and classical (peak to trough) cycles.
\b/ Timing is in months; first number corresponds to growth cycle turns and the second to classical cycles; (+) = Lag, (−) = Lead.

Sources: National Bureau of Economic Research, Center for International Business Cycle Research; authors.

Table 3.45   Two-Month Decline/Rebound Turning Point Rule with Threshold Levels Using the Composite Index of Leading Economic Indicators for Spotting Turning Points in Economic Cycles (1948–1991).

Economic Cycle \a/				Leading Indicator Signal and Timing \b/					
High	Peak	Low	Trough	High/Peak	High	Peak	Low/Trough	Low	Trough
July 1948	Nov. 1948			Aug. 1948	+1	−3			
		Oct. 1949	Oct. 1949				Aug. 1949	−2	−2
Mar. 1951	− − −			Mar. 1951	0	− −			
		July 1952	− − −				Sept. 1952	+2	− −
Mar. 1953	July 1953			Apr. 1953	+1	−3			
		Aug. 1954	May 1954				May 1954	− −	− −
Feb. 1957	Aug. 1957			Feb. 1956	−12	−18			
		Apr. 1958	Apr. 1958				June 1958	+2	+2
Feb. 1960	Apr. 1960			Aug. 1959	−6	−8			
		Feb. 1961	Feb. 1961				Feb. 1961	0	0
May 1962	− − −			May 1962	− −	− −			
		Oct. 1964	− − −				Feb. 1964	−8	− −
June 1966	− − −			May 1966	− −	− −			
		Oct. 1967	− − −				June 1967	−4	− −
Mar. 1969	Dec. 1969			Mar. 1969	0	−9			
		Nov. 1970	Nov. 1970				Jan. 1971	+2	+2
Mar. 1973	Nov. 1973			July 1973	+4	−4			
		Mar. 1975	Mar. 1975				Apr. 1975	+1	+1
Dec. 1978	Jan. 1980			Dec. 1978	0	−13			
		− − −	July 1980				July 1980	− −	0
− − −	July 1981			July 1981	− −	0			
		Dec. 1982	Nov. 1982				Oct. 1982	−2	−1
July 1984	− − −			June 1984	−1	− −			
		Jan. 1987	− − −				June 1985	−19	− −
Feb. 1989	July 1990			Mar. 1989	+1	−16			
				Averages	−1.1	−8.2	Averages	−2.8	+0.3

False Signals
Classical Cycles: 11 out of 29   (Percent Correct: 62.1%)
Growth Cycles: 7 out of 29   (Percent Correct: 75.9%)

Notes
\a/ Based on turning points in the growth (high to low) and classical (peak to trough) cycles.
\b/ Timing is in months; first number corresponds to growth cycle turns and the second to classical cycles; (+) = Lag, (−) = Lead.

Sources: National Bureau of Economic Research, Center for International Business Cycle Research; authors.

Finally, this evaluation was based on the current composite indicator, which has existed in its present form only since 1989; the data used was as revised and not based on its original reading. This is important since concurrent data may be more difficult to interpret, as suggested by Koenig and Emery.[103] Moreover, although the leading economic indicator has been recast with each revision, on the assumption that it represented the current best thinking of what leads the business cycle and based on the current best data for that role, secular changes in the economy might suggest "fixing" the historical data of the leading indicator. It is

Table 3.46 Three-Month Decline/Rebound Turning Point Rule Using the Composite Index of Leading Economic Indicators for Spotting Turning Points in Economic Cycles (1948–1991).

| Economic Cycle \a/ | | | | Leading Indicator Signal and Timing \b/ | | | | | |
High	Peak	Low	Trough	High/Peak	High	Peak	Low/Trough	Low	Trough
July 1948	Nov. 1948			Sept. 1948	+2	−2			
		Oct. 1949	Oct. 1949				Sept. 1949	−1	−1
Mar. 1951	− − −			Apr. 1951	+1	− −			
		July 1952	− − −				Feb. 1952	−5	− −
Mar. 1953	July 1953			May 1953	+2	−2			
		Aug. 1954	May 1954				Mar. 1954	−5	−2
Feb. 1957	Aug. 1957			Feb. 1957	0	−6			
		Apr. 1958	Apr. 1958				May 1958	+1	+1
Feb. 1960	Apr. 1960			Mar. 1960	+1	−1			
		Feb. 1961	Feb. 1961				Aug. 1960	−6	−6
May 1962	− − −			June 1962	+1	− −			
		Oct. 1964	− − −				Sept. 1962	−25	− −
June 1966	− − −			June 1966	0	− −			
		Oct. 1967	− − −				June 1967	−4	− −
Mar. 1969	Dec. 1969			July 1969	+4	−5			
		Nov. 1970	Nov. 1970				Jan. 1971	+2	+2
Mar. 1973	Nov. 1973			Aug. 1973	+5	−3			
		Mar. 1975	Mar. 1975				Apr. 1975	+1	+1
Dec. 1978	Jan. 1980			Jan. 1979	+1	−12			
		− − −	July 1980				Aug. 1980	− −	+1
− − −	July 1981			Nov. 1981	− −	+4			
		Dec. 1982	Nov. 1982				Nov. 1982	−1	0
July 1984	− − −			July 1984	0	− −			
		Jan. 1987	− − −				Jan. 1985	−24	− −
Feb. 1989	July 1990			July 1989	+5	−12			
				Averages	+1.8	−4.3	Averages	−6.1	−0.5

False Signals

Classical Cycles: 10 out of 28 (Percent Correct: 64.3%)
Growth Cycles: 6 out of 28 (Percent Correct: 78.6%)

Notes
\a/ Based on turning points in the growth (high to low) and classical (peak to trough) cycles.
\b/ Timing is in months; first number corresponds to growth cycle turns and the second to classical cycles; (+) = Lag, (−) = Lead.

Sources: National Bureau of Economic Research, Center for International Business Cycle Research; authors.

not clear, however, whether one approach is truly more desirable. In any event, the leading indicator will and should continue to evolve as the business cycle evolves.

One such evolution was called for in 1962, when Edgar Fiedler[104] proposed dividing the Commerce Department's composite index of leading indicators into two separate indicators—a long-term and a short-term leading indicator. The advantage of this method is that it can be used in a simple type of signaling system that harnesses the information from the long-term leading indicator

Table 3.47   Three-Month Decline/Rebound Turning Point Rule with Threshold · Levels Using the Composite Index of Leading Economic Indicators for Spotting Turning Points in Economic Cycles (1948–1991).

Economic Cycle \a/				Leading Indicator Signal and Timing \b/					
High	Peak	Low	Trough	High/Peak	High	Peak	Low/Trough	Low	Trough
July 1948	Nov. 1948			Sept. 1948	+2	−2			
		Oct. 1949	Oct. 1949				Sept. 1949	−1	−1
Mar. 1951	− − −			− − −	− −	− −			
		July 1952	− − −				− − −	− −	− −
Mar. 1953	July 1953			May 1953	+2	−2			
		Aug. 1954	May 1954				June 1954	−2	+1
Feb. 1957	Aug. 1957			Feb. 1957	0	−6			
		Apr. 1958	Apr. 1958				July 1958	+3	+3
Feb. 1960	Apr. 1960			Mar. 1960	+1	−1			
		Feb. 1961	Feb. 1961				Mar. 1961	+1	+1
May 1962	− − −			June 1962	+1	− −			
		Oct. 1964	− − −				Jan. 1963	−21	− −
June 1966	− − −			June 1966	0	− −			
		Oct. 1967	− − −				July 1967	−3	− −
Mar. 1969	Dec. 1969			July 1969	+4	−5			
		Nov. 1970	Nov. 1970				Feb. 1971	+3	+3
Mar. 1973	Nov. 1973			Aug. 1973	+5	−3			
		Mar. 1975	Mar. 1975				May 1975	+2	+2
Dec. 1978	Jan. 1980			Aug. 1979	+8	−5			
		− − −	July 1980				Aug. 1980	− −	+1
− − −	July 1981			Nov. 1981	− −	+4			
		Dec. 1982	Nov. 1982				Nov. 1982	−1	0
July 1984	− − −			July 1984	0	− −			
		Jan. 1987	− − −				Apr. 1986	−9	− −
Feb. 1989	July 1990			Dec. 1987	−14	−31			
				Averages	0.8	−5.7	Averages	−2.8	+1.4

False Signals

Classical Cycles: 6 out of 24   (Percent Correct: 75.0%)
Growth Cycles: 2 out of 24   (Percent Correct: 91.7%)

Notes
\a/ Based on turning points in the growth (high to low) and classical (peak to trough) cycles.
\b/ Timing is in months; first number corresponds to growth cycle turns and the second to classical cycles; (+) = Lag, (−) = Lead.

Sources: National Bureau of Economic Research, Center for International Business Cycle Research; authors.

and then sequentially uses the signal from the short-term indicator as confirmation. The British Central Statistical Office (CSO) calculates these types of indicator. While this may be an improvement over looking at a single leading indicator, according to Fiedler, it still is not the final answer to forecasting cyclical turning points.

Leo Barnes has developed one of the more elaborate decision rule systems.[105] Barnes's decision rules were called *parity cross-points* and were claimed to have a longer lead time in signaling cyclical turning points in the economy than could be attained by solely looking at the Commerce Department's leading indicator composites. Barnes' proposed forming ratios of the cyclical indicators relative to each other (i.e., the ratio of the leading to coincident indexes, the coincident to lagging indexes, and the leading to lagging indexes). He then suggested that when a ratio of the composites rose above (or fell below) 1.000 (parity), this was a *preliminary signal* of a turning point. A *definite signal* occurred when the ratios exceeded 1.010 or fell below 0.990, and finally, a *confirmation signal* occurred if the ratio remained above (or below) the *definite signal* threshold level for one additional month. Although this method worked in 1980 when Barnes presented his results, subsequent revisions to the cyclical indexes essentially vitiated the results. Nonetheless, the Barnes' system did contain the flavor of some more successful systems based on growth rates in those cyclical indicators.

One such decision rule system for interpreting movement in the composite cyclical indicator that does work is the Zarnowitz-Moore *sequential signals*. [106] This system uses growth rates—which are calculated as 6-month smoothed annual rates (SMSAR)—of the coincident and leading indicator composites. A subsequent modification by Moore[107] added an earlier signal, which was dubbed LLP1 for a recession and LLT1 for a recovery. The sequence of rules, as expanded by Moore, is as follows:

For Spotting Recessions

- *LLP1 Signal.* The first signal of a possible recession occurs when the long-leading composite indicator (Commerce Department series 990, which is compiled by CIBCR) growth rate (as measured on a SMSAR basis) slips below 2.3%.

- *P1 Signal.* The second sequential signal of recession occurs when the Commerce Department's composite leading indicator growth rate slips below 2.3% while the composite coincident growth rate is still positive. All growth rates are calculated on a SMSAR basis.

- *P2 Signal.* The third signal of recession occurs when the leading indicator growth rate slips below −1.0% and the coincident indicator growth rate slows to less than 2.3%.

- *P3 Signal.* The fourth and final signal of recession is a confirmation signal that often occurs after the turning point date. This signal occurs when the leading indicator growth rate is less than zero and the coincident indicator growth rate falls to less than −1.0%.

The timing of these signals compared with the NBER growth and classical business cycle turning point dates is shown in Table 3.48. The LLP1 signal can be canceled when the long-leading indicator growth rate exceeds 4.3%; the P1 signal can be canceled when the leading indicator growth rate exceeds 4.3%;

Table 3.48 Zarnowitz-Moore Sequential Signals: Four Signals of Slowdown and Recession (1948–1991).

Growth Cycle High	Business Cycle Peak	LLP1 Signal (LL<2.3)	P1 Signal (L<2.3, C>0)	P2 Signal (L<−1.0, C<2.3)	P3 Signal (L<0, C<−1.0)	Lead (−) or Lag (+), in Months, at Business Cycle Peaks				Lead (−) or Lag (+), in Months, at Growth Cycle Peaks			
						LLP1	P1	P2	P3	LLP1	P1	P2	P3
June 1948	Nov. 1948	N.A.	N.A.	N.A.	Jan. 1949	N.A.	N.A.	N.A.	+2	N.A.	N.A.	N.A.	+7
Mar. 1951	---	Nov. 1950	Apr. 1951	July 1951	---	---	N.A.	N.A.	---	−4	+1	N.A.	---
Mar. 1953	July 1953	Apr. 1953	May 1953	Aug. 1953	Sept. 1953	−3	−2	+1	+2	+1	+2	+4	+6
Feb. 1957	Aug. 1957	Sept. 1955	Feb. 1956	July 1956	Sept. 1957	−23	−18	−13	+1	−17	−12	+5	+7
Feb. 1960	Apr. 1960	July 1959	Nov. 1959	May 1960	Sept. 1960	−9	−5	+1	+5	−7	−3	−7	+7
May 1962	---	---	June 1962	---	---	---	---	---	---	---	+1	+3	---
June 1966	---	Feb. 1966	June 1966	Apr. 1967	---	---	---	---	---	−4	0	+10	---
Mar. 1969	Dec. 1969	Mar. 1969	June 1969	Dec. 1969	Feb. 1970	−9	−6	0	+2	0	+3	+9	+11
Mar. 1973	Nov. 1973	June 1973	Aug. 1973	Jan. 1974	Feb. 1974	−5	−3	+2	+3	+3	+5	+10	+11
Dec. 1978	Jan. 1980	Jan. 1978	Dec. 1978	Apr. 1979	Mar. 1980	−24	−13	−9	+2	−11	0	+4	+15
---	July 1981	---	July 1981	Sept. 1981	Oct. 1981	---	0	+2	+3	---	---	---	---
July 1984	---	---	June 1984	---	---	---	---	---	---	---	−1	---	---
Feb. 1989	July 1990	Mar. 1990	May 1989	Aug. 1990	Sept. 1990	−4	−14	+1	+2	+13	+3	+18	+19
					MEAN	−11.0	−7.6	−1.9	+2.4	−2.9	−0.1	+6.2	−10.4

Source: Center for International Business Cycle Research, Columbia University.

Table 3.49 Zarnowitz-Moore Sequential Signals: Four Signals of Recovery (1948–1991).

Growth Cycle Low	Business Cycle Trough	LLT1 Signal (LL>1.0)	T1 Signal (L>1.0, C<1.0)	T2 Signal (L>4.3, C>1.0)	T3 Signal (L>4.3, C>4.3)	Lead (−) or Lag (+), in Months, at Business Cycle Troughs				Lead (−) or Lag (+), in Months, at Growth Cycle Lows			
						LLT1	T1	T2	T3	LLT1	T1	T2	T3
Oct. 1949	Oct. 1949	Feb. 1949	Aug. 1949	Jan. 1950	Mar. 1950	−8	−2	+3	+5	−8	−2	+3	+5
July 1952	− − −	Feb. 1952	June 1952	June 1952	Aug. 1952	− −	− −	− −	− −	−5	−1	−1	+1
Aug. 1954	May 1954	Jan. 1954	May 1954	Nov. 1954	Dec. 1954	−4	0	+6	+7	−7	−3	+3	+4
Apr. 1958	Apr. 1958	Apr. 1958	June 1958	Oct. 1958	Nov. 1958	0	+2	+6	+7	0	+2	+6	+7
Feb. 1961	Feb. 1961	July 1960	Jan. 1961	June 1961	Aug. 1961	−7	−1	+4	+6	−7	−1	+4	+6
Oct. 1964	− − −	− − −	− − −	Dec. 1962	May 1963	− −	− −	− −	− −	− −	− −	−22	−17
Oct. 1967	− − −	Jan. 1967	June 1967	July 1967	Nov. 1967	− −	− −	− −	− −	−9	−4	−3	+1
Nov. 1970	Nov. 1970	Oct. 1970	Dec. 1970	May 1971	Dec. 1971	−1	+1	+6	+13	−1	+1	+6	+13
Mar. 1975	Mar. 1975	Apr. 1975	June 1975	Oct. 1975	Jan. 1976	+1	+3	+7	+10	+1	+3	+7	+10
− − −	July 1980	Sept. 1980	Sept. 1980	Dec. 1980	− − −	−8	+2	+5	− −	− −	− −	− −	− −
Dec. 1982	Nov. 1982	Mar. 1982	Sept. 1982	May 1983	June 1983	−8	−2	+6	+7	−9	−3	+5	+6
Jan. 1987	− − −	− − −	− − −	July 1985	− − −	− −	− −	− −	− −	− −	− −	−18	− −
Mar. 1991	Mar. 1991	May 1991	June 1991			+2	+3	− −	− −	− −	− −	− −	− −
					MEAN	−3.1	+0.7	+5.4	+7.9	−5.0	−0.9	−0.9	+3.6

Source: Center for International Business Cycle Research, Columbia University.

193

and finally, the P2 signal can be canceled when the leading indicator growth rate exceeds 1.0% and the coincident indicator growth rate exceeds 4.3%.

Similarly, the signals of recovery based on these composite indexes are:

For Spotting Recoveries

- *LLT1 Signal.* The initial signal of a recovery occurs when the long-leading indexes growth rate exceeds 1.0%.

- *T1 Signal.* The leading index growth rate exceeds 1.0%, while the coincident index growth rate is below 1.0%.

- *T2 Signal.* The leading index growth rate exceeds 4.3%, and the coincident indicator growth rate exceeds 1.0%.

- *T3 Signal.* The final confirmation signal of a turning point trough occurs when the leading and coincident indicator growth rates exceed 4.3%.

The timing performance of these signals is shown in Table 3.49 on page 193 and, on average, is consistent with a sequential nature.

The growth rates used throughout this system were not just plucked out of the air as might seem from this presentation. Instead, Zarnowitz and Moore determined the threshold growth rates based on two factors—the long-run growth in the economy and the variability of the irregular component of the indicators. For example, the 4.3% was equal to the upper band of the long-term trend in the economy (3.3%) plus the standard of the composite indicator (1.0%). Similarly, the lower band width used to signal a turning point was 0% growth minus 1.0%, which determined the -1.0% threshold used in the Zarnowitz and Moore system.

This system, which was originally just devised to call business cycle turning points, can now easily account for growth cycle turning points. But in an earlier attempt, Robert F. Deitch[108] modified the Zarnowitz-Moore signals explicitly to signal turning points in growth cycles. Deitch proposed incorporating the growth rate of the inverse of the lagging indicator into the system. The Deitch rules were applied as follows:

- *For Growth Cycle Highs.* When the 6-month smoothed rate of change in the inverse of the lagging indicator (1/LG) slips below 2.3%, this is the first signal of a growth cycle high—which is designated as H1. The second growth cycle peak signal, H2, occurs when the leading indicator (L) increases by less than 2.3%. The final signal (H3) occurs when the coincident indicator (C) increases by less than 2.3%. Deitch reported that the H1 signal led the growth cycle highs by an average of 8 months, the H2 signal led by an average of 1 month at turning points, and the H3 signal lagged by 5 months on average over the postwar period through 1983.

- *For Growth Cycle Lows.* The Deitch rules are applied in a similar manner for lower turning points except that the threshold level to exceed must be 4.3% (SMSAR). The L1 signal occurs when (1/LG) exceeds 4.3%; the L2 signal occurs when the leading indicator grows by more than 4.3%. The final confirmation signal of a turning point, L3, occurs when the coincident indicator growth exceeds 4.3%. These rules have led growth cycle lows, on average, by 4 months for L1 and 2 months for L2; and the confirming signal, L3, lagged the growth cycle low by an average of 4 months.

Another growth rate signaling system was proposed by the Institute for Trend Research (later it became ITR Associates) that used pressure cycles, as discussed earlier in this chapter, to identify cyclical turning points in a time series.[109] The ITR method is simple to apply, easy to interpret, and reproducible. More importantly, the Institute's founder, Chapin Hoskins, devised a series of rules to spot turning points in the economic cycle. Using the ITR basic concept, it is possible to date the growth and business cycles based on the Commerce Department's coincident indicator composite. The rules for determining a turning point are (1) a cyclical turn occurs when the 3/12 coincident indicator pressure curve crosses the 12/12 pressure curve, and (2) if the 12/12 pressure curve does not decline below zero (0%), then the decline is simply a growth cycle and not a business cycle contraction. On balance, this technique compares favorably with the NBER/CIBCR method; the average timing difference between the NBER growth business cycle turning points and the ITR method for deriving turning points is about 1 month, as indicated in Table 3.50. The recognition lag between the actual classical cycle turn and the confirmation turning point rule based on the 12/12 pressure curve (designated P12 in the table) could be shortened by using a 3/12 pressure curve (which is designated as P3 in the table). But from a real-time perspective, the user of this system would respond to the high and low signals, as noted in the earlier discussion of pressure curves, and the confirmation rule would not play a strategic role.

Neftçi Probability Approach

Explaining cyclical turning points in the economy and in financial markets has always held a special place in economic theory. Moreover, economic forecasters have considered turning points a particular challenge, especially since there is no clear theoretical consensus why business cycles occur. Some of the more traditional approaches to forecast or signal business cycle turning points have already been explored in this chapter. A second approach for spotting is based on probability. The turning point probability method, which

Table 3.50   Institute for Trend Research Turning Point Signals in the Composite Coincident Index (1948–1991).

Growth Cycle High	Business Cycle Peak	Growth Cycle Low	Business Cycle Trough	High Signal (P3−P12) <0	Peak Signal Confirmed (P12<0)	Low Signal (P3−P12) >0	Trough Signal Confirmed (P12>0)	Lead (−) or Lag (+), in Months, at Business/Growth Cycle Turns Timing			
								High	Peak	Low	Trough
June 1948	Nov. 1948	Oct. 1949	Oct. 1949	NA	NA	Jan. 1950	Aug. 1950	NA	NA	3	10
Mar. 1951	---	July 1952	---	May 1951	---	Sept. 1952	---	2	---	2	---
Mar. 1953	July 1953	Aug. 1954	May 1954	Sept. 1953	May 1954	Nov. 1954	June 1955	6	10	3	13
Feb. 1957	Aug. 1957	Apr. 1958	Apr. 1958	Feb. 1956	Dec. 1957	Sept. 1958	May 1959	−12	4	5	13
Feb. 1960	Apr. 1960	Feb. 1961	Feb. 1961	Oct. 1959	Feb. 1961	July 1961	Feb. 1962	−4	10	5	12
May 1962	---	Oct. 1964	---	Aug. 1962	---	Sept. 1963	---	3	---	−13	---
June 1966	---	Oct. 1967	---	May 1966	---	Jan. 1968	---	−1	---	3	---
Mar. 1969	Dec. 1969	Nov. 1970	Nov. 1970	Jan. 1969	Oct. 1970	Mar. 1971	Dec. 1971	−2	10	4	13
Mar. 1973	Nov. 1973	Mar. 1975	Mar. 1975	May 1973	Nov. 1974	Sept. 1975	June 1976	2	12	6	15
---	---	---	---	Dec. 1976	---	July 1977	---	---	---	---	---
Dec. 1978	Jan. 1980	July 1980	July 1980	Mar. 1979	June 1980	Dec. 1980	Sept. 1981	3	5	---	14
---	July 1981	Dec. 1982	Nov. 1982	Nov. 1981	Jan. 1982	Jan. 1983	Nov. 1983	---	6	---	12
July 1984	---	Jan. 1987	---	Sept. 1984	---	Nov. 1986	---	2	---	1	---
Feb. 1989	July 1990	---	---	Sept. 1988	Nov. 1990	Oct. 1991	---	−5	4	−2	---
							Mean	−0.8	6.8	1.5	12.8

was proposed by Salih Neftçi,[110] signals cyclical turning points by calculating the likelihood that an economic environment or regime has changed. A turning point probability signal is defined when the estimated probability reaches some preset threshold level of statistical confidence (say, 90% or 95%).

The Neftçi methodology statistically judges the likelihood of a turning point based on three pieces of information. The first item is the probability that the latest observation in the leading indicator is from the *recession* sample or the *recovery/expansion* sample. The second piece of information used is the chance of a recession (recovery) given the current length of the expansion (recession) relative to the historical average. Finally, these two sets of information are combined with last month's probability estimate in order to incorporate previous information.

The logic underlying this method is that business activity declines rapidly when a business cycle peak has been reached and that sensitive (leading) indicators show sharp declines in activity prior to a recession or shortly thereafter as well as sharp increases prior to a recovery or shortly thereafter. Sir John Hicks observed that "one of the most striking characteristics of actual cycles is that output, once it has passed the peak, falls off rather rapidly."[111] Similarly, John Maynard Keynes observed: "[T]he substitution of a downward for an upward tendency often takes place suddenly and violently."[112]

Neftçi formulated the problem of forecasting turning points as recognizing when this abrupt switch in probability distributions occurred for the composite index of leading indicators. This method, which has been applied to the recognition of turning points in the growth and classical cycles,[113] is implemented as follows:

1. *Set Up Probability Distributions.* The economic time series is segmented into two distributions—a downturn and an expansion sample. From these segments, two probability distributions can be fitted to the data based on the mean and standard deviation of each sample. Alternatively, as Neftçi originally presented the application, histograms can used as the underlying probability distributions (after some smoothing).

2. *Develop an a Priori Probability Distribution.* The user determines a subjective probability distribution that a recession (recovery) will develop so many months after the expansion (recession) begins. In this application, the prior probability is held constant, because the empirical evidence suggests that the probability of a turning point does not increase as calendar time lengthens. In particular, McCulloch[114] showed that once an expansion or recession has exceeded its historical minimum duration, the probability of a turning point is independent of its age. Alternatively, this prior probability can be optimized following the work of Diebold and Rudebusch.[115]

3. *Apply the Neftçi Recursive Formula.* Neftçi derived a probability formula using optimal stopping time theory. This formula predicts when an event will occur and not the level of the economic variable. The formula is:

$$\text{Prob}_t = \frac{[\text{Prob}_{t-1} + (\text{Prior}\,(1 - \text{Prob}_{t-1})\text{Prob1})]}{[\text{Prob}_{t-1} + (\text{Prior}(1 - \text{Prob}_{t-1})\text{Prob1}) + (1 - \text{Prob}_{t-1})\text{Prob2}(1 - \text{Prior})]}$$

where Prob is the probability of a recession (recovery) in the near term, Prior is the prior probability determined in step 2, Prob1 is the probability a new observation is in the downturn (upturn) distribution, and Prob2 is the probability that the new observation comes from the upturn or expansion case (downturn).

4. *Interpret the Results.* When the cumulative probability exceeded a preset level of confidence, say 90%, then a signal of a turning point occurred.

5. *Look for the Next Turning Point.* Once a turning point signal is given, the calculated probability is reset to zero and the search begins for the next turning point. Although this application lends itself to a two-state world, James Hamilton[116] has extended the methodology to *n* dimensional states (in Neftçi's original application, he posited two states—recession and expansion—but Hamilton's elaboration of the methodology allowed for a multidimensional world).

As an example of applying this technique, consider replicating Neftçi's original leading indicator example. The first step is to segment changes in the leading indicator into two samples—a recession and an expansion sample. Although Neftçi used a 3-month moving average on the histograms to determine a probability distribution, in this example, a normal distribution is fitted to the mean and standard deviation of the sample and the results are shown in Figures 3.25 and 3.26. The mean of the recession sample was −0.3%, whereas the mean of the expansion sample was +0.8%. This highlights the wide differences between the two samples, which is precisely what is sought after. Applying the Neftçi formula to leading indicators over the postwar business cycle history yielded one false signal. That signal, however, corresponded to the minirecession (or growth recession) in 1966. On balance, the Neftçi method worked well in spotting and confirming business cycle recessions—although its average lead time at business cycle peaks provided essentially little if any advance warning of a turn in the economy. But still, this technique would naturally require a recognition lag, which is kept to a minimum.

This probability-based decision rule for interpreting changes in the leading indicator is shown graphically in Figure 3.27, which shows the calculated monthly probabilities of recession and recovery for the 1990–1991 period. The individual cycle performance of this method is shown in Table 3.51.

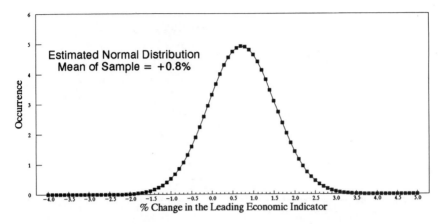

Figure 3.25 Probability Distribution of Upturn Observations in the Leading Index, Monthly Percentage Change.

The technique is a welcome addition to an economist's proverbial bag of tools since it can be combined with any indicator of interest. In later chapters, it will be demonstrated as a turning point signaling device for interest rate and regional business cycles.

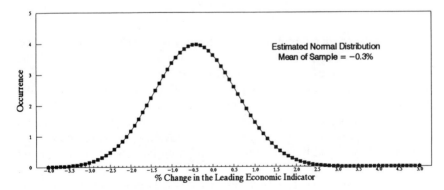

Figure 3.26 Probability Distribution of Downturn Observations in the Leading Index, Monthly Percentage Change.

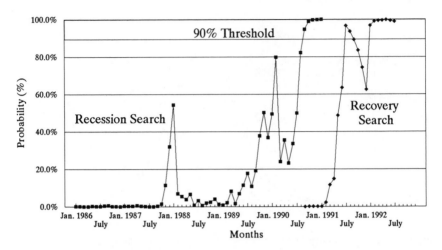

Figure 3.27   Probability of a Recession and Recovery (Based on "Sequential Analysis" on the Composite Leading Indicator).

Turning Point Accuracy with Probability Projections

Brier[117] proposed a statistic to measure the accuracy of turning point probability predictions within a specific time horizon. That measure is known as the *quadratic probability score* (QPS) and is defined as follows:

$$\text{QPS} = \frac{1}{T} \sum_{t=1}^{T} 2(p_t - r_t)^2$$

where p_t is the predicted probability of a turning point within a specified time horizon and r_t is the realization or outcome, which is assigned the value 1 if the turning point occurred within the time frame or 0 if it did not. The QPS statistic is the counterpart of mean square error and QPS can range between 0 and 2, with 0 implying a perfect forecast. This statistic has been popularized by Diebold and Rudebusch.[118] Diebold and Rudebusch used QPS to optimize a turning point probability model as suggested by Neftçi. Coons, in the chapter on financial cycles, also used QPS to optimize an interest rate turning point model.

It is also possible to define an accuracy statistic of probabilities as follows:

$$\text{Accuracy Rate} = 1 - \left\{ \frac{1}{T} \sum_{t=1}^{T} |p_t - r_t| \right\}$$

Table 3.51   Turning Point Signals Based on the Neftçi Method with a 90% Threshold and the Composite Index of Leading Economic Indicators (1948–1991).

Economic Cycle \b/				90% Probability Signal and Timing \c/					
High	Peak	Low	Trough	High/Peak	High	Peak	Low/Trough	Low	Trough
July 1948	Nov. 1948			Nov. 1948	+4	0			
		Oct. 1949	Oct. 1949				Nov. 1949	+1	+1
Mar. 1951	– – –			Apr. 1951	+1	– –			
		July 1952	– – –				Sept. 1952	+2	– –
Mar. 1953	July 1953			Aug. 1953	+5	+1			
		Aug. 1954	May 1954				Aug. 1954	0	+3
Feb. 1957	Aug. 1957			Jan. 1957	–1	–7			
		Apr. 1958	Apr. 1958				Aug. 1958	+4	+4
Feb. 1960	Apr. 1960			Feb. 1960	0	–2			
		Feb. 1961	Feb. 1961				June 1961	+4	+4
May 1962	– – –			– – –	– –	– –			
		Oct. 1964	– – –				– – –	– –	– –
June 1966	– – –			Sept. 1966	+3	– –			
		Oct. 1967	– – –				Dec. 1967	+2	– –
Mar. 1969	Dec. 1969			Nov. 1969	+8	–1			
		Nov. 1970	Nov. 1970				Apr. 1971	+5	+5
Mar. 1973	Nov. 1973			Feb. 1974	+11	+3			
		Mar. 1975	Mar. 1975				July 1975	+4	+4
Dec. 1978	Jan. 1980			July 1979	+7	–6			
		– – –	July 1980				Oct. 1980	– –	+3
– – –	July 1981			Sept. 1981	– –	+2			
		Dec. 1982	Nov. 1982				Jan. 1983	+1	+2
July 1984	– – –			– – –	– –	– –			
		Jan. 1987	– – –				– – –	– –	– –
Feb. 1989	July 1990			Aug. 1990	+18	+1			
				Averages	+5.6	–1.0	Averages	+2.5	+3.3

False or Missed Signals

Classical Cycles: 4 out of 18   (Percent Correct: 77.8%)
Growth Cycles: 5 out of 22   (Percent Correct: 77.3%)

Notes
\a/ Prior probability constant set equal to 0.02; data as existing through January 1992.
\b/ Based on turning points in the growth (high to low) and classical (peak to trough) cycles.
\c/ Timing is in months; first number corresponds to growth cycle turns and the second to classical cycles; (+) = Lag, (−) = Lead.

Sources: National Bureau of Economic Research; authors.

again where p_t is the predicted probability of a turning point within a specified time horizon and r_t is the realization or outcome, which is assigned the value 1 if the turning point occurred with the time frame or 0 if it did not. The accuracy rate statistic is bounded by 0% and 100%, which makes it an easier statistic to communicate than QPS. Another measure of accuracy is the global squared bias, or *calibration*, which is defined as $2(\bar{p} - \bar{r})^2$, where $\bar{p}$ and $\bar{r}$ are the means of the predicted (p) and realized (r) values. This measure too can range between 0 (best) and 2 (worst) and is a measure of the closeness of the predicted probabilities to observed relative frequencies.

DIFFUSION INDEXES

Arthur F. Burns observed that a business cycle expansion does not imply that every underlying economic activity is expanding nor does a business cycle contraction mean that every business cycle firm has declining sales. He further observed that economic activity has two types of cycles: *seen* and *unseen*. One cycle is in the fluctuation of the aggregate measure itself and consequently is seen. But a second cycle—the unseen or *diffusion* cycle—exists in the distribution of components within that aggregate based on the number of expanding or contraction segments.[119] This unseen cycle is important because it helps to monitor and forecast the path of the seen cycle. In particular, cyclical expansions or contractions "diminish in scope before they come to an end" and "contractions that ultimately become severe are widespread in their early stages."[120]

Bert Hickman has suggested that the diffusion concept is a more realistic alternative to the widely accepted accelerator principle of investment. Hickman noted:

> [W]hen aggregative retardation occurs, it is not exclusively or even primarily because all individual outputs are increasing more slowly—the image which is probably at the back of the mind when the accelerator is applied to aggregate output—rather, it is principally because fewer industries are expanding at all and more have begun to decline.[121]

Similar ideas have been offered by William Fellner in his *theory of diminishing offsets* and by Arthur Burns in his *loss of industrial balance* idea.[122] Hence, although it is not widely recognized, the diffusion concept has been intertwined with economic theory of the business cycle. This view appears easily meshed with the purchasing view of the business cycle, which was discussed earlier.

The concept of diffusion is made operational by defining it as *a time series representing the percentage of the components within an aggregate that are expanding*. An index of diffusion is calculated from the percentage of components expanding (E), the percentage of components that are unchanged (U), and the percentage of components that are contracting (C) as $E + (1/2 \times U)$, where $E + U + C = 100\%$. A related concept is the *net balance* statistic or the *net percent rising* (NPR), which is defined as: $E - C$.

About 15 regional purchasing manager surveys are taken around the country, and many of those surveys report their results using the NPR formula, which can range between $+100$ and -100. Since NPR simply takes the difference between the percentage of the responses reporting "higher" and the percentage reporting "lower" (higher-lower), the bounds are clear; if all the responses are higher, then $100\% - 0\%$, or $+100$, is the upper bound, while if all the responses are lower, then $0\% - 100\%$, or -100, determines the lower bound. On the other hand, the National Association of Purchasing Management's survey results are compiled into a diffusion index (DI) that is bounded by 0% and 100%; the DI is calculated as $100 \times (\text{HIGHER} + (\text{SAME}/2))$, where HIGHER represents the percentage of the sample reporting an increase, and SAME represents the percentage of the total reporting no change. The relationship between these two summary measures—the NPR and the DI, is straightforward.

Consider the basic information used to calculate both measures, that is, the share of the sample that is higher, lower, and unchanged. For example, assume that the Southwestern Michigan Purchasing Management Association reported a reading for their new orders series of $+20$ based on the following responses:

HIGHER	SAME	LOWER
30%	60%	10%

Then the NPR equals the percentage of the sample reporting higher minus the percentage reporting lower, that is, $30\% - 10\%$, or 20%, and that is expressed as a $+20$ reading. The DI, however, is $30\% + (60\% / 2)$, or 60%. The relationship between the two measures is:

$$\text{NPR} = 2 \times (\text{DI} - 50)$$

where NPR is the net percentage rising (e.g., $+20$) and DI is the NAPM-type diffusion index (e.g., 60%). Alternatively, the identity can be expressed as:

$$\text{DI} = 50 + (\text{NPR} / 2)$$

The choice of which formula to use for expressing the direction of survey change is arbitrary.

Other variants on these basic formulas exist. For example, Jack Bishop, who conducts the Purchasing Management Association of Chicago's (PMAC) monthly business conditions survey, has proposed the following summary statistic, which is bounded by 0% and 100%:

$$\text{DI} = \text{HIGHER} + (\text{SAME} \times (\text{HIGHER} / (\text{HIGHER} + \text{LOWER})))$$

The Bishop formulation weights the unchanged responses by the percentage of those recording changes (higher and lower) that were higher. Technically, the result is undefined at one point, when the percentage of the sample reporting HIGHER and LOWER are both zero. But, practically, the result might simply be set equal to 50% if that occurred. The differences in the Bishop formulation versus the standard summary statistic, as previously shown, are (1) the Bishop variant (BV) removes the assumption that the unchanged responses should be equally distributed, (2) the BV adds a *strength of change element* by weighting the responses in the direction of the maximum change, and (3) BV is more volatile as shown in Table 3.52. The equivalent BV reading based on the preceding example (and shown in Table 3.52) is 75%.

The relationship between the aggregate time series and the diffusion index is shown in Figure 3.28. There are four stages of the diffusion index and its corresponding phase in the aggregate cycle. Stage 1 occurs when the diffusion index moves up from 50% to 100% (or simply when the index is above 50% and rises), which implies that the aggregate series is increasing at an increasing rate. In stage 2, the diffusion index is declining from its upper bound of 100% to 50% (or simply the index moves from a higher to a lower number above 50%); this implies that the aggregate series is increasing at a decreasing rate. At stage 3, the diffusion index is below 50% and declining, which implies the aggregate series is decreasing at an increasing rate. Finally, stage 4 takes place

Table 3.52   Relationship between Different Index Formulations.

NAPM–type Formula	Bishop Formulation	Net Percentage Rising	Percentage of Sample Responding Higher	Same	Lower
20.0	0.0	−60	0	40	60
75.0	100.0	50	50	50	0
65.0	80.0	30	40	50	10
55.0	60.0	10	30	50	20
45.0	40.0	−10	20	50	30
35.0	20.0	−30	10	50	40
25.0	0.0	−50	0	50	50
70.0	100.0	40	40	60	0
60.0	75.0	20	30	60	10
50.0	50.0	0	20	60	20
40.0	25.0	−20	10	60	30
30.0	0.0	−40	0	60	40
65.0	100.0	30	30	70	0
55.0	66.7	10	20	70	10
45.0	33.3	−10	10	70	20
35.0	0.0	−30	0	70	30
60.0	100.0	20	20	80	0
50.0	50.0	0	10	80	10
40.0	0.0	−20	0	80	20
55.0	100.0	10	10	90	0
45.0	0.0	−10	0	90	10
50.0	not defined	0	0	100	0

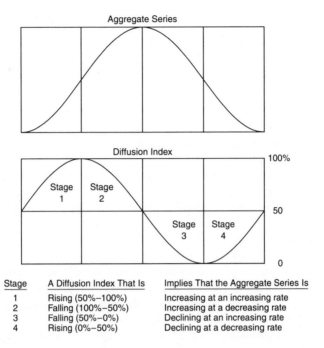

Stage	A Diffusion Index That Is	Implies That the Aggregate Series Is
1	Rising (50%–100%)	Increasing at an increasing rate
2	Falling (100%–50%)	Increasing at a decreasing rate
3	Falling (50%–0%)	Declining at an increasing rate
4	Rising (0%–50%)	Declining at a decreasing rate

Figure 3.28 Diffusion Index Properties. (*Source: Economic Review,* Federal Reserve Bank of Cleveland, January 1971, p. 6.)

when the diffusion index is moving up from its lower bound of 0% to 50%; this implies that the aggregate series is declining at a decreasing rate.

The major limitation with diffusion indexes is that their volatility can make interpretation difficult. A way around this problem is to lengthen the span of time over which the diffusion index is calculated, for example, using spans of 6 or 9 months rather than the typical 1-month comparisons (or one quarter, if the data is quarterly). Although this generally reduces the volatility, it increases the loss of current observations. This occurs because the index should be centered on the mid-month of the span to prevent cyclical timing distortions, and consequently the most recent observations are lost. Smoothing the one-month diffusion indexes is an alternative to lengthening the span of time for comparison (which sometimes is not possible; this is the case with the National Association of Purchasing Management's survey, which asks respondents to evaluate the current month's business conditions compared with the previous one). One such smoothing formulation is the *declining balance* method:

$$(12x_t + 11x_{t-1} + 10x_{t-2} + 9x_{t-3} + 8x_{t-4} + 7x_{t-5} + 6x_{t-6}$$
$$+ 5x_{t-7} + 4x_{t-8} + 3x_{t-9} + 2x_{t-10} + x_{t-11}) / 78$$

where x represents the one-month (or short-span diffusion index). A second method is the *binomial filter:*

$$(0.003906x_{t-4}) + (0.03125x_{t-3}) + (0.109375x_{t-2}) + (0.21875x_{t-1})$$
$$+ (0.2734x_t) + (0.21875x_{t+1}) + (0.109375x_{t+2})$$
$$+ (0.03125x_{t+3}) + (0.003906x_{t+4})$$

where the coefficients are derived from a binomial formula. The *Conference Board* method,[123] which is a variant on the declining balance method, calculates a smoothed diffusion index in two steps. First, it calculates a diffusion index for each subcomponent of its composite index by assigning a value of 1 if the change in the series is positive, .5 if stationary (no change), and 0 if it declined. Then, the declining balance method is applied, which smooths the ragged pattern.

An alternative method of constructing a diffusion index is as a *cumulative* diffusion index. This type of index accumulates monthly net balances starting from some initial (preselected) point in time. The Japanese Economic Planning Agency (EPA), uses this method for their coincident, leading, and lagging composite diffusion indicators of the Japanese economy. As noted earlier, the EPA even dates business cycles in terms of its cumulative composite coincident diffusion index.

The Conference Board has experimented with several other alternative forms for constructing diffusion indexes. Two methods worth noting are the *variable span* diffusion index and the *ranked* diffusion index.[124] The variable span diffusion index combines each component with individually tailored moving averages based on the component's month of cyclical dominance (MCD) statistic, which is the number of months necessary for the cyclical component to dominate the irregular component. The MCD weighting scheme, as built into the Census seasonal adjustment routine, uses moving averages from 1 month (no smoothing) up to 6 months for highly volatile series. For example, in constructing a variable span diffusion index for say, a 10-component index, might result in 2 components using 6-month moving averages, 3 with 5-month moving averages, and so forth. The resulting index, therefore optimizes the moving average weights for each component of the aggregate.

Ranked diffusion indexes, on the other hand, are more tedious to construct but in some instances may be a more useful smoothing device. The logic behind this method is to rank the change in the individual component using the previous n months (say, 6 months). Consider the following example, which shows the following period changes in a specific component:

Period	(T) Time	T − 1	T − 2	T − 3	T − 4	T − 5	T − 6
Change	20	18	22	13	26	20	17

Then these seven observations are rank ordered as follows:

Period	(T) Time	T − 1	T − 2	T − 3	T − 4	T − 5	T − 6
Rank	4.5	3	6	1	7	4.5	2

where the largest change has the highest rank (7) and the smallest change has the lowest rank (1). When there is a tie, the observations with the same change are assigned an average rank for the tied position, which in this case is $(4 + 5) / 2 = 4.5$. The current observation for this index then would be calculated as:

$$\sum_{i=0}^{i=n} r_{t-i} X_{t-i} / R$$

where R equals the sum of all the ranks (in this case, $R = 28$) and n equals the maximum number of terms in the moving rank (in this case, $n = 7$). Hence, the current observation in this example would equal $(^{4.5}/_{28})X_t + (^{3}/_{28})X_{t-1} + (^{6}/_{28})X_{t-2} + (^{1}/_{28})X_{t-3} + (^{7}/_{28})X_{t-4} + (^{4.5}/_{28})X_{t-5} + (^{2}/_{28})X_{t-6}$. This method assumes that the cumulative weight is invariant (e.g., 28) since the moving average span is fixed once it is determined by trial and error or some other technique.

In this section, several different forms of diffusion indexes were explored. It is natural to ask: Is one diffusion index formula better than any other? The Conference Board concluded its study with the expected observation that the more drastic the smoothing, the more likely it is that a turning point signal will be recognized with a greater lag. In the Conference Board test, the variable span and ranked diffusion indexes performed equally well.

Finally, the Conference Board has introduced a measure called the *sense of diffusion index*, which is a diffusion index of other diffusion indexes. This measure mainly serves as a confirming index of a turning point. The Board suggests that the sense of diffusion would help eliminate false turning point signals by providing confirming signals of cyclical turns when a majority of diffusion indexes send the same message.

First Differences and Diffusion

Michael Lovell[125] has shown that a diffusion index obtained from an aggregate time series is related to its first difference in the following manner: denote the aggregate series by X_t and the components within the aggregate as X_{it}. The mathematical *sign function*, which literally is the sign associated with a number or expression, can be used to designate one of three possible values $+1$, 0, or -1. Thus, the $\text{sign}(X_{it} - X_{it-1}) = 1$ if $(X_{it} - X_{it-1})$ is greater than 0 (>0); $\text{sign}(X_{it} - X_{it-1}) = -1$ if $(X_{it} - X_{it-1})$ is less than 0 (<0); and

$\text{sign}(X_{it} - X_{it-1}) = 0$ if $(X_{it} - X_{it-1}) = 0$. Using this concept, the diffusion index can be defined as:

$$\Sigma\{\text{sign}(\Delta X_{it}) / 2n + (\tfrac{1}{2})\},$$

and the ith change can be expressed as the difference between the sign function and the absolute value of the change in the component:

$$(X_{it} - X_{it-1}) = \text{sign}(\Delta X_{it}) - |\Delta X_{it}|$$

Therefore, the change in the aggregate series can be written as:

$$\Delta X_t = \Sigma(X_{it} - X_{it-1}) = \Sigma\,\text{sign}(\Delta X_{it}) - |\Delta X_{it}|$$

This then directly relates the change in the aggregate to the diffusion index. Furthermore, if all components of the aggregate were to move by the same amount, then the diffusion index and the change would move in lockstep.

Interpreting Movement in Diffusion Indexes

Three techniques will be looked at for interpreting movement in diffusion indexes (these methods could, in fact, be applied equally well to composite indexes as well). They are (1) the Conference Board's band approach, (2) the Chaffin-Talley statistical hypothesis test, and (3) the Anderson discriminant analysis approach. Each of these methods attempts to do the same thing—reduce the noise in the time series while accentuating the turning point signal.

Conference Board Band Approach.   The Conference Board has proposed an indifference band around the 50% or midline of its diffusion index to screen out false signals. The determination of the width of that band was done by a trial-and-error approach. The Board looked at a 1% band (49%–51%), a 2% band (48%–52%), a 3% band (47%–53%), and finally a 4% band (46%–54%). They concluded that the band width should depend on the volatility of the diffusion index, but the wider the band, the later the turning point recognition. For the Conference Board's principal diffusion index, they found that a band width greater than three index points "stretches recognition time without . . . achieving any additional economy."[126]

Although the band width concept is easy to use and communicate, potential users of this technique can see that it can be quite ad hoc in the determination of the optimal band. But there are some statistical alternatives to this early Conference Board approach.

Chaffin-Talley Statistical Band Approach. Chaffin and Talley[127] proposed a more formal approach to forming indifference bands around the midline of the movement of a diffusion index. In their review of diffusion indexes
as signaling turning point, they concluded: "[M]ost true leads for predicting
changes in the direction of the business cycle have occurred when the [diffu-
sion] index has had something of an extreme value."[128] Interestingly, this is the
same phenomenon that Neftçi has used to derive an optimal stopping rule for
interpreting changes in composite indexes, as discussed earlier in this chapter.
Both the Neftçi and Chaffin and Talley methods share a common ground. Unfortunately, the Chaffin and Talley turning point recognition method for diffusion index, as they applied it, had a high degree of false signals.[129]

The Chaffin and Talley approach is significant because it showed an early attempt to apply a formal statistical hypothesis test to interpret movement in diffusion indexes. Although those authors proposed this method as a way to eliminate
ad hoc smoothing, their signaling system may be improved by combining it with
mild smoothing methods.

Anderson Discriminant Analysis Method. The final method that will be
considered is discriminant analysis, which is a multivariate statistical technique used to classify an observation into one of two or more mutually exclusive and exhaustive categories based on a set of criteria. One of the many uses
of this method is to classify the creditworthiness of an applicant as a *good* or
bad credit risk. Or, more appropriately for this discussion, to distinguish
whether fluctuation in an economic indicator is more consistent with characteristics of a recession or an expansion. Note the conceptual similarity between this method and the Neftçi sequential analysis; the difference is that the
Neftçi method builds up information (dynamic), whereas discriminant analysis
evaluates each piece of information separately in time (static). Anderson[130]
applied discriminant analysis to interpret movement in a set of diffusion indicators in order to statistically determine whether the economy was heading
into a recession or an expansion. He calculated the measures of discrimination
using a simpler form of the technique known as the *weighted application blank.*
Although other more sophisticated versions of this method exist, the flavor of
the method is clearer using the weighted application blank—and it is easier to
replicate in other areas. An alternative to discriminant analysis is to use a regression model. George Ladd[131] has shown that discriminant analysis and linear probability functions (that is, a linear regression where the dependent
variable has the values of only 0 or 1) are closely related and that linear regression can be used to discriminate between samples.

The simpler form of discriminant analysis, which Anderson used, is applied
as follows for classifying an observation as more likely from a recession or expansion sample:

1. *Distinguish the Recession and Expansion Periods.* Mark off recession and expansion periods of the cycle for the time series under consideration based on a business, growth, or specific cycle chronology.

2. *Select Two Samples to Establish the Class Intervals.* Select data from the recession and expansion populations such that the samples are of nearly equal size. Develop a recession and expansion distribution using the data selected by either smoothing a histogram or fitting a distribution to the samples. The data not used for the samples make up the *holdout group* that tests the ex post accuracy of the discriminant function.

3. *Select the Series or a Transformation of the Series to Analyze.* Anderson's example of discriminant analysis was based on several diffusion indexes. The series he examined were diffusion indexes of wholesale prices, raw material prices, average workweek, initial claims, new orders for durable goods, industrial production, employment, and retail sales, which were jointly scored by this method to determine a turning point. Several observations can be drawn from Anderson's work: (1) The broader the coverage of the series and the more cyclical the economic indicators are, the higher the reliability of the turning point signal. (2) The collection of indicators need not be limited to only one kind of measure such as diffusion indexes. It may be useful to include diffusion indexes, changes in composite leading indicators, survey indicators, and so forth in the turning point screening process. (3) If the intent is to apply the method to a single indicator, numerous characteristics can be screened. An example of the third point will be shown.

4. *Determine a Frequency Distribution.* A frequency distribution brings order to an array of observations by consolidating the information into meaningful class intervals. The class intervals for the recession and expansion cases are generally determined by judgment but should be selected to maximize the difference between the expansion and contraction samples.

5. *Determine the Strong and/or Assigned Weights for the Class Intervals.* The difference between the percentage of the sample in the expansion class interval and the recession class interval determines the *Strong* and/or assigned weights. E. K. Strong[132] devised a simplifying rule for determining the weight to assign the class interval. Tables 3.53 through 3.55 can be used to select the Strong weight. While one can work with these weights, England[133] recommended converting the Strong weights to assigned weights to simplify the computation. England substituted alternative weights for the Strong weights using rules shown in Table 3.56.

6. *Determine the Discriminant Score for Each Observation in the Holdout Group.* A discriminant score is calculated for each of the remaining

Table 3.53   Strong Weights to Assign to Differences between Class Intervals (To Be Used When Both Percentages Lie between 8 and 92).

Difference in Percentages	Net Weight
69	27
68	26
67	25
66	24
65	23
64	22
62–63	21
61	20
60	19
58–59	18
56–57	17
54–55	16
52–53	15
50–51	14
48–49	13
45–47	12
42–44	11
39–41	10
36–38	9
33–35	8
29–32	7
24–28	6
21–23	5
16–20	4
12–15	3
8–11	2
3–7	1
0–2	0

Source: E. K. Strong, "An Interest Test for Personnel Managers," *Journal of Personnel Research,* Vol. 5, 1927.

observations of the holdout group by assigning a score based on the frequency distribution previously derived.

7. *Select a Cutting Score.* A cutting score is a threshold value that is used to classify an observation into one or another category. To select the value that is most effective in discriminating between the recession and expansion samples, a range statistical test is used, called the *index of greatest discrimination.* For each score in the holdout group, the

Table 3.54   Strong Weights to Assign to Differences between Class Intervals (To Be Used When Both Percentages Lie between 3 and 7, 93 and 97).

Difference in Percentages	Net Weight
69	27
68	26
67	25
66	24
64–65	23
63	22
62	21
60–61	20
58–59	19
57	18
55–56	17
53–54	16
50–52	15
48–49	14
45–47	13
42–44	12
39–41	11
35–38	10
31–34	9
27–30	8
23–26	7
19–22	6
15–18	5
11–14	4
7–10	3
4–6	2
2–3	1
0–1	0

Source: E. K. Strong, "An Interest Test for Personnel Managers," *Journal of Personnel Research,* Vol. 5, 1927.

percentage of observations at or above that given score is listed for both cases. The index of discrimination is the difference between the expansion and contraction scores. The cutting or threshold score is the score yielding the highest spread between the samples.

8. *Use the Weighting Scheme to Classify the Sample.* The end product of this exercise is a classification rule to interpret when an economic indicator has changed by a significant amount to be classified as most likely signaling a turning point in the cycle.

Table 3.55 Strong Weights to Assign to Differences between Class Intervals (To Be Used When Both Percentages Lie between 0 and 2, 98 and 100).

Difference in Percentages	Net Weight
69	28
68	27
67	26
66	25
65	24
63–64	23
62	22
60–61	21
59	20
57–58	19
55–56	18
53–54	17
51–52	16
49–50	15
46–48	14
43–45	13
40–42	12
36–39	11
32–35	10
28–31	9
24–27	8
19–23	7
15–18	6
11–14	5
7–10	4
4–6	3
2–3	2
1	1
0	0

Source: E. K. Strong, "An Interest Test for Personnel Managers," *Journal of Personnel Research,* Vol. 5, 1927.

Now, consider applying this simple form of discriminant analysis to the Japanese Economic Planning Agency's diffusion index of leading indicators. The criteria to be evaluated are (1) the level of the leading diffusion index, (2) the month-to-month change in the index, which is a way of capturing the Hicks and Keynes idea that activity falls off sharply at the onset of a recession, and (3) the average level of diffusion index over the previous two periods—a smoothing mechanism to eliminate false signals.

Table 3.56   Determining Assigned Weights from Strong Weights.

Strong Weight	Assigned Weight
−4 or less	0
+3, +2, +1, 0	1
+4 or more	2

Source: George England, *Development and Use of Weighted Application Blanks,* Wm. C. Brown Co., Dubuque, IA, 1961.

1. The recession and expansion periods in the Japanese EPA's diffusion index of leading indicators were marked off using the CIBCR turning point chronology (although the EPA's own chronology could have been used since the two generally are similar).

2. Expansion observations were taken from December 1954 through July 1964 (84 observations) and 80 recession observations were selected from the beginning of the time series until December 1974.

3. As previously noted, three criteria were selected to gauge which sample the observation was more likely from.

4. Initially, the class intervals for the frequency distributions were chosen as every 10 points, as shown in Table 3.57, using the diffusion index level criteria (criterion 1) for the EPA's leading diffusion index. This

Table 3.57   Frequency Distribution of the Level of the Japanese Economic Planning Agency's Leading Diffusion Indicator during the Sample Period.

Classes	Expansion	Contraction
90.0–100.0	16.6%	1.2%
80.0–89.9	19.0	3.7
70.0–79.9	15.5	7.5
60.0–69.9	22.6	10.0
50.0–59.9	7.1	11.3
40.0–49.9	4.8	3.7
30.0–39.9	3.6	21.3
20.0–29.9	6.0	11.3
10.0–19.9	4.8	23.7
0.0–9.9	0.0	6.3
Total	100.0%	100.0%

Table 3.58 Condensed Frequency Distribution and Weights.

Classes	Expansion (1)	Contraction (2)	Col. (1) − Col. (2)	Strong Weight	Assigned Weight
60.0–100.0	73.8%	22.5%	51.3	+15	2
40.0–59.9	11.9	15.0	−3.1	−1	1
0.0–39.9	14.3	62.5	−48.2	−13	0
Total	100%	100%			

was then condensed to highlight the differences between the expansion and recession periods as shown in Table 3.58.

5. The Strong and assigned weights are determined by reference to Tables 3.53 through 3.56. For the first criterion, these weights are shown in Table 3.58. A similar derivation is undertaken for the other two criteria, and the results are shown in Table 3.59.

6. Using the assigned weights for each criteria, each observation is evaluated and assigned a composite weight, which is the sum of the weights for each of the three criteria.

7. The cutting score is determined by tabulating the combined scores in the holdout group for recessions and expansions. In this example, the maximum is 6 (three criteria each with a maximum value of 2) and a minimum of 0. Table 3.60 shows the final distribution of combined

Table 3.59 Assigned Weights for Other Criteria.

Criterion 2: Change in the Diffusion Index	
Critical Class	Weight
+10 to +100	2
−9.9 to −100	0

Criterion 3: Average of Previous Two Months' Diffusion Indexes	
Critical Class	Weight
60.0 to 100.0	2
40.0 to 59.9	1
0.0 to 39.9	0

Table 3.60   Determination of Cutting Score That Yields the Maximum Discrimination between Periods of Expansion and Contraction in the Holdout Group.

Score	Expansion	Contraction	Index of Discrimination (Expansion–Contraction)
6	13.6	0.0	13.6
5	19.7	3.1	16.6
4	62.1	15.6	46.5
3	81.0	29.7	51.3 ← Maximum Difference
2	84.8	45.3	39.5
1	91.6	65.6	26.0
0	100.0	100.0	0.0

scores used to select the cutting or threshold score. In this case, the index of greatest discrimination is 3.

8. Classify the entire sample into a recession and expansion case depending on the combined score. If the combined score is 3 or greater, classify the observation as an expansion; a score of 2 or less is classified as a recession.

Despite this formalization, even this method runs the risk of calling false turning point signals. Using a 1-month change rule (a signal is flashed when the score moved above or below 3), only 45.2% of the turns were correct between 1954 and 1986. Waiting an additional month (a signal must be present for 2 consecutive months), increased the accuracy to 70%. In determining whether a turning point signal was a true call, a 3-month rule improved the accuracy to 73.7%; a 4-month rule, to 82.4%; and a 5-month rule, to 93.3%. Needless to say, however, the more certainty required of a turning point, the longer the recognition lag for spotting a turn. In Anderson's own example for the U.S. economy, he was forced to devise an operating rule to improve the reliability of the signal despite a broad-based selection of economic indicators to key off of.

Although this and Anderson's application showed mixed results, it is a challenging test of an indicator or indicator system. More formal discriminant methods are available, but the technique shown is easy to apply, conceptually easy to understand, and easy to interpret.

CROSS-CUT ANALYSIS OR FACTOR LISTING

Cross-cut analysis, which is also known as factor listing or scoresheet analysis, is a monitoring technique that assemblies current data and evaluates the economic information as *favorable* or *unfavorable,* sometimes with a scoring system of +3 to −3.[134] Leonard H. Lempert, Director of Statistical Indicators Associates (SIA), has used this technique with excellent results for many years. An example is shown in Table 3.61. Several characteristics of the business cycle are listed and then ranked according to recent cyclical trends.[135] Using this technique in April 1981, three months prior to the NBER's dated peak in the business cycle, Lempert warned that the 1980 recovery was fading fast.[136] This technique is a simplified variant on discriminant analysis, discussed earlier in the chapter. Instead of relying on a purely statistical interpretation, this method tends to use a more personal evaluation of business conditions, though formal rules could be set up to indicate when an indicator change should be −3 instead of −2, or −2 instead of −1, and so forth. The normal and lower bound method of monitoring movement, which also was discussed earlier in this chapter, is yet another refinement that could be incorporated into this scoresheet.

BUSINESS CYCLE SURVEYS

Werner H. Strigel of the IFO Institute for Economic Research in Munich, described business cycle surveys as "information instruments . . . born from the need of the moment" and consequently are a special type of economic statistic.[137] These opinion surveys provide useful input for monitoring and forecasting the business cycle because this information can be quickly collected and disseminated or can provide additional insight into an issue. An example of a survey that is quickly disseminated is the National Association of Purchasing Management's monthly survey of 300 purchasing managers. Generally, this survey is collected at mid-month and is reported on the first business day of the next month. This qualitative information is turned into diffusion indexes representing composite business conditions, employment, production, new orders, prices, delivery speed, and inventories. There are also numerous consumer confidence surveys and investment surveys that have been used to measure expectations and/or current behavior and opinion of businesses and consumers.

Expectations, according to George Katona, who was associated with the University of Michigan's Survey Research Center for 35 years, either are formed by extrapolating from past experience or are shaped by actions or intended actions of government or business. Nonetheless, Katona argues that purely econometric formulations of expectations are not sufficient to measure opinion. In particular,

Table 3.61   SIA's Indicator Forecasting Scoresheet, April 1981 (Scale Ranges from −3 for Most Unfavorable to +3 for Most Favorable).

	Score
1. Change in the Scope of Business Cycle	
A. Percentage of indicators expanding	+1
B. Duration of run indicators	+1
C. Trends in indicators	+1
Average Score	+1
2. Status of Composite Indexes	
A. Composite index of leading indicators	+2
B. Composite index of coincident indicators	+2 (U)
C. Composite index of lagging indicators	+1 (U)
Average Score	+2
3. Excesses and Corrections	
A. Unit labor costs	−1 (U)
B. Manufacturing and trade inventories	0 (U)
C. Ratio of inventories to sales	+1
D. Ratio of coincident to lagging indicators	+1
E. Capacity utilization	+1 (U)
F. Plant and equipment expenditures	+1 (U)
G. Commercial and industrial loans	+1 (U)
Average Score	+1
4. Monetary Conditions	
A. Treasury bill rate	0 (D)
B. Bank loan rate	0 (D)
C. Corporate bond yields	−1 (D)
D. Federal funds rate	0 (D)
E. Change in liquid assets	0 (D)
F. Money supply change	0 (D)
Average Score	0 (D)
5. Financial Activity	
A. Change in installment credit	0 (D)
B. Change in mortgage debt	−1 (D)
C. Change in business bank loans	+1
Average Score	0 (D)
6. Corporate Climate	
A. Aftertax corporate profits	+1 (U)
B. Common stock prices	+1 (D)
C. Ratio of prices to unit labor costs	+1 (U)
Average Score	+1 (U)

Table 3.61 *(Continued)*

	Score
7. Fixed Capital Investment	
A. Contracts and orders for plant and equipment	+1
B. Housing permits	0 (D)
C. Appropriations for new capital	+1 (U)
D. Anticipated plant and equipment spending	+1 (U)
E. Net business formation	−1
F. Capital appropriations backlog	+2
Average Score	+1
8. Demand for Goods	
A. New orders for durable goods	+1
B. Change in business inventories	0
C. Change in unfilled orders	+1
D. Industrial raw material prices	+1
E. Vendor performance (supplier delivery time)	+1
Average Score	+1
9. Labor Market Conditions	
A. Average workweek length	+1
B. Initial claims for state unemployment insurance	+1
C. Nonagricultural employment	+2 (U)
D. Unemployment rate	+2 (U)
E. Placements and hirings	0 (D)
F. Layoffs in manufacturing	+1
Average Score	+1
10. Outside Influences	
A. Impact of strikes and weather	0
B. Federal Reserve monetary policy stance	−1
C. Fiscal policy	−1
D. International developments	−1 (U)
E. Military developments	0
F. Other fiscal policy	−1
Average Score	−1
11. Magnitude of Change	
A. Stage of the business cycle	+1
B. Leading indicators	+1
C. Coincident indicators	+1
D. Lagging indicators	+1 (U)
Average Score	+1

Source: Statistical Indicator Reports, April 1981. Statistical Indicator Associates, North Egremont, MA.

U = Upward Change from Previous Scoresheet.
D = Downward Change from Previous Scoresheet.

he challenged the rational expectations hypothesis, which "dispenses with empirical research on expectations [but] does not represent an appropriate scientific procedure because businessmen, consumers, and workers often have a very limited horizon of knowledge about existing conditions and may not always form their expectations rationally."[138] Katona's point is well taken; surveys, in and of themselves, are useful tools for monitoring the business cycle. Tables 3.62 through 3.64 provide a listing of some of the major surveys in the United States, Canada, and the United Kingdom.

DETERMINING LEADS AND LAGS AMONG INDICATORS

This section will explore three typical techniques to determine whether a series leads, lags, or coincides with movement of another indicator. These methods are (1) the NBER turning point criteria, (2) statistical correlation, and (3) cross-spectral analysis. These techniques can compliment each other and should not be viewed as being mutually exclusive.

NBER Turning Point Criteria

The simplest technique is concerned only with turning points. These criteria are used to determine the timing relationship among series based on descriptive summary statistics. This approach can answer questions such as, How many months before or after a business or specific cycle turn occurred did another series exhibit a turning point? As suggested and demonstrated earlier, this is a rather straightforward application. Convention suggests that a turning point of between two months before and after a reference cycle turning point date is essentially coincident.

Correlation

A statistical correlation is a technique used to determine the average relationship between two (or more) series over the entire time series. The coefficient of correlation, r, ranges between -1 and $+1$, where 0 means no relationship, -1 is a perfect inverse relationship, and $+1$ is a perfect positive correlation. Alternatively, r^2, is often presented; this statistic can range between 0 and 1. The r^2 measure can be interpreted as the amount of variation accounted for from a linear relationship with another series. Instead of just looking at turning points, correlation answers the question: What is the typical relationship between series A and series B? Correlation, in and of itself, should not be thought of as suggesting that series A *causes* series B movement or vice versa; it is only a measure of the strength of comovement between the two series.

Table 3.62 U.S. Business Cycle Surveys (Selected Business, Investment, and Consumer Surveys).

Performed by	Since	Frequency	Sectors	Sample Size	Form of Publication
			Business Surveys		
National Association of Purchasing Management Tempe, AZ	1931	Monthly	Purchasing managers	300	"Report on Business"
Dun & Bradstreet New York	1947	Quarterly	Manufacturing, wholesale, retail nonfinancial services	3,000	"Dun and Bradstreet Looks at Business"
	1987	Quarterly	Business executives in 14 countries	9,000	"Dun and Bradstreet Looks at Business"
	1990	Monthly	Manufacturers	1,000	Press Releases
Federal Reserve Bank Philadelphia, PA	1967	Monthly	Regional manufacturers		"Business Outlook Survey"
Manpower Temporary Services, Inc. Milwaukee, WI	1977	Quarterly	Public and private industries in all regions	15,000	Hiring intentions survey; in-press release
National Federation of Independent Business (NFIB) Washington, DC	1973	Quarterly	Small business in manufacturing, wholesale, retail trade, services, construction, and transportation	2,000	Quarterly press release
The Conference Board New York	1976	Quarterly	All industries	1,600	"Report on Business Expectations"
Mitsubishi Bank, Ltd. New York	1988	Monthly	Air cargo companies, seaports, and trucking firms	65	Foreign trade survey press release

Table 3.62 (*Continued*)

Performed by	Since	Frequency	Sectors	Sample Size	Form of Publication
Investment Surveys					
U.S. Department of Commerce Washington, DC	1947	Quarterly	All industries	13,000	"Survey of Current Business"

Performed by	Since	Frequency	Sample Size	Form of Publication
Consumer Surveys				
ABC News/*Money* Magazine New York	1985	Weekly	1,000	Consumer Comfort Index report to clients
Sindlinger & Co. Wallingford, PA	1957	Weekly	2,000	Reports to clients
Conference Board New York	1968	Monthly	5,000	Reports to clients; press releases
University of Michigan Survey Research Institute Ann Arbor, MI	1946	Monthly	500	Reports to clients

Source: Centre for International Research on Economic Tendency Surveys (CIRET), Information Letter, Feb. 1, 1992; authors.

Table 3.63 Canadian Business Cycle Surveys (Selected Business, Investment, and Consumer Surveys).

Performed by	Since	Frequency	Sectors	Sample Size	Form of Publication
			Business Surveys		
Canadian Construction Association Ottawa	1974	Quarterly	Construction industry	150	"Construction"
Statistics Canada Ottawa	1975	Quarterly	Manufacturing	5,000	Report in "Statistics Canada Daily"
The Conference Board of Canada Ottawa	1977	Quarterly	All industries	240	"Business Attitudes and Investment Spending Intentions"
			Investment Surveys		
Statistics Canada Ottawa	1945	Twice a year	All industries and government	24,000	"Private and Public Investment in Canada"
Department of Industry, Trade and Commerce Ottawa	1970	Quarterly	All industries and government	300	"Survey of Capital Investment Intentions and Outlays"
The Conference Board of Canada Ottawa	1977	Quarterly	All industries	240	"Business Attitudes and Investment Spending Intentions

Performed by	Since	Frequency	Sample Size	Form of Publication
			Consumer Surveys	
The Conference Board of Canada Ottawa	1966	Quarterly	1,000	"Survey of Consumer Buying Intentions"

Source: Centre for International Research on Economic Tendency Surveys (CIRET), Information Letter, Feb. 1, 1992; authors.

223

Table 3.64 United Kingdom Business Cycle Surveys (Selected Business, Investment, and Consumer Surveys).

Performed by	Since	Frequency	Sectors	Sample Size	Form of Publication
Business Surveys					
Confederation of British Industry (CBI) London	1958	Monthly	Industry	2,000	"Industrial Trends Survey"
National Economic Development Office London	1983	Monthly	Wholesale and retail trade Construction	500	"Industrial Trends Survey" Results appear in "European Economy"
Royal Institute of British Architects London	1959	Quarterly	Construction	1,000	"Quarterly Statistical Bulletin"
Department of the Environment London	1970	Three times a year	Construction	1,000	"Housing and Construction Statistics"
The British Chambers of Commerce London	1985	Quarterly	Manufacturers and services	6,000	"The British Chambers of Commerce Quarterly Economic Survey"

Investment Surveys

Performed by	Since	Frequency	Sectors	Sample Size	Form of Publication
Confederation of British Industry (CBI) and Central Statistical Office (CSO) London	1958	Quarterly	Industry	2,000	"Industrial Trends Survey"
Departments of Trade and Industry Newport	1955	Quarterly	Manufacturers and services	2,600	"British Business"

Consumer Surveys

Performed by	Since	Frequency	Sample Size	Form of Publication
Conference Board and Research Surveys of Great Britain London	1986	Monthly	2,000	"U.K. Consumer Confidence Index"
Social Surveys Gallup Institute London	1961	Monthly	2,000	Results appear in "European Economy"

Source: Centre for International Research on Economic Tendency Surveys (CIRET), Information Letter, Feb. 1, 1992; authors.

However, since this method can assess the degree of association between the two series over time, it can be used to support the claim that series A should lead (or lag) series B by quantifying the timing relationship. Although this may seem like a trivial distinction, it is not. A high correlation between two series can be the result of a third factor or simple randomness that the technique cannot pick up.

As an example, consider assessing the timing relationship between the Federal Reserve Board's nominal exchange rate index and the pace of consumer price inflation. Using correlation over various timing relationships suggests that the highest relationship between those two series occurs after 21 months, as shown in Table 3.65. Consequently, exchange rate fluctuations are inversely

Table 3.65   Correlation between the CPI and the Exchange Rate Lead Time (Year-over-Year Percentage Change, 1970–1987).

CPI with Exchange Rate at Different Timing (Months)	Correlation
Coincident	+0.174
1	+0.145
2	+0.114
3	+0.076
4	+0.034
5	−0.012
6	−0.059
7	−0.109
8	−0.158
9	−0.208
10	−0.261
11	−0.320
12	−0.378
13	−0.442
14	−0.506
15	−0.557
16	−0.601
17	−0.637
18	−0.668
19	−0.688
20	−0.698
21	−0.700 ← Strongest
22	−0.695
23	−0.687
24	−0.679

related to consumer inflation, and the exchange rate leads movement in the CPI.

Cross-Spectral Analysis

Cross-spectral analysis[139] is the two-series counterpart of spectral analysis, which was discussed earlier in the chapter. Spectral techniques, whether for one or more series, decompose a time series into a series of frequencies representing fixed-length cycles. Cross-spectral analysis assesses the strength of this wavelength relationship between pairs of economic indicators. To determine the lead or lag between pairs of economic indicators, two cross-spectral statistics are used: *coherence* and *phase*. The coherence measure can take a value between 0 and 1; the concept is similar to the square of the correlation coefficient from a regression. Coherence measures the proportion of variance explained by one of the series (say, a leading indicator) at a given frequency of the second series (say, the coincident indicator). Phase measures the time difference between the leading and the coincident indicators and is measured in radians. The phase statistic can be converted into a time-oriented measure, rather than expressing it in radians, by applying the formula:

$$\text{Timing difference between series} = \frac{\text{Phase angle}}{2\pi} \times C$$

where C is the cycle length. While this transformation is more meaningful for determining timing differences between series, Hause[140] cautions that phase leads and lags measured using cross-spectral analysis will rarely provide direct estimates of the time domain relationships except under extremely restrictive assumptions. Consequently, care should be exercised in interpreting these statistics.

To apply cross-spectral analysis, it is desirable to have a minimum of 200 observations and the economic indicators must be stationary, that is, the mean and variance must be constant over time. If the series has a trend, it must be removed by calculating a first or higher-order difference (or the time trend can be removed by other means such as those described earlier in this chapter).

It is the intent of this book to show how to use the techniques, interpret them, and know the limitations and strengths of the methods, rather than to provide the theoretical foundations of the methods. But cross-spectral analysis provides a challenge to this goal because it is difficult to fully understand the method without knowing some of the theory. Therefore, the reader interested in this technique should go to some of the references for more details.

Consider applying cross-spectral analysis to determine whether there is any timing relationship between housing starts and the change in the population.

Table 3.66   Cross-Spectral Analysis Summary Table.

Cycle Length	Spectrum (X)	Spectrum (Y)	Coherence	Phase		Amplitude
				Angle	Lead/Lag*	
28.0	31811	204366	0.55	0.078	0.3	60047
14.0	46783	110720	0.41	0.095	0.2	46293
9.3	49907	59767	0.43	0.050	0.1	35712
7.0	31758	40906	0.58	−0.037	−0.0	27455
5.6	20722	33600	0.82	−0.051	−0.0	23833
4.7	21121	40561	0.75	0.066	0.0	25296
4.0	19999	48396	0.77	0.107	0.1	27305
3.5	18472	50020	0.83	−0.000	−0.0	27676

Negative (−) indicates that Y leads X, Positive indicates that X leads Y, Zero (0) indicates that X and Y are coincident.

To simplify the discussion of how to calculate the cross-spectrum, a computer program is included in the Appendix. Therefore, only the conceptual steps of the program will be highlighted.

1. Remove any trends in the data. In this example, the trend in population was removed by using a first difference, while housing starts were assumed to be trendless.

2. Select some arbitrary number of points (m) at which to evaluate the spectrum. Granger suggests that the number be less than a third of the entire sample size.

3. Individually, calculate the spectra for each series, housing starts (x) and the change in the population (y). The method used to calculate the spectra is more refined than was shown in the spectral analysis example discussed earlier. The major difference is that, in this example, weighting factors (for smoothing purposes) were used. Two common filters are the Tukey-Hanning and Parzen weights. For statistical reasons, the Parzen weights were used here. Table 3.66 presents the spectra for the two series. (For exposition purposes, the sample size selected only included 28 data points—less than the Granger recommended minimum.) The spectrum is estimated at points (π_j/m) for $j = 0, 1, \ldots, m$ using the formula:

$$\text{Spectrum}_j = \frac{C_0}{2\pi} + \frac{1}{\pi} \sum_{k=1}^{m} C_k \lambda_k \cos(\pi_j/m)k$$

where the Parzen filter, lamda (λ), is defined as:

$$\lambda_k = 1 - (6k^2 / m^2) (1 - (k / m)) \qquad \text{for } 0 \leq k \leq (m/2)$$
$$= 2(1 - (k/m))^3 \qquad \text{for } (m/2) \leq k \leq m$$

4. Calculate the cross-covariances. The cross-covariances (C_{xy} and C_{yx}) are calculated by using the following formulas:

$$C_{yx} = (1/n) \sum_{t=1}^{n-k} (x_t - \bar{x}) (y_{t+k} - \bar{y}) \text{ and,}$$

$$C_{xy} = (1/n) \sum_{t=1}^{n-k} (y_t - \bar{y}) (x_{t+k} - \bar{x})$$

5. Calculate the cospectrum (the real part) and the quadrature (the imaginary part) of the cross-spectrum using the following formulas:

$$\text{COSPEC}_j = (1/4\pi) [C_{xy}(0) + C_{yx}(0)]$$

$$+ (1/2\pi) \sum_{k+1}^{m} \lambda_k [C_{xy}(k) + C_{yx}(k)] \cos(\pi_j / m) k$$

and,

$$\text{QUAD}_j = (1/2\pi) \sum_{k=1}^{m} \lambda_k [C_{xy}(k) - C_{yx}(k)] \sin(\pi_j / m) k$$

6. Calculate the coherence (COH), amplitude (AMPL), and phase (PHASE) or lag statistics using these formulas:

$$\text{AMPL}_j = \sqrt{(\text{COSPEC}_j^2 + \text{QUAD}_j^2)}$$
$$\text{PHASE}_j = \arctan(-\text{QUAD}_j / \text{COSPEC}_j)$$
$$\text{COH}_j = \text{AMPL}_j^2 / (\text{SPECX}_j + \text{SPECY}_j)$$

where SPECX and SPECY are the individual spectra calculated using the spectrum formula given here.

7. Interpret the results. Assuming that the cross-spectral estimates are calculated using the BASIC language computer program included in the Appendix, consider the output from that program, as shown in Table 3.66. The two columns of particular interest in determining leads or lags at various frequencies are the coherence and lead/lag. A strong relationship at a particular wave length must be first established to determine a lead or lag relationship. In the example, high coherence was found at cycle lengths of 5.6 years (0.82) and 3.5 years (0.83). Then the next question to

ask is, What is the timing relationship? At both cycle lengths, this example suggested that housing starts and the change in the population were coincident indicators since the phase statistic converted into a time domain was essentially zero.

While cross-spectral analysis can be useful in searching for timing relationships among indicators at particular wave lengths, the method has limitations. Most economic time series have trends, but this method requires the elimination of the trend. As with any time series method that attempts to eliminate trends, the question remains, What if the trend changes? Will the trend adjustment cause a bias in the series toward finding or rejecting cycles? It is tough to answer some of these empirical questions. Although no technique is totally infallible, cross-spectral analysis can provide a useful check or cross-check on other cycle techniques.

SPECIAL ISSUES IN BUSINESS CYCLE MEASUREMENT

The final sections of this chapter will address numerous special measurement issues ranging from a statistical test to measure whether the business cycle has changed to measuring turning point error. Each section is independent of each other and provides a ready reference for the future.

Has the Business Cycle Changed Its Character? A Case Study Using Reference Cycle Stages and the Wilcoxon Test

Howard J. Sherman[141] has suggested that the dynamics of the U.S. business cycle were different in the postwar period through 1970 than in the 1970s and 1980s. Sherman uses traditional NBER stages to argue that business cycle fluctuations were mild during the 1950s and 1960s but rather severe during the 1970s and 1980s. A formal statistical test of his hypothesis seems the most effective way to judge the validity of this claim. The *Wilcoxon two-sample statistical test* (also known as the *Mann-Whitney* or *U test*) is a nonparametric or distribution-free test that can be used to test the differences between the means of two groups, which in this case are the business cycle growth rate averages in the pre-1970 and post-1970 periods. Briefly, the Wilcoxon test is applied as follows:

1. The null hypothesis (that is, the hypothesis to be tested) is that the average of sample 1 equals the average of sample 2.

2. The alternative hypothesis is that the average of sample 1 is not statistically similar.

3. The two samples are ranked in ascending order as if they were one sample.

4. The test statistic is calculated.

5. A conclusion is reached.[142]

Now, consider applying this test to the average real GNP growth during the seven complete cycles (from trough to trough) between 1949 and 1982. The individual growth rates per cycle are shown in Table 3.67. On the surface, Sherman's claim appears plausible. However, this test suggests otherwise. The application of the Wilcoxon test is as follows:

1. *State the Hypothesis to Test.* The null hypothesis is that pre-1970 real GNP growth rates were similar to the pace of U.S. economic activity during the 1970s and early 1980s.

2. *State the Alternative Hypothesis.* The alternative hypothesis is that the pre-1970 cycles had statistically different average growth from the post-1970 cycles.

3. *Determine a Level of Significance.* The level of significance is preset at 95% ($\alpha = 0.05$).

4. *Determine the Critical Region for the Test.* A two-tailed test is used in which the critical region has a probability of less than 0.025 ($\alpha/2$) or greater than 0.975.

5. *Compute the U Test Statistic.* To perform the statistical test, arrange the original data in ascending order:

Original Growth Rate	0.03	1.75	1.83	2.80	3.53	3.85	4.85
Rank	1	2	3	4	5	6	7

Table 3.67 Average Real GNP Growth during Postwar Business Cycles, 1949–1982.

Sample	Trough	Peak	Trough	Average Growth (%)
One	Oct. 49	July 53	May 54	+4.85
	May 54	Aug. 57	Apr. 58	+1.75
	Apr. 56	Apr. 60	Feb. 61	+3.53
	Feb. 61	Dec. 69	Nov. 70	+3.85
Two	Nov. 70	Nov. 73	Mar. 75	+1.83
	Mar. 75	Jan. 80	July 80	+2.80
	July 80	July 81	Nov. 82	+0.03

The growth rates associated with sample 1 (pre-1970) are underscored. Then compute the following:

n_1 = size of sample 1 = 4

n_2 = size of sample 2 = 3

w_1 = sum of the ranks of sample 1 = 2 + 5 + 6 + 7 = 20

$w_2 = \{[(n_1 + n_2)(n_1 + n_2 + 1)]/2\} - w_1$

$\quad = \{[(4 + 3)(4 + 3 + 1)]/2\} - 20 = 28 - 20 = 8$

$u_1 = w_1 - [n_1(n_1 + 1)]/2 = 20 - [(4)(5)]/2 = 10$

$u_2 = w_1 - [n_2(n_2 + 1)]/2 = 8 - [(3)(4)]/2 = 2$

$U = \min(u_1, u_2)$ = minimum of u_1 and u_2 = 2

6. *Draw a Conclusion.* Based on standard statistical evaluation tables, the probability that U is less than or equal to 2 given that the null hypothesis is true equals 0.057. Since this probability is greater than the level of significance (0.05), this implies that the null hypothesis can be accepted that the periods are *similar* (technically, this result fails to reject the null hypothesis). As such, the Sherman claim is rejected.[143]

Although this example demonstrated one specific application of statistical hypothesis testing, it also is useful to explore other statistical tests, such as the *Kruskal-Wallis test* (or *H test*). This statistical test is also a nonparametric method used to determine whether several samples have identical means. Although it is not possible to discuss every statistical hypothesis test, this section should motivate the reader to explore other standard hypothesis tests as a way of statistically determining various cycle claims.

Cycle Stages in Statistical Regressions

Phillip Cagan[144] suggested that cycle stages could be a useful way to investigate the causal effects within economic cycles using regressions. The advantage of using cycle stages in a regression instead of the time series in calendar time is that the cyclical stage average gives equal weight to each phase of the expansion and contraction. Alternatively, "the disadvantage of calendar time weighting is that a long, comparatively smooth business expansion tends to induce trendlike movements in most economic variables, which then appear to be correlated with each other even though their behavior is otherwise dissimilar."[145] However, stage averages should not be viewed as a substitute for examining calendar movement, but as a supplemental analytical approach. Indeed, cycle stages in regressions can be used to investigate all types of economic cycles, including the Kondratieff, Juglar, or Kitchin cycles.

TIME SERIES MODELING USING LEADING INDICATORS

Composite leading indicators can be used in models to forecast a coincident or lagging indicator and not only to call a turning point. The form of those models includes standard regressions as well as multiple autoregressive integrated moving averages (MARIMA), also known as state-space models. The basic logic for using leading indicators in a statistical model, which in its simplest form takes the form: $CI = fn(LI)$, where CI is the coincident indicator and LI is the leading indicator, is that the leading index is essentially a *reduced-form* variable to capture the relevant economic flows. Alternatively, leading indicators can be used to determine the cycle phase. This model uses the leading indicator to switch economic regimes. Consider a simple example where the aim is to forecast the 6-month smoothed growth rate of the U.S. composite index of coincident indicators.

1. *Segment the Historical Periods.* Using an average lead time of 6-months, a *dummy* or qualitative variable is calculated as follows: If the 6-month smoothed growth rate in the composite leading indicator exceeded 3.2% (the long-run trend of the economy), then let the qualitative variable equal 1, otherwise let it equal 0.

2. *Use the Dummy Variable in a Regression.* A naive type of model can demonstrate this method, where the explanatory variables are lagged growth rates of the coincident indicator and the one-period change in the growth rates of the same indicator. The estimated equation looks like this:

$$CI = 0.925 \times (1 - \text{Dummy}) \times CI_{t-1} + 0.600 \times (1 - \text{Dummy})$$
$$\times (CI_{t-1} - CI_{t-2}) +$$

$$0.985 \times (\text{Dummy}) \times CI_{t-1} + 0.193 \times (\text{Dummy})$$
$$\times (CI_{t-1} - CI_{t-2})$$

where the constant term was suppressed because it was statistically insignificant and the CI is the 6-month smoothed growth rate of the coincident indicator. (All the coefficients were statistically significant, and the R bar squared equaled 0.953.) This is only a sample equation, which demonstrated the use of switching variables. Moreover, a forecast could be made under a "recession scenario" (Dummy = 0) and an "expansion scenario" (Dummy = 1) to test the sensitivity of the business environment.

CYCLE DURATION: A STATISTICAL TEST OF SIGNIFICANCE

Is the length of the business cycle (or any cycle, for that matter) sufficient reason alone to expect a cyclical turning point? McCulloch[146] proposed a statistical hypothesis test to determine whether cycle length is a significant factor in determining the next turning point. Intuitively, it would seem that there is a higher chance of a recession as a business cycle expansion gets older. But this intuitive claim is not supported by the McCulloch test. de Leeuw[147] extended McCulloch's work and found some weak evidence that duration might matter though the evidence is not strong enough to reject the McCulloch finding.

Consider the following application of the McCulloch test, which statistically judges the claim whether the length of the postwar growth cycle is reason enough for expecting the end of a growth cycle expansion. This test can be thought of as judging whether there is a constant probability of a new downturn (upturn) as the cycle gets longer versus an increasing probability as the duration lengthens. The statistical test is applied by comparing the probability of grouped cycle averages using a likelihood ratio test, which has a chi-square distribution.[148]

To apply the McCulloch test, the following is done:

1. *Divide the Cycle Durations into Two or More Groups.* In this example, the growth cycle durations are split into two groups, which are divided in a somewhat arbitrary manner: cycle lengths between 8 and 20 months and those above 20 months. The break point of 20 months was selected because it was the median of the sample of nine cases, and everything less than 8 months was eliminated because the NBER assumes minimum duration criteria. In this case, the ranked duration lengths are 8, 15, 17, 17, 17, 20, 22, 28, 30, and 45, where the sample size is 5 for the cycles less than or equal to 20 and greater than or equal to 8, and the sample size is 4 for the cycles greater than 20 months in duration.

2. *Determine the Potential Maximum Number of Turning Points.* The maximum number of turning points equals the total number of months per cycle excluding any portion that is eliminated for minimum duration reasons but including those that lasted at least as long as the break point. In this case, the number of potential peaks between 8 months and 20 is

equal to 94 (i.e., $8 + 15 + 17 + 17 + 20 + (4 \times (20 - 7)) - (5 \times 7)$) and the number of potential peaks over 20 months is equal to 45 (i.e., $22 + 28 + 30 + 45 - (4 \times 20)$). Table 3.68 summarizes the calculations needed for the test.

3. *Test the Hypothesis that $p_1 = p_2$.* The null hypothesis is that the frequencies (p_1 and p_2, as calculated in Table 3.68) are identical, that is, H_0: $p_1 = p_2$, while the alternative hypothesis is H_1: p_1 is not equal to p_2. This hypothesis is tested using a likelihood ratio test: $-2 \ln \lambda$, where the logarithm of the likelihood ratio, $\ln \lambda$, is equal to $[m_{12} \ln(m_{12})] + [(n_{12} - m_{12}) \ln(n_{12} - m_{12})] - [n_{12} \ln(n_{12})] - \Sigma m_i \ln(m_i)$ $-\Sigma(n_i - m_i) \ln(n_i - m_i) + \Sigma n_i \ln(n_i)$. In this case, the logarithm of the likelihood ratio equals: $9 \ln(9) + 130 \ln(130) - 139 \ln(139)$ $-5 \ln(5) - 4 \ln(4) - 89 \ln(89) - 41 \ln(41) + 94 \ln(94) + 45 \ln(45) =$ -0.305. Then -2 multiplied by -0.305 equals 0.61.

4. *Draw a Conclusion.* The calculated statistic (0.61) is then tested against the chi-square distribution for one degree of freedom; that is, [(number of rows minus one) $\times$ (number of columns minus one)]. At a 5% level of significance, the chi-square value is 3.84, which far exceeds the calculated statistic. Therefore, this statistical test allows one to accept the null hypothesis that there is a constant probability of a new downturn (upturn) as the growth cycle duration increases, which means that the chance of a downturn is independent of the duration of the growth cycle.

Although this test makes an important point, it should not be viewed as saying that the age of the cycle is not important. As discussed earlier, cycle theories suggest why older cycles come to an end; this test only leads one to reject the hypothesis that cycle length alone can be used as a reason to expect the next downturn.

Table 3.68   McCulloch Test of Growth Cycle Duration.

Criteria	Actual Peaks	Potential Peaks, Nonterminations	Total	Frequency ($m/(n - m)$)
$8 < t < 20$	$m_1 = 5$	$n_1 - m_1 = 89$	$n_1 = 94$	$p_1 = 0.056$
$20 < t$	$m_2 = 4$	$n_2 - m_2 = 41$	$n_2 = 45$	$p_2 = 0.098$
	$m_{12} = 9$	$n_{12} - m_{12} = 130$	$n_{12} = 139$	$p_{12} = 0.069$

CAUSALITY TESTS

All the economic indicators that are classified by the NBER/Commerce Department or other private or governmental agencies as leading or lagging imply something about causality. Although most statistical techniques cannot make a statement about causality, Granger[149] proposed a *pseudocausality* test to measure the strength of the causal relationship between economic indicators. The Granger method statistically determines whether series X is more likely to cause an impact on series Y, or vice versa. An early application of this method by Sims[150] demonstrated: "[T]he hypothesis that causality is unidirectional from money to income agrees with the postwar U.S. data, whereas the hypothesis that causality is unidirectional from income to money is rejected."[151] Before describing this method, it should be noted that this technique is not without its critics who argue that a basic assumption of linear independence between series X and Y fails to account for any nonlinear relationship.[152] Although this criticism is correct, the technique is still valid within the bounds of its assumptions. As with any statistical test, the technique should be applied carefully, and the conclusions should not be overstated. This method, which also is known as the *Granger-Sims causality test,* provides a powerful technique in the search for leading economic indicators.

The following five steps summarize how to apply the causality test:

1. Remove any trend from the individual series.

2. Run an ordinary least squares regression of series X on series Y and vice versa using past and future values.

3. Rerun the regressions from step 2 without the future values.

4. Calculate the F-statistic to determine whether the future values have any influence on the dependent variables.

5. Draw a conclusion. According to the Granger-Sims test, the dependent variable does not *cause* (sometimes called *Granger cause*) the independent variable if the coefficients on the future values are not statistically different from zero.

To demonstrate the test, consider an example of the method presented by Bishop.[153] Bishop used this test to answer the question: Does the money supply influence prices and/or do prices influence the money supply? There were four possibilities to consider: (1) growth in the money supply (M) caused price movement (CPI); (2) the CPI caused $M;$ (3) M caused CPI and CPI caused M (bidirectional causality); or (4) there was no causal relationship between M and $CPI.$

Bishop estimated the following equations using ordinary least squares regressions:

1. $CPI_t = fn(M_t$: 8 past lags, present, 4 future)

2. $CPI_t = fn(M_t$: 8 past lags, present)

3. $M_t = fn(CPI_t$: 8 past lags, present, 4 future)

4. $M_t = fn(CPI_t$: 8 past lags, present)

where the eight quarter lags and four quarter future leads were chosen arbitrarily (though many studies have used these exact formulations); these equations also included seasonal dummies and a linear trend variable. The results are presented in Table 3.69. The test does not judge causality based on which of the equations for the *CPI* or *M* explain more of the overall variance but determines whether the future variables in the *CPI* or *M* equations have any statistical influence in explaining the dependent variable.

On the surface, the *M* equations have higher *R*-bar squared statistics. However, the appropriate way to determine the direction of Granger causality is to apply an *F*-test to the coefficients of the four-period ahead terms. The results of the *F*-test are shown in Table 3.70, which suggests that Granger unidirectional causality exists from the money supply to inflation (since the *F* statistic is statistically different from the "table value"), whereas the reverse is not true (suggesting that these terms are not statistically different from zero). Although the Granger test is not conclusive proof that a particular type of causal pattern exists, it can offer some evidence for that position. More importantly, Granger

Table 3.69   Summary of Bishop's Regressions (Estimation Interval: 1951–1976).

Regression	*F*-Test	R^2	Standard Error of Estimate
$CPI = fn(M, M$ with 8 qtr. lag)	1.57	0.19	0.00431
$CPI = fn(M, M$ with 8 qtr. lag, M with 4 future qtrs.)	1.82	0.27	0.00419
$M = fn(CPI, CPI$ with 8 qtr. lag)	14.06	0.66	0.00470
$M = fn(CPI, CPI$ with 8 qtr. lag, CPI with 4 future qtrs.)	12.87	0.71	0.00450

Source: "The Construction and Use of Causality Tests," *Agricultural Economics Research,* Vol. 31, No. 4 (October 1979), p. 5.

Table 3.70 F-Test on the Coefficients for the Future Values.

Causal Flow	Form of Regression	$F(4.83)$
M causes CPI	M regressed on CPI	5.09*
CPI causes M	CPI regressed on M	2.30

* Significant at the 0.05 level.

causality is one more tool of analysis that in combination with other techniques may lead a researcher ultimately to discover some new economic law.

TURNING POINT ERROR

Milton Friedman suggested that the true test of a theory is in how well it predicts the future. This same claim also might be made about statistical models and techniques. The techniques discussed in this chapter suggested ways to understand the workings of economic cycles in order to forecast them. But alas, even with perfect knowledge of past cyclical patterns and the reasons for their occurrence, there can be no guarantee of an accurate forecast—no matter which technique is used. Because no method of forecasting is foolproof, objective assessment of accuracy is important. One criterion to judge the performance of a forecasting methodology is to evaluate how well it forecasted historical turning

		PREDICTED	
		Turning Point	No Turning Point
A C T U A L	Turning Point	F 11	F 12
	No Turning Point	F 21	F 22

Interpretation: Each cell represents the occurance of each event. A perfect forecast implies that F[21] + F[12] = 0.

Figure 3.29 Measures of Turning Point Error.

points. Statistics have been developed to assess this accuracy. As shown in Figure 3.29, there are four possible combinations between a turning point prediction and an outcome: (1) predicting a turning when one does not occur (F_{21}), (2) predicting a turning point when one does occur (F_{11}), (3) predicting no turning point when one does occur (F_{12}), and predicting no turning point when none occurs (F_{22}). A perfect forecast is when $F_{21} = F_{12} = 0$. In assessing the accuracy of turning point error, three statistics can be used:

1. The *turning point error* is: $(F_{12} + F_{21}) / (F_{11} + F_{12} + F_{21} + F_{22})$.
2. The *error due to missed turning point* is: $(F_{12}) / (F_{11} + F_{12})$.
3. The *error due to falsely predicting a turn* is: $(F_{21}) / (F_{21} + F_{11})$.

Finally, other criteria exist for evaluating forecasts made with different techniques. Some of the more common measures of forecast accuracy include root mean square error, average absolute error, and Theil's U statistic. Implicit in all of these evaluation criteria is some penalty function, so be careful to recognize the underlying assumptions.

Appendix

CROSS-SPECTRAL ANALYSIS BASIC
COMPUTER PROGRAM

```
10 REM Cross-Spectral Analysis Program
20 N=28
30 DIM X(N),Y(N)
40 DATA 1553.7,1296.1,1365,1492.5,1634.9,1561,1509.7,1195.8,1321.9,1545.4,1499.5
50 DATA 1469,2084.5,2378.5,2057.5,1352.5,1171.4,1547.6,2001.4,2036.1
60 DATA 1760,1312.6,1100.3,1072.1,1712.5,1755.8,1735.9,1900
70 DATA 1602,1916,1526,1382,2263,2069,2028,1545,1816,2154,2307,2750,3131
80 DATA 3910,2970,3024,3033,2997,2883,2877,2953,2877,2385,2141,1944,2168
90 DATA 1823,2381
100 FOR I = 0 TO N-1
110 READ X(I)
120 NEXT I
130 FOR I = 0 TO N-1
140 READ Y(I)
150 NEXT I
160 NOB = N
170 M = INT((NOB/3)-1)
180 PI = 4*ATN(1)
190 PRINT
200 REM PRINT "m ="; M; "pi =";PI
210 GOSUB 300
220 GOSUB 410
230 GOSUB 640
240 GOSUB 720
250 GOSUB 920
260 GOSUB 1030
270 GOSUB 1140
280 GOSUB 1230
290 END
300 REM average
310 S1=0
320 S2=0
330 FOR J =  0 TO NOB-1
340 S1=S1+X(J)
350 S2=S2+Y(J)
360 NEXT J
370 XM=S1/NOB
380 YM=S2/NOB
390 REM PRINT "means";XM,YM
400 RETURN
410 REM variance-covariance calculations
420 FOR K = 0 TO M
430 C1 = 0
440 C2 = 0
450 C3 = 0
460 C4 = 0
470 FOR T = 1 TO (NOB-K)
480 C1 = C1 + ((X(T)-XM)*(Y(T+K)-YM))
490 C2 = C2 + ((Y(T)-YM)*(X(T+K)-XM))
500 C3 = C3 + ((X(T)-XM)*(X(T+K)-XM))
510 C4 = C4 + ((Y(T)-YM)*(Y(T+K)-YM))
```

```
520 NEXT T
530 CYX(K) - (1/NOB)*C1
540 CXY(K) - (1/NOB)*C2
550 CXX(K) - (1/NOB)*C3
560 CYY(K) - (1/NOB)*C4
570 REM cxy(-k) - cyx(k)
580 REM cyx(-k) - cxy(k)
590 REM PRINT "cyx";K;"-";CYX(K);
600 REM PRINT "cxy";k;"-";cxy(K)
610 REM PRINT "cxx";K;"-";CXX(K);
620 REM PRINT "cyy";K;"-";CYY(K)
630 NEXT K
640 REM calculate Parzen weights
650 FOR K - 0 TO INT(M/2)
660 W(K) - 1 - (6*(K^2)/M^2) * (1 - (K/M))
670 NEXT K
680 FOR K -(INT(M/2) + 1) TO M
690 W(K) - 2*((1 - (K/M))^3)
700 NEXT K
710 RETURN
720 REM calculate individual spectra
730 FOR J - 0 TO M
740 TERM1XX - 0
750 TERM1YY - 0
760 FOR K - 1 TO INT(M/2)
770 TERM1XX - TERM1XX+W(K)*CXX(K)*COS(((PI*K)/M)*J)
780 TERM1YY - TERM1YY+W(K)*CYY(K)*COS(((PI*K)/M)*J)
790 NEXT K
800 TERM2XX - 0
810 TERM2YY - 0
820 FOR K - (INT(M/2) + 1) TO M
830 TERM2XX - TERM2XX + W(K)*CXX(K)*COS(((PI*K)/M)*J)
840 TERM2YY - TERM2YY + W(K)*CYY(K)*COS(((PI*K)/M)*J)
850 NEXT K
860 SPECX(J) - (CXX(0)/(2*PI))+(1/PI)*TERM1XX+(2/PI)*TERM2XX
870 SPECY(J) - (CYY(0)/(2*PI))+(1/PI)*TERM1YY+(2/PI)*TERM2YY
880 REM PRINT "spectrum for x";J;SPECX(J)
890 REM PRINT "spectrum for y";J;SPECY(J)
900 NEXT J
910 RETURN
920 REM calculate cospectrum
930 FOR J - 0 TO M
940 TERM1S - 0
950 FOR K - 1 TO M
960 TERM1S - TERM1S +(W(K)*(CXY(K)+CYX(K))*COS(((PI*J)/M)*K))
970 NEXT K
980 TERM1S(J) - TERM1S
990 COSPEC(J) - (1/(4*PI))*(W(0)*(CXY(0)+CYX(0)))+((1/(2*PI))*TERM1S(J))
1000 REM PRINT "co-spectrum -";COSPEC(J);"for j -";J
1010 NEXT J
1020 RETURN
1030 REM calculate the quadrature spectrum
1040 FOR J - 0 TO M
1050 TERM2S - 0
1060 FOR K - 1 TO M
```

```
1070 TERM2S=TERM2S+(W(K)*(CXY(K)-CYX(K))*SIN(((PI*J)/M)*K))
1080 NEXT K
1090 TERM2S(J) = TERM2S
1100 QUAD(J) = (1/(2*PI))*(TERM2S(J))
1110 REM PRINT "quadrature spectrum = ";QUAD(J);"for j =";J
1120 NEXT J
1130 RETURN
1140 REM stats
1150 FOR J = 0 TO M
1160 AMPL(J) = (COSPEC(J)^2 + QUAD(J)^2)^.5
1170 PHASE(J) = ATN(-QUAD(J)/COSPEC(J))
1180 COH(J) = AMPL(J)^2/(SPECX(J)*SPECY(J))
1190 REM PRINT "amplitude =";AMPL(J);"phase =";PHASE(J);"coherence =";COH(J)
1200 REM priNT "c^2+q^2 =";COSPEC(J)^2+QUAD(J)^2;"leq Spcx*Spcy";SPECX(J)*SPECY(J)
1210 NEXT J
1220 RETURN
1230 REM Table of Results
1240 LPRINT " ";TAB(20);"Cross-Spectral Analysis Summary Table"
1250 LPRINT " ";TAB(20);"-----------------------------------"
1260 LPRINT
1270 LPRINT "Cycle";TAB(11);"Spectrum";TAB(22);"Spectrum";TAB(33);
1280 LPRINT "Coherence";TAB(45);"    Phase";TAB(63);"Amplitude"
1290 LPRINT "Length";TAB(11);"    (X)";TAB(22);"    (Y)";TAB(45);"Angle";
1300 LPRINT TAB(52);"Lead/Lag*"
1310 LPRINT "------";TAB(11);"--------";TAB(22);"--------";TAB(33);
1320 LPRINT "---------";TAB(45);"-----";TAB(52);"--------";TAB(63);"---------"
1330 FOR I = 1 TO M
1340 LPRINT USING "###.#";NOB/I;
1350 LPRINT TAB(8);
1360 LPRINT USING "#########";SPECX(I);
1370 LPRINT TAB(20);
1380 LPRINT USING "#########";SPECY(I);
1390 LPRINT TAB(34);
1400 LPRINT USING "#.##";COH(I);
1410 LPRINT TAB(42);
1420 LPRINT USING "###.###";PHASE(I);
1430 LPRINT TAB(54);
1440 LPRINT USING "###.#";(PHASE(I)/(2*PI*(I/NOB)));
1450 LPRINT TAB(60);
1460 LPRINT USING "#########";AMPL(I)
1470 NEXT I
1480 LPRINT:LPRINT:LPRINT
1490 LPRINT "* Negative (-) indicates that Y leads X,"
1500 LPRINT "  Positive indicates that X leads Y,"
1510 LPRINT "  Zero (0) indicates that X and Y are coincident."
1520 RETURN
```

Part Three

Economic History

4 U.S. Business Cycle History

Sir John Hicks wrote: "[W]e have no reason to have confidence in [a forecast] unless it is based on historical analysis, so, even if our business is with forecasts, of what is likely to happen, or with the probable results of policies to be adopted now, historical analysis comes first."[1] With this in mind, a review of economic history for the United States will be undertaken with the main emphasis on the post-World War II period. The placement of this material after the chapter on measurement techniques was intentional; many of the techniques discussed earlier will be used in the subsequent analysis.

The discussion of business cycle history will be approached mainly from a chronological perspective. However, a summary section will consider the typical sequences in the business cycle; this discussion will expand on the brief coverage devoted to this subject in Chapter 1. Some business cycle techniques discussed earlier will come into play such as business cycle stage analysis and sequential analysis.

LESSONS FROM THE PRE-WORLD WAR II CYCLES

The U.S. economy during the pre-World War II period has a long history of cyclical behavior. Since the 1870s and prior to World War II, the U.S. economy experienced 18 business cycles. Those cycles were very different from the post-World War II business cycles. During the pre-World War II period, the average expansion lasted 29 months, whereas the average duration of the contraction was 21 months. The ratio of expansion to contraction duration was 1.3. But during the post-World War II period, the average length of an expansion was about 50 months, whereas the contraction phase lasted about 10 months, on average (see Table 4.1). The average expansion length in the post-World War II period was 4.8 times as long as its prior contraction.

The difference between the prewar and postwar expansion-to-contraction ratios—1.3 versus 4.8, respectively—marks a distinct change in the character

Table 4.1 Business Cycle Duration and Relationship between Expansions and Contractions, 1870–1992.

Cycle		Duration of Expansion	Cycle		Duration of Contraction	Ratio, Expansion/Prior Contraction
Trough	Peak		Peak	Trough		
Dec. 1870	Oct. 1873	34	Oct. 1873	Mar. 1879	65	
Mar. 1879	Mar. 1882	36	Mar. 1882	May 1885	38	0.6
May 1885	Mar. 1887	22	Mar. 1887	Apr. 1888	13	0.6
Apr. 1888	July 1890	27	July 1890	May 1891	10	2.1
May 1891	Jan. 1893	20	Jan. 1893	June 1894	17	2.0
June 1894	Dec. 1895	18	Dec. 1895	June 1897	18	1.1
June 1897	June 1899	24	June 1899	Dec. 1900	18	1.3
Dec. 1900	Sept. 1902	21	Sept. 1902	Aug. 1904	23	1.2
Aug. 1904	May 1907	33	May 1907	June 1908	13	1.4
June 1908	Jan. 1910	19	Jan. 1910	Jan. 1912	24	1.5
June 1912	Jan. 1913	12	Jan. 1913	Dec. 1914	23	0.5
Dec. 1914	Aug. 1918	44	Aug. 1918	Mar. 1919	7	1.9
Mar. 1919	Jan. 1920	10	Jan. 1920	July 1921	18	1.4
July 1921	May 1923	22	May 1923	July 1924	14	1.2
July 1924	Oct. 1926	27	Oct. 1926	Nov. 1927	13	1.9
Nov. 1927	Aug. 1929	21	Aug. 1929	Mar. 1933	43	1.6
Mar. 1933	May 1937	50	May 1937	June 1938	13	1.2
June 1938	Feb. 1945	80				
Prewar Average		28.9	Prewar Average		21.8	1.3
Oct. 1945	Nov. 1948	37	Feb. 1945	Oct. 1945	8	4.6
Oct. 1949	July 1953	45	Nov. 1948	Oct. 1949	11	4.1
May 1954	Aug. 1957	39	July 1953	May 1954	10	3.9
Apr. 1958	Apr. 1960	24	Aug. 1957	Apr. 1958	8	3.0
Feb. 1961	Dec. 1969	106	Apr. 1960	Feb. 1961	10	10.6
Nov. 1970	Nov. 1973	36	Dec. 1969	Nov. 1970	11	3.3
Mar. 1975	Jan. 1980	58	Nov. 1973	Mar. 1975	16	3.6
July 1980	July 1981	12	Jan. 1980	July 1980	6	2.0
Nov. 1982	July 1990	92	July 1981	Nov. 1982	16	5.8
			July 1990	Mar. 1991	8	
Postwar Average		49.9	Postwar Average		10.4	4.8

Source: National Bureau of Economic Research.

of business cycles. The main reasons for the lengthening of the expansion compared with the contraction have been the institutional and structural changes to the economy since World War II as well as a greater emphasis by government on countercyclical policies. For example, the role of agriculture underscores how structural changes in the economy can change the nature and cause of the business cycle. Charles Kindleberger observed: "[U]p until the business cycle of 1857, or perhaps 1866, the harvest was the measure of business conditions."[2] But just as agriculture's importance dwindled with the rise of the industrial revolution, the economy continues to evolve and with it, the nature and characteristics of the business cycle change.

Business Cycles before World War I

Figure 4.1 portrays pre-World War I, interwar, and post-World War II business cycles as measured by year-over-year percentage change in real gross national product (GNP). While a complete review of every pre-World War I cycle will not be undertaken, several of those historical episodes are worth considering.

One interesting episode of the pre-World War I period was the 1882 recession. The 1882 recession had its origin in the 1880 boom when business activity was expanding at an annual rate of better than 20%. That strong pace of real growth was eventually followed by a very long recession, which began in 1882 and lasted 38 months.[3] The lesson from this recession was that each business cycle phase is

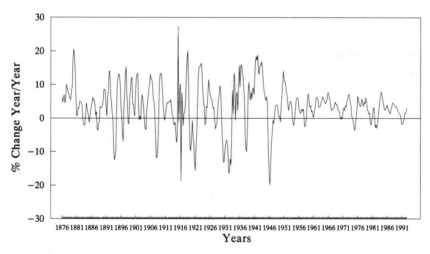

Figure 4.1 Real GNP, 1876–1992, 1987 Dollars, Two Series Linked (1876–1946) and (1947–1992). (*Sources:* National Bureau of Economic Research, U.S. Department of Commerce; authors.)

somewhat dependent on its preceding expansion or contraction—this particularly was true of the 1882 recession.

The seeds of that long 38-month recession were found in its prior cyclical expansion. Friedman and Schwartz describe that expansion, which lasted between March 1879 and March 1882, as "a combination of favorable physical and financial factors."[4] Those physical factors included (1) A protracted recession before the 1879 expansion that lasted 65 months and set the foundation for the subsequent strong rebound in output. This phenomenon has been repeated time and again—the sharper the contraction, the sharper the rebound in output. (2) Two successive years of bumper crops in the United States, combined with poor crop harvests abroad, resulted in very high exports. Table 4.2 shows export values during this period. Between the first quarter of 1879 and the second quarter of 1880, total exports rose by 43% and food exports alone rose by 40%; food exports accounted for half the increase in total exports over those six quarters. On the financial side, this surge in U.S. exports caused increased demand for dollars abroad to pay for those goods from the United States. In turn, the merchandise trade flows were balanced by a foreign inflow of gold to the United States, which "helped produce an expansion in the stock of money and in prices."[5] U.S. inflation, as measured by consumer prices, accelerated to about 4% in 1880, the first increase in inflation since 1864. In response to the rise in inflation, monetary policy became tighter and produced a recession in 1882. Business activity declined 25% during this recession causing many bank and nonbank failures (Table 4.3 shows the severity of the early recessions); it also caused a moderate deflationary trend that continued long after the end of that recession. Between 1882 and 1895, the price level declined by about 1% per year.[6]

Inflation and Interest Rates

Despite the roller-coaster pattern of real growth, interest rates during the latter part of the nineteenth century were generally declining or relatively low as shown in Figure 4.2. In the mid-1860s, inflation was high and so were interest rates (a result of the Civil War), but as the price level trended lower, so too did interest rates. Aside from a short-lived pickup of inflation in the early 1880s, the inflation rate remained below its mid-1860s peak (see Figure 4.3). The next serious bout of inflation was around 1918, which was a result of an unleashing of pent-up demand in the aftermath of World War I (see Figures 4.4 and 4.5). This inflationary period culminated in two back-to-back recessions that resembled the 1980 and 1981 recessions. These two recessions in 1918 and in 1920 ultimately wrung out the inflation—another similarity with the 1980s. The 1920 recession was particularly sharp—about 1.75 times as severe as the average decline in business activity between 1882 and 1926.

Table 4.2 U.S. Export Values (Seasonally Adjusted at Annual Rates, Millions of $).

Year and Quarter		Value
1879	1	$686.0 Trough
	2	713.6
	3	793.6
	4	793.2
1880	1	804.0
	2	982.4 Peak
	3	954.8
	4	852.8
1881	1	893.2
	2	934.0
	3	879.2
	4	686.4 Trough
1882	1	723.2
	2	744.0
	3	818.4
	4	781.2
1883	1	882.0 Peak
	2	815.6
	3	768.0
	4	729.2
1884	1	750.0
	2	717.2
	3	747.2
	4	770.0
1885	1	722.8
	2	708.4
	3	627.6 Trough
	4	683.6

Source: Ilse Mintz, *Cyclical Fluctuations in the Exports of the United States since 1879,* National Bureau of Economic Research, New York, 1967, p. 284.

The 1920–1928 Period

The NBER classifies three recessions in the 1920s before the 1929 depression. The recession in 1920 lasted 18 months and was the result of the two factors: (1) tighter monetary policy—a response to high inflation, and (2) a significant reduction in military expenditures after World War I. Another

Table 4.3 Measures of Amplitude of Cyclical Movement in the United States, 1873–1929.

	(1)	(2)	(3)	(4)	(5)	(6)	(7)	(8)	(9)
		NBER Reference Dates		Axe-Houghton Index of Trade and Industrial Activity		Babson Index of Physical Volume of Business Activity		AT&T Index of Industrial Activity	
Line	Peak	Trough	Peak	Fall	Rise	Fall	Rise	Fall	Rise
1	Oct. 1873	Mar. 1879	Mar. 1882	−24.6%	46.5%				
2	Mar. 1882	May 1885	Mar. 1887	−8.2	37.1				
3	Mar. 1887	Apr. 1888	July 1890	−11.7	32.1				
4	July 1890	May 1891	Jan. 1893	−29.7	16.8		22.7%		
5	Jan. 1893	June 1894	Dec. 1895	−20.8	37.3	−26.9%	35.9		
6	Dec. 1895	June 1897	June 1899	−8.8	58.9	−15.3	47.6		
7	June 1899	Dec. 1900	Sept. 1902	−17.1	36.3	−12.2	41.4	−9.2%	38.5%
8	Sept. 1902	Aug. 1904	May 1907	−31.0	39.4	−14.2	48.1	−17.6	54.4
9	May 1907	June 1908	Jan. 1910	−10.6	59.3	−22.7	43.6	−29.1	44.9
10	Jan. 1910	Jan. 1912	Jan. 1913	−19.8	25.6	−9.0	23.3	−7.8	30.8
11	Jan. 1913	Dec. 1914	Aug. 1918	−14.1	49.2	−18.9	56.8	−19.5	52.3
12	Aug. 1918	Mar. 1919	Jan. 1920	−32.7	23.2	−28.6	34.2	−21.5	28.9
13	Jan. 1920	July 1921	May 1923	−22.7	68.5	−32.3	65.0	−29.4	60.1
14	May 1923	July 1924	Oct. 1926	−10.0	36.1	−17.2	28.0	−20.5	39.4
15	Oct. 1926	Nov. 1927	Aug. 1929		21.6	−9.5	25.2	−5.8	24.9
			Average	−18.7%	39.1%	−18.8%	39.3%	−17.8%	41.6%

Source: Victor Zarnowitz, "Business Cycles and Growth: Some Reflections and Measures," National Bureau of Economic Research, Working Paper No. 655, April 1981, p. 37.

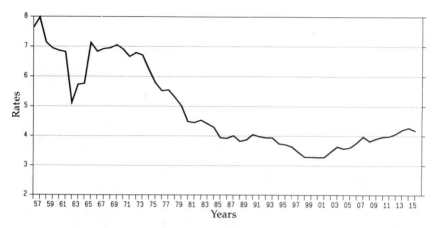

Figure 4.2 Interest Rates, 1857–1916, Railroad Bond Yields, Lowest Yielding Each January. (*Source:* F. R. Macauley, *The Movement of Interest Rates, Bond Yields, and Stock Prices in the United States since 1856,* New York: NBER 1936, pp. A111–112.)

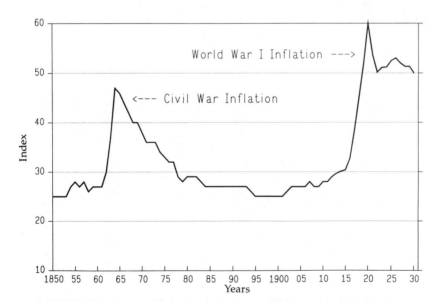

Figure 4.3 The Consumer Price Index (1967-100). (*Source: BLS Handbook of Labor Statistics, 1975.*)

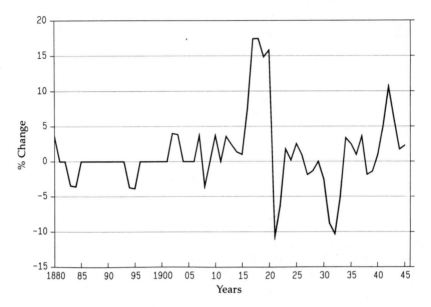

Figure 4.4   The Consumer Price Index (Annual Change, 1880–1945). (*Source: BLS Handbook of Labor Statistics, 1975.*)

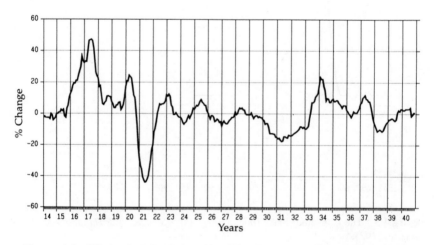

Figure 4.5   Wholesale Price Index (Year/Year Percentage Change 1914–1940).

often cited reason for the 1920 recession was a consumer reluctance to spend due to sharply higher prices. (Since then, econometric research and surveys have found that two influences make inflation a critical determinant of consumer spending: (1) Higher inflation can diminish real incomes, and (2) higher inflation also can create a psychological fear that in turn causes consumers to save more.) The 1923 recession was moderately brief and mild.[7]

The 1926 recession also was quite mild by most comparisons. Some contemporary observers such as L. P. Ayres even noted that the recession beginning in 1926 and lasting through late 1927 was a minor business downturn "which was not sufficiently important to be considered as marking the end of a cycle."[8] Kindleberger observed: "[I]n retrospect, [the 1926 recession] is thought to lack the characteristics of a normal business cycle and to reflect primarily the decision of Henry Ford to close down automobile production for six months to permit the changeover from the Model T . . . to the Model A in an effort to compete more effectively with Chevrolet."[9] Victor Zarnowitz has dubbed the period from 1923 until the 1929 depression as "a period of calmness before the storm."[10]

On balance, the Roaring Twenties were characterized by generally favorable business conditions. The period, however, began with a severe recession and ended on a similar note; the 1920s were punctuated by two mild recessions in 1923 and 1926. The generally favorable business conditions during the mid-years of the decade were due to (1) price stability during most of the 1920s, which was a result of rapid productivity growth; (2) the greater acceptance and use of consumer credit spurred consumer spending; (3) the rise of the automobile— passenger car production tripled over the course of the decade and by 1929 accounted for about 13% of total industrial output and employed 7% of the work force;[11] and (4) the Mellon tax cuts—the Revenue Acts of 1921, 1924, and 1926.

Between 1921 and 1926, the Mellon tax cuts provided a new thrust to the economy and made the 1923 and 1926 recessions less severe. Those federal income tax cuts were needed to reverse war-related tax increases legislated under the Revenue Act of 1917. Under the 1917 law, Congress lowered the individual income tax exemption and imposed an income tax surtax to raise revenue to finance the war effort. But after the war, Congress did very little to repeal those tax provisions. In 1921, Warren G. Harding was inaugurated as president; in that year, his Secretary of Treasury, Andrew Mellon, took the lead to repeal those repressive taxes. In a sequence of tax bills between 1921 and 1926, Congress lowered the tax burden. The 1921 Revenue Act reduced the marginal personal surtax rate from 65% to 50% and lowered the combined normal and surtax rates from 73% to 58%.[12] That 1921 tax bill also repealed the excess profits tax but increased the corporate tax rate from 10% to 12.5%. The Revenue Act of 1924 cut the combined normal and surtax top marginal personal tax rate from 58% to 46% and those rates again were lowered, this time to 25% by the Revenue Act of 1926. The 1926 act was made retroactive to 1925 earned income, which also contributed to the mildness of the 1926 recession.

The Great Depression and Its Aftermath

There was no single cause of the 1929 depression. Most observers point to the following factors:

1. As shown in Figure 4.6, the residential construction sector declined for several years prior to 1929—this sector accounted for about 5% of real GNP. Figure 4.6, which presents a 2-quarter smoothed annual rate (TQSAR) of growth in residential investment, highlights the lead time of the housing sector in the economic downturn. Although demand was weakening, the overextension of real estate credit aggravated the contraction.

2. Short-term interest rates were rising. The Federal Reserve hiked the discount rate several times before the 1929 business cycle peak in an attempt to stem the speculation in the stock market. The commercial paper rate rose from 4% in 1928 to 6% by early 1929 (see Figure 4.7).

3. Exports were declining.

4. Car production declined in early 1929 as sales began to decline.

Against this background of higher interest rates and weakening foreign, residential, and car demand, several factors contributed to the duration and depth of the 1929 recession that turned a potentially "ordinary" recession into a major depression.

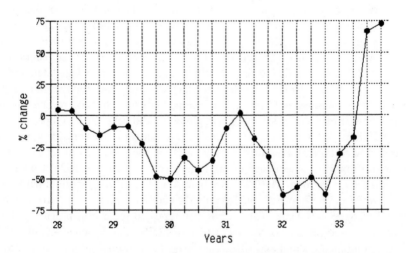

Figure 4.6   Residential Investment (TQSAR), Housing Weakened Dramatically Prior to Depression. (*Source:* National Bureau of Economic Research.)

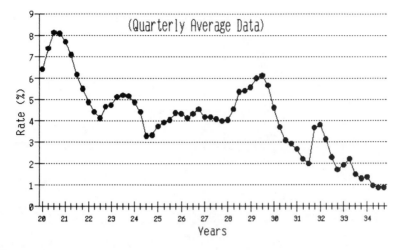

Figure 4.7 Commercial Paper Rate (Quarterly Average Data). (*Source:* National Bureau of Economic Research.)

The strong rise of consumer credit in the 1920s helped spur consumer spending. However, it also led to overextended consumers. As the debt burden of consumers began to rise, they began to slow their purchases of durable goods, particularly cars. Consumer installment debt provided greater strength to the economy on the upside and, consequently, reinforced the downturn when it occurred.

Another factor that added to the subsequent problems of the depression was a predepression shift within the banking system from demand deposits to time deposits. This shift toward time deposits provided banks more opportunity to underwrite real estate and speculate in the stock market. Further, the 1929 depression was aggravated by real shocks to the economy including the Smoot-Hawley Tariff and protectionist reaction worldwide.[13] In addition to these factors, the monetary policy implemented during the depression was inappropriate and led to a reduction in the money stock by one-third, which exacerbated the deflationary trend in the economy.

Although the 1929 stock market crash was a highly visible reaction to the speculation in the economy, the stock market actually reached its peak on September 7 (as measured by the Standard & Poor's 90 common stock price index) and was declining in an orderly manner. According to Friedman and Schwartz: "[T]he stock market crash coincided with a stepping up of the rate of economic decline. During the two months from the cyclical peak in August 1929 to the crash, production, wholesale prices, and personal income fell at annual rates of 20%, 7.5%, and 5%, respectively."[14]

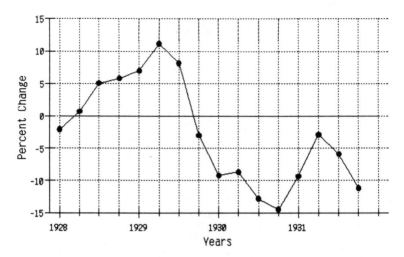

Figure 4.8 Real GNP (2-Quarter Smoothed Growth), 1929 Great Depression. (*Source:* National Bureau of Economic Research.)

Figure 4.8 provides an overview of how the depression unfolded as represented by real GNP growth. The economy was truly booming through the second quarter of 1929, but the collapse was sharp and persistent.

The stock market crash was soon followed by a reversal of the Federal Reserve's tighter monetary policy. Between late 1929 and the end of 1930, the Fed, through its open market operations, bought about $500 million of government securities to aggressively inject liquidity into the financial system. By early 1931, this had started to revive the economy.

But those "signs of recovery that appeared early in 1931 [soon] were washed away by new financial catastrophes originating in Europe."[15] A credit crisis developed in Europe ultimately leading England to discard the gold standard in late 1931. This departure from the gold standard resulted in a $600 million outflow of gold from the United States over a 3-month period and caused the Federal Reserve to tighten monetary policy to slow the gold drain:

> Because of the low level of money market interest rates in the United States, foreign central banks had for some time been selling dollar bankers' acceptances previously purchased for their accounts by the New York Federal Reserve Bank, the proceeds of which were credited to their dollar bank deposits. From the week of September 16, the unloading of the bills onto the Federal Reserve assumed panic proportions. Foreign central banks drew down their deposits to increase earmarkings of gold, much of which was exported during the following six weeks.[16]

On October 8, 1931, the New York Federal Reserve Bank's board of directors voted to raise the discount rate from 1.5% to 2.5%. A week later, George Harrison, governor of the New York Federal Reserve Bank, proposed a further hike in the discount rate to 3.5%. At that time, the New York Fed was more powerful than the Washington board of directors, and it remained so until the Banking Act of 1935 was signed into law. The 1935 act shifted the power to the Federal Reserve Board of Governors and away from the regional banks.

Maintaining the gold standard was the paramount monetary policy objective in 1931. The New York Fed felt that expansionary open market operations, if needed, would provide enough liquidity to the banking system to bolster the national economy. In April 1932, the Fed undertook a large-scale open market operation to provide that liquidity.

The United States stayed on the gold standard until 1933. In that year, President Franklin Roosevelt took the United States off of it, using a policy option given to the president by Congress in the Emergency Banking Act. In the following January, the Gold Reserve Act of 1934 became law. That law, among other things, raised the official price of gold from $20.67 to $35.00 an ounce, which in turn caused more mining of gold and hence, the stock of gold held by the Federal Reserve also rose. Between 1933 and 1937 there was a "surge in the monetary base [which] resulted from a huge addition to the nation's gold stock, the so-called gold avalanche."[17]

All these factors and many other legislative actions brought a halt to the 1929 depression, which according to the NBER chronology lasted 43 months and ended in March 1933.

The next phase of the business cycle began with the cyclical trough in March 1933 and extended until May 1937; the duration of that expansion was 50 months and was the longest expansion until that time. This recovery and expansion from the depth of the Great Depression was led by vigorous government spending. Even with the government spending stimulus, economic growth was anemic (see Figure 4.9).

The final pre-World War II business cycle recession lasted from May 1937 until June 1938, a span of 13 months.

Forecasting the Great Depression of 1929—Then and Now

In the early twentieth century, one of the most systematic attempts to forecast business cycle turning points in the United States was developed in 1919 by Warren M. Persons of Harvard University. Persons compiled a set of economic indicators, known as the Harvard ABC curves.[18] These indicators originally were based on five groups of 20 different series, which were later condensed into three groups for clarity. "All these groups revealed similar cyclical patterns, yet the cycles did not occur simultaneously but rather consecutively."[19]

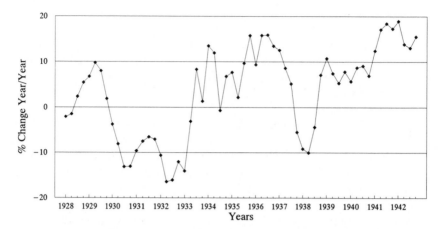

Figure 4.9   Real GNP Growth (2-Quarter Smoothed Annual Rate). (*Sources:* National Bureau of Economic Research, U.S. Department of Commerce; authors.)

These groups of indicators formed the basis of the first composite indicator forecasting system, as shown in Figures 4.10 through 4.12.[20]

Geoffrey Moore observed that the Harvard ABC "system came to grief in the Great Depression of 1929 because the interpreters of the curves took too optimistic a view and failed to foresee the debacle. Economists generally regard the episode as one of the great forecasting failures of all time."[21] However, recent work by Niemira and Klein found: (1) The ABC curves were not

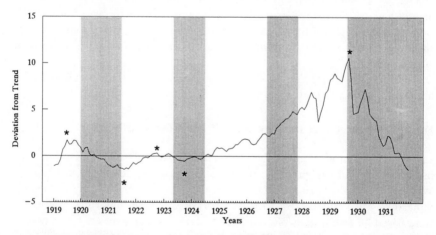

Figure 4.10   Harvard A Curve. * = Turning Point Derived from NBER Computer Analysis. Shaded Areas Represent Recessions as Designated by the National Bureau of Economic Research.

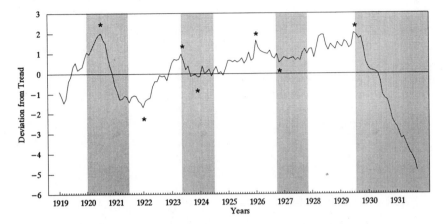

Figure 4.11 Harvard B Curve. * = Turning Point Derived from NBER Computer Analysis. Shaded Areas Represent Recessions as Designated by the National Bureau of Economic Research.

"good" or reliable cyclical indicators, (2) the relationship between the A, B, and C curves was not stable,[22] and (3) even allowing for all the limitations of these cyclical indicators, a purely statistical reading of those indicators based on a modern-day statistical technique, Neftçi's sequential analysis methodology (discussed in Chapter 3), would have led forecasters to conclude that a recession was imminent between 1928 and 1929. Obviously, the Neftçi methodology was

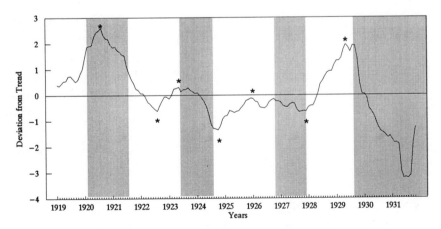

Figure 4.12 Group C Curve. * = Turning Point Derived from NBER Computer Analysis. Shaded Areas Represent Recessions as Designated by the National Bureau of Economic Research.

not available in the 1920s, but its application today to the original ABC data allows for an objective evaluation of those data. The Niemira and Klein conclusion supported an earlier evaluation of the Harvard barometers by Schumpeter, who wrote: "[T]he trouble was that the interpreters of the curves either would not believe their own methods or else would not take what they believe to be a serious responsibility in predicting depression."[23]

The sequential probabilities for the ABC curves are shown in Figures 4.13 through 4.15. The "A" curve, which was expected to act as a leading indicator of the other two group curves, in fact called a cyclical turning point in May 1928—15 months prior to the 1929 depression. The B and C curves could be viewed as a coincident and lagging indicators, respectively. The B curve signaled the turning point in December 1929, which was a 4-month recognition lag. The C curve, on the other hand, flashed a turning point signal in July 1929, 1 month before the turn dated by the NBER. Stability of the C curve in terms of cyclical timing was questionable to begin with since it lagged at the 1920 and 1923 peaks, based on sequential probabilities, but led at the 1926 peak. Thus, this turning point signaling system, using the Neftçi sequential signals, would have been far superior to the judgment used by the creators of the ABC curves in interpreting them especially since the creators remained optimistic for about a year after the onset of the depression.

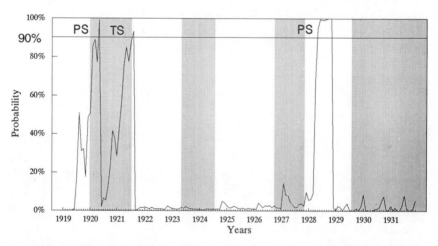

Figure 4.13 Turning Point Probability, Based on Harvard A Curve. PS = Peak Signal; TS = Trough Signal. (When the line exceeds the 90% threshold level, a turning point signal is said to be given. This figure shows successive peak and trough turning point signals based on the Harvard series.) Shaded Areas Represent Recessions as Designated by the National Bureau of Economic Research.

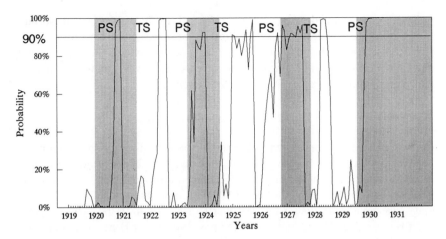

Figure 4.14 Turning Point Probability, Based on Harvard B Curve. TS = Trough Signal; PS = Peak Signal. (When the line exceeds the 90% threshold level, a turning point signal is said to be given. This figure shows successive peak and trough turning point signals based on the Harvard series.) Shaded Areas Represent Recessions as Designated by the National Bureau of Economic Research.

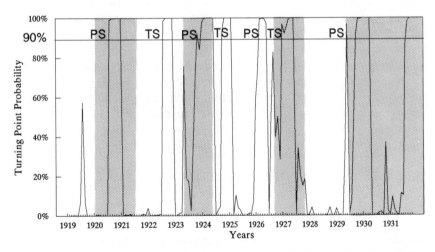

Figure 4.15 Turning Point Probability, Based on Harvard C Curve. TS = Trough Signal; PS = Peak Signal. (When the line exceeds to 90% threshold level, a turning point signal is said to be given. This figure shows successive peak and trough turning point signals based on the Harvard series.) Shaded Areas Represent Recessions as Designated by the National Bureau of Economic Research.

The lessons gained from the Niemira and Klein results are important for forecasting. The construction and testing of forecasting indicator systems is crucial to assess the reliability of the forecasting system. But even beyond that, a formal statistical framework for interpreting those signals is an important ingredient in any economic indicator system.

Observations on Pre-World War II Business Cycles

Charles Schultze observed that a few main features distinguish between the pre-World War II and post-World War II periods: (1) Nonconsumer spending caused a larger share of the business cycle fluctuation in the pre-World War II period than subsequent to that time; (2) the ratio of investment to GNP, on average, was smaller in the post-World War II period than in the earlier period; and (3) investment fluctuated less in the post-World War II period than before that period.[24] In many respects, these features should not be surprising since the backdrop of the pre-World War II period was the rise of the manufacturing sector. In the post-World War II period, the U.S. manufacturing sector matured and then declined, whereas the importance of the service sector began to increase in the economy. As the economy evolves, the cyclical characteristics also will evolve.

In a 10-country review of the changing nature of the business cycle before, during, and after World War II, Backus and Kehoe[25] found that with the exception of Japan, all the countries they studied—Australia, Canada, Denmark, Germany, Italy, Norway, Sweden, the United Kingdom, and the United States—showed a reduction in output volatility in the postwar period compared with the prewar or interwar periods. Moreover, they found a tendency toward lower correlations between output and money supply changes in the postwar period. Although these conclusions were not surprising, the generally uniform conclusions across the 10 countries, suggested a *common tendency* for the postwar period to show more stability compared with the prewar period.

PROFILES OF U.S. BUSINESSES AFTER WORLD WAR II

The 1945 Recession: Adjusting to Peacetime

The recession that began in February 1945 and lasted until October—a mere 8 months—was the result of a transition from war to a peacetime economy. The Office of War Mobilization and Reconversion projected that this transition would be costly to the economy and result in a sharp increase in the number of persons unemployed by between 7.4 and 8.3 million, but instead the transition was less traumatic and the number of unemployed persons rose to about 2.5 million. One reason that unemployment was not greater was due to the excess profits tax credit, which reduced the employers' cost of retaining workers after the war. If an employer retained a worker but did not utilize the person, part of the employee's wages could be deducted from the firm's taxable profits or else the business could take a tax credit. In essence, the government absorbed about 80% of the company's loss. Although this excess profits tax was repealed at the end of 1945, it helped avert more substantial layoffs when it was in force.

The relative ease of the transition was particularly amazing because "the peak in federal expenditures was reached in the first quarter of 1945, when they totaled $91 billion at a seasonally adjusted annual rate and accounted for 41 percent of GNP. Federal spending dropped slightly in the second quarter and plummeted thereafter, sinking to a level of $26 billion by the first quarter of 1946."[26] Offsetting some of this contraction in government spending was strong consumer pent-up demand, which was much stronger than forecasted. Consequently, the economy fared much better than had been feared, but the cost of this surge in demand was a surge in inflation. Contributing to the higher pace of inflation was the elimination of wartime wage controls, which were phased out starting in August 1945, though prices were not decontrolled until the summer of 1946. Legislation authorizing the Office of Price Administration, which oversaw the price and wage controls, was set to expire on June 30, 1946, but Congress extended its power until June 30, 1947, to ease this transition. By 1946, recession had given way to a concern about inflation. Although the transition was not without its problems, the peacetime economy was again set in motion.

U.S. Post-World War II Economic Growth: Trends and Cycles

In the subsequent analysis of the postwar period, the 1945 recession will be excluded from any summary measures of the period in as much as the characteristics of this transition recession were very different from the other business cycles in that period. Before discussing the postwar business cycle episodes, it is useful to review some trends and cyclical patterns present during the 1947–1992 period, which encompassed nine business cycle recessions.

Table 4.4 presents summary statistics on average growth rates for the major components of the U.S. gross domestic product (GDP) and the impact of recessions on those sectors. Real GDP and real Gross National Product (GNP) tend to fluctuate quite closely over time and are used interchangeably throughout this discussion as broad-based measures of economic activity. The difference between the two measures is that GDP measures the value of output produced in the United States, whereas GNP measures final demand of residents of the United States. Between 1947 and 1992, real GDP increased at an average 3.1% pace per year with a normal band of between + 1.5% and + 4.6% (the calculation of these "normal" bands is described in Chapter 3; it is one average deviation around the geometric average growth rate during this period). The most

Table 4.4   Key Economic Statistics in Perspective (Percentage Change at Annual Rates, in 1987 Dollars, unless Otherwise Noted).

Indicator	Average (1947–1992)	Normal Low	Normal High	Recession Impact Sharpest	Recession Impact Mildest
GDP	3.1	1.5	4.6	−4.1% 1973	−0.8% 1960
Consumption	3.2	2.0	4.4	−2.0% 1980	+1.8% 1969
Durable	4.4	−1.8	10.6	−11.9% 1980	+12.1% 1948
Nondurable	2.3	1.0	3.5	−3.2% 1973	+1.4% 1969
Services	3.7	2.8	4.6	−0.4% 1980	+3.3% 1953
Nonresidential Investment					
Structures	2.4	−1.9	6.7	−11.3% 1973	+5.7% 1960
Producers' Durable Equipment	3.4	−2.3	9.1	−20.6% 1948	−2.6% 1969
Residential Investment	2.6	−6.3	11.5	−30.4% 1973	+11.4% 1948
Government					
Federal	2.7	−2.0	7.4	−14.2% 1953	+4.9% 1960
State & Local	3.7	2.2	5.2	−0.9% 1980	+14.9% 1948
Net Exports					
Exports	4.4	−2.5	11.3	−13.5% 1957	+9.7% 1953
Imports	6.3	−0.3	13.0	−13.3% 1973	+3.7% 1957
Inventories	3.0	1.5	4.4	−2.2% 1948	+3.5% 1973
Addendum					
Real GNP	3.1	1.5	4.7	−4.4% 1973	−0.7% 1960
GDP Implicit Price Deflator	4.2	3.0	5.4	−2.5% 1948	+12.7% 1973
Nominal GDP	7.4	5.4	9.4	−3.3% 1948	+8.0% 1973
Disposable Personal Income					
Nominal	3.7	5.5	9.2	−2.1% 1948	+8.3% 1973
Real	3.2	1.6	4.8	−4.2% 1973	+2.7% 1969
Aftertax Profits					
Nominal	6.6	−5.6	18.8	−22.4% 1981	−0.9% 1990
Real	1.3	−9.9	12.5	−24.8% 1981	−4.1% 1990
GDP By Product Durability					
Goods	2.7	−0.1	5.5	−8.7% 1973	−1.6% 1969
Services	3.5	2.5	4.6	−0.6% 1957	+3.9% 1973
Structures	2.8	−1.7	7.3	−18.8% 1973	+9.0% 1948

Note: Recession impact measured over the real GDP specific cycle and on a cumulative basis (not at an annual rate).

severe recession was in 1973 and the least severe one was in 1960–1961, as measured from the specific cycle peak in real GDP to its trough. Imports, on average, were the fastest growing sector of the economy between 1947 and 1992, while nondurable consumption was the slowest growing sector.

On the income side, real disposable personal income increased at an average annual pace of 3.2%, while real aftertax profits rose by an average 1.3% per year. Corporate profits were quite volatile with a normal growth rate band between −9.9% and + 12.5%.

On the foreign trade side, real exports increased at an average 4.4% pace per year, while imports increased at an even faster rate of 6.3%—more than twice the pace of overall real GDP growth. A striking observation in the postwar period was the growing U.S. dependence on imports to meet domestic demand, even during recessions. The share of imports as a percentage of real GDP expanded in every business cycle downturn since 1948 (see Table 4.5). This rise in the GDP share of imports is one reason to expect less GDP contraction from future recessions since a slowdown or decline in imports will add to reported GDP (in the national income accounts, imports enter with a negative sign). Of course, this view is quite narrow and does not consider the relative impact on other sectors of the economy or the relative price effect.

Another secular change during this period was the rise of the service sector. In 1947, service-producing employment accounted for just under 60% of total employment but by 1992, that share rose to nearly 79%. A less dramatic, though still significant, rise was seen in service output as a share of real GDP. Services accounted for about 42% of GNP in the late 1940s but about 51% of GDP by 1992. To the extent that services have been less cyclical than goods, this often is cited as a reason for expecting less cyclicality in the economy beyond the 1990s. However, this view is now being challenged. A distinction between business services and consumer services is important to determine the degree of service sector cyclicality and its impact on the economy.[27] Consumer services tend to be more stable than business services.

Another stylized fact about postwar business cycles is that they have become less volatile than during the pre-World War II period. One reason for the changing nature of the cycle has already been noted—the economy's share of service employment has expanded over that period. Numerous other reasons are widely acknowledged for this change. Romer recalculated various prewar measures of activity and concluded that there was no strong evidence of the shift in volatility.[28] However, Balke and Gordon developed an improved set of prewar estimates that are superior to the Romer data and concluded that the prewar volatility was larger than in the postwar period.[29] Although the data controversy is not settled, the preponderance of the evidence suggests the postwar business cycle is more stable.

Table 4.5   Growth of U.S. Imports During Post-World War II Recessions.

Business Cycle	Imports as a % of Real GDP
1948–1949	3.30
1953–1954	3.93
1957–1958	4.70
1960–1961	4.79
1969–1970	6.82
1973–1975	7.24
1980	7.91
1981–1982	8.06
1990–1991	11.41

DeLong and Summers have argued that the key reasons for the greater stability in the postwar period were (1) the stabilizing effects of government, (2) increased availability of private credit, and (3) greater price rigidity, leading to less destabilizing swings from deflation and inflation.[30] But these explanations may be incomplete.

Zarnowitz cataloged a multitude of reasons the business cycle would be more stable in the postwar period[31] the list included (1) structural changes such as the shift toward more service employment, (2) the larger role of government stabilization policies, (3) institutional changes such as federal insurance programs, (4) increased use of discretionary monetary and fiscal policies, (5) learning from history, (6) smaller shocks to the economy, (7) better technology to control the inventory cycle, and (8) changes in the wage and price flexibility. Zarnowitz found at least some evidence that each of these factors have played a role.

Whether the business cycle has become less volatile or not between the pre- and post-World War II periods, may be a secondary point for understanding and forecasting the business cycle in the 1990s and beyond. Volatility is an issue *within* the post-World War II period as well. As shown in Figure 4.16, which is based on a moving 4-quarter standard deviation of growth of real GDP, volatility

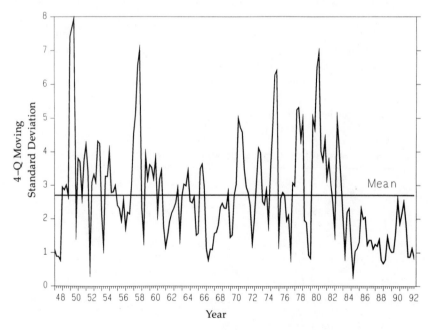

Figure 4.16   Real GDP Growth Volatility.

dropped appreciably between 1983 and 1992. Several key observations can be made:

1. In the 1980s, real GDP volatility moderated by nearly a percentage point over the 1970s.

2. The damped GDP volatility of the 1980s was helped by less volatility from export, import, and state and local government spending. Export volatility alone was less than a half of the 1970s and 1948–1992 experience.

3. Curiously, although many observers attribute the lessened volatility in real GDP to better control over inventories, inventory volatility has changed very little over the past 45 years (see Table 4.6).

Less volatility in the economy can result in better planning by business, though it is by no means clear that this is a structural shift to the economy. On the contrary, the greater stability in economic growth over the 1980s and early

Table 4.6 Volatility in Real GDP and Its Components, 1948–1992 (Percentage Points).

	1948–1992	1950–1959	1960–1969	1970–1979	1980–1992
GDP	2.71	3.51	2.37	3.12	2.18
Consumption	2.20	2.86	1.92	2.01	2.08
Nonresidential investment	7.25	10.90	5.45	6.09	6.11
Residential investment	13.48	12.69	11.75	14.29	12.00
Inventories[1]	1.96	2.52	1.54	1.75	1.90
Nonfarm inventories	2.23	3.11	1.85	1.95	1.97
Federal government spending	7.51	11.84	6.41	4.78	5.91
State and local government spending	2.59	3.46	2.93	2.35	1.61
Exports	13.96	16.67	19.54	13.62	6.05
Imports	13.62	19.43	13.02	13.74	8.70

Based on 4-quarter moving standard deviation of the annualized quarter-to-quarter percentage change.

[1] Inventories are measured as annualized quarter-to-quarter growth in the stock.

1990s may lead to more instability in the late 1990s as business adapts buying practices to what appears to be more stable demand. Similarly, the demilitarization during the 1990s, with the fall of Communism in Eastern Europe, is likely to shorten business cycle expansions until the economic adjustment to less military expenditures is fully implemented.

A final long-term observation is that government expenditures for war have a major impact on the economy's growth and even more importantly, these war expenditures can either moderate or accentuate business cycle swings. On balance, war expenditures tend to lengthen the business cycle expansion. Between 1854 and 1992, war expansions have lasted an average of 64 months, whereas peacetime cycles average 27 months; thus, war-related expansions have lasted about twice as long as peacetime expansions. The full cycle (T-P-T basis) has lasted 78 months for wartime business cycles and 46 months for peacetime cycles (see Table 4.7). While these comments center on war expenditures, military buildups such as in the early 1980s also could have a similar effect on lengthening the business cycle expansion.

Since trends hide the cyclical dynamic, it is again useful to look at the unfolding of the business cycle using stage analysis. Figure 4.17 shows the average growth profile for real GDP over the business cycle, together with its normal upper and lower growth band. As this figure indicates, real growth generally surges (stage II) after the end of a recession; growth remains well above trend until the final stage of the expansion is reached when the pace of the expansion slips slightly below the trend. At the peak of the cycle, growth decelerates sharply below trend; as the recession sets in, real GDP contracts sharply. Finally, a new trough is reached when real GDP is contracting at a slower rate (stage IX).

Besides understanding the typical dynamics of the business cycle, cycle patterns can be used to monitor the age of an expansion. The age of an expansion appropriately is measured by its business cycle characteristics and not by its

Table 4.7   U.S. Business Cycles during War Periods.

War	Business Cycle			Cycle Length (Months)
	Trough	Peak	Trough	
Civil War	June 1861	Apr. 1865	Dec. 1867	78
World War I	Dec. 1914	Aug. 1918	Mar. 1919	51
World War II	June 1938	Feb. 1945	Oct. 1945	88
Korean War	Oct. 1949	July 1953	May 1954	55
Vietnam War	Feb. 1961	Dec. 1969	Nov. 1970	117
			Average	78

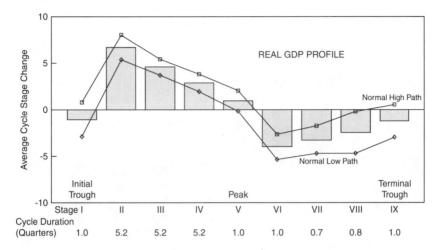

Figure 4.17 U.S. Business Cycle Stages, Average Growth and Duration per Stage, 1947–1992.

duration. Statistical tests or just eyeballing the data will help establish the probable phase of the cycle.[32] The correct question to ask in determining the cycle age is, Given recent economic growth, which stage of the cycle is it most consistent with? It also may be useful to look beneath the major aggregates for confirmation. For example, in the beginning phases of the cycle, real GDP advances at about 6.75% in stage II and 4.5% in stage III, on average, before decelerating to trend growth. More interesting, however, is to examine the diversity in growth between final sales and inventories.

Coming out of a recession, real final sales tend to increase at a 5.8% pace, while inventory growth is about three-fourths of that rate (see Figure 4.18). Demand remains robust as the economy shifts into stage III—the middle stage of the expansion. By stage IV of the business cycle, final sales grow at 2.8%, while inventory growth is 3.3%, on average, which is slightly faster than that sales gain. Initially, businesses allow inventories to build expecting that demand will pick up again. However, that business judgment turns out to be wrong, final sales continue to slow, and inventories then follow the lead of final sales. By the trough in the recession (stage IX), inventory liquidation ceases and sets in motion a turnaround in the economy. A statistical or judgmental tracking of these phases is likely to provide a greater understanding of the business cycle.

Delving beneath the final sales aggregate also could be useful. The consumer sector is one of the most important sectors of the economy and accounts for about two-thirds of real GNP/GDP. Figure 4.19 presents its typical cyclical profile over

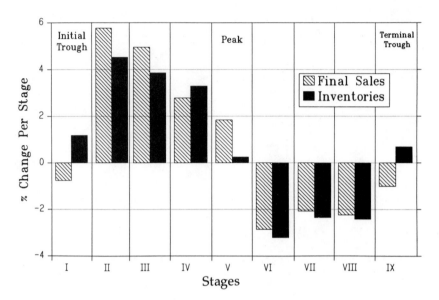

Figure 4.18 Business Cycle Stages—Relationship between Real Final Sales and Real Inventories.

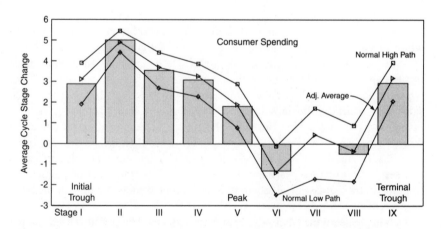

Figure 4.19 U.S. Business Cycle Stages, Average Growth per Stage for Real Consumer Spending, 1948–1990.

the postwar horizon. Consumption is an early mover (and probably a "prime mover") in the business cycle. Coming out of a recession, real consumer spending expands at an average 4.7% pace during stage II of the cycle. By stage III, the pace slows modestly—growing at 4.2%. By stage III of the expansion, however, the pace slips below average, growing at a 2.9% pace (the trend = 3.1%). Consumption turns negative only late into the recession (in stage VII) but turns positive, though at a subpar pace, by the trough of the business cycle.

Another key business cycle indicator is corporate profits. Real aftertax profits surge early in the recovery and begin to deteriorate by the late stages of the expansion, as shown in Figure 4.20. Stock prices are a leading indicator of the business cycle because they tend to anticipate profit performance.

The cyclical behavior or real wages, productivity, and labor's share of national income has been examined in depth over the past half century. Arthur Okun observed: "[I]t is fair to summarize the consensus as finding no detectable significant cyclical pattern in real wages. Meanwhile, the procyclical pattern of productivity movements has been solidly established in dozens of empirical studies. Relative to trend, labor's share of income is highest in slumps."[33] Robert Gordon, who examined the productivity issue further, concluded that there existed an "end-of-expansion" phenomenon whereby "firms tend consistently to hire more workers in the late stages of a business expansion than is justified by the

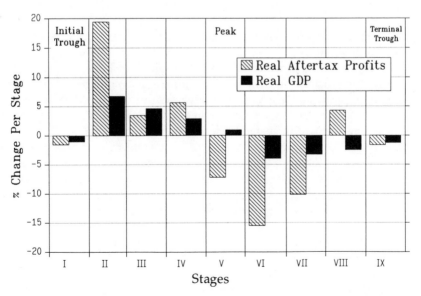

Figure 4.20 Business Cycle Stages, Relationship between Profits and GDP.

level of output."[34] As such, he argued, productivity weakens near the end of an expansion due to an overshooting in hiring needs.

An empirical study by Bernanke and Powell found (1) labor productivity is procyclical by industry and was so during the prewar and postwar periods, (2) productivity is a leading rather than a coincident indicator, and (3) weekly hours and employment are not only procyclical but hours lead growth while employment lags output.[35] The finding that employment is a lagging indicator runs counter to the "conventional wisdom," which classifies employment as being generally coincident with the business cycle. But the historical record seems consistent with the Bernanke and Powell finding; an actual decline in employment often does not show up until sometime after a business cycle peak. The employment diffusion index, however, can be a leading indicator of business/growth cycle peaks. This cyclical nature of employment diffusion provides evidence of Burns' "unseen" cycle, a concept discussed in Chapter 3.

In an excellent article, Ernst Boehm presented a framework to understand the business cycle dynamic.[36] Boehm extended the Burns and Mitchell hypothesis that the cause of a business cycle was determined by the price-cost-profit relationship. Boehm noted that "the price-cost cycle contributes appreciably to the explanation of the amplitude of business cycles as well as their duration. In particular, the empirical evidence shows that a major downswing in the price-cost cycle is generally associated with a classical recession. By contrast, the occasions when a growth slowdown does not lead to a classical recession are generally marked also by a relatively mild downturn in the price-cost cycle."[37] Boehm's empirical work suggested that the price-cost cycle leads business or growth cycles in Australia, Canada, the United Kingdom, and the United States.

Finally, one of the generally accepted facts about business cycles has been challenged in a debate over whether the business cycle upturn and downturn phases are symmetric. We have observed the empirical finding that post-World War II business cycles in the United States have expansion phases that outlive recessions by a ratio of about 4 to 1. This has naturally led to the conclusion that the business cycle is asymmetric. Blatt observed that Burns and Mitchell showed an asymmetry in the cycle duration still remained even after eliminating the long-term trend from business cycle measures.[38] However, empirical work on growth cycles suggests a symmetric cycle exists. The average high-to-low phase of the post-World War II growth cycles between 1948 and 1990, lasted 22 months and the average was identical for the low-to-high phase of the cycle. This empirical fact seems to suggest the existence of a symmetrical trend-adjusted or growth cycle.

Why should we care whether or not the business cycle has symmetry? A trend-adjusted cycle that is symmetric would suggest how long the duration of the current cycle phase might be. As simple as this observation is, the ramifications are important for understanding, econometric modeling, and forecasting the business cycle.

Neftçi sparked the debate in the literature on whether or not the business cycle is characterized by an asymmetric cycle based on duration. Neftçi designed a statistical test of this proposition based on Markov chains. He applied that method to the unemployment rate and concluded there was evidence for the asymmetry proposition; he argued that even adjusting the U.S. unemployment rate for a trend, the conclusion stood.[39] However, other researchers disagreed. Falk replicated the Neftçi results (correcting for an error in the derivation of a formula) and applied the same test to U.S. real GNP, productivity, and investment. Falk concluded that each of those series had a symmetric cycle. Furthermore, Falk extended the results to Canada, France, Italy, the United Kingdom, and West Germany. He concluded that only France and the United Kingdom growth cycles seemed to support an asymmetric cycle.[40]

DeLong and Summers also challenged the Neftçi finding. They examined the issue using a different statistical test. DeLong and Summers posited that if downturns were brief in duration while expansions were extended, that condition implied a negatively skewed frequency distribution of growth rates in output.[41] They calculated a coefficient of shewness (the third moment around the mean divided by the cube of the standard deviation) for real GNP and industrial production in the United States, Japan, Canada, West Germany, the United Kingdom, and France.[42] For U.S. real GNP, DeLong and Summers found little evidence of skewness, although there was some evidence of a slight positive skewness in the prewar period. Positive skewness was contrary to the conventional wisdom implying a rapid upswing and a protracted slowdown in economic activity during the prewar period. They concluded that the trend-adjusted cycle was asymmetric only for Canada and Japan, a different conclusion from that reached by Falk. However, the DeLong and Summers test can be sensitive to the time period examined as shown in Table 4.8.

Sichel refined the asymmetry debate to distinguish amplitude from duration, that is, he tested the claim that business cycle recessions were deeper than rebounds and not just shorter than the expansion phase. Based on his test for amplitude asymmetry, he concluded that U.S. real GNP and industrial production declined more during recessions (per period) than during the subsequent rebound. The unemployment rate also showed, according to Sichel, an asymmetric pattern.[43]

So what can be concluded? It appears that this flurry of research on business cycle symmetry generally is consistent with the conventional business cycle facts. Researchers have confirmed the obvious—the growth cycle usually is symmetric in total duration. On the other hand, the business cycle is characterized by a pronounced decline and, our research suggests, a more pronounced rebound.

Table 4.8   Skewness Coefficients for U.S. Real Gross National Product.

DeLong and Summers			Updated Results	
Period	Skewness	Standard Error	Skewness	Period
1950–1979	−0.33	0.29	−0.05	1947–1990
			−0.98	1949–1983
			+0.09	1950–1959
			−0.22	1960–1969
			+0.02	1970–1979
			−0.85	1980–1989

Sources: J. B. DeLong and L. H. Summers, "Are Business Cycles Symmetrical?" in *The American Business Cycle: Continuity and Change,* Chicago: University of Chicago Press, 1986, p. 171; authors.

Yet, none of this research distinguishes between the cyclical decline and the period when output returned to its *previous peak* and not the next peak in the cycle. Real U.S. GDP, on average, returned to its previous peak following a recession faster than it declined. Additionally, the median rebound in growth was 2.2 times faster than the decline per period (see Table 4.9). This supports an asymmetry in the business cycle amplitude, but it is different from the idea suggested by Sichel and others.[44] More importantly, the delineation of the recovery as the period when the economy reached its low until when it returned to its previous peak leads to two rules of thumb for business cycle forecasting based on real GDP:

1. The milder the recession is cumulatively, then the milder will be the subsequent cumulative rebound, as measured from the business cycle trough to the *return to previous peak.*

2. The business cycle recovery, on average, takes about 80% as long as the preceding recession.

These stylized cycle and trend facts should be kept in mind in the following discussion of individual business or growth cycles during the postwar period, to observe similarities and differences among business cycles.

Transition to a Peacetime Economy: 1946–1948

As the U.S. economy continued to adjust to peacetime activities, the major problem that it faced during the 1946–1948 period was a bout of high inflation. In 1945, inflation—as measured by the Consumer Price Index—rose

Table 4.9 Business Cycle Rebounds (Amplitude and Speed of Business Recoveries based on Real GDP).

U.S. Recessions	Peak to Trough				Trough to Return-to-Previous Peak				
	Decline (Annual Rate)	Number of Qtrs.	Cumulative Decline	Change per Period	Rebound (Annual Rate)	Number of Qtrs.	Cumulative Rebound	Change per Period	Speed of Rebound*
1948–1949	-1.1%	4	-1.1%	-0.3%	15.9%	1	3.8%	3.8%	13.7%
1953–1954	-2.2	4	-2.2	-0.5	4.9	2	2.4	1.2	2.2
1957–1958	-6.5	2	-3.3	-1.7	6.8	3	5.1	1.7	1.0
1960–1961	-1.1	3	-0.8	-0.3	3.4	1	0.8	0.8	3.1
1969–1970	-1.2	3	-0.9	-0.3	5.1	1	1.2	1.2	4.3
1973–1975	-3.3	5	-4.1	-0.8	5.9	3	4.4	1.5	1.8
1980	-9.9	1	-2.6	-2.6	4.6	3	3.4	1.1	0.4
1981–1982	-2.8	4	-2.8	-0.7	4.7	3	3.5	1.2	1.6
1990–1991	-2.9	3	-2.2	-0.7	1.9	6	2.9	0.5	0.7
Average 1948–1991	-3.4	3.2	-2.2	-0.9	5.9	2.6	3.1	1.4	3.2
Median 1948–1991	-2.8	3	-2.2	-0.7	4.9		3.4	1.2	2.2

* The "speed of rebound" statistic is calculated as the per period rebound in real GDP (on its specific cycle) to the previous peak divided by the per period contraction in real GDP.

Table 4.9 (Continued)

Business Cycle Expansions (Amplitude and Speed of Business Expansions based on Real GDP).

U.S. Expansions	Trough to Next Peak				Return-to-Previous Peak to Next Peak				Speed of Change*
	Gain (Annual Rate)	Number of Qtrs.	Cumulative Increase	Change per Period	Gain (Annual Rate)	Number of Qtrs.	Cumulative Gain	Change per Period	
1949–1953	7.8%	14	30.2%	2.2%	7.2%	13	25.5%	2.0%	0.52
1954–1957	3.4	13	11.6	0.9	3.2	11	9.0	0.8	0.68
1958–1960	5.1	8	10.4	1.3	4.1	5	5.1	1.0	0.60
1961–1969	4.5	35	47.1	1.3	4.5	34	45.9	1.3	1.62
1970–1973	4.1	14	15.0	1.1	4.0	13	13.6	1.0	0.84
1975–1980	4.0	20	21.5	1.1	3.6	17	16.3	1.0	0.66
1980–1981	2.8	5	3.5	0.7	0.2	2	0.1	0.1	0.05
1982–1990	3.5	31	30.6	1.0	3.4	28	26.1	0.9	0.80
Average 1948–1991	4.4	17.5	21.2	1.2	3.8	15.4	17.7	1.0	0.72
Median 1948–1991	4.3		18.3	1.1	3.8		15.0	1.0	

* The "speed of change" statistic is calculated as the per period increase in real GDP (on its specific cycle basis) from when it "returned to previous peak" divided by cumulative rebound.

2.2% (on a December-to-December basis), though this was artificially restrained due to wartime price controls. In 1946, however, inflation surged 18.1% (from December to December), with a huge 31.3% increase in food prices. The inflation picture was still troublesome in 1947 as the CPI rose 8.8% (from December to December). By 1948, consumer inflation moderated to a 3% gain. Despite this surge in inflation, interest rates were not directly affected; the link was exceedingly weak due to the government's desire to ease the transition. The 3-month Treasury bill rate (on a discount basis) rose from 0.375% in 1946 to 0.594% in 1947 and 1.040% in 1948. Although interest rates did move higher, short-term interest rates did not reflect the diminishing value of the dollar due to higher inflation. Corporate bond yields (Moody's Aaa) averaged 2.53% in 1946; they notched up to 2.61% in 1947 and 2.82% in 1948. The Federal Reserve intentionally made credit available.

In addition to the strong wage and price pressures because of the removal of controls, inflation was exacerbated due to adverse weather in 1947 that resulted in a poor corn harvest and high prices. Moreover, that poor harvest had a much larger *real* impact on the economy in the 1940s than would be true today. The civilian population living on farms accounted for about 17% of the population in the late 1940s, whereas by the late 1980s, it accounted for about 2% of the population.

Real GNP growth remained anemic until the second quarter of 1947 (as shown in Figure 4.21). While this was to be expected, the adjustment process extended over a 2-year period before steady and healthy growth resumed.

The 1948 Recession: An Export Boom-Bust Cycle

The U.S. economy peaked in November 1948, marking the onset of the first truly postwar recession. Three factors were responsible: (1) slower federal government spending, (2) a boom-bust cycle in exports, and (3) an inventory correction.

While many observers of this period considered the 1948 recession an "inventory cycle," the fact is that the inventory correction was not the principal cause of this recession but a contributing factor. Moreover, an inventory correction occurred in 1947—a year before the recession. In 1947, a swing in real inventories lowered economic growth by 2.2 percentage points accounting for just about the entire decline in real GDP. In 1948, inventory growth resumed and added 1.1% to growth.

The principal cause of the 1948 recession was a dramatic boom-bust cycle in exports. Real exports surged by 100% in 1946 and 18.6% in 1947, which was followed by a bust. In 1948, real exports declined 23.3%. The 1947 bulge in exports added 1.2 percentage points to real GDP alone but lowered growth by 1.1 percentage points in the subsequent year. On the other hand, domestic demand, as measured by real gross domestic purchases, rose a strong 6% in 1948.

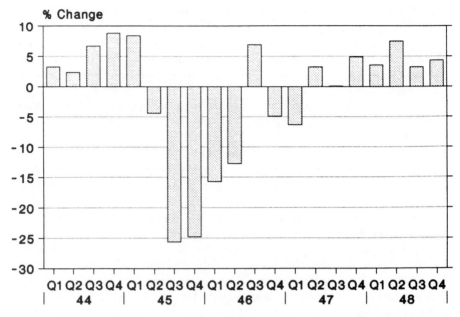

Figure 4.21 Real GNP Growth (Quarterly Growth at Annual Rates). (*Source:* National Bureau of Economic Research.)

This boom-bust export cycle was triggered by a surge in European demand as they recovered from war (and pent-up demand was unleashed) and by a harsh European winter in 1947. This European demand for U.S. goods subsequently vanished when funds to pay for foreign goods dried up. The surge in U.S. export demand was financed in part by U.S. government loans to Europe and by gold shipments.

In 1947, strong foreign demand "reversed the easing tendencies that were beginning to appear in some lines of business" in the United States.[45] Foreigners "drew on their dollar resources so rapidly that they soon were all but exhausted."[46] As a result, foreign demand took a nosedive despite the attempt by Congress to provide additional interim foreign aid. That action only temporarily boosted real export growth. Although export growth turned positive in early 1949, the foreign aid was too little and too late to save the U.S. economy from a recession. By that time, business already realized that the strong foreign demand present in 1947 had evaporated and with it their need to build or maintain inventories for a high growth environment. A sharp slowing in the pace of federal government purchases further contributed to the 1948 recession.

The slowdown in final demand was exacerbated by an inventory correction. The acceleration of inventory expansion through 1948 reached a pace of around

5% by midyear. Inventory growth was far in excess of final demand, which was slowing. As a result, business first slowed the pace of inventory expansion and by the second quarter of 1949 they were reducing their inventory.

Another factor weighing heavy on the economy was the effect of lingering high inflation. As noted earlier, consumer inflation rose 8.8% in 1947 (on a December-to-December basis) but did moderate to a 3% pace in 1948. On a monthly basis, consumer inflation was growing at a pace of more than 11% in early 1948. These relatively high inflation rates tempered consumer spending to some degree.[47] In 1947, consumer spending grew 1.8%, its slowest pace since 1942—a year when inflation was also a problem—and it improved modestly in 1948 when inflation averaged 2.3%. By July 1949, consumer prices declined sharply—down about 3%.

Two conflicting policy actions were taken in 1948. In August, Congress responded to the high inflation by granting the Federal Reserve temporary authorization to increase reserve requirements and control consumer credit. In September 1948, the Federal Reserve implemented a policy to regulate the size of the down payment and maturities of installment credit. These credit regulations were eased in March 1949 and were eliminated at the end of June. But countering this move to restrict credit expansion, Congress passed a tax cut in 1948 (over President Truman's veto). This tax cut turned out to be a "good" fiscal policy for 1949 since the stimulative effect of the cut helped to shorten the 1948–1949 contraction and limited the cumulative real GDP decline to 1.1%—the third mildest contraction during the 1947–1992 period. The jobless rate rose to nearly 8% by the end of the recession, substantially higher than the prerecession low of less than 4%.

The trough of the recession was in October 1949. On balance, this recession was relatively mild and lasted 11 months—close to the postwar average. The mild nature of this recession was helped by tax policy, lower inflation, and the first major postwar automotive restyling by the big three auto companies,[48] which caused a surge in new car sales.

The 1951 Slowdown: Higher Taxes, Inflation, and a Steel Strike

The U.S. economy continued to expand into 1950. By midyear, however, the economy faced an economic crisis. North Korean military forces invaded South Korea on June 25, 1950. This triggered a surge in second- and third-quarter consumption as consumers feared shortages and a return to wartime rationing. Consumption also was boosted by a payment in early 1950 of over $2 billion of National Service Life Insurance dividends to veterans. By the third quarter of 1950, real consumer spending was growing at a rapid 10.4% pace, while overall real GDP growth was expanding at a sizzling 13% pace during the second half of the year. President Truman recommended a tax increase in July 1950 to dampen demand and that proposal was swiftly approved by September. Taxes were raised by $5 billion. A second revenue bill, the Excess Profits Tax Act, was approved in January 1951, but its provisions were made retroactive to July 1, 1950. The surge in demand catapulted consumer prices over 12% by early 1951. To counter inflation, Congress passed the Defense Production Act on September 8, 1950, giving the president the power to impose general wage and price controls. The president imposed those controls on January 26, 1951. But by that time, the buying binge and inflation bulge had subsided. The pace of real consumption slowed by the fourth quarter of 1950 to about 4%. Inventory investment, however, picked up the slack. Korean war related federal government spending also accelerated by year-end 1950. Responding to the need for defense goods, industrial production surged by mid-1950 despite an auto strike against Chrysler that began in January. Increasing interest rates (which were low by current standards) also contributed to the slowing of business activity. As shown in Figure 4.22, commercial paper rates rose throughout 1951.

This period also saw a new arrangement between the Federal Reserve and the Treasury. The conflict between the Fed and the Treasury climaxed in August 1950 when the Federal Reserve raised the discount rate to quell inflation while being forced to buy nearly $8 billion of government debt because the markets were unwilling to purchase the debt that was perceived to be at too low an interest rate. These two actions were contradictory and possibly contributed to a growth cycle slowdown instead of a recession. The Federal Reserve, under Chairman McCabe, decided it could no longer have monetary policy subordinate to debt management. The friction came to a head on March 4, 1951, when

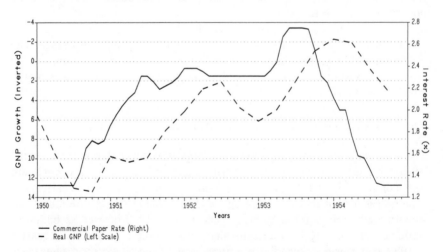

Figure 4.22   Real GNP Growth and 6-Month Commercial Paper Rates. (Solid line (—) Represents Interest Rate (right scale); Dashed Line (- - -) Represents Real GNP % (left scale, inv.).)

the Federal Reserve and the Treasury issued an "accord" whereby the Federal Reserve gained independence and would minimize its role in the monetization of government debt.

With the end of the forward buying, a growth cycle peak occurred in March 1951 and that slowdown continued until July 1952. The slowdown was accentuated by a steel strike in the summer of 1952. A nationwide steel strike involving 560,000 workers began on April 29, 1952, and lasted 59 days. The auto industry was forced to curtail production due to steel shortages, and car sales declined. Following the steel strike, the pace of employment and industrial production again accelerated, in part as industry rebuilt their steel inventories and car sales rebounded in the fourth quarter of 1952.

The 1953–1954 Recession: A Defense-Less Economy and Slower Consumer Spending

The Korean War armistice was signed on July 27, 1953, and that month also marked a peak in U.S. economic activity; the subsequent recession extended through May 1954. Based on cyclical depth and duration, the 1953 recession was "average." The reference cycle decline lasted 10 months, while the cumulative decline in real GDP was 2.2%, slightly milder than the median decline during postwar recessions. The principal catalyst for the contraction was an unwinding of the defense buildup. As shown in Figure 4.23, defense spend-

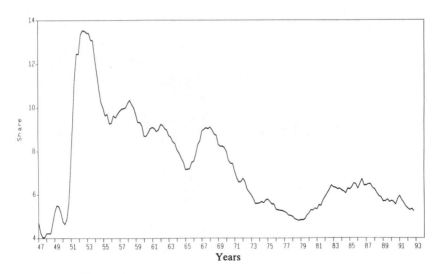

Figure 4.23   Defense Share of Gross Domestic Product.

ing as a share of GDP stood around 13% during the Korean War and dropped sharply after the war ended. That decline also meant that businesses needed less inventories; the pace of inventories followed defense spending downward. The second factor in the recession was a slowdown in consumer spending. Hickman observed that consumer spending played an active role in the contraction and subsequent rebound: "Developments in the consumer sector cannot be viewed merely as passive responses to autonomous changes in government expenditures or taxes."[49] A real consumer spending slowdown preceded the 1953 recession and that slowdown was widespread across all types of goods—durables, nondurables, and services (see Figures 4.24–4.26). It is difficult to point to one overriding reason for that consumer behavior. The slowdown in consumer spending appeared to be a natural reaction to the healthy increase in consumption prior to 1953.[50] The net result, however, was that the slowing accentuated the recessionary forces.

The 1953–1954 recession was marked by a "v"-shaped real GNP/GDP cycle. The unemployment rate, a lagging indicator of the business cycle, rose to a high of about 6% by late 1954. The early turnaround in the pace of consumer spending was a trigger for the recovery. Additionally, a pickup in export activity contributed to the end of the contraction. Both fiscal and monetary policies were supportive. In March 1954, the Excise Tax Reduction Act was enacted, which cut taxes by $1.0 billion. This legislation removed the Korean War excise tax. In August 1954, a second tax bill became law. That bill—the Internal Revenue Code of 1954—cut taxes by $1.4 billion and completely overhauled the Internal

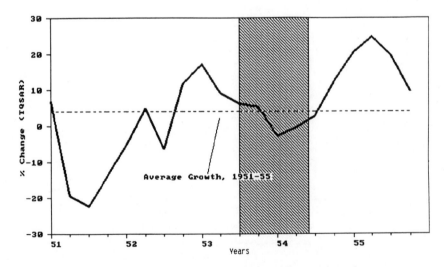

Figure 4.24 Consumer Durable Goods Expenditures.

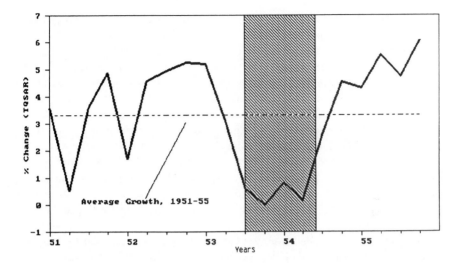

Figure 4.25   Consumer Nondurable Goods Expenditures.

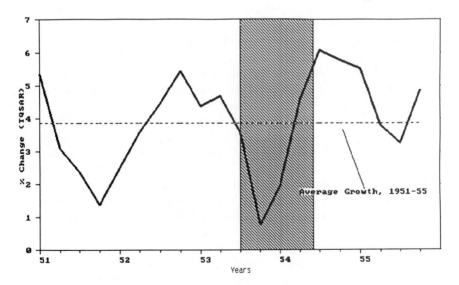

Figure 4.26   Consumer Service Expenditures.

Revenue Code of 1939. Personal taxes were cut by about $3 billion, but they were partially offset by higher contributions to Social Security insurance.

Monetary policy serendipitiously turned easy at the onset of the recession. In early 1953, the Federal Reserve was concerned about a serious inflation threat, especially from hefty increases in the price of consumer services, and a surge in business loan demand that had occurred late in the prior year. The Fed gradually tightened the supply of credit. This policy was upset in May, however, as the Treasury offered $1.2 billion of long-term government bonds at 3.25%—much higher than the prevailing rate. The Federal Reserve reversed its leaning toward a tighter policy in May; the Fed felt that the Treasury debt issue put too much upward pressure on interest rates. The timing of the change in monetary policy was fortuitous, since it turned out to be coincident with the peak in business activity. Consequently, the swift policy shift lessened the impact of the recession.

The economy rebounded from the 1954 recession and grew robustly in 1955 with back-to-back 6% real GDP growth (based on 2-quarter smoothed growth rates) through the first two quarters of 1955. Automotive sales were again a major catalyst for the rebound. A 36-month installment auto loan contract was introduced for the first time in 1955, and the industry's big three all introduced major model style changes—the first since 1949. Strong demand for cars and surging gains in industrial production, which rose to nearly 20% by early 1955 triggered a pickup in producer prices. The Federal Reserve responded by slowing the pace of money growth in early 1955, and interest rates rose. Residential investment, which had already turned up before the end of the 1954 recession, was dealt a blow by two governmental agencies. In April 1955, the Federal Housing Administration (FHA) and the Veterans Administration (VA) prohibited closing costs from being underwritten by their loans, and in July, the FHA and VA raised the minimum down-payment requirement. Housing investment decelerated by the third quarter of 1955 and contracted by the fourth quarter.

On the political front, President Eisenhower had a heart attack in September 1955 and an operation for ileitis in June 1956. The political background did not seem to have much direct impact on economic activity or consumer confidence.

Real GDP growth decelerated by 1956 and skidded to a meager 1% by the third quarter of 1956. The third quarter sluggishness was accentuated by a nationwide steel strike involving 500,000 workers that began on July 1 and lasted 36 days. In June 1956, Congress enacted the Federal Aid Highway Act of 1956, which increased excise taxes on gasoline and other motor fuels by $2.5 billion. That legislation earmarked those excise taxes for the Highway Trust Fund to finance construction of a nationwide highway system.

Several forces helped the economy in late 1956. Industrial production rebounded sharply following the steel strike and accelerated car production for the new model year. Exports in 1956 were stronger and steadier than during 1955 running at a high double-digit pace. Interest rates dipped in mid-1956, which further supported economic growth, but soon they resumed their upward trek through late 1957.

Aftertax profits, which had been increasing at hefty 20% to 40% per quarter (at an annual rate) between the end of the recession and the end of 1955, began to weaken substantially in 1956. By the third quarter, aftertax profits declined by nearly 8% (TQSAR) but recovered slightly in the subsequent two quarters. By the second quarter of 1957, however, a profit recession was in full force.

The 1957–1958 Recession: Higher Interest Rates and Lower Investment

The economy entered its second recession of the 1950s in August 1957; this contraction was characterized by its relative short duration, which was 8 months, but its relatively sharp decline. Real GDP cumulatively declined by 3.3%. Higher interest rates, a response to rising inflation, were a principal catalyst for the slowdown in nonresidential investment that preceded the 1957 recession. In addition to that factor, federal government spending and exports were slowing from the beginning of 1957. These factors coalesced and produced a recession by midyear. The Federal Reserve banks raised the discount rates from 3% to 3.5% in August 1957 and kept a tight posture to monetary policy until November, when the discount rate was cut to 3%. The discount rate was again cut in January 1958, and this was followed by still further easing moves that included a reduction in the reserve requirements that banks must hold and a cut in the discount rate to 1.75% by April 1958. The 3-month Treasury bill rate fell to around 1% (on a discount basis) by the end of the recession from about 3.5% in October 1957. The Federal Reserve easing of monetary policy triggered a rebound in economic activity.

The 1960–1961 Recession: A Steel Strike and a Matter of Balance

The U.S. economy entered its first recession of the 1960s in April 1960 but the precipitants of that contraction were set in motion before that time. The federal government's intent on balancing the budget resulted in declining federal government expenditures throughout 1959.[51] Adding to the woes of the economy were a series of increases in Social Security taxes in 1959 and 1960, a hike in the gasoline excise tax in 1959, and a hike in the excise tax rate for tires, tubes, and heavy trucks. In 1961, the unemployment insurance tax was raised from 3% to 3.1%. In addition to the changes in taxes, a major steel strike on July 15, 1959, further weakened the economy. The steel strike involved 519,000 workers and lasted 116 days; an agreement was reached on January 5, 1960. But by then, the contractionary forces already were evident. Nonetheless, the cumulative decline in real GDP during the 1960–1961 recession was a modest 1% making this recession the mildest of the postwar period through 1992.

One reason it was mild was that interest rates were already declining at the onset of the recession. The 10-year government bond yield, which moved up from its low of under 3% at the end of the 1957–1958 recession to 4.7% by the beginning of 1960, reversed course in the beginning of 1960. The Federal Reserve cut the discount rate from 4% to 3.5% in June 1960 and by September, they cut it to 3%. As a result, the interest rate decline helped to soften the effect of the recession.

The 1962 Slowdown: A Brief Pause

Following the 1960 recession, the economy continued to grow until 1969. Growth, however, was delineated by periods of acceleration and deceleration. The period beginning in May 1962 and extending until October 1964 marked a slowdown phase in the economy, or a growth recession, characterized by two growth rate cycles in real final sales. The first slowdown in real final sales lasted between the second quarter of 1962 and the first quarter of 1963. Final sales slowed from about 5.5% to about 3%. A second final sales cycle began at that point and the pace of real final sales accelerated to 7% by the first quarter of 1964, then slowed to about 3.5% by the end of 1964. In part due to a concern about the slowdown in the economy, Congress enacted the Revenue Act of 1962 on October 16 of that year. This law provided investment tax credits to businesses for the purchases of equipment. Further stimulative fiscal policy measures came from the Revenue Act of 1964 (enacted February 26, 1964); this law lowered individual and corporate tax rates. On the inflation front, concern about wage and price behavior led the Kennedy Administration in January 1962 to set out *responsible guideposts* for wage and price increases. Whether this policy was successful or not was questionable since the guidelines were ignored in most negotiations. Nonetheless, consumer prices were moderate during the period, generally running about 1% to 1.5% between 1962 and 1964 while wages, as measured by average weekly earnings, grew by 4% in 1962, 3% in 1963 and 3.2% in 1964. In perspective, the 1962 slowdown was very modest and without much of the character of other slowdowns such as in 1951, 1966, or 1984.

The 1966–1967 Growth Recession: Credit Crunch Time

The 1961 business cycle expansion faced its second test of survival in 1966. Several factors prompted a credit crunch between 1965 and 1966 that culminated in mid-1966: (1) a sharp increase in government long-term borrowing, as a result of spending needs to fund the Vietnam War (U.S. combat troops were sent into Vietnam in July 1965), (2) an economy growing near full employment, and (3) tighter monetary policy.

Fiscal policy was stimulative during this period with the Excise Tax Reduction Act of 1965 (enacted June 21, 1965) that cut excise tax rates on automobiles and air conditioners. But tax policy turned more restrictive later as the Tax Adjustment Act of 1966 (enacted March 15, 1966) and the Investment Credit Suspension Act of 1966 (effective October 10, 1966) were passed into law. However, the investment tax credit was restored on June 13, 1967 and made retroactive to March 9, 1967.

With the economy near full-employment and inflationary pressures building, the Federal Reserve raised the discount rate from 4% to 4.5% on December 3, 1965. Short-term interest rates moved up by about 200 basis points between 1964 and 1966; the prime rate rose from 4.5% to 5% effective December 6, 1965, notched up to 5.5% on March 10, 1966, up to 5.75 percent on June 19, 1966, and peaked at 6% on August 16, 1966. The pace of the money supply (M2) slowed dramatically in 1966, while real M2 was essentially flat during the year. The short-term corporate debt ratio to total debt increased during 1965 and 1966 and nonfinancial corporate liquidity fell as corporate profits declined—classic ingredients of a credit crunch.

Although the Federal Reserve held the discount rate constant for the remainder of the growth cycle, monetary policy continued to lean against the wind. The Federal Reserve raised the interest rate ceilings that banks could pay on time deposits by one percentage point in an attempt to calm the investment spending boom.[52] This monetary policy tool resulted in an uneven impact on various sectors of the economy; savings and loans experienced fund withdrawals—the phenomenon known as disintermediation—and the housing industry was impacted sharply. To alleviate some of these sector disruptions, Congress passed the Interest Rate Adjustment Act of 1966 in September, which authorized the Federal Reserve to set differential interest rate ceilings by the size of the deposit. Acting under this new legislation, the Federal Reserve Board immediately cut the maximum rate on time deposits of less than $100,000 from 5.5% to 5%, while holding the large CD rate at 5.5%.

Inflation rose from the 1% to 2% range in 1965 to the 3% to 4% range during 1966. Consumer inflation peaked in September 1966 at 3.9%, measured as a 6-month smoothed annualized rate (SMSAR). The inflationary spiral unwound until May 1967 when it reached its low at 2.1%. That deceleration in inflation occurred on lessened demand pressures; real GDP growth decelerated from 8% in the first quarter of 1966 to 2.5% in the first half of 1967.

The 1966 growth recession lasted from June 1966 to October 1967 (16 months), shorter than the 29-month slowdown that began in 1962 but more pronounced than its immediate predecessor. On balance, the 1966 growth recession was an investment-led slowdown in economic activity whose growth was quickly restored by the reinstatement of the 7% investment tax credit, the end of an auto strike that lasted from September 14 through October 22, 1967, and declining interest rates. The Federal Reserve cut the discount rate on April 7, 1967, from 4.5% to 4%.

The 1969 Recession: Fiscal Policy and Labor Unrest in the Auto Industry

By 1967, unchecked government spending associated with the Vietnam War and the Great Society programs resulted in higher inflation and a record foreign trade deficit (at least up until that time). After the British devalued their currency, the Federal Reserve moved to tighten credit to dampen domestic inflation and to strengthen the dollar. In November 1967, the Fed raised the discount rate to 4.5% and increased demand deposit reserve requirements by 0.5%. The Federal Reserve again raised the discount rate in March 1968 to 5% and notched it up to 5.5% in April. Also in 1968, Congress passed the Revenue and Expenditure Control Act (enacted June 28, 1968). That tax measure imposed a 10% personal and corporate income tax surcharge.[53] Individual withholding taxes were increased effective on July 1, 1968 but the tax was retroactive to April 1, 1968. Although this surcharge was set to expire on June 30, 1969, it was later extended until the end of 1969. In addition to more restrictive fiscal policy, monetary policy was restrictive during 1969, and the Fed again raised the discount rate to 6% on April 4, 1969, due to a concern about inflation. Indeed, in 1969, the CPI posted a hefty 6.2% increase, year-end to year-end.

Real GDP growth slowed gradually but consistently over the early stage of the 1969 recession but in 1970, a 2-month auto industry strike tipped the economy deeper into recession. This strike against General Motors lasted from September 14 through November 11, 1970. The recession officially began in December 1969 and lasted until November 1970, which was an *average* 11 months in duration but was milder than most postwar recessions.

Adding to the woes of the economy in 1970 was a major bankruptcy. On June 21, 1970, Penn Central Railroad—the nation's largest railroad after the merger of the Pennsylvania Railroad and the New York Central—declared bankruptcy and defaulted on $82 million of its commercial paper. Arthur Burns, the Chairman of the Federal Reserve, worried that "a wave of fear would pass through the financial community, engulf other issuers of commercial paper, and cast doubt on a wide range of other securities."[54] To head off this potentially serious financial problem, the Federal Reserve, acting in a rapid sequence, cut the discount rate from 6% to 5.75% on November 13, then notched it lower to 5.5% on December 4, 5.25% on January 8, 1971, 5% on January 22, and 4.75% on February

19. The recovery that ensued in 1971 was modest; after an initial spurt in real GDP growth of about 4% (TQSAR) in the first quarter of 1971, real growth moderated through the year. Exports remained relatively flat in the early stages of the recovery, state and local government spending slowed, while structures and producers' durable equipment spending were slow to recover. Even consumption growth was relatively modest in the first year of recovery. The 10-year government note yield, which declined from a peak of just under 8% during the 1969 recession to about 5.75% by early 1971, backed up to about 6.75% by mid-1971 and then reversed direction again to just under 6% by year-end. Eventually, lower interest rates and inflation ignited a substantial pickup in economic activity in 1972 but that also followed a major fiscal policy shift at mid-year.

On August 13–15, 1971, President Nixon held a top-level meeting with 16 of his economic advisors at Camp David. The policy that came from that meeting was to have a major impact on the economic landscape for years to come. The President and his advisors decided to implement wage and price controls—the first time such a policy had been implemented since 1951. On Sunday evening, August 15, 1971, President Nixon, acting under the Economic Stabilization Act of 1970, announced to the public that he was instituting a system of wage and price controls.[55] To alleviate selling pressure on the dollar, President Nixon further announced that the United States was abandoning dollar-gold convertibility and no longer would buy gold at $35 per ounce to support the U.S. greenback. Nixon supported the Smithsonian agreement, which pegged the dollar to the yen and deutsche mark and readjusted the price of gold. This was the first step toward floating exchange rates. Additionally, the program imposed a 10% surcharge on imports. The program was initially well received by the public. On the Monday following the President's announcement, the stock market reflected the euphoria that the public shared as well. The Dow Jones Industrial Average rose 32.9 points on August 16, the biggest one-day point increase up until that time.[56]

The wage and price control program evolved over time and ultimately consisted of four phases, which turned out to be relatively ineffective against the rapid commodity-based inflation from food and energy price shocks. In the months immediately prior to the controls, consumer price inflation was running at an average of 4.2% (SMSAR) for the first 8 months of 1971; the price and wage program, at best, lowered the pace to 3.3% during phase II of the program (see Table 4.10).

In December, the Revenue Act of 1971 was enacted into law. That law lowered taxes by $8 billion by (1) implementing, 1 year ahead of schedule, increases in personal exemptions and standard federal income tax deductions, (2) repealing excise taxes on automobiles (retroactive to August 15, 1971) and small trucks and buses (retroactive to September 22, 1971), and (3) reinstating a 7% investment tax credit.

Table 4.10 Wage and Price Control Sequences, 1971–1974.

Stage	Period	Span (months)	Consumer Price Indexes, Percentage Change**			
			Total CPI	Food	Energy	Total Less Food & Energy
Precontrols	Aug. 1970 – July 1971	12	4.7	2.9	3.7	5.5
Freeze	Aug. 15, 1971 – Nov. 1971	3	3.6	3.5	4.7	3.2
Phase II	Nov. 1971 – Jan. 1973	13	3.3	4.7	3.0	2.9
Phase III	Jan. 1973 – June 1973	5	6.1	14.6	7.1	3.2
Second Freeze	June 13, 1973 – Aug. 1973	2	7.4	19.9	7.9	3.5
Phase IV	Aug. 1973 – Apr. 30, 1974*	9	9.8	18.1	26.2	5.6
Postcontrols	May 1974 – Apr. 1975	12	11.2	10.2	19.2	10.9

* Authorization for wage and price controls under the Economic Stabilization Act expired.
** Average 6–month smoothed growth rates.

The 1973–1975 Recession: Oil and Commodity Prices Soar and Price Controls Are Removed

The economic expansion remained in place until 1973. By March 1973, fixed exchange rates were abandoned and the dollar was allowed to float ("managed float"). The dollar depreciated, and on November 12, 1973, central bankers met in Basel and terminated the convertibility of gold for dollars and allowed the dollar to freely float. In that same year, a burst of food and energy inflation was the ultimate catalyst for a major disruption in the economy. In 1973, food prices rose 20.3% on a December-to-December basis and only moderated to a still hefty 12% in 1974. On top of that, oil prices exploded.

In October 1973, the Organization of Petroleum Exporting Countries (OPEC)—which controlled more than 80 percent of the world's oil exports—raised the price of a barrel of oil within 2 months from $6 to $23. The result was a surge in U.S. inflation and long lines at gas stations, as motorists attempted to beat the "no gasoline today" signs. Energy prices rose 17% on a December-to-December basis, in 1973 and ballooned by 21.6% in 1974 and 11.4% in 1975. Zarnowitz and Moore[57] described the 1973–1975 recession: "[P]robably more than in most [prior] business cycles . . . the 1973–1974 slowdown-and-recession sequence was influenced by cost increases affecting food, fuel, and raw materials, and by supply restrictions, which tend to produce rising prices along with falling output."[58]

Following the food and energy price explosions of the early 1970s, consumer buying patterns shifted. A "buy-in-advance" of higher inflation mentality became more widespread among consumers for big-ticket items such as cars, houses, and household durable goods. According to University of Michigan surveys, about 45% of consumers held the buy-in-advance view by 1978, which was up substantially from about 30% during the 1972–1973 commodity price boom period.

As shortages developed, businesses began to place multiple orders for goods they needed for production. As a result, new orders surged—even after the recession occurred. This traditional leading indicator peaked about midway through the 1973–1975 recession. Businesses were fooled by this ephemeral demand, and when the activity began to slow more sharply in the manufacturing sector in late 1974, the ordering bubble was burst; in turn, the inventory cycle amplified the contraction. Real inventory spending remained strong through 1974, running between 4% and 6% (TQSAR) throughout the year. The inventory liquidation did not occur until early 1975.

The wage and price control program was terminated on April 30, 1974, and over the subsequent year, the CPI grew by slightly more than 11%. As such, long-term interest rates moved in a countercyclical pattern—rising during the recession—while short-term rates remained high halfway through the 1973–1975 recession.

In late 1974, two banks collapsed: the U.S. National in San Diego and the Franklin National in New York. Franklin National Bank, the twentieth largest U.S. bank, failed on October 8, 1974; it was the largest bank failure up until that time. The failure occurred at the same time as two international bank failures—the Herstatt in Germany and the Israel-British Bank in Israel and London. The international scope of the failures raised concern about disruptions in the foreign exchange market, loan syndication, and the interbank market.

Moreover, during the 1974–1975 recession, Federal Reserve Board Chairman Arthur Burns faced a new challenge—the collapse of real estate investment trusts (REITs). The First Mortgage Real Estate Investment Trust was about to go bankrupt and potentially cause a major ripple effect on that rapidly growing and increasingly troubled (due to the recession) segment of investment market. Burns and the Fed put together a 100-bank consortium to provide a $400 million revolving credit line to the First Mortgage Real Estate Investment Trust. But this turned out to be just the tip of the iceberg. Other REITs began to file for bankruptcy. The REIT market soon came tumbling down, and banks took major losses. The real estate market did not improve until late 1975.

On balance, the 1973–1975 recession was the most severe downturn in the postwar period, with real GDP contracting, cumulatively, by 4.1%. Its duration of 16 months was one of the longest contractions in the postwar period. The ensuing recovery was strong but punctuated by a *pause* in mid-1976.[59]

In that same year—1976, the role of the traditional banking relationship began to change. Exxon bypassed its banks and directly sold $54.9 million of pollution-control bonds. Although there was a long period before more direct offerings occurred, this marked a turning point in the banking industry. In 1982, Exxon again went to the market directly with a $500 million taxable bond offering. Today, major corporations routinely bypass the investment banker and go directly to the market themselves weakening the relationship of the bank credit and business activity.

The 1980 Recession: Oil Price Explosion and Credit Controls

Fiscal policy began to shift toward more restraint in 1978 but that was short lived. The Revenue Act of 1978, which was enacted into law in November 1978, reduced taxes on individuals and businesses by about $21 billion. This gave a new lift to the economy, despite the impact of the second oil price shock, which hit the world economies in late 1978 and acted as a "tax hike." The surge in world oil prices was tied to the overthrow of the Shah of Iran and the shutting off of Iranian oil exports to the United States, which resulted in more than a doubling of oil prices. Crude oil prices rose from $13 per barrel to $34 per barrel, which again caused major disruptions to the U.S. economy. Consumer energy prices bulged 37.5% in 1979 (on a December-to-December basis), 18% in 1980, and 11.9% in 1981. On April 2, 1980, the Crude Oil Windfall Profits Tax Act of 1980 was enacted, which was expected to raise $13 billion from the windfall price hike to domestic producers of crude oil.

In addition to the oil price surge, a worldwide crop shortage in 1978 caused food prices to rise rapidly. Food prices rose 11.8% in 1978 based on the December-to-December growth in the CPI for food, and the double-digit pace continued for two more years. Food prices rose 10.2% in 1979 and 1980. As a result of these commodity price shocks from food and energy, which feedback into the nonfood, nonenergy areas, overall inflation soared 11.3% in 1979, 12.2% in 1980, and 9.5% in 1981.

On October 6, 1979, Federal Reserve Chairman Paul Volcker implemented a new operating procedure for monetary policy that shifted the focus away from controlling the federal funds rate to controlling bank reserves. The Federal Reserve described this change as a "watershed event."[60] The discount rate also was raised from 11% to 12% and increased the marginal reserve requirement. Federal Reserve Chairman Paul Volcker described these actions as a sign of the Fed's resolve not to finance an accelerating inflation rate.

But inflation did not abate and the Carter administration, nudged by George Meany, the president of the AFL-CIO, began seriously to consider the imposition of credit controls to rein in the growth of credit and inflation.[61] The Federal Reserve raised the discount rate from 12% to 13% on February 15, 1980. Market speculation continued about the probable imposition of credit controls, and on March 14, 1980, President Carter, acting under the Credit Control Act of 1969 (Public Law 91-151), issued Executive Order 12201 to invoke selective credit controls as a means ultimately to restrain inflation. With that order, the President authorized the Federal Reserve to implement credit controls.

The Federal Reserve then issued its Credit Restraint Program (CRP), which was a combination of provisions available to the central bank under the Credit Control Act and its own charter. The CRP imposed six provisions on the banking industry: (1) voluntary credit restraint to limit loan growth, (2) a 15% deposit requirement on certain types of consumer loans, (3) a 2 percentage point increase in the marginal reserve requirement to 12% on managed liabilities, (4) the imposition of a 10% deposit requirement on nonmember banks of the Federal Reserve, (5) the imposition of a 15% deposit requirement on money market mutual funds, and (6) a 3 percentage point surcharge on discount window borrowing for banks with at least $500 million of deposits. The program's objective was to raise the cost of funds for banks thereby slowing bank credit growth.

The banks immediately reacted by raising the prime lending rate by 50 basis points to 19%, the third increase in that rate in four business days. At the same time, evidence was building that the economy was weakening sharply. Schreft observed: "[Although] consumer credit controls were largely symbolic and without [regulatory] teeth . . . they induced consumers to alter their buying behavior."[62]

In the commodity arena, a silver crisis was brewing that would test the CRP. The Hunt brothers—Nelson and William—and an institution controlled by the Hunt family and various Arab investors—the International Metals Investment Company (IMIC)—had taken big positions in the silver market. Between October 1979 and January 1980, the Hunts began to take delivery of silver as their futures contract holdings matured. By January 1980, they increased their holdings in silver to about 120 million ounces with huge futures holdings still outstanding. On January 17, 1980, the price of silver hit about $50 per ounce before the bull market for that commodity evaporated. By the end of January, silver prices fell to about $34 and the decline escalated between March 10 and March 27, when the silver price tumbled from $29.75 to $10.80 per ounce. The rapid decline in prices caused margin calls on the Hunt's future contract positions.

On March 13, 1980, IMIC, the Hunt-controlled company, advised Merrill Lynch that it was unable to meet a $45 million margin call on its silver position. Four days later, the Hunt brothers similarly advised Bache, the broker having the largest exposure to the Hunt silver holdings, that they were unable to meet a $44 million margin call. Although IMIC and the Hunts provided silver bullion to the brokerages in lieu of the money to cover the margin calls, this caused Bache and Merrill Lynch to draw on their bank credit to meet exchange requirements. The Federal Reserve allowed those brokerages to draw on those credit lines even though the Federal Reserve Board's Special Credit Restraint Program was in effect. Andrew Brimmer, a former governor of the Federal Reserve, who was then on the board of the COMEX (the futures exchange that was principally involved), wrote: "[T]he potential [silver] crisis was checked by a timely decision by the Federal Reserve Board to permit commercial banks to lend to commodity speculators—although the grant of such loans was clearly inconsistent with the credit controls the Federal Reserve Board then had in place."[63]

By April, there was clear evidence that the recession was unfolding, and with it, interest rates began to decline. The prime rate, which stood at 20% on April 2, was cut to 19.5% on April 18, the first of a sequence of reductions that brought it down to 11% on July 25. The Federal Reserve's policy committee, the Federal Open Market Committee, met on April 22 and observed that "the anti-inflationary measures announced on March 14 appeared to have curbed considerably spending in anticipation of price increases."[64] Real consumer spending peaked in November 1979 and reached its low in May 1980. Car sales tumbled by 34.5% between January and May 1980. But the CRP was having an undesired side effect of causing a sharp retrenchment by the consumer, and thus on May 7, the Federal Reserve eliminated the 3% discount rate surcharge. On July 3, President Carter rescinded the Federal Reserve's Authority under the Credit Control Act and the Federal Reserve announced the phaseout of the controls program.

Interest rates dropped further throughout July, which stimulated housing and consumption, and the economy rebounded. Unfortunately, inflationary pressures also intensified.

The 1981–1982 Recession: Slaying Inflation and Its Consequences

By late 1980, it was clear that the brief recession of that year had not done much to restore the price-cost-profit relationship. The economy was still undergoing adjustment to the commodity price explosion, and interest rates again backed up by late 1980. The 3-month Treasury bill rate, on a discount basis, continued to rise into 1981 and peaked at slightly over 16% by midyear and only began to edge lower as the economy entered a recession. Long-term interest rates rose sharply and the 10-year government note yield peaked at about 15% shortly after the start of the 1981 economic contraction. The unemployment rate rose from the low 7% range at the beginning of the recession and peaked at just a bit below 11% shortly after the end of the recession.

Real consumer spending, which turned negative early in the recession, got a lift from fiscal policy. On August 13, 1981, the Economic Recovery Act was enacted, which accelerated depreciation, and individual income tax rates were reduced by 25% over 33 months; the first round, a 5% income tax cut, was implemented October 1, 1981. The second stage of the Economic Recovery Act cut income taxes by 10% on July 1, 1982. As such, consumption tended to expand throughout most of the recession.

The pace of consumer prices slowed sharply over the 1981–1982 recession from over 10% in mid-1981 to less than 5% by the end of the recession. As inflation and inflationary expectations subsided in October 1982, the Federal Reserve abandoned bank reserve targeting.

The 1984–1986 Growth Recession: A Manufacturing Sector Recession as the Economy Adjusted to a Strong Dollar

Between 1980 and 1985, the Federal Reserve's trade-weighted dollar exchange rate index rose nearly 64% ultimately causing a major contraction in the manufacturing sector of the economy through the export channel. Real merchandise exports were down about $25 billion over that period.

On September 22, 1985, the "Group of Five" (G-5) finance ministers—the United States, the United Kingdom, Germany, France, and Japan—met at the Plaza Hotel in New York and implemented an "orderly depreciation" of the dollar. The so-called Plaza Accord was in place until February 21–22, 1987, when the G-7 finance ministers (the G-5 nations plus Italy and Canada) met at the Louvre in Paris to declare that the dollar had fallen enough and they agreed to stabilize the currency. Over the 18-month period between September 1985 and February 1987 the dollar fell about 30%, based on the Federal Reserve's trade-weighted average exchange value index.

With a slowdown in the economy between mid-1984 and late 1986, highly leveraged real estate transactions turned sour. The savings and loan crisis that began to unfold in 1985 ultimately forced the federal government into a massive bailout of the industry. In 1989, the Financial Institutions Reform, Recovery, and Enforcement Act (FIRREA) was enacted to fund the huge liabilities of the failed or insolvent savings and loans that were closed or sold by the government. In addition, commercial banks felt many of the same real estate loan pressures as the savings and loans as well as repayment problems associated with the Latin American debt repayment situation. In 1984, 14.05% of all commercial banks were unprofitable and that number rose to 20.66% by 1987.

Congress passed the Balanced Budget and Emergency Deficit Control Act in 1985 to demonstrate a commitment to reduce the federal budget deficits. The passage of that law helped to lower long-term interest rates on the expectation that the federal budget deficit would be brought down to zero by fiscal year 1991, and hence, the federal government's borrowing needs would be lessened. However, the so-called Gramm-Rudman-Hollings law turned out to be more symbolic than real in cutting the deficit.

In late 1985, world crude oil prices began to slip as some OPEC countries produced more oil than then allowed under the OPEC agreement. Saudi Arabia attempted to bring concurrence on oil production quotas within OPEC. Saudi Arabia's Oil Price Minister Ahmed Zaki Yamani stepped up his country's oil production to force the OPEC countries to adhere to OPEC quotas and to prop up the price of oil. But in the interim, that action dramatically lowered oil prices and pushed world crude oil prices from about $26 per barrel in January to a low of $9.35 per barrel by August 1, 1986. Interest rates followed the price of oil down. Oil prices rebounded from their mid-1986 lows as at least some OPEC members pledged to cut production to conform with the 1984 production quotas. World oil prices settled around the mid $13 range through the remainder of the year, with an occasional upward blip from that price. Interest rates essentially held steady through the end of 1986. Short-term interest rates remained relatively stable in 1987, while long-term rates backed up.

The sharp decline in the foreign exchange value of the dollar was a catalyst for economic growth causing a surge in exports. By contributing 1 to 2 percentage points to real GDP growth between 1986 and 1988, these exports pulled the manufacturing sector out of its own recession.

The 1988–1989 Slowdown: Prelude to Recession with Weaker Exports and Car Demand

The growth rate peak in the economic activity that occurred in mid-1988, was set in motion by two key factors: (1) a substantial (though expected at the time) slower pace of export growth, and (2) tighter monetary policy. From a cyclical perspective, the 1988 second-quarter peak in export growth was followed by a peak in industrial production and employment. The next leg of the slowdown was due to the feedback effects of relatively less foreign demand and higher interest rates, which continued to rise throughout 1989. The growth cycle peak has been fixed at February 1989 by CIBCR.

Several special factors impacted the economy in the latter part of 1989. A strike at Boeing that lasted 48 days and involved 57,000 workers resulted in a sharp decline in Boeing aircraft shipments. That strike also had a noticeable impact on overall exports and industrial production. However, by the second quarter of 1990, Boeing's aircraft production returned to normal. Weather was also unkind to the economy in late 1989. Hurricane Hugo impacted the South during the third quarter; in October an earthquake occurred in California. Additionally, December was the fourth coldest December in the 95 years since the Weather Bureau (National Weather Service) had been keeping records. But by January 1990, the economy and weather turned mild. January temperatures across the nation were the warmest on record for that month. These abnormally wide fluctuations in temperatures caused havoc with economic statistics that adjusted for "normal" seasonal patterns, making it difficult to get a true assessment of the underlying strength or weakness in the economy.

In addition to these special factors, the slowdown was taking its toll on car sales. As the 1990 models filled the car showrooms, consumers showed less interest in purchasing them. Car production, however, just kept growing until the end of 1989 when inventories reached a 91-day supply—substantially higher than the 60 to 65 day target that is considered normal. By January 1990, the car manufacturers cut production dramatically and cleared out a lot of the inventory by offering sweetened buyer incentives. Seasonally adjusted domestic car production fell 35% between December and January.

As the economy moved beyond the first quarter of 1990, the economic cycle was beginning to show tentative signs of resuming growth. But that situation changed dramatically in early August.

The 1990–1991 Recession: Troubles in the Middle East Tip the Scale

The economy weakened rapidly in the face of worldwide political uncertainty, triggered by Iraq's invasion of Kuwait on August 2, 1990. The world price of crude oil, which was less than $19 per barrel in July, soared in response to the hostile move and heightened world tension (see Figure 4.27). Oil prices peaked at about $40 per barrel in early October. The crude oil price increase was immediately passed along to the consumer as the Automobile Association of America's (AAA) retail gasoline survey dramatically showed. The average price of a gallon of unleaded gasoline at the pump was $1.075 on August 1, the

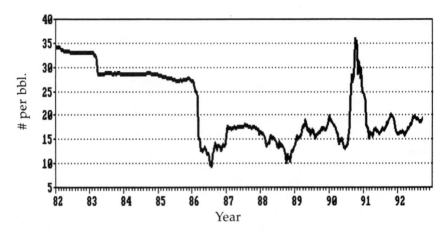

Figure 4.27 Average World Crude Oil Price. (*Source:* American Petroleum Institute.)

day before Iraq invaded Kuwait, and jumped to $1.115 on the day following the invasions.[65] It subsequently rose to $1.387 per gallon by December 4, 1990. Consumer confidence tumbled as the level of economic uncertainty soared. The National Bureau of Economic Research Business Cycle Dating Committee ultimately selected July 1990 as the peak in the business cycle.

On November 5, 1990, President Bush signed into law a major deficit reduction package—the Omnibus Budget Reconciliation Act of 1990 (OBRA), which was estimated to reduce the budget by $500 billion over five years. That legislation included a hike of 5 cents in the gasoline tax, effective December 1, 1990, that was expected to raise $4.4 billion. Additionally, a 25% increase in the tobacco excise tax went into effect on January 1, 1991, and the beer, wine, and distilled spirits tax was raised. Also, the Budget Enforcement Act of 1990 (Title XIII of the Omnibus Budget Reconciliation Act) placed annual caps on discretionary spending and required that any subsequent changes to entitlement programs and fiscal policy not increase the federal deficit. These actions—which ultimately hampered countercyclical action by the federal government—were an attempt to rein in the projected deficit of more than $300 billion.

On the evening of January 16, 1991 (Eastern time), the United States, in coordination with its allies and after failure of all attempts to negotiate a settlement, followed through on its threat to force Iraq to comply with the United Nations' resolutions calling for Iraq's withdrawal from Kuwait. And so began the Gulf War, which lasted until February 27 when President Bush declared the war over. The Allies were the ultimate victors in the conflict, and Iraqi troops pulled out of Kuwait. At home, consumers' confidence rebounded. But that euphoria was short-lived as the recession's effects were reaffirmed. Although the NBER officially declared the end of the classical recession as March 1991, making the 1990–1991 recession only 8 months long, the growth recession lingered.

The motor vehicle industry stood out during this recession. Between the second quarter of 1990 and the first quarter of 1991, real motor vehicle output declined by a hefty $40 billion, or accounted for nearly 38% of the overall decline in real GDP. Moreover, economic growth between 1991 and 1992 was meager and fluctuated with the increases or decreases in motor vehicle production. In the second quarter of 1991, real car and truck output increased by nearly $16 billion accounting for about 78% of the total rise in real GDP. Fourth-quarter real motor vehicle production (the real output change was $0.8 billion) dipped and was widely perceived as an economywide "dip." After that production adjustment, motor vehicle output reaccelerated by early 1992. Between the fourth quarter of 1991 and the second quarter of 1992, motor vehicle production accounted for a little less than a fourth of all real growth. This highlighted the importance of the motor vehicle sector for the economy; few other industries could have such a concentrated and rapid impact on overall growth.

Uncertain times continued into 1991 and 1992 on both the domestic and international arenas. On August 19, 1991, a Soviet coup attempt occurred, which ultimately failed and set into motion major change in Eastern Europe. The ripple effect was felt in the United States primarily through accelerating cuts in planned U.S. defense expenditures. Moreover, tighter bank lending standards, which evolved during the 1990–1991 recession, remained in place at banks. This further depressed the already tenuous economic recovery. But throughout this time, monetary policy continued to ease in small steps. Between June 1989 and September 1992, the Federal Reserve eased interest rates 23 times, mostly through small declines in the federal funds rate (see Table 4.11).

Those Cyclical and Secular Forces

Mark Watson[66] argued that the 1990 recession differed from past recessions. Watson wrote: "[M]any characteristics of the current recession are unique; the most obvious is the sudden outbreak of hostilities in the Middle East and coincident increase in uncertainty and fall in consumer sentiment." In particular, he argued that historical interest rate relationships such as the yield curve or the 6-month commercial paper-Treasury bill ("risk") spread behaved very differently this time. As a result, he contended that the 1990 recession would not have been predicted based on historical relationships. Moreover, Watson concluded that "monetary policy . . . was less important during the current recession."

This conclusion was based on work by Stock and Watson that developed the National Bureau of Economic Research's *experimental composite cyclical indicators*. Reviewing the individual behavior of the Stock and Watson leading indicator components, Watson found that the "unusual behavior" of some of those

Table 4.11 Tracking Federal Reserve Policy 1989–1992.

Date of Action	Action Taken	Effective Federal Funds Rate			Change since Last Action
		Day of Action	Next Business Day	Change	
02/24/89	Discount rate raised to 7.0% from 6.5%	9.79%	9.92%	0.13 pp.	pp.
06/05/89	Federal funds rate notched down	9.64	9.58	-0.06	-0.34
07/06/89	Federal funds rate notched down	9.46	9.23	-0.23	-0.35
07/26/89	Federal funds rate notched down	8.86	9.00	0.14	-0.23
10/16/89	Federal funds rate notched down	8.63	8.70	0.07	-0.30
11/06/89	Federal funds rate notched down	8.74	8.64	-0.10	-0.06
12/20/89	Federal funds rate notched down	8.42	8.27	-0.15	-0.37
07/13/90	Federal funds rate notched down	8.18	8.07	-0.11	-0.20
10/29/90	Federal funds rate notched down	7.87	7.84	-0.03	-0.23
11/15/90	Federal funds rate notched down	8.12	7.85	-0.27	0.01
12/07/90	Federal funds rate notched down	7.25	7.18	-0.07	-0.67
12/18/90	Discount rate cut to 6.5%	7.37	7.13	-0.24	-0.05
01/08/91	Federal funds rate notched down	5.94	5.88	-0.06	-1.25
02/01/91	Discount rate cut to 6.0%	6.30	6.10	-0.20	0.22
04/30/91	Discount rate cut to 5.5%	5.98	5.90	-0.08	-0.20
08/09/91	Federal funds rate notched down	5.71	5.65	-0.06	-0.25
09/13/91	Discount rate cut to 5.0%	5.31	5.56	0.25	-0.09
10/30/91	Federal funds rate notched down	4.44	5.23	0.79	-0.33
11/06/91	Discount rate cut to 4.5%	4.87	4.94	0.07	-0.29
12/06/91	Federal funds rate notched down	4.52	4.52	0.00	-0.42
12/20/91	Discount rate cut to 3.5%	4.11	4.26	0.15	-0.26
04/09/92	Federal funds rate notched down	3.76	3.44	-0.32	-0.82
07/02/92	Discount rate cut to 3.0%	3.46	3.56	0.10	0.12
09/04/92	Federal funds rate notched down	3.02	3.02	0.00	-0.54

pp. = percentage points

Table 4.12   Interest Rate Spreads over the Business Cycle.

A. Commercial Paper Minus Treasury Bill Spread (Basis Points)

Cyclical Peak	Months prior to cyclical peak			
	9	6	3	0
July 1953	NA	NA	NA	NA
Aug. 1957	NA	NA	NA	NA
Apr. 1960	16	20	17	61
Dec. 1969	66	148	117	95
Nov. 1973	39	65	156	98
Jan. 1980	49	65	157	82
July 1981	69	102	72	135
Average	47.8	80.0	103.8	94.2
Standard Deviation	19.3	42.8	53.4	24.2
Normal High	57.5	101.4	130.5	106.3
Normal Low	38.1	58.6	77.1	82.1
July 1990	62	41	45	38

B. Ten−Year Treasury Minus One−Year Treasury Spread (Basis Points)

Cyclical Peak	Months prior to cyclical peak			
	9	6	3	0
July 1953	NA	NA	47	55
Aug. 1957	5	−4	12	−8
Apr. 1960	1	−27	−31	24
Dec. 1969	−22	−47	−66	−52
Nov. 1973	45	−4	−142	−84
Jan. 1980	−113	−66	−214	−126
July 1981	−74	−151	−64	−144
Average	−26.3	−49.8	−65.4	−47.9
Standard Deviation	52.6	50.4	82.6	69.7
Normal High	−0.0	−24.6	−24.1	−13.0
Normal Low	−52.6	−75.0	−106.7	−82.7
July 1990	2	29	39	53

C. Ten−Year Treasury / One−Year Treasury Ratio

Cyclical Peak	Months prior to cyclical peak			
	9	6	3	0
July 1953	NA	NA	1.119	1.231
Aug. 1957	1.015	0.988	1.034	0.980
Apr. 1960	1.002	0.944	0.938	1.059
Dec. 1969	0.994	0.933	0.916	0.936
Nov. 1973	1.073	0.994	0.839	0.889
Jan. 1980	0.907	0.928	0.828	0.896
July 1981	0.941	0.893	0.955	0.908
Average	0.989	0.947	0.947	0.986
Standard Deviation	0.053	0.035	0.096	0.114
Normal High	1.015	0.964	0.995	1.043
Normal Low	0.962	0.929	0.899	0.928
July 1990	1.003	1.037	1.046	1.067

indicators relative to past business cycles would not have led observers to expect a recession. First, Watson argued that the Treasury yield curve (10 minus 1 year maturities) was positive 9, 6, and 3 months before the July 1990 peak. This was different from the five previous recessions (with the single exception of 3 months before the 1960 recession). But despite Watson's assertion that the Treasury yield curve spread was different, extending his analysis back into the 1950s shows the current yield curve experience was more similar to those recessions (see Table 4.12 on page 301). Second, the risk spread was relatively narrow 3 to 6 months before the 1990 recession compared with the experience in the prior 30 years. Moreover, Watson dismissed the possible explanation that financial markets have undergone structural changes, altering the relationship between monetary policy and interest rate spreads.

Watson seemed correct in asserting that the 1990 recession had some different properties from past recessions, which always is true to some degree with every recession. The difference in 1990 from earlier recessions, however, was more due to a clash between secular and cyclical forces. The forces included:

1.   The U.S. economy was less interest rate sensitive in the 1990 recession than in earlier cycles, although this conclusion is still controversial.

2.   The interest rate impacts that do occur have been occurring later.

3.   *Economic hardship,* that is permanent job loss as a share of total job loss, was more pervasive during the early 1990s than in previous recessions. The ratio reached a record high of 45.2% in May 1992 (the historical data series began in 1967). In the previous recession, the economic hardship ratio climbed to 43.2% shortly after the end of the 1981–1982 recession.

4.   In effect, the post-1991 U.S. economy was in a "postwar environment," without support programs to soften the transition. Private sector defense-related employment peaked in October 1986 at 1.44 million workers. By June 1990—just before the 1990–1991 recession and a major slide in that industry's employment, the private defense-related work force stood at 1.41 million workers. But then a major contraction set in, tied to developments in Eastern Europe that all but eliminated the Soviet and Eastern European threat to world security. Through mid-1992, the defense industry's private sector work force was reduced by 250,000 persons. Although defense-related employment accounted for only 1% of the total U.S. work force in 1990, it accounted for a whopping 13.4% of the nation's job loss between June 1990 and June 1992. Moreover, estimates of the total employment impact of lower defense expenditures were substantial. The Congressional Budget Office (CBO) cited a projection of potentially more than 800 thousand defense-related jobs being lost by 1995. By that

benchmark, about one-third of the industry's employment adjustment has been made. Between the first quarter of 1991 when defense spending peaked with the advent of the war with Iraq and the second quarter of 1992, real defense spending was cut $27.3 billion, equivalent to a constant drag of 0.5 percentage points on real GDP growth.

5. The tremendous government debt situation constrained fiscal policy.

6. The favorable tax treatment in the early 1980s led to an excess capacity of commercial building, which without a strong recovery remained difficult to soak up.

LESSONS FOR THE 1990s

Although the framework for this historical discussion has been the chronology of the business cycle, it may be increasingly important to view the 1990s much more in the Schumpeterian framework—that is, as a sum of short, intermediate, and long cycles. The long cycle is, in large part, determined by demographic factors. The intermediate cycle is heavily influenced by building activity, and the short cycle swings to inventory fluctuation. Maurice Lamontagne, a former cabinet minister and senator in Canada, believed that Canadian policy makers and advisors who focused on a single cycle committed serious economic forecasting and policy errors. He argued that economic forecasts must recognize and analyze cycles of differing duration based on what determines them and then must orient policy measures appropriate to their causes.[67] The U.S. economic experience in the early 1990s underscores Lamontagne's point; the "long cycle" is a paramount and very real concern for the United States. The long cycle of the 1990s is being driven not only by demographics but also by the federal government's deficit control.

Appendix

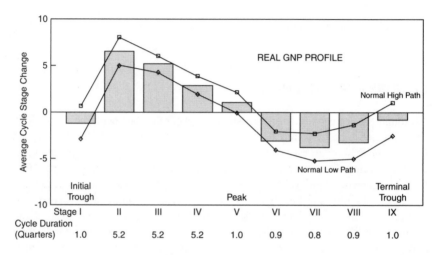

Figure A.1 Business Cycle Stages Average Growth and Duration per Stage for Real GNP, 1948–1990.

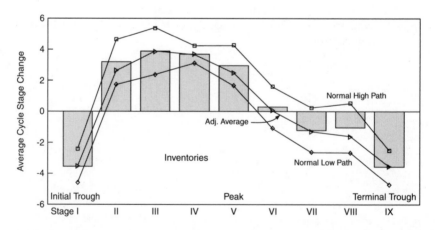

Figure A.2 U.S. Business Cycle Stages Average Growth per Stage for Real Inventories, 1948–1990.

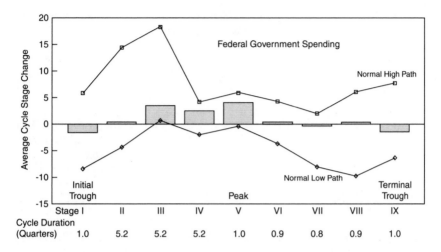

Figure A.3 Business Cycle Stages Average Growth and Duration per Stage for Real Federal Government Spending, 1948–1990.

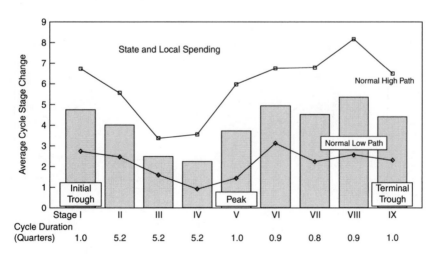

Figure A.4 Business Cycle Stages Average Growth and Duration per Stage for Real State and Local Spending, 1948–1990.

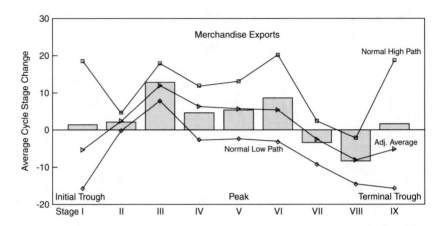

Figure A.5 U.S. Business Cycle Stages Average Growth per Stage for Merchandise Exports, 1948–1990.

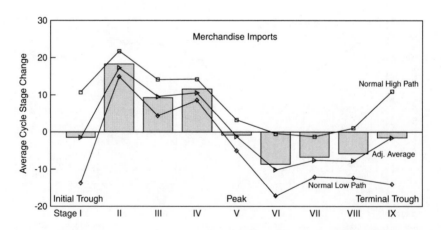

Figure A.6 U.S. Business Cycle Stages Average Growth per Stage for Merchandise Imports, 1948–1990.

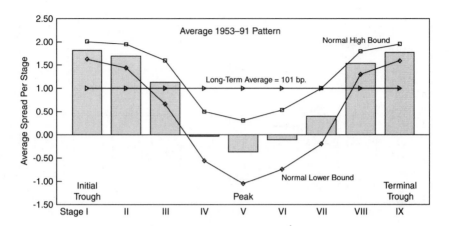

Figure A.7 Yield Curve over the Business Cycle.

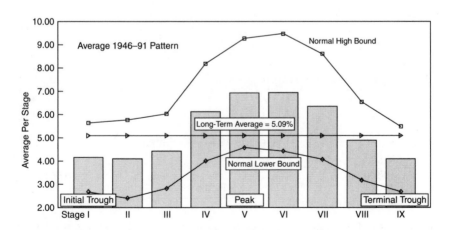

Figure A.8 Three-Month Treasury Bill Rate over the Business Cycle.

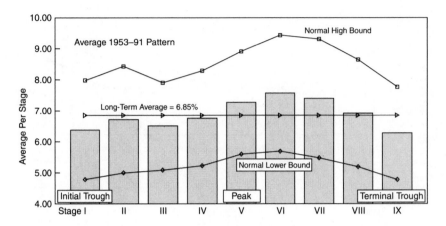

Figure A.9 Ten-Year Government Bond Rate over the Business Cycle.

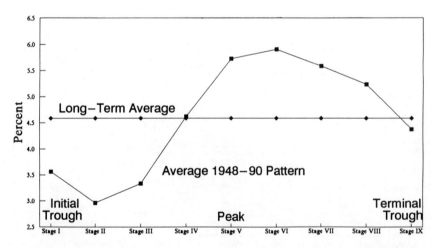

Figure A.10 Consumer Inflation over the Business Cycle Cyclical Patterns Adjusted for Long-Term Average.

Part Four

Application of Cycle Techniques

5 Industry Cycles

Monitoring and forecasting industry cycles provides a means of disaggregating the business cycle into its component parts. It opens up a new avenue for exploring timing relationships between industries and also gives the business manager insight into the industry turning points without requiring detailed and time-consuming analysis or vast expense. Moreover, a company that quickly recognizes a change in the phase of the industry cycle could unleash either a recession or a recovery marketing strategy to optimize their sales. A key reason to study the industry cycle is to understand how to use the forces within different stages of the cycle to moderate fluctuations in a company's sales. Marketing efforts are likely to be different during a recession than during an expansion and early recognition of the changing environment could be crucial to a business. Even if demand for a product is not very cyclical, a firm's clients could be impacted by the industry cycle stage, which could affect whether the producing company is paid in a timely fashion or paid at all.

Examples abound on the usefulness of leading industry indicators. For example, leading retail industry indicators could alert a retailer of the need to change pricing points or the product mix. Additionally, advance warning can help a company change advertising efforts. Marketing research has found that companies that step up their advertising during a recession (countercyclical advertising) yielded substantially larger sales gains and produced a stronger company when the recovery eventually came, compared with companies that trimmed their advertising expenditures to save money.[1] In other research, it was found that consumer demand for autos is about 15% more price sensitive during recessions.[2] These examples illustrate the importance of knowing how one's business or industry should respond to changes in advertising, prices, and so forth during different phases of the cycle. But in addition to knowing how to respond to the changing business environment, it is important to know *when to change* and that is where industry leading indicators play a role.

Finally, government policymakers also might find industry indicators a useful fiscal policy tool. It is possible to envision an industry-specific tax policy that would allow firms to fund a tax-free contingency reserve (possibly a business counterpart of an Individual Retirement Account) that could be drawn on only when an industry's leading indicator signals a downturn. The applications in both the public and private sectors are unlimited.

THE LOGIC FOR INDUSTRY LEADING INDICATORS

There is an old story that exemplifies the logic for, and the usefulness of, specific industry leading economic indicators. It seems that Andrew Carnegie, the steel tycoon, had his own leading economic indicator. Carnegie reasoned that if he watched the smoke from local steel factories, he could gauge the strength or weakness of business. If the smoke was billowing strong, strong business conditions would surely follow and vice versa.

This story highlights three key strengths of leading economic indicators. They are (1) easy to interpret, (2) easy to communicate, and (3) relatively inexpensive to formulate. Another reason to consider using leading industry economic indicators is that a flood of information has been swamping business. A leading indicator, however, can convey a message quickly and efficiently without requiring management to digest a lengthy report. But no single leading indicator is perfect, and this has led to the compilation of groups of indicators into *composite* or *diffusion indicators*.[3] The selection of the indicators for a cyclical index generally is based on what has been dubbed an *eclectic economic theory*. Frank de Leeuw (1991), who is the chief statistician of the U.S. Department of Commerce, has provided an interesting explanation of the theoretical underpinnings for the selection of leading economic indicators of national business, which also apply to the industry analysis. In essence, de Leeuw suggests five rationales for the selection of leading economic indicators; Indicators should (1) lead the production process (e.g., new orders), (2) reflect rapid economic adjustment (e.g., weekly hours), (3) reflect market expectations (e.g., consumer buying plans), (4) serve as policy levers (e.g., monetary and fiscal policy indicators), and (5) have a mathematical lead (e.g., a growth rate versus a level). Although the de Leeuw rationales are guiding principles, in practice, the selection process is as much a trial-and-error process as anything. An indicator that theoretically *should* lead another series might not, for numerous reasons ranging from the poor quality of the data to a faulty theory.

More generally, the term can mean different things to different people. To a person who uses state space or multivariate ARIMA statistical models, a leading indicator is a supplemental series used in conjunction with the internal dynamics of the series itself to help forecast it. In this context, a leading indicator is used to forecast all points. To an economist in Germany, the term *leading indicator* often means a survey-based or qualitative indicator. For example, Schmid

(1986) has proposed a survey-based leading indicator of the savings and loan industry. However, the approach that will be discussed in this chapter will be the traditional or National Bureau of Economic Research (NBER) approach to leading indicators. Leading indicators in the NBER context are turning point indicators, which could be qualitative or quantitative.

FORMULATING A CYCLICAL INDICATOR SYSTEM FOR INDUSTRY

The first step in the process of formulating a cyclical indicator is to answer the paramount question that Jim Stock and Mark Watson (1989) posed about leading indicators, which for this application can be stated as: *What are industry leading indicators supposed to lead?* The answer is much easier to answer for industry analysis than for the composite cyclical indicator of the Bureau of Economic Analysis. The starting point, as shown in Figure 5.1, is to select a target variable or set of variables that are most relevant as performance measures of one's business or industry.

Previous work on industry cycles examined either industrial production, employment in the specific industry, or the current or constant dollar value of the industry's shipments or sales. For some purposes, a specific target variable makes sense. For example, PaineWebber's leading indicator of automobile sales was intended to forecast the auto sales cycle. Another example of leading indicators to forecast a specific economic indicator was the *Builder Index* developed by the National Association of Home Builders (NAHB). Although the NAHB no longer maintains that indicator, it was intended to lead fluctuation in housing starts and had an average 6-month lead time. A more comprehensive indicator approach was applied by Richard D. Karfunkle,[4] who examined the textile industry while employed at E.I. Du Pont de Nemours & Company. He measured the textile industry cycle using consensus turning point dates based on several coincident indicators for the industry (an application of the cluster method discussed in Chapter 3).

Karfunkle, who was guided by the NBER's work, selected seven textile series as his set of coincident indicators consisting of (1) the *Textile World Index* of textile manufacturing activity, (2) textile mill products manufacturers' sales, (3) cotton consumption, (4) number of textile mill products production workers, (5) number of apparel production workers, (6) wages of textile mill products production workers, and (7) wages of apparel production workers. He then compiled a summary measure of industry activity as a diffusion index of those series that was conceptually similar to the method used by the Japanese Economic Planning Agency in measuring its economic cycle (as discussed in Chapter 1).

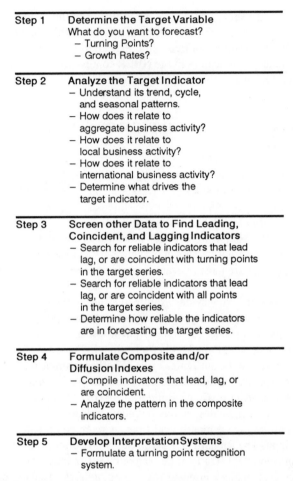

Step 1	Determine the Target Variable
	What do you want to forecast?
	– Turning Points?
	– Growth Rates?
Step 2	Analyze the Target Indicator
	– Understand its trend, cycle, and seasonal patterns.
	– How does it relate to aggregate business activity?
	– How does it relate to local business activity?
	– How does it relate to international business activity?
	– Determine what drives the target indicator.
Step 3	Screen other Data to Find Leading, Coincident, and Lagging Indicators
	– Search for reliable indicators that lead lag, or are coincident with turning points in the target series.
	– Search for reliable indicators that lead lag, or are coincident with all points in the target series.
	– Determine how reliable the indicators are in forecasting the target series.
Step 4	Formulate Composite and/or Diffusion Indexes
	– Compile indicators that lead, lag, or are coincident.
	– Analyze the pattern in the composite indicators.
Step 5	Develop Interpretation Systems
	– Formulate a turning point recognition system.

Figure 5.1   Steps in Formulating a Leading Economic Indicator System.

Although composite and diffusion indexes both provide a useful way of summarizing economic activity, the composite indicator approach may prove more stable in determining turning point dates on an ongoing basis. An example of this approach is in Niemira (1982).

Niemira compiled composite indexes of leading and coincident business activity for the chemical industry. This industry cycle was defined as a composite indicator of three key industry economic indicators whose turning points were roughly coincident with each other. In the NBER parlance, the term *roughly* means within plus or minus 3 months of the clustered turning point date. The chemical industry cycle turning points were based on a composite index of industry activity including (1) chemical industrial production, (2) chemical industry employment, and (3) the chemical industry's real value of shipments. These series are reported monthly by the U.S. Departments of Labor and Commerce and the Federal Reserve Board. In addition to these series, a weekly indicator for freight carloadings in the chemical industry, which was averaged for the month and seasonally adjusted, appeared promising as an industry coincident indicator. Indeed, for the aggregate economy, total freight carloadings were classified as a coincident indicator by the NBER in the period preceding World War II. After World War II, however, freight carloadings became a less reliable barometer of general business conditions due to the declining trend of rail freight traffic. On an industry basis, and in particular for the chemical industry, there appeared to be some evidence for the inclusion of this series within the composite coincident indicator. Nonetheless, because of the relative shortness of the historical data for the chemical carloadings data (when the work was done in 1981), this series was not included in the composite chemical industry coincident indicator at the time.

Table 5.1 presents the cyclical turning points for each of the industry coincident indicators compared with the turning point dates selected in the composite industry index. These dates for the composite index, as well as the components were selected by use of the NBER computer methodology as described in Chapter 3.

One advantage of developing an industry specific turning point chronology based on a composite index is reflected in Table 5.1, which shows that not every industry economic indicator has the same cyclical turning points. Hence, selecting turning points in a composite index is equivalent to determining turning points from a *consensus of indicators*. More specifically, if industrial production alone was used as the measure of the industry cycle, then this measure implied that the industry was not affected by the general business downturn experienced in 1969–1970. If, however, either employment or the value of shipments deflated by the producer price index for chemicals was used as a measure of the industry cycle, then both of these series indicated a downturn had occurred. Another advantage of using several indicators jointly as a measure of the industry activity is that the turning point dates are less sensitive to data revisions—a benefit for analytical purposes.

ANALYZING THE INDUSTRY CYCLE

The next step in the process is to analyze the industry cycle. A comparison of the industry cycle with the aggregate cycle should be made. Table 5.2 shows this comparison for the chemical cycle. However, the similarity in the cyclical

Table 5.1 Turning Points of Chemical Industry Indicators, 1949–1980.

Industry Cycle		Industrial Production		Employment		Real Shipments	
Peak	Trough	Peak	Trough	Peak	Trough	Peak	Trough
	July 1949		July 1949		Aug. 1949	—	—
July 1953	May 1954	July 1953	Jan. 1954	Aug. 1953	May 1954		Dec. 1953
Oct. 1957	Apr. 1958	Oct. 1957	Apr. 1958	Jan. 1958	July 1958	Mar. 1957	Mar. 1958
June 1960	Feb. 1961	June 1960	Dec. 1960	June 1960	Feb. 1961	Dec. 1959	Jan. 1961
Mar. 1970	Mar. 1971	NCD	NCD	July 1969	Feb. 1971	Oct. 1969	Nov. 1970
July 1974	Mar. 1975	Aug. 1974	Mar. 1975	Sept. 1974	July 1975	Feb. 1974	Mar. 1975
Jan. 1980	July 1980	Jan. 1980	July 1980	Apr. 1980	Aug. 1980	Mar. 1979	June 1980

NCD = No Corresponding Date.

Table 5.2   Relationship between the Business Cycle and the Chemical Industry Cycle, 1949–1980.

Business Cycle		Chemical Industry Cycle		Timing Relationship	
Peak	Trough	Peak	Trough	Peak	Trough
	Oct. 1949		July 1949		−3 mo.
July 1953		July 1953		0 mo.	
	May 1954		May 1954		0
Aug. 1957		Oct. 1957		+2	
	Apr. 1958		Apr. 1958		0
June 1960		June 1960		+2	
	Feb. 1961		Feb. 1961		0
Dec. 1969		Mar. 1970		+3	
	Nov. 1970		Mar. 1971		+4
Nov. 1973		July 1974		+8	
	Mar. 1975		Mar. 1975		0
Jan. 1980		Jan. 1980		0	
	July 1980		July 1980		0
			Average	+2.5 months	+0.1 months

Note: Plus sign (+) indicates a lag; negative sign (−) indicates a lead.

turning points between the industry and the nation raises a question as to the usefulness of a distinct and specialized set of industry leading indicators: *Why not simply use the aggregate leading indicators?* The answer is that business cycles represent widely diffused changes in the underlying industries; this does not imply that every industry must be affected or affected at precisely the same time or to the same degree. This point becomes clearer from Table 5.3, which shows the 1980 cyclical troughs in the two-digit SIC components of industrial production. Some industries were not affected by the 1980 recession while others lead or lag the consensus or clustered July 1980 turning point date. Examining this lead-lag relationship among industries can provide additional insight into the structure of the industrial sector.

Numerous business cycle monitoring and forecasting methods, such as recession-recovery monitoring and stage analysis, should be applied to the coincident measure of industry activity to help understand the industry's cyclical nature. This descriptive analysis of the industry could further help illuminate how the industry operates. Additionally, application of some of these business cycle methods can address questions of probable future cycle length and pattern. A knowledge of a *typical* and *stable* cyclical pattern also will help to highlight unusual cyclical behavior, which the analyst must evaluate by other means.

Table 5.3   Diffusion of Cyclical Turning Points by Industrial Sector.

	Industry Specific	Turning Point Date
Nondurable	Food (SIC 20)	NCD
Manufacturers	Tobacco Products (SIC 21)	NCD
	Textile Mill Products (SIC 22)	July 1980
	Apparel Products (SIC 23)	July 1980
	Paper and Products (SIC 26)	July 1980
	Printing and Publishing (SIC 27)	NCD
	Chemicals and Products (SIC 28)	July 1980
	Petroleum Products (SIC 29)	Aug. 1980
	Rubber and Plastic Products (SIC 30)	July 1980
	Leather and Products (SIC 31)	Sept. 1980
Durable	Ordnance, Private and Gov't (SIC 19,91)	NCD
Manufacturers	Lumber and Products (SIC 24)	May 1980
	Furniture and Fixtures (SIC 25)	July 1980
	Clay, Glass, Stone Products (SIC 32)	July 1980
	Primary Metals (SIC 33)	July 1980
	Fabricated Metal Products (SIC 34)	July 1980
	Nonelectrical Machinery (SIC 35)	June 1980
	Electrical Machinery (SIC 36)	July 1980
	Transportation Equipment (SIC 37)	Aug. 1980
	Instruments (SIC 38)	Sept. 1980
	Miscellaneous Manufactures (SIC 39)	Sept. 1980
Nonmanufacturing	Mining (SIC 10-14)	NCD
	Utilities	NCD

NCD = No Corresponding Date.

INTERINDUSTRY COMPARISONS USING THE INDICATOR APPROACH

Another advantage of developing a comprehensive set of industry composite indicators is to explore cyclical timing relationships among industries. With the U.S. Commerce Department's Input-Output (I-O) tables for the U.S. economy as a guide to the degree of interdependence among industries, some of the major demanding industries can be identified.

In a preliminary review, Niemira (1982) examined three production cycles relative to the chemical industry. The hypothesis examined was whether industries that demand chemical products had a cyclical turn prior to that exhibited by the chemical industry. Of the three production cycles examined, textiles (SIC 22) and rubber and plastics (SIC 30) were major users of chemical products while the third, lumber (SIC 24) was not a major user, according to the I-O tables. On average, the rubber and plastic products production cycle was coincident with turning points in the chemical industry (Table 5.4); the textile production cycle led the chemical cycle at peaks but was coincident at troughs (Table 5.5). Finally, the lumber production cycle led the chemical cycle peaks by about 14 months on average with a median lead of 13 months and also led at troughs in the chemical cycle by roughly 3 months (Table 5.6). What this preliminary review hinted at for this industry was that an interest-sensitive industry that fluctuated with housing demand provided early warning of the future direction of the economy and the chemical industry. In this case, industries that demanded chemical products (derived demand) did not provide a clue for the chemical industry cycle. Nonetheless, it still may be useful to form and analyze a composite derived-demand index for this or other industries using the I-O data to weight individual industry demand.

IN SEARCH OF LEADING INDICATORS

The third step in formulating an indicator system is to screen the data for possible reliable leading, coincident, and lagging indicators of your target variable. Often it is better to apply economic theory loosely. For example, if the purpose

Table 5.4 Relationship of the Chemical Industry Cycle and the Production Cycle for Rubber and Plastic Products (SIC 30) (1949–1980).

Chemical Industry Cycle		SIC 30 Production Cycle		Timing Relationship	
Peak	Trough	Peak	Trough	Peak	Trough
	July 1949		July 1949		0 mo.
July 1953		May 1953		−2 mo.	
	May 1954		Dec. 1953		−5
Oct. 1957		Aug. 1957		−2	
	Apr. 1958		May 1958		+1
June 1960		Jan. 1960		−5	
	Feb. 1961		Dec. 1960		−2
Mar. 1970		NCD		NCD	
	Mar. 1971		NCD		NCD
July 1974		July 1974		0	
	Mar. 1975		Mar. 1975		0
Jan. 1980		Aug. 1979		−5	
	July 1980		July 1980		0
			Average	−2.8 mo.	−1.0 mo.

NCD = No corresponding date.

Note: Plus sign (+) indicates a lag; negative sign (−) indicates a lead.

Table 5.5   Relationship of the Chemical Industry Cycle and the Production Cycle for Textile Mill Products (SIC 22) (1949–1980).

Chemical Industry Cycle		SIC 22 Production Cycle		Timing Relationship	
Peak	Trough	Peak	Trough	Peak	Trough
	July 1949		May 1949		−2 mo.
July 1953		May 1953		−2 mo.	
	May 1954		Jan. 1954		−4
Oct. 1957		Feb. 1956		−20	
	Apr. 1958		Apr. 1958		0
June 1960		Jan. 1960		−5	
	Feb. 1961		Dec. 1960		−2
Mar. 1970		July 1969		−8	
	Mar. 1971		Jan. 1971		−2
July 1974		Nov. 1973		−8	
	Mar. 1975		Jan. 1975		−2
Jan. 1980		Sept. 1979		−4	
	July 1980		July 1980		0
			Average	−7.8 mo.	−1.7 mo.

NCD = No corresponding date.

Note: Plus sign (+) indicates a lag; negative sign (−) indicates a lead.

Table 5.6   Relationship of the Chemical Industry Cycle and the Production Cycle for Lumber and Products (SIC 24) (1949–1980).

Chemical Industry Cycle		SIC 24 Production Cycle		Timing Relationship	
Peak	Trough	Peak	Trough	Peak	Trough
	July 1949		Feb. 1949		−5 mo.
July 1953		Jan. 1953		−6 mo.	
	May 1954		Aug. 1954		+3
Oct. 1957		June 1955		−28	
	Apr. 1958		Dec. 1957		−4
June 1960		May 1959		−13	
	Feb. 1961		Dec. 1960		−2
Mar. 1970		Mar. 1969		−12	
	Mar. 1971		June 1970		−9
July 1974		Sept. 1973		−10	
	Mar. 1975		Dec. 1974		−3
Jan. 1980		Dec. 1978		−13	
	July 1980		May 1980		−2
			Average	−13.7 mo.	−3.1 mo.

NCD = No corresponding date.

Note: Plus sign (+) indicates a lag; negative sign (−) indicates a lead.

was to forecast turning points in consumer spending, it might seem natural to use income or employment to forecast it. In reality, however, you may be disappointed. More often than not, consumption leads income and employment at turning points. So it may be necessary to rethink the consumption process. Economists tend to think of consumption and buying as identical. In part, this is true because personal consumption and income data are reported on a *cash basis* instead of an *accrual basis*. But from a marketing standpoint, consumption is always the final phase of the shopping-buying-consumption chain. Hence, a natural leading indicator of consumption is anything that motivates shopping, which can include the consumers' response to difficult or favorable economic times. Unfortunately, the lead time may be quite short between shopping and buying—even for a durable good. For example, the National Automobile Dealers Association (NADA) found that the time span between shopping for and buying a new car is only a few days. Even when data exist on buyer traffic, they may not provide a useful measure for forecasting turning points. For example, the National Association of Home Builders' buyer traffic survey tends to lag reported new home sales by about one month. Since no data series is perfect, *flexibility is a key requirement in the search for reliable cyclical indicators.*

As noted earlier, there are several types of leading indicators. Leading indicators can exist because they are reported "early." To some extent, this is true of the National Association of Purchasing Management's monthly *Purchasing Managers Index* (PMI) as compared with turning points in industrial production. In other cases, leading indicators exist by design. A growth rate in the target series *mathematically* will lead turning points in the series itself. Ideally, the search process should look for indicators having a conceptual lead with the target variable but that may be a luxury in practice. Moreover, do not dismiss reliable lagging indicators in a search for leading indicators since, as Geoffrey Moore (1969) has observed, the inverse of a lagging indicator can serve as a long-leading indicator.

Over the past 40 years, Geoffrey Moore has been one of the major proponents of the indicator technique. Geoffrey Moore's Center for International Business Cycle Research (CIBCR) at Columbia University is a major source of research on composite indicators. Moore has developed numerous industry, national, and international leading indicators that could be used as an input into a company or industry indicator. An example of using a leading indicator within another one is Statistics Canada's composite leading indicator. The Canadian government indicator uses the U.S. leading indicator as one of its components.

The fourth step in the process is to develop a summary leading indicator. In Karfunkle's textile industry research, he compiled a leading diffusion indicator using (1) textile mill products manufacturers' new orders, (2) textile mill products manufacturers' new orders-to-inventory ratio, (3) textile mill products manufacturers' sales-to-inventory ratio, (4) textile weavers' stock prices, (5) textile mill products production workers' average weekly hours, (6) textile mill products total accessions, (7) textile mill products workers' layoffs, (8) apparel production workers' average weekly hours, and (9) general merchandise retail sales-to-inventories ratio. Karfunkle's diffusion indicators were formed as an average duration-of-run index (discussed in Chapter 3).

In screening indicators for the chemical industry leading index, Niemira used the NBER's *two-thirds rule* to select leading indicators. The two-thirds rule was applied as follows: "[A] series was considered an acceptable indicator of revivals if its specific cycle troughs led the corresponding reference troughs at two-thirds or more of the reference troughs it covered; or if it was 'roughly coincident' (turned within 3 months of the reference trough) at two-thirds or more of the troughs; or even if it lagged at two-thirds or more of the troughs."[5] Similarly, the process was also applied to the determination of peaks. This rule provided an objective means of determining the timing classification of an indicator. Based on this criterion, four indicators were found to be reliable leading indicators of the chemical industry: (1) the Standard & Poors Chemical Stock Price Index, (2) the average workweek for the chemical industry, (3) capacity utilization in the chemical industry, and (4) profit margins in the chemical industry. Once these indicators were identified, a composite leading indicator of the chemical industry was compiled.

When that chemical industry composite index was originally compiled, the layoff rate for the industry was used instead of the average workweek. But since that time, the Bureau of Labor Statistics (BLS) discontinued industry layoff rates, which necessitated replacing that component with the average workweek for the industry. The selection of those four indicators was guided by the U.S. long-list of leading indicators, as well as the availability of data. The list of industry indicators examined included those actually selected and an inventory-to-sales ratio for the industry, the change in assets from the Quarterly Financial Report, and some other economic measures that since have been discontinued by the BLS.

The inclusion of the capacity utilization rate for the chemical industry may be questioned. Capacity utilization had a timing relationship with its industry cycle that was similar to its aggregate counterpart, which was leading at peaks, coincident at troughs, and unclassified overall. Nonetheless, that component was included because of its reliability as a leading indicator at peaks.[6]

The chemical industry's leading economic indicator (CILEI) anticipated the peaks in the industry cycle by 10 months on average, with a median lead of 11 months (see Table 5.7). At troughs, the CILEI led by roughly 3 months on average, with a median lead of 4 months. However, CILEI had three *extra turns* that corresponded to growth cycle turning points. Indeed, even the U.S. Commerce Department's aggregate leading indicator has been susceptible to false signals. Therefore, a useful extension of this industry cycle research

Table 5.7   Chemical Industry Cycle and Leading Indicator Turning Points, 1957–1980.

Chemical Industry Cycle		Leading Indicator		Timing Relationship	
Peak	Trough	Peak	Trough	Peak	Trough
Oct. 1957		Apr. 1956		−18 mo.	
	Apr. 1958		Nov. 1957		−5 mo.
June 1960		July 1959		−11	
	Feb. 1961		Dec. 1960		−2
Mar. 1970		Apr. 1969		−11	
	Mar. 1971		Nov. 1970		−4
July 1974		May 1974		−2	
	Mar. 1975		Jan. 1975		−2
Jan. 1980		Apr. 1979		−9	
	July 1980		July 1980		0
			Average	−10.2 months	−2.6 months

Note: Plus sign (+) indicates a lag; negative sign (−) indicates a lead.

Extra Cycles in Leading Indicator

Peak	Trough
Aug. 1961	June 1962
Feb. 1966	July 1967
Mar. 1976	Jan. 1978

is to develop decision rules for interpreting changes in the industry leading indicator.

ADD-ON STRUCTURES FOR INTERPRETING THE INDICATORS

The fifth and final step in formulating an indicator system is to implement a statistical turning point recognition rule. Although it may seem obvious in retrospect that a leading indicator has peaked or bottomed out, it is far less obvious on a real-time basis. A classic example of when judgmental interpretation of the cyclical indicators failed on a real-time basis was in the 1920s with the infamous Harvard ABC curves, which were an early set of cyclical indicators. The Harvard economists who interpreted the curves failed to foresee the Great Depression and consequently the system was viewed as a great failure. But in a recent review of those indicators, Klein and Niemira found that a purely statistical interpretation of those ABC curves would have called a turning point in the economy about a year before the onset of the Great Depression (see Chapter 4). The moral of that exercise for forecasting is that although a statistical system for interpreting the data may seem unnecessary, it is actually essential. Judgment—while important for forecasting—can cloud the interpreter's understanding of what is really happening.

There are three common *add-on structures* for making the most of a leading indicator, and the choice of which technique to use is in part dependent on the audience. Those techniques include (1) *the growth rate rules,* such as those developed by Moore and Zarnowitz (1982) for interpreting the U.S. cyclical indicators, (2) *the probability-based rules,* as reflected in the work of Neftçi (1982) and Hamilton (1989), and (3) the *growth rate projections* based on leading indicators following the work of Stock and Watson (1989) or using pattern recognition models such as a neural network. But no method needs to be used exclusively.

CONCLUSION

There is a footnote to the story of the Carnegie indicator, which is that it probably would not have stood the test of time. Not only is the steel industry very different today than it was in Andrew Carnegie's day, but the Environmental Protection Agency (EPA) probably would have lessened the usefulness of the Carnegie indicator anyway. Thus, leading indicators as well as econometric models must be updated from time to time. With careful formulation, testing, and periodic updating of a leading indicator, the result is likely to be well received by a company's management. Moreover, the payoff from this industry work for policymakers and market participants is a knowledge of intertemporal relationships or channels among industries, which could provide an invaluable forecasting aid. Although many economists have observed a changing industrial structure in the U.S. economy,[7] this may or may not have any noticeable impact on the cyclical relationship between the production processes of the manufacturing and nonmanufacturing industries. This issue remains an area for future industry cycle research.

Finally, some of the most successful applications of leading indicators for an individual's own company are not documented in the literature. For example, Donald Hilty, the corporate economist of Chrysler Corporation, has developed a leading economic indicator for Chrysler's business. His indicator is compiled as a diffusion index and the bottom line message is presented as a system of colors—red, green, and yellow.[8] Chrysler's former chairman, Lee Iacocca, watched the indicator closely, and the message from the leading indicator is disseminated widely within the corporation.

What ultimately should be recognized is that leading indicators are a *reduced form economic model.* They provide a model that can be much more persuasive to the noneconomist. Moreover, *industry* cyclical indicators make sense because:

> [R]ecessions impact some industries, products and regions of the country hard and bypass others entirely. Among the industries and products most affected are: automobiles, home furnishings, large appliances, travel and airlines, convenience foods, aluminum, steel, petrochemicals and synthetic fibers. Relatively unaffected are: liquor and wine, tobacco, small appliances, packaged goods, computer and service industries.[9]

Industry leading indicators offer a customized microeconomic forecasting tool.

REFERENCES

Buell, R. S., and Maurer, R. A., 1985, "A Leading Indicator of Drilling Activity," *Society of Petroleum Engineers* (SPE), No. 14466.

Coons, James W., 1990, "Predicting Turning Points in the Interest Rate Cycle," Huntington National Bank, Columbus, OH, manuscript, October.

de Leeuw, Frank, 1991, "Toward a Theory of Leading Indicators," in *Leading Economic Indicators: New Approaches and Forecasting Records,* K. Lahiri and Geoffrey Moore, eds., Cambridge: Cambridge University Press, 15–56.

Hamilton, James D., 1989, "A New Approach to the Economic Analysis of Nonstationary Time Series and the Business Cycle," *Econometrica,* Vol. 57, No. 2 (March), 357–384.

Holmes, R. A., 1986, "Leading Indicators of Industrial Employment in British Columbia," *International Journal of Forecasting,* Vol. 2, 87–100.

Journal of Commerce, 1991, "Early Warning System Helps Workers Guard Jobs," August 22, Section B, p. 1B.

Karfunkle, Richard, 1969, "Statistical Indicators of the Textile Cycle," *Business Economics,* May, 13–17.

Layton, Allan P., Defris, Lorraine V., and Zehnwirth, Ben, 1986, "An International Comparison of Economic Leading Indicators of Telecommunications Traffic," *International Journal of Forecasting,* Vol. 2, 413–425.

Maurer, Ruth A., 1985, "Indicators for the Energy and Minerals Industries," Colorado School of Mines, Working Paper ME-WP No. 1012, June.

McLaughlin, Robert L., 1971, "Leading Indicators: A New Approach for Corporate Planning," *Business Economics,* May.

Moore, Geoffrey H., 1969, "Generating Leading Indicators from Lagging Indicators," *Western Economic Journal,* June, 137–144.

Moore, Geoffrey H., and Zarnowitz, Victor, 1982, "Sequential Signals of Recession and Recovery," *Journal of Business,* Vol. 55 (January) 57–85.

Neftçi, Salih, 1982, "Optimal Prediction of Cyclical Downturns," *Journal of Economic Dynamics and Control,* 225–241.

Niemira, Michael P., 1982, "Developing Industry Leading Economic Indicators," *Business Economics,* January, 5–16.

Niemira, Michael P., 1990, "A New Leading Indicator of Service Inflation," *The Service Economy,* Coalition of Service Industries, October, 1–5.

Niemira, Michael P., 1991, "Using Composite Leading Indicators of Consumption to Forecast Sales and to Signal Turning Points in the Stock Market," in *Leading Economic Indicators: New Approaches and Forecasting Records,* K. Lahiri and Geoffrey Moore, eds., Cambridge University Press, 335–371.

Niemira, Michael P., 1991, "An International Application of Neftçi's Probability Approach for Signaling Growth Recessions and Recoveries Using Turning Point Indicators," in *Leading Economic Indicators: New Approaches and Forecasting Records,* K. Lahiri and Geoffrey Moore, eds., Cambridge: Cambridge University Press, 91–108.

Niemira, Michael P., 1990, "Forecasting Turning Points in the Stock Market Cycle and Asset Allocation Implications," *Studies in Modern Business Cycles: Recent Work in Analyzing Business Cycles,* Philip A. Klein, ed., Armonk, NY: M. E. Sharpe, 109–127.

Niemira, Michael P., and Fredman, Giela T., 1991, "An Evaluation of the Composite Index of Leading Indicators for Signaling Turning Points in Business and Growth Cycles," *Business Economics,* October, 49–55.

Niemira, Michael P., and Klein, Philip A., 1991, "Forecasting the Great Depression Using Cyclical Indicators: Another Look," manuscript, February.

Phillips, Keith R., 1990, "The Texas Index of Leading Economic Indicators: A Revision and Further Evaluation," *Economic Review,* Federal Reserve Bank of Dallas, July, 7–20.

Roth, Howard L., 1986, "Leading Indicators of Inflation," *Economic Review,* Federal Reserve Bank of Kansas City, November, 3–20.

Schmid, Dieter, 1986, "A New Qualitative Leading Indicator for Forecasting New Savings and Loan Industry," *Leading Indicators of Demand in the Building Industry,* CIRET Study 37, Munich, 119–147.

Stock, James H., and Watson, Mark W., 1989, "New Indexes of Coincident and Leading Economic Indicators," in *NBER Macroeconomics Annual 1989,* O. Blanchard and S. Fischer, eds., Cambridge, MA: MIT Press, 351–394.

6 Regional Business Cycles

INTRODUCTION

Regional sensitivity to national recessions and expansions has differed widely in the postwar period.[1] Evolving from this business cycle fact was the concept of *rolling recessions* popularized in the 1980s by Wall Street economists. In that view, business cycles were not necessarily destined because unsynchronized regional recessions were continually occurring. But regions are linked, and weakness developing in one region can spread quickly to another. Hence, despite the appeal of the rolling regional recession idea, it is probably not totally defensible based on business cycle history. On the other hand, some regions may have a tendency to be at the forefront of cyclical change—for better or worse. For example, one study sponsored by the U.S. Employment Development Administration in the late 1970s found that states located in the Northeast had a tendency to lead at business cycle downturns, states in the West tended to lag, and Southern states tended to skip mild slowdowns but to lead at severe downturns.[2] Why is this the case?

The answer may lie with regional growth *trends*. Regions where trend growth is rapid have tended to be less sensitive to the national cycle and vice versa. Moreover, Richard Syron (1978) observed that even given structural changes in the economy, there is still no convergence in economic growth across regions of the United States:

> The trend over the last 30 years has been for a smaller proportion of the workforce to be employed in heavy industries that are tied to a particular locality because of the availability of raw materials. Advances in transportation and communications would also be expected to result in increased integration of regional economies. However, despite these developments there does not appear to be any trend toward a convergence in regional sensitivity to business cycles. If anything, regions seem to be becoming more dissimilar. It is also interesting to note that the variation in regional responsiveness is not positively related to the severity of a recession. A threshold effect seems to exist with relatively mild recessions affecting only slower-growing regions, which may also have a high

share of cyclically sensitive industries, while once a downturn becomes sufficiently severe it affects all industries and parts of the country.[3]

Since regions behave differently, state and local governments as well as local businesses should examine the character of their own regional cycle. Only
then is it possible to compare and contrast the cyclical nature of different regions of the country. Unfortunately, at the regional level, measurement problems are more pronounced. In the first of two contributed articles in this
chapter, Zoltan Kenessey, who has been associated with the Federal Reserve
Board's industrial production series for about 15 years, addresses the regional
measurement issue. At the Federal Reserve Board, Kenessey spearheaded a
move to develop regional *total production indexes,* and he presents the history,
methodology, and a catalog of the regional total production measures available
(to date).

The second contribution takes a slightly different approach. Keith Phillips,
an economist with the Dallas Federal Reserve Bank, developed a coincident
indicator of the Texas economy and then formulated a leading economic indicator for the state of Texas. To help interpret changes in the leading indicator,
Phillips then used Neftçi's sequential probabilities (see Chapter 3). That approach allowed him to quantify the risk of a turning point in the Texas economy. His article also catalogs regional leading economic indicators that have
been developed for various states, cities, and regions in the United States.

Both contributions are excellent regional applications of the themes of this
book. While these articles are different from each other, they share a common thread: developing indicators to measure and monitor regional economic
performance.

Regional Monthly Production Indexes in the United States

Zoltan Kenessey*

HISTORICAL BACKGROUND

The Federal Reserve System, the central banking institution of the country, sets and carries out monetary policy in the United States. It is also instrumental in operation of the payment mechanism, in the examination of banks, and in fiscal-agency functions for the U.S. Treasury. The Federal Reserve is organized as a regional organization, and its functions are executed with the help of 12 district banks and their 25 branches located in various U.S. cities. In assessing the system's national role, economists often overlook the implications of the regional features of the U.S. central banking system.

From its inception in 1913, the Federal Reserve has maintained a keen interest in the business conditions of the country, with particular regard to cyclical movement in the economy. A key coincident indicator of the U.S. economy is the monthly Index of Industrial Production, which has been compiled at the Board of Governors of the Federal Reserve System in Washington, DC since the 1920s and goes back to 1919. Naturally, the Board provides and analyzes banking and monetary statistics covering the gamut of the flow of funds, and the statistical activities in these fields (while not covered in this review) provide a wealth of information regarding national and regional financial developments.

The following information is confined to the work on production indexes and describes both recent initiatives and long-standing efforts in this area. To place this work in context, first an outline is given about the Federal Reserve as a regional organization.

The work on the regional production indexes is presented against the backdrop of four analytical applications of these indicators:

1. Comparisons of regional growth with national rates and performance of other regions.

* Dr. Kenessey is currently the Director of the International Statistical Institute, in Voorburg, The Netherlands. This article developed from work when he was a Senior Economist at the Board of Governors of the Federal Reserve System in Washington, DC. Over his long career, which also included work at the United Nations, Dr. Kenessey was in charge of the industrial output section of the Federal Reserve Board. While at the Federal Reserve, he spearheaded an effort to develop a timely service production index. (The views expressed in this article are his and should not be attributed to the Federal Reserve Board, the Federal Reserve Banks, or to their staff.)

2. Analysis of regional and national business cycle movements.

3. Study of the uneven growth between the Pacific and Atlantic coastal areas, on the one hand, and the American heartland, on the other.

4. Evaluation of the regional shifts to services and issues of deindustrialization.

Because the analytical possibilities of the production indexes cannot be evaluated without understanding the statistical and methodological issues behind these indicators, the concluding part of the review deals with conceptual and data questions. These include value-added estimates in the regional context; forecasting accuracy of the different regional indexes; relevance of regional input-output for the index work; the use of regional electric energy data (collected originally by the 12 Federal Reserve banks for the National Industrial Production Index); the use of gross state product data for weighting the regional indexes; the issue of capital-energy complementarity. Also, in view of the large share of service production at the national level (and overwhelming significance in some regions and states), reliance on regional industrial production indicators alone may not provide sufficient analytical basis any more. Therefore, recent efforts to develop comprehensive regional production indexes (which cover the output of all goods and all services) are also described.

The literature regarding the new developments in regional production indexes in the United States is not widely known within or outside the country, so an extensive listing of references follows this article. Many of these sources, especially the more recently published materials, can be obtained from the 12 Federal Reserve banks.

THE FEDERAL RESERVE: A REGIONAL ORGANIZATION

The Federal Reserve System, as established in 1913, includes 12 districts, each of which is served by a Reserve bank. The districts are numbered from 1 to 12, in the order of the Federal Reserve banks located in the following cities: Boston, New York, Philadelphia, Cleveland, Richmond, Atlanta, Chicago, St. Louis, Minneapolis, Kansas City, Dallas, and San Francisco.

The territory of the 12 districts varies a great deal: the area served by the Federal Reserve Bank of San Francisco (Twelfth District) is by far the largest, but the geographic scope of the Minneapolis, Kansas City, or Dallas Fed is also much more extensive than that of the Boston, New York, Philadelphia, or Cleveland Federal Reserve Bank. The determination of the district boundaries in 1913 was largely based on the economic and financial importance (rather than the geographic size) of the new districts at that time. Also, attaching prime importance to economic interconnections rather than administrative boundaries, the new districts, in many cases, cut across state lines. Such circumstances explain the large size of the districts west of the Mississippi and the small area of the districts in New England. Today, in contrast, not only by area but also by population and total output, the Twelfth District is the largest (owing mainly to the phenomenal development of California). According to population, in descending order, today the 12 districts rank as follows: San Francisco, Chicago, Atlanta, New York, Richmond, Dallas, Cleveland, Kansas City, St. Louis, Boston, Philadelphia, Minneapolis. The population of the Twelfth District (the largest) is almost six times greater than that of the Ninth (the least populated).

In total output (aggregate gross state output by district) the ranking is slightly different: San Francisco, New York, Chicago, Atlanta, Richmond, Dallas, Cleveland, Boston, Kansas City, St. Louis, Philadelphia, Minneapolis. Finally, in terms of per capita output, Boston and New York lead, followed by San Francisco and Dallas. Philadelphia, Cleveland, Richmond, Chicago, Minneapolis, and Kansas City occupy middle or near middle ranks, while Atlanta and St. Louis are at the bottom (Kenessey, 1986).

In comparison with European countries, the territory of the districts (with the exception of the Philadelphia district) is often rather large: six of them (San Francisco, Dallas, Kansas City, Minneapolis, Chicago, and Atlanta) are larger than France, which has the largest territory in Western Europe. In population, moreover, only the San Francisco district is somewhat over 40 million inhabitants, and only Chicago is somewhat over 30 million. Both districts remain well behind populous European states such as Germany, Italy, the United Kingdom, France, or Spain. On the other hand, even the least populous districts have more inhabitants than the smaller European states such as Switzerland or Denmark. The climatic differences among the 12 districts are also significant. For example, the average temperature in Dallas is about 48% higher than in Minneapolis. In comparison, the average temperature in Rome is about 42% higher than in Stockholm. In both cases, however, the temperatures listed exaggerate the climatic variations because a large part of the inhabitants of both continents live within a smaller range of temperatures, with the U.S. average being somewhat higher (perhaps by 10%–12%) than the Western European.

These data illustrate the point that each Federal Reserve bank serves a sizable part of the U.S. economy and these parts—while having dominant common features—also vary in a number of regards. Both the common and the particular characteristics of the districts may enter the picture when they—as mentioned—participate in the setting and implementation of monetary policy, and carry out a number of other functions as well (Strong, 1922).

In respect of national economic policy, the Federal Reserve banks set the discount rate and evaluate the economic conditions that, in turn, guide the determination of the open market operations of the System:

Open market operations are the principal instrument used by the Federal Reserve to implement national monetary policy. According to statute the Federal Open Market Committee is responsible for determining what transactions the Federal Reserve will conduct in the open market. . . . The FOMC comprises the seven members of the Board of Governors and five Reserve Bank presidents, one of whom is the president of the Federal Reserve Bank of New York. The other Bank presidents serve one-year terms on a rotating basis. (Board of Governors, 1984, pp. 6–7)

Whether they happen to be committee members or not, all 12 bank presidents attend the meetings of the FOMC as voting or nonvoting participants of its discussion (usually 8 meetings are held each year). To carry out this responsibility, they rely on their own research staff, which helps in the evaluation, analysis, and forecasting of economic events. The availability of national and regional statistical information is quite important for this process (Bell & Crone, 1986). Given the usefulness of production indicators as coincident cyclical indicators, there has been a long-standing interest by the Board of Governors and members of the FOMC in the U.S. Index of Industrial Production (reports of the FOMC, without fail, contain references to the movements observed by the index). The expansion in regional production indexes, while less important for gauging the overall U.S. business cycle, has helped the banks determine the movements in their own districts relative to the nation's as a whole and in comparison with other districts. The information available from such indexes can also throw light on the changes observed in the operations of the banks, such as distribution of coin and currency, operation of the payments mechanism, examination of banks, and fiscal-agency functions for the U.S. Treasury.

PRODUCTION INDEXES: EARLY FEDERAL RESERVE EFFORTS

The Federal Reserve Bank of Atlanta was among the first to create its regional production index. Growing out of work in the 1950s, a district manufacturing output index was introduced in 1970 (Pyun, 1970, p. 75). The concepts and methods applied were similar to those used for the national industrial production index (NIPA); physical product data, however (which covers about half the U.S. index), were not used. The two types of data—labor series (manhours worked and electricity used kilowatt hours)—were the two basic ingredients incorporated in all other regional production indexes as well. For both labor and electricity productivity, factors were estimated and the series were corrected by them to provide more reliable regional output estimates. Census value-added data were used as weights for the industries included (Strobel, 1978). The original indexes were later revised and certain modifications were accepted in the process. The Atlanta indexes, owing to their careful preparation and to the extensive period of development dedicated to them, exercised considerable influence on similar work in other districts.

In the Dallas district, the index work also goes back to the 1950s; the Texas Industrial Production Index (TIPI) has been estimated since 1958 (Sullivan, 1975). Unlike most other regional indexes, TIPI includes mining and utilities as well as manufacturing, because of their large share in the Texas economy. Over the years, the methodology of TIPI changed in various ways (Fomby, 1983), albeit for a considerable period, it was rather analogous to the Atlanta approach. In the early 1980s, sophisticated research was carried out regarding TIPI, and some interesting econometric investigations were published concerning regional production indicators (Fomby, 1986).

In San Francisco, a manufacturing production index of the district was issued in December 1973 on a 1967 = 100 basis back to January 1963. A Cobb-Douglas production function was chosen to describe the movement of manufacturing output in this region. The San Francisco index, while retaining similarity with the work in other districts, departed from them by introducing a three-factor production function. Explaining the departure, Walsh and Butler suggested:

> [T]he two inputs on which we have observations, labor and electricity consumption, exhaust only about half of the production receipts in typical industries. Of the other half, about four-fifths would typically accrue to factors other than capital, and one-fifth would accrue to capital. . . . Our solution to the problem was simply to abandon the usual two-factor model and go to an explicit three-factor formulation. (Walsh & Butler, 1973)

As explained later in this article, the Chicago indexes also have recently been extended from their earlier two-factor format, by introducing a third basic component in a different way (by adding a payroll variable). Naturally, research on extending production functions to include variables other than labor and capital has been undertaken by prominent researchers elsewhere (Jorgenson, Gollop, & Fraumeni, 1987).

In the 1970s and early 1980s, the Federal Reserve Bank of Boston published monthly regional production indexes for manufacturing and several of its components. The indexes were meant to be analogous to the U.S. indexes constructed by the Board of Governors in Washington, DC, and in part, relied on the movements shown in the U.S. index to estimate the changes in production of New England (Connolly, 1978). The New England Index covered six states: Connecticut, Maine, Massachusetts, New Hampshire, Rhode Island, and Vermont.

In the 1970s, the Planning Board of Puerto Rico (Junta Central de Planificacion, JUCEPLAN) initiated studies to improve measurement of monthly output changes on the island, owing to dissatisfaction with the available limited indicator estimated by a private service locally. At the request of JUCEPLAN, the staff of the Board of Governors was involved in the evaluation of statistical sources available for this purpose and in the development of blueprints for a new measure. The statistical basis for estimating a production index for the island is essentially the same as in other areas of the United States; hence, the construction of the index would be feasible, and initial work has been carried out to this end. However, the firm establishment of the index would have required budgetary resources that were not available at the time (Kenessey, 1979).

In the late 1970s and early 1980s, in conjunction with the review of the kilowatt hour survey that the district banks maintain for use of the data in the national industrial production index, experimental regional indexes were estimated for the 12 districts. The intent of the effort was to illustrate the potential regional usefulness of the KWH data collected by the banks. The indexes were of the Laspeyres type and used 1972 as the base year. Productivity factors for 2-digit SIC categories computed at the national level were assumed to have validity in all 12 districts. These indexes were uniform in their methodology and comparable across districts (Kenessey, 1986). An attempt was also made to estimate annual output indexes for the 12 districts, covering the 1963–1986 period (Kenessey, 1987a).

These early indexing efforts were often abandoned as budgetary stringencies appeared. The question arises: Should we pay any attention to these attempts at all? Our positive reply to the question rests on two significant strains of experience obtained during the early years. The first is that the early efforts have proven the statistical feasibility of estimating regional production indexes on the basis of available regional indicators, particularly labor and KWH series. The weights required for the indicators are also available from the gross state product estimates now produced for every state by the Bureau of Economic Analysis (Giese, 1989). The second is the wealth of research results accumulated in the early years of regional index work, especially in Atlanta, Dallas, and San Francisco. Whether the publication of the indexes was interrupted (as in Atlanta, or San Francisco) or has been continued (as in Dallas) the methodological experience gained in all the efforts provides valuable reasons for both current and future work in this field. Indeed, the present discussions and new developments in various districts (Chicago, Richmond, Philadelphia, Cleveland) cannot be understood except in the context of these early efforts. Hence, the concluding methodological section of this review refers to the early and current efforts as interrelated and inseparable.

RECENT EXTENSION OF PRODUCTION INDEXES

Among the recent wave of new regional production indexes, the establishment of the Ohio manufacturing index by the Federal Reserve Bank of Cleveland was the first. This index used a Cobb-Douglas type production function and, in the main, followed the methodology of the Atlanta index (Bryan & Day, 1987).

The second development, and of greater impact, has been the work initiated at the Federal Reserve Bank of Chicago (Schnorbus & Israilevich, 1987). The bank's new indicator, the *Midwest Manufacturing Index (MMI)* covers the entire Seventh District, which comprises the states of Michigan, Iowa, southern Wisconsin, and the larger (and more industrialized) parts of Illinois and Indiana. The new MMI followed the methodology of the Atlanta method and utilized labor series (total worker hours), electricity use data (KWH), as well as value added and payroll data for constructing weights and so forth for the 17 two-digit manufacturing industries of the district. In the summer of 1989, MMI was revised in three main respects:

1. The base year was updated from 1973 to 1983.
2. The weights for each of the 17 component industries were determined by a new empirical model.
3. A U.S. version of MMI was created for comparisons with manufacturing output movements at the national level (Schnorbus & Israilevich, 1989).

The third major indexing initiative occurred at the Federal Reserve Bank of Richmond. In 1988, the work in Richmond resulted in an aggregate index for the Fifth District as a whole, as well as in state indexes of manufacturing for Maryland (including Washington, DC), North Carolina, South Carolina, Virginia, and West Virginia. The publication of state indexes is a helpful addition, inasmuch as the political authorities, of course, are organized according to political boundaries, and both legislative and executive branches of the concerned states can make good use of the new series. Apart from this novelty, the indexes are similar to the others: The data used are mainly labor series, kilowatt hour data, and value-added information; and linear homogeneous production functions are accepted to represent the relationship between output and the two key inputs, labor and capital (Bechter, Chmura, & Ko, 1988).

The fourth important regional indexing event in the Federal Reserve System has been the introduction of the Mid-Atlantic index by the Federal Reserve Bank of Philadelphia. Since 1989, this index has tracked the course of output in Delaware, New Jersey, New York, and Pennsylvania. The Third District (the area of the Bank) only covers the eastern two-thirds of Pennsylvania, the southern part of New Jersey, and the entire state of Delaware. Since data on value added, employment, and average weekly hours are available for entire states, it was preferable to provide coverage for the whole of the four states mentioned. Also, the KWH data is collected by Federal Reserve districts and the series collected by the Philadelphia Bank do not cover western Pennsylvania and northern New Jersey. Since the KWH data for the latter are collected by the Federal Reserve Bank of New York but cannot be separated from the rest of that district's data,

New York was included into the indicator. On the other hand, KWH data for western Pennsylvania could be obtained from the Federal Reserve Bank of Cleveland. In essence, the Mid-Atlantic Manufacturing Index covers two Federal Reserve districts: the Second (New York) and the Third (Philadelphia). Nineteen manufacturing industries are included, and the Atlanta methodology is followed (Hamer, 1989). Regarding this region, mention should be made also of the work at The Pennsylvania State University on a separate manufacturing index for that state (Anderson, 1989).

Finally, the Federal Reserve Bank of Dallas has recently updated TIPI (Berger & Long, 1989). An important feature of this recent review was the benchmarking of TIPI to new data available from the Bureau of Economic Analysis (BEA) of the U.S. Department of Commerce on gross state product. Previously TIPI, like the other regional indexes, relied on data from the U.S. Bureau of the Census (from the Censuses and Annual Surveys of Manufacturers) for benchmarking its series.

Also, consideration has been given to the resumption of production index work in Atlanta. At the minimum, it is planned that the Federal Reserve Bank of Atlanta will assist in the establishment of a production index for Florida, one of the key states and most dynamic economies in the district. Also, with the help of the Federal Reserve Bank of Richmond, preparatory work is under way to construct a monthly production indicator of the District of Columbia (Kenessey, 1989b).

ANALYTICAL USES OF THE INDEXES

Like other multipurpose statistical measures, the regional production indexes have a variety of uses. Users in government, business, academia, and the media approach these output indicators from many viewpoints and with divergent analytical purposes. The widest use of the production indexes is the gauging of the current health of a region's economy, especially in respect of the ups and downs of the business cycle. In addition, recent utilization of the regional indexes included the evaluation of relative performance of regions, comparisons of the cyclicality of various regions, the study of differences in coastal and inland development, and research regarding regional deindustrialization in the United States. The general question of spatial decentralization of manufacturing in the U.S. was raised some time ago (Norton & Ries, 1979).

Almost every regional index has been compared with the manufacturing output index for the United States. In view of the methodological differences, these comparisons have certain inherent limitations, so recently the Federal Reserve Bank of Chicago created an index for the total United States conforming to the methodology of the Midwest Manufacturing Index (Schnorbus &

Israilevich, 1989). Owing to the differences in their methodologies, the various regional indexes are not entirely comparable with each other either, therefore, such comparisons have some limitations as well. To the degree that the indexes aim at estimating changes in real value added in manufacturing as available from Census data, the overall scope of the estimates may be very close. However, the need to deflate the nominal value-added data with specific regional price measures (which are not necessarily available in the optimal form for such regional purposes) may also limit the comparability of these estimates. So far, the highest degree of comparability seems to exist for the five state indexes created at the Federal Reserve Bank of Richmond.

Cyclicality in the regional economies and their interconnections with the national cycle are among the key questions studied by users of output indexes. On the one hand, comparisons of the charts of the regional output indexes (and statistical measures of variability, etc.) permit the evaluation of the differences in cyclical movements among them. On the other hand, the strength of the interconnection in the movements can be studied by statistical techniques as well (Sherwood-Call, 1988). Tests of such national-state comovements suggest that the linkages to the national fluctuations are rather different for various states.

The contrasting economic development, in the mid-to-late 1980s, between the more prosperous coastal areas and the sluggish inland economic regions of the United States has received a fair amount of attention in the media and in the U.S. Congress (Joint Economic Committee, 1986). On a broader plane, the earlier tendency of gradual reduction in regional (state) per capita income differences in the 1980s has been replaced by increasing state income divergence. Various explanations have been offered for these developments. However, it was suggested "that the regional variation in output growth was not due to differences in productivity growth, but instead to variation in the rates of growth of capital and labor. We thus found no evidence to support the hypothesis that an aging public infrastructure, obsolete capital stock or higher rate of unionization have slowed total factor productivity in the Snow Belt" (Hulten & Schwab, 1984, p. 152). Although there is little doubt about the recent growth in regional economic disparities (Kenessey, 1987b), explanations for these differences vary (Carlino, 1986). Moreover, while regions are obviously impacted by the general thrust in national economic growth, the regions and districts also have their own ups and downs.

At the national and at the regional level, the deindustrialization issue has remained controversial (Norton, 1986). Constant dollar Gross Product Originating data by Industry do not suggest a decline in the share of manufacturing output within total U.S. GNP/GDP. As far as individual regions are concerned, there is little doubt that some older manufacturing regions have grown more slowly than other areas of the country. The pertinent questions have been extensively studied, especially for the Chicago district (Schnorbus & Giese, 1987). In the Chicago studies, findings based on the Midwest Manufacturing Index played a crucial role. While the shift to services is generally viewed as unavoidable, concerns about this development are also voiced in the districts (Perna, 1987).

CONCEPTUAL AND STATISTICAL QUESTIONS

Several conceptual and statistical issues are involved in the estimation and evaluation of regional production indexes. Only four broad issues are discussed in this review: (1) the type of production function used, (2) the weights applied, (3) the problems of electricity use, and (4) the prospects for total production indexes. Many other questions, including such important ones as aggregation, sampling, interindustry linkages, and seasonal adjustment are not touched on. Even the matters discussed are considered only with regards to the regional production indexes previously described.

PRODUCTION FUNCTIONS

As mentioned earlier, the regional manufacturing indexes generally followed the formulation initially applied to the Atlanta indexes. This nonparametric approach assumes that the movement of manufacturing production can be represented by changes in manufacturing *value added* for which the Surveys and Censuses of Manufactures provide *annual* data. To develop monthly estimates in the movement of manufacturing value added, *monthly* data on *labor* inputs, known from the survey of the Bureau of Labor Statistics (BLS), and monthly data on capital inputs (proxied by electricity consumption by industry data, collected by the districts) are combined. It is assumed that there are only these two factors of production—capital and labor. Further assumptions are that markets are competitive, firms maximize profits, constant returns to scale exist, and total output is the aggregate of industry outputs. For each industry, the annual payroll data on labor compensation are divided by the value added for the industry, and the resultant ratio provides the share for the labor factor; the share of the capital factor is assumed to equal one minus labor's share. The annual nominal value-added data are deflated by price indexes to obtain annual value added in real terms. Thus annual output equals real value added, which equals the joint contribution (sum) of the two factors of output (labor and capital). Essentially, the method assumes that value added of each factor of production can be represented as the *sum of payments* to labor and capital. Consequently, such methods have been called "sum-of-payments methods" (Fomby, 1986).

The labor and capital shares of output are assumed to be relatively stable, although provisions are made to allow gradual shifts between them. This is achieved in the monthly estimating of value added via the factor inputs. Monthly capital and labor productivity factors are applied to the capital and labor inputs. Monthly productivity factors are inferred from the relationship between annual factor inputs and the value-added data. The trends in these productivity factors, which are determined from annual observations, need to be interpolated for the 12 months within each year, and extrapolated after the latest available annual observation for the subsequent months, until new annual data become available. Typically, the annual growth rates in productivity of labor and capital are evenly distributed for the intervening 12 months. A similar smooth trend is assumed to hold for the changes in the share weights of labor and capital, known only annually. The interpolation of these weights can allow for shifts between them; in most cases, however, the extrapolation of such shifts is considered hazardous, and constant share weights are maintained for the period of extrapolation. The seasonally adjusted monthly labor and KWH series for each industry, combined with the monthly share and productivity factors yield the estimate, for the given month, of the real value added for that industry, which is then divided by the average monthly value of the same measure for the base period (e.g., 1987). The index for overall manufacturing is compiled by aggregating, with value-added weights, the individual industry indexes into the total index. The various regional indexes differ in some respects from each other, but for most, the preceding outline describes the basic steps involved in estimating them. The 1975 revision of the Dallas Fed's TIPI incorporated a Cobb-Douglas empirical production function for estimating it. That formulation provided for explicit variations in factor proportions. In the 1983 revision of TIPI, however, an Atlanta type sum-of-payments approach was introduced again.

The nonparametric Atlanta approach, which was used for most indexes, has been fairly successful and reliable. An influential study (Fomby, 1986, first distributed as a working paper in 1983) indicated that this method outperformed other nonparametric approaches, as well as parametric methods. The return to the Atlanta method was a result of these findings. Studies undertaken since then suggest that, in spite of its simplicity, the Atlanta method remains the best performer among both parametric and nonparametric methods, as long as only capital and labor factors are used in estimating the indexes. A Chicago Federal Reserve study reinforced this finding that the Atlanta method was a superior formulation for an index based on two factors of production. (Israilevich, Schnorbus, & Schneider, 1989). However, by adding a third variable (payroll earnings by industry, a series also available on a monthly basis), parametric models yielded better results. The Chicago review also suggested:

> Finally, and most importantly, the study finds that no single method can be found that produced the lowest mean absolute errors for all industries in the set. In other words, even better results can be obtained by modeling each industry individually

to find the lowest prediction error, and then combining all the industry series into an aggregate manufacturing index, based on weights derived from each industry's share of total value added. (Israilevich, Schnorbus, & Schneider, 1989, pp. 19–20)

The Chicago study involved data for a 1972–1983 in-sample period and projections for two out-of-sample years: 1984 and 1985. The projected values for these two years were compared with known values for them. Another study recently conducted at the Dallas Fed explored systematic multivariate time series models for forecasting the Texas economy (Gruben & Long, 1988).

WEIGHTING

As mentioned earlier, the Annual Surveys and Censuses of Manufacturers provide value-added data for manufacturing by states, which can be aggregated into district series. An alternative set of value-added data is available from the BEA gross state product (GSP) series. The conceptual groundwork for GSP goes back some years (Kendrick & Jaycox, 1965), and in recent years there have been many improvements in the data (Renshaw, Trott, & Friedenberg, 1988). In the recent revision of the Texas Industrial Production Index, these series have been used for the index. Also, a Chicago inquiry explored the data problems related to the value-added series available from Census.

An additional statistical problem is that auxiliary establishments of manufacturing enterprises (corporate headquarters, research laboratories, computer centers, warehouses) "are wrongly apportioned to states and regions on the basis of operating establishment site while neglecting the location of the auxiliary establishment. . . . We believe that this contribution to manufacturing output should be counted at the site of the auxiliary activity" (Israilevich & Testa, 1989, p. 3). On the basis of a review of the concentration of auxiliary establishments in certain metropolitan areas, the authors "expect that, in measuring manufacturing output, the North and Midwest actually have greater levels than currently reported while manufacturing activity in the South is overstated" (Israilevich & Testa, p. 5).

ELECTRICITY USE

Electricity consumption in industry has been used to estimate the output of many industries in the Federal Reserve Board's Industrial Production Index (IP) since the 1971 major revision of the index: In terms of the value-added weights of 1977, about 31% of the index is compiled with electricity data. As mentioned, these data are collected from the public utilities and many self-generators by the 12 Federal Reserve banks on a monthly basis. Given their involvement in the work with these series, it is not surprising that all regional indexing efforts by the districts rely, in part, on these data series. The use of capital stock for estimating capital services in the production process has been favored, but lack of such data for the indexes prevented their use. Also, the regional builders of production indexes widely accepted the results of a study in the 1970s that indicated the change in electric power use can be a useful proxy regarding the services of capital in the process of production (Moody, 1974).

In connection with electricity use, the debate regarding the relationship between energy and capital (whether they are substitutes or complements) is of some interest (Solow, 1987). Some authors found that capital and energy are complements, others suggested that they are substitutes. The idea that they are complements in the short run but substitutes in the long run was also broached. From the viewpoint of production indexes, perhaps the suggestion that the number of variables studied (only capital, labor, and energy—or adding a fourth variable, materials) also matters when searching for answers to these questions. It has been also suggested that the relationships between energy and capital are sensitive to the composition of capital according to its two reported subdivisions: equipment and buildings, as these two types of capital are differently related to energy. Indeed, a recent study, based on cross-sectional data for 40 states in the United States reported: "Our empirical results do not support the aggregation of building and machinery capital into a single index of capital" (Garofalo & Malhotra, 1988). Thus the complex relationships between energy and capital are not yet fully understood, and the role of these two factors in the productivity slowdown is still further analyzed (Kilpatrick & Naisbitt, 1988). In our view, the importance of including more than just capital and labor in estimating output is perhaps the most important suggestion available from a number of studies. Whether electricity is the best indicator for estimating capital services or is preferably used as an energy variable is not as important as how many inputs are used in the production function. In general terms, the attention to including intermediate inputs in accounting for growth has been of considerable relevance for this turn of research interests (Hulten, 1978).

INDEXES OF TOTAL PRODUCTION

In view of the cyclical sensitivity of manufacturing, the attention paid both at national and regional levels to industrial production indexes is quite understandable. At the same time, the shift to service production indicates the importance of following output changes in services as well. In October 1989, 110.1 million people were estimated to be on nonagricultural payrolls, according to the establishment survey of BLS. Manufacturing and mining employment amounted to 20.4 million (18.5% of the total). In comparison, the six major service sectors (transportation; communication; public utilities; wholesale trade; retail trade; finance, insurance, and real estate; services; government) employed 84.1 million persons (76.4% of the total). At the regional level, particularly in certain states, the share of service employment can be even higher. Thus both nationally and in the regions, the monthly changes in service production deserve as much scrutiny as the movements in industrial production.

At the national level, the Federal Reserve Board has produced an Experimental Service Production Index (SP), which was circulated to interested users for comments over a 3-year period. Also, experimental indicators were estimated for comparisons with SP for all goods as well. The *all goods index* was based, in the main, on the Federal Reserve's Index of Industrial Production (IP), which goes back to 1919. The comprehensive system of indexes for all goods and all services comprised monthly production measures for four megasectors, as follows:

1. Primary Sector
   Agriculture
   Mining
2. Secondary Sector
   Construction
   Manufacturing
3. Tertiary Sector
   Transportation, communications, utilities
   Wholesale trade
   Retail trade
4. Quaternary Sector
   Finance, insurance, real estate
   Services
   Government

The primary and the secondary megasectors add up to the goods production area, while the tertiary and quaternary sectors aggregate into total services output. The indexes for all goods and all services together are the measure of total production.

Additionally, work has been done to develop regional total production indexes that cover all goods and all services. Two indexes of this sort, one for the state of Florida (Kenessey, 1989a) and another for the District of Columbia (Kenessey, 1989b) have been developed. The methodology of these two regional indexes was very similar to the original national IP methods, which have been used for SP at the national level as well.

For estimating the total production index and its megasector components, in general, three types of monthly indicators (basic series) are used. First, if available, and appropriate, physical unit measure output indicators are used (number of stocks traded on the stock exchange, number of homes sold, number of hospital admissions, etc.). Second, in numerous other cases, physical unit series are used as proxies to estimate changes in output. Most of these indicators are production worker hours and electricity use by various industries. Both labor series and kilowatt hour indicators are adjusted by production factor coefficients (PFCs) to allow for productivity change and thus assure the proper functioning of these input series as proxies of output change. Third, in order to allow for the impact of use of equipment and structures on the movement of production, capital use indicators are added to the previously mentioned first and second series. To each megasector, and every major industry within the four megasectors, value-added weights, taken from the BEA National Income and Product Accounts (NIPA) series, are assigned and thus the production changes in industries have a proportional impact on the changes in the total output. The indexes are calculated as Laspeyres type indexes, with 1987 envisaged as their base period. The not seasonally adjusted and seasonally adjusted indexes are compiled and for the latter the Census X-11 seasonal adjustment technique is utilized.

SUMMARY

The history of production index estimates within the Federal Reserve System goes back to 1919. The need for business cycle analysis, and for understanding of business conditions in general, led the Federal Reserve Board and the 12 Federal Reserve banks to follow movements of both financial and nonfinancial indicators of the economy from the inception of the system.

At the national level, IP has been widely followed and the experimental SP index has also stimulated interest both within and outside government. At the Federal Reserve banks, after the early beginnings of regional index developments in the 1960s and 1970s, new indexes were introduced in Chicago (Midwest Manufacturing Index in 1987), in Cleveland (Ohio Manufacturing Index in 1987), in Richmond (Fifth District Manufacturing Index, as well as indexes for five states within the district in 1988), and in Philadelphia (Mid-Atlantic

Manufacturing Index, which covers the Second and Third Districts, in 1988). Also, the Texas Industrial Production Index was revised in 1989.

The regional indexes, in the main, follow the methodology developed at the Federal Reserve Bank of Atlanta in the 1960s and 1970s. However, extensive efforts in Chicago and Dallas have significantly contributed to the understanding of the conceptual and statistical intricacies of the indexes. Research has been done to extend the regional work from manufacturing to services as well, in order to provide monthly measures of total production initially for some states and later for entire districts.

REFERENCES

Anderson, W. D., 1989, "The Pennsylvania Manufacturing Activity Index: Methodologies and Applications," *Pennsylvania Economic Studies,* No. 5, 1–31, The Pennsylvania State University, University Park, PA.

Bechter, D. M., 1988, *The Federal Reserve Today,* Federal Reserve Bank of Richmond, 1–32.

Bechter, D. M., Chmura, C., & Ko, R. K., 1988, "Fifth District Indexes of Manufacturing Output," *Economic Review,* Vol. 74, No. 3, 23–31, Federal Reserve Bank of Richmond.

Bell, J., and Crone, T., 1986, "Charting the Course of the U.S. Economy: What Can Local Manufacturers Tell Us?" *Business Review,* July/August, 3–16, Federal Reserve Bank of Philadelphia.

Berger, F. D., & Long, W. T., III, 1989, "The Texas Industrial Production Index," *Economic Review,* November, 21–28, Federal Reserve Bank of Dallas.

Board of Governors of the Federal Reserve System, 1984, *The Federal Reserve System—Purposes and Functions,* Washington, DC.

Bryan, M. F., & Day, R. L., 1987, "Views from the Ohio Manufacturing Index," *Economic Review,* Vol. 23, No. 3, 20–30, Federal Reserve Bank of Cleveland.

Carlino, G. A., 1986, "Do Regional Wages Differ?" *Business Review,* July/ August, 17–25, Federal Reserve Bank of Philadelphia.

Connolly, J. S., 1978, "The Revised New England Production Index," *New England Economic Indicators,* August.

Fomby, J. B., 1983, "The Revision of the Texas Industrial Production Index," *Methodology of the Texas Industrial Production Index,* Federal Reserve Bank of Dallas.

Fomby, J. B., 1986, "A Comparison of Forecasting Accuracies of Alternative Regional Production Index Methodologies, *Journal of Business and Economic Statistics,* Vol. 4, No. 2, 177–186.

Fosler, R. S. (ed.), 1988, "The New Economic Role of the American States," *Strategies in a Competitive World Economy,* Committee for Economic Development. Oxford: Oxford University Press.

Garofalo, G. A., and Malhotra, D. M., 1988, "Aggregation of Capital and Its Substitution with Energy," *Eastern Economic Journal,* Vol. XIV, No. 3, 251–262.

Giese, A. S., 1989, "A Window of Opportunity Opens for Regional Economic Analysts: BEA Releases Gross State Product Data," Working Paper, February, 3–23, Federal Reserve Bank of Chicago.

Gruben, W. C., & Long, W. T., 1988, "Forecasting the Texas Economy: Applications and Evaluation of a Systematic Multivariate Time Series Model," *Economic Review,* January, 11–28.

Hamer, T. O., 1989, "A New Regional Economic Indicator: The Mid-Atlantic Manufacturing Index," *Business Review,* January/February, 3–14.

Hulten, C. R., 1978, "Growth Accounting with Intermediate Inputs," *Review of Economic Studies,* October, 511–578.

Hulten, C. R., & Schwab, R. M., 1984, "Regional Productivity Growth in U.S. Manufacturing: 1951–78," *American Economic Review,* Vol. 74, No. 1, 152–162.

Israilevich, P. R., Schnorbus, R. H., & Schneider, P. R., 1989, "Reconsidering the Regional Manufacturing Indexes," *Economic Perspectives,* Vol. XIII, No. 4, 13–21, Federal Reserve Bank of Chicago.

Israilevich, P. R., & Testa, W. A., 1989, "The Geography of Value Added," *Economic Perspectives,* Vol. XIII, No. 5, 2–12, Federal Reserve Bank of Chicago.

Joint Economic Committee of the Congress of the United States, 1986, *The Bi-coastal Economy,* Staff Study, Washington, DC.

Jorgenson, D. W., Gollop, F. M., and Fraumeni, B., 1987, *Productivity and U.S. Economic Growth,* Cambridge, MA: Harvard University Press.

Kenessey, Z., 1979, *An Industrial Production Index for Puerto Rico,* Study for the Puerto Rico Planning Board, February.

Kendrick, J. W., & Jaycox, G. M., 1965, "The Concept and Estimation of Gross State Product," *Southern Economic Journal,* October, 153–168.

Kenessey, Z., 1986, "Regional Industrial Production Indexes in the U.S.," *System Committee on Regional Analysis,* Federal Reserve Bank of Chicago, October.

Kenessey, Z., 1987a, "Annual Output Indexes for Federal Reserve Districts, 1963–1986," *System Committee on Regional Analysis,* Federal Reserve Bank of St. Louis, October.

Kenessey, Z., 1987b, "Regional Output Disparities in the U.S.," *System's Business Analysis Committee,* Federal Reserve Bank of Kansas City, November.

Kenessey, Z., 1989a, *The Development of a Comprehensive Monthly Measure of Production for Florida, Regional Manufacturing Indexes,* Federal Reserve Bank of Philadelphia, September.

Kenessey, Z., 1989b, *The Construction of a Monthly Production Index for the District of Columbia,* University of the District of Columbia, November.

Kilpatrick, A., & Naisbitt, B., 1988, "Energy Intensity, Industrial Structure and the 1970s' Productivity Slowdown," *Oxford Bulletin of Economics and Statistics,* Vol. 50, No. 3, 229–241.

Moody, C. E., Jr., 1974, "The Measurement of Capital Services by Electrical Energy," *Oxford Bulletin of Economics and Statistics,* Vol. 36, No. 1, 45–52.

Norton R. D., 1986, "Industrial Policy and American Renewal," *Journal of Economic Literature,* Vol. XXIV, March, 1–40.

Norton, R. D., and Ries. J., 1979, "The Product Cycle and the Spatial Decentralization of American Manufacturing," *Regional Studies,* Vol. 73, 141–151.

Perna, N. S., 1987, "The Shift from Manufacturing to Services: A Concerned View," *New England Economic Review,* January/February, 30–38, Federal Reserve Bank of Boston.

Pyun, C. S., 1970, "A New Measure of Industrial Activity: District Manufacturing Production Index," *Monthly Review,* June, 74–78, Federal Reserve Bank of Atlanta.

Renshaw, V., Trott, E. A., & Friedenberg, H. L., 1988, "Gross State Product by Industry 1963–86," *Survey of Current Business,* May, 30–46, U.S. Department of Congress, Bureau of Economic Analysis, Washington, DC.

Schnorbus, R. H., & Giese, A. S., 1987, "Is the Seventh District's Economy Deindustrializing?" *Economic Perspectives,* Vol. 11, No. 6, 3–9, Federal Reserve Bank of Chicago.

Schnorbus, R. H., & Israilevich, P. R., 1987, "The Midwest Manufacturing Index: The Chicago Fed's New Regional Economic Indicator," *Economic Perspectives,* Vol. XI, No. 5, 3–7, Federal Reserve Bank of Chicago.

Schnorbus, R. H., & Israilevich, P. R., 1989, "The MMI Gets a Different Look," *Chicago Fed Letter,* No. 24, August, Federal Reserve Bank of Chicago.

Sherwood-Call, C., 1988, "Exploring the Relationships Between National and Regional Economic Fluctuations," *Economic Review,* Vol. 3 (Summer), 15–25, Federal Reserve Bank of San Francisco.

Solow, J. L., 1987, "The Capital-Energy Complementarity Debate Revisited," *American Economic Review,* September, 605–614.

Strobel, F. R., 1978, *Sixth District Manufacturing Production Indexes,* Technical Note and Statistical Supplement, April, Federal Reserve Bank of Atlanta.

Strong, B., 1922 (1989 reprint), "Federal Reserve Control of Credit," reprinted in *Quarterly Review,* Special Issue: 75th Anniversary; 6–14, Federal Reserve Bank of New York.

Sullivan, B. P., 1975, *Methodology of the Texas Industrial Production Index,* Federal Reserve Bank of Dallas.

Walsh, J., & Butler, L., 1973, "The Construction of Industrial Production Indices for Manufacturing Industries in the Twelfth Federal Reserve District," Working Paper No. 15, December, Federal Reserve Bank of San Francisco.

Regional Indexes of Leading Economic Indicators

Keith R. Phillips*

Since 1983, there has been a growing interest in the construction of regional leading indexes. An important reason for this movement has been the vastly different economic performances of regions in the United States during the 1980s. During this period, national indicators were often of little use to the regional forecaster.

The construction of a leading index offers the regional analyst a low-cost method of economic prediction. While the initial creation of a leading index can be time consuming, usually little maintenance is required. Leading indexes generally are constructed to provide stability in the relationship between the index and the business cycle. For example, the type of leading index produced by the U.S. Department of Commerce, Bureau of Economic Analysis (BEA), has been shown to be quite stable over time and across countries.[1a]

A leading index is often easier for users to understand than econometric models. While an econometric forecasting model is often complex, a leading index can be broken down easily to the net contribution of its components. Having a better feel for the sources of the forecast, the user can interject personal knowledge and expertise to achieve an individualized outlook.

The leading indicator approach also has limitations. Leading indicators do not offer the precision of an econometric model.[2a] Leading indicators are generally constructed to lead business cycle turning points and not to forecast growth rates or intracyclical movements in the economy.

The use of regional composite indexes is widespread across the United States. Some examples of leading indexes currently being produced are listed in Table 6.1. The list is not comprehensive.[3a] As seen in Table 6.1, leading indexes are being produced extensively at both the state and metropolitan levels. Most of the indexes are released either monthly or quarterly.

In examining leading indexes at the regional level, the BEA leading index is the primary role model. This is true of the variables contained in the indexes as well as the construction of the indexes. Many of the regional indexes, however, contain unique variables and approaches in their construction.

* Keith R. Phillips is an economist with the Federal Reserve Bank of Dallas. He joined the bank in January 1984. His areas of concentration include regional economics and economic forecasting. In September 1988, Mr. Phillips was awarded the Bank's President's Award for Excellence for the development of the Texas indexes of leading and coincident indicators. Mr. Phillips is responsible for regional forecasting at the Dallas Fed and is a contributing member of the Western Blue Chip Economic Forecasting Group.

Table 6.1 Regional Leading Indexes.

Region	Source	Periodicity
Southeast, aggregate, and each of the states Alabama, Arkansas, Florida, Georgia, Kentucky, Louisiana, Mississippi, North Carolina, South Carolina, Tennessee, Virginia, and West Virginia	Economic Forecasting Center College of Business Administration Georgia State University University Plaza Atlanta, GA 30303-3083	M
North Alabama	Mary Sonneburg Center for High Technology Management and Economic Research University of Alabama–Huntsville Morton Hall 220 Huntsville, AL 35899	Q
Arizona	Tracy L. Clark Center for Business Research College of Business Arizona State University Tempe, AZ 85287-4406	M
Colorado	Kendall Wilson Center for Business and Economic Research Regis College 50th and Lowell Denver, CO 80221-1099	M
Georgia	Mary Evans Georgia Business and Economic Conditions Selig Center for Economic Growth College of Business Administration University of Georgia Athens, GA 30337	Bi-M
Idaho	Kelly Matthews First Security Bank of Idaho P.O. Box 7069 Boise, ID 83730	M
Indiana	Developed by the Community Research Institute Fort Wayne, IN Published in *The Journal Gazette* Fort Wayne, IN	M

Table 6.1 *(Continued)*

Region	Source	Periodicity
Kansas	Jarvis Emerson Department of Economics Waters Hall, Room 327 Kansas State University Manhattan, KS 66506	M
Kentucky	Developed jointly by School of Business University of Louisville College of Business and Economics University of Kentucky Published in the *Louisville Courier-Journal*	M
Mississippi	Mississippi's Business Center for Policy Research and Planning Mississippi Institutes of Higher Learning 3825 Reigewood Jackson, MS 39211	M
New Hampshire	Dennis Delay Public Service of New Hampshire P.O. Box 330 Manchester, NH 03105	Q
New York (Capital Region)	Center for Economic Growth One KeyCorp Plaza Albany, NY 12207	M
Southeast North Carolina	William W. Hall, Jr. Center for Business and Economic Services University of North Carolina–Wilmington 601 South College Road Wilmington, NC 28403	Q
Oklahoma	Louisa Dickson Southwestern Bell 707 N. Robinson, Room 716 Oklahoma City, OK 73102	Q
Pennsylvania	Center for Research of the College of Business Administration The Pennsylvania State University University Park, PA 16802	M
South Carolina	Division of Research College of Business Administration University of South Carolina Columbia, SC 29208	Q
Tennessee	Vicki Cunningham Center for Business and Economic Research The University of Tennessee–Knoxville Knoxville, TN 37996-4170	M

Table 6.1 *(Continued)*

Region	Source	Periodicity
Texas	Keith Phillips Research Department Federal Reserve Bank of Dallas Station K Dallas, TX 75222	M
Utah	Kelly Matthews Economics Department First Security Corporation P.O. Box 30006 Salt Lake City, UT 84130	M
Virginia	Alan M. Gayle Crestar Bank P.O. Box 26665 Richmond, VA 23261-6665	M
Central Virginia	Roy Savoian, Dean Walter G. Mason Center for Business and Economic Research School of Business Lynchburg College 1501 Lakeside Drive Lynchburg, VA 24501	Q
Wisconsin	Department of Industry, Labor and Human Relations 201 E. Washington Avenue P.O. Box 7944 Madison, WI 53707	M
Atlanta, Baltimore, Boston, Chicago, Cincinnati, Cleveland, Dallas, Denver, Detroit, Houston, Kansas City, Los Angeles, Miami, Milwaukee, Minneapolis, New York, Philadelphia, Phoenix, Pittsburgh, St. Louis, San Diego, San Francisco, Seattle, and Washington, DC	Maggie O'Donovan Grant Thorton 605 Third Ave. New York, NY 10158	Q

Table 6.1 *(Continued)*

Region	Source	Periodicity
Dallas/Ft. Worth	Produced by Data Resources Inc. Published by *The Dallas Morning News*	M
Long Island	Produced and Published by *Long Island Business News*	M
New Orleans (six-parish area)	Karen Barkel Division of Business and Economic Research College of Business Administration University of New Orleans–Lakefront New Orleans, LA 70148	Q
Peoria, IL	Bernard Groitein, Director Center for Business and Economic Research College of Business Administration Bradley University 1501 W. Bradley Avenue Peoria, IL 61625	Q
Toledo, OH	Produced jointly by the College of Business Administration University of Toledo and the Toledo Chamber of Commerce Published in the *Toledo Business News*	Q

Common regionally measured leading index components include average weekly hours of production workers in manufacturing, new unemployment compensation claims, housing permits and starts, and new business formations and incorporations. Other regionally measured components include the net gain in business telephone access lines, average overtime hours in manufacturing, real retail sales, indexes of stock prices of regionally based companies, auto registrations, sales tax receipts, bank deposits, help-wanted indexes, the prime rate, and various survey variables such as business expectations and orders. Examples of nationally measured variables included in regional indexes are the BEA leading index, the M2 money supply, and the value of the dollar.

In the selection of leading index components for Delaware County, Mathis and Zech (1988) use principles from regional theory. The authors note that regional growth is dependent on business investment and growth in exports. In calculating their regional leading index, they first define regional export industries by the use of location quotients. They then collect nationally measured sales-to-inventory ratios for the export industries to include as components of the regional leading index.[4a] They also use investment variables such as regional business formation and an index of regional business expectations. Although this procedure has weaknesses, it represents a unique approach to regional index construction.

Most of the regional indexes currently produced are composite indexes compiled in the same way that the BEA compiles its leading index. Several of the indexes, however, are diffusion indexes. Diffusion indexes simply measure the percentage of the components that are increasing. Diffusion indexes tend to have longer lead times than composite indexes but are generally more volatile. In examining a leading index for Delaware County, Gerring, Mathis, and Zech (1989) found that a composite index has advantages over both a diffusion index and a method based on a vector autoregressive model.

WHAT DOES A REGIONAL LEADING INDEX LEAD?

The first step in the construction of a regional leading index is deciding what the leading index should lead. The BEA's leading index was constructed to lead business cycle peaks and troughs as designated by the National Bureau of Economic Research (NBER).[5a] Unfortunately, most regions do not have officially designated business cycle turning points.

In constructing the Kentucky leading index, Glennon and Adams (1985) first defined a state reference cycle by taking 40 economic variables and measuring the percentage that reached a peak or trough within every 3-month period since 1960. Peaks and troughs in this measure were then used to date peaks and troughs in the Kentucky business cycle.

Although business cycle turning points are important in constructing leading indexes, it can often be more useful to have a business cycle variable that is defined over the entire cycle. A useful method in defining regional business cycles is to use monthly series that, at the national level, are defined by the BEA as coincident to the business cycle. These regional variables can then be combined into a coincident index in the same manner as the BEA constructs its coincident index. (For a list of coincident indicators, see *Business Conditions Digest,* March 1990, pp. 6–9. For a detailed description of how to combine the movements of coincident indicators into a single index, see *Handbook of Cyclical Indicators* (1984), pp. 65–70 or Chapter 3 of this book. For an example of the construction of a regional coincident index, see Phillips (1988).)

The Texas coincident index was constructed by combining changes in Texas nonagricultural employment and industrial production. Nonagricultural employment, however, is often used by regional analysts to best approximate the regional business cycle. Other analysts, however, have developed more complicated measures of the regional business cycle. For example, Georgia State University combines five series into a coincident index for each of the 12 states in the Southeast.

METHODS OF REGIONAL LEADING
INDEX CONSTRUCTION

As mentioned earlier, most regional indexes are constructed using a methodology similar to that of the BEA leading index. In constructing the U.S. leading index, the BEA scores variables in terms of seven criteria: (1) economic significance, (2) statistical adequacy, (3) cyclical timing, (4) business cycle conformity, (5) smoothness, (6) timeliness, and (7) revisions. Although the scoring system is primarily qualitative, the BEA tries to ensure the evaluation of the important aspects of economic series in a consistent and somewhat replicable manner. A detailed explanation of the scoring system is explained in Zarnowitz and Boschan (1975), and an example of a similar scoring technique applied to the construction of a regional index is given in Kozlowski (1977).

In following the rather simple procedure outlined by the BEA, several problems often arise in the selection of regional leading index components. The limited number of candidate series is often a problem. Whereas the BEA selects the best leading indicators from hundreds of candidate series, the regional analyst is often pressed to find even 10 or 20 candidate series.

Frequently, another limiting factor is the time periods for which the candidate series are available. The BEA scoring procedure concentrates on the relationship between the candidate series and peaks and troughs of the business cycle. To do a thorough evaluation, the series must be considerably long and cover many business cycles. Since many of the candidate series at the regional level are not available for lengthy time periods, the analyst may seek a different approach to measuring the relationship between the candidate series and the business cycle.

In constructing the Texas Index of Leading Economic Indicators, I utilized a procedure that examines the relationship between the candidate series and the business cycle over all points. The procedure is part of the identification stage of a single-input transfer function model. Specifically, I looked at the cross-correlations between the Texas coincident index and lags of the candidate series. To eliminate any spurious correlation, all variables were made stationary, and then the candidate series was made white noise by using an autoregressive moving average (ARMA) model. The same ARMA model was then used to prewhiten the coincident index.

This procedure is described in Vandaele (1983, pp. 267–299) and is easily performed with statistical computer packages such as SAS. Examples of this technique are shown in Figures 6.1 and 6.2. Figure 6.1 shows the correlation coefficients between lags of an index of real stock prices of Texas companies and the Texas coincident index. Also shown are a plot of the correlations and significance lines representing two standard errors of the estimates. Both series are in first differences of natural logs. Since the differencing of the stock price index was sufficient to make this series white noise, no further ARMA process was necessary.

Lag	Covariance	Correlation	-1 9 8 7 6 5 4 3 2 1 0 1 2 3 4 5 6 7 8 9 1
0	-1.801E-05	-0.03794	. * .
1	-5.474E-05	-0.11532	. ** .
2	.000043545	0.09174	. ** .
3	.000048557	0.10230	. ** .
4	-3.756E-05	-0.07914	. ** .
5	.000020971	0.04418	. * .
6	.000021611	0.04553	. * .
7	.000037609	0.07923	. ** .
8	.000055633	0.11721	. ** .
9	.000119825	0.25245	. *****
10	.000061893	0.13040	. *** .
11	.000036148	0.07616	. ** .
12	.000070244	0.14799	. *** .
13	.000059562	0.12548	. *** .
14	-8.861E-06	-0.01867	. .
15	.000019414	0.04090	. * .
16	.000021387	0.04506	. * .
17	-3.041E-05	-0.06407	. * .
18	-3.572E-05	-0.07526	. ** .
19	-2.686E-05	-0.05658	. * .
20	-1.394E-05	-0.02937	. * .
21	-2.200E-05	-0.04635	. * .
22	-2.571E-05	-0.05417	. * .
23	-6.098E-05	-0.12848	.*** .
24	-4.840E-05	-0.10198	. ** .

'.' MARKS TWO STANDARD ERRORS

Figure 6.1 Correlations between Changes in the Texas Coincident Index and Lags of Changes in an Index of Real Stock Prices of Texas Companies.

As shown in Figure 6.1, the stock price index appears to have a significant statistical relationship with the Texas coincident index. The figure also shows that the relationship occurs at a lead time of 9 months. To judge the timing of the candidate series, the lead time shown in this procedure was used with lead times calculated solely at turning points. Because the correlation was significant and the lead time was at least 2 months in both the cross-correlation analysis and at turning points, the Texas stock price index was given a high score for business cycle conformity and cyclical timing.

Figure 6.2 shows the correlations between the Texas help wanted index and the Texas coincident index. Both series are in first difference of natural log form, and both are filtered by an ARMA (1,2). Although the help wanted index had a significant effect at a lead time of zero, it also had significant effects at lead times of 4 to 6 months. Based on the information in Figure 6.2, and lead times calculated solely at business cycle turns, the help wanted index was given a high score for business cycle conformity and cyclical timing.

LAG	COVARIANCE	CORRELATION	-1 9 8 7 6 5 4 3 2 1 0 1 2 3 4 5 6 7 8 9 1
0	.000105995	0.28432	. |*****
1	.000044371	0.11902	. |** .
2	.000049014	0.13147	. |*** .
3	.000039412	0.10572	. |** .
4	.000077218	0.20712	. |****
5	.000076586	0.20543	. |****
6	.000085848	0.23027	. |*****
7	.000027467	0.07368	. |* .
8	.000023197	0.06222	. |* .
9	-8.094E-07	-0.00217	. | .
10	1.099E-06	0.00295	. | .
11	-2.853E-05	-0.07654	. **| .
12	-.00001187	-0.03184	. *| .
13	.000010951	0.02937	. |* .
14	-1.302E-05	-0.03493	. *| .
15	-3.007E-05	-0.08067	. **| .
16	-5.806E-05	-0.15573	.***| .
17	-6.923E-05	-0.18570	****| .
18	-3.714E-05	-0.09963	. **| .
19	.000014475	0.03883	. |* .
20	.000031489	0.08446	. |** .
21	.000029073	0.07798	. |** .
22	.000011059	0.02966	. |* .
23	-2.113E-05	-0.05667	. *| .
24	-7.355E-05	-0.19730	****| .

'.' MARKS TWO STANDARD ERRORS

Figure 6.2 Correlations between Changes in the Texas Coincident Index and Lags of Changes in the Texas Help Wanted Index (both series have been filtered by an ARMA (1,2) process).

When the Texas leading index was created, the Texas help wanted index was available for only 7 years and the Texas stock price index was available for 8 years. These time periods covered less than two complete business cycles. Assuming that the intracyclical relationship between the candidate series and the coincident index is strongly related to their relationship at turning points, the use of the transfer function thus provided valuable information in the evaluation of leading index components.

QUESTIONS CONCERNING THE USE OF REGIONAL LEADING INDEXES

Once a leading index is constructed, the regional analyst must address several questions. The first question is simply what constitutes a signal. At the national level, many analysts have found that three consecutive increases (decreases) in the BEA leading index provide a strong signal of an expansion (contraction) in economic activity. The problem with the 3-month rule is that it does not consider the magnitude of change in the leading index and it generally restricts the probability horizon to just two outcomes—zero or one.

As an improvement on the 3-month rule, Neftçi (1982) estimates a sequential probability formula that uses changes in the BEA leading index to compute the probability of recession. Diebold and Rudebusch (1989) show that this sequential probability method is better than the 3-month rule in predicting turning points. Although the sequential probability method has not been widely used at the regional level, its application is quite simple.

Another question the regional analyst must address is, Do changes in the leading index signal classical business cycle turning points or growth cycle turning points? Growth cycles are marked by periods in which economic growth goes above or below its long-run trend. An extensive discussion of growth cycles is given in Klein and Moore (1985), and the application of the probability of recession to growth cycles is given in Niemira (1990). The use of growth cycles at the regional level generally has been limited to the observance that declines in regional indexes often lead periods of slow growth.

To define growth cycles in the Texas economy during the 1980s, I first examined movements in the smoothed Texas coincident index. The index revealed several distinct periods where growth in the economy slowed to a rate close to zero. During these periods, the average growth rates in the index were significantly different from zero (at the 5% level of significance).

Using this general procedure, the exact month of the turning point is not apparent. Using a more specific procedure, such as that described in Klein and Moore (1985), however, would not ensure specific turning point dates since the Klein and Moore procedure also involves some subjectivity.

EXAMPLE: A REGIONAL INDEX OF LEADING ECONOMIC INDICATORS

In constructing the Texas Index of Leading Economic Indicators, 14 candidate variables were examined and 9 were selected. Table 6.2 shows the components and their weights. Seven of the nine variables are estimated with state data, one variable is national, and one is an international variable weighted by regional factors. Economic processes covered by the components include employment, prices, and production. Other indicators that were investigated but rejected by the BEA-type scoring procedure (utilizing the transfer function approach) include Texas housing permits and new business incorporations.

Table 6.2   Components of the Texas Index of Leading Economic Indicators.

Variable	Weight
Texas	
Average weekly hours of production workers in manufacturing	1.03
Help wanted index	1.05
Real Texas77 stock price index	1.02
New unemployment compensation claims (inverted)	1.03
Real retail sales (3-month moving average)	0.97
Number of well permits issued	0.50
Real price of crude oil	0.50
National	
BEA index of leading economic indicators	0.98
International	
Texas trade-weighted real value of the dollar (inverted)	0.92

Note: In computing the index, the weights are divided by 8.

Turning points in the Texas leading index (TLI) have had a strong relationship with turning points in the Texas coincident index. As indicated in Figure 6.3, the TLI turned down 4 months before the August 1981 peak in the coincident index, and it rebounded 5 months before the trough in March 1983. The leading index then peaked in April 1984, 16 months before the coincident index peak in August 1985. This lead time may be deceiving, however, because the decline in the leading index was likely signaling a growth recession that began in late 1984.

Following the decline in the leading index from April 1984 until December 1984, the index began a pattern of gains and declines with a gradual upward drift. This seems consistent with the general pattern of weak growth in the coincident index. Beginning in late 1985, however, the leading index plunged and the Texas economy soon followed.

The leading index rebounded in July 1986, 8 months before the beginning of the state's economic recovery. The index rose fairly steadily until September 1987, when it declined for 5 consecutive months. The decline in the TLI late in 1987 signaled a growth recession that began in April 1988.

The TLI, through a pattern of ups and downs, gradually climbed from early 1988 to the middle of 1989. This pattern was followed by a gradual upward climb in the coincident index from March 1989 to August 1990. The leading

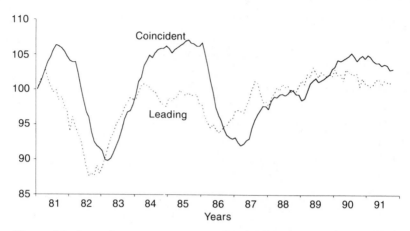

Figure 6.3   Texas Composite Economic Indexes (Index, January 1981 = 100).

index then flattened beginning in mid-1989 and the economy entered another growth recession beginning in August 1990.

While the overall pattern of the leading index from 1988 to 1991 seems to conform well to the pattern of growth in the coincident index, this period highlights the erratic and seemingly confusing signals that can be given by a leading index when the economy is growing slowly and unevenly. During such periods, users must not attach too much importance to any 1- or 2-month change in the leading index.

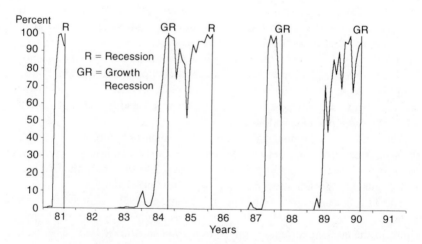

Figure 6.4   Probability of Recession in Texas.

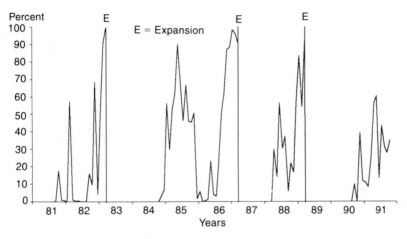

Figure 6.5 Probability of Expansion in Texas.

To better quantify the information given by changes in the leading index, a sequential probability estimation was performed.[6a] Figures 6.4 and 6.5 show the probabilities of recession and expansion in Texas from January 1981 to November 1991. As seen in Figure 6.4, the Texas leading index is a better indicator of growth recessions than classical business cycle recessions. The probability of recession reached at least 90% before every recession and growth cycle recession over this limited time period. If used as a predictor of classical business cycle recessions, however, the leading index would have given many false signals throughout the late 1980s.

As seen in Figures 6.4 and 6.5, the TLI has had a strong relationship with the Texas business cycle. Past performance suggests that movements in the TLI can give important insight into future directional changes in the state's economy. It is unclear, however, whether the leading index can distinguish between periods of very little growth and periods of actual decline. As the index is constructed over time and across several more business cycles, this question can be studied further.

SUMMARY

Regional leading indexes are gaining popularity across the United States. There are several reasons for this trend including past performance of the BEA leading index and the relative simplicity of the indexes. Most of the regional indexes currently being produced are modeled after the BEA leading index. Many of the indexes, however, contain unique variables and approaches.

Although the use of regional leading indexes has proliferated in the late 1980s, very little has been done to evaluate their performance. Kozlowski (1987), however, does give some support to the use of regional indexes. Kozlowski evaluated the predictive ability of three state and four metropolitan indexes, which were produced by different sources, and overall found them to perform well.

It is likely that the use of regional leading indexes will continue to grow. The differential pattern of economic performance in the Northeast versus the Midwest in the early 1990s exemplifies the need for regional business cycle forecasting. Regional analysts have gained much from research on the BEA leading index and can take advantage of techniques such as the sequential probability approach and the study of growth cycles. In the future, however, more research needs to be done on the specific problems and challenges of creating and using regional leading indexes.

NOTES

1a. See Klein and Moore (1985).

2a. Although most leading indexes do not forecast growth rates in the business cycle, a recently developed leading index does. The value of the National Bureau of Economic Research Experimental Leading Index corresponds to a 6-month forecast of overall economic activity. For more information on this experimental leading index, see Stock and Watson (1989).

3a. The list was derived mainly from a phone survey given to the members of the Association for University Business and Economic Research. While many of the sources are members of this association, others were referred to me by the members and some I had encountered in my past research.

4a. A weakness with the procedure is that it uses national sales/inventory ratios, measured at the two-digit SIC level. Industry mixtures within these broad classifications, however, can be quite different in the region than in the nation. And even if the industry mix is identical, inventories and sales at the local level can be quite different from the national level. Thus, the national inventory/sales ratios may be poor leading indicators of the regional economy. If tested using the BEA scoring procedure, however, measures of export industries such as inventory/sales ratios, real product prices, and capacity offer the regional analyst an expanded set of possible leading index components.

5a. The National Bureau of Economic Research, a private, nonprofit economic research organization, determines business cycle turning points sometime after they have occurred by studying the movements in many economic variables. Although the process is subjective, much of the selection is done by computer program. For further information on this process, see Klein and Moore (1985) and Bry and Boschan (1971).

6a. For an explanation of the derivation of the sequential probability method with some useful refinements, see Diebold and Rudebusch (1989).

REFERENCES

Bry, Gerhard, and Charlotte Boschan, 1971, *Cyclical Analysis of Time Series: Selected Procedures and Computer Programs,* NBER Technical Paper No. 20.

Diebold, Francis X., and Glenn D. Rudebusch, 1989, "Scoring the Leading Indicators," *Journal of Business* 62, 3, 369–391.

Gerring, Lori, Edward J. Mathis, and Charles E. Zech, 1989, "Sub-regional Level Forecasting—A Comparison of Three Methodologies," *Journal of Business Forecasting*, Winter 1989–1990, 17–22.

Glennon, Dennis, and Margaret O. Adams (1985), "Leading Indicators of the Kentucky Economy," Center for Business and Economic Research, University of Kentucky at Lexington, *Kentucky Economy Review and Perspective*, Vol. 9, No. 1, (Spring), 3–6.

Handbook of Cyclical Indicators, 1984, a supplement to *Business Conditions Digest*, U.S. Department of Commerce, Bureau of Economic Analysis.

Klein, Philip A. and Moore, Geoffrey H., 1985, *Monitoring Growth Cycles in Market-Oriented Countries, Developing and Using International Economic Indicators*, NBER Studies in Business Cycles, No. 26.

Kozlowski, Paul J., 1977, "A Local Index of Leading Indicators: Construction, Uses, and Limitations," technical paper of W. E. Upjohn Institute for Employment Research, October.

Kozlowski, Paul J., 1987, "Regional Indexes of Leading Economic Indicators: An Evaluation of Forecasting Performance,"*Growth and Change*, Summer.

Mathis, Edward J., and Charles E. Zech, 1988, "How to Develop a Diffusion Index for Sub-Regional Level Forecasting," *Journal of Business Forecasting*, Winter 1988–1989, 18–26.

Neftçi, Salih N., 1982, "Optimal Prediction of Cyclical Downturns," *Journal of Economic Dynamics and Control*, 4, 225–241.

Niemira, Michael P., 1990, "An International Application of Neftçi's Probability Approach for Signalling Growth Recessions and Recoveries Using Turning Point Indicators," in *Leading Economic Indicators: New Approaches and Forecasting Records*, Kajal Lahiri and Geoffrey Moore, Cambridge: Cambridge University Press.

Phillips, Keith R., 1988, "New Tools for Analyzing the Texas Economy: Indexes of Coincident and Leading Economic Indicators,"*Federal Reserve Bank of Dallas Economic Review*, July, 1–13.

Stock, James H. and Mark W. Watson, 1989, "Indexes of Coincident and Leading Economic Indicators," in *NBER Macroeconomics Annual 1989*, 351–394.

Vandaele, Walter, 1983, *Applied Time Series and Box-Jenkins Models*, New York: Academic Press.

Zarnowitz, Victor, and Charlotte Boschan, 1975, "Cyclical Indicators: An Evaluation and New Leading Indexes," *Business Conditions Digest*, May, series ES1, no. 75-5.

7 International Business Cycles

THE INDICATOR APPROACH TO MONITORING INSTABILITY

One of Wesley Clair Mitchell's basic tenets was that to understand business cycles, we must first obtain "the main facts of economic history." Tjalling Koopman's original view, as expressed in his famous review of Burns and Mitchell's *Measuring Business Cycles,* was that the National Bureau of Economic Research was engaged in an enormously wasteful undertaking by commencing its analysis of business cycles by collecting something like 1,300 time series. But the forecasting ability of the system of roughly 20 to 25 leading, lagging, and coincident indicators that eventually emerged has long since proved its usefulness in monitoring ongoing macroeconomic activity. Its overall reliability no doubt contributed to his ultimate conclusion that analyzing many time series in this way might be a "reasonably efficient" way to commence the study of business cycles.

Certainly the technique for dating business cycles considered in Chapter 3, and the indicator-based system for forecasting that this approach led to, is today one of the most widely used methods for following macroeconomic performance, both alone and by inclusion of indicators in various econometric models. As suggested also in Chapter 3, reasonably reliable leading or lagging indicators do not behave as they do because of statistical flukes or natural oddities. They are not like reading tea leaves or sheep entrails. Indicators behave as they do for sound economic reasons, and the system of indicators—leading, coincident, and lagging—reflects much of how and why enterprise-based economic activities plan for and adjust to economic change. In effect, the historical process by which the U.S. indicator system was developed, though strongly empirical in its approach, was always one in which economic theory and empirical observation were closely interrelated.

DEVELOPING INTERNATIONAL CYCLICAL INDICATORS

This basic conclusion was never clearer than it became when researchers began asking two critical questions:

1. Do the same indicators that seem so reliable when applied to *classical business cycles* behave equally well when applied to *growth cycles?*

2. Could indicator systems, based on roughly equivalent measures of economic activity, be set up to monitor instability in other market-oriented countries?

The answer to the first question emerged as an encouraging "yes" as the result of the efforts of Geoffrey H. Moore, Philip A. Klein, and others who launched the International Economic Indicators Project (a study of international growth cycles) in the early 1970s while they were still at the National Bureau of Economic Research. Work in other parts of the industrial, market-oriented world was not long in following.

In general, postwar efforts at broadening the work on indicators internationally concentrated on growth cycles; these cycles appeared to many to be the most common manifestation of instability in many major industrial market-oriented economies because the decades following World War II were often characterized by rapid growth. Even in the United States, there were those who thought that the business cycle was obsolete as recently as the decade of the 1960s, when no classical cycle turning points are shown. A conference was held in London entitled "Is the Business Cycle Obsolete?"[1], out of which came a conference volume devoted to considering why most industrialized market countries seemed to have escaped the decade without the classical recessions so typical of prewar times. Early work on the International Economic Indicators project suggested that at least two U.S. "growth cycles" can be discerned for this decade. The Project took its cue from the early work in this field done by Ilse Mintz.[2] She studied aggregate instability in West Germany and found that during the years 1950–1967, during which there were no classical cycles, there were at least four "growth recessions." Growth cycles can be viewed as cycles in detrended data, or as deviations from trend. Classical cycles is the phenomenon to which the term business cycles has customarily been applied. They are characterized by alternating periods of absolute expansion and contraction in the *level* of economic activity. Growth cycles, in contrast, represent alternating periods of above and below average trend rates of growth.

The techniques for constructing growth cycles from time series are somewhat complicated. We now have computer programs that may be applied to the basic time series and from which a preliminary growth cycle peak and trough chronology for each relevant series is derived. These programs were derived from the computer programs originally utilized in connection with the Burns-Mitchell work on "classical cycles." Basically, the growth cycle program attempts to keep the same rules for telling the difference between cyclical changes in time series and noncyclical changes, making only the changes necessary to adapt to the dimensions of the growth cycle. These adaptations feature a technique for estimating the underlying trend rate of growth from which the deviations making up the growth cycle phases may be calculated. The trend is nonlinear rather than linear, but this "flexible trend" nonetheless is designed to cover a period long relative to the growth cycles themselves.[3] We shall shortly see some of the many uses to which growth cycle analysis, including its leading indicators, can be put.

As noted earlier, because of the impressive post-World War II growth rates in much of the world, Moore and his associates, early in their work on monitoring international instability, decided to concentrate on developing a system for monitoring growth cycles. Early work on international instability showed that, at least for the United States, the same indicators that proved reliable in monitoring classical cycles could serve as a useful guide in initial efforts to set up growth cycle indicator systems to date and monitor growth cycles elsewhere. The reasons are not surprising. The discussion in Chapter 3 suggests that indicators reflect significant types of economic processes and that the interrelations among these processes are perforce temporally connected. Thus, from the perspective of economic theory, the timing of the indicators makes cyclical sense. It was not illogical, therefore, to expect that the temporal patterns found at classical turning points might behave in the same way at growth cycle turning points. What may have been surprising, however, was that when the indicator system developed for U.S. "classical" cycles was fashioned from rough equivalents of the same indicators for other market-oriented countries, it often behaved better than had originally been the case at classical cycles in the United States. Partly this result was understandable from the new insights that focus on growth cycles provided. In earlier times, leading U.S. indicators had sometimes been charged with providing "false signals" of peaks that subsequently failed to materialize. The new insight was the realization that the temporal interrelationships monitored by the indicator systems can be so sensitive that leading indicators can anticipate coming weaknesses in the macroeconomy—growth recessions if you will—as well as actual declines in aggregate economic activity. Thus, far from becoming obsolete, the U.S. economy was experiencing growth recessions during the 1960s, even though, as we have learned all too well, "classical cycles" are still with us as well.

SETTING UP AN INTERNATIONAL ECONOMIC INDICATOR SYSTEM

Early on, those who had been working closely with cyclical indicators in the United States, realized that the most propitious and useful kind of international economic indicator system to set up would be one that enabled researchers to make maximum use of international comparability in assessing the results. At the Center for International Business Cycle Research (CIBCR), established by Geoffrey Moore and his associates first at Rutgers University and later at Columbia University, the task was defined to be finding rough equivalents in other countries of the series that had proven to be reliable U.S. indicators for classical cycles.

Elsewhere, as interest in tracking growth cycles grew, the approach was not always the same. At the Organization for Economic Cooperation and Development (OECD)—the 24-nation organization with headquarters in Paris—a working party made up of at least one delegate from each member country, was set up to investigate monitoring growth cycles internationally. Meeting several times in the early 1980s, the group decided, in its initial deliberations, to monitor fluctuations in "output—broadly defined." Many countries determined to do this by utilizing the index of industrial production alone as the gauge for macroeconomic performance. In a world where services account for ever-increasing percentages of GNP, this was not considered adequate at the CIBCR, which acted as consultant to the OECD in these deliberations. In the CIBCR's work on growth cycles it was agreed from the outset that "macroeconomic performance" should include measures of income, output, employment, and/or unemployment, sales, and so forth, as had in fact always been the case in studying classical cycles at the NBER. Moreover, the Mitchell approach had from the outset underscored the necessity of dating cycles meaningfully, in a way that appeared most to further understanding of the underlying cyclical processes. This requirement has always been complicated by the fact, recognized very early by Mitchell, that the various measures of "aggregate economic activity" customarily encompassed in the notion of business cycles might not (often, do not) turn simultaneously at the ends of either expansions or contractions.

The OECD also decided to permit each country to decide for itself what measures of economic activity might—in each country viewed alone—be most sensitive cyclically to the growth cycle fluctuations being monitored. This approach led various countries to use diverse measures of aggregate economic activity in the leading indexes developed as an outgrowth of these OECD efforts. The diversity in series might well be expected to reduce international comparability somewhat, although to our knowledge, no study on this question has yet been undertaken.

On the other hand, the work at the OECD focused international attention on the benefits of developing a leading indicator system. One was set up at the OECD.[4] This system, which is now updated monthly in the OECD's *Main Economic Indicators,* suggested the extent to which by the 1980s interest in tracking international instability by means of leading indicators had been accepted as a viable and promising approach. Data from the OECD indicator data bank are included in various national efforts around the world in monitoring growth cycles.

Although there is much to be said for developing the best and most sensitive indicator system from the data available for each individual country, the logic of the indicator system suggests that rough equivalents to leading and lagging indicators in one market country ought to bear the same temporal relationship in other countries. Whatever else may be said, examination of the international indicators section of the OECD's *Main Economic Indicators* indicates the diverse efforts of the member countries of the OECD have produced a set of leading indexes that at the very least appear roughly to lead at turning points in the individual country indexes of industrial production. As noted earlier, no systematic study has yet compared these results with other efforts, either those of the CIBCR or of individual countries, to see how their ability to monitor modern growth cycles in many countries may differ.

As for the CIBCR, Table 7.1 shows the most recent chronology of growth cycle peaks and troughs for 11 countries, and groups of countries, monitored monthly by the Center's *International Economic Indicators.*[5]

How well does the CIBCR's system of leading and lagging indicators bear the expected relationship to the growth cycle chronologies established? It shows the median timing at growth cycle peaks of the peaks in each individual indicator, based on the closest available national series—a rough foreign equivalent of each series found on the 1966 list of U.S. indicators for classical cycles. (Not every country indicator could match some of the U.S. indicators.) In short, the table shows the timing of each available equivalent indicator for each of the other countries, at all the peaks covered by existing data that the CIBCR growth cycle program could determine. (Computer-selected turning points are always reviewed judgmentally.)

Table 7.2 shows that the median timing for leading indicators, roughly coincident indicators, and lagging indicators follows the expected temporal relationship (the leaders turn before the coincident series which turn before the lagging indicators) for every country currently monitored by the Center with the single exception of New Zealand, where the median timing for the leaders and the coincident series is zero for both.

By examining the table more closely it will become apparent that among all the indicators classified as leading, there are very few in which the median timing is not negative—that is, turning before the peak month in each country. We have long followed the practice, both for classical as well as for growth cycles, of declaring an indicator as "roughly coincident" if it turns within 3 months of the reference peak or trough. In Table 7.2, there are few series classified as coincident in which the median timing falls outside these limits (personal income for Germany with a median timing of −6 months would be one such exception).

Finally, perusal of the laggers suggests very few median timings for these indicators that do not lag the growth cycle peaks. The lagging indicators are obviously less well developed—there are still countries in which none have yet been identified. Moreover, the laggers for most countries have not been kept up to date as assiduously at the CIBCR as have the leaders and the coincident indicators. (There is, however, much to be said for developing lagging indicators internationally. Not only do they provide "long leaders" when examined in inverted form, as discussed in Chapter 3, but they are often smoother than leading indicators, thereby rendering changes in their direction—genuine phase-changes— somewhat more reliable in the short run than might be the case otherwise.)

Table 7.3 is similar to Table 7.2 except it presents the median timings at growth cycle troughs. While there are more exceptions to the expected timing relationship in all three of the indicator groups, it is, in general, fair to say that the initial hypothesis concerning indicators of troughs paralleled the hypotheses concerning forecasting of peaks: that series with reasonably reliable timing relationships to U.S. classical troughs might be expected, in the case of trough equivalents in other countries, to show the same relationship at the identifiable growth cycle troughs. This hypothesis has been verified. Parenthetically, we may say that many series, even in the United States, show more reliable timing patterns at peaks than they do at troughs.

CONCLUSION

In the years since NBER work on the international economic indicators began (1973), much work has been devoted to the analysis of growth cycles in other parts of the world. The European Economic Commission, working with a variety of national survey agencies, has contributed much to the "qualitative data" available for monitoring both classical and growth cycles, although the need has been perhaps greater for series with which to develop leading indexes for growth cycles. The EEC's business and consumer surveys concerning orders, output, sales, purchase prices, and a variety of other economic variables were previously discussed in Chapter 3.

In individual countries, the Japanese, the British, the Canadians, the Australians, and the Dutch, among others, all produce some kind of periodical report indicating the current status of their growth cycle, as reflected in a variety of variables they monitor regularly, and the status of their own national leading (and sometimes lagging) indicators for these growth cycles. The international

Table 7.1 Growth Cycle Peak and Trough Dates, Eleven Countries, 1948–1987 (Revised December 1990).

Peak or Trough	North America		Europe				Pacific	
	United States	Canada	United Kingdom	West Germany	France	Italy	Japan	Australia
P	7/48							
T	10/49	5/50						
P	3/51	4/51	3/51	2/51				4/51
T	7/52	12/51	8/52					11/52
P	3/53	3/53					12/53	
T	8/54	10/54		2/54			6/55	
P	2/57	11/56	12/55	10/55	8/57	10/56	5/57	8/55
T	4/58	8/58	11/58	4/59	8/59	7/59	1/59	1/58
P	2/60	10/59						8/60
T	2/61	3/61						9/61
P	5/62	3/62	3/61	2/61			1/62	
T	10/64	5/63	2/63	2/63			1/63	
P					2/64	9/63	7/64	
T					6/65	3/65	2/66	
P	6/66	3/66	2/66	5/65	6/66			4/65
T	10/67	2/68	8/67	8/67	5/68			1/68
P	3/69	2/69	6/69	5/70	11/69	8/69	6/70	5/70
T	11/70	12/70	2/72	12/71	11/71	9/72	1/72	3/72
P	3/73	2/74	6/73	8/73	5/74	4/74	11/73	2/74
T	3/76	10/75	8/75	5/75	6/75	5/75	3/75	10/75
P		5/76				12/76		8/76
T		12/77				10/77		10/77
P	12/78	10/79	6/79	2/80	8/79	2/80	2/80	
T		5/80			8/81*			
P		6/81			3/83*			6/81
T	12/82	11/82	6/83	7/83	1/85*	4/83*	6/83	5/83
P	6/84*	11/85*				6/85*	5/85*	11/85
T	1/87*	11/86*				8/88*	5/87*	3/87
P	2/89*							6/89*

Note: The chronologies for groups of countries are based on composite indexes of output, income, employment, and trade, weighted by each country's GNP in 1980, expressed in U.S. dollars. The chronologies begin at different dates because appropriate data are not available earlier. Since the chronologies are not updated frequently, the absence of a recent date does not necessarily mean that a turn has not occurred. G-7 country group includes United States, Canada, United Kingdom, West Germany, France, Italy, and Japan.

* Based on trend-adjusted coincident index.

Source: For the United States, National Bureau of Economic Research; for other countries, Center for International Business Cycle Research.

Region			2	4	5	10		
Taiwan R.O.C.	South Korea	New Zealand	North America	Countries Europe	Countries Pacific	Countries excl. U.S.	G-7 Countries	11 Countries
			10/49					
			4/51					
			7/52					
			3/53					
			8/54					
			2/57	5/57		5/57	3/57	3/57
			4/58	3/59	1/59	2/59	5/58	5/58
			2/60				2/60	2/60
			2/61				2/61	4/61
			4/62	3/61	3/61	3/61	2/62	2/62
6/63			11/63	2/63	1/63	2/63	2/63	2/63
					9/64	2/64		
					3/66			
4/65		6/66	3/66	3/66			6/66	3/66
8/67	9/66	4/68	10/67	6/68		5/68	10/67	10/67
11/68	10/69	7/70	8/69	4/70	6/70	6/70	10/69	10/69
1/71	3/72	11/72	11/70	2/72	1/72	2/72	11/71	11/71
12/73	10/73	2/74	11/73	11/73	10/73	11/73	11/73	11/73
2/76	6/76	3/75	5/75	8/75	2/75	8/75	5/76	5/76
6/76		12/76						
7/77		2/78						
8/78	2/79	1/80	12/78	11/79	2/80	2/80	2/80	2/80
	10/80	11/80	6/80					
		7/81	7/81					
10/82		5/83	12/82	6/84	5/83	5/83	12/82	2/83
5/84*	2/84	8/84	6/84		5/85	5/85	5/85	5/85
8/85*	10/85		1/87		5/87	5/87	5/87	5/87

Table 7.2   Median Lead (−) or Lag (+) of Individual Indicators at Growth
Cycle Peaks, in Months, Eleven Countries.

Indicators: U.S. Classification and U.S. Titles[a]	United States	Canada	United Kingdom	West Germany
LEADING INDICATORS				
Average workweek, mfg.	−3	−3	0	−8
New unemployment claims[b]	−1	−1	NA	+2
New orders, consumer goods[c]	−2	−2	NA	NA
Formation of bus. enterprises	−11	NA	−8	−8
Contracts and orders, plant and equipment[c]	+1	+3	−3	−6
Building permits, housing	−6	−3	−11	−10
Change in bus. inventories[c]	0	0	−4	−4
Indus. materials price change	−8	−2	+3	−5
Stock price index	−4	−3	−5	−6
Profits[c]	−4	−5	−4	−8
Ratio, price to labor cost	−8	+1	−14	−9
Change in consumer debt[c]	−6	−2	−16	−21
Median	−4	−2	−5	−6
COINCIDENT INDICATORS				
Nonfarm employment	+1	+2	+2	+3
Unemployment rate[b]	0	+1	+1	+3
Gross national product[c]	0	0	−13	0
Industrial production	+3	0	0	0
Personal Income[c]	−1	+1	−4	−6
Mfg. and trade sales[c]	−1	−2	−3	−3
Median	0	0	−2	0
LAGGING INDICATORS				
Long duration unemployment[b]	+6	+1	+6	NA
Plant and equipment investment[c]	+5	+4	+5	−2
Business inventories[c]	+6	+9	+10	+15
Productivity change, nonfarm[b]	+11	+15	+8	+11
Business loans outstanding[c]	+6	+3	+4	NA
Interest rates, bus. loans	+7	+5	+5	+2
Median	+6	+4	+6	+6

NA = no indicator available.

[a] The series available for each country are sometimes only roughly equivalent in content to the U.S. series. In some cases, two series are used to match the U.S. series and the median includes all observations for both series. The periods covered vary for each indicator and each country, but all are within the years 1948–1987.

[b] Inverted.

[c] In constant prices.

France	Italy	Japan	Australia	Taiwan[d]	South Korea[e]	New Zealand	All Countries
LEADING INDICATORS							
−4	0	−4	−2	−8	−7	0	−3
−41	NA	NA	NA	NA	NA	NA	−1
−11	−8	NA	NA	+6	NA	0	−2
NA	−4	−10	−8	NA	NA	NA	−8
NA	NA	−5	−2	NA	1	0	−2
−9	−2	−12	−5	−3	NA	+2	−6
+2	NA	−1	NA	NA	NA	−6	−1
−2	0	−4	−5	NA	NA	−3	−3
−3	−6	−8	−7	0	−6	−7	−6
NA	NA	−10	−2	NA	NA	NA	−4
−4	+2	−2	−14	NA	NA	0	−4
NA	NA	−9	−10	NA	NA	−3	−9
−4	−5	−6	−5	−4	−2	0	−4
COINCIDENT INDICATORS							
+6	+6	+2	+3	+1	+5	+9	+3
0	+1	0	+1	+3	−6	0	+1
−1	+1	−5	0	−10	+2	0	0
0	0	0	0	0	+2	NA	0
NA	NA	−9	−3	−4	NA	−4	−4
−2	−1	−8	−2	+2	0	0	−2
0	+1	−2	0	−1	+2	0	0
LAGGING INDICATORS							
NA	NA	NA	+7	NA	NA	NA	+6
NA	NA	0	+2	+6	NA	NA	+4
+8	+6	+4	+8	+24	NA	NA	+8
NA	NA	+8	+12	+10	NA	NA	+11
NA	NA	−6	+8	+5	NA	NA	+4
+6	+3	+7	+3	+7	NA	NA	+5
+7	+4	+4	+8	+7	NA	NA	+6

[d] Additional leading indicators for Taiwan and medians at peaks and troughs are exports[c], −9, −3; money supply[c], −4, −4. Additional coincident indicators are: freight traffic, 0, −4; bank clearings[c], −4, −8.

[e] Additional leading indicators for South Korea are: accession rate, −1, −5; letter of credit arrivals[c], −2, −8; inventories to shipments[b], −1, −3.

Table 7.3   Median Lead (−) or Lag (+) of Individual Indicators at Growth Cycle Troughs, in Months, Eleven Countries.

Indicators: U.S. Classification and U.S. Titles[a]	United States	Canada	United Kingdom	West Germany
LEADING INDICATORS				
Average workweek, mfg.	−2	−5	−2	−1
New unemployment claims[b]	−5	−2	NA	−3
New orders, consumer goods[c]	−2	0	NA	NA
Formation of bus. enterprises	−1	NA	−10	−4
Contracts and orders, plant and equipment[c]	−5	0	−1	0
Building permits, housing	−9	−9	−10	+2
Change in bus. inventories[c]	−2	0	−6	−1
Indus. materials price change	−4	−4	+3	+1
Stock price index	−4	−6	−8	−8
Profits[c]	−2	−2	−3	−12
Ratio, price to labor cost	−7	0	−9	−6
Change in consumer debt[c]	−4	−11	−15	−18
Median	−4	−2	−7	−3
COINCIDENT INDICATORS				
Nonfarm employment	+1	0	+2	+6
Unemployment rate[b]	+1	+2	+1	0
Gross national product[c]	−1	−1	0	0
Industrial production	0	0	0	0
Personal income[c]	0	0	−3	+6
Mfg. and trade sales[c]	0	0	−1	0
Median	0	0	0	0
LAGGING INDICATORS				
Long duration unemployment[b]	+4	+2	+3	NA
Plant and equipment investment[c]	+7	+6	+8	0
Business inventories[c]	+6	+8	+6	+16
Productivity change, nonfarm[b]	+10	+8	+12	+3
Business loans outstanding[c]	+6	+3	+6	NA
Interest rates, bus. loans	+11	+5	−1	+18
Median	+6	+6	+6	+10

NA = no indicator available.

[a] The series available for each country are sometimes only roughly equivalent in content to the U.S. series. In some cases, two series are used to match the U.S. series, and the median includes all observations for both series. The periods covered vary for each indicator and each country, but all are within the years 1948–1987.

[b] Inverted.

[c] In constant prices.

France	Italy	Japan	Australia	Taiwan[d]	South Korea[e]	New Zealand	All Countries
LEADING INDICATORS							
−3	+4	−4	−4	−12	−10	+3	−3
NA	NA	NA	NA	NA	NA	NA	−3
−12	−9	NA	NA	−13	NA	−3	−6
NA	−7	−14	−8	NA	NA	NA	−8
NA	NA	0	0	NA	−2	−4	0
−7	−2	−6	−7	−7	NA	−2	−7
+1	NA	−4	NA	NA	NA	−2	−2
−1	+1	−7	+1	NA	NA	+3	+1
−9	−8	−4	−4	0	−1	−10	−6
NA	NA	−10	−2	NA	NA	NA	−2
−3	+1	−2	−9	NA	NA	+5	−3
NA	NA	−6	−6	NA	NA	−6	−6
−5	−8	−5	−4	−6	−4	−2	−4
COINCIDENT INDICATORS							
+7	+8	+2	+4	0	+7	0	+2
+1	+7	+2	0	0	0	0	+1
−4	−1	−2	0	0	+2	+2	0
−3	0	0	0	0	0	NA	0
NA	NA	+1	+1	+1	NA	+3	+1
0	−7	−1	−2	−4	0	−4	−1
0	0	0	0	0	0	0	0
LAGGING INDICATORS							
NA	NA	NA	+5	NA	NA	NA	+4
NA	NA	+4	+6	+6	NA	NA	+6
+4	+5	+5	+16	+19	NA	NA	+6
NA	NA	+8	+16	+8	NA	NA	+8
NA	NA	0	−7	−6	NA	NA	+2
+8	+9	+18	+16	+15	NA	NA	+11
+6	+7	+5	+11	+8	NA	NA	+6

[d] Additional leading indicators for Taiwan and medians at peaks and troughs are exports[c], −9, −3; money supply[c], −4, −4. Additional coincident indicators are: freight traffic, 0, −4; bank clearings[c], −4, −8.

[e] Additional leading indicators for South Korea are: accession rate, −1, −5; letter of credit arrivals[c], −2, −8; inventories to shipments[b], −1, −3.

consensus is clearly on the side of monitoring growth cycles rather than classical cycles, although the world, as the review of recent business cycle history in Chapter 4 underscores, has suffered recessions as well as slowdowns in the postwar period. While there is much yet to learn about growth cycles, in many parts of the world, efforts are underway to find better ways to date growth cycles and to apply indicators more accurately for tracking those growth cycles.

GENERAL REFERENCES

Boehm, Ernst, and Moore, G. H., 1985, "New Economic Indicators of Australia, 1949–84," *Australia Economic Review,* 4th Quarter, 34–56.

Boschan, Charlotte, and Ebanks, Walter W., 1978, "The Phase-Average Trend: A New Way of Measuring Economic Growth," *Proceedings of the Business and Economics Statistics Section,* American Statistical Association, 332.

International Economic Indicators, CIBCR, Columbia University, NY.

Klein, Philip A., 1981, *Analyzing Growth Cycles in Post-War Sweden,* Swedish Industrial Publications, Economic Research Reports Stockholm.

Klein, Philip A. (Ed.), 1990, *Analyzing Modern Business Cycles,* Essays Honoring Geoffrey H. Moore, Armonk, NY: M.E. Sharpe.

Klein, Philip A., and Moore, Geoffrey H., 1985, *Monitoring Growth Cycles in Market-Oriented Countries, Developing and Using International Economic Indicators,* National Bureau of Economic Research Studies in Business Cycles, No. 26, Cambridge, MA: Ballinger Publishing Company.

Mintz, Ilse, 1969, "Dating Post-war Business Cycles, Methods and Their Application to Western Germany, 1950–67," National Bureau of Economic Research, Occasional Paper 107, New York, NY.

Nilsson, Ronny, 1987, "OECD Leading Indicators," *OECD Economic Studies,* No. 9, Autumn 105–145.

OECD Leading Indicators and Business Cycles in Member Countries, 1960–1985, 1987, OECD, Paris, January.

SELECTED COUNTRY REFERENCES

Canadian Business Cycle References:

Daly, D. J. "Business Cycles in Canada: Their Postwar Persistence," in *Is the Business Cycle Obsolete?,* Martin Bronfenbrenner, ed., New York: John Wiley & Sons, 45–65.

Lamontagne, Maurice, 1984, *Business Cycles in Canada,* Toronto: James Lorimer & Company.

Murphy, Lawrence J., Laurie, Nathan M., Simard, Claude, and Durand, René, 1977, *Perspectives on the Canadian Economy: An Analysis of Cyclical Instability and Structural Change,* The Conference Board in Canada, Technical Paper No. 2, Ottawa.

Japanese Business Cycle References:

Fujino, Shozaburo, 1966, "Business Cycles in Japan, 1868–1962," *Hitotsubashi Journal of Economics,* Vol. 7, No. 1 (June), 56–79.

Horiye, Yasuhiro, Naniwa, Sadao, and Ishihara, Suzu, 1987, "The Changes of Japanese Business Cycles," *BOJ Monetary and Economic Studies,* Vol. 5, No. 3 (December), 49–100.

Yoshikawa, Hiroshi, and Ohtake, Fumio, 1987, "Postwar Business Cycles in Japan: A Quest for the Right Explanation," *Journal of the Japanese and International Economies,* Vol. 1, 373–407.

United Kingdom Business Cycle References:

Britton, Andrew, 1986, *The Trade Cycle in Britain, 1958–1982,* Cambridge: Cambridge University Press.

O'Dea, D. J., 1975, *Cyclical Indicators for the Postwar British Economy,* Cambridge: Cambridge University Press.

8 The Inflation Cycle

SOME FACTS ABOUT THE INFLATION PROCESS

Arthur Okun, a former Chairman of the Council of Economic Advisers, observed that inflation has a "typical" and an "atypical" nature.[1] The typical characteristics are intertwined with the business cycle, whereas the atypical part is determined by psychology. Basically, two schools of thought (with numerous variants) explain the inflationary process. One approach is the monetary school and the other approach links inflation to economic slack in the economy. Typically, econometric formulations of the inflationary process based on the slack concept rely on measures such as capacity utilization, some price markup variable, employee compensation, and the change in productivity to explain the pace of inflation. From a cyclical perspective, however, compensation and productivity measures tend to lag inflation turning points.[2]

The monetary school argues that the rate of inflation equals the trend rate of growth in the money supply.[3] From an econometric standpoint, that hypothesis is usually formulated as a distributed lag on the growth in the money supply. While the use of a monetary aggregate to forecast inflation makes sense, empirical research has shown that the rate of change in M1 is very volatile and is a poor cyclical leading indicator of inflation because there are too many false signals.[4] More recently, the Federal Reserve has suggested the money-inflation link was a long-term phenomenon, which could be proxied by a concept called P-star (a variant on the "MV = PQ" identity as discussed in Chapter 2). The Federal Reserve's P-star or "M2 per unit of potential GNP model" takes the form: $p - p^* = (v - v^*) + (q^* - q)$, where p is the price level, v is velocity of M2, and q is real output. The starred variables are "long-run" values for those measures. A discussion of this model contained in a Federal Reserve working paper noted:

> [T]he use of M2 as a short-run or a long-run monetary target has some important limitations. [This model] links prices to only their recent behavior, M2, potential output, and long-run velocity; the forecasts of short-term inflation from such a model clearly miss much of the importance in the inflation process over the short

run. Wage trends, interest rates, foreign exchange movements, and the gap between real and potential output . . . are not captured by M2 and P*.[5]

Hence, although money will determine the long-term pace of inflation, in the short run, it fails to capture the cyclical dynamic.

Finally, the atypical, or psychological, aspect of inflation can be measured by surveys. However, an examination of inflation expectations conducted at the New York Federal Reserve found that expectations are more reactive to inflationary pressures than predictive of them.[6] This was exemplified during 1988. An upward spike in the University of Michigan's and the Conference Board's measures of consumer inflation expectations occurred when news reports circulated that a drought affected food prices and would add substantially to inflation. The result was that inflation expectations rose concurrently with the rise in food inflation.

So what is left of the theory of inflation? The *mark-up theory of pricing*[7] provides a guiding principle for insight and prospective on the inflation cycle. This simple theory has formed the foundation for a number of econometric model formulations of price determination and the inflation process. Moreover, the cyclically adjusted cost-plus markup view also offers an eclectic theory for selecting leading indicators of inflation. But before discussing leading indicators of inflation, it is important to consider how consumer inflation actually unfolds over its cycle.

The Unfolding of the Inflation Cycle

One of the easiest ways to summarize the typical pattern of the inflation cycle is to apply the National Bureau of Economic Research descriptive statistics method of dividing a cycle, as measured from the initial trough to peak to terminal trough, into standardized sections of development (as discussed in Chapter 3). The initial trough is dubbed stage I, the peak is stage V, and the final trough is stage IX; each of these three stages is 3 months in duration centered on the turning point. Stages II through IV are the expansion phases, which subdivide the entire expansion into three parts that are as equal in length as possible. A similar breakdown is calculated for stages VI through VIII, which comprise the contraction phase of the cycle.

Although this segmentation may seem technical, the whole story is captured in Figure 8.1, which presents the average growth pattern for the consumer inflation cycle over the ten inflation cycles since 1949. As depicted in that chart, inflation averages 1.4% (SMSAR) at its initial trough, then edges up to about 2% in stage II. The pace of inflation accelerates further to 3.25% in stage III. At this point, shock or cost-push inflation pressures typically drive inflation up another two points to 5.25% in stage IV. During stage IV, inflation generally shows the

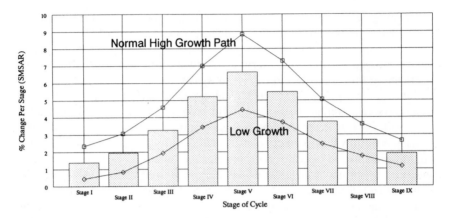

Figure 8.1   Consumer Inflation Cycle; Nine Stages of the Ten Cycles between 1949 and 1991.

greatest acceleration. The inflation rate cycle culminates with a peak in stage V as the CPI accelerates still further and averages around + 6.6%. The unwinding of the inflationary buildup, designated by stages VI through IX, is relatively symmetric with the buildup phase. This is an important observation since the growth cycle also appears relatively symmetric in duration, suggesting a causal link.

Yet, based on this framework alone, it is difficult to predict how long each phase of the inflation cycle will last, since the duration of these phases can vary substantially. As shown in Table 8.1, between 1945 and 1991 the average duration of the acceleration phase of the inflation cycle was 30.6 months (with a standard deviation of 19.8 months), while the deceleration phase lasted an average 21.5 months (with a standard deviation of 8.4 months). To reduce the uncertainty associated with the duration of the inflation cycle, several inflation monitoring and forecasting tools will be introduced and discussed, including a composite leading indicator of consumer inflation, a composite leading indicator of service-sector inflation, a consumer price diffusion index, and a consumer price volatility measure. These measures can help broaden the understanding of past, present, and future inflation.

Inflation "Trend Cycles" and the Business Cycle

Burns and Mitchell asked whether there was evidence that business cycles occurring during the upwave of long price cycles tend to have a different character from those occurring during the downwave. Their hypothesis was that when the inflation *trend* is in an upward phase, expansions tend to be longer and contractions tend to be shorter in duration. Additionally, Burns and

Table 8.1 Consumer Inflation Cycle Based on Six-Month Smoothed Growth Rates, 1946–1992.

Turning Point Dates and Value at Turning Point				Change in Percentage Points		Duration in Months	
Peak	Value	Trough	Value	P→T	T→P	P→T	T→P
Nov. 1946	+23.2%	July 1949	−3.0%	−26.2	—	32.0	—
Feb. 1951	+12.4	Mar. 1953	0.0	−12.4	15.4	25.0	19.0
Aug. 1953	+1.5	Oct. 1954	−1.4	−2.9	1.5	14.0	5.0
Mar. 1958	+4.2	May 1959	+0.4	−3.8	5.6	14.0	41.0
Oct. 1959	+2.3	June 1961	+0.6	−1.7	1.9	20.0	5.0
Oct. 1966	+4.1	May 1967	+2.1	−2.0	3.5	7.0	64.0
Apr. 1970	+6.3	Aug. 1972	+2.9	−3.4	4.2	28.0	35.0
Sept. 1974	+12.5	Apr. 1976	+4.9	−7.6	9.6	19.0	25.0
Mar. 1980	+15.2	Mar. 1983	+1.9	−13.3	10.3	36.0	47.0
Feb. 1984	+5.0	Apr. 1986	+0.4	−4.6	3.1	26.0	11.0
Oct. 1990	+6.9	Jan. 1992*	+2.8	−4.1	6.5	15.0	54.0
Average	+8.5%		+1.1%	−7.5%	+6.2%	21.5 mo.	30.6 mo.
Median	+6.3%		+0.6%	−4.1%	+6.1%	25.0 mo.	30.0 mo.
Standard Deviation	6.3		2.1	7.0	4.2	8.4	19.8

*Current cycle is low to date, which might not be cyclical trough.

Mitchell hypothesized that an uptrend in inflation tends to enlarge the amplitude of the business cycle expansion and conversely, during the downwave of inflation, the business cycle amplitude tends to be dampened.[8] Although the evidence they presented to support their hypothesis was not overwhelmingly strong, the hypothesis is worth examining further over the postwar period. The examination will focus on the consumer price cycle instead of the wholesale price cycle, to which Burns and Mitchell directed their attention to as a representation of the Kondratieff long price wave. Using the Consumer Price Index instead of the Producer Price Index (PPI) may be a better test of this hypothesis since the U.S. economy has shifted toward more of a service economy over the years since Burns and Mitchell first posited their view; to ignore service prices, which the PPI does, would ignore about half of the consumers' basket of items purchased.

To test whether the Burns and Mitchell observation, which was made in the 1940s, has stood the test of time, inflation *trend cycles*[9] were marked off during the postwar period when the cumulative sum (CUSUM) of squares statistical test[10] signaled that parameter instability existed (that is, when the CUSUM statistic exceeded a 5% significance band) in a simple trend regression between the 6-month smoothed rate of change in the CPI and a linear time trend. A result of this test implied that the inflation trend cycle was different during the 1963–1984 period from the remainder of the 1947–1991 period. Hence, this established two *low inflation trend* periods, from 1948 to 1962 and from 1985 to 1991, with an average inflation rate of 2.6% (and a standard deviation of 2.6 percentage points). The *high inflation trend* period, which was marked off between 1963 and 1984, had an average inflation rate of 5.8% (with a standard deviation of 3.5 percentage points). Both sample periods had 264 observations, and both had an overall period peak to trough range of about 15 percentage points. Hence, this working definition of a trend cycle in inflation seemed to provide a reasonable segmentation of the postwar history and the next step was to test the Burns and Mitchell hypothesis.

As shown in Table 8.2, at a 95% statistical confidence level using a standard statistical hypothesis for the differences of expansion or contraction sample means, these results imply that *high inflation phases of the inflation cycle tend to be associated with longer business cycle recessions and shorter business cycle expansions.* This conclusion is in stark contrast with the Burns and Mitchell hypothesis and furthermore, rejects the implicit view that *money illusion* can exist very long without a negative repercussion on the economy. Additionally, this establishes a direct empirical link between inflation and the business cycle, which is intuitive and theoretically has been shown in the business cycle literature.

SPECIALIZED TOOLS TO MONITOR AND FORECAST INFLATION

Inflation Monitoring with Diffusion and Volatility Measures

Inflation monitoring should encompass more than just looking at the pace of CPI growth. The growth in the CPI alone fails to answer some key questions about the character of the inflation, such as (1) where is inflation headed? (2) how widespread are the price increases? and (3) how are those price swings disrupting the real and financial sectors of the economy?

To address these questions, two inflation measures could be calculated—inflation diffusion and volatility. A *consumer inflation diffusion index* can be calculated, as shown in Figure 8.2 (with an inverted scale), that measures whether increases in consumer price categories were higher or lower. The diffusion index shown is calculated using the individual differences of 41 components of the CPI, which are based mostly on the Bureau of Labor Statistics' two-digit expenditure classes and measured on a SMSAR basis, minus the overall pace of inflation. This *difference-from-total* diffusion index concept appears better suited for this analysis than using a standard diffusion index, which simply would measure the number of components that were up or down in any given

Table 8.2 A Statistical Test of the Burns and Mitchell Inflation Hypothesis, 1948–1991.

Sample 1: "Low Inflation Trend Cycle Period"
Business Cycles between 1947 and 1962, 1985
and 1991

Peak	Trough	Contraction Duration	Expansion Duration
Nov. 48	Oct. 49	11 mo.	37 mo.
July 53	May 54	10	45
Aug. 57	Apr. 58	8	39
Apr. 60	Feb. 61	10	24
July 90			92
	Mean	9.8 mo.	47.4 mo.
	Standard Deviation	1.1	23.3

Sample 2: "High Inflation Trend Cycle Period"
Business Cycles between 1963 and 1984

Peak	Trough	Contraction Duration	Expansion Duration
Dec. 69	Nov. 70	11 mo.	106 mo.
Nov. 73	Mar. 75	16	36
Jan. 80	July 80	6	58
July 81	Nov. 82	16	12
	Mean	12.3 mo.	53.0 mo.
	Standard Deviation	4.1	34.7

Hypothesis Test for Contractions

H_0: Mean$_1$ = Mean$_2$
H_1: Mean$_1$ ≠ Mean$_2$
Significance Level: 0.05
Critical region: $T < -3.182$ and $T > 3.182$
Degrees of Freedom: 3.43
$T_c = -1.178$ (where T_c represents the test statistic)
Conclusion: Fails to Reject Null Hypothesis

Hypothesis Test for Expansions

H_0:   Mean$_1$ = Mean$_2$
H_1:   Mean$_1$ ≠ Mean$_2$
Significance Level: 0.05
Critical region: $T < -2.571$ and $T > 2.571$
Degrees of Freedom: 5.06
$T_e = -0.277$ (where T_e represents the test statistic)
Conclusion: Fails to Reject Null Hypothesis

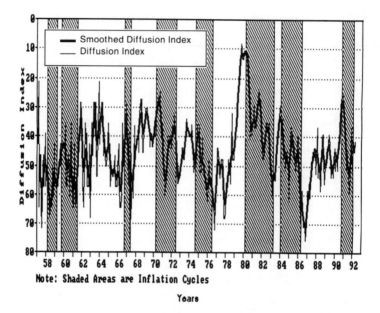

Figure 8.2   Consumer Price Diffusion Index, Scale Inverted. Shaded Areas Are Inflation Cycles.

period. Historically, since 70% to 80% of the CPI's components tend to increase in any given month, recognizing any change in the breadth of inflation would be difficult with a standard diffusion index. Based on this difference-from-total price diffusion index, a key observation is that inflation tends to be more widespread in the later stages of the inflation cycle. This is reasonable to expect from a theoretical perspective as well.[11] Moreover, this diffusion index, which tends to peak after the CPI and reach a trough near the low in the inflation cycle, can be used in a sequential fashion along with the CPI itself to monitor the unfolding of the inflation process.

Another key measure of inflation is volatility. Volatility, as measured by a 12-month moving standard deviation, captures the degree of "risk" associated with inflation. Generally, the higher the volatility, the higher the degree of uncertainty for such activities as holding business inventories or for investors planning on "real returns." A 12-month moving standard deviation of the CPI (on a SMSAR basis) tends to peak near the high in the inflation cycle and trough near the low in the inflation cycle, as shown in Figure 8.3.

On balance, these two additional measures of inflation provide a way to look beneath the reported CPI trends and assess whether the inflationary price spiral is or is not heating up and what its major consequences may be. The typical cyclical pattern is that the CPI diffusion index tends to be at a low and the

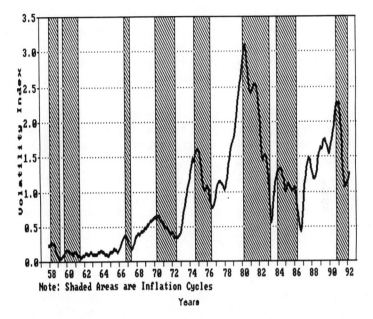

Note: Shaded Areas are Inflation Cycles

Years

Figure 8.3 Consumer Price Volatility Index. Shaded Areas Are Inflation Cycles.

volatility index near a high at cyclical peaks in inflation and just the reverse at cyclical troughs. In addition to these measures, leading indicators of inflation can provide a window on the future direction of inflation.

A Composite Index of Leading Indicators of Inflation

After examining the dimensions of inflation (rate, breadth, and volatility), it is then natural to ask; Where is inflation headed? In the early 1980s, a composite leading indicator of inflation was compiled at Chemical Bank, which later evolved at PaineWebber and Mitsubishi Bank. To demonstrate the usefulness of a composite leading indicator, consider the *Mitsubishi Bank Leading Indicator of Inflation*. This composite leading indicator of inflation was formed from seven inflation-sensitive components using techniques discussed in Chapter 3. This index was based on the cyclical relationship between the individual leading indicator components and the consumer inflation cycle, as measured by a 6-month smoothed growth rate (SMSAR) in the CPI-U. The components include:

1. The employment-to-population ratio was included as a gauge of labor market wage pressures. As the ratio rises, so, too, do wage pressures and vice versa.

2. The National Association of Purchasing Management (NAPM) surveys purchasing managers whether they are paying more, less, or about the same for supplies. This survey-based indicator was included to capture inflationary pressures at an early stage of processing.

3. NAPM also asks their business survey committee to report how quickly orders are being filled (supplier lead times). As business activity picks up, delivery lead times tend to increase. Initially, this has little impact on inflation. However, if order backlogs are high for extended periods of time, then the likelihood that businesses can pass along price hikes increases.

4. Over the postwar period, the share of imports rose steadily over every business cycle. Hence, "imported inflation" is a greater concern for the domestic economy. To proxy this impact, the Federal Reserve Board's nominal exchange rate is included in the composite index, although this measures only the exchange rate effect.

5. To measure the slack in the economy, the Federal Reserve Board's manufacturing capacity utilization rate was included. This is a common component of most econometric models of price change and had an average lead of 13 months with turning points in inflation. When the economy approaches a capacity constraint, there is a tendency for higher unit costs of production because less efficient plant and equipment is brought on stream to meet demand.

6. The *Journal of Commerce* spot price index also is included in the composite as a sensitive measure of raw material prices. This index includes the price of oil, which is about 7% of the index, and directly will capture "oil shocks."

7. The final component of the index is the U.S. Department of Agriculture's index of agricultural prices paid to farmers. That measure is a gauge of potential food inflation and is particularly important since food consumption accounts for one-fifth of the total consumer budget.

These seven indicators were compiled into an index using a modified version of the NBER/Commerce Department methodology, described in Chapter 3. The one modification was to optimize individual component weights using the Holmes technique.[12] The resulting leading indicator of inflation is shown in Figure 8.4.

A slightly different barometer of future inflationary pressure is calculated by Columbia University's Center for International Business Cycle Research. Their leading indicator of inflation, which tends to move in lockstep with the preceding composite measure, includes (1) the employment-to-population ratio, (2) the growth in total debt, (3) the *Journal of Commerce* spot price index,

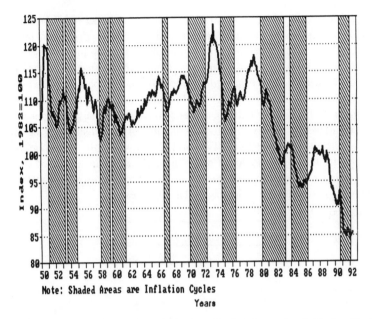

Figure 8.4   Leading Indicator of Inflation. Shaded Areas Are Inflation Cycles.

(4) nonfuel import prices, (5) Dun & Bradstreet's business survey of expected selling price changes, (6) the NAPM buying price index, and (7) the NAPM supplier leadtime measure. In most cases, the CIBCR and Mitsubishi Bank leading indicators of inflation have the same strengths, weaknesses, and forecast message. But the chief weakness of these indicators, as formulated, is that the lead time between turning points in the inflation cycle and the leading indicator of inflation is variable, which makes forecasting from these indicators difficult. To address this problem, two methods will be discussed, which use a fixed period forecast horizon.

TWO APPROACHES FOR FORECASTING INFLATION USING COMPOSITE LEADING INDICATORS

Economic models as well as leading inflation indicators tend to have a difficult time accurately forecasting a specific level of inflation when the pace of inflation changes abruptly. Nonetheless, quantitative inflation forecasts are important for monetary policy, investment strategy, and so on. The typical inflation model based on leading indicators tends to use a lagged dependent variable or is formulated as a state space model (multivariate ARIMA model). However, experience shows that the lagged dependent variable in whatever model formulation is often the dominant explanatory variable in forecasting the next period's inflation rate. Conceptually, this may surrender the power of the leading indicator of inflation to the autoregressive or habit-persistence term. An alternative to the standard model formulation is a *multiple state* forecasting model based on the composite leading indicator of inflation. This model formulation does not subjugate the role of leading indicators to the habit-persistence term since a lagged dependent variable is not included. This type of forecasting model for consumer price inflation can be specified as follows: STATE = $fn(LII_{t-n})$, where the lead time, $t - n$, of the composite leading indicator of inflation (LII) was selected based on its historical timing relationship with the 6-month smoothed growth rate (SMSAR) and STATE represents the following inflation states:

State	Inflation Rate
6	8% or more
5	6%–8%
4	5%–6%
3	4%–5%
2	2%–4%
1	0%–2%
0	less than 0%

The forecasting model estimated included two lagged terms of the LII at 9 and 12 months and a time trend, which was set equal to 1 in January 1947. Between 1960 and 1991, the estimated relationship between the leading indicator of inflation and the state of inflation was:

$$\text{State} = -28.51 + 0.0148 \times \text{Trend} + 0.0871 \times LII_{-9} + 0.161 \times LII_{-12}$$
$$(-32.08) \quad (31.41) \qquad\qquad (3.213) \qquad\qquad (5.844)$$

where the numbers in parenthesis, under the coefficients, are t-statistics. This equation explained 78% of all variability over that period. The estimated and actual inflation states are presented in Figure 8.5.

An alternative to the multiple state model is to reformulate the composite index of leading indicators using a new composite index methodology. This example demonstrates how a *neural network* can be used to compile leading indicators. This methodology requires the components of the leading indicator to be recompiled using a *neural network projection* of the leading indicator component with a 9-month lead time on the 6-month smoothed growth rate of the CPI. A neural network is an artificial intelligence simulation technique to identify patterns between data inputs and the resulting outputs. A neural network

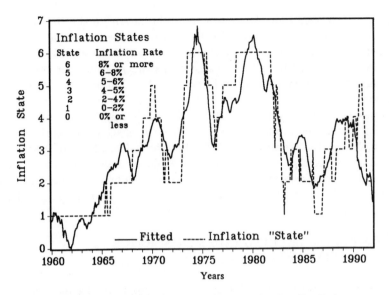

Figure 8.5 Forecasting Inflation States Using Leading Index.

model learns by example, not by a specific rule or instruction. This computational technique shares similarities with other sequential econometric methods, yet it may be a more powerful computational tool to determine which factors determine an output since it is nonparametric. The model's computational nomenclature and framework are borrowed from the field of biology. The model is composed of three levels or *layers* of neurons—the input, the hidden layer, and the output. It is obvious what the input and output are, while the hidden layer might be thought of as the level where *data sifting* takes place, or the level where the process of association is determined between the input and the output. A neuron is said to *fire* or be active if the stimulus is greater than some threshold level. This threshold level has a parallel to economic concepts such as *Weber's law,* the *just perceivable difference, focus-loss,* and the relative income hypothesis. Hence, threshold levels for action and reaction are deeply rooted in economic theory, which makes this technique appealing for economic modeling and forecasting.[13]

Once the seven component projections were calculated using the neural network, which determined the best-fitted relationship based on a minimization of the mean square error, then the individual component projections were combined using correlation weights (the Holmes technique). The final inflation projection for 9 months hence was derived from a neural network of the combined leading indicator forecasts and a trend component to capture the secular forces present since 1950. The advantage of this new method is that there is no lagged dependent variable in the formulation and it does not employ statistical data mining to formulate a composite forecast indicator. Instead, this approach recognizes the need for a broad-based composite indicator because there is no single explanation for bouts of inflation.[14] An additional advantage of this methodology is that it fixed the forecast horizon at 9 months. This new leading indicator of inflation, which has a 9-month lead time by design, forecasted the cyclical fluctuation in inflation reasonably well, as shown in Figure 8.6. The root mean squared error over the 1948–1992 period was 1.1 percentage points and in more recent periods, the error has remained about the same. Although this indicator forecasts the overall direction of inflation with a reasonably high degree of success, at times, it is useful to examine sector-specific inflation.

A COMPOSITE LEADING INDEX OF SERVICE SECTOR INFLATION

The radio commentator, Paul Harvey, once said: "In times like these, it helps to recall that there have always been times like these." And so it is true with service inflation. Since 1940, consumer service prices have outpaced commodity prices,

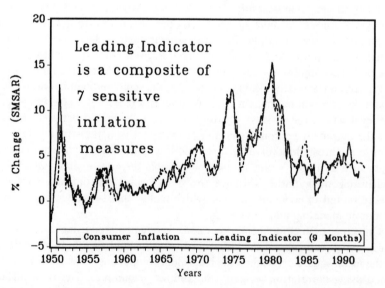

Figure 8.6   Consumer Inflation versus New Leading Indicator of Inflation, a Composite of Seven Sensitive Inflation Measures.

measured on a year-to-year basis, a whopping 81.1% of the time (measured between March 1940 and July 1990). Moreover, service price increases have exceeded commodity prices by one percentage point or more in 64.1% of the months that the Department of Labor has data for that period. Carrying this one step further, service prices have exceeded commodity prices by two percentage points or more 38.4% of the time. These simple statistics raise the question: Why do service prices often exceed commodity prices? And are there leading indicators of service inflation similar to the leading indicators for overall inflation?

The Service/Goods Inflation Nexus: A Review of the Issues

Rappoport[15] examined several claims why inflation rates in the service sector generally have exceeded those of goods prices. He concluded (1) there was very little evidence that mismeasurement of inflation in the services explained the higher pace of service inflation, (2) sector differences in productivity could not completely explain the differences in the sector inflation rates, but (3) there was some evidence that tightening in the female labor market relative to the male work force contributed to relatively higher service sector inflation rates.

Rappoport's view of the role productivity plays in explaining price differentials was supported by Kutscher and Mark,[16] who attacked the common perception that the shift to a larger share of service sector employment in the economy was the main reason for the productivity slowdown since 1970. Kutscher and Mark concluded that the shift accounted for at most 0.1 percentage point lower rate of productivity per year. A study by Runyon[17] also found little support for the view that the employment shift to services was the main cause of poor aggregate productivity, which in turn led to higher inflation in the economy than otherwise. Furthermore, generalizations about low productivity in the service industries may be misleading since Kutscher and Mark as well as a study by Kendrick[18] have found that many service industries are highly capital intensive and productivity varies widely among these services.

The Rappoport finding attributing higher service sector inflation rates to the relative tightness in the female work force seems unconvincing. In particular, the male-female unemployment rate differential remained essentially stable from about 1965 to 1979, while service sector inflation was far from stable during that period.

Bert Hickman[19] provided one of the clearest descriptions why the service-commodity price gap exists. Hickman wrote that service prices "are subject to special influences which set them somewhat apart from industrial prices, especially with regard to sensitivity to current shifts of cost or demand. . . . [Consequently,] as a class . . . they are slow to respond to changes in cost or demand, because some are subject to public regulation (utilities) and others are influenced by market imperfections of some sort or another (rent, medical care, personal services, etc.)."[20] But this does not mean that service prices are immune from the business cycle.

In Search of Leading Indicators of Service Price Cycles

Is it possible to develop a leading indicator of the service sector price cycle? Niemira[21] undertook such an endeavor. The search for leading indicators of the service sector price cycle were based on an eclectic theoretical foundation using the perspective of Linder's theory of consumption[22] and the Burns and Mitchell concept of price diffusion. In essence, Linder argued that the consumer attempts to maximize utility subject to the traditional budget or income constraint and a time constraint. This time constraint is an important extension of traditional theory since it incorporates a time-savings attribute into the consumer's decision process in the purchase of goods and services. As the time constraint becomes more binding, the demand for services is stronger and with it there is an upward pressure on service prices. But a second concept, price diffusion, plays a role in the formation of service prices. Service prices tend to respond slowly to price pressures from sources outside the service sector, but once those price pressures are more widely diffused, service prices play catch-up. This lagging relationship suggests that commodity prices themselves are a leading indicator of service prices. (This does not mean, however, that the service sector *demand* simply marches to the tune of the goods producing sectors—our focus is simply prices.)

Simple correlation analysis and traditional National Bureau of Economic Research (NBER) cycle dating techniques were used to test the cyclical significance of a potential leading indicator of service prices. Several tentative conclusions were drawn: (1) The service-sector unemployment rate tends to be a lagging indicator of service sector price movement, and (2) the rate of change in service sector employment tends to lead turning points in the service inflation cycle. One reason employment changes would lead price changes in the service sector might be that as the demand for labor in the service sector heats up, wages and output prices are likely to rise. Yet, the sector unemployment rate did not appear to capture this price fluctuation since the unemployment rate is affected by longer term demographics and economic shifts within the economy.

Another sector-specific indicator examined was average hourly earnings for services. This indicator was coincident with turning points in the service price cycle. It is interesting that wage increases in the service sector are, on balance, passed through to output prices rather rapidly. It was found that changes in average hourly earnings in *manufacturing,* however, led changes in service prices by 10 months on average and led turning points by an average of 3 months. Two commodity prices for food and energy also led service sector inflation.[23] Food prices led service prices by an average of 8 months while energy prices had an average 11-month lead time.

An Experimental Leading Indicator of Service Sector Inflation

Since no single leading indicator of service inflation that was examined totally explained service sector price fluctuations, a composite index was formed from four series that had a consistent lead relationship over service prices. This *experimental* composite index was compiled from (1) average hourly earnings in manufacturing, (2) service sector employment, (3) the CPI for food, and (4) the CPI for energy commodities.[24] The performance of this experimental leading indicator of service inflation is shown in Figure 8.7. The composite anticipates cyclical movement in service prices by an average of about 10 months.

While this initial work offered some promising evidence on what may or may not be important determinants of service sector price swings, it is far from complete. More research is needed to determine a comprehensive theory and a broader based set of economic indicators to serve as harbingers of service

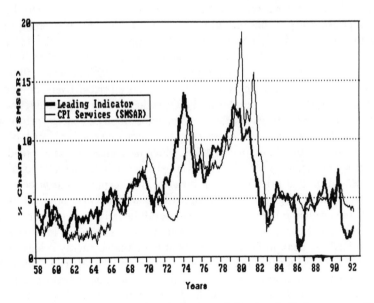

Figure 8.7 Experimental Leading Indicator of Service Inflation versus Service Inflation.

sector inflation. Nonetheless, the work by Niemira has taken one step in that direction and provides a handful of indicators to monitor as a guide to the future direction of service prices.

TWELVE LITTLE KNOWN FACTS ABOUT THE
INFLATION CYCLE

Armed with the inflation tools just presented, it is useful to summarize some of the major cyclical characteristics of consumer inflation:

1. *The Inflationary Process Has Two Parts: The Catalyst and the Feedback Effects.*

The Catalyst—Food and/or Energy Prices. Inflationary or deflationary shocks have played a major role in causing swings in the consumer inflation rate. Food and energy price surges, generally, have been those shocks. Over the 10 inflation cycles since 1949, only five had a cyclical peak in the inflation rate of more than 5%. All but one of these high inflation periods were associated with higher food and/or energy prices. The one exception was the February 1951 cyclical inflation peak of 12.4% (6-month smoothed annualized rate, SMSAR). In that period, prices were driven up by speculative forward buying as a hedge against possible rationing of commodities. This was prompted by the outbreak of the Korean War in June 1950 and memories of World War II rationing and was stopped by the imposition of wage and price controls in January 1951. Nonetheless, all the remaining cases—1970, 1974, 1980, and 1990—were associated with higher food or energy prices. Even the cyclical trough in the inflation rate in April 1986 was due to energy price declines.

The Feedback Effects. Historically, when higher food and energy prices were the impetus for a new inflationary spiral, a broader based rise in prices took hold soon thereafter. Our CPI diffusion index, which measures how widespread consumer price changes are for about 40 commodities and services, picks up this effect. Based on that price diffusion measure, the second-round price effects can be traced following a shock from higher food and/or energy prices. Table 8.3 presents the cyclical relationship between overall inflation, the food and energy price cycles, and consumer price diffusion. Typically, a surge in food prices tends to lead the peak in inflation by about 6.5 months, energy prices tend to peak roughly coincident with the peak in inflation, and the diffusion index tends to peak about a year after energy prices peak. There are some classic exceptions, such as the 1974–1976 period when the diffusion index peaked after the subsequent trough in inflation. This was an unusual situation because wage and price controls were present during the 1971–1974 period and the adjustment process was stretched out longer than otherwise.[25]

Table 8.3 A Comparison of Turning Point Dates in the Inflation Cycle, 1958–1992.

Inflation Cycle	Date	Food			Energy			Diffusion		
		Date	Timing	Value	Date	Timing	Value	Date	Timing	Value
Peak	Mar. 1958	Mar. 1958	0 mo.	8.7%	Aug. 1958	+5 mo.	2.1%	June 1958	+3 mo.	67.9%
Trough	May 1959	Apr. 1959	−1	−3.6	Dec. 1958	−5	−1.1	Mar. 1960	+10	35.7
Peak	Oct. 1966	Mar. 1966	−7	7.6	Apr. 1967	+6	3.8	May 1967	+7	75.0
Trough	May 1967	May 1967	0	−1.0	Apr. 1968	+11	0.5	June 1967	+1	22.7
Peak	Apr. 1970	Dec. 1969	−4	8.6	Jan. 1971	+9	5.9	Apr. 1971	+12	60.0
Trough	Aug. 1972	Jan. 1971	−19	1.0	June 1972	−2	1.3	Sept. 1973	+13	34.0
Peak	Sept. 1974	Aug. 1973	−13	25.0	Mar. 1974	−6	41.6	Nov. 1976	+26	72.0
Trough	Apr. 1976	June 1976	+2	1.0	May 1976	+1	3.3	Sept. 1979	+41	8.1
Peak	Mar. 1980	June 1978	−21	13.8	Sept. 1979	−6	43.2	Mar. 1983	+36	60.0
Trough	Mar. 1983	Feb. 1983	−1	1.1	Apr. 1982	−11	−8.0	Jan. 1984	+10	29.3
Peak	Feb. 1984	Feb. 1984	0	5.4	Feb. 1984	0	2.8	Jan. 1985	+11	62.2
Trough	Apr. 1986	Oct. 1985	−6	1.3	Apr. 1986	0	−23.7	Mar. 1985	−13	36.6
Peak	Oct. 1990	Sept. 1988	−25	6.9	Oct. 1990	0	26.9	Sept. 1991	+11	59.8
Trough	Jan. 1992	May 1992	+4	0.4	July 1991	−6	−6.7	Dec. 1991	−1	36.6
	Overall Average		−6.5 mo.	5.4%		−0.3 mo.	6.6%		11.9 mo.	47.1%
	Peak Average		−10.0	10.9		1.1	18.0		15.1	65.3
	Trough Average		−3.0	0.0		−1.7	−4.9		8.7	29.0

2. *A Pickup in Inflation Is Associated with a Higher Savings Rate.* This is known as the *Katona effect* and is named after George Katona who observed this phenomenon in consumer survey research. In 1981 testimony before the Joint Economic Committee of Congress, the late George Katona, director of the Survey Research Center of the University of Michigan, summarized his research (based on 25–30 years of consumer survey work) on the effect of inflation on consumer spending and confidence. Katona noted:

> American people have generally felt worse off when inflation accelerated. This was true even of people whose incomes rose much more than prices; such people complained that they could not make use of the well-deserved fruits of their labor. In addition, inflation made people feel uncertain and fearful that later they would have trouble purchasing necessities. Therefore, in response to inflation people reduced their discretionary expenditures and increased the amounts they saved.[26]

Although Katona noted that this savings rate response was less true of the 1970s when the "buy now, before prices rise more" psychology took hold, it did characterize the rest of postwar experience. Moreover, the Katona savings-inflation hypothesis is relevant today since the inflationary environment more closely resembles the 1950s and 1960s than the 1970s. Our research suggests: (1) There generally is a relationship between the rate of consumer inflation and the savings rate, but the cyclical timing between the two series has shifted; that is, the effect of higher inflation was more coincident with the rise in savings in the early 1950s but tends to lag the turning points in inflation in the more recent periods, and (2) every one percentage point increase (decrease) in the CPI inflation rate causes an increase (decrease) of 0.5 percentage points in the savings rate.

3. *Growth Cycles Peak before Inflation.* The National Bureau of Economic Research (NBER) has designated the growth slowdown phases of the economic cycle, which are shown in Table 8.4 with the CPI turning point dates. Of the 11 cycles shown, inflation peaked after the growth cycle peak in 7 of these cycles. However, if the amplitude in the growth cycle was modest (such as in 1962) then there was little effect on the pace of inflation. On average, the inflation cycle turning point dates occurred 5 months after the growth cycle turns, though the standard deviation was a hefty 10 months.

4. *Fluctuation in the CPI and PPI Is Generally Coincident.* Since 1983, large monthly changes in the Producer Price Index (PPI) have tended to pass through to the CPI in the same month. A simple statistical correlation supports this since the highest correlation (0.68) occurs in the concurrent month between changes in these two statistics.

5. *Retail Prices Are Less Volatile than Wholesale Prices.* Volatility in the PPI is four times larger than that of the CPI. Using a moving 12-month standard

Table 8.4   U.S. Inflation and Growth Cycles in the Post-World War II Period.

Inflation Cycles	Growth Cycles	Timing, in Months
High: Nov. 1946	High: July 1948	−20
Low: July 1949	Low: Oct. 1949	−3
High: Feb. 1951	High: Mar. 1951	−1
Low: Mar. 1953	Low: July 1952	8
High: Aug. 1953	High: Mar. 1953	5
Low: Oct. 1954	Low: Aug. 1954	2
High: Mar. 1958	High: Feb. 1957	13
Low: May 1959	Low: Apr. 1958	13
High: Oct. 1959	High: Feb. 1960	−4
Low: June 1961	Low: Feb. 1961	4
High: —	High: May 1962	—
Low: —	Low: Oct. 1964	—
High: Oct. 1966	High: June 1966	4
Low: May 1967	Low: Oct. 1967	−5
High: Apr. 1970	High: Mar. 1969	13
Low: Aug. 1972	Low: Nov. 1970	21
High: Sept. 1974	High: Mar. 1973	18
Low: Apr. 1976	Low: Mar. 1975	13
High: Mar. 1980	High: Dec. 1978	15
Low: Mar. 1983	Low: Dec. 1982	3
High: Feb. 1984	High: July 1984	−5
Low: Apr. 1986	Low: Jan. 1987	−9
High: Oct. 1990	High: Feb. 1989	20
	Average	5.0
	Standard Deviation	10.3

deviation of monthly changes in the CPI and the PPI, the average standard deviation is 0.20 percentage points (for month-to-month percentage change) for the PPI versus 0.05 percentage points for the CPI. One reason this occurs is coverage differences; the PPI for finished goods does not include services while the CPI does. Another reason is that retail prices tend to be more "sticky."

6. *A Slower Pace of Money Growth Contains Numerous False Signals in Predicting Inflation Peaks and Troughs.* In a recent analysis of the predictive ability of inflation indicators, Howard Roth concluded that M1 signaled too many turning points that were not associated with the inflation cycle.[27] The record is no better for M2. The record does not make at all clear that money growth always will cause an acceleration or deceleration in inflation.

7. *Service Prices Are Cyclical and Tend to Lag Overall Inflation and Business Cycle Turning Points.* Service prices tend to lag the overall inflation cycle by an average of 1 month, with some notable exceptions. Although service prices tend to increase at a higher trend rate then commodity prices or the overall pace of inflation, the cyclical amplitude changes in service and commodity prices tend to be similar. During the seven periods of accelerating inflation since 1958, service prices rose an average 5.5 percentage points from their cyclical lows while overall inflation rose 5.6 percentage points and commodity prices rose 6.5 percentage points. During the eight periods of decelerating inflation since 1957, service prices slowed an average 4.9 percentage points while overall inflation slowed 5.6 percentage points and commodity prices slowed by 5.5 percentage points.

With regard to the business cycle, the Commerce Department classifies service prices as a lagging indicator. Reinforcing the significance of this point, the Commerce Department also includes service prices as a component of their composite index of lagging indicators.

8. *Service Prices Are Less Sensitive to Supply-Side Price Shocks than Are Commodity Prices.* Supply-side price shocks tended to impact service prices indirectly through the overall increase in inflation. This was particularly evident in 1986 when oil prices fell sharply and service prices did not show much response.

9. *Service Prices Tend to Lag Turning Points in Commodity Prices.* On average, service prices tended to peak 1 month after commodity prices peaked and reached a low about 6 months after commodity prices did (see Table 8.5). This tendency suggests that service prices are "sticky" on the way down. Moreover, the correlation for all periods (not just turning points) between service and commodity prices revealed a 9-month lead time of commodity over service prices.

10. *Wages Are a Lagging Indicator of Inflation.* Despite the popular view that "where wages go, so goes inflation," the facts do not support that conclusion. It might be argued that during the late 1970s, cost-of-living adjustments (COLAs) were responsible for the wage rate "catch-up" and hence caused the lagging relationship between wages and inflation. However, this is not a new phenomenon. In a 1969 review of this relationship, Geoffrey H. Moore, who was then the Commissioner of the Bureau of Labor Statistics, observed that compensation rates tended to follow inflation.[28] Moore's study is worth noting since it was done in the pre-COLA boom period.

Statistical analysis as well as turning point analysis suggests that wages in fact, do tend to lag inflation. The strength of the statistical relationship between compensation and inflation implies that (1) changes in inflation "cause"

Table 8.5   Relationship between Turning Points in Price Cycles, 1958–1992.

Total CPI-U		Service Prices			Commodity Prices		
Month	Rate[a]	Month	Rate[a]	Timing[b]	Month	Rate[a]	Timing[b]
Peaks							
Mar. 1958	4.2%	Nov. 1957	4.7%	−4 mo.	Mar. 1958	3.9%	0 mo.
Oct. 1959	2.3	Oct. 1959	4.2	0	Dec. 1960	1.8	+14
Oct. 1966	4.1	Nov. 1966	5.7	+1	Apr. 1966	3.2	−6
Apr. 1970	6.3	Mar. 1970	8.9	−1	Dec. 1969	5.4	−4
Sept. 1974	12.5	Dec. 1974	11.9	+3	Mar. 1974	13.0	−6
Mar. 1980	15.2	June 1980	19.2	+3	Mar. 1980	13.7	0
Feb. 1984	5.0	Sept. 1984	5.7	+7	Feb. 1984	4.3	0
Oct. 1990	6.9	Aug. 1990	6.3	−2	Oct. 1990	6.4	0
Average	7.1%		8.3%	+0.9 mo.		6.5%	−0.3 mo.
Median	5.7%		6.0%	+0.5 mo.		4.9%	0.0 mo.
Troughs							
May 1959	0.4%	Dec. 1958	1.9%	−5 mo.	Mar. 1959	−0.8%	−2 mo.
June 1961	0.6	Oct. 1962	1.4	+16	Nov. 1961	−0.2	+5
May 1967	2.1	Nov. 1967	3.7	+6	Apr. 1967	0.7	−1
June 1972	2.9	Feb. 1973	3.1	+8	Nov. 1971	2.4	−7
June 1976	4.9	Dec. 1976	7.2	+6	Apr. 1976	2.9	−2
Mar. 1983	1.9	Dec. 1982	2.2	−3	Mar. 1983	1.6	0
Apr. 1986	0.4	Mar. 1987	3.9	+11	Apr. 1986	−4.0	0
Jan. 1992*	2.8	May 1992*	3.9	+4	Jan. 1992*	0.9	0
Average	2.0%		3.4%	+5.4 mo.		0.4%	−0.9 mo.
Median	2.0%		3.4%	+6.0 mo.		0.8%	−0.5 mo.

* Current cycle is low to date, which might not be the cyclical trough.

[a] All rates are calculated as 6-month smoothed growth rates (SMSAR) in seasonally adjusted data.

[b] Timing is measured from the turning point in the total CPI; a minus represents a lead in months, while a positive sign represents a lag.

changes in wages and not the reverse,[29] and (2) inflation leads wage rate changes by 3 to 6 months.

11. *The Stock Market Cycle Is Dependent on the Stage of the Inflation Cycle.* The stock market cycle is composed of two phases: (1) the money illusion phase and (2) the "no illusion" phase. Both parts are influenced by inflation. In the money illusion phase of the stock cycle, stock prices continue to rise even as early evidence of a pickup in inflation develops. The reason this happens is that as inflation increases, equity analysts raise their estimates of company earnings and propel the stock market upward. This phenomenon can be traced through the Institutional Brokers Estimate System, I/B/E/S, earnings' revisions index. I/B/E/S constructed an earnings revisions index as a ratio of the percentage of estimates raised relative to the percentage of estimates lowered, and it also serves as a leading indicator of cyclical turning points in the inflation cycle. In the second phase—the "no illusion" phase—higher inflation cuts into real growth and causes a negative impact on stock prices.

12. *Interest Rates Lag the Business Cycle but Are Coincident with the Inflation Cycle.* Short-term interest rates, as measured by the 3-month Treasury bill rate, have a tendency to lag the business cycle but to lead inflation peaks by an average of five months and to be coincident at inflation troughs. There are some noticeable exceptions to this generalization as suggested in Table 8.6.

In summary, the leading indicator of inflation may have broader uses. The buildup of inflationary pressures puts upward pressure on interest rates and consequently, tends to lower stock prices. Hence, another use of the leading indicator of inflation is as leading indicator of interest rates and stock prices. James Coon explores this point in Chapter 9, in his contribution on using a composite leading indicator of inflation to forecast turning points in the interest rate cycle. The discussion of stock market cycles in Chapter 10 is also enlightening.

Table 8.6 Relationship of the Treasury Bill Cycle with the Inflation Cycle.

| | Three-Month Treasury Bill Cycle | | | | Relationship with Inflation Cycle | | | |
	Turning Point	Rate	High to Low (%)	Low to High (%)	At Peaks	Timing	At Troughs	Timing
High:	Apr. 1953	2.19			Aug. 1953	−4 mo.		
Low:	June 1954	0.64	−70.7				Oct. 1954	−4 mo.
High:	Oct. 1957	3.58		459.4	Mar. 1958	−5		
Low:	June 1958	0.83	−76.8				May 1959	−11
High:	Dec. 1959	4.49		441.0	—	—		
Low:	July 1961	2.24	−50.1				—	—
High:	Sept. 1966	5.36		139.3	Oct. 1966	−1		
Low:	June 1967	3.53	−34.1				May 1967	1
High:	Jan. 1970	7.87		122.9	Apr. 1970	−3		
Low:	Feb. 1972	3.20	−59.3				Aug. 1972	−6
High:	Aug. 1974	8.96		180.0	Sept. 1974	−1		
Low:	Dec. 1976	4.35	−51.4				Apr. 1976	8
High:	Mar. 1980	15.20		249.4	Mar. 1980	0		
Low:	June 1980	7.07	−53.4				Mar. 1983	NCD
High:	May 1981	16.30		130.6	Feb. 1984	NCD		
Low:	Oct. 1986	5.18	−68.2				Apr. 1986	6
High:	Mar. 1989	8.82		70.2	Oct. 1990	−19		
Low:*	July 1992	3.20	−63.7				Jan. 1992	6
	Average		−58.7%	224.1%	Mean	−4.7 mo.		0.0 mo.
					Median	−3.0 mo.		−1.0 mo.

NCD = No Corresponding Date.

* To date, not necessarily cyclical low.

Note: The 3-month Treasury bill rate is expressed on a discount basis.

9 Financial Cycles

Arthur Burns observed: "If the onset of the contraction is marked by a financial crisis or if one develops somewhat later, there is a substantial probability that the decline of aggregate activity will prove severe and perhaps abnormally long as well."[1] This observation has and continues to underlie numerous theories of the interaction of the business and financial cycles.

From the early days of economics, the role of financial institutions in the amplification of the business cycle was recognized in some fashion. For example, Mullineux observed that as early as 1816, M. Carey wrote in his *Essays on Banking,* "[B]anks contributed to and significantly amplified commercial and financial crises because, rather than checking the spirit of overtrading, they fostered and extended it by discounting freely on demand. Then at the first sign of crisis they abruptly changed their practice and adopted a dramatically opposite stance and diminished their loans violently and rapidly."[2] In 1867, John Mills, who also attempted to connect the business cycle with financial cycles, divided the credit cycle into four phases: (1) collapse (panic), (2) depression (post-panic), (3) activity (recoil period), and (4) excitement (speculative period).[3] He linked each stage of the credit cycle to a psychological impact on business. The monetary theories of the business cycle that derived from this thinking were discussed in Chapter 2 and will not be repeated.

As the credit cycle has evolved with changes in financial institutions, its effects have unfolded in different ways. In the 1960s, for example, credit crunches occurred in the savings and loan (S&L) industry due to disintermediation (the withdrawal of funds from S&L's to higher paying financial instruments) but in the 1980s, financial deregulation contributed to the boom-bust financial cycle. In most cases, the real estate market has been the primary conduit through which the credit cycle impacted the economy.

Financial theories of the business cycle encompass several perspectives: (1) the credit cycle (supply and demand for funds), (2) the monetary cycle (the policy induced cycle), and (3) the interest rate cycle (a combination of policy, demand for funds, credit quality, and inflation expectations). This chapter has two parts: the first part briefly discusses financial cycle research (the credit, monetary, and interest rate cycles); the second part is a contributed article by James Coons, the chief economist of Huntington National Bank. The Coons article describes a unique application of leading inflation indicators for signaling turning points in the interest rate cycle. It exemplifies several key cyclical themes found throughout this book, including (1) the use of leading indicators for forecasting, (2) a specialized application of Neftçi's sequential analysis, and (3) the linking of a theory of the financial cycle to the real world.

THE CREDIT CYCLE

Researchers of financial business cycles often ask this central question: Is bank credit fluctuation the source of the business cycle? The starting point to understand this view is based on how banks operate during the business cycle, which can be summarized by two competing theories: (1) the Banks' Willingness to Lend theory, and (2) the Bank Portfolio Holding theory.

The Banks' Willingness to Lend Theory

This theory attributed to Stiglitz and Weiss,[4] argues that as interest rates rise, relatively secure borrowers, who are unwilling to pay the higher borrowing costs, curtail their borrowing. Those companies still willing to borrow at the higher interest rates are less creditworthy and are more risky for the bank. Rather than making loans to the higher risk companies, banks restrict credit. This view has a long history. Thorstein Veblen, Wesley Mitchell, and Hyman Minsky are among the many writers holding this view as part of a larger business cycle hypothesis. The Minsky theory is one of the more influential contemporary theories of how financial markets create cycles.[5] Minsky's theory has been called the *financial instability hypothesis* (FIH). Minsky describes his FIH as follows: "[T]he structural characteristics of the financial system change during periods of prolonged expansion and economic boom and that these changes cumulate to decrease the domain of stability of the system. Thus, after an expansion has been in progress for some time, an event that is not of unusual size or duration can trigger a sharp financial reaction. . . . Once the sharp financial reaction occurs, institutional deficiencies will be evident."[6]

The Minsky hypothesis has been flushed out by Revell,[7] who argues that competition within the financial system ultimately leads to bad banking practices. Under self-imposed or government regulation, according to Revell's hypothesis, the industry captures "supernormal profits" or "surplus profits." Once deregulation occurs, however, new entrants into the financial system must differentiate their product by innovation or lower prices. These new competitors attract less creditworthy borrowers and added risk. In turn, the competition leads the established banks to counter the moves by the new financial institutions, which ultimately lowers the credit quality and profits of the industry. At the first hint of problems, withdrawals from an unsound institution occur, which could have ripple effects throughout the industry.

Revell further suggested that a very competitive banking cycle is intertwined with the economic cycle. By lending to the most profitable ventures in the economy, the banking industry becomes overexposed to sectors of the economy that currently are doing well. When fortunes in those sectors turn, the banking system is faced with mounting bad debt. Mullineux cites the 1987–1988 collapse in the Texas real estate market as a recent example of the banking industry's overexposure to the energy industry. This may also be true of the Japanese banking system in the late 1980s and early 1990s, which has gone through deregulation and whose fortunes were tied to its real estate and equity markets.

Metcalfe[8] and Kindleberger[9] echo these views as well. In essence, they argue that "crises originate with events that significantly increase profit expectations in one sector of the economy and stimulate an increased demand for finance. . . . The extension of bank credit then increases the money supply and self-exciting euphoria develops. . . . More and more firms and households are tempted into speculative finance and are led away from rational behavior, and manias or bubbles result."[10] Kindleberger asked why the control of the money supply fails to limit this speculation. He answers, "[U]nder euphoric conditions with a rush out of money into real or other financial assets, the markets monetize credit and create new money (or give rise to higher velocity)."[11]

Henry Kaufman[12] also has recognized the risks of too much deregulation of the banking system in the United States. Kaufman argues that financial institutions are unique and that deregulation of the financial system stemmed from a false belief that the free market would discipline the system in its twin responsibilities as an entrepreneurial and fiduciary institution. But Kaufman argues that since banks are bailed out, the *prosper or perish rules* of the marketplace are not fully implemented, which raises an inconsistency in the financial system. He concludes that "some reregulation of the financial institutions seems unavoidable in the future."[13]

The Bank Portfolio Holding Theory

This theory, attributed to Bernanke and Blinder,[14] suggests that even if credit rationing does not take place, bank portfolio shifting will impact the economy. If banks shy away from making bank loans, they will allocate that money to security holdings—especially, government bonds. This view was also supported by earlier work by Wood,[15] who found that bank holdings of securities rise relative to loans during expansions but fall during recessions.

In either theory of the credit cycle, the next step is to show that a relationship between the growth in bank credit and the economy exists. On this point, the evidence is mixed. King[16] found little support for this hypothesis, whereas Bernanke[17] and Lown[18] found evidence that the credit cycle leads the business cycle.

THE MONETARY CYCLE

A second approach to link the financial and real sectors has been popularized by Friedman and Schwartz.[19] In their view, the business cycle dances to the fluctuation (growth rate) in the money supply. In essence, they argue:

> [T]here seems to us, accordingly, to be an extraordinarily strong case for the propositions that (1) appreciable changes in the rate of growth of the stock of money are a necessary and sufficient condition for appreciable changes in the rate of growth of money income; and that (2) this is true both for long secular changes and also for changes over periods roughly the length of business cycles."[20]

William Poole[21] reexamined this claim using a "readily reproducible" method, discussed in Chapter 3. Poole concluded: "[T]he evidence for the necessity of a decline in money growth for a business cycle peak is clear."[22] And indeed, this result still holds.

Meiselman[23] has taken this idea one step further and suggested that a political monetary cycle exists in the United States, where the money supply (M1) is accelerated ahead of presidential elections to help the political party controlling the White House stay in control after the next election. He argued that there are three distinct phases of monetary growth: Phase I, the deceleration phase, typically lasts about two quarters, and occurs about a year and a half before the presidential elections. Phase II, the monetary acceleration phase, begins early in the election year. Meiselman felt that the monetary growth profile during Phases I and II was essentially identical under Republican and Democratic administrations. Finally, Phase III is marked by a slowdown in monetary growth but the degree and duration of the slowdown, he argued, is different under Republican and Democratic administrations. Meiselman acknowledged it was difficult to make a strong statistical case for his view and simply reviewed the "micro facts," which he argued were consistent with that view.

THE INTEREST RATE CYCLE—TERM STRUCTURE
OVER THE BUSINESS CYCLE

The last type of financial cycle is the interest rate cycle, which directly incorporates all the relevant market forces and is similar to any *price cycle* since an interest rate is the *price* of borrowing or lending money. The theoretical underpinnings of this approach are found in Keynes's *theory of liquidity preference,* which essentially showed that interest rates are determined simultaneously with consumption, investment, government spending, and net exports. An elaboration on this approach is found in the *loanable funds theory.*

The relationship between the interest rate yield and its term of maturity, holding all other factors constant, is known as the *term structure of interest rates* or the *yield curve.* The shape of the yield curve varies over the business cycle as expectations for growth and inflation change. Using the business cycle stage framework and cycle averages for U.S. government debt securities, Figures 9.1 and 9.2 trace the typical yield curve shape over the business cycle. In Figure 9.1, the yield curve patterns are shown for the period leading up to a peak in the business cycle. In Stage I, the yield curve is upward sloping, that is, the yield on longer term government securities are higher than the shorter term maturities. As the economy moves away from the trough in the business cycle, the yield curve ratchets higher (in Stage II) almost uniformly across all maturities. However, as the economy moves into the middle stage of the expansion period (Stage III), the shape of the yield curve begins to change. The yields on the shorter maturities (U.S. government bills and notes) tend to rise while the long end of the yield curve tends to fall slightly. But as the short end of the term structure continues to move higher (Stage IV), the long end remains relatively stable causing a partial inversion of the yield curve, that is, some of the shorter maturity instruments are yielding a higher rate than the long end of the curve. This process continues through the peak in the business cycle (Stage V). In Stage V, the whole yield curve tends to be inverted as the short end rises more than the long end, but the long end shows the largest rise of the business cycle

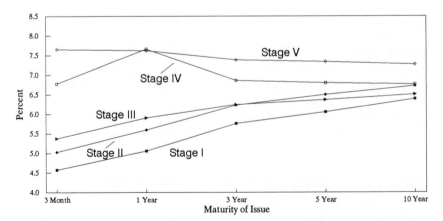

Figure 9.1 The Yield Curve over the Business Cycle, Stages I (Initial Trough) through V (Peak), 1954–1991 Averages.

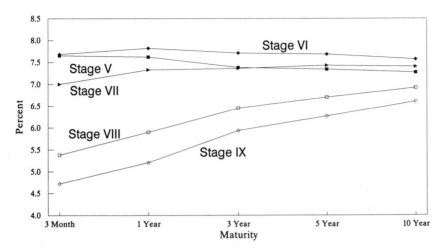

Figure 9.2 The Yield Curve over the Business Cycle, Stages V (Peak) through IX (Terminal Trough), 1954–1991 Averages.

during this phase. The long end of the yield curve tends to move higher after the peak in the economy (Stage VI) but maturities less than one year tend to show little change. Then with the recognition of a recession, Federal Reserve policy tends to push down short-term interest rates and in Stage VII, short-term rates drop about 70 basis points on average, while the long end falls about 20 basis points (see Figure 9.2). As Federal Reserve policy becomes more aggressive in lowering rates and getting the economy moving again, short-term rates decline by about 150 basis points in Stage VIII. At the business cycle trough (Stage IX), short-term rates drop by about another 80 basis points while long-term rates drop by about 30 basis points. And with that, the process starts all over again.

But care should be exercised in reading too much into these cyclical patterns. Sidney Homer[24] correctly observed that although bond yields tend to fluctuate with the business cycle, such a pattern can be relied on only when the cyclical forces are "powerful." Homer noted that at other times the bond market "was capable of a wide variety of patterns that do not correlate with business trends and are influenced no doubt partly by long-term secular fundamentals and partly by transitory political or economic events."[25]

CREDIT CRUNCHES AND FINANCIAL CRISES

Intertwined with the theories of business and financial cycles is the role of credit crunches and financial crises. The concept of the financial crisis is older than the credit crunch hypothesis but shares a common implication for the economy. In the Jevons sense and again with Minsky, Wolfson, and others, financial crises were *striking events,* [26] that distinguished them from the typical characterization of a credit crunch.

Martin Wolfson[27] reviewed the major tenets of financial crisis theories against the empirical record, which ultimately led him to formulate his *business cycle model of financial crises.* Several of his key observations were:

1. Financial crises tend to occur after a peak in the business cycle.

2. Debt payment difficulties tend to occur as corporate profits peak.

3. At business cycle peaks, debt increases relative to equity and the debt maturity shortens.

4. Financial crises have been triggered by a "surprise event," which could be either a sudden change in an institutional arrangement (such as a change in a banking regulation) or an event that causes lenders to fear the loss of their funds.

5. The financial crises were alleviated by the central bank's functioning as the lending of last resort.

Wolfson's theory is particularly insightful in that it links the cyclical nature of finance with the business cycle.

One of the more challenging theories for the occurrence of credit crunches was put forth by Albert Wojnilower,[28] who posited that demand for credit at upper turning points (if not at other times as well) was essentially inelastic with respect to the level of interest rates. Hence, "the growth of credit is therefore essentially supply-determined—if not always, then at least at those times that are cyclically important."[29] He further argues that access to the credit markets is more important to the supply of credit than merely access to the money markets. This point is well taken since more corporations have tapped the credit markets directly than have borrowed at a bank. Following this line of reasoning, Wojnilower contended that credit bottlenecks were the trigger for recessions.

Sinai[30] and Eckstein and Sinai[31] provided another perspective on the credit crunch thesis with essentially the same conclusion that credit crunches lead to recessions. Sinai defined a credit crunch as follows:

> [A] period of an intensifying squeeze on liquidity, where the credit demand of households, businesses and governments increasingly outstrip the ability of the financial system to provide sufficient funds. Both internal and external sources of finance slowly, but continuously, diminish for each sector or become available only at a prohibitive cost. The liquidity squeeze takes its toll sector by sector, until eventually all sectors sharply curtail their desired expenditures.[32]

To monitor the financial environment, Sinai developed a *crunch barometer*[33] based on flow of funds data that allowed him to distinguish phases of the credit cycle.

The interaction of the credit crunch and the business cycle also was used by investment strategists' Richard Hoffman and Steven Resnick.[34] Hoffman and Resnick divided the credit cycle into four stages: (1) the boom, (2) the period of tightening liquidity, (3) the credit crunch, and (4) reliquification. They observed that: (1) stock prices tended to contract late in the boom phase of the credit cycle or shortly into the tightening liquidity phase, and (2) the corporate financing gap (as measured by the ratio of fixed and inventory investment to cashflow) tended to be an excellent coincident indicator of a peak in short-term interest rates and the onset of a credit crunch.

FINANCIAL INDICATORS: FROM THEORY TO PRACTICE

In the final analysis, one of the significant challenges that a forecaster faces is to take a financial theory of the business cycle and make it operational. Over the years, several financial indicators have been suggested to do just that. For example, Starleaf and Stephenson,[35] in a representative approach, developed a *monetary full employment interest rate* to measure the relative ease or tightness of actual monetary policy. Blinder and Goldfeld[36] broadened this idea to include a fiscal policy barometer, while Carlson[37] made the monetary-fiscal policy barometer concept more concrete and usable. Carlson developed an annual monetary-fiscal policy chronology based on whether policy was tight, neutral, or easy. Brimmer and Sinai[38] provided another example of the monetary-fiscal policy barometer approach. These authors defined their monetary policy barometer as the ratio of free reserves to total bank reserves, while their fiscal policy barometer was based on the ratio of the full employment or standardized federal budget deficit to nominal GNP. Keen[39] derived a quarterly policy tightness-looseness chronology based on three barometers: (1) monetary policy, (2) credit conditions, and (3) fiscal policy. The Keen approach used relative-strength measures (based on deviations between a short- and long-duration moving average) to determine the status of the policy barometer; it is probably the most practical application of the IS-LM framework.

In an update of the Keen results, Niemira[40] found that *tight* credit conditions were associated with 83% of the recessions between 1957 and 1989 and lasted an average of 12.8 months. Tight credit conditions also were associated with the slowdowns in 1966 and 1984. Tight monetary policy, on the other hand, was associated with two-thirds of the recessions between that same period, and the average duration of tight monetary policy had been 8 months. Finally, tight fiscal policy was associated with 67% of all the recessions over that period and lasted

13.3 months. Although not all these conditions were present for each recession, at least one of these policy barometers was tight prior to every recession, and the duration of the tightness and policy mix could determine the duration and severity of the recession.

This approach is a practical encapsulation of economic theory (the IS-LM framework) into a set of economic indicators, but as always, the chosen economic variable may be appropriate at certain times but quite inappropriate at others. Hence, a better solution for examining the policy mix over time might be to derive a policy barometer based on what was relevant to policy at a given time and to switch measures when necessary. Although it may be convenient to have a consistent policy barometer over time, the fact of the matter is that policy interests change. This requires a composite of numerous measures or a policy-switch parameter to capture the relevant measure of policy tightness or ease. The benefit in using policy barometers is that this approach adds another dimension to conveniently measure, monitor, and forecast the business cycle.

In the following article by James Coons, the focus turns to forecasting turning points in the interest rate cycle. The article is representative of cycle thinking and forecasting. The approach, as is true throughout this book, treats turning points as *special*. Moreover, while the economic indicator approach may appear to be based on an ad hoc reasoning, there is a good deal of theory and evidence behind these techniques.

Predicting Turning Points in the Interest Rate Cycle

James W. Coons*

INTRODUCTION

There is an old story that Albert Einstein, in his travels, came across three men with widely different IQs. The first man had an IQ of 300. Einstein said, "That's great, Let's talk about my new theory of relativity." After awhile, he came across a fellow with an IQ of 150. Einstein said, "That's good, we can talk about global politics." The third fellow he encountered had an IQ of 65. Einstein paused and then asked, "So, where do you think interest rates will be a year from now?"

While interest rate forecasting has proven so difficult that it may be best left to simple minds, for many, it remains an unavoidable evil. Unanticipated swings in interest rates can have severe and undesirable effects on the wealth of individuals and firms alike.

Unfortunately, useful information on the future course of interest rates is difficult to acquire and recognize on a regular basis. McNees (1986) calculated that predictions by major commercial forecasting firms of the 3-month treasury bill yield 6 months hence were as far as 200 basis points away from the actual levels 67% of the time. I am not aware of any study of cyclical turning point forecast accuracy (indeed, part of the problem is that we do not approach interest rate forecasting this way); however, Belongia (1987) found that *The Wall Street Journal* forecast panel correctly predicted the direction of change in the 3-month treasury bill yield over 6-month horizons less than half of the time.

An important factor behind the myopia of interest rate forecasters is their pursuit of an unreasonable objective with the wrong tools. The typical interest rate forecast is expressed as point estimates of future interest rate levels even though, as Zarnowitz and Lambros (1987) point out, predictions are inherently probabilistic statements. The most commonly used forecasting tools, such as regression analysis, are designed to predict conditional means, not the timing of turning points.

* James W. Coons is Vice President and Chief Economist for Huntington National Bank, Columbus, Ohio. His duties include forecasting developments in the economy and financial markets and assisting in the formulation of investment strategy for the bank. An earlier version of this article received the Library Award at the American Bankers Association's Stonier Graduate School of Banking.

Wecker (1979) demonstrates that conventional forecasting methods are ill suited to addressing changes in direction, although he and Kling (1987), Kling and Bessler (1989), Stock and Watson (1988, 1989), Hamilton (1990), and Highfield (1990) adapt time series methods to turning point detection. Yet conventional applications of time series techniques tend merely to extend recent trends. As in the case of interest rates, the fundamental shifts are of paramount concern.

This article discusses an application of sequential analysis to predicting turning points in the interest rate cycle during 1953–1989. Neftçi (1982) developed a sequential filtering technique that has been applied by Palash and Radecki (1985), Mills (1988), Diebold and Rudebusch (1989), and Niemira (1991) to generate signals of impending turns in the business cycle. Shyy (1989) examined turning points in foreign exchange rates, Niemira (1990) applied it to the stock market, and Phillips (1990) studied the Texas business cycle. As far as I know, this is the first application of a sequential filter to predicting turning points in the interest rate cycle.

THE COMPOSITE INTEREST RATE INDEX

Although a unique set of factors determines each individual interest rate, Cagan (1966, 1972) and others have noted the high degree of comovement among rates over the course of the economic growth cycle. One reason for this correlation is the common dependence of all interest rates on inflation expectations—a dependence that appears to dominate most other factors most of the time. In a clever examination of inflation-indexed bonds traded in the United Kingdom market, Woodward (1990) observed that real rates during the 1980s were quite stable, particularly on an after-tax basis. Changes in inflation expectations were responsible for most of the fluctuation in nominal yields. As a result, the interest rate cycle is assumed to be driven mainly by inflation expectations.

A proxy for the interest rate cycle, a composite interest rate index (CIRI) is constructed from the yields on six separate financial instruments that differ in credit quality and term to maturity. The six component rates are the yields on the 3-month treasury bill, 180-day commercial paper, the 1-year, 5-year, and 10-year treasury notes, and Moody's composite index of corporate bond yields.

The index is a weighted average of the symmetrical percentage changes in the six interest rate series. The weights are standardization factors, computed as the average of the absolute values of the symmetrical percentage changes during the sample period. The value of the CIRI for April 1953 is set to 100, and the index is cumulated using the standardized percentage changes. The dates of peaks (troughs) in the interest rate cycle are identified as the month in which the CIRI reaches its highest (lowest) value in the neighborhood of each growth cycle turning point.

As represented by the CIRI, the interest rate cycle corresponds closely to the growth cycle (Figure 9.3). On average, the CIRI turned at the same time as the growth cycle at troughs; the timing of turns was widely dispersed, however, from as early as 22 months to as late as 21 months. The CIRI turned an average of 5 months after growth cycle peaks, and the leads/lags fell in a more narrow range.

The sample period includes nine peak-to-peak cycles, which lasted an average of 42 months. The nine falling regimes averaged 15 months in length, but they were as long as 31 months and as short as 3 months (Table 9.1). Rising rate regimes were longer because growth expansions were longer than growth recessions. The 10 rising rate regimes were as long as 45 months, as short as 8 months, and averaged 28 months in length.

The timing of turning points in the six components of the CIRI are tightly nested around turning points in the composite index. More than half the component series reversed direction in the same month as the CIRI. In excess of 70% turned within 1 month and 79% within 2 months, suggesting that the composite index provides representative estimates of interest rate cycle turning point dates.

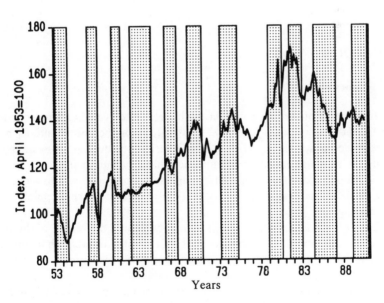

Figure 9.3 Growth Cycles and a Composite Interest Rate Index. Shaded Areas Designate Growth Recessions.

Table 9.1   Duration of Interest Rate Regimes and Cycles.

Falling Regimes			Rising Regimes			Full Cycles
Peaks	Troughs	No. of Months	Troughs	Peaks	No. of Months	No. of Months Peak to Peak
Oct. 57	June 58	8	July 54	Oct. 57	39	
Dec. 59	May 61	17	June 58	Dec. 59	18	26
Jan. 62	Dec. 62	11	May 61	Jan. 62	8	25
Sept. 66	Apr. 67	7	Dec. 62	Sept. 66	45	56
Jan. 70	Mar. 71	14	Apr. 67	Jan. 70	33	40
Aug. 74	Dec. 76	28	Mar. 71	Aug. 74	41	55
Mar. 80	June 80	3	Dec. 76	Mar. 80	39	67
Sept. 81	May 83	20	June 80	Sept. 81	15	18
June 84	Jan. 87	31	May 83	June 84	13	33
Mar. 89			Jan. 87	Mar. 89	26	57
Mean		15.4	Mean		27.7	41.9
Std. Dev.		9.0	Std. Dev.		12.7	16.4
Max.		31	Max.		45	67
Min.		3	Min.		8	18

Notes: The Composite Interest Rate Index (CIRI) is compiled by the Huntington National Bank.

THE SEQUENTIAL FILTER

The Framework

The forecasting of turning points in the interest rate cycle is approached as a sequential decision-making exercise. Observations on the state of interest rates are examined in sequence. With each observation, the decision is made to terminate the sampling process and announce that a turning point has occurred, or to postpone a decision and continue the sampling process. The sequential filter identifies the statistically optimal time to predict a turning point, based on a leading time series.

Moore (1988) and Cullity (1987) have documented the record of the leading inflation index (LII), compiled by the Center for International Business Cycle Research (CIBCR), as a leading indicator of interest rates. On average during the sample period, the LII led turns in the CIRI by six months at troughs and seven months at peaks. The reference dates for the CIRI and the LII are listed and compared in Table 9.2. Figure 9.4 shows the LII against alternating phases of the interest rate cycle.

Table 9.2   Turning Points in the Interest Rate Cycle and the Leading Inflation Index.

Troughs			Peaks		
CIRI	LII	Lead/Lag (−)	CIRI	LII	Lead/Lag (−)
July 54	Mar. 54	−4	Oct. 57	Dec. 55	−22
June 58	Apr. 58	−2	Dec. 59	July 59	−5
May 61	Feb. 61	−3	Jan. 62	Mar. 62	2
Dec. 62	July 62	−5	Sept. 66	Apr. 66	−5
Apr. 67	May 67	1	Jan. 70	Sept. 69	−4
Mar. 71	Nov. 70	−4	Aug. 74	Mar. 74	−5
Dec. 76	June 75	−18	Mar. 80	Apr. 79	−11
June 80	July 80	1	Sept. 81	Nov. 80	−10
May 83	Dec. 82	−5	June 84	June 84	0
Jan. 87	Aug. 85	−17	Mar. 89	June 88	−9
Mean		−5.6	Mean		−6.9
Std. Dev.		6.3	Std. Dev.		6.4
Max.		1	Max.		2
Min.		−18	Min.		−22

Notes: The Composite Interest Rate Index (CIRI) is compiled by the Huntington National Bank. The Leading Inflation Index (LII) is from the CIBCR.

The LII regularly leads the interest rate cycle, but recognizing the LII as a leading indicator merely replaces one turning point detection problem with another. A turning point in the LII signals an imminent shift in interest rates, but what criteria identify such a turning point? The successful use of the LII, or any other indicator, requires the efficient extraction of information from the series. In fact, ad hoc rules for interpreting leading indicators fail to incorporate the risk-reward tradeoff and produce unreliable predictions.[1a]

Neftçi's (1982) contribution was to characterize turning point forecasting as an optimal stopping time problem. It is a stopping time problem because the object of prediction is the time of an event, not the level or rate of change of a time series. The solution is optimal in the sense that the sequential filter balances the reward of correctly anticipating a turning point with the risks of sounding a false alarm or issuing a late signal. Simply stated, the sequential filter is a prediction rule that translates a leading time series into probabilities of a near-term turning point in a target time series.

A crucial assumption is that the indicator series behaves differently in upturns than in downturns. The probability distribution that generates the indicator series during upturn regimes must be independent of the corresponding

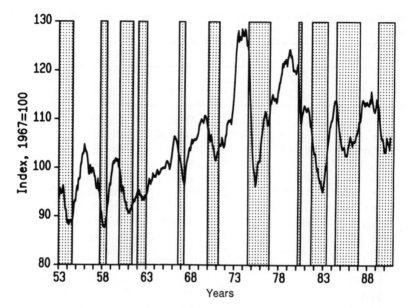

Figure 9.4 Interest Rate Cycles and the Leading Inflation Index (LII). Shaded Areas Designate Falling Interest Rate Regimes.

distribution for downturn regimes. The sharpness of peaks and troughs in the leading inflation index and the more rapid pace of decreases than of increases suggest compliance with the assumption.

The sequential filter operates by discerning changes in the stochastic process of the indicator series—in this case, the LII. The switches between probability distributions correspond to regime shifts and, therefore, to turning points. Detection of the otherwise unobservable shifts between the distributions is the mechanism by which the sequential filter produces turning point signals.

The Model

From Shiryayev (1978), the probability of a near-term regime shift is:

$$P_t = \frac{A}{A + B},$$

(1a)

where:

$$A = \{P_{t-1} + pa\,(1 - P_{t-1})\}\,p0_t,$$

(1b)

$$B = (1 - P_{t-1})\,p1_t\,(1 - pa),$$

(1c)

P_t is the posterior probability that the stochastic process underlying the leading time series shifted from month $t - 1$ to month t, P_{t-1} is the posterior probability calculated in the prior month, and pa is the a priori probability of a regime switch. Also referred to as the prior probability of a regime change, pa is assigned by the analyst, based on knowledge about the target series, contemporaneous patterns in other indicators, or other information.

The remaining terms, $p0_t$ and $p1_t$, are conditional probabilities that depend on past values of the leading series. When the most recent turning point was a trough, then $p0_t$ and $p1_t$ are the conditional probabilities that month t was in a downturn regime and an upturn regime, respectively. When the most recent turning point was a peak, $p0_t$ and $p1_t$ are the conditional probabilities that month t was in an upturn regime and a downturn regime, respectively.

An optimal stopping time rule is used to extract turning point signals from the estimated probabilities. As Neftçi (1982) shows, the optimal stopping time depends on the analyst's willingness to risk a false alarm. Specifically, an imminent turning point is detected when:

$$P_t \geq 1 - f, \text{ where } 0 \leq f \leq 1, \tag{2}$$

where f is the acceptable probability of a false signal. Following convention, the false signal risk factor is set to 5%.

As a result, turning points are signaled when P_t is equal to or greater than 95%. In that month, testing for the next turning point begins, based on the $1 - P_t$ probability that a regime switch has not yet occurred. This means that the recursive calculation of P_{t+1} for the next turning point will be initialized with $1 - P_t$. In this way, the model explicitly reflects the uncertainty with which turning points are identified in practice.

Other models have incorporated the assumption that turning points are immediately recognizable with certainty by using $P_{t-1} = 0$ to initialize the recursion after each turning point. Even in the case of business cycles, for which widely accepted turning point dates are available, the assumption is not strictly valid. Definitive reference dates are determined and announced at least 6 months after the fact. In the case of interest rates, no official arbiter of turning points exists.

The Application

The first step in the application of the sequential filter is the estimation of conditional probability distributions, from which the $p0_t$ and $p1_t$ are drawn. The distributions are estimated by separately fitting normal distributions to the sample means and variances for rising and falling regimes.

Following Diebold and Rudebusch (1989), the a priori probability of a regime switch is assigned the value that minimizes the quadratic probability score

(QPS) over a one-period horizon. The QPS is the equivalent of mean squared error for probability forecasts, measuring the closeness of calculated probabilities to observed outcomes.

A constant prior is, of course, insensitive to regime duration. In fact, however, the frequency of regime changes, which is the same as the reciprocal of the average regime duration, is the constant probability with the lowest QPS.[2a] As a result, while the prior does not vary with the duration of a regime, it does reflect the historical frequency of turning points. I use the constant probability that produces the minimum QPS for all turning points as the prior, assuming that a rising regime is no more or less likely to end than a falling regime.

THE RESULTS

Calculating the Probabilities

The probabilities of an imminent turning point are calculated for each month from July 1954 to August 1990. The probabilities are lagged one month to account for the recognition lag. In general, the probabilities begin each regime at very low levels, rising rapidly and exceeding the critical 95% level in the neighborhood of turning points.

Borrowing the graphical approach of Highfield (1990), Figures 9.5, 9.6, and 9.7 illustrate the sequential-filter-designated regime of each monthly observation of the CIRI. Plus signs represent observations in rising rate regimes. Boxes represent observations in falling rate regimes.

The designations correspond well with the actual regimes. Notable exceptions are early signals of the October 1957 peak, the March 1980 peak, and the January 1987 trough, late signals of the April 1967 trough, and June 1980 peak, and a 13-month false rising regime signal during the August 1974 to December 1976 falling regime.

Scoring the Results

The results are scored with four measures: quadratic probability score (QPS), the basis point index (BPI), the percentage of signals that were correct, and the number of correct signals as a percentage of actual regimes, or definition.[3a] Correct signals are those that accurately identify the direction of change in the CIRI. The BPI is the sum of changes in the CIRI between turning point signals, adjusted for the direction of the change. It is a proxy for the gains that could have been achieved by acting on the signals. The potential BPI is the sum of changes in the CIRI between actual turning points. Definition measures the balance between the frequency and accuracy of the signals and the actual turning points.

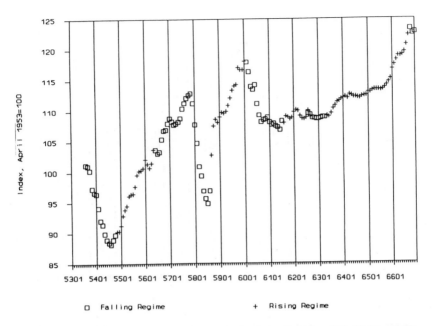

Figure 9.5 Composite Interest Rate Index (Regimes Based on LII: 53:07–66:12).

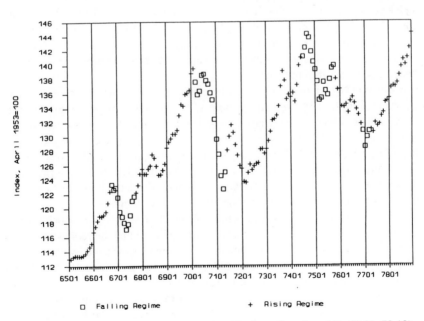

Figure 9.6 Composite Interest Rate Index (Regimes Based on LII: 65:01–78:12).

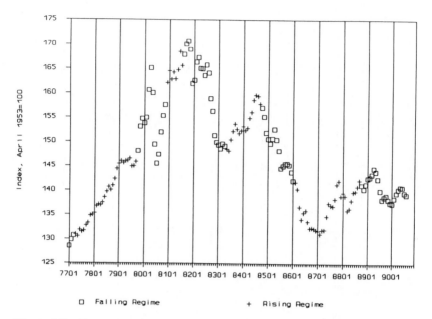

Figure 9.7   Composite Interest Rate Index (Regimes Based on LII: 77:01–90:08).

The scores for the filtered LII are compared with those for the predictions from five different benchmark methods: the LII 1% growth rate rule (1% rule), sequential probabilities computed directly from values of the CIRI using 5% and 32% priors, and direction reversals in the prime commercial bank and Federal Reserve discount rates.

Cullity (1987) applied the 1% rule to map the 6-month smoothed percentage change in the LII into turning points. The initial move of the growth rate above 1% or below −1% signals a switch to a rising or falling rate regime, respectively. The CIRI probabilities were calculated using the same method as the LII probabilities but were based on conditional distributions computed from observations on the CIRI itself, rather than the LII. Changes in the direction of the prime and discount rates are assumed to reflect judgments regarding the future course of interest rates by key economic agents.

By construction, the sequential filter of the CIRI itself will produce turning point signals after the fact. Nonetheless, the signals should be more stable with respect to actual turning point dates than the signals generated by other methods. Priors of 5% and 32% were tested, because they have the lowest QPSs for forecast horizons of 1 and 7 months, respectively.

A QPS can range from 0, for perfect accuracy, to 2, for complete inaccuracy. The QPS for a zero probability, the equivalent of never predicting a turning point, had a lower QPS than any of the benchmark methods. The constant probability of 100%, the equivalent of predicting a turning point every month, was nearly perfectly inaccurate over the 1-month horizon, as indicated by the QPS of 1.91.

The constant probability of 5% produced the lowest QPS by a wide margin for the 1-month horizon. Among the benchmark methods, the filtered CIRI with the 5% prior had the lowest QPS, followed by the filtered LII. For a forecast horizon of 7 months, the filtered LII had the lowest QPS, albeit the scores for the 1% rule and the filtered CIRI with both 5% and 32% priors were close. With the exception of the constant probabilities, the filter of the LII performed best according to the QPS.

The differences among scores on the other measures are more revealing (see Table 9.3). The sequential filter of the LII produced 22 turning point signals, 18 of which were correct. The LII probabilities had the highest BPI—28% larger than the BPI of the 1% rule and 15.5% larger than for the sequential filter of the CIRI with the 32% prior. The signals from the filtered LII captured 44.4% of the possible gains over the interest rate cycle, the most of any method.

The prime rate produced the most signals, but only half were correct. Even so, the prime rate rule demonstrated substantial definition by producing more correct signals than there were actual regimes. The lateness of the prime rate signals detracted from all its scores, especially during predicted regimes that corresponded to relatively small changes in rates within actual regimes.

The sequential filter of the CIRI with the 32% prior scored well in all respects, capturing 38.5% of the potential BPI and producing 23 correct

Table 9.3 Quadratic Probability Scores for Selected Turning Point Detection Methods at All Turning Points, August 1953 to April 1989.

Method		Forecast Horizon	
		1 Month	7 Months
Filtered LII 5% Pr		0.39	0.50
LII 1% Rule		0.51	0.63
Filtered CIRI 32% Pr		0.69	0.64
Filtered CIRI 5% Pr		0.25	0.61
Prime Rate		0.66	0.98
Discount Rate		0.62	0.96
Constants	0%	0.093	0.634
	5%	0.089	0.576
	32%	0.238	0.433
	100%	1.907	1.366

signals—4 more than the actual number of regimes and 1 more than the LII. The remarkable performance by the sequential filter of the target series itself exemplifies the power and usefulness of the technique.

Post-October 1979 Performance

The rapid pace of change in financial markets might have altered the behavior of interest rates and turning point detection methods in important ways. To measure the effect of such changes on the performance of the signaling methods, I calculated the measures in Table 9.4 for the post-October 1979 period on an ex ante as well as ex post basis. The performance measures are summarized in Table 9.5.

The LII distributions for the two periods are little different. In fact, while the post-October 1979 probabilities changed slightly, no turning point dates were altered and all the scores were the same on both an ex post and ex ante basis. In contrast, the CIRI distributions for the pre-October 1979 period were noticeably more diffused than for the entire sample. The difference is reflected in changes to probabilities, signal dates, and scores.

Ex post, the CIRI filtered with a 32% prior had the highest scores. The signals captured 53.6% of the potential change in the BPI and produced 9 correct signals out of 10—3 more than the actual number of regimes—despite the greater volatility of interest rates during the period. The definition of prime rate signals exceeded even that of the CIRI with the 32% prior, but the numerous incorrect signals reduced the BPI. The LII signals had the second highest BPI, capturing 32.7% of the potential. The BPI for the filtered CIRI with the 5% prior was actually negative.

The ranking of methods did not change on an ex ante basis, although the performance of the CIRI filter with the 32% prior deteriorated. The potential BPI fell to 36%. The number of signals increased by 5 to 16, but the number correct increased by only 1. The definition improved, matching that of the prime rate rule.

Interestingly, the scores of the CIRI with the 5% prior were sharply higher on an ex ante basis. The BPI as a percentage of potential jumped from negative territory to 24.4%, due to an increase in the timeliness of the signals. Seven of the 10 signals were earlier than on an ex post basis, advancing by an average of 3 months.

Variable Priors

A final test was performed by using the posterior probabilities derived from the sequential filter of the CIRI with the 5% prior as the priors for the filter of the LII. The scores are shown in Table 9.6. The BPI for the entire sample

Table 9.4 Summary of Scores for Selected Turning Point Detection Methods, July 1954 to December 1989.

Method	Basis Point Index (BPI)[a]	Potential BPI Change (%)	Number of Regimes	Correct Predicted Regimes as a Percentage of Total	
				Predicted Regimes (%)	Actual Regimes (%)
Filtered LII 5% Pr	153.19	44.4	22	81.8	94.7
LII 1% rule	119.67	34.7	20	80.0	84.2
Filtered CIRI 32% Pr	132.65	38.5	30	76.7	121.1
Filtered CIRI 5% Pr	45.58	13.2	20	60.0	63.2
Prime rate	52.35	15.2	42	52.4	115.8
Discount rate	61.64	17.9	21	61.9	68.4
Potential[b]	344.69	100.0	19	—	100.0

[a] The BPI is the absolute value of the change in the CIRI between turning point signals.

[b] Based on turning points in the interest rate cycle, determined from the CIRI and economic growth cycle reference dates.

Table 9.5 Summary of Scores for Selected Turning Point Detection Methods, October 1979 to December 1989.

Method	Basis Point Index (BPI)[a]	Potential BPI Change (%)	Number of Regimes	Correct Predicted Regimes as a Percentage of Total	
				Predicted Regimes (%)	Actual Regimes (%)
Ex Post					
Filtered LII 5% Pr	45.82	32.7	7	71.4	71.4
LII 1% rule	25.61	18.3	5	80.0	57.1
Filtered CIRI 32% Pr	75.15	53.6	11	81.8	128.6
Filtered CIRI 5% Pr	−9.35	−6.7	10	40.0	57.1
Prime rate	24.95	17.8	16	62.5	142.9
Discount rate	5.43	3.9	7	42.9	42.9
Ex Ante					
Filtered LII 5% Pr	45.82	32.7	7	71.4	71.4
Filtered CIRI 32% Pr	50.47	36.0	16	62.5	142.9
Filtered CIRI 5% Pr	34.17	24.4	10	70.0	100.0
Potential[b]	140.19	100.0	7	—	100.0

[a] The BPI is the absolute value of the change in the CIRI between turning point signals.

[b] Based on turning points in the interest rate cycle, determined from the CIRI and economic growth cycle reference dates.

Table 9.6   Summary of Scores for the Sequential Filter of the LII Using Posterior CIRI Probabilities as Priors.

Scoring Measures	1954 to 1989	October 1979 to December 1989	
		Ex Post	Ex Ante
Basis point index (BPI)	159.3	59.80	58.07
Potential BPI (%)	46.2	42.7	41.4
Number of predicted regimes	41	13	24
Correct signals as a % of all predicted signals	65.9	53.8	58.3
Correct signals as a % of all actual regimes	142.1	100.0	200.0

period was 4% larger than for the filter of the LII using the constant 5% prior. The total number of signals nearly doubled to 41. The number of correct signals increased by 5, to 27, lowering the percentage correct to 65.9%, but raising the definition to 142.1%—the highest among all benchmark methods.

On an ex post basis for the post-October 1979 period, the performance remained below that of the CIRI with the 32% prior, but well ahead of the performances of all other methods. The BPI was the second highest, but 6 of the 13 signals, including the 4 most recent ones, were incorrect. On an ex ante basis, the performance improved somewhat. The BPI topped that of the CIRI with the 32% prior by 15.1%. The variable prior approach issued 24 signals. Only 58.3% were correct, but there were two correct signals for each actual regime, indicating substantial definition.

CONCLUSION

The application of the sequential filter to detecting turning points in the interest rate cycle produced promising results. The sequential filter of the LII outperformed the 1% rule, but the 1% rule posted high scores for such a simple and easily applied method. Remarkably, the filter of the composite interest rate index itself scored well over the entire sample and outdistanced other methods in the period of volatile rates since late 1979.

The stability of the conditional probability distributions for the LII between the entire sample and the pre-October 1979 sample was reassuring. The instability of the distributions for the CIRI and the dramatic difference between the performance of the signals produced with the 5% prior on an ex post and ex ante basis question its reliability.

A feature of the signals not addressed, but of importance in some applications, is the lead-lag time. The scoring measures used do not differentiate between early and late signals. The LII signals occurred earlier on average than CIRI signals, but the timing relative to the actual turning point dates was much more variable. The filtered LII signals occurred in the same months as troughs and 2.9 months in advance of peaks, on average, whereas filtered CIRI signals (32% prior) occurred an average of 2.4 months after troughs and 1.5 months after peaks.

In addition, some information generated by the sequential filter was lost in the translation to binary turning point signals. Monthly revisions to turning point probabilities are an advantage over the binary readings of the 1% rule and prime and discount rate reversal rules, which are not reflected in the scoring measures.

Finally, the use of the posterior probabilities computed directly from the target series as priors for a filter of a leading series enhances the performance of the technique.

NOTES

1a. In fact, economic forecasters appear to rely on suboptimal methods. In a clever application of Bayes' theorem, Herman O. Stekler, "An Analysis of Turning Point Forecasts," *American Economic Review*, Vol. 62 (September 1972), 724, showed that forecasters have routinely underutilized information about the timing of business cycle peaks that is contained in common economic indicators.

2a. Consider a time series, x_t, $t = 1, \ldots, n$, that is a binary representation of turning points in some other time series. $x_t = 1$ for t that are in a different regime than $t - 1$. $x_t = 0$ for all t that are in the same regime as $t - 1$.

The average regime duration is

$$D = \frac{n}{\sum\limits_{t=1}^{n} x_t}. \tag{1}$$

The frequency of regime change is the inverse of the average duration, or

$$F = \frac{\sum\limits_{t=1}^{n} x_t}{n}. \tag{2}$$

From Diebold and Rudebusch (1989), the QPS of a time-invariant probability. P, is

$$QPS = \frac{2}{n} \sum\limits_{t=1}^{n} (P - x_t)^2 \tag{3}$$

Differentiating (3), with respect to P, shows that QPS reaches a minimum with respect to P when

$$\frac{4}{n} \sum_{t=1}^{n} (P - x_t) = 0. \tag{4}$$

After several tranformations, (4) is

$$\frac{\sum_{t=1}^{n} P}{n} = \frac{\sum_{t=1}^{n} x_t}{n} \tag{5}$$

Substituting (2) for the righthand side of (5), QPS is at a minimum when

$$\frac{\sum_{t=1}^{n} P}{n} = F, \tag{6}$$

or since P is a constant, when $P = F$. In other words, the frequency of regime changes is the constant probability forecast with the lowest QPS.

3a. The methods were also tested on their ability to identify the contemporaneous interest rate regime during the July 1953 to December 1989 period. The actual state-of-rates was assigned the value of one during rising regimes and zero during falling regimes. Predicted series were constructed by assigning the value of one to periods between predicted troughs and peaks and zero to the periods between predicted peaks and troughs.

The LII predictions had the highest correlation with the actual state-of-rates, 0.56, but that was essentially matched by the 0.54 correlation of the predictions from the CIRI probabilities with the 32% prior. The next closest correlation was 0.48, with the 1% rule predictions. The correlations of the discount rate, prime rate, and predictions from the CIRI probabilities with the 5% prior were 0.42, 0.37, and 0.31, respectively.

REFERENCES

Belongia, Michael T., 1987, "Predicting Interest Rates," *Federal Reserve Bank of St. Louis Review,* Vol. 69 (March), 9.

Cagan, Phillip, 1966, "Changes in the Cyclical Behavior of Interest Rates," National Bureau of Economic Research, Occasional Paper 100.

Cagan, Phillip, 1972, "The Recent Cyclical Movements of Interest Rates in Historical Perspective," *Business Economics,* Vol. 7 (January), 43–52.

Cullity, John P., 1987, "Signals of Cyclical Movements in Inflation and Interest Rates," *Financial Analyst's Journal,* Vol. 43 (September/October), 40.

Diebold, Francis X., and Rudebusch, Glenn D., 1989, "Scoring the Leading Indicators," *Journal of Business,* Vol. 62 (June), 369.

Hamilton, James D., 1991, "Analysis of Time Series Subject to Change in Regime," *Journal of Econometrics,* Vol. 45 (July–August), 39–70.

Highfield, Richard A., 1990, "Bayesian Approaches to Turning Point Prediction," Johnson Graduate School of Management, Cornell University, manuscript, July.

Kling, John L., 1987, "Predicting the Turning Points of Business and Economic Time Series," *Journal of Business,* Vol. 60 (February), 201.

Kling, John L., and Bessler, David A., 1989, "Calibration-Based Predictive Distributions: An Application of Prequential Analysis to Interest Rates, Money, Prices, and Output," *Journal of Business,* Vol. 62 (April), 477.

McNees, Steven K., 1986, "Forecasting Accuracy of Alternative Techniques: A Comparison of U.S. Macroeconomic Forecasts," *Journal of Business and Economic Statistics,* Vol. 4 (January), 5.

Mills, Leonard, 1988, "Can Stock Prices Reliably Predict Recessions?" *Federal Reserve Bank of Philadelphia Business Review,* (September/October), 3.

Moore, Geoffrey H., 1988, "An Improved Leading Index of Inflation," Center for International Business Cycle Research, Columbia University Graduate School of Business, manuscript (October).

Neftçi, Salih N., 1982, "Optimal Prediction of Cyclical Downturns," *Journal of Economic Dynamics and Control,* Vol. 4 (March), 225.

Niemira, Michael P., 1990, "Forecasting Turning Points in the Stock Market Cycle and Asset Allocation Implications," in *Analyzing Modern Business Cycles,* Philip A. Klein, ed., Armonk, NY: M. E. Sharpe, 109.

Niemira, Michael P., 1991, and Fredman, Giela. "An Evaluation of the Composite Index of Leading Indicators for Signaling Turning Points in Business and Growth Cycles," *Business Economics* (October), 49–55.

Palash, Carl J., and Radecki, Lawrence J., 1985, "Using Monetary and Financial Variables to Predict Cyclical Downturns," *Federal Reserve Bank of New York Quarterly Review,* Vol. 10 (Summer), 36.

Phillips, Keith R., 1990, "The Texas Index of Leading Economic Indicators: A Revision and Further Evaluation," *Federal Reserve Bank of Dallas Economic Review* (July), 17–25.

Shiryayev, A. N., 1978, *Optimal Stopping Rules,* New York: Springer-Verlag, 1978.

Shyy, Gang, 1989, "Bullish or Bearish: A Bayesian Dichotomous Model to Forecast Turning Points in the Foreign Exchange Market," *Journal of Economics and Business,* Vol. 41 (January), 49.

Stekler, Herman O., 1972, "An Analysis of Turning Point Forecasts," *American Economic Review,* Vol. 62 (September), 724.

Stock, James H., and Watson, Mark W., 1988, "A Probability Model of the Coincident Economic Indicators," National Bureau of Economic Research, Working Paper 2772, November.

Stock, James H., and Watson, Mark W., 1989, "New Indexes of Coincident and Leading Economic Indicators," in *NBER Macroeconomics Annual 1989,* Oliver Jean Blanchard and Stanley Fischer, eds., Cambridge, MA: MIT Press, 351.

Wecker, William, 1979, "Predicting the Turning Points of a Time Series," *Journal of Business,* Vol. 52, 35.

Woodward, G. Thomas, 1990, "The Real Thing: A Dynamic Profile of the Term Structure of Real Interest Rates and Inflation Expectations in the United Kingdom, 1982–1989," *Journal of Business,* Vol. 63 (July), 373–398.

Zarnowitz, Victor, and Lambros, Louis A., 1987, "Consensus and Uncertainty in Economic Prediction," *Journal of Political Economy,* Vol. 95 (June), 591.

10 Stock Market Cycles

Beryl Sprinkel observed that "stock price trends are particularly difficult to predict, since they appear to have no close and simple relation to the general pattern of business and profits. It is true that economic activity and stock prices go in the same direction about two-thirds of the time, but it is the other third that is most interesting and potentially most profitable."[1] Indeed, since Sprinkel made that statement in the early 1960s, his observation has held. Between 1946 and 1991, there have been 13 stock market cycles and 9 business cycle recessions; in 8 of those 9 recessions, the stock market responded to the general business conditions, which implies that 62% of the time the stock market moves with the economy. Curiously then, this raises the question: Why does the stock market go its own way and how can turning points be anticipated? Before addressing that issue, consider the profile of the typical stock market cycle.

PROFILE OF THE STOCK MARKET CYCLE

The contraction (bear market) and expansion (bull market) phases of the stock market price cycle can be demonstrated using the Burns and Mitchell cycle stages framework (see Chapter 3). As shown in Figure 10.1, the stock market, as represented by monthly fluctuation in the Standard & Poors 500 stock price index,[2] posts its best gains in the early stages of a bull market; those gains decrease in amount as the bull market ages. When the stock market enters a bear market, stock market losses are relatively small at first but escalate toward the middle stage of a declining market. Bear markets, on average, decline by 20% from a monthly average peak to trough, while a bull market typically posts a gain of about 60% (see Table 10.1). On average, bull markets outlive bear markets by a ratio of 3:1. This contrasts with business cycle expansions that on average, outlive recessions by a ratio of almost 4:1.

In examining the stock market cycle, several methods will be discussed from the fixed length cycle to a comprehensive indicator "buy" and "sell" signaling system. But first, it is useful to review the linkage between stock prices and the business cycle.

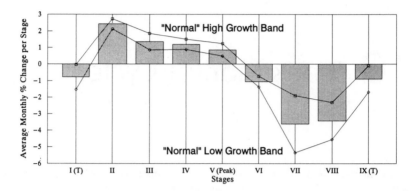

Figure 10.1   The Stock Market Cycle. (The S&P 500 stock price index was divided into stages of the cycle, according to the standard Burns & Mitchell (NBER) technique, which collapses the cycle into relevant growth phases and highlights the cycle dynamic.)

THE STOCK MARKET AND THE ECONOMY

In reviewing the relationship of stock prices and the economy, Pearce[3] noted that the stock prices play many roles, such as (1) reflecting profit expectations, (2) reacting to interest rate changes, and (3) incorporating market psychology. Although stock prices embody those aspects of the economic environment, they also have a secondary impact on the economy through the consumption and investment channels. Although the significance of that function is open to debate, the main suggestions are that consumption is impacted by the stock market through (1) consumer wealth (yet, this view has been tarnished somewhat after the 1987 stock market crash when consumption did not collapse[4]) and/or, (2) consumer confidence. The linkage between the stock market and business investment generally is assumed to be through (1) the cost of capital, or (2) the replacement cost of existing capital. In essence, the cost-of-capital view is that when stock prices are high, companies are more inclined to issue stock to finance their capital expenditures. Although tax issues play an important role in this process, that factor is beyond the scope of this discussion. The second approach—often attributed to James Tobin and dubbed *Tobin's q*—essentially argues that investment will occur when q, which is defined as the ratio of the value of total market debt and equity divided by the cost of replacing the existing capital stock at current prices, is greater than one. If stock prices are increasing fast enough to push that ratio above one, then according to the theory, net investment will increase. However, there is no consensus on the strength and timing of the investment-stock price impact.[5]

Table 10.1   Turning Points and Duration of Stock Market Cycles (Based on Monthly Average S&P 500 Stock Price Index).

| Stock Market Cycle | | Value at | | % Change | | Duration (Months) | | Ratio, Bull/Bear |
Peak	Trough	Peak	Trough	P-->T	T-->P	P-->T	T-->P	Market Duration
May 1946	June 1949	18.70	13.97	−25.3		37	43	1.2
Jan. 1953	Sept. 1953	26.18	23.27	−11.1	87.4	8	34	4.3
July 1956	Dec. 1957	48.78	40.33	−17.3	109.6	17	19	1.1
July 1959	Oct. 1960	59.74	53.73	−10.1	48.1	15	14	0.9
Dec. 1961	June 1962	71.74	55.63	−22.5	33.5	6	43	7.2
Jan. 1966	Oct. 1966	93.32	77.13	−17.3	67.8	9	26	2.9
Dec. 1968	June 1970	106.48	75.59	−29.0	38.1	18	31	1.7
Jan. 1973	Dec. 1974	118.42	67.07	−43.4	56.7	23	21	0.9
Sept. 1976	Mar. 1978	105.45	88.82	−15.8	57.2	18	32	1.8
Nov. 1980	July 1982	135.65	109.38	−19.4	52.7	20	15	0.8
Oct. 1983	July 1984	167.65	151.08	−9.9	53.3	9	37	4.1
Aug. 1987	Dec. 1987	329.36	240.96	−26.8	118.0	4	30	7.5
June 1990	Oct. 1990	360.39	307.12	−14.8	49.6	4		
	Average			−20.2	64.3	14.5	28.8	2.9
	Standard Deviation			9.0	25.8	8.9	9.5	2.3

In the final analysis, the economic cycle sometimes can provide an understanding of why stock prices move as they do, but in many cases, stock prices march to a different drummer and at their own pace. This realization has triggered numerous hypotheses on what determines stock prices, some of which will be discussed.

FORECASTING THE STOCK MARKET USING FIXED-LENGTH CYCLES

The Foundation for the Study of Cycles (FSC) has found that a 40.68-month stock market cycle existed over time.[6] The obvious advantage of knowing that a cycle can be approximated by a fixed-length period is knowing when to look for the next turning point. And so it is with this 40.68-month cycle: It provides an indication of timing—if not amplitude. Consider the historical record of the 40.68-month stock price cycle, which is converted into a true month by making a few simplifying assumptions. First, a peak-and-trough date was selected from the actual cycle and used as an initial condition for a peak and a trough date in the fixed-length cycle. The selection of these starting points was determined by the closeness of the individual cycle length (either peak-to-trough or trough-to-peak) to its postwar average. Second, the 40.68-month period was adjusted to a daily rate and that fixed daily span was extended forward and backward from the fifteenth day of those two turning point dates (for January 1953 and October 1960). This approach resulted in a cycle that had an average turning point that led the actual peak in the S&P 500 stock price cycle by 2.1 months for the 14 stock market peaks since 1946—though its standard deviation was 9.5 months. At troughs in the stock market cycle, the average turning point in the fixed-length cycle occurred 1.7 months before the actual cycle trough with a standard deviation of 10.8 months (see Table 10.2). However, the long lead time at peaks since 1980 hints at a lengthening of that cycle. After some experimentation, it appears that a 41.6-month cycle (Table 10.3) fits the turning point dates better in the postwar period than the 40.68-month cycle (which was determined by the FSC using a stock price series that extended over 200 years beginning in June 1789) with a commensurate improvement in the return.[7] Nonetheless, the existence of a 41-month stock market cycle has been around for quite awhile; it was first uncovered in 1912 by the Rothchilds, and in 1923, Crum and Kitchin reported a similar result.[8]

The stock market cycle seems to be approximated reasonably well by this fixed-length cycle, considering that there is no theoretical reason to expect such a repetitive cycle duration. On the other hand, since the discussion of this cycle is known widely and has been discussed for years, it may have become a self-fulfilling prophesy. Whatever the reason, the overall closeness of

Table 10.2 The Stock Market Cycle versus a 40.68-Month, Fixed-Length Cycle (Based on Monthly Average S&P 500 Stock Price Index).

Actual Cycle		40.68–Month Cycle		Timing (in Months) at		Fixed–Cycle Value		% Change	
Peak	Trough	Peak	Trough	Peak	Trough	Peak	Trough	P––>T	T––>P
Apr. 1946	Feb. 1948	June 1946	July 1947	2	−7	18.58	15.77	−15.1	
June 1948	June 1949	Sept. 1949	Nov. 1950	15	17	15.49	19.83	28.0	−1.8
Jan. 1953	Sept. 1953	Jan. 1953	Mar. 1954	0	6	26.18	26.57	1.5	32.0
July 1956	Dec. 1957	May 1956	June 1957	−2	−6	46.54	47.55	2.2	75.2
July 1959	Oct. 1960	Aug. 1959	Oct. 1960	1	0	59.40	53.73	−9.5	24.9
Dec. 1961	June 1962	Dec. 1962	Feb. 1964	12	20	62.64	77.39	23.5	16.6
Jan. 1966	Oct. 1966	Apr. 1966	May 1967	3	7	91.60	92.59	1.1	18.4
Dec. 1968	June 1970	July 1969	Sep. 1970	7	3	94.71	82.58	−12.8	2.3
Jan. 1973	Dec. 1974	Nov. 1972	Jan. 1974	−2	−11	115.05	96.11	−16.5	39.3
Sept. 1976	Mar. 1978	Mar. 1976	Apr. 1977	−6	−11	101.08	99.05	−2.0	5.2
Nov. 1980	July 1982	June 1979	Aug. 1980	−17	−23	101.73	123.50	21.4	2.7
Oct. 1983	July 1984	Oct. 1982	Dec. 1983	−12	−7	132.66	164.36	23.9	7.4
Aug. 1987	Dec. 1987	Feb. 1986	Mar. 1987	−18	−9	219.37	292.47	33.3	33.5
June 1990	Oct. 1990	May 1989	July 1990	−13	−3	313.93	360.03	14.7	7.3
		Sept. 1992	Nov. 1993						
		Jan. 1996	Feb. 1997						
			Average	−2.1	−1.7			6.7	20.2
		Standard Deviation		9.5	10.8			16.1	20.3

431

Table 10.3 The Stock Market Cycle versus a 41.60-Month, Fixed-Length Cycle (Based on Monthly Average S&P 500 Stock Price Index).

Actual Cycle		41.60–Month Cycle		Timing (in Months) at		Fixed–Cycle Value		% Change	
Peak	Trough	Peak	Trough	Peak	Trough	Peak	Trough	P––>T	T––>P
Apr. 1946	Feb. 1948	Apr. 1946	Apr. 1947	0	–10	18.66	14.60	–21.8	4.7
June 1948	June 1949	Aug. 1949	Aug. 1950	14	14	15.29	18.43	20.5	42.1
Jan. 1953	Sept. 1953	Jan. 1953	Jan. 1954	0	4	26.18	25.46	–2.8	81.7
July 1956	Dec. 1957	June 1956	May 1957	–1	–7	46.27	46.78	1.1	21.8
July 1959	Oct. 1960	Oct. 1959	Oct. 1960	3	0	57.00	53.73	–5.7	22.2
Dec. 1961	June 1962	Mar. 1963	Mar. 1964	15	21	65.67	78.80	20.0	8.9
Jan. 1966	Oct. 1966	July 1966	July 1967	6	9	85.84	93.01	8.4	–2.0
Dec. 1968	June 1970	Dec. 1969	Dec. 1970	12	6	91.11	90.05	–1.2	22.5
Jan. 1973	Dec. 1974	Apr. 1973	Apr. 1974	3	–8	110.27	92.46	–16.2	14.0
Sept. 1976	Mar. 1978	Sept. 1976	Sept. 1977	0	–6	105.45	96.23	–8.7	19.9
Nov. 1980	July 1982	Feb. 1980	Jan. 1981	–9	–18	115.34	132.97	15.3	25.1
Oct. 1983	July 1984	June 1983	June 1984	–4	–1	166.39	153.12	–8.0	60.1
Aug. 1987	Dec. 1987	Nov. 1986	Nov. 1987	–9	–1	245.09	245.01	–0.0	38.1
June 1990	Oct. 1990	Mar. 1990	Mar. 1991	–3	5	338.47	372.28	10.0	
		Aug. 1993	Aug. 1994						
		Dec. 1996	Dec. 1997						
	Average			1.9	0.6			0.8	27.6
	Standard Deviation			7.1	9.5			11.9	22.5

432

the fixed-length cycle with the actual performance makes this a cycle worth watching.

Finally, it is possible to calculate a quadratic probability score (QPS) and an accuracy rate at different lead times for the fixed-length cycle. Based on the 41-month stock market cycle, the probability of a turning point increases by $1/41$ in each period. From this information, the QPS for this fixed-length cycle is determined (see Figure 10.2), and then it is presented as an accuracy rate (see Chapter 3). The accuracy rate, as shown in Figure 10.3, suggests that the 41-month stock market cycle tends to provide a turning point signal with the highest accuracy 5 months before an actual market turn.

WHAT DRIVES THE STOCK MARKET?

The traditional dividend discount model (DDM) suggests that stock prices are equal to the present value of expected future dividends.[9] Hence, changes in the earnings ability of a company or the discount rate of the dividend stream will change the value of the asset. On the latter point, stock market duration, which measures how sensitive the stock market is to interest rates changes (duration is more commonly used in relationship with fixed-income instruments) can be

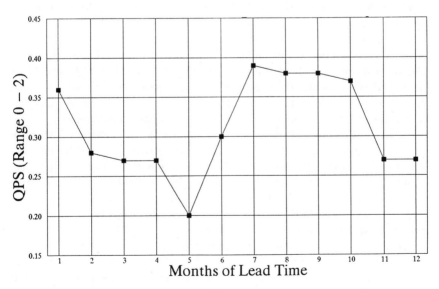

Figure 10.2 Quadratic Probability Scores for 41-Month, Fixed-Length Stock Market Cycle.

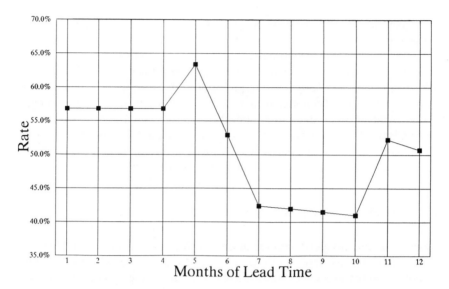

Figure 10.3 Accuracy Rate at Different Lead Times for 41-Month, Fixed-Length Stock Market Cycle.

approximated using the DDM model. With a few simplifying assumptions, it can be shown that duration equals the inverse of the dividend yield. This implies that the higher the dividend yield, the greater the interest rate risk and vice versa. Then stock market duration can be compared with bond market duration to measure the relative interest rate sensitive of these financial groups. The key problem in applying this type of framework is that "many market participants have difficulty developing credible estimates for near-term payouts, much less for distant flows of dividends or earnings."[10] Of course, DDM is only one (although it may be the most popular) valuation technique.

Variants on this basic structure exist for valuing the stock market. The price-to-earnings ratio (P/E) is a popular statistic that has been used to value the market. Basu,[11] for example, showed that stocks with low P/E's tend to outperform high P/E stocks over the long run. Turning the P/E framework into a forecasting tool is easy using expected earnings.[12]

Moving from a definitional role of what determines stock prices to a technical role, Renshaw[13] examined the duration of stock market runs as a forecaster of future stock price movement. He concluded that once stock prices reverse direction and move higher by more than 5% on an annual basis, then stock prices tend to continue to move higher by another 5% in the subsequent year before the risk of a market reversal grows.

A causal argument for stock market fluctuation was proffered by Loungani, Rush, and Tave (LRT),[14] who suggested that stock market dispersion is a leading indicator of stock prices two years hence. They first defined stock market dispersion along the lines of Lilien,[15] as follows:

$$\text{Dispersion} = [\Sigma\ c_i(g_{it} - g_t)^2/n_i]^{(1/2)}$$

where g_{it} is the growth rate of stock prices for industry i at time t, g_t is the overall growth in stock prices, n is the number of industries, and c_i are industry weights derived from shares of total employment. The dispersion measure would be zero if all industries grow by the same magnitude as the total. On the other hand, a high value of the dispersion measure would imply uneven growth.

The LRT stock market dispersion index was derived from 45 annual stock price indexes compiled by Standard and Poors.[16] Their study empirically found that this measure was negatively correlated with economic activity, which would suggest that as divergence increases—or in Hickman's view, as diffusion narrows—this ultimately signals a slowdown in economic activity and with it corporate profits and stock prices.

This dispersion concept, which measures the standard deviation of growth rates, is closely related to the diffusion index idea and the diffusion theories of Hickman, Burns, and Fellner discussed in Chapter 3. However, some conceptual differences favor the Hickman et al., concept over the LRT measure. For example, during the 1980s, a moving standard deviation of real GDP indicated that the dispersion within the economy was smaller. This however, was more likely a result of various fast-growing sectors in the economy beginning to slow instead of the slowest growing sectors accelerating their growth. Hence, while dispersion may suggest "better balanced growth," diffusion would suggest that it was less broad-based.

Tufte[17] has suggested the existence of an electoral-stock market cycle, where government policies are pursued to provide the best economic environment at election time. In a review of the history of stock prices and the presidential election cycle, Stovall[18] concluded:

1. During the twentieth century, the strongest gain in stock prices has occurred in the third year of the presidential term—up 11% (14.9% since 1945).

2. Since 1901, stock prices under Democratic administrations have outperformed Republican administrations (34.9% vs. 30.5%).

3. The reverse is true since 1945 when stock prices did better under Republicans than Democrats (34.3% vs. 30.2%).

4. During the twentieth century, investors have tended to get a better return from fixed-income investments than in the stock market during the first two years of a presidential term.

But the record is by no means clear-cut. As shown in Table 10.4, the large standard deviations associated with the returns by political party suggest that there is little statistical difference between returns under a Republican or Democratic administration (which could be shown more formally by applying a statistical test). Hence, it is reasonable to conclude that the impact of the presidential party on stock prices is less fact than fancy.

Since the time of Beryl Sprinkel's studies of money and stock prices,[19] the linkage has been examined and essentially rejected. Rozeff[20] concluded: "[It] is simply not true that past money supply data can provide a profitable guide to investment timing or improve a portfolio's rate of return."[21] A similar conclusion was reached by Auerbach.[22] Auerbach, who was equally as forceful in his conclusion, observed that the studies showing a strong relationship between money supply changes and the future behavior of stock prices "appear to be incorrect."[23] Cooper[24] examined the link between money and stock prices using spectral analysis between 1947 and 1970 and found that the money supply lagged stock prices by 1 to 3 months. Nonetheless, Milton Friedman[25] has repackaged the Sprinkel idea in terms of real price changes with the same basic assertion of a linkage. The weight of the evidence, however, is on the side of rejecting the Friedman/Sprinkel hypothesis.

As might be expected, this review has barely skimmed the surface of the literature. However, it suggests that there are a host of reasons for stock market behavior, and most hypotheses seem to have some validity. This brief review has focused attention on three approaches to explain stock price movement: (1) definitional, (2) technical, and (3) causal. The following section explores and demonstrates the use of causal leading indicators for forecasting turning points in the stock price cycle based on inflation and the prospects for economic growth. Inflation appears to be a critical determinant of stock prices through the interest rate and profit channels. Initially, a little inflation appears "good" for the stock market since earnings estimates are inflation dependent (and analysts tend to raise their earnings projections with a slight pickup in inflation), but at some point the "earnings illusion" disappears as asset allocation shifts hurt stock prices. This simple view has led Niemira[26] to forecast turning points in the stock market cycle based on a leading indicator of inflation and sequential probabilities.

FORECASTING TURNING POINTS IN THE STOCK MARKET USING COMPOSITE INDICATORS

Indicator systems, such as described in Kwon[27] and Boehm and Moore,[28] have been used to forecast turning points in the stock market cycle. But inevitably, no system is perfect, as reflected by the missed and extra turning points in the

Table 10.4 Stock Price Performance over the Presidential Cycle, 1901–1991, Based on the Year-End DJIA.

	First Year	Second Year	Third Year	Fourth Year	All Four Years
Republicans					
McKinley/T. Roosevelt	−8.7	−0.4	−23.6	41.9	−1.6
T. Roosevelt	38.2	−1.9	−37.7	46.6	23.8
Taft	15.0	−17.9	0.4	7.6	2.0
Harding/Coolidge	12.7	21.7	−3.3	26.2	67.5
Coolidge	30.0	0.3	28.8	48.2	148.9
Hoover	−17.2	−33.8	−52.7	−23.1	−80.0
Eisenhower (1st term)	−3.6	44.0	20.0	2.3	71.1
Eisenhower (2nd term)	−12.8	34.0	18.4	−9.3	23.3
Nixon	−15.2	4.8	6.1	14.6	8.1
Nixon/Ford	−18.7	−27.8	38.3	17.9	−1.5
Reagan (1st term)	−9.2	19.6	20.3	−3.7	25.7
Reagan (2nd term)	27.7	22.8	2.3	11.9	79.0
Bush	27.0	−4.3	20.3	4.2	52.2
Average	5.0	4.7	2.9	14.3	32.2
Standard Deviation	19.9	22.3	25.7	20.9	52.3
Average since 1945	−0.7	13.3	18.0	5.4	36.8
Standard Deviation	18.3	22.6	10.8	9.2	28.8
Democrats					
Wilson (1st term)	−10.3	−5.1	81.7	−4.2	8.1
Wilson (2nd term)	−21.7	10.5	30.5	−32.9	24.3
F. D. Roosevelt (1st term)	66.7	4.1	38.5	24.8	200.2
F. D. Roosevelt (2nd term)	−32.8	28.1	−2.9	−12.7	−27.1
F. D. Roosevelt (3rd term)	−15.4	7.6	13.8	−12.1	16.2
F. D. Roosevelt/Truman	26.6	−8.1	2.2	−2.1	16.4
Truman	12.9	17.6	14.4	−8.4	64.6
Kennedy/Johnson	18.7	−10.8	17.0	14.6	41.9
Johnson	10.9	−16.9	15.2	4.3	8.0
Carter	−17.3	−3.1	4.2	14.9	−4.0
Average	3.8	2.4	21.5	−1.4	34.9
Standard Deviation	28.0	13.2	23.3	15.9	59.9
Average since 1945	10.4	−4.3	10.6	4.7	25.4
Standard Deviation	14.9	11.8	6.1	9.2	24.7
Overall Average	4.5	3.7	11.0	7.6	32.5
Overall Average since 1945	3.9	6.0	14.9	5.2	30.2

Boehm and Moore turning point system for the U.S. stock market (Table 10.5). Yet, by the same token, these systems provide a disciplined approach to trading, which often yields superior investment returns to a *buy-and-hold* strategy.

Nonetheless, over the long haul, even a buy-and-hold stock strategy produced a decent return. Between 1953 and mid-1992, the average monthly return on stocks has been almost twice the return on bonds or cash equivalents (as measured by the 3-month Treasury bill). This is shown in Figure 10.4. The moral is that if a person were to use a buy-and-hold strategy and if the next 40 years' experience is similar to the last, then investing in the stock market for the long run should provide superior returns.

However, it is not always clear when to commit new money to the stock market, and so the various indicator systems can be useful. Martin Pring[29] advocated a basic six-stage business cycle framework to understand the investment sequences between stocks, bonds, and commodities. While such a conceptual framework is helpful in thinking about the investment process, he recognized that in the real world market turning points may occur simultaneously with

Table 10.5   Boehm-Moore Turning Point Signals Compared with the Stock Market Cycle, Based on the S&P 500.

		Boehm-Moore Signals	
Peak	Trough	Peak	Trough
May 1946	June 1949	—	Mar. 1949
Jan. 1953	Sept. 1953	June 1953	Feb. 1954
July 1956	Dec. 1957	Dec. 1955	May 1958
July 1959	Oct. 1960	Oct. 1959	Aug. 1960
Dec. 1961	June 1962	—	—
Jan. 1966	Oct. 1966	May 1966	Feb. 1967
Dec. 1968	June 1970	May 1969	Nov. 1970
Jan. 1973	Dec. 1974	Aug. 1973	May 1975
Sept. 1976	Mar. 1978	—	—
Nov. 1980	July 1982	June 1981	Apr. 1982
Oct. 1983	July 1984	—	—
Aug. 1987	Dec. 1987	—	—
June 1990	Oct. 1990	—	—
		Extra Turns	
		Mar. 1951	Mar. 1952
		Mar. 1978	Oct. 1980
		Apr. 1989	May 1989

Source: Boehm and Moore (1991).

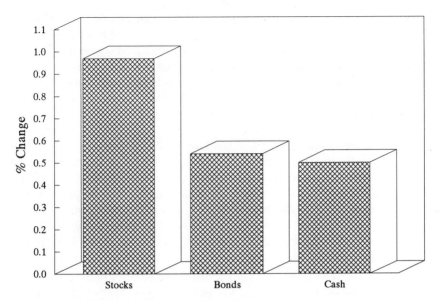

Figure 10.4 Stocks, Bonds, and Cash Equivalents (Average Monthly Return with Dividends or Capital Gains/Loss).

each other or in a different sequence. To determine the phase of the investment cycle, Pring suggested monitoring a host of indicators (often based on 12-month moving averages). He called one of those indicators the *Torque Index,* and defined it as the ratio of housing starts to the National Association of Purchasing Management's supplier delivery times. Pring suggested that the Torque Index, which was expressed as a 6-month moving average of a 12-month moving average (a 6 × 12 moving average), was a key leading indicator of stock market tops. However, Pring recognized and correctly cautioned that the accuracy of that indicator—or, just about any individual indicator—was not sufficiently consistent to solely base an investment strategy on it. A solution to this problem is to use broadly diversified composite indicators, as was done in the preceding studies by Kwon, Boehm and Moore, and Niemira.

To demonstrate the value of composite indicators in signaling turning points, consider the following indicator system that incorporates a barometer of the economy and an inflation measure. The approach can be elaborated on by including additional asset classes for the domestic and international markets, but the basic framework is what is significant for this discussion. This two-asset turning point signaling system incorporates our leading indicator of inflation (described in Chapter 8) and the Commerce Department's composite index of lagging indicators. To measure the efficiency of this investment system, two total return measures were calculated for stocks (based on the S&P 500) and cash equivalents (based on the 3-month Treasury bill rate). When a stock market sell signal was issued, the money was assumed to be rolled over entirely into 3-month Treasury bills. Furthermore, it was assumed that since the composite index of lagging indicators is reported with a 1-month lag, a buy/sell signal from the indicator system would occur (in real time) with a 1-month lag as well. Here are the rules that were applied:

- *The Long-Leading Indicator.* The inverse of the composite index of lagging indicators serves as a long-leading indicator of the economy and consequently can be used to signal changes in the economy (see Figure 10.5). The difference between a 3-month pressure curve and a 6-month pressure curve of the inverse of the lagging indicator, which will be dubbed LAG36, proved to be a simple and efficient method to call a turning point. When the difference was positive, that was favorable for investing in the stock market and vice versa.

- *Inflation Expectations.* The second indicator captured inflation expectations 6 months ahead, based on our leading indicator of inflation and shown in Figure 10.6. This was formulated as

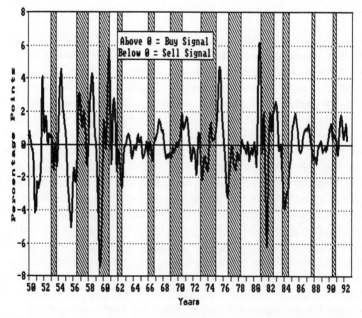

Figure 10.5 Long-Leading Indicator and the Stock Market Cycle. Shaded Areas Represent Bear Markets.

CPI_FORECAST$_{t+6}$ − CPI_FORECAST$_t$, where CPI_FORECAST is the inflation forecast based on the leading indicator. This term will be referred to as INFEXP. When inflation expectations were rising (that is, INFEXP was positive), that was unfavorable for stock market investing.

A *buy signal* occurred if both the long-leading indicator (LAG36) and the inflation expectations (INFEXP) measures signaled it was time to switch funds into the stock market, that is, if LAG36 > 0 and INFEXP < 0. In other words, a buy signal occurred when the prospect for the economy was improving and inflation expectations were subsiding. Similarly, a *sell signal* occurred if the reverse condition was in force, that is, LAG36 > 0 and INFEXP < 0.

Between 1951 and 1991, these "buy and sell" signals proved to be profitable. The investment performance from this strategy yielded a total return of 13.6%, at an annual rate, during that 40-year period, or in more recent times, it yielded a 15.9% gain between 1967–1991. The yield from this two-asset trading system was roughly two to five percentage points higher than simply following a buy-and-hold stock strategy. Table 10.6 presents the individual buy/sell episodes; the average holding period was 14.9 months.

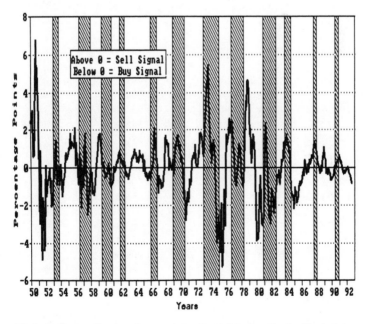

Figure 10.6 Inflation Expectations and the Stock Market Cycle. Shaded Areas Represent Bear Markets.

Table 10.6   Investment Performance of Two-Asset Turning Point Signaling System, 1950–1991.

Buy+1	Sell+1	Stock Total Return Index	Annualized Return (%)	Cash Total Return Index	Annualized Return (%)	Holding Periods (Months)
	195007	59.60		95.56		
195111		84.74	30.2	97.44	1.5	16
	195305	101.01	12.4	100.18	1.9	18
195403		113.43	14.9	101.52	1.6	10
	195504	169.39	44.8	102.67	1.0	13
195610		220.27	19.1	106.29	2.3	18
	195902	287.04	12.0	112.96	2.6	28
196002		301.90	5.2	117.21	3.8	12
	196103	360.06	17.7	120.58	2.6	13
196105		375.24	28.1	121.05	2.4	2
	196110	388.42	8.6	122.24	2.4	5
196303		393.03	0.8	127.23	2.9	17
	196310	445.09	23.8	129.65	3.3	7
196502		550.47	17.3	136.14	3.7	16
	196503	552.34	4.2	136.59	4.1	1
196511		597.96	12.6	140.28	4.1	8
	196603	582.75	−7.4	142.48	4.8	4
196701		570.10	−2.6	148.58	5.2	10
	196804	672.09	14.1	157.37	4.7	15
197006		570.28	−7.3	181.26	6.7	26
	197109	782.41	28.8	193.13	5.2	15
197408		657.45	−5.8	231.15	6.4	35
	197604	948.24	24.6	255.94	6.3	20
198003		1180.34	5.7	345.95	8.0	47
	198103	1580.21	33.9	390.72	12.9	12
198202		1427.68	−10.5	445.54	15.4	11
	198306	2225.69	39.5	507.57	10.3	16
198502		2608.28	10.0	594.82	10.0	20
	198606	3729.48	30.8	655.25	7.5	16
198609		3653.31	−7.9	664.59	5.8	3
	198708	5193.53	46.8	700.39	5.9	11
199001		5836.30	4.9	837.94	7.7	29
	199102	6467.28	9.9	908.66	7.8	13
199107		6879.94*	16.0*	930.81*	6.0	

* Through June 1992.

Table 10.6 *(Continued)*

	Cumulative Returns		
	1951–1961 (%)	1967–1991 (%)	1951–1991 (Standard Deviation— Percentage Points)
Stock/Cash Mix	13.36	15.85	13.45
Stocks Only	11.68	10.61	15.32
Cash Only	5.85	7.81	3.32
Average Holding Period	14.9 months		

Note: All returns are expressed at annual rates.

CONCLUSION

In a review of some of the current stock market research, Granger[30] asked the question: *Are stock prices forecastable?* His review concluded that there was some hope that stock prices were forecastable if a long horizon was considered, disaggregate data was exploited, outlier and exceptional events were removed, and nonlinear regime *switching models* were used. The composite indicator system that was demonstrated in this chapter falls into the regime switching model class, and a long horizon was considered. This system is not a get-rich overnight system but demonstrates that a disciplined approach to trading can be derived based on macroeconomic indicators.

Part Five

Conclusion

11 The Future of the Business Cycle—Alive and Well but Different

LESSONS FROM THE PAST AND PRESENT

This exploration into cycles has returned to where it started, which is a cycle of sorts. But the journey, we hope, was one with an upward trend. Richard Goodwin observed: "[A] cycle is simply the form in which growth takes place."[1] Goodwin was echoing Joseph Schumpeter's perspective: *Progress is fluctuation.*[2] This view reflects the fundamental characteristic of modern industrial market economies. It has been evident for some time that one consequence of rapid growth often is that we must cope with more instability.

The nature of modern industrial economies makes stable growth a difficult objective to achieve. We have seen that volatile investment is a major factor in the modern cycle. How could it be otherwise? The task confronting modern entrepreneurs is formidable. To begin with, they must anticipate with some precision what the demand for their product will be in the future, and they must try to coordinate the growth in their capacity with the expected growth in that demand. Even more, they must recognize that, among other things, they may be wrong in their estimation of how long it will take to modify their capacity, and they may fail to calculate accurately the technological changes, that can change the capacity-output ratio itself, as well as the length of time required to adjust capacity. Finally, they may have been wrong in their original estimate of the growth in demand for their final product, or they could have been correct in that original estimate (they might have correctly interpreted all the factors that were originally available to them in estimating how demand might grow) but consumer demand still could shift markedly higher or lower, given abrupt changes in aggregate domestic and international economic conditions.

Hence, it is remarkable that the rate of growth of capacity and final demand are as well coordinated as they are. This highlights one of the marvels of the free market system. The free market allocation mechanism is impressive, even though, at times, it might be strained to maintain stable growth when coordinating thousands of individual investment decisions.

Throughout this book, we have examined growth using various tools of analysis including economic theory, measurement techniques, and forecasting methods. Early on, we recognized that in seeking theories to explain instability in industrialized market economies, the first task was to determine the common denominator, over time and across countries, that would yield a generalized explanation of our business cycle history. Obviously, each cycle is *unique,* if for no other reason than that it occurs at a singular period in time and, therefore, occurs with a unique set of external factors impinging on the performance of the economy. Those external factors were never exactly repeated over history and are unlikely to be repeated in the future. In seeking useful business cycle theory, we must tread a careful line. On the one hand lies "mere description," which has no true explanatory power but aims simply at recording every economic fact that might conceivably impinge on the currently unrolling business cycle. On the other side, we find a sweeping generalization that can apply to many business cycles but has little explanatory power because it fails to focus on the real variables in real cycles with sufficient specificity to be useful in either diagnosis or the development of appropriate policy. Therefore, the development of business cycle theory requires "meaningful generalization." This theory must isolate those interrelationships among cycles that are recurring from those factors that make each cyclical episode a unique phenomenon.

Our review of business cycle theory shows that we have learned a good deal about the nature and causes of instability in the modern market economy. The business cycle has been with us virtually since the founding of the United States, and therefore, in spite of the changes in the economy, some underlying and endemic mechanisms must be at work creating greater instability than ideally we would want. What earlier in our history were often called "financial panics" gave way to the recessions and depressions of the twentieth century. Whatever they are called, any careful examination of the major statistical series reflecting aggregate economic activity in the United States shows the recurring pattern of expansion and contraction that has been the subject of this book.

Not only has the economy changed and business cycles, to a certain extent, with it, but over the years, cycle thinking has evolved. In the mid-1800s, Jevons thought of the business cycle as a succession of periodic crises often produced by exogenous change. In Mitchell's day and since, cycles have been thought of in a time series sense as an ongoing nonperiodic phenomenon, partly exogenous and partly endogenous in origin, and having a specific beginning, middle, and end. The terminology over the years has changed but the parts are consistently an initial trough (also the terminal trough of the previous cycle), a cumulative expansion, a peak, a cumulation contraction, and a terminal trough.

The techniques for identifying and dating business cycle turning points (originally developed by Burns and Mitchell) have evolved. But the logic itself for dating the business cycle has endured. This logic makes clear that while many individual series contribute to the business cycle chronology, the chronology need not fully reflect any particular time series. In this manner, the chronologies that play so prominent a role in our monitoring and forecasting techniques are like any average. Moreover, a side benefit of the years of NBER business cycle research in culling thousands of economic time series is the emergence of relatively few series as our "most reliable indicators" of business cycle expansions and contractions.

With the formalization of techniques for cycle dating, the search for cycles spread beyond macrocycles and rightly so. The phenomenon of business instability is a generalized one, and it permeates the economy affecting the behavior and functions of many of its parts. Research on measuring instability leads constantly to refinements in techniques for measuring and forecasting business cycles, which can lead to new theories and new insights. In all likelihood, the business cycle and specific cycles will continue to evolve. Yesterday's cycle has some similarities with today's cycle, but there are many differences as well. The role of the forecaster and analyst is to ferret out what is *enduring* and to distinguish it from what is not and to understand how those enduring factors are *evolving*.

Too often, a lack of historical perspective leads analysts to assert that these are unique economic times. But as Paul Harvey, the radio commentator, aptly put it: "In times like these, it is helpful to recognize that there have been times like these." In a sense, this study of business cycles is an exercise in giving theoretical meaning to "times like these."

Otto C. Lightner, in his *History of Business Depressions,* described the late 1880s and early 1890s in a uniquely present-day tone. He wrote:

> [I]t cannot be said that the eight years preceding 1893 were any better than normal at the most. The slow times that set in during [President] Cleveland's first administration continued to some degree during the whole of Harrison's, and while they could not be called depressed times, yet they were years in which very little headway was being made.[3]

Change a few names and dates and it might be an equally valid description of the 1990s.

In sum, Wesley Mitchell voiced a comment, which essentially is a theme throughout this book:

> Business history repeats itself, but always with a difference. This is part of what is implied by saying that the process of economic activity within which business cycles occur is a process of cumulative change. . . . A thoroughly adequate

theory of business cycles, applicable to all cycles, is consequently unattainable. Even if some one cycle could be fully accounted for, the account would necessarily be inaccurate for cycles that were the outgrowth of earlier or of later conditions. Nor are all the differences between the successive cycles of one country and between the contemporary cycles of several countries minor. Even such an elementary matter as the order in which the phases of a business cycle succeed one another is not invariable. A revival of business activity does not always develop into prosperity—sometimes it relapses into depression. Such deviations from the usual course of events occurred in the United States in 1892, 1895, and 1910. A situation of intense strain, presenting the phenomena of crises, sometimes occurs in a period of depression, instead of following a period of prosperity; for example the American stringency of 1896. . . . Every business cycle, strictly speaking, is a unique series of events and has a unique explanation, because it is the outgrowth of a preceding series of events, likewise unique.[4]

A recent development that Mitchell anticipated and is, therefore, in the Mitchellian tradition, has been addressed in this book as well—the difference between classical cycles and slowdowns (growth cycles). This important distinction may have numerous implications for the future. At upper turning points, the distinction between growth and classical cycles has enabled us to gain considerable insight concerning the factors that turn slowdowns into full-fledged downturns, and the factors that make this less likely. But a new dynamic may be unfolding between the growth and classical cycles. The NBER determined the classical business cycle trough was reached in March 1991, although it seems likely that the growth cycle low was reached much later, in the summer of 1992. Ten years earlier, the lag between the growth and business cycle troughs coming out of the 1982 recession was only one month. This raises an interesting question whether the 1982 recovery marked a turning point in the relationship between growth and classical cycle troughs in the United States. Undoubtedly, future research will shed some light on this issue.

THE FUTURE OF THE BUSINESS CYCLE

The 1990–1991 U.S. business cycle contraction was the thirty-first classical recession since 1854; its subsequent recovery, the thirty-second expansion on record, began in April 1991 and was characterized by weak and halting growth. Although economic data are not as consistent and detailed in most other countries, the business cycle chronologies extend back to the eighteenth century for France, the United Kingdom, and Germany. There is considerable evidence that business cycles have manifested themselves in all market-oriented industrialized economies, virtually from inception. Moreover (and thought provoking indeed, is this observation), they seem to occur regardless of whether the governments are interventionist or not.

Although business cycles appear endemic, we need not conclude that we have learned nothing useful. The ability of most market-oriented economies to control at least partially the degree of instability they suffer most of the time adds credence to the view that the study of business cycles since 1940 has enabled us to improve macro performance. While there is much room for improvement, progress has been made.

One sign that we have learned much that is useful about instability in the modern world is our recognition that much of Mitchell's analysis of "what happens during the business cycle" is as accurate a depiction of the cycles of today as it was for the economy he was describing. Our efforts to isolate what cycles have in common from that which is distinctive has borne fruit at least to this extent.

As we contemplate the future course of macroeconomic activity, at least four underlying forces are likely to shape the business cycle of the future: (1) the maturity of the economy (Rostow's view), (2) the degree of globalization of the economy, (3) the demographic change, and (4) the rapidity at which the post-cold-war environment unfolds. Of these, only the final point is a transitional concern.

Dealing with these in reverse order, we note that transitional or not, the last point hearkens back to the challenge raised 60 years ago by Alvin Hansen. Although his "secular stagnation thesis" has been out of favor for many years, the notion that "mature capitalist economies" find it difficult to employ fully their resources—human and nonhuman—is a recurring challenge. Nonetheless, it is perhaps worth recalling that of the factors giving rise to employment opportunities in mature capitalist countries, Hansen gave considerable weight to war. While he had not perhaps contemplated "cold war," it is nonetheless true that the cold war provided a large employment opportunity for the United States, and perhaps to a lesser extent other Western industrialized countries. Accordingly, it is not inappropriate to note that the existence of the cold war left Hansen's secular stagnation thesis untested. Today, the end of the cold war enables us finally to see whether we can maintain high employment in capitalist economies devoted to peacetime activities. Our concern with defense industry plant closings suggests that the question remains open at this point. Whether these reallocation problems represent merely transitional problems or more serious challenges to full resource use remains to be seen.

Demographic challenges, another tenet of the Hansen secular stagnation hypothesis, are a major obstacle not only to the stability of the world's economies in the years to come, but to their ability to survive. At various points in this book, we have alluded to the relations between First and Third World countries. The tension created for Third World countries between population viewed as *hands* and population viewed as *mouths* is well documented. In contemplating growth and stability for the industrialized countries of the next century, major attention will need to focus on these demographic challenges. The relationship between the structural requirements imposed on the labor force by advancing technology and the characteristics of that labor force need to be related carefully to consideration of demographic policy in all countries. Moreover, the aging and growth of the population in mature economies such as Japan and the United States, has implications for domestic consumption, investment, and government spending with clear spillover effects on demand for goods from the rest of the world. This problem is far larger than a simple focus on growth and stability, but nonetheless demography will impinge on these problems in many ways.

Finally, Rostow's view is closely related to the Hansen thesis already considered. Increasingly, the ability of an economy to thrive will be bound up with the ability of other economies to thrive. In contemplating growth and stability for any open economy, the problems posed by the diverse stages of maturity reached by various market economies will require careful attention. The business cycle of tomorrow will share much with cycles of the past but the dynamics, including the volatility, duration, and diffusion, may be more influenced by these secular changes.

We end where we began, with an observation by Arthur Burns from his presidential address to the American Economic Association:

> We are living in extraordinarily creative but also deeply troubled times. One of the triumphs of this generation is the progress that our nation has made in reducing economic instability. In the years ahead, no matter what we do as a people, our economy will continue to undergo changes, many of which were neither planned nor anticipated. However, the course of events, both domestic and international, will also depend—and to a large degree—on our resourcefulness and courage in deliberately modifying the structure of our economy so as to strengthen the forces of growth and yet restrain instability.[5]

Although these words were spoken in 1959, the message rings true nearly 35 years later.

Appendixes

APPENDIXB

Appendix A
Real GNP, Billions of
1987 Dollars

Year	Q1	Q2	Q3	Q4
1875	116.04	117.61	115.58	116.33
1876	123.11	123.17	122.82	124.40
1877	128.67	129.77	135.13	135.75
1878	138.87	139.44	143.98	143.47
1879	146.46	151.16	156.90	169.91
1880	176.78	178.73	177.69	179.88
1881	177.82	180.25	183.19	185.03
1882	186.61	189.17	191.74	192.40
1883	188.26	186.71	187.84	188.16
1884	190.56	195.16	193.74	191.74
1885	191.68	192.67	193.77	195.93
1886	198.17	201.33	205.87	206.29
1887	208.81	210.01	207.47	210.30
1888	202.13	202.26	204.72	207.58
1889	209.39	208.16	210.84	215.00
1890	219.49	225.58	229.19	232.02
1891	226.44	226.78	243.53	250.50
1892	257.90	258.70	259.53	262.34
1893	261.88	258.70	237.01	229.24
1894	231.64	232.85	242.44	253.84
1895	258.78	263.72	273.21	278.68
1896	267.04	264.45	261.05	259.26
1897	275.88	282.61	295.06	298.96
1898	297.35	293.00	290.46	294.02
1899	314.61	317.04	324.92	329.84
1900	327.57	330.24	330.56	331.76
1901	354.49	370.73	373.43	376.39
1902	367.85	368.43	375.59	374.69
1903	386.36	394.48	396.16	384.06
1904	382.86	382.11	382.51	393.36
1905	398.89	408.16	416.20	433.32
1906	451.11	456.08	464.52	476.48
1907	476.86	478.73	473.49	447.26
1908	421.06	422.15	432.38	447.07
1909	465.40	477.37	490.37	500.04
1910	501.11	496.09	493.34	496.60
1911	504.77	510.25	516.23	519.20
1912	527.61	535.38	541.82	548.26
1913	545.24	542.22	546.28	539.31
1914	534.74	535.68	523.47	499.80
1915	504.08	681.84	517.51	541.74
1916	556.00	554.35	556.75	557.31
1917	543.32	562.66	566.24	586.86

Year	Q1	Q2	Q3	Q4
1918	613.94	663.87	680.08	652.70
1919	611.73	609.03	613.11	612.85
1920	607.72	577.21	567.46	536.42
1921	512.01	525.23	540.70	558.33
1922	577.11	605.05	623.48	647.14
1923	671.83	688.49	676.85	677.70
1924	696.24	674.36	667.37	701.45
1925	717.69	726.27	744.88	760.48
1926	767.51	769.86	788.02	792.56
1927	789.68	794.46	782.07	767.16
1928	773.04	782.60	800.58	808.83
1929	825.23	859.18	864.63	823.92
1930	794.06	789.55	750.95	716.14
1931	717.64	730.17	701.50	665.50
1932	641.51	610.18	588.89	585.31
1933	551.28	591.02	638.01	593.13
1934	625.83	661.70	633.58	633.50
1935	673.96	676.18	694.88	733.45
1936	736.98	783.19	805.60	832.28
1937	829.48	850.53	847.32	786.55
1938	753.32	765.24	809.95	842.35
1939	834.31	822.16	852.96	908.09
1940	881.86	893.93	930.42	971.08
1941	991.49	1046.91	1102.05	1138.93
1942	1179.43	1192.52	1246.16	1316.14
1943	1364.62	1394.35	1440.59	1481.30
1944	1493.35	1502.08	1526.55	1559.06
1945	1590.82	1573.19	1460.94	1360.27
1946	1303.59	1260.02	1281.31	1265.41
1947	1244.90	1252.90	1260.70	1275.60
1948	1290.90	1302.90	1310.90	1323.50
1949	1312.10	1308.60	1318.90	1307.60
1950	1357.00	1400.10	1453.00	1492.30
1951	1511.20	1557.10	1594.90	1606.20
1952	1617.30	1621.80	1631.30	1666.80
1953	1696.20	1704.80	1696.20	1679.60
1954	1669.90	1667.50	1686.90	1708.80
1955	1753.30	1769.10	1788.80	1804.80
1956	1799.20	1810.60	1814.60	1837.40
1957	1849.30	1848.80	1864.60	1841.00
1958	1800.80	1815.40	1851.40	1891.20
1959	1915.10	1947.70	1941.80	1953.60
1960	1988.10	1983.30	1985.80	1974.00

Year	Q1	Q2	Q3	Q4
1961	1991.10	2018.90	2048.40	2090.10
1962	2117.30	2140.60	2157.70	2157.70
1963	2187.40	2215.30	2253.60	2271.10
1964	2329.30	2347.30	2375.40	2380.60
1965	2429.20	2462.50	2503.80	2560.30
1966	2613.90	2618.50	2642.80	2657.90
1967	2674.30	2685.50	2717.90	2732.90
1968	2770.30	2815.60	2836.00	2840.70
1969	2883.60	2886.00	2901.70	2892.30
1970	2885.60	2877.90	2913.10	2889.70
1971	2959.80	2965.40	2981.30	2997.50
1972	3058.40	3110.50	3148.40	3197.80
1973	3279.40	3295.60	3297.20	3322.10
1974	3298.40	3304.40	3272.20	3254.60
1975	3177.40	3213.90	3275.50	3323.60
1976	3386.80	3400.50	3412.70	3448.90
1977	3503.90	3561.80	3610.80	3599.30
1978	3629.10	3737.90	3769.80	3819.30
1979	3821.20	3829.80	3862.00	3868.30
1980	3884.60	3782.30	3780.50	3846.20
1981	3901.60	3882.80	3904.90	3848.50
1982	3793.00	3810.30	3789.40	3791.70
1983	3816.50	3916.70	3978.80	4046.60
1984	4119.10	4169.40	4193.00	4216.40
1985	4238.10	4270.50	4321.80	4349.50
1986	4406.40	4394.60	4422.30	4430.80
1987	4463.90	4517.80	4563.60	4633.00
1988	4667.10	4710.30	4738.70	4789.00
1989	4830.70	4851.60	4853.40	4875.10
1990	4907.80	4915.50	4898.90	4861.40
1991	4822.00	4831.80	4843.70	4848.20
1992	4890.70	4899.10	4945.60	4991.81

Sources: National Bureau of Economic Research; U.S. Department of Commerce; authors.

Appendix B
Consumer Price Index (CPI-U)

Year	Jan.	Feb.	Mar.	Apr.	May	June	July	Aug.	Sept.	Oct.	Nov.	Dec.
1947	21.5	21.6	22.0	22.0	22.0	22.1	22.2	22.4	22.8	22.9	23.1	23.4
1948	23.7	23.7	23.5	23.8	24.0	24.1	24.4	24.4	24.4	24.3	24.2	24.0
1949	24.0	23.9	23.9	23.9	23.9	23.9	23.7	23.7	23.7	23.7	23.7	23.6
1950	23.5	23.6	23.6	23.6	23.8	23.9	24.1	24.2	24.3	24.5	24.6	25.0
1951	25.4	25.8	25.9	25.9	26.0	25.9	25.9	25.9	26.0	26.2	26.3	26.5
1952	26.5	26.4	26.4	26.5	26.5	26.5	26.7	26.7	26.6	26.7	26.7	26.7
1953	26.6	26.6	26.6	26.7	26.7	26.8	26.8	26.9	26.9	26.9	26.9	26.9
1954	26.9	27.0	26.9	26.9	26.9	26.9	26.9	26.9	26.8	26.7	26.8	26.8
1955	26.8	26.8	26.8	26.8	26.8	26.7	26.8	26.7	26.9	26.8	26.9	26.9
1956	26.8	26.9	26.9	26.9	27.0	27.2	27.3	27.3	27.3	27.5	27.5	27.6
1957	27.7	27.8	27.9	27.9	28.0	28.1	28.2	28.3	28.3	28.3	28.4	28.5
1958	28.6	28.7	28.9	28.9	28.9	28.9	28.9	28.9	28.9	28.9	28.9	29.0
1959	29.0	29.0	29.0	29.0	29.0	29.1	29.1	29.2	29.2	29.4	29.4	29.4
1960	29.4	29.4	29.4	29.5	29.6	29.6	29.6	29.6	29.6	29.8	29.8	29.8
1961	29.8	29.8	29.8	29.8	29.8	29.8	29.9	29.9	30.0	30.0	30.0	30.0
1962	30.0	30.1	30.2	30.2	30.2	30.2	30.2	30.3	30.4	30.4	30.4	30.4
1963	30.4	30.5	30.5	30.5	30.5	30.6	30.7	30.8	30.7	30.7	30.8	30.9
1964	30.9	30.9	30.9	31.0	31.0	31.0	31.0	31.0	31.1	31.1	31.2	31.3
1965	31.3	31.3	31.3	31.4	31.5	31.6	31.6	31.6	31.6	31.6	31.7	31.8
1966	31.9	32.1	32.2	32.3	32.4	32.4	32.5	32.7	32.8	32.9	32.9	32.9
1967	32.9	33.0	33.0	33.1	33.1	33.3	33.4	33.5	33.6	33.7	33.9	34.0
1968	34.1	34.2	34.3	34.4	34.5	34.7	34.9	35.0	35.1	35.3	35.4	35.6
1969	35.7	35.8	36.1	36.3	36.4	36.6	36.8	36.9	37.1	37.3	37.5	37.7
1970	37.9	38.1	38.3	38.5	38.6	38.8	38.9	39.0	39.2	39.4	39.6	39.8

Year												
1971	39.9	39.9	40.0	40.1	40.3	40.5	40.6	40.7	40.8	40.9	41.0	41.1
1972	41.2	41.4	41.4	41.5	41.6	41.7	41.8	41.9	42.1	42.2	42.4	42.5
1973	42.7	43.0	43.4	43.7	43.9	44.2	44.2	45.0	45.2	45.6	45.9	46.3
1974	46.8	47.3	47.8	48.1	48.6	49.0	49.3	49.9	50.6	51.0	51.5	51.9
1975	52.3	52.6	52.8	53.0	53.1	53.5	54.0	54.2	54.6	54.9	55.3	55.6
1976	55.8	55.9	56.0	56.1	56.4	56.7	57.0	57.3	57.6	57.9	58.1	58.4
1977	58.7	59.3	59.6	60.0	60.2	60.5	60.8	61.1	61.3	61.6	62.0	62.3
1978	62.7	63.0	63.4	63.9	64.5	65.0	65.5	65.9	66.5	67.1	67.5	67.9
1979	68.5	69.2	69.9	70.6	71.4	72.2	73.0	73.7	74.4	75.2	76.0	76.9
1980	78.0	79.0	80.1	80.9	81.7	82.5	82.6	83.2	83.9	84.7	85.6	86.4
1981	87.2	88.0	88.6	89.1	89.7	90.5	91.5	92.2	93.1	93.4	93.8	94.1
1982	94.4	94.7	94.7	95.0	95.9	97.0	97.5	97.7	97.7	98.1	98.0	97.7
1983	97.9	98.0	98.1	98.8	99.2	99.4	99.8	100.1	100.4	100.8	101.1	101.4
1984	102.1	102.6	102.9	103.3	103.5	103.7	104.1	104.4	104.7	105.1	105.3	105.5
1985	105.7	106.3	106.8	107.0	107.2	107.5	107.7	107.9	108.1	108.5	109.0	109.5
1986	109.9	109.7	109.1	108.7	109.0	109.4	109.5	109.6	110.0	110.2	110.4	110.8
1987	111.5	111.9	112.3	112.8	113.1	113.6	113.9	114.4	114.8	115.1	115.5	115.7
1988	116.0	116.2	116.6	117.2	117.5	118.0	118.6	119.1	119.7	120.1	120.4	120.8
1989	121.3	121.8	122.4	123.2	123.8	124.1	124.5	124.6	124.9	125.5	125.9	126.4
1990	127.5	128.1	128.7	129.0	129.2	130.0	130.6	131.7	132.6	133.5	133.8	134.2
1991	134.7	134.9	135.1	135.4	135.7	136.1	136.2	136.6	137.1	137.4	137.9	138.2
1992	138.3	138.7	139.4	139.7	139.9	140.3	140.5	140.9	141.2	141.8	142.1	142.2

Source: Bureau of Labor Statistics, U.S. Department of Commerce.

461

Appendix C
Standard & Poors 500 Stock
Price Index, Monthly Average

Year	Jan.	Feb.	Mar.	Apr.	May	June	July	Aug.	Sept.	Oct.	Nov.	Dec.
1901	7.07	7.25	7.51	8.14	7.73	8.50	7.93	8.04	8.05	7.91	8.08	7.95
1902	8.12	8.19	8.20	8.48	8.46	8.41	8.60	8.83	8.85	8.57	8.24	8.05
1903	8.46	8.41	8.08	7.75	7.60	7.18	6.85	6.63	6.47	6.26	6.28	6.57
1904	6.68	6.50	6.48	6.64	6.50	6.51	6.78	7.01	7.32	7.75	8.17	8.25
1905	8.43	8.80	9.05	8.94	8.50	8.60	8.87	9.20	9.23	9.36	9.31	9.54
1906	9.87	9.80	9.56	9.43	9.18	9.30	9.06	9.73	10.03	9.97	9.93	9.84
1907	9.56	9.26	8.35	8.39	8.10	7.84	8.14	7.53	7.45	6.64	6.25	6.57
1908	6.85	6.60	6.87	7.24	7.63	7.64	7.92	8.26	8.17	8.27	8.83	9.03
1909	9.06	8.80	8.92	9.32	9.63	9.80	9.94	10.18	10.19	10.23	10.18	10.30
1910	10.08	9.72	9.96	9.72	9.56	9.10	8.64	8.85	8.91	9.32	9.31	9.05
1911	9.27	9.43	9.32	9.28	9.48	9.67	9.63	9.17	8.67	8.72	9.07	9.11
1912	9.12	9.04	9.30	9.59	9.56	9.58	9.59	9.81	9.86	9.84	9.73	9.38
1913	9.30	8.97	8.80	8.79	8.55	8.12	8.23	8.45	8.53	8.26	8.05	8.04
1914	8.37	8.48	8.32	8.12	8.17	8.13	7.68	NA	NA	NA	NA	7.35
1915	7.48	7.38	7.57	8.14	7.95	8.04	8.01	8.35	8.66	9.14	9.46	9.48
1916	9.33	9.20	9.17	9.07	9.27	9.36	9.23	9.30	9.68	9.98	10.21	9.80
1917	9.57	9.03	9.31	9.17	8.86	9.04	8.79	8.53	8.12	7.68	7.04	6.80
1918	7.21	7.43	7.28	7.21	7.44	7.45	7.51	7.58	7.54	7.86	8.06	7.90
1919	7.85	7.88	8.12	8.39	8.97	9.21	9.51	8.87	9.01	9.47	9.19	8.92
1920	8.83	8.10	8.67	8.60	8.06	7.92	7.91	7.60	7.87	7.88	7.48	6.81
1921	7.11	7.06	6.88	6.91	7.12	6.55	6.53	6.45	6.61	6.70	7.06	7.31
1922	7.30	7.46	7.74	8.21	8.53	8.45	8.51	8.83	9.06	9.26	8.80	8.78
1923	8.90	9.28	9.43	9.10	8.67	8.34	8.06	8.10	8.15	8.03	8.27	8.55
1924	8.83	8.87	8.70	8.50	8.47	8.63	9.03	9.34	9.25	9.13	9.64	10.16
1925	10.58	10.67	10.39	10.28	10.61	10.80	11.10	11.25	11.51	11.89	12.26	12.46
1926	12.65	12.67	11.81	11.48	11.56	12.11	12.62	13.12	13.32	13.02	13.19	13.49
1927	13.40	13.66	13.87	14.21	14.70	14.89	15.22	16.03	16.94	16.68	17.06	17.46
1928	17.53	17.32	18.25	19.40	20.00	19.02	19.16	19.78	21.17	21.60	23.06	23.15
1929	24.86	24.99	25.43	25.28	25.66	26.15	28.48	30.10	31.30	27.99	20.58	21.40
1930	21.71	23.07	23.94	25.46	23.94	21.52	21.06	20.79	20.78	17.92	16.62	15.51
1931	15.98	17.20	17.53	15.86	14.33	13.87	14.33	13.90	11.83	10.25	10.39	8.44

Year												
1932	8.30	8.23	8.26	6.28	5.51	4.77	5.01	7.53	8.26	7.12	7.05	6.82
1933	7.09	6.25	6.23	6.89	8.87	10.39	11.23	10.67	10.58	9.55	9.78	9.97
1934	10.54	11.32	10.74	10.92	9.81	9.94	9.47	9.10	8.88	8.95	9.20	9.26
1935	9.26	8.98	8.41	9.04	9.75	10.12	10.65	11.37	11.61	11.92	13.04	13.04
1936	13.76	14.55	14.86	14.88	14.09	14.69	15.56	15.87	16.05	16.89	17.36	17.06
1937	17.59	18.11	18.09	17.01	16.25	15.64	16.57	16.74	14.37	12.28	11.20	11.02
1938	11.31	11.04	10.31	9.89	9.98	10.21	12.24	12.31	11.75	13.06	13.07	12.69
1939	12.50	12.40	12.39	10.83	11.23	11.43	11.71	11.54	12.77	12.90	12.67	12.37
1940	12.30	12.22	12.15	12.27	10.58	9.67	9.99	10.20	10.63	10.73	10.98	10.53
1941	10.55	9.89	9.95	9.64	9.43	9.76	10.26	10.21	10.24	9.83	9.37	8.76
1942	8.93	8.65	8.18	7.84	7.93	8.33	8.64	8.59	8.68	9.32	9.47	9.52
1943	10.09	10.69	11.07	11.44	11.89	12.10	12.35	11.74	11.99	11.88	11.33	11.48
1944	11.85	11.77	12.10	11.89	12.10	12.67	13.00	12.81	12.60	12.91	12.82	13.10
1945	13.49	13.94	13.93	14.28	14.82	15.09	14.78	14.83	15.84	16.50	17.04	17.33
1946	18.02	18.07	17.53	18.66	18.70	18.58	18.05	17.70	15.09	14.75	14.69	15.13
1947	15.21	15.80	15.16	14.60	14.34	14.84	15.77	15.46	15.06	15.45	15.27	15.03
1948	14.83	14.10	14.30	15.40	16.15	16.82	16.42	15.94	15.76	16.19	15.29	15.19
1949	15.36	14.77	14.91	14.89	14.78	13.97	14.76	15.29	15.49	15.89	16.11	16.54
1950	16.88	17.21	17.35	17.84	18.44	18.74	17.38	18.43	19.08	19.87	19.83	19.75
1951	21.21	22.00	21.63	21.92	21.93	21.55	21.93	22.89	23.48	23.36	22.71	23.41
1952	24.19	23.75	23.81	23.74	23.73	24.38	25.08	25.18	24.78	24.26	25.03	26.04
1953	26.18	25.86	25.99	24.71	24.84	23.95	24.29	24.39	23.27	23.97	24.50	24.83
1954	25.46	26.02	26.57	27.63	28.73	28.96	30.13	30.73	31.45	32.18	33.44	34.97
1955	35.60	36.79	36.50	37.76	37.60	39.78	42.69	42.43	44.34	42.11	44.95	45.37
1956	44.15	44.43	47.49	48.05	46.54	46.27	48.78	48.49	46.84	46.24	45.76	46.44
1957	45.43	43.47	44.03	45.05	46.78	47.55	48.51	45.84	43.98	41.24	40.35	40.33
1958	41.12	41.26	42.11	42.34	43.70	44.75	45.98	47.70	48.96	50.95	52.50	53.49
1959	55.62	54.77	56.15	57.10	57.96	57.46	59.74	59.40	57.05	57.00	57.23	59.06
1960	58.03	55.78	55.02	55.73	55.22	57.26	55.84	56.51	54.81	53.73	55.47	56.80
1961	59.72	62.17	64.12	65.83	66.50	65.62	65.44	67.79	67.26	68.00	71.08	71.74
1962	69.07	70.22	70.29	68.05	62.99	55.63	56.97	58.52	58.00	56.17	60.04	62.64
1963	65.06	65.92	65.67	68.76	70.14	70.11	69.07	70.98	72.85	73.03	72.62	74.17

Year	Jan.	Feb.	Mar.	Apr.	May	June	July	Aug.	Sept.	Oct.	Nov.	Dec.
1964	76.45	77.39	78.80	79.94	80.72	80.24	83.22	82.00	83.41	84.85	85.44	83.96
1965	86.12	86.75	86.83	87.97	89.28	85.04	84.91	86.49	89.38	91.39	92.15	91.73
1966	93.32	92.69	88.88	91.60	86.78	86.06	85.84	80.65	77.81	77.13	80.99	81.33
1967	84.45	87.36	89.42	90.96	92.59	91.43	93.01	94.49	95.81	95.66	92.66	95.30
1968	95.04	90.75	89.09	95.67	97.87	100.53	100.30	98.11	101.34	103.76	105.40	106.48
1969	102.04	101.46	99.30	101.26	104.62	99.14	94.71	94.18	94.51	95.52	96.21	91.11
1970	90.31	87.16	88.65	85.95	76.06	75.59	75.72	77.92	82.58	84.37	84.28	90.05
1971	93.49	97.11	99.60	103.04	101.64	99.72	99.00	97.24	99.40	97.29	92.78	99.17
1972	103.30	105.24	107.69	108.81	107.65	108.01	107.21	111.01	109.39	109.56	115.05	117.50
1973	118.42	114.16	112.42	110.27	107.22	104.75	105.83	103.80	105.61	109.84	102.03	94.78
1974	96.11	93.45	97.44	92.46	89.67	89.79	82.82	76.03	68.12	69.44	71.74	67.07
1975	72.56	80.10	83.78	84.72	90.10	92.40	92.49	85.71	84.67	88.57	90.07	88.70
1976	96.86	100.64	101.08	101.93	101.16	101.77	104.20	103.29	105.45	101.89	101.19	104.66
1977	103.81	100.96	100.57	99.05	98.76	99.29	100.18	97.75	96.23	93.74	94.28	93.82
1978	90.25	88.98	88.82	92.71	97.41	97.66	97.19	103.92	103.86	100.58	94.71	96.11
1979	99.71	98.23	100.11	102.07	99.73	101.73	102.71	107.36	108.60	104.47	103.66	107.78
1980	110.87	115.34	104.69	102.97	107.69	114.55	119.83	123.50	126.51	130.22	135.65	133.48
1981	132.97	128.40	133.19	134.43	131.73	132.28	129.13	129.63	118.27	119.80	122.92	123.79
1982	117.28	114.50	110.84	116.31	116.35	109.70	109.38	109.65	122.43	132.66	138.10	139.37
1983	144.27	146.80	151.88	157.71	164.10	166.39	166.96	162.42	167.16	167.65	165.23	164.36
1984	166.39	157.25	157.44	157.60	156.55	153.12	151.08	164.42	166.11	164.82	166.27	164.48
1985	171.61	180.88	179.42	180.62	184.90	188.89	192.54	188.31	184.06	186.18	197.45	207.26
1986	208.19	219.37	232.33	237.98	238.46	245.30	240.18	245.00	238.27	237.36	245.09	248.61
1987	264.51	280.93	292.47	289.32	289.12	301.38	310.09	329.36	318.66	280.16	245.01	240.96
1988	250.48	258.13	265.74	262.61	256.12	270.68	269.05	263.73	267.97	277.40	271.02	276.51
1989	285.41	294.01	292.71	302.25	313.93	323.73	331.93	346.61	347.33	347.40	340.22	348.57
1990	339.97	330.45	338.47	338.18	350.25	360.39	360.03	330.75	315.41	307.12	315.29	328.75
1991	325.49	362.26	372.28	379.68	377.99	378.29	380.23	389.40	387.20	386.88	385.92	388.51
1992	416.08	412.56	407.36	407.41	414.81	408.27	415.05	417.93	418.48	412.50	422.84	435.64

Source: Standard & Poors.

Appendix D
Three-Month Treasury Bill Rate, Discount Basis, Monthly Average

Year	Jan.	Feb.	Mar.	Apr.	May	June	July	Aug.	Sept.	Oct.	Nov.	Dec.
1946	0.38	0.38	0.38	0.38	0.38	0.38	0.38	0.38	0.38	0.38	0.38	0.38
1947	0.38	0.38	0.38	0.38	0.38	0.38	0.66	0.75	0.80	0.85	0.92	0.95
1948	0.97	1.00	1.00	1.00	1.00	1.00	1.00	1.06	1.09	1.12	1.14	1.16
1949	1.17	1.17	1.17	1.17	1.17	1.17	1.02	1.04	1.07	1.05	1.08	1.10
1950	1.07	1.12	1.12	1.15	1.16	1.15	1.16	1.20	1.30	1.31	1.36	1.34
1951	1.34	1.36	1.40	1.47	1.55	1.45	1.56	1.62	1.63	1.54	1.56	1.73
1952	1.57	1.54	1.59	1.57	1.67	1.70	1.81	1.83	1.71	1.74	1.85	2.09
1953	1.96	1.97	2.01	2.19	2.16	2.11	2.04	2.04	1.79	1.38	1.44	1.60
1954	1.18	0.97	1.03	0.96	0.76	0.64	0.72	0.92	1.01	0.98	0.93	1.14
1955	1.23	1.17	1.28	1.59	1.45	1.41	1.60	1.90	2.07	2.23	2.25	2.54
1956	2.41	2.32	2.25	2.60	2.61	2.49	2.31	2.60	2.84	2.90	2.99	3.21
1957	3.11	3.11	3.08	3.06	3.06	3.29	3.16	3.37	3.53	3.58	3.29	3.04
1958	2.44	1.54	1.30	1.13	0.91	0.83	0.91	1.69	2.44	2.63	2.67	2.77
1959	2.82	2.70	2.80	2.95	2.84	3.21	3.20	3.38	4.04	4.05	4.15	4.49
1960	4.35	3.96	3.31	3.23	3.29	2.46	2.30	2.30	2.48	2.30	2.37	2.25
1961	2.24	2.42	2.39	2.29	2.29	2.33	2.24	2.39	2.28	2.30	2.48	2.60
1962	2.72	2.73	2.72	2.73	2.68	2.73	2.92	2.82	2.78	2.74	2.83	2.87
1963	2.91	2.92	2.89	2.90	2.92	2.99	3.18	3.32	3.38	3.45	3.52	3.52
1964	3.52	3.53	3.54	3.47	3.48	3.48	3.46	3.50	3.53	3.57	3.64	3.84
1965	3.81	3.93	3.93	3.93	3.89	3.80	3.83	3.84	3.92	4.02	4.08	4.37
1966	4.58	4.65	4.58	4.61	4.63	4.50	4.78	4.95	5.36	5.33	5.31	4.96
1967	4.72	4.56	4.26	3.84	3.60	3.53	4.20	4.26	4.42	4.55	4.72	4.96
1968	4.99	4.97	5.16	5.37	5.65	5.52	5.31	5.08	5.20	5.35	5.45	5.94
1969	6.13	6.12	6.01	6.11	6.03	6.43	6.98	6.97	7.08	6.99	7.24	7.81

1970	7.87	7.13	6.63	6.50	6.83	6.67	6.45	6.41	6.12	5.90	5.28	4.87
1971	4.44	3.69	3.38	3.85	4.13	4.74	5.39	4.93	4.69	4.46	4.22	4.01
1972	3.38	3.20	3.73	3.71	3.69	3.91	3.98	4.02	4.66	4.74	4.78	5.07
1973	5.41	5.60	6.09	6.26	6.36	7.19	8.01	8.67	8.29	7.22	7.83	7.45
1974	7.77	7.12	7.96	8.33	8.23	7.90	7.55	8.96	8.06	7.46	7.47	7.15
1975	6.26	5.50	5.49	5.61	5.23	5.34	6.13	6.44	6.42	5.96	5.48	5.44
1976	4.87	4.88	5.00	4.86	5.20	5.41	5.23	5.14	5.08	4.92	4.75	4.35
1977	4.62	4.67	4.60	4.54	4.96	5.02	5.19	5.49	5.81	6.16	6.10	6.07
1978	6.44	6.45	6.29	6.29	6.41	6.73	7.01	7.08	7.85	7.99	8.64	9.08
1979	9.35	9.32	9.48	9.46	9.61	9.06	9.24	9.52	10.26	11.70	11.79	12.04
1980	12.00	12.86	15.20	13.20	8.58	7.07	8.06	9.13	10.27	11.62	13.73	15.49
1981	15.02	14.79	13.36	13.69	16.30	14.73	14.95	15.51	14.70	13.54	10.86	10.85
1982	12.28	13.48	12.68	12.70	12.09	12.47	11.35	8.68	7.92	7.71	8.07	7.94
1983	7.86	8.11	8.35	8.21	8.19	8.79	9.08	9.34	9.00	8.64	8.76	9.00
1984	8.90	9.09	9.52	9.69	9.83	9.87	10.12	10.47	10.37	9.74	8.61	8.06
1985	7.76	8.27	8.52	7.95	7.48	6.95	7.08	7.14	7.10	7.16	7.24	7.10
1986	7.07	7.06	6.56	6.06	6.15	6.21	5.83	5.53	5.21	5.18	5.35	5.53
1987	5.43	5.59	5.59	5.64	5.66	5.67	5.69	6.04	6.40	6.13	5.69	5.77
1988	5.81	5.66	5.70	5.91	6.26	6.46	6.73	7.06	7.24	7.35	7.76	8.07
1989	8.27	8.53	8.82	8.65	8.43	8.15	7.88	7.90	7.75	7.64	7.69	7.63
1990	7.64	7.74	7.90	7.77	7.74	7.73	7.62	7.45	7.36	7.17	7.06	6.74
1991	6.22	5.94	5.91	5.65	5.46	5.57	5.58	5.33	5.22	4.99	4.56	4.07
1992	3.80	3.84	4.04	3.75	3.63	3.66	3.21	3.13	2.91	2.86	3.13	3.22

Source: Federal Reserve.

Appendix E
Ten-Year U.S. Government
Note Yield, Monthly Average

Year	Jan.	Feb.	Mar.	Apr.	May	June	July	Aug.	Sept.	Oct.	Nov.	Dec.
1953	NA	NA	NA	2.83	3.05	3.11	2.93	2.95	2.87	2.66	2.68	2.59
1954	2.48	2.47	2.37	2.29	2.37	2.38	2.30	2.36	2.38	2.43	2.48	2.51
1955	2.61	2.65	2.67	2.75	2.76	2.78	2.90	2.97	2.97	2.88	2.89	2.96
1956	2.90	2.84	2.96	3.18	3.07	3.00	3.11	3.33	3.38	3.34	3.49	3.59
1957	3.46	3.34	3.41	3.48	3.60	3.80	3.93	3.93	3.92	3.97	3.72	3.21
1958	3.09	3.05	2.98	2.88	2.92	2.97	3.20	3.54	3.76	3.80	3.74	3.86
1959	4.02	3.96	3.99	4.12	4.31	4.34	4.40	4.43	4.68	4.53	4.53	4.69
1960	4.72	4.49	4.25	4.28	4.35	4.15	3.90	3.80	3.80	3.89	3.93	3.84
1961	3.84	3.78	3.74	3.78	3.71	3.88	3.92	4.04	3.98	3.92	3.94	4.06
1962	4.08	4.04	3.93	3.84	3.87	3.91	4.01	3.98	3.98	3.93	3.92	3.86
1963	3.83	3.92	3.93	3.97	3.93	3.99	4.02	4.00	4.08	4.11	4.12	4.13
1964	4.17	4.15	4.22	4.23	4.20	4.17	4.19	4.19	4.20	4.19	4.15	4.18
1965	4.19	4.21	4.21	4.20	4.21	4.21	4.20	4.25	4.29	4.35	4.45	4.62
1966	4.61	4.83	4.87	4.75	4.78	4.81	5.02	5.22	5.18	5.01	5.16	4.84
1967	4.58	4.63	4.54	4.59	4.85	5.02	5.16	5.28	5.30	5.48	5.75	5.70
1968	5.53	5.64	5.74	5.64	5.87	5.72	5.50	5.42	5.46	5.58	5.70	6.03
1969	6.04	6.19	6.30	6.17	6.32	6.57	6.72	6.69	7.16	7.10	7.14	7.65
1970	7.80	7.24	7.07	7.39	7.91	7.84	7.46	7.53	7.39	7.33	6.84	6.39
1971	6.24	6.11	5.70	5.83	6.39	6.52	6.73	6.58	6.14	5.93	5.81	5.93
1972	5.95	6.08	6.07	6.19	6.13	6.11	6.11	6.21	6.55	6.48	6.28	6.36
1973	6.46	6.64	6.71	6.67	6.85	6.90	7.13	7.40	7.09	6.79	6.73	6.74

Year												
1974	6.99	6.96	7.21	7.51	7.58	7.54	7.81	8.04	8.04	7.90	7.68	7.43
1975	7.50	7.39	7.73	8.23	8.06	7.86	8.06	8.40	8.43	8.14	8.05	8.00
1976	7.74	7.79	7.73	7.56	7.90	7.86	7.83	7.77	7.59	7.41	7.29	6.87
1977	7.21	7.39	7.46	7.37	7.46	7.28	7.33	7.40	7.34	7.52	7.58	7.69
1978	7.96	8.03	8.04	8.15	8.35	8.46	8.64	8.41	8.42	8.64	8.81	9.01
1979	9.10	9.10	9.12	9.18	9.25	8.91	8.95	9.03	9.33	10.30	10.65	10.39
1980	10.80	12.41	12.75	11.47	10.18	9.78	10.25	11.10	11.51	11.75	12.68	12.84
1981	12.57	13.19	13.12	13.68	14.10	13.47	14.28	14.94	15.32	15.15	13.39	13.72
1982	14.59	14.43	13.86	13.87	13.62	14.30	13.95	13.06	12.34	10.91	10.55	10.54
1983	10.46	10.72	10.51	10.40	10.38	10.85	11.38	11.85	11.65	11.54	11.69	11.83
1984	11.67	11.84	12.32	12.63	13.41	13.56	13.36	12.72	12.52	12.16	11.57	11.50
1985	11.38	11.51	11.86	11.43	10.85	10.16	10.31	10.33	10.37	10.24	9.78	9.26
1986	9.19	8.70	7.78	7.30	7.71	7.80	7.30	7.17	7.45	7.43	7.25	7.11
1987	7.08	7.25	7.25	8.02	8.61	8.40	8.45	8.76	9.42	9.52	8.86	8.99
1988	8.67	8.21	8.37	8.72	9.09	8.92	9.06	9.26	8.98	8.80	8.96	9.11
1989	9.09	9.17	9.36	9.18	8.86	8.28	8.02	8.11	8.19	8.01	7.87	7.84
1990	8.21	8.47	8.59	8.79	8.76	8.48	8.47	8.75	8.89	8.72	8.39	8.08
1991	8.09	7.85	8.11	8.04	8.07	8.28	8.27	7.90	7.65	7.53	7.42	7.09
1992	7.03	7.34	7.54	7.48	7.39	7.26	6.84	6.59	6.42	6.59	6.87	6.77

Source: Federal Reserve.

Appendix F
Industrial Production Index

Year	Jan.	Feb.	Mar.	Apr.	May	June	July	Aug.	Sept.	Oct.	Nov.	Dec.
1919	8.00	7.60	7.40	7.50	7.60	8.10	8.50	8.70	8.50	8.40	8.30	8.40
1920	9.20	9.20	9.00	8.50	8.80	8.90	8.60	8.70	8.40	8.00	7.40	6.90
1921	6.50	6.40	6.20	6.20	6.40	6.30	6.30	6.50	6.60	7.00	6.90	6.80
1922	7.10	7.40	7.80	7.50	7.90	8.30	8.30	8.10	8.60	9.10	9.50	9.70
1923	9.50	9.60	10.00	10.20	10.30	10.20	10.10	10.00	9.70	9.70	9.70	9.50
1924	9.70	9.90	9.70	9.40	9.00	8.60	8.50	8.80	9.10	9.30	9.50	9.70
1925	10.00	10.00	10.00	10.10	10.10	10.00	10.30	10.10	10.00	10.40	10.60	10.70
1926	10.50	10.50	10.70	10.70	10.60	10.70	10.70	10.90	11.10	11.10	11.00	11.00
1927	10.90	11.00	11.10	10.90	11.00	10.90	10.80	10.80	10.60	10.40	10.40	10.40
1928	10.70	10.70	10.80	10.80	10.90	11.00	11.10	11.40	11.50	11.70	11.90	12.10
1929	12.30	12.20	12.30	12.50	12.70	12.80	13.00	12.90	12.80	12.60	11.90	11.40
1930	11.40	11.40	11.20	11.10	10.90	10.60	10.10	9.90	9.70	9.50	9.20	9.00
1931	9.00	9.00	9.20	9.20	9.10	8.90	8.80	8.50	8.10	7.80	7.70	7.60
1932	7.40	7.20	7.10	6.70	6.40	6.20	6.00	6.20	6.60	6.80	6.80	6.70
1933	6.60	6.60	6.20	6.70	7.80	8.90	9.80	9.40	8.90	8.40	7.90	8.00
1934	8.20	8.60	9.00	9.00	9.20	9.00	8.40	8.30	7.80	8.20	8.30	8.80
1935	9.50	9.70	9.60	9.50	9.50	9.60	9.60	10.00	10.20	10.50	10.70	10.90
1936	10.70	10.40	10.60	11.20	11.50	11.70	11.90	12.10	12.30	12.50	12.80	13.20
1937	13.20	13.30	13.70	13.70	13.70	13.50	13.60	13.50	13.10	12.10	10.90	10.00
1938	9.70	9.60	9.60	9.50	9.20	9.30	9.90	10.40	10.70	11.00	11.40	11.50
1939	11.50	11.60	11.70	11.60	11.60	11.80	12.20	12.40	13.10	13.80	14.10	14.10
1940	14.00	13.50	13.20	13.50	13.90	14.30	14.50	14.60	14.90	15.10	15.50	16.00
1941	16.40	16.90	17.40	17.40	18.20	18.40	18.60	18.80	18.80	19.00	19.10	19.40
1942	19.80	20.10	20.30	19.80	19.80	19.90	20.30	21.00	21.50	22.20	22.70	23.20
1943	23.40	24.00	24.20	24.50	24.70	24.60	25.30	25.90	26.50	26.90	27.30	26.90
1944	27.20	27.40	27.40	27.40	27.20	27.10	27.10	27.40	27.30	27.40	27.10	27.00
1945	26.80	26.70	26.50	26.00	25.30	24.80	24.20	21.70	19.70	18.90	19.60	19.70

1946	18.60	17.70	19.60	19.20	18.50	19.60	20.30	21.10	21.50	21.80	22.00	22.10
1947	22.40	22.50	22.60	22.50	22.60	22.60	22.40	22.60	22.70	22.90	23.30	23.30
1948	23.50	23.50	23.30	23.30	23.70	24.00	24.00	23.90	23.70	23.90	23.60	23.40
1949	23.20	22.90	22.50	22.40	22.10	22.00	22.00	22.20	22.40	21.60	22.20	22.60
1950	22.90	23.00	23.80	24.60	25.20	25.90	26.70	27.60	27.40	27.60	27.50	28.00
1951	28.10	28.30	28.40	28.50	28.40	28.20	27.80	27.50	27.70	27.70	27.90	28.10
1952	28.40	28.50	28.60	28.40	28.10	27.80	27.40	29.20	30.20	30.50	31.10	31.30
1953	31.40	31.60	31.80	32.00	32.20	32.00	32.40	32.20	31.60	31.30	30.60	29.80
1954	29.60	29.70	29.50	29.30	29.50	29.60	29.60	29.60	29.60	30.00	30.50	30.90
1955	31.60	32.00	32.70	33.10	33.70	33.70	34.00	33.90	34.10	34.70	34.80	34.90
1956	35.10	34.80	34.80	35.10	34.80	34.50	33.40	34.80	35.60	35.90	35.60	36.10
1957	36.00	36.30	36.30	35.80	35.70	35.80	36.00	36.00	35.70	35.10	34.30	33.70
1958	33.00	32.30	31.90	31.40	31.70	32.60	33.00	33.70	34.00	34.40	35.40	35.50
1959	36.00	36.70	37.20	38.00	38.60	38.60	37.70	36.40	36.40	36.10	36.30	38.60
1960	39.60	39.20	38.90	38.60	38.50	38.10	37.90	37.90	37.50	37.40	36.90	36.20
1961	36.30	36.20	36.40	37.20	37.70	38.30	38.70	39.10	39.00	39.80	40.40	40.70
1962	40.40	41.10	41.30	41.40	41.30	41.20	41.60	41.70	41.90	42.00	42.20	42.20
1963	42.50	42.90	43.20	43.60	44.10	44.30	44.10	44.20	44.60	44.90	45.10	45.10
1964	45.50	45.80	45.80	46.50	46.80	46.90	47.20	47.50	47.70	47.00	48.50	49.10
1965	49.60	49.90	50.60	50.80	51.20	51.60	52.10	52.30	52.40	52.90	53.20	53.80
1966	54.40	54.70	55.50	55.50	56.10	56.30	56.60	56.70	57.20	57.60	57.20	57.30
1967	57.60	57.00	56.60	57.20	56.70	56.70	56.50	57.60	57.50	58.00	58.80	59.50
1968	59.40	59.60	59.80	59.90	60.60	60.80	60.70	60.90	61.10	61.20	62.00	62.20
1969	62.60	63.00	63.50	63.20	63.00	63.60	63.90	64.10	64.10	64.10	63.50	63.30
1970	62.10	62.10	62.00	61.90	61.80	61.60	61.70	61.60	61.20	60.00	59.60	61.00
1971	61.50	61.30	61.30	61.60	61.90	62.20	62.00	61.70	62.70	63.10	63.40	64.10
1972	65.60	66.00	66.50	67.60	67.50	67.70	67.60	68.50	69.20	70.20	71.10	71.70
1973	71.80	72.80	72.80	73.00	73.40	73.90	74.40	74.30	74.90	75.20	75.20	74.00
1974	73.00	72.70	73.00	72.90	73.80	74.00	73.60	73.40	73.70	73.20	71.10	68.10

Year	Jan.	Feb.	Mar.	Apr.	May	June	July	Aug.	Sept.	Oct.	Nov.	Dec.
1975	66.30	65.30	64.10	64.70	64.50	65.30	65.70	66.90	67.60	67.90	68.60	69.10
1976	69.90	71.10	70.90	71.20	72.00	72.10	72.50	72.90	73.10	73.40	74.60	75.20
1977	75.50	75.90	76.60	77.70	78.30	78.90	78.90	79.00	79.40	79.40	79.50	79.10
1978	78.80	79.00	80.00	82.00	82.30	83.10	83.30	83.60	84.10	84.50	85.20	85.40
1979	85.10	85.80	86.10	85.20	86.20	86.10	85.60	85.30	85.50	86.00	85.70	85.60
1980	85.90	86.20	86.20	84.50	82.50	81.50	81.20	82.40	83.50	84.00	85.50	85.90
1981	85.20	85.40	85.70	85.00	85.60	86.10	87.10	86.90	86.50	85.80	84.80	84.10
1982	82.40	84.20	83.70	83.20	82.70	82.40	82.00	81.60	81.00	80.30	80.00	79.30
1983	80.80	80.70	81.30	82.30	83.20	83.70	85.30	86.50	87.90	88.60	88.80	89.20
1984	91.00	90.90	91.90	92.40	93.00	93.50	93.90	94.00	93.90	93.20	93.30	92.80
1985	93.10	93.80	94.10	94.50	94.70	94.40	94.10	94.50	95.00	94.20	94.60	95.60
1986	96.10	95.50	94.60	94.80	94.80	94.40	94.80	95.00	95.10	95.60	96.20	96.70
1987	96.50	97.60	98.20	98.30	99.20	100.10	100.80	101.00	100.90	102.30	102.20	102.60
1988	103.50	103.50	103.90	104.30	104.80	105.00	106.10	106.40	106.20	106.50	106.90	107.40
1989	107.70	107.60	107.70	108.60	108.30	108.40	107.80	108.20	108.20	107.70	108.10	108.60
1990	107.50	108.50	108.90	108.80	109.40	110.10	110.40	110.50	110.60	109.90	108.30	107.20
1991	106.60	105.70	105.00	105.50	106.40	107.30	108.10	108.00	108.40	108.40	108.10	107.40
1992	106.60	107.20	107.60	108.10	108.90	108.50	109.40	109.10	108.90	109.70	110.10	110.50

Source: Federal Reserve.

Appendix G
Electronic Bulletin Boards

Having the most recent and up-to-date as well as complete historical data is important for analysis and forecasting. In the age of information technology, *electronic bulletin boards* exist to meet data users' needs. Some bulletin boards are fee-based, whereas others are free to access. The following electronic bulletin boards are among those currently available:

1. *Source*   U.S. Department of Agriculture
   Service   Commercial Information Delivery Service (CIDS)
   Voice Number   202-720-5505
   Data Number   Must subscribe first
   Cost   Fee-based
   Information   Contains government information about developments and statistics dealing with the agriculture industry.

2. *Source*   U.S. Department of Commerce
   Service   Bureau of Economic Analysis BBS
   Voice Number   301-763-7554
   Data Number   301-763-7554
   Cost   Free
   Information   Contains business and industry information collected by the U.S. Census Bureau and the Bureau of Economic Analysis.

3. *Source*   U.S. Department of Commerce, Bureau of the Census
   Service   State Data Center/Business-Industry Data Center
   Voice Number   301-763-1580
   Data Number   301-763-7554
   Cost   Free
   Information   Selected Bureau of the Census economic reports, geographic electronic mapping and any press reports dealing with Census Bureau surveys.

4. *Source*   U.S. Department of Commerce
    Service   Economic Bulletin Board (EBB)
    Voice Number   202-482-1986
    Data Number   202-482-3870
    Cost   Fee-based
    Information   Best source of current economic and financial data across a wide spectrum of government agencies.

5. *Source*   U.S. Department of Commerce
    Service   Climate Dialup Services (CDUS)
    Voice Number   301-763-4670
    Data Number   301-899-0827 (300-1200 baud), 301-899-1173 (1200 baud)
    Cost   Fee-based
    Information   Provides daily/weekly/monthly weather information collected by the National Weather Service.

6. *Source*   U.S. Department of Commerce
    Service   NGDC Solar Terrestrial Data
    Voice Number   303-497-6346
    Data Number   303-497-7319
    Cost   Free
    Information   Sunspot numbers from the 1800s, Ottawa flux data, geomagnetic indices, irradiance data.

7. *Source*   U.S. Department of Energy
    Service   Energy Information Admin. Electronic Publishing System (EPUB)
    Voice Number   202-586-8800
    Data Number   202-586-2557
    Cost   Free
    Information   Contains selected energy-related data from numerous energy publications.

8. *Source*   Federal Reserve Bank of Dallas
    Service   Fed Flash
    Voice Number   214-922-5171/73
    Data Number   214-922-5199
    Cost   Free
    Information   Contains data on national and regional economic and financial data.

9. *Source*   Federal Reserve Bank of Minneapolis
    Service   KIMBERELY
    Voice Number   612-340-2489

Data Number   612-340-2443

Cost   Free

Information   Contains economic and financial data on banking, interest rates, and the economy.

10.   *Source*   Federal Reserve Bank of St. Louis

   Service   Federal Reserve Economic Data (FRED)

   Voice Number   314-444-8562

   Data Number   314-621-1824

   Cost   Free

   Information   Contains data and information on banking, interest rates, and the economy with extensive historical data.

Notes

CHAPTER 1

1. Arthur F. Burns, "Progress Towards Economic Stability," *American Economic Review*, Vol. 50, No. 1 (March 1960), 1.

2. For a report on the Bureau's history, see Solomon Fabricant, *Toward a Firmer Basis of Economic Policy: The Founding of the National Bureau of Economic Research*, Cambridge, MA: NBER, 1984.

3. Arthur F. Burns and Wesley C. Mitchell, *Measuring Business Cycles*, New York: NBER, 1946, 3.

4. This vagueness was intentional; see ibid., 90.

5. Philip A. Klein, "The Neglected Institutionalism of Wesley Clair Mitchell: The Theoretical Basis for Business Cycle Indicators," *Journal of Economic Issues*, Vol. XVII, No. 4 (December 1983), 867–899.

6. *Measuring Business Cycles*, 40–41.

7. This amplitude adjustment is proposed by E. Haywood, "The Deviation Cycle: A New Index of the Australian Business Cycle 1950–1973," *Australian Economic Review*, Fourth Quarter, 1973, 31–39.

8. Ilse Mintz, *Dating Postwar Business Cycles: Methods and Their Applications to Western Germany, 1950–67*, New York: NBER, 5.

9. Geoffrey H. Moore, "Growth Cycles: A New-Old Concept," *Morgan Guaranty Survey*, August 1979, 12–14.

10. Victor Zarnowitz, "Business Cycles and Growth: Some Reflections and Measures," Working Paper No. 665, National Bureau of Economic Research, April 1981.

11. Maurice Lee, *Economic Fluctuations: Growth and Stability*, Homewood, IL: Irwin, 1959, 250.

12. John R. Meyer and Daniel H. Weinberg, "On the Classification of Recent Cyclical Experience," *National Bureau of Economic Research, Inc. 55th Annual Report*, September 1975, 1–8.

13. Ibid., 8.

14. M. Baba, N. Nomura, and S. Tahara, "Major Features of New Business Cycle Indicators in Japan," in *Leading Indicators and Business Cycle Surveys*, Hampshire, England: Gower Publishing Co., 1984, 609.

15. Irving Fisher, "Our Unstable Dollar and the So-Called Business Cycle," *Publication of the American Statistical Association*, 1925, 191–192.

16. Thomas J. Sargent, *Macroeconomic Theory*, New York: Academic Press, 1979.

17. James H. Stock, "Measuring Business Cycle Time," *Journal of Political Economy*, Vol. 95, No. 6, (1987), 1240–1261.

18. Ibid., 1243.

19. The Wilcoxon (Mann–Whitney) statistical test is described in Chapter 3. The method determines the probability of U (the test statistic) given the null hypothesis that the mean of the recession and expansion segments of the business cycle are equal; in this case it was 0.00, which is less than 0.05 (the level of significance). Hence, this test fails to accept the hypothesis that the recession and expansion segments have identical means. More generally, this can be interpreted as rejecting the Stock view.

20. Specifically, the Wilcoxon test accepts the null hypothesis that the mean growth rates in stages II and III, stages VI and VII, and stages VII and VIII are equal. It fails to accept that hypothesis for stages III and IV. This test was applied for the seven cycles between 1949 and 1982. It was felt that testing adjacent phases of the cycle using that nonparametric test would capture the essence of the Stock concern. Our finding does not negate the importance of the NBER work. All it suggests is that the use of some convenient rules for dividing the business cycle into stages should be refined. Possibly the use of discriminant analysis to divide growth rates into three stages of expansion and contraction could refine the original method.

21. William G. Tomek and Kenneth L. Robinson, *Agricultural Product Prices* (2nd ed.) Ithaca, NY: Cornell University Press, 1981, 179.

22. Alan Blinder and Douglas Holtz-Eakin, "Inventory Fluctuations in the United States since 1929," in *The American Business Cycle: Continuity and Change,* Robert J. Gordon, ed., Cambridge, MA: NBER, 1986, 183–214.

23. Lloyd A. Metzler, "The Nature and Stability of Inventory Cycles," *Review of Economics and Statistics,* Vol. XXII, No. 2 (August 1941), pp. 113–129, reprinted in *Business Fluctuations, Growth, and Economic Stabilization: A Reader,* John J. Clark and Morris Cohen, eds., New York: Random House, 1963, 113–142.

24. L. R. Klein and J. Popkin, "An Econometric Analysis of the Postwar Relationship between Inventory Fluctuations and Change in Aggregate Economic Activity," *Inventory Fluctuations and Economic Stabilization* (Part III), Joint Economic Committee, 1961, 71–86.

25. Alan Blinder, *Inventory Theory and Consumer Behavior,* Ann Arbor: University of Michigan Press, 1990.

26. John Hoagland, Lee Buddress, and Michael Heberling, "Pyramid Power of Purchases" (mimeo.), paper presented at the National Association of Purchasing Management Annual Meeting, New Orleans, LA, April 30, 1990. This paper also makes an interesting point regarding industries that are large buyers of inputs. The authors suggest that these large purchasers of raw material and supplies are likely to trigger this inventory cycle. The manufacturing industries that are major purchasers are (in order of importance, based on 1982 data) (1) petroleum refining—15% of all manufacturing purchases; (2) motor vehicles—4.7% of factory purchases; (3) meatpacking; (4) steel mills; (5) organic chemicals; (6) plastic products; (7) motor vehicle parts; (8) electronic computing; (9) aircraft; and (10) fluid milk industry.

27. Hal Mather, *How to Really Manage Inventories,* New York: McGraw-Hill, 1984. Mather's book provides a significant challenge to economists' view of inventories. It seems that too often economists do not really understand the "real world" inventory process. Moreover, Mather argued that as more companies apply a "just-in-time" inventory control system, the fluctuations from the inventory cycle will be greatly dampened. This seems to be consistent with the recent historical experience.

28. Ibid., 11.

29. Joseph A. Schumpeter, "The Analysis of Economic Change," reprinted in *Business Fluctuations, Growth, and Economic Stabilization: A Reader,* John J. Clark and Morris Cohen, eds., New York: Random House, 1963, 47.

30. In *The American Business Cycle: Continuity and Change,* 267–357.

31. J. J. van Duijn, *The Long Wave in Economic Life,* London: George Allen & Unwin, 1983.

32. Manuel Gottlieb, *Long Swings in Urban Development,* New York: NBER, 1976, 1.

33. Carl A. Dauten and Lloyd M. Valentine, *Business Cycles and Forecasting,* Pelham Manor, NY: South-Western Publishing, New York, 1974.

34. B. P. Klotz and L. Neal, "Spectral and Cross Spectral Analysis of the Long Swing Hypothesis," *Review of Economics and Statistics,* Vol. LV, 291–298.

35. G. Ronald Witten, "Riding the Real Estate Cycle," *Real Estate Today,* August 1987, 42–48.

36. Wesley C. Mitchell, *Business Cycles: The Problem and Its Setting,* New York: NBER, 1927, 227.

37. N. D. Kondratieff, "The Long Waves in Economic Life," *Review of Economic Statistics,* 111.

38. Edwin Mansfield, "Long Waves and Technological Innovation," *American Economic Review,* May 1983, 144.

39. Solomos Solomou, *Phases of Economic Growth, 1850–1973: Kondratieff Waves and Kuznets Swings,* Cambridge, England: Cambridge University Press, 1987.

40. Paul A. Volcker, *The Rediscovery of the Business Cycle,* New York: Free Press, 1978, 43–44.

41. Joseph A. Schumpeter, "The Analysis of Economic Change," *Review of Economics and Statistics,* Vol. XVII, No. 4 (May 1935), 2–10, reprinted in *Business Fluctuations, Growth, and Economic Stabilization: A Reader,* John J. Clark and Morris Cohen, eds., New York: Random House, 1963, 55.

42. Joseph A. Schumpeter, *Business Cycles,* New York: McGraw-Hill, 1939, 173–174.

43. Jay W. Forrester, "A New View of Business Cycle Dynamics," *Journal of Portfolio Management,* Fall 1976, 22.

44. Arthur F. Burns and Wesley C. Mitchell, *Measuring Business Cycles,* New York: NBER, 1946, 460.

45. This is based on Walt W. Rostow, *The World Economy,* Austin: University of Texas Press, 1978, 103–110. An earlier account is W. W. Rostow, *The Process of Economic Growth* (2nd ed.), W.W. Norton, New York, 1962.

46. See, for example, Michael Beenstock, *The World Economy in Transition* (2nd ed.), London: George Allen & Unwin, 1984, 153–157. Also some criticism is summarized in J. J. van Duijn, *The Long Wave in Economic Life,* London: George Allen & Unwin, 1983, 45–56.

47. John Hicks, *A Market Theory of Money,* Oxford: Clarendon Press, 1989.

48. Ibid., 93.

49. Ibid., 94.

50. Mary S. Morgan, *The History of Econometric Ideas,* Cambridge: Cambridge University Press, 1990.

51. Ibid., 55.

52. Martin H. Wolfson, *Financial Crises,* M. E. Sharpe, New York: Armonk, 1986.

CHAPTER 2

1. Robert A. Heilbroner, *The Worldly Philosophers,* New York: Simon & Schuster, 1953.

2. See Arthur F. Burns, *The Business Cycle in a Changing World,* New York: NBER, 1969, Chapter 1, especially pp. 16–17.

3. In a parallel example, accountants can always show that a firm's assets equal its liabilities plus net worth. It is true for a bankrupt firm, a sluggish firm, or a rapidly growing firm. It is, in short, a truism for any firm at a given time but tells little about the health of the firm.

4. Gottfried Haberler, *Prosperity and Depression,* Geneva: League of Nations, 1937.

5. Ibid., cf. Chapter 7.

6. All Jevons's work on the subject was reprinted in *Investigations in Currency and Finance,* London: Macmillan, 1884.

7. H. S. Jevons, *The Causes of Unemployment, The Sun's Heat and Trade Activity,* London: 1910, also "Trade Fluctuations and Solar Activity," *Contemporary Review,* August 1909.

8. Henry L. Moore, *Economic Cycles: Their Law and Cause,* New York: Macmillan, 1914. See also H. L. Moore, *Generating Economic Cycles,* New York: Macmillan, 1923.

9. Quoted in Wesley C. Mitchell, *What Happens during Business Cycles,* 57.

10. Cf. A. C. Pigou, *Industrial Fluctuations,* London: Macmillan, 1927.

11. Cf. Dennis Robertson, *A Study of Industrial Fluctuations,* P. S. King, 1915.

12. See Mordecai Ezekial, "The Cobweb Effect," *Quarterly Journal of Economics,* February 1938, 255–280. Reprinted in Am. Econ. Ass., *Readings in Business Cycle Theory,* Philadelphia: Blakiston, 1944, 422–442.

13. Quoted in Haberler, op. cit., p. 83. His study was originally published in Russian (1894). This is from the German version, *Studien fur Geschichte der Handelskrisen in England,* Jena: 1901.

14. See A. C. Pigou, *Industrial Fluctuations,* London: Macmillan, 1927, especially Chapter VII.

15. See R. G. Hawtrey, *Good and Bad Trade,* London: Constable, 1913; *Monetary Reconstruction,* (2nd ed.) 1926 (originally published 1923); *Currency and Credit,* London: Longmans, Green, 1919, 1923, 1928; *Monetary Reconstruction,* New York: Longmans, Green, 1926; *Trade and Credit,* 1928; *Trade Depression and the Way Out,* 1931, 1933; *The Art of Central Banking,* London: Longmans, Green, 1933; *The Gold Standard in Theory and Practice* (3rd ed.), 1933; *Capital and Employment,* London: Longmans, Green, 1937. His monetary theory of the cycle is summarized in "The Trade Cycle," (originally Chapter 5 in *Trade and Credit,* reprinted as Chapter 16 in Am. Econ. Ass., *Readings in Business Cycle Theory,* Philadelphia: Blakiston, 1944, 330–349). For a fuller discussion of this work, cf. Haberler, op. cit., Chapter 2.

16. For a fuller discussion of many of these points, cf. Robert A. Gordon, *Business Fluctuations,* New York: Harper and Brothers, 1961, 352–356.

17. See Jean Lescure, *Des Crises Generales et Periodiques de Surproduction* (3rd ed.), Paris: Librarie du Recueil Sirey, 1923.

18. Mitchell's assertion that the causes of business fluctuations could be determined only by first examining the empirical record carefully (i.e., examining the behavior over time of a large number of time series,) led to considerable initial criticism.

19. Cf. Tjalling Koopmans, "Measurement without Theory," *Review of Economics and Statistics,* Vol. XXIX (August 1947). Reprinted in Am. Econ. Ass., *Readings in Business Cycles,* Vol. X, R. A. Gordon and L. R. Klein, eds., Homewood, IL: Irwin, 1956, 186–203. Vining's rejoinder, entitled "Koopmans on the Choice of Variables to Be Studied and Methods," appeared in the *Review of Economics and Statistics,* Vol. XXXI (May 1949), and is reprinted in Gordon and Klein, op. cit., 204–217. A further reply by Koopmans and a Rejoinder by Vining appeared in the *Review of Economics and Statistics,* May 1949, and are reprinted in Gordon and Klein, op. cit., 218–230. A final comment by Koopmans, taken from a collection of his essays published in 1957, is included in Gordon and Klein, op. cit., 231, and presumably gives his final minimal approval to the Burns-Mitchell approach.

20. Wesley C. Mitchell, *Business Cycles and Their Causes*, Berkeley: University of California Press, 1959 (reprint of Part III of *Business Cycles*, originally written in 1913), 61.

21. That Mitchell was correct in this view, expressed so long ago, has recently been retested. A recent study suggests that businesses keep on a small percentage (about 4%) of their work force despite a lack of work. This *labor hoarding hypothesis* was empirically confirmed in a study by Jon A. Fay and James L. Medoff, "Labor and Output over the Business Cycle: Some Direct Evidence," *American Economic Review*, Vol. 75, No. 4 (September 1985), 638–655.

22. Wesley C. Mitchell, *Business Cycles: The Problem and Its Setting*, New York: NBER, 1927. This view is still argued convincingly—to many students of the cycle—in our own time. See Geoffrey H. Moore, "Productivity, Costs, and Prices; New Light from an Old Hypothesis," *Business Cycles, Inflation, and Forecasting*, National Bureau of Economic Research, Cambridge, MA: Ballinger Press, 1980, 275–291.

23. Arthur F. Burns, Wesley C. Mitchell, and the National Bureau, *29th Annual Report of the National Bureau of Economic Research*, New York, 1949, 23.

24. Robert E. Lucas, Jr., "Methods and Problems in Business Cycle Theory," *Journal of Money, Credit, and Banking*, Vol. XII, No. 4 (November 1980, Part 2), 698.

25. Metzler's theory was considered in "The Nature and Stability of Inventory Cycles," *Review of Economics and Statistics*, Vol. XXIII (August 1941), reprinted in Gordon and Klein, op. cit., 100–129. Later, careful empirical work on the role of inventories in business cycles was conducted by two researchers at the National Bureau of Economic Research: Moses Abramowitz, *Inventories and Business Cycles, With Special Reference to Manufacturers' Inventories*, New York: NBER, 1950; Thomas M. Stanback, Jr., *Postwar Cycles in Manufacturers' Inventories*, New York: NBER, 1962.

26. Wicksell published extensively during the first 40 years or so of the twentieth century. One of his first publications was *Geldzins und Guterpreise*, Jena, 1898. Translated as *Interest and Prices*, London, 1936. See also *Lectures on Political Economy*, London, 1934 and "The Influence of the Rate of Interest on Prices," *Economic Journal*, June 1907. For an analysis of Wicksell, see Haberler, op. cit., 34–36.

27. Hayek has written extensively. See, for example, his *Monetary Theory and the Trade Cycle*, New York: Harcourt Brace, 1933; *Prices and Production*, London: George Routledge & Sons, 1935; *Profits, Interest, and Investment*, London: George Routledge & Sons, 1939.

28. See *The Theory of Money and Credit*, London: 1934. Translated from the German, *Geldwertstabilisierung und Konjunkturpolitik*, Jena: 1928.

29. Tugan-Baranowski's principal work was published in Russian in 1894 and was translated into German under the title, *Studien fur Geschichte Handelkrisen in England*, Jena: 1901.

30. Cf. Haberler, op. cit., 83.

31. See "Vorbemerkungen zu einer Theorie der Ueberproduktion," in *Jahrbuch fur Gesetzgebung, Verwaltung, und Volkswirtschaft*, 1902; also "Krisen" in *Handworterbuch der Staatswissenschaften*, 1925; also Haberler, op. cit., 72–80.

32. See Gustav Cassel, *Theory of Social Economy* (Vol. II, rev. ed.), London: 1932 (originally published 1918). Translated from the German.

33. Ibid., 556.

34. Joseph A. Schumpeter's work included *The Theory of Economic Development*, Cambridge, MA: Harvard University Press, 1934. Translated from the German; originally published in 1911. He published a two-volume work, *Business Cycles*, New York: McGraw-Hill, 1939. A short explanation of his theory of innovations is in "The Analysis of Economic Change," *Review of Economics and Statistics*, 1935, 2–10, reprinted in Am. Econ. Ass., *Readings in*

Business Cycle Theory, G. Haberler, ed., 1944, 1–19. For a statement of the full implications of his theory for the future of capitalist economies, see his *Capitalism, Socialism, and Democracy,* New York: Harper, 1947.

35. Joseph A. Schumpeter, *Business Cycles,* New York: McGraw-Hill, 1939, 102.

36. See Schumpeter, *Capitalism, Socialism, and Democracy,* op. cit.

37. Underconsumptionists would include Lauderdale, Sismondi, and Lederer, and among twentieth-century Americans, Gordon Hayes, in addition to the economists discussed in the text.

38. Douglas was very popular in Canada, where his advocacy of "social credit" received a good deal of attention. See C. H. Douglas, *Social Credit,* New York: W.W. Norton, 1933.

39. John M. Keynes, *The General Theory of Employment, Interest, and Money,* New York: Harcourt Brace, 1936, 371.

40. See W. T. Foster and W. Catchings, *Money,* Boston: Houghton Mifflin, 1923; *Profits,* Boston: Houghton Mifflin, 1925; and *The Road to Plenty,* Boston: Houghton Mifflin, 1928.

41. Hobson's views are set out in a lengthy series of books. See in particular John A. Hobson, *The Industrial System,* London: Longmans, Green, 1909; *The Economics of Unemployment* (rev. ed.), London: George Allen & Unwin, 1931; and *Imperialism* (1st, 2nd, 3rd ed.), Reissued, Ann Arbor: University of Michigan Press, 1965 (originally published 1902, 1905, 1938).

42. Marx's views are found in his famous book, *Capital (Das Kapital),* originally published in German in 1867. A convenient English edition is the Modern Library Edition (New York) (no date given).

43. Karl Marx and Friedrich Engels, *Manifesto of the Communist Party,* originally published in London in 1848. Here, *The Marx-Engels Reader,* Robert C. Tucker, ed., New York: W.W. Norton, 1972, 340.

44. John M. Keynes's views on macroinstability are found in his well-known book, *The General Theory of Employment, Interest, and Money,* New York: Harcourt Brace and Company, 1936. See especially Chapter 22, "Notes on the Trade Cycle."

45. Keynes, *General Theory,* op. cit., 27–28. Italics in original.

46. Actually Keynes took the concept of the multiplier from work by R. F. Kahn. Kahn was concerned with the employment-multiplying consequences of an initial change in employment. Keynes turns this "employment multiplier" into an "investment multiplier." See R. F. Kahn, "The Relation of Home Investment to Unemployment," *Economic Journal,* June 1931. See also Keynes, *General Theory,* op. cit., 112–119.

47. Paul A. Samuelson, "Interactions between the Multiplier Analysis and the Principle of Acceleration," *Review of Economics and Statistics,* May 1939, 75–78. Reprinted in *Readings in Business Cycles Theory,* op. cit., 261–269.

48. See J. M. Clark, "Business Acceleration and the Law of Demand: A Technical Factor in Economic Cycles," *Journal of Political Economy,* 1917. Reprinted in *Readings in Business Cycle Theory,* op. cit., 235–260.

49. William J. Fellner, "The Capital Output Ratio in Dynamic Economics," in *Money, Trade, and Economic Growth* (Essays in honor of John H. Williams), New York: Macmillan, 1951, 105–134. See especially Part V, 124–126.

50. Michael Kalecki, *Essays in the Theory of Economic Fluctuations,* and *Studies in Economic Dynamics,* 1943.

51. Nicholas Kaldor, "A Model of the Trade Cycle," *Economic Journal,* March 1940, 72–92.

52. Richard M. Goodwin, "A Model of Cyclical Growth," in *The Business Cycle in the Post-War World,* Erik Lundberg, ed., London: Macmillan, 1955. Reprinted in Gordon and Klein, *Readings in Business Cycles,* op. cit., 6–22.

53. The original Domar essays were "Expansion and Employment," *American Economic Review, 37* (March 1947), 34–55, and "The Problem of Capital Accumulation," *American Economic Review,* 38 (December 1948), 777–794. They were reprinted in Domar's *Essays in the Theory of Economic Growth,* Oxford University Press, 1957.

54. Harrod developed a multiplier-accelerator model of the cycle in *The Trade Cycle,* 1936; see also "An Essay in Dynamic Theory," *Economic Journal,* XLIX (March 1939), subsequently expanded in *Towards a Dynamic Economics,* Macmillan, 1949.

55. John R. Hicks, *A Contribution to the Theory of the Trade Cycle,* Oxford: Oxford University Press, 1950. We can here comment only on a sample of these theories.

56. For a full and especially clear discussion of Domar's model, see Wallace G. Peterson, *Income, Employment, and Economic Growth,* New York: W.W. Norton (rev. ed.), 1967, 414–428.

57. An introductory article on the subject is James Gleick, "Solving the Mathematical Riddle of Chaos," *New York Times Magazine,* June 10, 1984, 31–71. See also William J. Baumol and Richard E. Quandt, "Chaos Models and Their Implications for Forecasting," *Eastern Economic Journal,* Vol. XI, No. 1 (January–March 1985), 3–15. For a survey article, see Murray Frank, "Chaotic Dynamics in Economic Time-Series," *Journal of Economic Surveys,* Vol. 2, No. 2 (1988), 103–133.

58. William A. Brock and Chera L. Sayers, "Is the Business Cycle Characterized by Deterministic Chaos?" *Journal of Monetary Economics,* Vol. 22 (1988), 71–90.

59. Milton Friedman, *Studies in the Quantity Theory of Money,* Chicago: University of Chicago Press, 1956, and "The Quantity Theory of Money—A Restatement," *Journal of Political Economy,* LXVII (August 1959), 327 ff.; *The Demand for Money: Some Theoretical and Empirical Results,* New York: Columbia University Press, for National Bureau of Economic Research, 1959. See also *The Relationship of Prices to Economic Stability and Growth,* U.S. Congress, Joint Economic Committee, Compendium, 1958; *The Optimum Quantity of Money and Other Essays,* Chicago: Aldine Publishing, 1969; *A Theoretical Framework for Monetary Analysis,* Occasional Paper, New York: NBER, 1971.

60. With Milton Friedman, she wrote two pioneering studies of the relationship of changes in the money supply and changes in aggregate economic activity. The first, Milton Friedman and Anna Jacobson Schwartz, *A Monetary History of the United States, 1867–1960,* Princeton, NJ: Princeton University Press, for the National Bureau of Economic Research, 1963; and the second, *Monetary Trends in the U.S. and the United Kingdom, Their Relation to Income, Prices, and Interest Rates, 1867–1975,* Chicago: University of Chicago Press, for the National Bureau of Economic Research, 1982.

61. Brunner and Meltzer, *Monetary Economics,* Oxford & New York: Blackwell, 1989.

62. Phillip Cagan, *Determinants of the Effects of Changes in the Stock of Money, 1875–1960,* New York: Columbia University Press, for National Bureau of Economic Research, 1965; *The Demand for Currency Relative to Total Money Supply,* New York: NBER, 1958.

63. The theory is associated with Robert G. King and Charles I. Plosser, who presented their views in an article entitled "Money, Credit, and Prices in a Real Business Cycle," *American Economic Review,* June 1984, 363–380. Another version of real business cycles appears in Carl E. Walsh, "New Views of the Business Cycle: Has the Past Emphasis on Money Been Misplaced?" *Business Review,* Federal Reserve Bank of Philadelphia, January–February, 1986, 3–14. A recent study of real business cycles is Enrique G. Mendoza, "Real Business Cycles in a Small Open Economy," *American Economic Review,* Vol. 81, No. 4 (September 1991), 797–818. The abstract suggests the approach: "The model is parameterized, calibrated, and simulated to explore its ability to rationalize the observed pattern of postwar Canadian business fluctuations. The result shows that the model mimics many of the stylized facts . . ." (p. 797). Cf. also Robert G. King, Charles I. Plosser, James H. Stock, and Mark W. Watson, "Stochastic Trends

and Economic Fluctuations," *American Economic Review,* 81, 4 (September 1991), 819–840. This article testing the real business cycle approach concludes, "[P]ermanent productivity shocks typically explain less than half the business-cycle variability in output, consumption, and investment" (p. 819).

64. Richard M. Goodwin, "A Model of Cyclical Growth," in *The Business Cycle in the Postwar World,* Eric Lundberg, ed., London: Macmillan, 1955. Reprinted in Gordon and Klein, *Readings in Business Cycles,* 6–22.

65. Arthur Laffer, *Supply-Side Economics,* Pacific Palisades, CA: Goodyear, 1982.

66. Keynes, op. cit., 325.

67. The seminal paper on this notion is Michael Kalecki's "Political Aspects of Full Employment," *Political Quarterly,* Vol. 14 (1943), 322–330.

68. "The Political Business Cycle," *Review of Economic Studies,* Vol. 42 (April 1975), 169–190.

69. MacRae's approach is similar to that of Nordhaus. MacRae, however, develops a model in which the objective is to minimize the vote loss from inflation and unemployment. See C. Duncan MacRae, "A Political Model of the Business Cycle," *Journal of Political Economy,* Vol. 85, No. 2 (1977), 239–263.

70. See Paul Mosley, "Towards A 'Satisfying' Theory of Economic Policy," *Economic Journal,* Vol. 86 (March 1976), 59–72.

71. See Edward R. Tufte, *Political Control of the Economy,* Princeton, NJ: Princeton University Press, 1978. One possible test of this *fixed-length cycle* is to use spectral analysis to test for the presence of a two- or four-year cycle. A simpler method that could be applied is known as periodogram analysis. He describes this technique in Chapter 3 and applies it to the unemployment rate. That effort suggests that a four-year cycle in unemployment might well exist.

72. One study that finds no evidence of the political business cycle is by Richard K. Abrams, Richard T. Froyen, and Roger N. Waud, "The State of the Federal Budget and the State of the Economy," Research Working Paper 80-08, Reserve Bank of Kansas City, September 1980. An application of spectral analysis that also casts doubt on this hypothesis is found in Donald R. Knopp and John P. Walter, "The Political Business Cycle," *Business Economics,* September 1980, 97–99.

73. See Bennet MacCallum, "The Political Business Cycle: An Empirical Test," *Southern Economic Journal,* Vol. 44, No. 3 (January 1978), 504–515. MacCallum, argues that the empirical record does not support the hypothesis.

74. David I. Meiselman, "Is There A Political Monetary Cycle?" *Cato Journal,* Vol. 6, No. 2 (Fall 1986), 563–579.

75. John Muth, "Rational Expectations and the Theory of Price Movements," *Econometrica,* Vol. 29, No. 3 (July 1961), 315–335.

76. Ibid., 316.

77. See Robert E. Lucas, "Understanding Business Cycles," in *Stabilization of the Domestic and International Economy* (Vol. 5), Karl Brunner and Allan Meltzer, eds., Carnegie-Rochester Series on Public Policy, Amsterdam: North-Holland Publishing, 1977, 7–29. Reprinted in Robert Lucas, *Studies in Business Cycle Theory,* Cambridge, MA: MIT Press, 1981.

78. For example, a book by K. Holden, D. A. Peel, and J. Thompson, *Expectations: Theory and Evidence,* New York: St. Martin's Press, 1985, surveyed some 100 studies of the rational expectations hypothesis including consumer surveys, business surveys, and both aggregate and micro investigations, as well as surveys studies in both the United States and the United Kingdom.

79. Ibid., 174.

80. Arthur Okun, "Rational-Expectations-with Misperceptions as a Theory of the Business Cycle," *Journal of Money, Credit, and Banking,* XII, 4 (November 1980, Part 2), 817–825. For

an excellent survey of the empirical work on rational expectations models, see A. W. Mullineux, *The Business Cycle after Keynes: A Contemporary Analysis,* Totowa, NJ: Barnes and Noble, 1984.

81. For a good summary of extant business cycle theories and the current state of the debate, see Victor Zarnowitz, "Recent Work on Business Cycles in Historical Perspective: A Review of Theories and Evidence," *Journal of Economic Literature,* XXIII, 2 (June 1985), 523–580.

CHAPTER 3

1. Thomas J. Sargent and Christopher A. Sims, "Business Cycle Modeling without Pretending to Have Too Much A Priori Economic Theory," *New Methods in Business Cycle Research: Proceedings from a Conference,* Federal Reserve Bank of Minneapolis, October 1977, 45–109.

2. Arnold Zellner, ed., *Seasonal Analysis of Economic Time Series,* Economic Research Report, ER-1, Department of Commerce, December 1978. Moving averages tend to be a staple of commodity and stock market technical analysis as well as seasonal adjustment. For example, see Frank Hochheimer, "Moving Averages: An Explanation and Computerized Testing of Simple, Linear, and Exponentially Smoothed Moving Averages," in *Technical Analysis in Commodities,* P. J. Kaufman, ed., New York: John Wiley & Sons, 1980, 39–51.

3. The Spencer moving average was used in the Census II X-9 version of the seasonal adjustment program in the X-11 version of the program, however, the Spencer curve was replaced with a Henderson curve that can be a 5- 9- 13- or 23-term moving average).

4. Sidney Alexander, "Rate of Change Approaches to Forecasting—Diffusion Indexes and First Differences," *Economic Journal,* June 1958, 288–301.

5. This is based on George R. Arrington, "Building a Variable-Length Moving Average," *Technical Analysis of Stocks and Commodities,* June 1991, 18–23.

6. This calculation is described in Victor Zarnowitz and Geoffrey H. Moore, "Sequential Signals of Recession and Recovery," *Journal of Business,* Vol. 55, No. 1 (January 1982), 62.

7. Shirley Kallek, "An Overview of the Objections and Framework of Seasonal Adjustment," *Seasonal Analysis of Economic Time Series,* Economic Research Report, ER-1, Department of Commerce, December 1978, 3–25.

8. A. B. Larson, "The Hog Cycle as Harmonic Motion," *Journal of Farm Economics,* Vol. 46 (May 1964), 357–386; Gordon C. Rausser and Thomas F. Cargill, "The Existence of Broiler Cycles: An Application of Spectral Analysis," *American Journal of Agricultural Economics,* Vol. 50 (1970), 109–121; and F. V. Waugh and M. M. Miller, "Fish Cycles: A Harmonic Analysis," *American Journal of Agricultural Economics,* Vol. 52 (August 1970), 422–430.

9. This is based on a method discussed in Frederick E. Croxton and Dudley J. Cowden, *Applied General Statistics,* New York: Prentice-Hall, 1942, 555–559.

10. An early application of this method to business cycle analysis is found in C. W. J. Granger and M. Hatanaka, *Spectral Analysis of Economic Time Series,* Princeton, NJ: Princeton University Press, 1964. For an introductory article on the method, see William T. Taylor, "Leading Indicators from Fourier Spectral Analysis," *Technical Analysis of Stock and Commodities,* April 1985, 5–10. Also, the following article is highly recommended: Hung Chan and Jack Hayya, "Spectral Analysis in Business Forecasting," *Decision Sciences,* Vol. 7, 137–151. Finally, the following is another useful article: O. Brandes, J. Farley, M. Hinich, and U. Zackrisson, "The Time Domain and the Frequency Domain in Time Series Analysis," *Swedish Journal of Economics,* 1968, 25–42.

11. C. W. J. Granger and M. Hatanaka, *Spectral Analysis of Economic Time Series,* Princeton, NJ: Princeton University Press, 1964, 61. However, an argument is made that the number of observations available in most economic time series should not hinder the economist from

applying spectral analysis. See Marc Nerlove, "Spectral Analysis of Seasonal Adjustment Procedures," *Econometrica,* Vol. 32, No. 3 (July 1964), reprinted in *Selected Readings in Econometrics from Econometrica,* John W. Hooper and Marc Nerlove, eds., Cambridge, MA: MIT Press, 1970, 442–471.

12. Simone Clemhout and Salih N. Neftçi, "Policy Evaluation of Housing Cyclicality: A Spectral Analysis," *Review of Economics and Statistics,* August 1981, 385–394. Contrary to this finding, Rosen found an average 3½-year cycle existed in housing starts by using simple inspection (time-oriented) methods. See Kenneth T. Rosen, *Affordable Housing: New Policies for the Housing and Mortgage Markets.* Cambridge, MA: Ballinger Publishing Co., 1984.

13. The Bartels test is described in Anthony F. Herbst, *Analyzing and Forecasting Futures Prices,* New York: John Wiley & Sons, 1992; C. E. Armstrong, "Cycle Analysis—A Case Study Part 25: Testing Cycles for Statistical Significance," *Cycles,* October 1973, 231-235.

14. The Foundation for the Study of Cycles was founded by Edward R. Dewey and later carried on by Gertrude Shirk, Jeffrey Horovitz, and Richard Mogey. For information about the Foundation and/or its research, contact them at 900 W. Valley Road, Suite 502, Wayne, PA 19087. Wesley C. Mitchell, the first research director of the National Bureau of Economic Research, was once a director of the Foundation as well. The Foundation attempts to analyze and collect information on cycles in all fields. See Edward R. Dewey, *Cycles: Selected Writings,* Irvine, CA: Foundation for the Study of Cycles,

15. "The Problem of Secular Trend," *Review of Economic Statistics,* October 15, 1934.

16. Geoffrey H. Moore, "Measuring Recessions," reprinted in *Business Cycle Indicators, Vol. 1,* Princeton, NJ: Princeton University Press, 1961, 120–161.

17. An interesting example of arguing from a cyclical perspective can be found in R. Alton Gilbert and Mack Ott, "Why the Big Rise in Business Loans at Banks Last Year?" *Review,* Federal Reserve Bank of St. Louis, March 1985, 5–13. The authors use recovery patterns to argue visually that business loans were increasing faster than historical recovery patterns suggested were normal. They proceed to compare recovery patterns for nominal GNP with the current cycle and rule this out as a cause of faster growth in business loans since the GNP growth pattern was rather consistent with past experience. While the authors do not resort to statistical methods to test their claim, this approach more than adequately answered the question: Is the faster-than-normal expansion in business loans a result of a faster-than-normal business expansion?

18. Although this case is presented as an example, the fact of the matter is that the median is a better gauge of the central tendency here.

19. Robert L. McLaughlin, "A Model of an Average Recession and Recovery," *Journal of Forecasting,* Vol. 1-1 (1982), 55–65.

20. Robert L. McLaughlin, "The Strawman," *Micrometrics,* a supplement to *Turning Points* July 9, 1982.

21. Richard C. Katz, "Time Quartile Analysis: A Forecasting Technique," *Journal of Portfolio Management,* Winter 1977, 65–70.

22. Arthur F. Burns and Wesley C. Mitchell, *Measuring Business Cycles,* New York: NBER, 1946.

23. This concept is similar to a sign function, which takes on three values, $+1$, 0, or -1.

24. *Cyclical Analysis of Time Series: Selected Procedures and Computer Programs,* New York: NBER, 1971.

25. E. Haywood, "The Deviation Cycle: A New Index of the Australian Business Cycle 1950–73," *Australia Economic Review,* Fourth Quarter, 1973, 31–39. The conceptual argument for dating the business cycle in "cycle-sensitive" measures is a throwback to an earlier idea of

segmenting the overall cycle into its trend, cycle, seasonal, and irregular components. To the extent that some sectors of the economy are more or less cyclical, or more or less secular, this allows sectors to be segmented along those lines. This cycle-sensitive concept has been employed over the years, and the argument for it is summarized in Geoffrey H. Moore, *Leading Indicators for the 1990s*, Homewood, IL: Dow Jones-Irwin, 1990.

26. Wesley Clair Mitchell, *Business Cycles and Their Causes*, Philadelphia: Porcupine Press, 1989 (originally published 1941), 7.

27. The Organization for European Cooperation and Development (OECD), a group with 24 member countries, has decided to use industrial production as the sole series to determine the reference cycle in its member countries. For an interesting account of the difficulties in selecting a consistent methodology for multicountry cyclical analysis, see Benoit Reynard and John Dryden, "Cyclical Analysis and Leading Indicators—The OECD Experience," Paper presented at the 17th CIRET Conference, Vienna, Austria, September 11–14, 1985.

28. See, for example, Geoffrey H. Moore, "What is a Recession?" in *Business Cycles, Inflation, and Forecasting*, Cambridge, MA: Ballinger Publishing Co., 1980, 13–19; or, Robert E. Hall, "The Business Cycle Dating Process," *NBER Reporter*, Winter 1991/92, 1–3. In dating the 1990 recession peak, for example, nonagricultural employment less Census workers was used as a bellwether series to date the peak, in addition to the total measure of employment. The issue was that short-term Census Bureau employment for the decennial Census inflated the payroll data during the Census-taking period and depressed the data thereafter. Consequently, it would have been inappropriate to date the peak in the employment series without accounting for this special factor. It should be recalled that the definition of the turning point generally excludes strikes and other special factors.

29. One such critic of the selection process was George W. Cloos, "How Good Are the National Bureau's Reference Dates?" *Journal of Business*, Vol. 36, No. 1 (January 1963), 14–32.

30. Julius Shiskin, "The Changing Business Cycle," *New York Times*, December 1, 1974, Section 3, 12.

31. *The Business Cycle in a Changing World*, New York: NBER, 1969, 37.

32. See, for example, Nicholas M. Kiefer, "Economic Duration Data and Hazard Functions," *Journal of Economic Literature*, Vol. XXVI (June 1988), 649–679. Other articles that illustrate the use of probability models for estimating duration of a change in one's unemployment status include Stephen Nickell, "Estimating the Probability of Leaving Unemployment," *Econometrica*, Vol. 47, No. 5 (September 1979), 1249–1266; and Tony Lancaster, "Econometric Methods for the Duration of Unemployment," *Econometrica*, Vol. 47, No. 4 (July 1979), 939–956.

33. Frederick R. Macauley, *The Smoothing of Time Series*, New York: NBER, 1931.

34. For a further discussion of this technique, see Frederick E. Croxton and Dudley J. Cowden, *Applied General Statistics*, New York: Prentice-Hall, New York, 1942. Also see Leroy M. Piser, "The Adjustment of Time Data for the Influence of Easter," *Journal of the American Statistical Association*, Vol. XXIX (June 1934), 190–191.

35. The discussion of the computer program is based on Julius Shiskin, Allan H. Young, and John C. Musgrave, *The X-11 Variant of the Census Method II Seasonal Adjustment Program*, Technical Paper No. 15, Bureau of the Census, February 1967. For a description of the earlier Census Method II program, see Julius Shiskin, "Electronic Computers and Business Indicators," *Journal of Business*, October 1957, and reprinted in *Business Cycle Indicators: Vol. 1. Contributions to the Analysis of Current Business Conditions*, Geoffrey H. Moore, ed., Princeton, NJ: Princeton University Press, 1961, 517–597. An excellent description of the Census program is also found in Spyros Makridakis and Steven C. Wheelwright, *Forecasting Methods and Applications*, New York: John Wiley & Sons, 1978. For application of the

seasonal adjustment routine with special reference to problems associated with the money supply, see Alfred Broaddus and Timothy Q. Cook, "Some Factors Affecting Short-Run Growth Rates of the Money Supply," *Economic Review*, Federal Reserve Bank of Richmond, Vol. 63, No. 6 (November/December 1977), 2–18; and Thomas A. Lawler, "Seasonal Adjustment of the Money Stock: Problems and Policy Implications," *Economic Review*, Federal Reserve Bank of Richmond, Vol. 63, No. 6 (November/December 1977), 19–27.

36. The following were actual trading day prior weights used in the retail sales data for 1976: Sundays sales, 0.379; Monday sales, 0.914; Tuesday sales, 1.048; Wednesday sales, 0.963; Thursday sales, 1.054; Friday sales, 1.347; and Saturday sales, 1.294.

37. In particular, see the appendix to Estela Bee Dagum, "Comments on 'A Survey and Comparative Analysis of Various Methods of Seasonal Adjustment,'" by John Kuiper, in *Seasonal Analysis of Economic Time Series*, Economic Research Report, ER-1, Bureau of the Census, December 1978, 85–92.

38. A detailed discussion of this method is beyond the scope of this book. However, the interested reader should see William S. Cleveland, Douglas M. Dunn, and Irma J. Terpenning, "SABL: A Resistant Seasonal Adjustment Procedure with Graphical Methods for Interpretation and Diagnosis," in *Seasonal Analysis of Economic Time Series*, Economic Research Report, ER-1, Bureau of the Census, December 1978, 201–236. A less technical discussion is found in Hans Levenbach and James P. Cleary, *The Beginning Forecaster: The Forecasting Process through Data Analysis*, Lifetime Leading Publications, Belmont, CA, 1981, Chapter 19.

39. John Kuiper, "A Survey and Comparative Analysis of Various Methods of Seasonal Adjustment," in *Seasonal Analysis of Economic Time Series*, Economic Research Report, ER-1, Bureau of the Census, December 1978, 59–76.

40. Leroy M. Piser, "A Method of Calculating Weekly Seasonal Indexes," *Journal of the American Statistical Association*, Vol. XXXVII (September 1932), 307–309. This Piser method is also clearly demonstrated in Croxton and Cowden, *Applied General Statistics*, New York: Prentice-Hall, 1942, 528–538.

41. Louis Zeller, "Weekly Seasonal Adjustment Program for the IBM S/360 Computer," manuscript, Board of Governors of the Federal Reserve System, February 15, 1972.

42. For a wonderful and generally ignored investigation of the impact of abnormal weather on store sales, see Fabian Linden, "Weather in Business," *Conference Board Business Record*. Vol. 16 (1959), 90–94, 101; and Fabian Linden, "Consumer Markets: Merchandising Weather," *Conference Board Business Record*. Vol. 19, No. 6 (1962), 15–16.

43. W. J. Maunder, *The Uncertainty Business*, Methuen & Co., London, 1986. Also see W. J. Maunder, "National Economic Indicators: The Importance of the Weather," in *Essays in Honour of Ronald Lister*, L. D. B. Heenan and G. W. Kearsley, eds., Dunedin, New Zealand: University of Tago, 1982, 41–60. A final article worth reading is W. J. Maunder, "Weekly Weather and Economic Activities on a National Scale: An Example Using United States Retail Trade Data," *Weather*, Vol. 28 (1973), 2–18.

44. "The drought afflicting California is starting to send an uneasy rumble through the municipal bond market . . ." was the theme of a 1990 story: "Drought May Hurt Some California Bonds," *New York Times*, November 1, 1990, D-1.

45. For discussion of the permanent nature of shocks to the economy—a view held by the real business cycle school, see Mark Rush, "Real Business Cycles," *Economic Review*, Federal Reserve Bank of Kansas City, February 1987, 20–32.

46. Arthur F. Burns, *The Business Cycle in a Changing World*, New York: NBER, 1969.

47. Ibid., p. 6. Very short-term cycles in business activity exist even on a weekly basis and they are not necessarily location dependent. For example, a major U.S. air freight carrier has observed a *worldwide* weekly freight pattern. Tuesdays are the weekly low for activity,

whereas Saturdays are the weekly peak in business. Moreover, as long as economies are linked, the movable holidays in one country could impact another through the timing of the trade flow. The movable holiday Chinese New Year, which is tied to a lunar cycle, can impact U.S. imports in given months, ountries observing the holiday make a mad dash to ship goods out before the holiday and then take a 10- to 14-day holiday when business virtually comes to a halt. But over long periods of time, these seasonal shifts may wash out in the data, and hence, the presence of "seasonal unit roots" (unstable seasonal patterns) may be rejected. The rejection of seasonal unit roots may not necessarily imply the absence of a seasonal effect from this type of shift.

48. See Robert B. Barsky, and Jeffrey A. Miron, "The Seasonal Cycle and the Business Cycle," *Journal of Political Economy,* Vol. 97, No. 3 (1989), 503–534.

49. See Jeffrey A. Miron, "The Economics of Seasonal Cycles," National Bureau of Economic Research, Working Paper No. 3522, November 1990.

50. See three papers by J. J. Beaulieu and J. A. Miron: (1) "Seasonal Unit Roots in Aggregate U.S. Data," unpublished manuscript, Boston University, January 1991; (2) "A Cross-Country Comparison of Seasonal Cycles and Business Cycles," National Bureau of Economic Research, Working Paper No. 3459, October 1990; (3) "The Seasonal Cycle in U.S. Manufacturing," National Bureau of Economic Research, Working Paper No. 3450, September 1990.

51. Barsky and Miron (1989), 523.

52. Easter can fall between late March and late April.

53. See Robert E. Hall, *Booms and Recessions in a Noisy Economy,* New Haven, CT: Yale University Press, 1991. Hall observed: "[T]racking down noise has evolved into a major research program involving dozens of macroeconomists. It cannot be separated from the topic of propagation mechanisms, because noise is the residual in a structural equation" (p. 2). He also acknowledged that some of the most important moving forces within aggregate economic activity are *not* fundamental.

54. Ibid.

55. See John Hoagland, Lee Buddress, and Michael Heberling, "The Pyramid Power of Purchases," unpublished manuscript, East Lansing: Michigan State University, April 1990.

56. See Hal Mather, *How to Really Manage Inventories.* New York: McGraw-Hill, 1984.

57. Although inadequate inventory management may have been a factor in past business cycles, it is less of an issue today with a *just-in-time* (JIT) inventory goal or policy. In a private conversation with Hal Mather, he observed that what he wrote in 1984 was far less true of companies in the 1990s. A measure of the effectiveness of JIT is reflected in the National Association of Purchasing Management's lead-time statistic, which was relatively trendless into and during the 1990 recession. However, notwithstanding today's better inventory management systems, the order/purchasing/shipment cycle can still be a powerful force in the economy. For example, the automotive industry can quickly raise or cut their production by 30% to 40% over a three-month period, which can create major havoc with the purchasing and supplier process.

58. To some extent, these national average temperature and precipitation data are flawed for this purpose. These data are really weighted by 48 contiguous states and are not population weighted, which would make far more economic sense. Unfortunately, the effort to produce population-weighted data was abandoned by the government in a budget cutback. Additionally, the insured loss data indirectly capture some of the adverse weather effects—although many caveats should be noted: (1) These data do not include uninsured losses, and flood damage included represents a relatively small percentage of the population having that type of insurance coverage. (2) The insurance data also include man-made disasters such as the

1967 riots. Hence, while it may be useful to account for man-made disasters in this study, the purview of this study extends to other types of "shocks."

59. Separately, two other tests were applied. First, a probit model was estimated to measure whether the precipitation and temperature data by month were helpful in explaining the business or growth cycle turning point date. By and large, those results were not encouraging.

60. See John R. Herman and Richard A. Goldberg; *Sun, Weather, and Climate,* Mineola, NY: Dover Publications, 1985.

61. Ibid., 269.

62. Ibid., 270.

63. Ibid., 269.

64. For an interesting account of Jevons's work, see Mary S. Morgan, *The History of Econometric Ideas,* New York: Cambridge University Press, 1990.

65. James Arthur Estey, *Business Cycles: Their Nature, Cause, and Control,* (3rd ed.), Englewood Cliffs, NJ: Prentice-Hall, 1956, 175.

66. See, for example, Lovell's summary of the statistical flaw in Jevons's analysis. He wrote that the coincidence that Jevons had found between a monthly series on bankruptcies (which was used to determine the cycle in business activity) and sunspot activity was "regrettable" since the bankruptcy data was interrupted between 1785 and 1790. "If he had filled in the gap in his data by consulting issues of *Gentleman's Magazine* or the *London Chronicle* for those years, it seems certain" that his conclusion would have been different. See Michael Lovell, *Macroeconomics: Measurement, Theory, and Policy,* New York: John Wiley & Sons, 1975, 400.

67. See, for example, C. Aziariadis and R. Guesnerie, "Sunspots and Cycles," *Review of Economic Studies,* Vol. LIII (1986), 725–737. Aziariadis and Guesnerie wrote: "[O]ne may view 'sunspots' as a convenient label for a host of psychological factors (animals spirits, fears, Bayesian learning theories, etc.) that are unrelated to the preferences, endowment or production set of any individual, and yet come to influence the forecasts and actions of economic decision-makers" (p. 725).

68. See Michael Zahorchak, *Climate: The Key to Understanding Business Cycles,* Linden, NJ: Tide Press, 1983.

69. Ibid., 195.

70. See Edward R. Dewey, "Economic and Sociological Phenomena Related to Solar Activity and Influences," *Cycles,* September 1968, and reprinted May/June 1990, 151–162.

71. Ibid., 151.

72. Shirley Kallek, "An Overview of the Objectives and Framework of Seasonal Adjustment" *Seasonal Analysis of Economic Time Series,* Arnold Zellner, ed., U.S. Department of Commerce, December, 1978, 4–5.

73. Joseph Schumpeter, *History of Economic Analysis,* New York: Oxford University Press, 1954.

74. For a discussion of the theory, also see T. W. Swan, "Economic Growth and Capital Accumulation," *The Economic Record,* Vol. 32 (November 1956), 334–343, reprinted in *Macroeconomic Theory: Selected Readings,* Harold R. Williams and John D. Huffnagle, eds., Englewood Cliffs, NJ: Prentice-Hall, 1969, 477–486.

75. See Alvin H. Hansen, *Business Cycles and National Income,* New York: W.W. Norton, 1964, 557–558.

76. Porter H. Sutro devised this long-leading indicator. A discussion of the Sutro index is found in Alfred L. Malabre, Jr., "The Outlook—Will a Recession Arrive Along with Elections?" *The Wall Street Journal,* December 19, 1983, 1.

77. Wallace H. Duncan, "Business Cycles—A New Leading Indicator," *Review,* Federal Reserve Bank of Dallas, March 1977, 1–6. Also see Wallace H. Duncan, "Cyclical Changes in the Composition of Output: A Tool for Forecasting the National Economy," *Business Economics,* January 1982, 21–23.

78. Galen G. Blomster, "The 'Naive, Yield Curve Model,'" Northwestern National Bank of Minneapolis, November 5, 1981. The relationship estimated between 1970 and 1991 was PCHYA (Real Final Sales) = 0.57737 + 1.04280 × (AAA Corporate Bond Yield minus Three − Month Treasury Bill Rate, Coupon Equivalent) Where PCHYA (Real Final Sales) is the year-over-year percentage change in real final sales. This statistical relationship explained 64% of the fluctuation in the dependent variable.

79. Robert L. McLaughlin, "The Paired Index as a Leading Indicator," *Proceedings of the American Statistical Association, Business and Economic Statistics Section,* 1970, 7–14.

80. Arthur F. Burns, "New Facts on Business Cycles," reprinted in *Business Cycle Indicators, Vol. 1,* Geoffrey H. Moore, ed., New York: NBER, 1961, 36.

81. Alvin H. Hansen, *Business Cycles and National Income,* New York: W. W. Norton, 1964, 581–583. Also see Geoffrey H. Moore, "The Analysis of Economic Indicators," in *Business Cycles, Inflation, and Forecasting,* Ballinger Publishing Co., 1980, 301–319. A discussion of the ABC curves also can be found in Edwin Frickey, "Revision of the Index of General Business Conditions," *Review of Economic Statistics,* May 1932, 80–87. For an account of the development of the Commerce Department's involvement in cyclical indicators, see Joseph W. Duncan and William C. Shelton, *Revolution in United States Government Statistics: 1926–1976,* U.S. Department of Commerce, October 1978, 197–200.

82. Thomas Sargent and Christopher Sims, "Business Cycle Modeling without Pretending to Have Too Much *A Priori* Economic Theory," in *New Methods in Business Cycle Research: Proceedings from a Conference,* Federal Reserve Bank of Minneapolis, October 1977, 45–110.

83. Milton Friedman, "Wesley C. Mitchell as an Economic Theorist," *Journal of Political Economy,* December 1950, 465–493.

84. Numerous models have been developed to show the leading indicators as an expectational variable, which affects the economic process it leads. For example, see Walter W. Ebanks, "Economic Indicator Forecasting: A Formal Treatment," *American Statistical Association Proceedings of the Business and Economics Division,* 1978, 213–219. Many of the survey-based leading indicators have been used in models of the economy, such as W. Naggl, "The Anticipations Model: A Short-Term Forecasting Model Based on Anticipations Data," in *Leading Indicators and Business Cycle Surveys,* Karl H. Oppenlander and G. Poser, eds., Aldershot, England: Gower, 1984, 161–192. For an overview of the expectational theories, see J. T. Brimer, "The Behavioral Approach to Expectations," Paper presented at the 17th CIRET Conference, Vienna, Austria, September 11–14, 1985.

85. Geoffrey H. Moore, "Generating Leading Indicators from Lagging Indicators," *Western Economic Journal,* June 1969, 137–144. For an earlier paper on this idea, see John H. Merriam, "New Economic Indicators," *Western Economic Journal,* June 1968, 195–204. Other useful references include Charles J. Haulk, "Lagging Indicators: Guide to the Future?" *Economic Review,* Federal Reserve Bank of Atlanta, May/June 1978, 55–56; and John P. Cullity, "Current Research on Lagging Indicators in Major Industrial Countries," unpublished manuscript, Center for International Business Cycle Research, September 5, 1980.

86. This simple framework is based on Paul J. Kozlowski, *A Local Index of Leading Indicators: Construction, Uses, and Limitations,* Kalamazoo, MI: W. E. Upjohn Institute for Employment Research, October 1977.

87. For example, a composite index for the chemical industry cycle provides a better gauge of the cyclical characteristics of the industry than any single measure. The composite indicator is one

way to summarize disparate information and minimize the noise in the statistical indicators. See M. P. Niemira, "Developing Industry Leading Economic Indicators," *Business Economics,* Vol. XVII, No. 1 (January 1982), 5–16.

88. See Appendix A, "Technical Notes on Amplitude-Adjusted General Indexes, Adjusted Rates of Change, and Diffusion Indexes," in Julius Shiskin, *Signals of Recession and Recovery,* New York: NBER, 1961.

89. Geoffrey H. Moore and Julius Shiskin, *Indicators of Business Expansions and Contractions,* New York: NBER, 1967.

90. This additional weighting scheme once used by the Commerce Department may not add anything to the predictive power of the leading indicators according to a study by Auerbach. He concluded, "[T]he extensive effort devoted to assigning and updating weights for the series included has essentially no effect on the resulting index; it is indistinguishable from one with equal weights." Alan J. Auerbach, "The Index of Leading Indicators: 'Measurement without Theory,' Thirty-Five Years Later," *Review of Economics and Statistics,* Vol. LXIV, No. 4 (November 1982), 594.

91. Julius Shiskin, "Reverse Trend Adjustment of Leading Indicators," *Review of Economics and Statistics,* Vol. 49 (1967), 45–49.

92. This method of using correlations has been proposed by R. A. Holmes, "Leading Indicators of Industrial Employment in British Columbia," *International Journal of Forecasting,* Vol. 2., No. 1 (1986), 87–100. Other applications of this technique include the Paine-Webber Leading Indicator of Automobile Sales.

93. Michael P. Niemira and Giela T. Fredman, "An Evaluation of the Composite Index of Leading Indicators for Signaling Turning Points in Business and Growth Cycles," *Business Economics,* October 1991, 49–55.

94. Charlotte Boschan and Walter W. Ebanks, "The Phase-Average Trend: A New Way of Measuring Economic Growth," *Proceedings of the Business and Economic Statistics Section,* American Statistical Association, 1978, 332. Another description of the method is found in Philip A. Klein and Geoffrey H. Moore, *Monitoring Growth Cycles in Market-Oriented Countries: Developing and Using International Economic Indicators,* Cambridge, MA: Ballinger Publishing Co., 1985, 32.

95. Ilse Mintz, *Dating Postwar Business Cycles: Methods and Their Application to Western Germany, 1950–67,* New York: NBER, 1969, 15–20. Milton Friedman has noted that the use of percentage changes over deviations from trend is preferred since it requires no decision about the type of trend present in the data. See Milton Friedman, "The Lag in Effect of Monetary Policy," *Journal of Political Economy,* Vol. 69 (October 1961), 447–466. As previously noted, this was also the conclusion of Burns and Mitchell.

96. Bryon Higgins, "Monetary Growth and Business Cycles: The Relationship between Monetary Decelerations and Recessions," *Economic Review,* Federal Reserve Bank of Kansas City, April 1979, 12–23. Also see William Poole, "The Relationship of Monetary Decelerations to Business Cycle Peaks: Another Look at the Evidence," *Journal of Finance,* Vol. XXX (June 1975), 697–712.

97. Stephen Beveridge and Charles R. Nelson, "A New Approach to Decomposition of Economic Time Series into Permanent and Transitory Components with Particular Attention to the Measurement of the 'Business Cycle,'" *Journal of Monetary Economics,* Vol. 7 (1981), 151–174.

98. Ibid., 167.

99. Beatrice N. Vaccara and Victor Zarnowitz, "How Good Are the Leading Indicators?" *1977 Proceedings of the Business and Economic Statistics Section,* American Statistical Association, 1977.

100. Ibid., 50.

101. Geoffrey H. Moore, "Growth Cycles: A New-Old Concept," in *Business Cycles, Inflation, and Forecasting* (2nd ed.), Cambridge, MA: Ballinger Publishing Co., 61–64.

102. For a brief review of some interpretation rules, see Howard Keen, Jr., "Leading Economic Indicators Can Be Misleading, Study Shows," *Journal of Business Forecasting,* Winter 1983–1984, 13–14. Keen also considers a two-month change rule with negative and decelerating growth to be a signal of a recession. He concluded that this rule had the best performance among a few simple rules he tested.

103. Evan F. Koenig and Kenneth M. Emery, "Misleading Indicators? Using the Composite Leading Indicators to Predict Cyclical Turning Points," *Economic Review,* Federal Reserve Bank of Dallas, July 1991, 1–14.

104. Edgar Fiedler, "Long-Lead and Short-Lead Indexes of Business Indicators," *Proceedings from the Business and Economics Section,* American Statistical Association, 1961, 287–301. Another attempt to update the Fiedler work for the United States was done by Jason Benderly and Jeffrey A. Shapiro, "Short-Term versus Long-Term Leading Indicators and Implications for the Inflation Outlook," unpublished manuscript, Washington Analysis Corporation, April 25, 1979. More recently, CIBCR took up this idea and compiled a long- and short-term leading indicator of the business cycle, which is published monthly in the *Survey of Current Business.*

105. Leo Barnes, "Business Forecasting with Higher Order Indicators—A Neglected Art," *Business Economics,* September 1980, 22–31.

106. Victor Zarnowitz and Geoffrey H. Moore, "Sequential Signals of Recession and Recovery," *Journal of Business,* Vol. 55, No. 1 (January 1982), 57–85, and reprinted in Geoffrey H. Moore, *Business Cycles, Inflation, and Forecasting,* (2nd ed.), Ballinger Publishing Co., Cambridge, MA, 23–60. Also see Geoffrey H. Moore, "Recession/Recovery: An Early Warning System," *Morgan Guaranty Survey,* November 1982, 11–14; Michael P. Niemira, "Sequential Signals of Recession and Recovery: Revisited," *Business Economics,* January 1983, 51–53.

107. Geoffrey H. Moore, "Signals of Recession," *Recession-Recovery Watch,* Vol. 12, No. 3 (August 1990), 1–7.

108. Robert F. Deitch, "Anticipating Growth Recessions and Recoveries: A New Sequential Signalling System," Paper presented at the Fifth International Symposium on Forecasting, June 11, 1985.

109. A discussion of this method can be found in David L. Hurwood, Elliot S. Grossman, and Earl L. Bailey, *Sales Forecasting,* Conference Board, Report No. 730, 1978, 63–67. See also Dale W. Sommer, "Cycle Forecasting Spots Trends," *Industry Week,* April 25, 1977, 71–75.

110. Salih N. Neftçi, "Optimal Prediction of Cyclical Downturns," *Journal of Economic Dynamics and Control,* 1982, 225–241. An aspect of this idea is looked at further in Salih Neftçi, "Are Economic Time Series Asymmetric over the Business Cycle?" *Journal of Political Economy,* Vol. 92, No. 2 (1984), 307–328. An application of the method to several leading indicators is found in Carl J. Palash and Lawrence J. Radecki, "Using Monetary and Financial Variables to Predict Cyclical Downturns," *Federal Reserve Bank of New York Quarterly Review,* Summer 1985, 36–45. A related paper by William E. Wecker, "Predicting the Turning Points of a Time Series," *Journal of Business,* Vol. 79, No. 1, (1979), 35–50, takes a different approach from Neftçi's though Wecker also uses probability distributions in determining turning points.

111. John Hicks, *A Contribution to the Theory of the Trade Cycle,* Oxford: Clarendon Press, 1950.

112. John Maynard Keynes, *The General Theory of Employment, Interest and Money,* London: Macmillan, 1936.

113. An example of this approach applied to the international growth cycle is found in Michael P. Niemira, "An International Application of Neftçi's Probability Approach for Signaling Growth Recessions and Recoveries Using Turning Point Indicators," in *Leading Economic Indicators: New Approaches and Forecasting Records*, Kajal Lahiri and Geoffrey H. Moore, eds., Cambridge University Press, New York, 1991, 91–108.

114. J. Huston McCulloch, "The Monte Carlo Cycle in Business Activity," *Economic Inquiry*, Vol. 13, No. 3 (September 1975), 303–321.

115. Francis X. Diebold and Glenn D. Rudebusch, "Turning Point Prediction with the Composite Leading Index: An Ex Ante Analysis," in *Leading Economic Indicators: New Approaches and Forecasting Records*, Kajal Lahiri and Geoffrey H. Moore, eds., New York: Cambridge University Press, 1991, 231–256.

116. Hamilton, who has written extensively on this subject, has generalized the Neftçi framework for *n* different regimes and shows that Neftçi's application is a special case. See James D. Hamilton, "Analysis of Time Series Subject to Changes in Regime," *Journal of Econometrics*, Vol. 45 (1990), 39–70; James D. Hamilton, "A New Approach to the Economic Analysis of Nonstationary Time Series and the Business Cycle," *Econometrica*, Vol. 57 (March 1990), 357–384; James D. Hamilton, "Rational-Expectations Econometric Analysis of Changes in Regime," *Journal of Economic Dynamics and Control*, Vol. 12 (1988), 385–423. Also see an application of this technique for calling turning points in the foreign exchange market, Charles Engel and James D. Hamilton, "Long Swings in the Dollar: Are They in the Data and Do Markets Know It?" *American Economic Review*, Vol. 80, No. 4 (September 1990), 689–713.

117. G. W. Brier, "Verification of Forecasts Expressed in Terms of Probability," *Monthly Weather Review*, Vol. 75 (1950), 1–3.

118. F. X. Diebold and G. D. Rudebusch, "Scoring the Leading Indicators," *Journal of Business*, Vol. 62 (1989), 369–391. Also see Diebold and Rudebusch, "Turning Point Prediction," ibid.

119. Arthur F. Burns, "New Facts on Business Cycles," in *The Business Cycle in a Changing World*, New York: NBER, 1969, 54–100.

120. Geoffrey H. Moore, "Diffusion Indexes, Rates of Change, and Forecasting," in *Business Cycle Indicators, Vol. 1*, Geoffrey H. Moore, ed., New York: NBER, 1961, 287.

121. Bert G. Hickman, "Diffusion, Acceleration and Business Cycles," in *Business Fluctuations, Growth, and Economic Stabilization: A Reader*, John J. Clark and Morris Cohen, eds., New York: Random House, 1963, 346, reprinted from *American Economic Review*, Vol. XLIX, No. 4 (September 1959).

122. See Bert G. Hickman, *Growth and Stability of the Postwar Economy*, Washington, DC: Brookings Institution, 1960, 283–285.

123. Morton Ehrlich, "Using the Conference Board's Diffusion Indexes," *Conference Board Record*, July 1966, 12–15.

124. Leo B. Shohan, *The Conference Board's New Diffusion Indexes*, New York: National Industrial Conference Board, 1963.

125. Michael C. Lovell, *Macroeconomics: Measurement, Theory, and Policy*, New York: John Wiley & Sons, 1975, 397.

126. Shohan, ibid., 21.

127. Wilkie W. Chaffin and Wayne K. Talley, "Diffusion Indexes and Indifference Bands," *Proceedings of the American Statistical Association* (Business and Economics Division), 1974, 408–411.

128. Ibid., 408.

129. Wilkie W. Chaffin and Wayne K. Talley, "Diffusion Indexes and a Statistical Test for Predicting Turning Points in Business Cycles," unpublished manuscript, 1986.

130. Leonall C. Anderson, "A Method of Using Diffusion Indexes to Indicate the Direction of National Economic Activity," *Proceedings of the American Statistical Association*, 1966, 424–434.

131. George W. Ladd, "Linear Probability Functions and Discriminant Functions," *Econometrica*, Vol. 34, No. 4 (October 1966), 873–885. Arthur Goldberger has raised two problems with using linear regression formulations for discriminant analysis: (1) the error term does not have a constant variance, and (2) the independent variable may exceed one or be less than zero while probabilities are restricted to be within zero and one. Goldberger suggests alternatives to these problems. In particular, he suggests the use of probit analysis, which is a functional form limited to the range of probabilities. Arthur Goldberger, *Econometric Theory*, New York: John Wiley and Sons, 1964, 249.

132. E. K. Strong, Jr., "An Interest Test for Personnel Managers," *Journal of Personnel Research*, Vol. 5 (1927).

133. George England, *Development and Use of Weighted Application Blanks*, Dubuque, IA: Wm. C. Brown Co., 1961.

134. A brief discussion of the early use of this technique is found in Frederick E. Croxton and Dudley J. Cowden, *Applied General Statistics*, New York: Prentice-Hall, 1942, 820–822.

135. This particular scoresheet was first derived by Julius Shiskin, "The 1961–69 Economic Expansion in the United States: The Statistical Record," *Business Conditions Digest*, Bureau of the Census, January 1970. Also see Julius Shiskin and Leonard H. Lempert, "Indicator Forecasting," in *Methods and Techniques of Business Forecasting*, William F. Butler, Robert A. Kavesh, and Robert B. Platt eds., Englewood Cliffs, NJ: Prentice-Hall, 1974, 37–75.

136. *Statistical Indicator Reports*, April 1, 1981. Special thanks to Leonard Lempert for providing selected issues of *Statistical Indicator Reports*.

137. Werner H. Strigel, "The Figure and Pulse of the Economy," in *In Search of Economic Indicators*, Werner H. Strigel, ed., New York: Springer-Verlag, 1977, 22.

138. George Katona, "Expectations in Economics," in *Expectations and the Economy*, Joint Economic Committee, U.S. Congress, December 11, 1981, 27.

139. Probably the classic discussion of this technique as applied to business cycle indicators is C. W. J. Granger and M. Hatanaka, *Spectral Analysis of Economic Time Series*, Princeton, NJ: Princeton University Press, 1964. Other representative articles using cross-spectral analysis include Thomas J. Sargent, "Interest Rates in the 1950s," *The Review of Economics and Statistics*, Vol. 50 (May 1968), 164–172; G. Gudmundsson, "Time-series Analysis of Imports, Exports and Other Economic Variables," *Journal of the Royal Statistical Society*, Vol. 134 (1971), 383–412; Saul H. Hymans, "On the Use of Leading Indictors to Predict Cyclical Turning Points," *Brookings Papers on Economic Activity*, No. 2, 1973, 339–375. The Hymans article is particularly interesting in his use of cross-spectral analysis to form a composite leading indicator where the frequencies (wave lengths) are weighted by their power spectra and each leading indicator component also is entered with its highest lead time (as determined by the phase statistic) and then weighted by the square root of its coherence. For an application to commodity price cycles, see Walter C. Labys and C. W. J. Granger, *Speculation, Hedging and Commodity Price Forecasts*, Lexington, MA: D. C. Heath, 1970. Granger has contributed a lot of articles using this method applied to everything from interest rates to stock prices.

140. John C. Hause, "Spectral Analysis and the Detection of Lead-Lag Relations," *The American Economic Review*, Vol. 61 (1971), 213–217.

141. "Changes in the Character of the U.S. Business Cycle," *Review of Radical Political Economics,* Vol. 18, Nos. 1 and 2 (1986), 190–204.

142. Numerous excellent books on statistical hypothesis testing exist. This discussion is based on Ronald E. Walpole, *Introduction to Statistics,* (2nd ed.), New York: Macmillan, 1974. Another introductory text is John E. Freund and Frank J. Williams, *Elementary Business Statistics: The Modern Approach,* (3rd ed.), Englewood Cliffs, NJ: Prentice-Hall, 1977.

143. Other statistical tests may be used that are more powerful than the *U* test to prove or disprove such a hypothesis, but this example demonstrates a *method* that the researcher can use.

144. *The Channels of Monetary Effects on Interest Rates,* New York: NBER, 1972.

145. Ibid., 57.

146. J. Huston McCulloch, "The Monte Carlo Cycle in Business Activity," *Economic Inquiry,* Vol. XIII (September 1975), 303–321.

147. Frank de Leeuw, "Do Expansions Have Memory?" Discussion Paper 16, U.S. Department of Commerce, Bureau of Economic Analysis, unpublished manuscript, March 1987.

148. A discussion of the qualifications of this statistical test is beyond the scope of this book. The reader is encouraged to look at the original papers. For example, an area of disagreement among users of this technique is the number of groups to use and which (if any) cycles should be eliminated.

149. C. W. J. Granger, "Investigating Causal Relations by Econometric Models and Cross-Spectral Models," *Econometrica,* Vol. 37, No. 3 (July 1969), 424–438.

150. Christopher Sims, "Money, Income, and Causality," *American Economic Review,* Vol. 62 (1972), 540–552.

151. Ibid., 540.

152. For a discussion of the "fatal flaws" with these causality tests, see Roger K. Conway, P.A.V.B. Swamy, John F. Yanagida, and Peter von zur Muehlen, "The Impossibility of Causality Testing," *Agricultural Economics Research,* Vol. 36, No. 3 (Summer 1984), 1–19.

153. Robert V. Bishop, "The Construction and Use of Causality Tests," *Agricultural Economics Research,* Vol. 31, No. 4 (October 1979), 1–6.

CHAPTER 4

1. Sir John Hicks, *Causality in Economics,* New York: Basic Books, 1979, 63.

2. Charles Kindleberger, *The World in Depression, 1929–1939,* Berkeley: University of California Press, 1986, 72. Another reference on the history of business cycles, is Otto C. Lightner, *The History of Business Depressions,* New York: Burt Franklin, 1970.

3. This was the third longest contraction on record. The longest was the recession that began in October 1873 and lasted until March 1879—65 months. However, Milton Friedman and Anna Schwartz argue: "[T]he steady decline in prices from 1873 to 1879 probably led contemporary observers and has certainly led later observers to overstate the severity of the contraction in terms of real output." *A Monetary History of the United States, 1867–1960,* Princeton, NJ: Princeton University Press, 1963, 97. The second longest was the 1929 depression, which lasted 43 months.

4. Ibid., 97.

5. Ibid., 98.

6. Based on data from the *Handbook of Labor Statistics 1975—Reference Edition,* U.S. Department of Labor, Bureau of Labor Statistics, 1975, 313.

7. Victor Zarnowitz, "Business Cycles and Growth: Some Reflections and Measures," NBER Working Paper No. 665, April 1981.

8. Leonard P. Ayres, *Turning Points in Business Cycles,* New York: Macmillan, 1939, 45.

9. Kindleberger, *The World in Depression,* 43.

10. Zarnowitz, "Business Cycles," 40.

11. Maurice W. Lee, *Economic Fluctuations: Growth and Stability,* Homewood, IL: Irwin, 1959.

12. The maximum marginal personal income tax rate was 15% in 1916, but jumped to 67% in 1917, 77% in 1918, and then remained at 73% between 1919 and 1921. For more details see Christopher Frenze, *The Mellon and Kennedy Tax Cuts: A Review and Analysis,* A Staff Study by the U.S. Congress, Joint Economic Committee, June 18, 1982.

13. Gottfried Haberler, "The Great Depression of the 1930s—Can it Happen Again?" in *The Business Cycle and Public Policy 1929–80,* U.S. Congress, Joint Economic Committee, November 28, 1980, 1–19.

14. Friedman and Schwartz, *A Monetary History,* 106.

15. Albert G. Hart, Peter Kenen, and Alan D. Entine, *Money, Debt and Economic Activity* (4th ed.), Englewood Cliffs, NJ: Prentice-Hall, 410.

16. Friedman and Schwartz, *A Monetary History,* 316.

17. Robert A. Degen, *The American Monetary System,* Lexington, MA: Lexington Books, 1987, 80.

18. See Warren M. Persons, "Indices of Business Conditions," *Review of Economic Statistics,* Vol. 1 (1919), 5–107, and "An Index of General Business Conditions," *Review of Economic Statistics,* Vol. 1 (1919), 111–205.

19. Gunter Gabish and Hans-Walter Lorenz, *Business Cycle Theory: A Survey of Methods and Concepts,* New York: Springer-Verlag, 1987, 6.

20. In Germany, the Institute for Business Cycle Research under the direction of E. Wagemann, also set out to form a similar, though more comprehensive, indicator system in 1928. Wagemann criticized the Harvard ABC curves, not on theoretical grounds but on comprehensiveness. Another early attempt to form a composite cyclical leading indictor was done in 1931 by Bradford Smith, who devised an index to forecast changes in the American Telephone and Telegraph Company's index of business activity with a one-year lead time. See Bradford B. Smith, "A Forecasting Index for Business," *Journal of the American Statistical Association,* Vol. XXVI, No. 174 (June 1931), 115–127.

21. Geoffrey Moore, "The Analysis of Economic Indicators," *Scientific America,* January 1975, reprinted in *Business Cycles, Inflation, and Forecasting,* Cambridge, MA: Ballinger Publishing Co., 1980, 302.

22. Michael P. Niemira and Philip A. Klein, "A New Look at Forecasting the Great Depression," Paper presented at the EURO IX-TIMS XXVIII International Conference, Paris, July 6–8, 1988.

23. Joseph Schumpeter, *History of Economic Analysis,* New York: Oxford University Press, 1954, 1165.

24. Charles L. Schultze, "A Century of U.S. Economic Fluctuations: Why Has Performance Improved?" in *Other Times, Other Places,* Washington, DC: Brookings Institution, 1986, 57–84.

25. David K. Backus and Patrick J. Kehoe, "International Evidence on the Historical Properties of Business Cycles," *American Economic Review,* Vol. 82, No. 4 (September 1992), 864–888.

26. Bert G. Hickman, *Growth and Stability of the Postwar Economy,* Washington, DC: Brookings Institution, 1960, 44.

27. This distinction between producer and consumer services is widely recognized and accepted, for example, see Thomas M. Stanback, Jr., *Understanding the Service Economy: Employment, Productivity, Location,* Baltimore: Johns Hopkins University Press, 1979. More recent research done at the Bank of Japan echoes this distinction in assessing the macroeconomic effect of the rise of services on cyclical fluctuations. See *Expansion of Japan's Tertiary Sector: Background and Macroeconomic Implications,* Bank of Japan, Research and Statistics Department, December 1989.

28. Christina Romer, "Is the Stabilization of the Postwar Economy a Figment of the Data?" *American Economic Review,* June 1986, 314–334, and "Remeasuring Business Cycles," National Bureau of Economic Research, Working Paper No. 4150, August 1992. In that paper, Romer suggested new turning point dates for the pre-World War II period. Those alternative dates were based on recalculated historical data and a working definition of a turning point in terms of a cumulative loss in output rule as follows: (1) A cycle exists if the cumulative loss in the log of output between the peak and the return to peak exceeds 0.44 (the loss is 44% per months of industrial production loss), (2) the later of multiple extreme values is chosen as the turning point if the cumulative gain or loss in industrial production between an absolute extreme and a local extreme is less than 0.11, and (3) a turning point date of a cycle should be one month after the local extreme plateau if the gain or loss in industrial production is less than 0.008. Based on these rules, Romer determined that the average length of a contraction during the 1887–1917 period was 9.7 months instead of the NBER date average of 17.7 months. The 1918–1940 average length of a contraction was 13.7 months compared with the NBER date average of 18.0 months. The Romer conclusion was that over time there has not been a shortening in the contraction of cycles relative to expansions. The Romer dates are given below in year and month.

NBER Reference Dates		Romer Reference Dates	
Peak	Trough	Peak	Trough
1887:3	1888:4	1887:2	1887:7
1890:7	1891:5		
1893:1	1894:6	1893:1	1894:2
1895:12	1897:6	1895:12	1897:1
1899:6	1900:12	1900:4	1900:12
1902:9	1904:8	1903:7	1904:3
1907:5	1908:6	1907:7	1908:6
1910:1	1912:1	1910:1	1911:5
1913:1	1914:12	1914:6	1914:11
		1916:5	1917:1
1918:8	1919:3	1918:7	1919:3
1920:1	1921:7	1920:1	1921:7
1923:5	1924:7	1923:5	1924:7
1926:10	1927:11	1927:3	1927:12
1929:8	1933:3	1929:9	1932:7
1937:5	1938:6	1937:8	1938:6
		1939:12	1940:3

29. N. S. Balke and R. J. Gordon, "The Estimation of PreWar Gross National Product: Methodology and New Evidence," *Journal of Political Economy,* Vol. 97, No. 1 (1989), 38–92.

30. J. Bradford DeLong and Lawrence H. Summers, "The Changing Cyclical Variability of Economic Activity in the United States," in *The American Business Cycle: Continuity and Change,* R. J. Gordon, ed., Chicago: University of Chicago Press, 1986, 679–727.

31. Victor Zarnowitz, "Facts and Factors in the Recent Evolution of Business Cycles in the United States," National Bureau of Economic Research, Working Paper No. 2865, February 1989.

32. A formal statistical test could be used to determine the phase of the cycle. For example, if the average pace of change per stage and its associated deviation are known, it is easy to apply a goodness-of-fit test to determine the likely stage of the current business cycle.

33. Arthur M. Okun, *Prices & Quantities: A Macroeconomic Analysis,* Washington, DC: Brookings Institution, 1981, 16.

34. Robert J. Gordon, "The 'End-of-Recession' Phenomenon in Short-Run Productivity Behavior," *Brookings Papers on Economic Activity,* No. 2, 1979, 448.

35. Ben S. Bernanke and James L. Powell, "The Cyclical Behavior of Industrial Labor Markets: A Comparison of the Prewar and Postwar Era," in *The American Business Cycle: Continuity and Change,* R. J. Gordon, ed., Chicago: University of Chicago Press, 1986, 583–621.

36. Ernst Boehm, "Understanding Business Cycles Today: A Critical Review of Theory and Fact,"*Analyzing Modern Business Cycles,* Philip A. Klein, ed., Armonk, New York: M. E. Sharpe, 1990, 25–56.

37. Ibid., 48.

38. J. M. Blatt, "On the Frisch Model of Business Cycles," *Oxford Economic Papers,* Vol. 32, No. 3 (1980), 467–479. This seemingly innocuous conclusion led to a reexamination of that empirical fact about the business cycle.

39. Salih Neftçi, "Are Economic Time Series Asymmetric over the Business Cycle?" *Journal of Political Economy,* Vol. 92, No. 2 (1984), 307–328.

40. Barry Falk, "Further Evidence on the Asymmetric Behavior of Economic Time Series over the Business Cycle," *Journal of Political Economy,* Vol. 94, No. 5 (1986), 1096–1109.

41. J. Bradford DeLong, and Lawrence H. Summers, "Are Business Cycles Symmetrical?" in *The American Business Cycle: Continuity and Change,* R. J. Gordon, ed., Chicago: University of Chicago Press, 1986, 166–179.

42. The coefficient of skewness, which provides a relative measure of skewness, is calculated as:

$$(\Sigma \, (x_i - \bar{x})^3 \, / \, N) \, / \, \sigma^3 \qquad \text{for } N = 1 \text{ to } i$$

43. Daniel E. Sichel, "Business Cycle Asymmetry: A Deeper Look," Economic Activity Working Paper No. 93, Federal Reserve Board of Governors, Washington, DC, 1989.

44. The studies that trend-adjust time series are always open to the criticism of applying an ad hoc adjustment, no matter how much they claim that it does not alter the results. Instead, it seems more defensible simply to use growth rates and argue that periods before and after a recession share a common trend that does not have to be removed to understand the cyclical dynamic. While the trend growth in the 1950s may be different from that in the 1980s, adjacent cycle phases should be little impacted. Our view rests on the assumption that the cycle does not affect the trend. However, one school of thinking suggests that the cycle can indeed affect the trend. If that is true, then any trend-adjustment method is open to even more criticism.

45. Carl A. Dauten and Lloyd M. Valentine, *Business Cycles and Forecasting,* Pelham Manor, NY: South-Western Publishing Co., 1974, 301.

46. Ibid.

47. This is known as the *Katona* effect. See George Katona, "Expectations in Economics," in *Expectations and the Economy,* Joint Economic Committee, U.S. Congress, December 11, 1981.

48. Robert J. Gordon, "Postwar Macroeconomics: The Evolution of Events and Ideas," in *The American Economy in Transition,* Martin Feldstein, ed., Chicago: University of Chicago Press, 1980, 115.

49. Hickman, 1960, 301.

50. Hickman's view of this slowing in consumer spending is tied to his view, which was very persuasively argued, that diffusion is a key determinant of the business cycle expansions and contractions, much like the accelerator effect. Hickman (1960, p. 105) raised the question: "[W]hy should a mere retardation in the rate of increase in retail sales cause an absolute decline of consumer goods production?" His answer was: "[P]robably the principal reason is the fact that there is a close positive correlation between the rate of change of aggregate retail sales and the proportion of individual items for which sales are increasing."

51. President Eisenhower was a staunch supporter of balanced and small federal budgets. See Edward R. Tufte, *Political Control of the Economy,* Princeton, NJ: Princeton University Press, 1978, 15–18.

52. The Fed acted under Regulation Q, a Federal Reserve ruling that controlled the maximum allowable interest rate that member banks could pay on time and savings deposits.

53. For a discussion of the effectiveness of the 1968 surcharge, see William L. Springer, "Did the 1968 Surcharge Really Work?" *American Economic Review,* Vol. 65, No. 4, 644–659. Springer concluded that the surcharge was less effective in curbing consumption than a permanent tax.

54. Arthur Burns, *Reflections of an Economic Policy Maker,* Washington, DC: American Enterprise Institute, 1978, 111.

55. George Katona in a statement on survey expectations in economics, told Congress: "[T]he 1951 [price controls] were introduced too late when they were no longer needed and the 1971 measures were introduced too early, long before rapid inflation set in." See *Expectations and the Economy,* Joint Economic Committee, U.S. Congress, December 11, 1981, 29–30. Several papers on the various phases of the wage and price control program are in *American Economic Review,* Papers and Proceedings, May 1974, 82–104.

56. For an interesting behind-the-scenes discussion of the events that led up to the policy and its aftermath, see Herbert Stein, *Presidential Economics* (Rev. and Updated), New York: Simon and Schuster, 1985.

57. Victor Zarnowitz and Geoffrey Moore, "The Recession and Recovery of 1973–76," *Explorations in Economic Research,* National Bureau of Economic Research, Vol. 4, No. 4 (Fall 1977), 471–557.

58. Ibid., 473.

59. Real GDP growth on a quarter-to-quarter annualized rate basis reflected this slowing more dramatically than the two-quarter annualized growth calculation. On a quarter-to-quarter basis, real GDP soared 8% in the first quarter of 1976 then slowed sharply to 1.5% in the second quarter and 1.4% in the third quarter before growth accelerated to 4.2% by the fourth quarter.

60. "U.S. Monetary Policy in Recent Years: An Overview," *Federal Reserve Bulletin,* January 1985, 14.

61. For an excellent account of the credit controls experience and history in 1980, see Stacey L. Schreft, "Credit Controls: 1980," *Economic Review,* Federal Reserve Bank of Richmond, November/December 1990, 25–55.

62. Ibid., 41.

63. Andrew F. Brimmer, "The Federal Reserve as Lender of Last Resort: The Containment of Systemic Risks," Paper presented at the American Economic Association, December 29, 1984, 41.

64. Board of Governors of the Federal Reserve Board, "Record of the Policy Actions of the Federal Open Market Committee," *Federal Reserve Bulletin,* Vol. 66, No. 6 (June 1980), 486.

65. Based on the American Automobile Association's (AAA) "fuel gauge," a survey of self-service, regular unleaded gasoline prices.

66. Mark Watson, "Using Econometric Models to Predict Recessions," *Economic Perspectives,* the Federal Reserve Bank of Chicago, November/December 1991, 14–25.

67. Maurice Lamontagne, *Business Cycles in Canada,* Canadian Institute for Economic Policy Series, Toronto: James Lorimer, 1984.

CHAPTER 5

1. Several articles reviewed the literature on countercyclical advertising. For example, "Advertising during a Recession," *Direct Marketing,* September 1991, 17–18, 23. Another marketing article is Nariman K. Dhalla, "Advertising as an Antirecession Tool," *Harvard Business Review,* January/February 1980, 158–165.

2. This is based on research done at Mitsubishi Bank (New York).

3. Diversification of economic indicators provides a more reliable economic indicator. See Niemira and Fredman (1991).

4. Richard D. Karfunkle, "Textile Cycle Indicators," American Statistical Association, Proceedings of the Business and Economics Division 1965, 114–125; and "Statistical Indicators of the Textile Cycle," *Business Economics,* May 1969, 13–17.

5. Geoffrey H. Moore, "Statistical Indicators of Cyclical Revivals and Recessions," *Business Cycle Indicators,* Vol. 1, Princeton, NJ: Princeton University Press, 1961, 203.

6. See Hans Tson Soderstrom, "Cyclical Fluctuations in Labor Productivity and Capacity Utilization Reconsidered," *Swedish Journal of Economics,* Vol. 74, No. 2, June 1972, 220–237.

7. See Richard E. Caves, "The Structure of Industry," in *The American Economy in Transition,* Martin Feldstein, ed., Chicago: University of Chicago Press, 1980, 501–545.

8. Robert McLaughlin, publisher of *Turning Points* (Cheshire, CT), has used a "color system" since 1969 for summarizing the state of the economy.

9. "Advertising during a Recession," 18.

CHAPTER 6

1. From a policy perspective, it is important to understand the nature of regional cycles. Are local cycles simply a result of the industry mix of a region? For a discussion of this issue see Richard A. Siegel, "Do Regional Business Cycles Exist?" *Western Economic Journal,* Vol. 5, No. 1 (1966), 44–57. Sherwood-Call observed that states tended to have a stronger link with the national cycle if the state was (1) large, (2) had a similar industrial mix, (3) was more heavily dependent on manufacturing, and (4) was not heavily dependent on farming and the oil industry. See Carolyn Sherwood-Call, "Exploring the Relationship between National and Regional Economic Fluctuations," *Economic Review,* Federal Reserve Bank of San Francisco, Summer 1988 (No. 3), 15–26.

2. Georges Vernez, Roger Vaughan, Burke Burright, and Sinclair Coleman, *Regional Cycles and Employment Effects on Public Works Investments,* Rand Corporation, Santa Monica, CA, January 1977.

3. Richard Syron, "Regional Experience during Business Cycles—Are We Becoming More or Less Alike?" *New England Economic Review,* Federal Reserve Bank of Boston, November/ December 1978, 32.

CHAPTER 7

1. Martin Bronfenbrenner (ed.), *Is the Business Cycle Obsolete?* New York: Wiley-Interscience, 1969.

2. Ilse Mintz, *Dating Postwar Business Cycles, Methods and Their Applications to Western Germany, 1950–67,* NBER, New York: Columbia University Press, 1969.

3. Cf. Charlotte Boschan and Walter W. Ebanks, "The Phase-Average Trend: A New Way of Measuring Economic Growth," *Proceedings of the Business and Economics Statistics Section,* American Statistical Association, (1978), 332.

4. *OECD Leading Indicators and Business Cycles in Member Countries, 1960–1985,* OECD, Paris, January 1987. This publication described the growth cycle leading indicator system.

5. CIBCR, *International Economic Indicators,* Monthly, Center for International Business Cycle Research, Graduate School of Business, Columbia University, New York.

CHAPTER 8

1. *Prices and Quantities: A Macroeconomic Analysis,* Brookings Institution, Washington, DC, 1981.

2. Geoffrey H. Moore, *The Anatomy of Inflation,* Bureau of Labor Statistics, Report 373, 1969. Also see *Interpreting Early Warnings of Inflation: A Study of Statistical Indicators,* Congressional Budget Office, September 1977.

3. One example of this line of thinking is John A. Tatom, "Does the Stage of the Business Cycle Affect the Inflation Rate?" *Review,* Federal Reserve Bank of St. Louis, Vol. 60, No. 9 (September 1978), 7–15.

4. Howard Roth, "Leading Indicators of Inflation," *Economic Review,* Federal Reserve Bank of Kansas City, November 1986, 3–20.

5. Hallman, Jeffrey, Richard D. Porter, and David H. Small, "M2 Per Unit of Potential GNP as an Anchor for the Price Level," *Federal Reserve Board of Governors, Staff Working Paper,* April 1989.

6. M. A. Akhtar, Cornelis A. Los, and Robert B. Stoddard, "Surveys of Inflation Expectations: Forward or Backward Looking," *Federal Reserve Bank of New York Quarterly Review,* Vol. 8, No. 4 (Winter 1983–84), 63–66.

7. This idea stems from R. L. Hall and C. J. Hitch, "Price Theory and Business Behavior," *Oxford Economic Papers,* Vol. 2 (May 1939), 12–45.

8. Arthur F. Burns and Wesley C. Mitchell, *Measuring Business Cycles,* New York: NBER, 1946, 433.

9. Arthur Burns used the term *trend cycle* in his work but calculated the trend cycle in a very different manner than that proposed here.

10. The cumulative sum of squares statistic, CUSUM, is defined as follows:

$$\frac{\sum_{i=k+1}^{i=t} w_i^2}{\sum_{i=k+1}^{i=n} w_i^2}$$

where $t = k + 1, \ldots, n$ and the expected value of the test statistic is $(t - k)/(n - k)$. The statistic is cumulative in the sense that the first k observations are initially used in the calculation and each new observation $(k + 1, k + 2, \ldots, n)$ is then included in the subsequent estimate.

11. This idea that price level variability affects output has been suggested by numerous economists including Marshall and Keynes. For example, see Alfred Marshall, "Answers to Questions on the Subject of Currency and Prices Circulated by the Royal Commission on the Depression of Trade and Industry," in *Official Papers by Alfred Marshall,* London: Macmillan, 1926. Also see John M. Keynes, *Tract on Monetary Reform,* New York: Harcourt Brace, 1924. In a brief survey of other research, Froyen and Waud noted that the recent evidence tends to support the view that price uncertainty and/or variability affects output. See Richard T. Froyen and Roger N. Waud, "Real Business Cycles and the Lucas Paradigm," *Economic Inquiry,* Vol. XXVI (April 1988), 183–201.

12. R. A. Holmes, "Leading Indicators of Industrial Employment in British Columbia," *International Journal of Forecasting,* Vol. 2, No. 1 (1986), 87–100.

13. For an introduction to the method, see Maureen Caudill, *Neural Network Primer,* San Francisco, CA: Miller Freeman Publications, 1990, J. Stanley, *Introduction to Neural Networks,* Nevada City, CA: California Scientific Software, 1989.

14. The rationale for composite indicators is discussed in great clarity in Victor Zarnowitz, *Business Cycles: Theory, History, Indicators, and Forecasting,* National Bureau of Economic Research, Chicago: University of Chicago Press, 1992. For an understanding of international price cycle similarities and sequences, see Philip A. Klein, "Leading Indicators of Inflation in Market Economies," *International Journal of Forecasting,* Vol. 2 (No. 4), 1986, 403–412.

15. Peter Rappoport, "Inflation in the Service Sector," *Federal Reserve Bank of New York Quarterly Review,* Winter 1987, 33–45.

16. Ronald E. Kutscher and Jerome A. Mark, "The Service-Producing Sector: Some Common Perceptions Reviewed," *Monthly Labor Review,* April 1983, 21–24.

17. Herbert Runyon, "The Services Industries: Employment, Productivity and Inflation," *Business Economics,* January 1985, 55–63.

18. John W. Kendrick, "Service Sector Productivity," *Business Economics,* April 1987, 18–24.

19. Bert G. Hickman, *Growth and Stability of the Postwar Economy,* Brookings Institution, Washington, DC, 1960.

20. Ibid., 399.

21. Michael P. Niemira, "In Search of Leading Indicators of Service Sector Inflation: An Empirical Investigation," Paper presented at the Western Economic Association in Vancouver, BC, July 1987.

22. For a discussion of this theory, see Thomas M. Stanback, Jr., *Understanding the Service Sector Economy: Employment, Productivity, Location,* Baltimore: Johns Hopkins University Press, 1979.

23. Food and energy prices often are the catalyst for a price-cost spiral and, hence, a pickup in these commodity prices could signal a general rise in inflation.

24. Because of the sticky nature of service prices on the downside, energy prices are assumed to impact service prices only when they are rising.

25. Technically, according to the Burns and Mitchell cyclical turning point scheme, the peaking of the diffusion index after the inflation turning point low would have disqualified this as a true turning point for that 1974 inflation peak. However, because wage and price controls disrupted the price environment, it was kept.

26. *Expectations and the Economy,* Joint Economic Committee, U.S. Congress, December 11, 1981, 28.

27. Roth (1986).

28. Geoffrey H. Moore, *The Anatomy of Inflation,* Bureau of Labor Statistics, Report 373, 1969.

29. Statistical tests can only suggest but not prove the direction of the causal flow between wages and inflation. These tests hence are generally referred to as "pseudo-causality" tests.

CHAPTER 9

1. Arthur Burns, *The Business Cycle in a Changing World,* National Bureau of Economic Research, 1969, 37.

2. A. W. Mullineux, *Business Cycles and Financial Crises,* Ann Arbor: University of Michigan Press, 64.

3. John Mills, "Credit Cycles and the Origin of Commercial Panics," *Transactions of the Manchester Society.* 1867.

4. Joseph E. Stiglitz and Andrew Weiss, "Credit Rationing in Markets with Imperfect Information," *American Economic Review,* Vol. 71 (June 1981), 393–410.

5. Hyman P. Minsky, *Can "It" Happen Again?* Armonk, NY: M. E. Sharpe. 1982.

6. Ibid., 118.

7. J. Revell, "The Complementary Nature of Competition and Regulation in the Financial Sector," in *UK Banking Supervision: Evolution, Practice and Issues,* E. P. M. Gardener, ed., London: George Allen & Unwin. 1986.

8. J. L. Metcalfe, "Self Regulation, Crises Management and Preventive Medicine: The Evolution of UK Bank Supervision," in *UK Banking Supervision: Evolution, Practice and Issues,* E. P. M. Gardener, ed., London: George Allen & Unwin, 1986.

9. Charles P. Kindleberger, *The International Economic Order,* Cambridge, MA: MIT Press, 1988.

10. Mullineux, Business Cycles, 83.

11. Kindleberger, *International Economic Order,* 111.

12. Henry Kaufman, *Interest Rates, the Markets, and the New Financial World,* New York: Times Books, 1986.

13. Ibid., 78.

14. Ben S. Bernanke and Alan S. Blinder, "Credit, Money, and Aggregate Demand," *American Economic Review,* Vol. 78 (May 1987), 435–439. Also see Reijo Heiskanen, "The Bank Credit Market and Business Fluctuations," *Economic Review,* Kansallis-Osake-Pankki (Kansallis Banking Group), Finland, No. 1 (1991), 12–16.

15. J. H. Wood, *Commercial Bank Loan and Investment Behaviour,* London: John Wiley & Sons, 1975.

16. Stephen R. King, "Monetary Transmission: Through Bank Loans or Bank Liabilities?" *Journal of Money, Credit, and Banking,* Vol. 18 (August 1986), 290–303.

17. Ben S. Bernanke, "Alternative Explanations of the Money-Income Correlations," *Carnegie-Rochester Conference Series on Public Policy,* 1986, 49–99.

18. Cara S. Lown, "Banking and the Economy," *Economic Review,* Federal Reserve Bank of Dallas, September 1990, 1–14; and "The Credit-Output Link versus the Money-Output Link: New Evidence," *Economic Review,* Federal Reserve Bank of Dallas, November 1988, 1–10.

19. Milton Friedman and Anna J. Schwartz, "Money and Business Cycles," *Review of Economics and Statistics,* Vol. 45 (February 1963), 32–64.

20. Ibid., 53.

21. William Poole, "The Relationship of Monetary Decelerations to Business Cycle Peaks: Another Look at the Evidence," *Journal of Finance,* Vol. XXX, No. 3 (June 1975), 697–712.

22. Ibid., 710.

23. David I. Meiselman, "Is There a Political Monetary Cycle," *Cato Journal,* Fall 1986, 563–579.

24. Sidney Homer, *The Great American Bond Market: Selected Speeches of Sidney Homer,* Homewood, IL: Dow Jones-Irwin, 1978.

25. Ibid., "Techniques for Forecasting Interest Rate Trends," 243.

26. This is how Sir John Hicks described it when distinguishing between the Jevons and Mitchell ideas of cycles. The Jevons idea of a cycle—in this case, a financial cycle—was embodied in the contemporary work of Hyman Minsky and his followers. Jevons and his contemporaries of the late 1800s viewed the cycle as a sequence of events (not as a statistical series). See John Hicks, *A Market Theory of Money,* 1989, Oxford: Clarendon Press.

27. Martin H. Wolfson, *Financial Crises,* Armonk, NY: M. E. Sharpe, 1986; and "Theories of Financial Crises," in *Financial Dynamics and Business Cycles: New Perspectives,* Willi Semmler, ed., Armonk, NY: M. E. Sharpe, 1989.

28. Albert M. Wojnilower, "The Central Role of Credit Crunches in Recent Financial History," *Brookings Papers on Economic Activity,* No. 2 (1980), 277–339.

29. Ibid., 277.

30. Allen Sinai, "Credit Crunches—An Analysis of the Postwar Experience," in *Parameters and Policies in the U.S. Economy,* Otto Eckstein, ed., New York: North-Holland Publishing, 1976, 244–274.

31. Otto Eckstein and Allen Sinai, "The Mechanisms of the Business Cycle in the Postwar Era," *The American Business Cycle: Continuity and Change,* Robert J. Gordon, ed., Chicago: University of Chicago Press, 1986, 39–105.

32. Sinai, "Credit Crunches," 244.

33. This idea was developed and described by Sinai in a series of articles appearing in the *Data Resources Review,* including "Crunch Impacts and the Aftermath," June 1980, 37–60, and "Credit Crunch Possibilities and the Crunch Barometer," June 1978, 9–18.

34. This caricature of the credit cycle and its implication was prevalent throughout Merrill Lynch's *Investment Strategy* publication in the late 1970s and early 1980s. Richard J. Hoffman was Merrill Lynch's chief investment strategist at the time and Steven R. Resnick was Merrill Lynch's senior investment strategist.

35. Dennis R. Starleaf and James A. Stephenson, "A Suggested Solution to the Monetary-Policy Indicator Problem: The Monetary Full Employment Interest Rate," *Journal of Finance,* Vol. 24 (September 1969), 623–641.

36. Alan S. Blinder and Stephen M. Goldfeld, "New Measures of Fiscal and Monetary Policy, 1958–73," *American Economic Review,* Vol. 66, No. 5 (December 1972), 780–796.

37. Keith M. Carlson, "The Mix of Monetary and Fiscal Policies: Conventional Wisdom Vs. Empirical Reality," *Review,* Federal Reserve Bank of St. Louis, October 1982, 7–21.

38. Andrew F. Brimmer and Allen Sinai, "The Monetary-Fiscal Policy Mix: Implications for the Short Run," *American Economic Review,* May 1986, 203–208.

39. Howard Keen, Jr., "Summary Measures of Economic Policy and Credit Conditions as Early Warning Forecasting Tools," *Business Economics,* October 1985, 38–43.

40. Michael P. Niemira, "The Policy Stance and Economic Growth: What Is the Relationship," *Monthly Business Conditions,* Mitsubishi Bank, June 1989.

CHAPTER 10

1. Beryl W. Sprinkel, *Money and Stock Prices,* Homewood, IL: Richard D. Irwin, 1964, 1.

2. Standard & Poors Corporation introduced the market-weighted S&P 500 in 1957 and designed it to mirror overall common stock price performance. Through market capitalization, the S&P 500 accounts for about three-quarters of total market capitalization.

3. Douglas K. Pearce, "Stock Prices and the Economy," *Economic Review,* Federal Reserve Bank of Kansas City, November 1983, 7–22.

4. Pearce observed that empirical studies he reviewed generally found the stock market impact on consumption amounted from 3% to 7% of the capital gain or loss. In reality, it is unclear how the gain or loss should be measured. Do consumers continually revalue their stock market holdings, implicitly or explicitly, or do they gain or lose from the "last time" they looked at the price of their holdings of individual stocks or stock mutual funds.

5. A mid-range estimate (but by no means a consensus), however, would suggest that every 10% increase (decrease) in stock prices results in a 7% to 11% increase in investment.

6. Although the Foundation for the Study of Cycles has published numerous articles on the subject, a representative article is Gertrude Shirk, "Cycles in Stock Prices—The 40.68-Month Cycle," *Cycles,* March 1987, 28–33. Gertrude Shirk, who has since retired as Executive Director of the Foundation, used a form of spectral analysis to determine the periodicity. For more information about their research, contact the Foundation for the Study of Cycles, 900 W. Valley Road, Suite 502, Wayne, PA 19087. This example and presentation differ from the spectral analysis work that the Foundation does.

7. Over the longer run, there may be some evidence of a *shortening* in this stock market cycle regardless of whether the recent cycle average pattern is more similar to a 40.68 or a 41.60 month cycle. In 1956, the FSC wrote about a 46-month cycle in stock prices. See Edward R. Dewey, "The 46-Month Cycle in Stock Prices," *Cycles,* August 1956; reprinted in Edward R. Dewey, *Cycles—Selected Writings,* Foundation for the Study of Cycles, 1970, 459–465. Today, however, using essentially the same statistical technique, they have found that the average cycle is about 5 months shorter in duration.

8. Richard Mogey, "Status of the 40.68-Month Cycle in Stock Prices," *Cycles,* December 1988, 292–294. Richard Mogey, the Executive Director of the Foundation for the Study of Cycles, discussed in that article the relationship of the 40.68 month stock price cycle with 5.92-year and 9.44-year cycles.

9. James L. Farrell, "The Dividend Discount Model: A Primer," *Financial Analysts Journal,* November/December 1985, 16–19.

10. Martin L. Leibowitz, *A New Perspective on Asset Allocation,* The Research Foundation of The Institute of Chartered Financial Analysts, Charlottesville, VA, 1987, 12.

11. S. Basu, "Investment Performance of Common Stocks in Relation to Their Price-Earnings Ratios: A Test of the Efficient Market Hypothesis," *Journal of Finance,* June 1977, 663–682.

12. Two earnings-consensus-gathering organizations are I/B/E/S and Zacks. Both have written about using earnings expectations for valuations. See for example, Greg Forsythe "Using Expected Earnings Growth in a Valuation Measure," *Zacks Investment Research,* March 1, 1990, 8. Also see "Using Consensus Growth Rate Forecasts to Evaluate P/E Ratios," *I/B/E/S Monthly Comments,* August 1987, 21.

13. Edward F. Renshaw, "The Anatomy of Stock Market Cycles," *The Journal of Portfolio Management,* Fall 1983, 53–57.

14. Prakash Loungani, Mark Rush, and William Tave, "Stock Market Dispersion and Business Cycles," *Economic Perspectives,* Federal Reserve Bank of Chicago, January/February 1991, 2–8.

15. David Lilien, "Sectoral shifts and Cyclical Unemployment," *Journal of Political Economy,* Vol. 90 (August 1982), 777–793.

16. Prakash Loungani, Mark Rush, and William Tave, "Stock Market Dispersion and Unemployment," *Journal of Monetary Economics,* Vol. 25 (June 1990), 367–388.

17. Edward R. Tufte, *Political Control of the Economy,* Princeton University Press, Princeton, 1978.

18. Robert H. Stovall, "Forecasting Stock Market Performance via the Presidential Cycle," *Financial Analysts Journal,* May–June 1992, 5–8. Yale Hirsch, who is noted for his excellent statistical work on the stock market and is the publisher of *The Stock Trader's Almanac,* examined this cycle based on the S&P composite since the 1832 election and essentially concluded the same thing as Stovall, who based his results on the DJIA. See Yale Hirsch, *Don't Sell Stocks on Monday,* New York: Penguin Books, 1986.

19. See Beryl W. Sprinkel, *Money and Stock Prices;* or "Monetary Growth as a Cyclical Indicator," *Journal of Finance,* September 1956, 333–346.

20. Michael S. Rozeff, "The Money Supply and the Stock Market: The Demise of a Leading Indicator," *Financial Analysts Journal,* September/October 1975, 18–26.

21. Ibid., 26.

22. Robert D. Auerbach, "Money and Stock Prices," *Monthly Review,* Federal Reserve Bank of Kansas City, September–October 1976, 3–11.

23. Ibid., 11.

24. Richard Cooper, "Efficient Capital Markets and the Quantity Theory of Money," *Journal of Finance,* June 1974, 887–908.

25. Milton Friedman, "Money and the Stock Market," *Journal of Political Economy,* 1988, Vol. 96, No. 2, 221–245.

26. Michael P. Niemira, "Forecasting Turning Points in the Stock Market Cycle and Asset Allocation Implications," *Analyzing Modern Business Cycles: Essays Honoring Geoffrey H. Moore,* Philip A. Klein, ed., M. E. Sharpe, Armonk, New York, 1990, 109–127.

27. P. Young Kwon, "Stock Prices, Profits, and Interest Rates during Business Cycles," Paper presented at the Atlantic Economic Association, February 14, 1982.

28. Ernest A. Boehm and Geoffrey H. Moore, "Financial Market Forecasts and Rates of Return Based on Leading Index Signals," *International Journal of Forecasting,* Vol. 7 (1991), 357–374.

29. Martin J. Pring, *The All-Season Investor,* New York: John Wiley & Sons, 1992.

30. Clive W. J. Granger, "Forecasting Stock Market Prices: Lessons for Forecasters," *International Journal of Forecasting,* Vol. 8 (1992), 3–13.

CHAPTER 11

1. Richard M. Goodwin, *Chaotic Economic Dynamics,* Oxford: Clarendon Press, 1990, 21.

2. Joseph A. Schumpeter, *Capitalism, Socialism, and Democracy,* New York: Harper & Brothers, 1949.

3. Otto C. Lightner, *The History of Business Depressions,* New York: Burt Franklin, 1970, 186 (originally published 1922).

4. Wesley Clair Mitchell, *Business Cycles and Their Causes,* Philadelphia: Porcupine Press, 1989, Preface pp. ix–x (originally published 1913).

5. Arthur F. Burns, "Progress Towards Economic Stability," *The American Economic Review,* Vol. L, No. 1 (March 1960), 19.

Index